Blackcurrant Jam

Orange Marmalade

Step-by-Step to

Home Cooking

Marshall Cavendish

CONTENTS

INTRODUCTION

Imagine a complete, individual cookery course in your own home, plus a superb collection of recipes, and you have *Step-by-Step Home Cooking*, a compact, informative cookbook which takes you right through the meal from start to finish - a permanent source of reference at your fingertips, where you want it, when you want it.

The key to good cooking is understanding the fundamentals, so *Step-by-Step Home Cooking* is divided into four sections – Soups and Sauces, Meat, Salads and Vegetables and Desserts – which begin at the beginning, with the basic techniques. All information is given in clear, everyday language and in logical order. The mouthwatering recipes included in each section are easy to follow and proceed from the simple to the more adventurous. All have been tested in our own kitchens and there are more than 1000 full-colour photographs that make the techniques even easier to follow and the recipes a feast for your eyes even before they are cooked.

An invaluable source of reference, *Step-by-Step Home Cooking* is a book you can't afford to be without.

Time symbols: an indication of preparation and cooking time is given for each recipe. This is calculated for beginners new to the techniques involved; experienced cooks can allow less time.

    ⧗ less than 1 hour
    ⧗⧗ 1-2½ hours
    ⧗⧗⧗ over 2½ hours

Weights and measures: both metric and Imperial measurements are given throughout, with Imperial figures appearing in square brackets. Metric and Imperial measures are not exact equivalents, so be sure to work with only one set of figures or the other.

Published by
Marshall Cavendish Books Limited
58 Old Compton Street
London W1V 5PA

© Marshall Cavendish Limited 1977–1983

First printing 1978
Second printing 1981
Third printing 1983

This material was first published by
Marshall Cavendish
in the partwork *Good Cooking*

Printed by L.E.G.O., Vicenza, Italy

ISBN 0 85685 454 9

Soups

home-made stock bases

Home-made stock is one of the 'basics' of good cookery. It is easy and satisfying to make and it can do a great deal to enhance simple everyday cooking, and to give soups and sauces authentic flavour.

WHAT IS STOCK?

Basically, stock is a liquid obtained by simmering meat or fish bones and trimmings in water with herbs, vegetables and seasonings. When all the goodness and flavour have been extracted, the liquid is strained and reduced to concentrate flavour. The resulting stock is then used as a base for soups, sauces, casseroles, aspics, stews and gravies.

Why make stock yourself when you can buy stock cubes? The answer is flavour. Without good stocks, many of the world's greatest dishes would not be worth tasting.

Making your own stock is, of course, more time-consuming than simply dissolving a stock cube in boiling water but the extra effort involved is not very great, and there is a world of difference in taste and texture. Stock cubes contain large amounts of salt and monosodium glutamate (an artificial flavouring) to give them a longer shelf life. These strong flavours concentrate during cooking and can easily spoil a delicate sauce or soup.

Types of stock

Stocks are divided into two types – brown and white. Brown stocks are richly coloured because the ingredients are lightly fried before liquid is added, while white stocks are more delicate in colour and in flavour.

Stocks are also divided into categories according to the quality of ingredients used. First stocks are the finest, made from fresh ingredients and usually used for sauces, soups and aspics where a really top-quality stock is essential. Second stocks are made from bones which have already been used once in stockmaking (with the addition of a few fresh ingredients to bolster flavour). Not so fine in flavour as first stocks, they are perfectly suitable for stews and casseroles and simple sauces.

Like most thin soups, spicy hot and sour soup is cooked very quickly so a good, well-flavoured brown stock is needed.

1

Types of stock & their uses

Stock	Uses
Brown stock: so called because ingredients are coloured by browning in fat before water is added. It is usually made exclusively from beef bones and meat, plus celery, onions or leeks, carrots and herbs. You may however, find some recipes which include veal or chicken.	The ideal choice for brown sauces. Also for kidney, tomato and vegetable soups requiring good colour and strong flavour, for moistening red meat casseroles and pies and, if very meaty and well-flavoured, for aspics, clear hot and cold jellied soups.
Game stock: a brown stock made from game carcasses and meat scraps plus beef bones (fresh or saved from making brown stock) plus vegetables, particularly celery, and complementary herbs.	Distinctive game flavour. Use for game soups, sauces to serve with game and to moisten game pies, pâtés and casseroles.
White stock: usually made from the bones and meat scraps of one or several of the following: veal, chicken, rabbit, pork, mutton, lamb, and ham, plus celery, root vegetables and herbs. Omit mutton, lamb and ham for a general-purpose white stock and only use pork sparingly.	Delicate meaty flavour and pale colour if based on veal or chicken. Use for cream soups, fine white sauces and aspics. A stock containing a lot of lamb or mutton is ideal for Scotch and barley broths. Use ham stocks for soups and purées made with peas or other pulses.
Household stock: white stock made from bones of a cooked ham, lamb or veal joint or chicken carcass plus any raw or cooked trimmings. Giblets, bacon rinds and scraps plus vegetables and herbs are also added.	Pale in colour. Not as fine in flavour as white stock but very economical and useful for vegetable broths, simple white sauces and casseroles made with pork or veal.
Chicken stock: white stock made with boiling fowl and knuckle of veal for maximum flavour. Cheaper versions use carcass, skin and giblets plus poultry scraps; or giblets only. Always include celery, a few root vegetables and herbs.	Good poultry flavour, pale colour. An excellent general-purpose stock for all types of soups, sauces for vegetables and white meat dishes, moistening white meat casseroles and pies and boiling rice for savoury dishes or for risottos.
Fish stock: a white stock made with heads, bones and trimmings of white fish, lemon, celery, a few root vegetables and herbs. Turbot heads, halibut, sole and plaice bones are best. Add cheap fresh white fish to bolster flavour if bones are few.	Almost colourless. Delicately flavoured. Quickly made. Wine can replace some of the water. Use immediately for fish soups, poaching fish, fish aspics and sauces or rice to accompany fish dishes.
Vegetable stock: really neither white nor brown. A good way to use up scraps. Can be made from one or several of the following: celery stalks, trimmings from leeks and carrots, outer cabbage leaves, watercress stalks, mushroom peelings, outer lettuce leaves, young pea or broad bean pods and some vegetable cooking liquids.	Mostly used in vegetarian cookery. Colour and flavour can be strengthened by lightly browning vegetables in butter before water is added. Blend all ingredients in a liquidizer to make an instant soup. Or strain off vegetables and use liquid for soups, braising vegetables, cooking pulses and for boiling rice.

CHOOSING INGREDIENTS

The very best first stocks are made from fresh meaty bones (or fish and fish bones) and vegetables bought specifically for the purpose. But there is no need to buy special ingredients for an economic stock for everyday use. Household stock is made by using leftovers which might otherwise go to waste – a cooked joint bone or chicken carcass and vegetable peelings (wrapped and refrigerated these scraps will keep for up to five days).

Do not, however, be tempted to treat your stockpot like a dustbin – throwing all your scraps into it indiscriminately will only produce poor results.

When choosing ingredients for stock, bear in mind the final dishes you plan to use it in. If, for instance, you are planning a chicken casserole, there is no point in including beef bones or cabbage – these distinctive flavours will not harmonize with or complement a chicken dish.

Meat and bones

There is great scope here for obtaining ingredients very cheaply, or even free. When you visit your butcher look out for large bones and odd pieces of meat (often left lying on the slab behind the counter). Most butchers are only too glad to sell them very cheaply and may even give them to you free of charge. Remember when buying bones that they have to fit into a pan so ask for them to be cut up. And, if you buy meat and ask the butcher to bone and trim it for you remember to take bones and trimmings home with you – useful additions for the stockpot.

What kind of meat and bones can you use? All sorts of bones can be used. Those with meat attached give extra flavour and make your stock more nutritious.

Beef bones and trimmings are excellent. Ham, gammon, mutton and lamb bones have distinctive flavour but they are useful for some specific purposes (see Types of Stock and their Uses). Pork bones and meat should be used sparingly as they give stock a slightly sweet flavour. Veal bones, pigs' trotters and calves' heads are excellent if you want a really gelatinous stock, so always include one of these if you want to make aspics or jellied soup. Chicken carcasses and game birds are also good for flavour, particularly if scraps of meat are attached. Bones must always be washed before use and veal must be blanched (plunged into boiling water) for five minutes and then rinsed before use because it releases a mass of grey scum which makes the stock cloudy.

Fish
The bones, heads and trimmings of all raw white fish can be used to make stock. Do not use oily fish (eg mackerel, herring) it is too strong in flavour. Bones and scraps from cooked fish are unsuitable as they have very little flavour to give.

Vegetables
The most commonly used vegetables are onions or leeks, carrots and celery. Always use fresh vegetables or vegetable peelings, never leftover cooked vegetables as these will make stock cloudy. Potatoes and other starchy vegetables, such as peas and beans, may also make stock cloudy and are best avoided.

Mushroom peelings add colour as well as flavour, as do tomatoes, but the latter may sour the stock if kept for more than a day, so it is better to add them only to the final dish. Turnips and members of the cabbage family can be used for vegetable stock but their flavours are too pronounced for meat or fish stock.

Herbs and seasonings
Aromatic and full of flavour, herbs are an essential ingredient of good home-made stock. Salt and peppercorns are also used and, occasionally, mace. Herbs are usually added to stock in the form of a bouquet garni – a little collection of complementary herbs tied together in a bunch if fresh, in a little muslin bag if dried or powdered.

The classic bouquet garni which is suitable for use in all stocks is made up of a sprig of fresh or dried thyme, a dried bay leaf and a few sprigs of fresh parsley. If using powdered herbs, use 5 ml (1 teaspoon) of each. Use a whole dried bay leaf and try to avoid using dried parsley – it is musty and poor in flavour compared to fresh.

You can vary the herbs in a bouquet garni to suit the ingredients in the stock. Do not be tempted to use too many different herbs – their flavours simply cancel each other out and mask rather than enhance the main ingredients.

Rosemary added to a classic bouquet garni is excellent for stocks containing mutton or lamb.
Tarragon either alone or with the classic bouquet garni is good in chicken stock.
Marjoram adds a distinctive flavour to game stocks. A few juniper berries can also be added.
Lemon balm or lemon verbena add pungency to mild chicken or fish stocks.
Fennel is also good for bolstering mild fish stock. Use alone or add it to the classic bouquet garni.

TIMING
Contrary to popular opinion, stock is extremely easy to make. Initial preparation of ingredients and skimming will take you about half an hour. After this, the stock can be left to simmer gently with little or no attention from the cook. Although cooking time can be long (up to five hours for some stocks), it can be stopped and restarted when it suits you. Straining, de-greasing and final flavouring of the stock will take about another 45 minutes or so in all, but once again these jobs can be broken up and done when most convenient. The end product is well worth the effort.

EQUIPMENT
To make stock you will need the following equipment:
- large pan
- skimmer or perforated spoon
- colander
- absorbent kitchen paper
- piece of butter muslin

Making a bouquet garni

1 Collect together a sprig of fresh thyme, a few sprigs of fresh parsley and a bay leaf.

2 Tie into a bunch with cotton, leaving a long end which can be tied to the pan handle.

OR if using dried herbs, place with fresh parsley on a small square of muslin or cheesecloth.

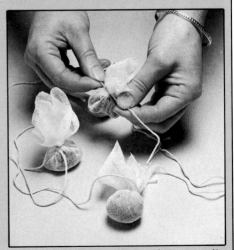

AND gather the edges of the muslin together and tie firmly with cotton, leaving a long end.

Large pan: the pan can be either a conventional saucepan or a double-handled stockpot. It must be heavy-based, lidded and at least 4.6 L [8 pt] capacity. A large size is essential: during cooking, stock reduces by about half, so you have to start with a lot of liquid in order to obtain a reasonable amount of stock.

Skimmer or perforated spoon: this is used to remove scum and sometimes fat from the surface of the stock. A draining spoon used for lifting vegetables out of water can be used but a flat skimmer especially designed for stock is best. You can simply slide the skimmer across the surface of the stock, rather than dipping in, which is necessary with a spoon shape.

Colander: this is used to strain the stock after cooking. As bones and meat tend to be heavy and very hot, a metal colander is best as it will not buckle or warp under the strain and heat.

Kitchen paper: this is used to mop up the fat from the surface of the stock. Double thickness paper is best as it is more absorbent. A slice of white bread can be used instead.

Butter muslin: essential for the final straining of the stock as its fine mesh will trap any scum or particles of food which may have slipped through the colander.

BASIC METHODS

With the exception of brown stock, where initial preparation differs slightly, all stocks are made following the method shown in the step-by-steps on this page. To make brown stock, follow the initial preparation stages shown in the step-by-step on page 6, then continue as for other stocks. Here are a few important points which are relevant to the making of all types of stock.

Bringing to the boil

Bringing the stock to the boil slowly is essential to force out impurities which rise as scum. If you bring the stock to the boil too fast the scum will be driven back into the liquid and will spoil the stock.

Skimming

Once the scum of impurities has formed it must be removed, otherwise it will be re-absorbed by the stock. Lift off the scum using a skimmer or a perforated spoon.

Seasoning

Herbs and seasonings are always added after this initial skimming. Do not season heavily at this stage as the liquid will reduce during cooking and concentrate flavour.

Simmering

Reduce heat to low and half cover the pan with a lid. It is important that the stock simmers (cooks just below boiling point) during the remaining cooking time or fat and scum will amalgamate with the stock and make it cloudy. Let it simmer very gently – just a bubble or two breaking the surface – until the liquid is reduced by almost half. This may take up to five hours (although fish stock should never be cooked for longer than 30 minutes). Skim as necessary during cooking and top up with boiling water if the liquid looks as if it will fall below the level of the ingredients.

Straining and de-greasing

Strain the stock through a colander into a large bowl or another pan, pressing the juices through with a spoon or vegetable press. Discard vegetables and herbs. Keep meat (if used) for potting or making into a cottage pie or Bolognese sauce. Keep bones for making second stock.

If the stock is for immediate use, remove the grease by floating a piece of absorbent kitchen paper or a slice of white bread on the surface. This will absorb the liquid fat. If time allows, a much easier and more effective way of removing all fat is to allow the stock to become quite cold so that the fat hardens into a solid surface layer and can then be lifted off quite easily with a knife.

Final straining and flavouring

After de-greasing, strain stock again, this time through a colander lined with butter muslin, to remove any impurities and small particles of meat or vegetables which may have slipped through during initial straining, otherwise the stock may quickly sour. Reheat the stock and, if flavouring is too weak for your purposes, boil over high heat to evaporate some of the liquid and to concentrate flavour. Correct seasoning, if necessary, by adding salt and pepper.

STORING STOCKS

Meat stock can be covered and kept in a refrigerator for up to 10 days but

1 Cut vegetables into chunks. Put in a heavy pan with washed meat or fish bones.

5 Half cover the pan and simmer for as long as specified in the recipe used.

OR cool stock a little then skim off fat with a skimmer or spoon.

4

Step-by-step white stock

2 Add cold water to the pan and bring to the boil as slowly as possible.

3 When the thick foam forms into a definite scum, remove with a spoon or skimmer.

4 When the scum has stopped rising in large quantities, add herbs and seasonings.

6 Skim and top up with boiling water if the liquid falls below the level of the ingredients.

7 Pour the stock through a colander into a clean bowl or pan. Reserve ingredients.

8 If stock is for immediate use, mop up fat with kitchen paper or a slice of bread.

OR leave until completely cold, then scrape off solid fat.

9 Strain de-greased stock through a sieve lined with fine muslin or cheesecloth.

10 Reheat. If the flavouring is weak, boil rapidly to reduce and concentrate flavour. Season to taste.

it should be boiled up every 3–4 days to keep it sweet. Fish stock should be used (or frozen) within 24 hours. Vegetable stock will keep for a maximum of 3 days but must be boiled up daily.

All stocks freeze well but they are bulky so it is a good idea to reduce your stock more than usual, concentrating its flavour well before freezing. You can always dilute it again. Pour into ice cube trays, calculating the number of cubes per 150 ml [¼ pt], and freeze. When frozen, turn into plastic bags and label. Frozen meat stock will keep for two months, frozen fish and vegetable stock for 1 month.

BROWN STOCK

This is the ideal stock to use in dishes which require a good colour and strong flavour. If you cannot find Spanish onions, very large, well-flavoured onions will do.

MAKES ABOUT 1.25 L [3 pt]
2.25 kg [5 lb] shin or neck beef bones with meat attached, chopped and washed
2 Spanish onions, sliced
3 large carrots, chopped
2 celery stalks, thickly sliced
salt
bouquet garni
bay leaf
6 black peppercorns

1 Put the bones in a large pan, extract fat and fry for 15 minutes, stirring occasionally, to brown bones evenly. Add a little dripping if necessary.

2 Add the prepared vegetables and cook gently until just coloured.

3 Pour on 3.25 L [6 pt] cold water and bring slowly to the boil.

4 Remove scum with a slotted spoon.

5 Add a little salt, the herbs and the peppercorns. Half cover the pan and simmer very gently for about 4 hours, skimming and topping up with boiling water as necessary.

6 Strain, de-grease, strain again, reduce and adjust seasoning to taste as necessary.

Variations
● Second brown stock: brown stock

Step-by-step brown stock

1 Cook the washed bones in a large pan over very low heat until fat is extracted.

2 Slightly increase heat and fry for 15 mins. Stir to brown evenly. Add a little fat if bones produce none.

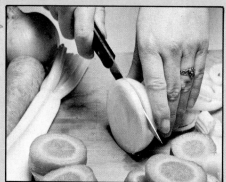

3 Meanwhile, prepare the vegetables: peel and slice onions, scrub carrots and celery and then cut them into chunks.

4 Add vegetables to the pan and cook for 10 minutes or until pale golden in colour. Continue from step 2 of white stock.

bones and meat can be re-used. To bolster flavour, add fresh vegetables and herbs and any joint bones and any chicken carcasses saved.
● Cheap brown stock: you can simply use saved joint bones and chicken carcasses in place of fresh shin or neck of beef bones. Reduce water by half.

WHITE STOCK

White stock, with its more delicate flavour, is the perfect base for cream soups and special sauces.

MAKES ABOUT 1.25 L [3 pt]
2.25 kg [5 lb] knuckle of veal, chopped and blanched
2 Spanish onions, sliced
3 large carrots, chopped
2 celery stalks, thickly sliced
1 medium-sized leek, thickly sliced
salt
6 white peppercorns
bouquet garni

1 Blanch the bones by plunging into boiling water for 5 minutes. Rinse in cold water.

2 Put the blanched bones in a large pan. Add vegetables, pour on to it 3.25 L [6 pt] cold water and bring to the boil slowly.

3 Remove scum with a slotted spoon.

4 Add salt, peppercorns and herbs and bring back to the boil.

5 Reduce heat, half cover the pan and simmer very gently for about 4 hours, skimming and topping up with boiling water as necessary.

6 Strain, de-grease, strain again, reduce and adjust seasoning to taste as necessary.

Variations
● Second white stock: bones used for white stock can be re-used with fresh vegetables and herbs. Add a chicken carcass to bolster flavour.

● Cheap white stock: replace fresh veal knuckle with leftover veal, chicken, beef or rabbit bones, or a mixture of all of these. Leftover pork, lamb or mutton bones can also be included but they must form only a very small proportion of the total bones if you want to make a general-purpose white stock.

HOUSEHOLD STOCK

Based on leftovers, this stock is very economic to make. Use it for casseroles, broths and other dishes which do not require a strongly coloured or flavoured stock. You could use a cooked joint bone, the carcass of a cooked bird, raw bones, cooked or raw meat trimmings, giblets, bacon rinds. But do not include too many different types of meat or bones or the flavours will cancel each other out. Be sure that cooked bones have not begun to develop 'off' flavours.

MAKES ABOUT 1.25 L [3 pt]
2.25 kg [5 lb] selection of bones and meat trimmings
2 large onions, peeled and sliced
1 carrot, sliced
1 leek, cleaned and sliced
2 celery stalks, thickly sliced
bouquet garni
6 black peppercorns
salt

1 Chop the bones into convenient-sized pieces.

2 Add the vegetables.

3 Pour on 3.25 L [6 pt] cold water and bring slowly to the boil.

4 Remove scum with a slotted spoon.

5 Add a little salt, the herbs and the peppercorns. Half cover the pan and simmer very gently for about 3 hours, skimming and topping up with boiling water as necessary.

6 Strain, de-grease, strain again, reduce and adjust seasoning to taste as required.

Variations

● Brown household stock: to give the stock extra colour, fry the bones for 15 minutes, stirring occasionally, to brown evenly. Add extra fat if necessary. Then continue from step 2 of household stock.

CHICKEN STOCK

This is one of the most useful of all stocks, frequently specified in recipes.

MAKES 1.25 L [3 pt]
1.40–1.60 kg [3–3½ lb] boiling fowl
700 g [1½ lb] knuckle of veal, chopped and blanched
2 large carrots, cut into quarters
2 Spanish onions, cut into quarters
1 leek, thickly sliced
1 celery stick, sliced
bouquet garni
6 white peppercorns
salt

1 Put the chicken, giblets (excluding liver) and veal in a large pan. Add vegetables, pour on 3.25 L [6 pt] water and bring slowly to the boil.

2 Remove scum with a slotted spoon.

3 Add bouquet garni, pepper and a little salt and bring back to the boil.

4 Reduce heat, half cover the pan and simmer very gently for 2½–3 hours until the meat falls away from the bone. Skim and top up with boiling water if the level of the liquid falls below the top of ingredients.

5 Strain, de-grease, reduce, strain again, and adjust seasoning to taste.

Variations

● Second chicken stock: re-use the carcass with fresh vegetables (1 carrot, 1 leek, 1 onion, 50 g [2 oz] mushroom stalks or peelings), herbs and 1.40 L [2½ pt] water to make a second stock.

● Giblet stock: wash the liver, gizzard and heart. Wash and scald the feet if you have them, scrape away the scales and nip off claws with pliers. Put everything in a saucepan together with a piece of celery, half an onion and a bouquet garni. Stew gently for ¾–1 hour. Strain, de-grease and use for gravies or soups.

GAME STOCK

Use pheasant, partridge, pigeon or any other game carcass to accompany game dishes. If bones weigh less than the amount specified here, just reduce the amount of water you use.

MAKES 850 ml [1½ pt]
700 g [1½ lb] game carcasses
1 small onion, cut into quarters
1 carrot, cut into quarters
1 celery stick, sliced
parsley sprig
bouquet garni
4 black peppercorns
salt
1 L [2 pt] second brown stock (see page 58).

1 Break up carcasses, put into a large pan and just cover with cold water. Leave for 1 hour. Add vegetables.

2 Bring slowly to the boil and remove scum with a slotted spoon.

3 Add herbs, pepper, salt and stock and bring back to the boil.

4 Reduce heat, half cover the pan and simmer very gently for 2 hours or until all flesh has separated from the bones.

5 Strain, de-grease, strain again, reduce and adjust seasoning to taste.

FISH STOCK

This is exceptionally quick to make. The reason for the short cooking time is that the fish bones and trimmings give up their flavour much faster than meat bones. Simmer for no longer than 30 minutes or the bones will give the stock a bitter, gluey flavour. Any non-oily white fish trimmings can be used but the inclusion of a halibut or turbot head produces the best stock. Always use fish stock within 24 hours.

MAKES ½ L [1 pt]
675 g (1½ lb) white fish trimmings
1 medium-sized onion or leek, sliced
1 celery stalk, sliced
juice of half a lemon
a few parsley stalks
small bouquet garni
6 white peppercorns
salt

1 Wash the fish trimmings well under cold running water. Put in a

large pan, add vegetables, cover with 1 L [2 pt] cold water and bring slowly to the boil.

2 Remove scum with a slotted spoon.

3 Add remaining ingredients, bring back to the boil, half cover with a lid and leave to simmer for 20–30 minutes.

4 Strain the stock into another saucepan through a sieve lined with butter muslin or cheesecloth. Press the bones with the back of a wooden spoon to extract all the juices, then discard the bones.

5 Boil the strained stock over high heat until it has been reduced by half and the flavour has been concentrated.

6 Adjust the seasoning and use immediately, or freeze when cold.

VEGETABLE STOCK

Here is an excellent way to use up vegetable peelings and scraps. Avoid using too much of strongly flavoured vegetables such as cabbage and greens as these will overpower the delicate flavour of the stock.

MAKES 850 ml (1½ pt]
    350 g [¾ lb] **vegetable peelings, such as outer stalks of celery, watercress stalks, carrot peelings, tomato and mushroom peelings and stalks, green parts of leeks**
3 white peppercorns
small bouquet garni
salt

1 Rinse the peelings under cold running water. Put them in a pan, add the peppercorns, bouquet garni and salt, 1.15 L [2 pt] cold water and bring to the boil.

2 Reduce heat, half cover with a lid and leave to simmer gently for 1–1½ hours.

3 Strain, reduce and adjust seasoning to taste.

Variation
● Brown vegetable stock: vegetables can be browned by frying in butter before you add the water. The sweetness in the vegetables will caramelize, adding flavour and colour.

MAKING THIN SOUPS

The simplest way to use stock is to make thin soups. These are made by cooking ingredients in stock. The liquid is not thickened except where one of the ingredients does this naturally (as when a potato disintegrates into the soup).

A really well-flavoured stock is essential to a thin soup because cooking time is usually very short (often only a few minutes), so the added ingredients do not have much chance to impart their flavour to the liquid. Brown, white, chicken and fish stocks are all suitable for making thin soups, and first stocks with their finer flavour are best.

AVGOLEMONO

Any white stock (chicken or veal) can be used. Leftover cooked rice can also be used – add it to the pan at the last minute, giving it just enough time to warm through.

This soup can be eaten either hot or cold. Served hot it has a very delicate flavour; served cold the taste is more lemony. If served cold, add a touch of elegance by garnishing with paper-thin slices of lemon and sprigs of dill weed.

SERVES 4 – 6
1.15 L [2 pt] white stock
50 g [2 oz] long-grain rice
3 eggs
juice of 2 small lemons
freshly ground black pepper

1 Bring the stock to the boil.

2 Sprinkle in the rice and simmer gently for about 15 minutes or until the rice is tender. To test this, fish out a grain of rice and bite it. If it is still hard, further cooking is required.

3 Meanwhile, break the eggs into a bowl, add the lemon juice and beat (stir vigorously) with a fork.

4 When the rice is cooked, remove the pan from the heat.

Home-made stocks are satisfying to make and not too taxing on the cook. Meat stocks do require long cooking but this can be stopped and started again as suits you. Pictured just before straining are: Top left, subtly flavoured chicken stock; Bottom left, quickly-cooked fish stock; Right, rich and beefy brown stock.

5 Stir a ladleful of hot stock into the egg mixture.

6 Add the egg mixture to the pan of stock, whisking in with a rotary or balloon whisk.

7 Reheat soup over low heat, stirring gently until it is the consistency of thin cream. Do not allow the soup to boil or the eggs will scramble.

8 Season and serve.

TASTY CHICKEN AND MUSHROOM SOUP

Dried Chinese mushrooms which are available from Chinese supermarkets are best for this soup as they have a strong, distinctive flavour. If dried are unobtainable use sliced fresh mushrooms instead.

SERVES 4–6
1.15 L [2 pt] chicken stock
50 g [2 oz] dried sliced Chinese mushrooms or 4 button mushrooms thinly sliced
125 g [5 oz] cooked chicken breast
salt
freshly ground black pepper
sprigs of watercress to garnish

1 Reconstitute the dried mushrooms by soaking in hot water for 20 minutes or until swollen.

2 Skin the chicken breast and cut into slivers.

3 Bring the stock to the boil. Add the

Chicken stock is the basis for this Chinese-style chicken and mushroom soup.

drained mushrooms and chicken.

4 Simmer for 5 minutes. Season to taste and garnish with watercress.

Variations

● For a luxurious version of chicken and mushroom soup, add 60 ml [4 tablespoons] of dry sherry just before serving.
● Instead of chicken meat use turkey or pork. Just before the end of cooking, add a few slices of cucumber.

STRACCIATELLA

It is essential to stir while adding the egg or it will set in a solid lump rather than being dispersed in fine threads (or rags, to give the literal Italian translation). Serve immediately or the egg will overcook and become rubbery in texture.

SERVES 4–6
1.15 L [2 pt] chicken stock
30 ml [2 tablespoons] grated Parmesan cheese
2 eggs

1 Break the eggs into a bowl. Add the cheese and beat (stir vigorously) with a fork until well blended.

2 Bring the stock to the boil over medium heat.

3 As soon as the stock reaches boil-

ing point, add the egg and cheese, pouring in a thin stream and stirring the stock vigorously to break the egg into strands.

4 Remove from heat and serve immediately.

HOT AND SOUR SOUP

Because this soup is Chinese in origin many of the ingredients are rather exotic. If you are unable to obtain bamboo shoots, use a small can of drained asparagus tips instead. Ordinary open mushrooms can be used instead of the dried Chinese kind and sunflower oil can be substituted for sesame oil.

SERVES 4
850 ml [1½ pt] beef stock
50 g [2 oz] dried sliced Chinese mushrooms or 4 fresh mushrooms sliced
30 ml [1 tablespoon] soy sauce
2.5 ml [½ teaspoon] chilli sauce
salt
freshly ground black pepper
100 g [¼ lb] rump steak
100g [4 oz] canned bamboo shoots
4 spring onions
30 ml [1 tablespoon] dry sherry

1 Soak the mushrooms in hot water for 20 minutes. Drain and discard the liquid.

2 Bring the stock to the boil. Add the soy sauce, chilli sauce, salt and pepper. Remove from heat.

3 Using a sharp knife, cut the meat into very thin strips.

4 Drain the bamboo shoots and cut into small pieces.

5 Trim the spring onions and cut in half.

6 Return the stock to the heat and bring back to the boil.

7 Add the meat, reduce heat and simmer for 5 minutes.

8 Add the bamboo shoots and onions and simmer for a further 4 minutes.

9 Remove from heat, stir in the sherry and serve immediately.

Soups

hearty soups

A meal cooked using only one pan and served in the dish in which it was cooked has an obvious advantage when it comes to washing up. Meal-in-a-bowl soups are easy and economic to make; and they are hot, tasty and filling—ideal family fare on a cold day.

There are two types of hearty soups. The end result is much the same in both cases, really a cross between a soup and a stew comprising a thin but richly-flavoured liquid filled with meat, vegetables and other delicious ingredients of your choice.

There is only one major difference between the two types of soup—the cooking time. Broths are based on meaty bones and water, so long simmering is essential to extract maximum flavour from the meat to produce a tasty liquid. The liquid element in stock-based soup is, of course, very tasty right from the start, so cooking time is relatively brief – just long enough to cook the ingredients that are served in it.

The liquid is not thickened with flour, cream or eggs in either broths or stock-based soups, but some of the ingredients (such as potato) may disintegrate during cooking and thus thicken the liquid a little. The soups are made substantial by the inclusion of the many solid ingredients which are cooked and served in it. You can use all sorts of vegetables, pulses (dried peas, beans and lentils), pasta, rice, barley, tapioca, meat (including sliced Frankfurters and other sausages), cheese and even poached eggs. These soups are, therefore, an excellent and economic way of using up leftovers or quantities of fresh food too small to make a dish on their own.

These hearty soups are excellent for inexpensive family meals, particularly if they are served with crusty bread and butter. They are so filling that all you need serve afterwards is cheese and a salad or fruit. You can also adapt these soups for the first course of a meal: for the same number of people, use the quantity of bones and liquid specified in a recipe but reduce the other ingredients by half to make the soup slightly less substantial.

BROTHS

Although broths require long slow cooking, they need comparatively little attention from the cook so they are a good dish to make when you plan to spend an afternoon in the kitchen doing other jobs such as making pastry or on wash day.

It is important to choose bones with a high proportion of meat attached to them in order to flavour the liquid well and provide chunks of meat to eat in the final dish. Rinse the bones quickly under a cold running tap to wash away any dirt or scum. Then cut away and discard (or render down) as much fat as possible.

The vegetables used in broths should always be fresh. Trim and chop them finely and add them to the pan near the beginning of cooking time.

Cut surfaces and lengthy cooking time do not matter when making broths because, although these factors inevitably mean that flavour and nutrients will escape from the

Minestrone, based on home-made beef stock, is rich and nourishing.

11

ingredients themselves, they are trapped in the liquid.

Cereals, pulses and pasta, if used, are cooked in the broth only for as long as is needed to make them tender. There is no point in adding them to the pan any earlier because, unlike meat and vegetables, they do not add any flavour to the liquid—they only increase the bulk of the final dish.

Broths, like stocks, should be meticulously skimmed during the early stages of cooking and any fat that floats to the surface should be removed before serving. This is particularly important when a fatty cut of meat, such as mutton scrag, is used or the final dish will be unpleasantly oily.

Broths are not strained before serving. They are served complete with all the ingredients that went into their making—except, of course, the bones. Lift the bones out when the broth is cooked, and discard them (or save for making a second stock) after removing the meat. The meat should be well cooked after long simmering and fall easily from the bone. Cut the meat into bite-sized pieces, discarding any gristle, fat or skin that might be attached. Return the meat to the pan and reheat gently before serving.

STOCK-BASED SOUPS

These soups are very simple and comparatively quick to prepare: cooking time is determined by how long it takes to tenderize the hardest ingredient. The choice of ingredients is almost limitless and includes left-over cooked foods as well as fresh ones. But for really tasty results two things are essential. First, the stock must be really well flavoured (and that means a good home-made stock as described in the last chapter. Secondly, the ingredients must be added to the pan in the right order and at suitable intervals so that everything is tender, hot and ready to serve at the same time. Those requiring the longest cooking time, such as pulses, must be added right from the start. Add hard root vegetables next, cut into 2.5 cm [1"] dice, then pasta or rice, followed by the softer fresh vegetables, again cut into 2.5 cm [1"] dice, and, finally, any cooked ingredients (such as left-over vegetables, bite-sized pieces of meat and slices of sausage) which simply need heating through.

Step-by-step broth

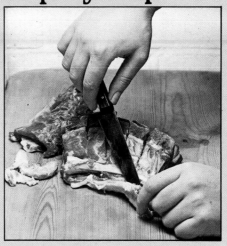

1 Rinse bones under cold running water. Using a sharp knife cut away as much fat as possible.

2 Put the meaty bones in a large flameproof casserole or saucepan and cover with cold water.

4 Add salt (and barley if used), cover the pan with a lid and simmer gently for 30 minutes.

5 Thoroughly scrub or peel the vegetables and cut them into dice about 2.5 cm [1"] square.

7 Turn off heat. Lift bones from the pan and discard after removing meat. Cut the meat into pieces.

8 Float kitchen paper or a slice of bread on the surface of the broth to mop up liquid surface fat.

3 Bring slowly to the boil. Using a flat skimmer, remove scum and rising fat as it forms.

6 Add the vegetables to the pan and continue simmering, covered, for a further 1½ hours.

9 Put bite-sized pieces of meat into the pan and gently reheat the broth. Garnish and serve.

SCOTCH BROTH

Here is a traditional and very popular broth. The secret for success lies in removing as much of the fat as possible from the meat, both before and after cooking. Cook and serve Scotch broth straight from the saucepan or, if you wish to take the dish to the table, in a large flameproof casserole.

SERVES 6
**700 g [1½ lb] mutton scrag
  or middle neck of lamb
5 ml [1 teaspoon] salt
40 g [1½ oz] pearl barley
3 small carrots
3 small leeks
2 small turnips
1 onion
2 celery stalks
freshly ground black pepper
15 ml [1 tablespoon]
  parsley**

1 Rinse the meaty bones under a cold running tap and shake to drain.

2 Cut away as much fat as possible and discard. Chop the bones, if the butcher has not done this, so they will fit into your pan.

3 Put the bones into the pan and cover with 1.7 L [3 pt] cold water.

4 Bring slowly to the boil. When scum and surface fat form, skim them away with a flat skimmer or perforated spoon. Skim for several minutes as the fat rises.

5 When all the scum has been removed, add the salt and barley. Cover the pan with the lid and simmer for 30 minutes.

6 Prepare the vegetables by scrubbing or peeling. Chop them into 2.5 cm [1″] dice.

7 Add the vegetables and cover the pan with a lid and continue simmering for a further 1½ hours.

8 When the broth is cooked, turn off heat and lift the bones on to a plate, using a perforated spoon.

9 Using a fork, detach the meat from the bones and shred or cut it into bite-sized pieces. Discard bones and any fat or gristle.

10 Remove as much surface fat as possible from the broth, mopping it up with absorbent kitchen paper or slices of bread.

11 Return the meat to the pan. Reheat gently and adjust seasoning to taste.

12 Sprinkle the broth with chopped parsley just before serving.

COCK-A-LEEKIE

This is another substantial Scottish soup suitable for a family meal. Not all the chicken meat is used in the final soup. After cooking, breast meat can be saved and used for a salad or another dish. For maximum economy, a small proportion – about 75 g [3 oz] – of chicken skin can be included in the soup, but only use the thinnest and whitest skin and chop it into strips smaller than a matchstick. Prunes are traditionally served in the dish and add an unusual element to a white soup. Include some of the green part of the leeks to add welcome colour to this soup.

SERVES 6
**1.8 kg [4 lb] boiling fowl
12 large prunes
1.4 kg [3 lb] leeks
2 celery stalks
bouquet garni
salt and pepper**

1 Put the prunes in a small saucepan. Cover with cold water and bring to the boil.

2 Remove the pan from the heat, cover with a lid and set aside until cold.

3 Place the chicken in a large flameproof casserole or saucepan and add 2.2 L [4 pt] cold water. Use more water if necessary because the chicken should be completely covered.

4 Place the pan over a moderately high heat and bring to boil.

5 Using a flat skimmer or perforated spoon, skim off any scum that rises to the surface.

6 Reduce heat, cover the pan with a well-fitting lid and simmer for an hour.

Herb dumplings in beef broth make an economical and filling meal-in-a-bowl. Oxtail broth, served without the meat, is an economical soup.

7 Meanwhile, wash and prepare the vegetables. Retaining 5 cm [2"] of the green stem, cut the leeks into 2.5 cm [1"] lengths. Cut the celery into 12 mm [½"] lengths.

8 When the hour is up, add the vegetables and bouquet garni to the pan.

9 Half cover the pan with a lid and simmer for a further 50 minutes.

10 Drain the prunes, slit them open and discard stones.

11 Add the prunes to the pan. Half cover it with the lid and continue simmering for 10 minutes or until the chicken is well cooked and falls easily from the bones. You can test this by lifting the chicken from the pan. If a leg joint is easily pulled off the body, the chicken is ready and will be easy to dismember.

12 Turn the heat off and lift the chicken out of the pan on to a plate.

13 When the chicken has cooled a little, skin and dismember it using your hands.

14 Discard the bones and all the skin except the best-looking bit over the breast.

15 Set the breast meat aside to use in another dish, and the leg meat, too, if you wish.

16 Cut the remaining pieces of meat into bite-sized pieces.

17 Roll the breast skin tightly and cut into thin slivers with scissors.

18 Using absorbent kitchen paper or a slice of bread, remove surface fat from the soup. Remove and discard the bouquet garni.

19 Add the bite-sized pieces of chicken and slivers of breast skin to the pan.

20 Reheat gently. Check seasoning and serve.

Making croûtons

Crispy cubes of freshly fried bread floated on the top of the soup as it is served make it look more attractive and add crunchy texture. Home-made croûtons are very much nicer than any cracker or soup-sprinkle that you can buy – and they are much more economical.

Stale bread makes better croûtons than fresh bread and this is a good use for the ends of loaves. Three or four thick slices will make enough croûtons for four people.

Fry the croûtons in shallow fat until golden, then drain them thoroughly on kitchen paper. Serve immediately or keep warm in a low oven until required.

You will need about 50 g [2 oz] of fat to fry croûtons made from four slices of bread. If you have sufficient quantity of bacon dripping this will give the croûtons a lovely flavour. Other suitable fats are butter (add 5 ml [1 teaspoon] of oil to prevent the butter from burning) and tasteless vegetable oil.

Plain, unflavoured croûtons are always popular but you can flavour them if you wish.

Make a garlic paste by chopping a clove of garlic finely, then mashing it in 5 ml [1 teaspoon] of salt with the edge of a round-bladed knife. Work in 15 ml [1 tablespoon] of butter to make sufficient paste to spread on four slices.

Commercial anchovy paste can be used in place of garlic salt and butter but it must be spread thinly or flavour will be overpowering. Fish-flavoured croûtons are not suitable for all soups.

OXTAIL BROTH

In this recipe vegetables and meat are gently fried in oil before the water is added. This gives the broth extra flavour and a rich brown colour. Because oxtail is inclined to be very fatty it is important to remove as much fat as possible after cooking. It is therefore best to chill the broth completely so that all the fat solidifies and can be lifted off the soup.

SERVES 4
1 oxtail, weighing about 700 g [1½ lb]
1 large onion
1 small turnip
1 celery stalk
2 cloves
15 ml [1 tablespoon] vegetable oil
salt
6 peppercorns
1 bay leaf
2 small carrots
15 ml [1 tablespoon] parsley

1 Rinse the oxtail under cold running water and shake dry. Using a sharp knife, divide it into joints and remove fat.

2 Scrub the vegetables, halve the onion and turnip and chop the celery into four pieces. Stud the onion with the cloves.

3 Warm the oil in a large flameproof casserole or saucepan over medium heat.

4 When the oil is hot add the vegetables and fry, turning, until lightly browned all over.

5 Add the oxtail pieces to the pan and fry until browned.

6 Pour on 1.15 L [2 pt] cold water and bring to the boil.

7 Remove scum and fat with a skimmer or perforated spoon.

8 Reduce heat and add some salt,

1 Spread the flavouring, if used, on four thick slices of bread.

2 Pile up the slices and remove the crusts.

3 Cut the crustless bread into cubes and set aside.

4 When the fat is hot add the croûtons, spread in a single layer.

5 Fry for about 2 minutes, turning to brown on all sides.

6 Lift out of the pan and thoroughly drain on kitchen paper.

15

peppercorns and bay leaf. Cover pan with a well-fitting lid and simmer gently for 3 hours.

9 Strain the broth through a colander into a large bowl. Discard the vegetables and seasonings and transfer the bones to a plate.

10 Using a fork or knife, remove the meat from the bones. Discard bones, fat and any gristle.

11 Reserve half the meat for another dish. Cut the remainder into bite-sized pieces.

12 When the shreds of meat are cold, put them into a rigid airtight container and refrigerate until required.

13 Cover the broth when cool and refrigerate for 8 hours or overnight.

14 Lift the cold fat from the surface of the broth and discard. Turn the broth into a pan and reheat gently.

15 Peel and trim the carrots and cut them into matchstick-sized pieces (called julienne strips).

16 Add the shreds of meat and julienne strips to the pan and cook for 3-4 minutes.

17 Chop the parsley and garnish the broth before serving.

BEEF SOUP WITH HERB DUMPLINGS

The addition of home-made dumplings makes this a very filling meal-in-a-bowl for a cold day. The dumplings shown here are beautifully light because breadcrumbs are used in place of some of the flour. In order to bind (hold together) the breadcrumbs thoroughly into the pastry, egg is used instead of water.

Make 4-5 small ones or one large one for each person. Add 20 minutes to the cooking time for larger ones.

Add shreds of meat reserved after making the broth or from leftovers.

SERVES 6
1.15 L [2 pt] beef stock
125 g [¼ lb] cooked beef cut into bite-sized pieces
75 g [3 oz] onion
75 g [3 oz] carrot

50 g [2 oz] potato
1 celery stalk
salt and pepper

For the dumplings:
50 g [2 oz] self-raising flour
50 g [2 oz] fresh breadcrumbs
50 g [2 oz] shredded suet
15 ml [1 tablespoon] freshly chopped mixed herbs
1 small egg
salt and pepper

1 Make the suet pastry for the dumplings by the usual method, adding the herbs and breadcrumbs with the dry ingredients. Beat the egg with a fork and add it in place of the usual water.

2 Put the dough on to a floured board. Divide it into pieces smaller than a walnut and roll each piece into a ball between your floured palms.

3 Put the beef stock into a flameproof casserole or saucepan and bring to simmering point.

4 Scrub or peel and trim the vegetables. Chop the onions, dice the carrots and potatoes, and slice the celery. Add to the pan and simmer for 5 minutes.

5 Add the dumplings, cover the pan with a lid and simmer for a further 10 minutes.

6 Two or three minutes before the end of cooking time, add the meat in shreds. Then check seasoning.

MINESTRONE

Pulses (dried peas, beans and lentils) must be soaked overnight and partially cooked before adding to the soup because they take so long to tenderize. Never cook pulses with salt because it hardens their skins; add salt only to the final dish just before serving.

When serving the soup, pass round a small bowl of grated Parmesan cheese so that each person can sprinkle more cheese on top of his soup. Offer diners croûtons, too, if you wish.

SERVES 6
50 g [2 oz] dried haricot beans
2 rashers bacon
1 clove garlic
1 medium-sized onion

3 tomatoes
1 large carrot
1 celery stalk
1.15 L [2 pt] beef or chicken stock
50 g [2 oz] pasta shapes
30 ml [2 tablespoons] Parmesan cheese
salt and pepper

1 Put the beans in a large bowl. Cover them with plenty of cold water and leave to soak overnight.

2 Drain the beans. Put them into a pan with fresh cold water and bring to the boil. Cover and simmer for 1 hour.

3 Chop the bacon into matchstick-sized pieces and put into a large flameproof casserole or saucepan. Place over low heat and cook until the fat starts to run.

4 Prepare the vegetables. Chop the garlic finely and cut the onion into thin slices.

5 Add the garlic and onion to the pan, cover and allow them to soften without colouring (this is called sweating). Shake the pan occasionally or stir to prevent sticking.

6 Add the stock to the pan, increase heat and bring to the boil.

7 Quarter the tomatoes and dice the other vegetables.

8 Add the carrots and drained, partly cooked beans. Reduce heat, cover the pan and simmer for 20 minutes.

9 Add the celery and tomatoes and continue simmering for a further 10 minutes.

10 Then bring the soup back to the boil and add the pasta shapes. Lower the heat and simmer until they are soft. The timing will depend on the size of the pasta – be guided by the packet instructions. For small shapes 8 minutes should be enough, for larger ones 12 minutes.

11 Stir in 30 ml [2 tablespoons] Parmesan cheese, season to taste with salt and freshly ground pepper and serve.

Moules à la marinière

Moules à la marinière

Shellfish add a touch of luxury to any meal; mussels are a great treat and fortunately they do not cost a great deal—rather the reverse.

This dish comes from France's Atlantic coast and is excellent, providing that the mussels are fresh and thoroughly cleaned. Gritty mussels are unpleasant to eat, while sand left in the soup will collect in the liquor, turning it grey. Dead mussels can give you nasty food poisoning, so be sure that they are alive, by the means described here.

Serve moules à la marinière as a meal-in-a-bowl for two people or a first course for four. For a meal-in-a-bowl buy 1 kg [2¼ lb] of mussels per person if sold by weight, or 1 L [1 qt] if sold by volume.

If a large number of mussels in the fishmonger's tray are open or the shells are broken, do not buy them because these will be dead. (Live mussels usually keep their shells closed when they are out of water.)

When you get home, clean the mussels thoroughly. This is not difficult but it does take time. Keep the cleaned mussels immersed in a bowl of water until required for cooking, changing the water several times.

Eat mussels on the day of purchase whenever possible. If you have to leave them overnight, add some salt to the water. If wished you can add a little flour or oatmeal, too, to feed the mussels so they become plump and white. Cover the bowl with a clean cloth and put in a cool place.

After cooking, check again that your mussels are fresh. Heat should force the shells open so discard any that remain closed.

It is usual to remove half the shell from each mussel before serving. This is to reduce the amount of shell in the soup bowls. Put an empty plate in the centre of the table for the remaining halves of the shells as each person discards them.

Serve in soup bowls with the mussels piled up, and provide spoons for the soup liquid. To eat the mussels, you pick the shell up in your fingers and tip the mussel into your mouth, discarding the empty shell. It is therefore a good idea to provide big napkins to wipe sticky fingers, and finger-bowls would also be useful.

SERVES 2
2 kg [2 quarts] mussels
1 onion
1 shallot (or a second onion)
1 garlic clove
4 parsley stalks
thyme sprig or dried thyme
salt and pepper
40 g [1½ oz] butter
200 ml [7 fl oz] dry white wine
  or dry cider
75 ml [3 fl oz] water
15 ml [1 tablespoon] chopped
  parsley

1 Mussels should be absolutely fresh. Tap any open mussel. Discard it if it does not shut.

5 When ready to cook, drain the mussels. Chop the garlic, onion and shallot very finely.

6 Melt butter in a large saucepan over low heat. Add vegetables, cover and sweat for 10 minutes.

10 Reduce the heat and cook for a further 3 minutes to make sure the mussels are cooked.

11 Strain the liquor through a colander into a second saucepan. Discard the herbs.

2 Using your hands, pull away beards (any hanging seaweed gripped between the two shells).

3 Scrub the mussels under cold running water. Scrape away encrustations with a sharp knife.

4 Keep the mussels in a bowl of cold water until ready to cook. Change the water several times.

7 Tie parsley stalks and thyme with a piece of fine string. Or tie up dried thyme in buttermuslin.

8 Add the herbs, wine or cider and water to the pan. Heat through slowly until almost boiling.

9 Add the mussels, cover and shake gently over fierce heat for 2 minutes to open the shells.

12 Discard any mussels that are still tightly shut. Remove half a shell from each that is open.

13 Add the mussels on their half shells to the liquor in the pan. Reheat gently and season to taste.

14 Ladle soup into a tureen or bowls, heaping up the mussels in the centre. Garnish with parsley.

19

French onion soup makes an economical and satisfying start to the meal.

French onion soup

This classic soup is unusual because it introduces cheese at the beginning of the meal. Serve the soup in a large oven proof tureen or six individual oven proof bowls, each topped with an island of sizzling toasted cheese. Each person submerges his own cheese island under the soup as he eats it, pressing the bread against the bottom of the bowl with the edge of a soup spoon to cut it into bite-sized pieces. If you do not have time to make beef stock, you could use canned consommé. For an extra rich soup add 15 ml [1 tablespoon] of brandy per serving. Stir in the brandy just before the end of cooking.

SERVES 6
350 g [¾ lb] onions
75 g [3 oz] margarine
1 L [2 pt] well-flavoured beef
  stock
bay leaf
salt and pepper
6 thick slices of French bread
100 g [¼ lb] Emmenthal cheese
30 ml [2 tablespoons] Parmesan
  cheese

1 Skin and finely chop the onions.

2 Melt the margarine in a heavy-based pan. Add the onions and cook over a low heat, stirring occasionally, until browned.

3 Add the stock and bay leaf. Season with salt and pepper. Cover pan and simmer gently for 30 minutes.

4 Grate the Emmenthal cheese, put it in a bowl, add the Parmesan cheese and mix the two together.

5 Heat the grill and heat the oven to 200°C [400°F] gas mark 6.

6 Toast the bread lightly on each side.

7 Remove the bay leaf and pour the soup into an oven proof soup tureen or six individual bowls.

8 Cover each slice of bread with cheese and float the bread on top of the soup.

9 Carefully put the soup tureen or bowls into the oven·and cook for 10–15 minutes, or until the cheese is melted and sizzling.

Green pea and bacon soup

Serve this hearty soup with crisp French bread.

Dried green peas are very hard when they are bought so they must be soaked overnight before they can be used. Green peas are available either whole or split. Both can be used to make this soup.

You can use 75 g [3 oz] diced cooked ham instead of bacon rashers. Add it at step 9.

If you make the soup in advance, up to step 8 in the recipe, it will keep, covered, in the refrigerator for 3 days. It will not keep quite so long after the milk has been added so if you have any soup left over, eat it within 2 days.

SERVES 6
200 g [7 oz] dried green peas
1.7 L [3 pt] ham or bacon
   stock
1 large onion
1 small carrot
a small piece of turnip
4 bacon rashers
50 g [2 oz] butter
bouquet garni
150 ml [¼ pt] milk

1 Soak the dried peas in water for at least 8 hours or overnight. The water must be cold and must cover the peas.

2 Peel and chop the onion into small pieces.

3 Scrub and chop the carrot. Peel and chop the turnip.

4 Remove and discard bacon rind.

Cut bacon into small pieces using kitchen scissors.

5 Melt the butter in a large heavy-based saucepan over low heat. Do not allow it to brown.

6 Add the bacon and chopped vegetables. Cook until the bacon and onion are just transparent.

7 Drain any surplus water off the peas and add to the pan with the stock and bouquet garni. Bring to the boil and cover.

8 Simmer over low heat for 2-2½ hours until the vegetables are reduced to a pulp.

9 Just before serving, remove the bouquet garni, check seasoning, add cooked ham if used, stir in the milk and reheat if necessary.

Soups

purée soups

For generous flavour, nourishment, good texture and simplicity of method, purée soups are a beginner's delight. You will find the inviting smells and superb flavour of a home-made soup tremendously satisfying.

Creamy vegetable purée soups are amazingly quick to make, and really economical too. A soup tureen makes an excellent investment for the shoestring cook – guests will be lured to the dining table by warm, inviting smells, and the delicious taste of a simple soup is so utterly different from canned products, as well as being really wholesome and nourishing. Purée soups make a very satisfying start to a meal, and the simple addition of swirls of cream or a garnish, such as crisply fried golden croûtons, will turn a simple soup into real dinner party fare.

VEGETABLE PUREE SOUPS

Basically, vegetable purée soups are made with vegetables and the liquid in which they were cooked. Ingredients are reduced to a purée by pushing through a vegetable mill, rubbing through a sieve or blending in a liquidizer. The resulting purée is usually substantial enough to serve as it is and needs no thickening agent in the form of a roux or eggs or cream. Flavour and texture, however, can be improved if a little fat is used to sweat the vegetables before the liquid is added and to enrich them just before serving.

The vegetables

It is important to use fresh vegetables but because the vegetables are reduced to a pulp, purée soups offer an excellent and economic opportunity to use slightly overripe vegetables or foods which might otherwise go to waste, such as the outer leaves of lettuce, slightly tough end-of-season peas, watercress stalks or mushroom peel. You can make delicious soups using either a single vegetable or a judicious mixture of several vegetables.

Tubers such as potatoes and Jerusalem artichokes, root vegetables such as carrots, parsnips and turnips, cauliflower and pulses (dried peas, beans and lentils) will all purée to a thick soup after cooking.

Vegetables such as mushrooms, tomatoes, onions, celery, cucumbers, asparagus, spinach, lettuce and watercress do not have much substance in themselves. If used alone, very large quantities would be needed to create the right consistency for a purée soup. An additional vegetable (such as a potato) therefore is usually added to give the starchy ingredient which is necessary for thickening.

The liquid

Stock is probably the most frequently used liquid. Chicken or other white stocks are the most suitable because brown stocks can be too strong and might overpower the flavour of the vegetable. By all means use vegetable stock where suitable. For example, for pea soup make stock from the pea pods (see the chapter on stocks). The liquid from canned peas also makes excellent stock.

Vegetable cooking water may be used as a liquid base. Taste it first to check that the flavour is not overpowering as this could ruin a delicate soup. The water in which a cauliflower has been cooked, for instance, makes a valuable addition to parsnip soup.

Milk can be used, either on its own or with other liquids, but take care not to dilute it too much as this can cause curdling.

THE BASIC METHOD

Preparing the vegetables for a purée soup should be quick and easy. Clean all vegetables and, if necessary, peel them. There is no need to spend a lot of time peeling vegetables that are to be sieved because the skins will be caught in the bowl of the sieve. Roughly slice or chop the vegetables; it doesn't matter how small you chop them up as any goodness that escapes during cooking is captured in the soup. Using small pieces of food speeds up cooking time and saves fuel costs.

Sweating

Once you have prepared the vegetables, the next and very important step when making a hot vegetable purée soup is to sweat the vegetables as this will make them really tender and tasty.

To sweat vegetables, melt a little butter – about 25 g [1 oz] to 450 g [1 lb] vegetables – in a heavy-based saucepan. Oil can be used if preferred; vegetable or sunflower oil are best – olive oil would probably give too distinctive a flavour. Dripping, especially bacon dripping, can be used to advantage when you are making, say, a pea soup because the flavours are complementary. Margarine can be substituted for butter but it has nothing like the good, rich flavour of butter. Add the vegetables to the melted fat and shake the pan or stir to coat the vegetables all over. Cover and cook gently over low heat for 5-10 minutes to soften the vegetables and allow them to absorb the fat without burning.

Never be tempted to try to speed up this process by increasing the heat. Fast cooking would fry the vegetables and give them a hard outer skin which would stop the fat from being absorbed. Frying would also spoil the colour of the soup.

Plain and chilled soup: fat tends to coagulate when cold, spoiling texture and appearance, so sweating is always omitted when the soup is to be served chilled. The process is usually omitted, too, when a very plain and easily digested soup is being prepared as the fat would make it too rich. In these cases the prepared vegetables are cooked directly with the liquid.

Adding the liquid

After the vegetables have sweated for about 5 to 10 minutes and have absorbed most of the fat, pour on the cold liquid. Season lightly with salt and pepper and complementary herbs and spices, if used. Bring to simmering point, cover and simmer until ingredients are quite tender – about 15-25 minutes, depending on the vegetables used. Do not overcook, especially if you are using green vegetables or the flavour and colour will be lost.

Making the purée

There are three methods of puréeing the soups: using a vegetable mill, a sieve or a liquidizer. These pieces of equipment vary in price and in the final texture they achieve. However, they are all equally efficient so choose the machine to suit your needs and your pocket.

A vegetable mill is probably the most versatile method of puréeing because the resulting texture can be matched to suit the chosen ingredients by using the fine, medium or coarse attachment. A celery soup, for example, would require the fine grid to make it really smooth whereas the turnip and cucumber soup would be better if given a slightly coarser texture by milling the vegetables through the coarse grid.

Using a liquidizer is probably the quickest and easiest way of reducing the vegetables with their cooking liquid to a purée (although it may be necessary to sieve the soup after blending to remove fibres). A liquid-

Step-by-step vegetable purée soup

1 Melt butter in a pan. Add prepared vegetables, cover and sweat gently over low heat for 5-10 minutes.

2 After sweating, season and add liquid. Cover the pan and simmer for 15-25 minutes until tender.

3 To purée vegetables using a vegetable mill, hold over another saucepan and turn the handle.

4 To purée vegetables using a sieve, pour contents of pan into sieve, and press vegetables through.

5 To purée vegetables using a liquidizer, pour contents of pan into the goblet and blend.

6 Reheat soup gently over low heat. Adjust seasoning and enrich if desired. Do not allow to boil.

izer produces a consistently smooth result but in some cases this will be rather too textureless for a purée soup.

Serving
If the soup is to be served hot, reheat gently after puréeing and adjust seasoning to taste. Add more liquid if the consistency is too thick. If too thin, the soup can be simmered, uncovered, to reduce the quantity by evaporation – but this process is not effective when much thickening is needed. Enrich if you wish.

Enriching
This is an optional extra, done just before serving, to add a creamy texture and improve flavour. Simply stir small pats of butter, a little cream or sour cream into the soup. If the soup is to be served hot, stir over a low heat until warmed through but on no account allow it to boil or it may curdle, particularly if thin cream is used. For a more dramatic effect, dish the soup into individual bowls or a soup tureen and then add the cream by dribbling swirls over the top of the soup.

Serving cold soups
If the soup is to be served cold remember that the consistency can afford to be slightly thinner because soup thickens on cooling. The seasoning should be rather stronger since flavours appear to diminish when ingredients are chilled. Cool the soup, cover and chill thoroughly for about 3 hours before serving. Don't be tempted to speed up the chilling process by floating ice cubes in the soup – it will only dilute the flavours and make a watery soup.

STORING
Purée soups can be kept both in the refrigerator and freezer.
In the refrigerator: allow soup to cool and pour into a container with an airtight lid. Covered, the soup will keep for up to 4 days.
In the freezer: allow soup to cool. Pour soup into ice-cube trays. Freeze if necessary then empty cubes into plastic bags, seal and store in freezer. Alternatively, pour soup into an airtight container, leaving 12 mm [½"] head-space, and cover with the lid and freeze. Either way, the soup should keep for up to 2 months.

COMBINATION SOUPS
One vegetable alone makes a delicious soup, but a mixture of two or more vegetables can also be excellent and the addition of herbs and spices can improve both types. Here are a few ideas.
● Make a colourful soup from celeriac and tomatoes. Sieve the soup to remove tomato seeds and flavour with chopped chives and a little grated orange zest.
● Combine parsnip and apple and flavour with a little sage.
● Make a creamy soup from onion and cauliflower, and add a touch of colour by flavouring and garnishing with paprika or ground nutmeg.
● Fresh sorrel leaves make a delicious, strongly flavoured soup. Adding a little potato thickens the soup and will make it go further; stir in a generous amount of thin cream before serving.
● For potage bonne femme, a classic and economic French soup, use a mixture of leeks, carrots and potatoes, with a pinch of sugar to bring out the sweetness of the carrots.
● For a delicately flavoured and coloured courgette purée soup, do not peel the courgettes. Cook them in light chicken stock and flavour with chervil or dillweed.
● For Irish potato soup, simmer equal quantities of potatoes and onions in milk.
● For an instant iced tomato soup to rival gazpacho, crush a small garlic clove with salt. Put into a liquidizer with canned tomatoes and their liquid. Add a pinch of sugar, salt and pepper and a good squeeze of lemon juice. Sieve after liquidizing to eliminate tomato seeds.

Amounts to use for single vegetable purée soups		
Vegetable	**Liquid**	**Butter**
Carrots 450 g [1 lb]	550 ml [1 pt]	25 g [1 oz]
Celery 450 g [1 lb]	1.15 L [2 pt]	25 g [1 oz]
Courgettes 225 g [½ lb]	550 ml [1 pt]	40 g [1½ oz]
Leeks 450 g [1 lb]	550 ml [1 pt]	25 g [1 oz]
Mushrooms 225 g [½ lb]	550 ml [1 pt] half stock and half milk	25 g [1 oz]
Onions 450 g [1 lb]	550 ml [1 pt]	40 g [1½ oz]
Peas 700 g [1½ lb]	550 ml [1 pt]	25 g [1 oz]
Potatoes 450 g [1 lb]	550 ml [1 pt]	40 g [1½ oz]
Spinach 450 g [1 lb]	550 ml [1 pt]	25 g [1 oz]
Tomatoes 450 g [1 lb]	550 ml [1 pt]	25 g [1 oz]
Watercress (4 bunches) 450 g [1 lb]	1.15 L [2 pt]	

FRUIT PUREE SOUPS

Fruit purée soups are Scandinavian in origin and are very popular in those countries. Although it may sound strange at first to some tastes, in fact fruit purée soups have a deliciously delicate flavour and make a superbly refreshing beginning and, sometimes, end to a meal. Similar in method and resulting texture to vegetable purée soups, fruit purée soups are made from fresh, and sometimes from dried, fruit.

Fruit

For best results use fresh, ripe fruit. Apples, pears, cherries, apricots, plums, pumpkins, peaches, blackberries, raspberries, loganberries, strawberries and melons can all be used.

Of the dried fruit, apricots and prunes give best results; apples and pears can also be used.

Making fruit soup rarely involves sweating the fruit because the soup is always served cold and the fat tends to rise to the top and spoil it, and most fruit don't need the extra softening.

The liquid

Water, red or white wine, or a mixture of water and wine are the most commonly used liquids. Apple juice can be used in place of the white wine. Chicken stock or beef stock are sometimes used, usually with apple or pumpkin.

Thickening fruit soups

Fruit soups made with a single fruit which has a high water content (for example, cherries, plums and apricots) are thickened with cornflour. This is done after the fruit has been cooked. For every 450 g [1 lb] fruit and 1.15 L [2 pt] liquid you will need 30 ml [2 tablespoons] cornflour.

Flavouring

If you are serving the soup as a first course it may be flavoured with nutmeg, cinnamon, cloves, lemon peel or ginger and occasionally curry powder. Stir in fresh or sour cream or yoghurt just before serving.

If you are serving the soup as a pudding, stir in sweetened whipped cream and dust with nutmeg or cinnamon just before serving.

PREPARING THE FRUIT

Prepare the fruit by cleaning, peeling, coring, seeding or stoning until only fruit pulp is left. If you are puréeing the cooked fruit through a sieve or a vegetable mill, you can leave the skins and stones of apricots and plums intact as they will add extra flavour to the liquid and be strained off during puréeing.

Soak dried fruit overnight in the liquid to be used in the recipe.

Cooking the fruit

Put fruit in the saucepan and add the liquid and complementary flavourings. When both wine and water are used in the recipe, only the water is added at this stage. Wine is added after the fruit is puréed so that it is not simmered for a long time.

Bring to simmering point and simmer, covered, until ingredients are quite tender – about 10-25 minutes, depending on fruit used.

Making the purée

With the exception of berry fruit, purée in the same way as for vegetables using a liquidizer or vegetable mill. Only very fleshy berry fruit, such as strawberries, can be puréed in a vegetable mill. Smaller berry fruit such as blackberries, raspberries and loganberries are almost fleshless so purée these by sieving or by liquidizing and then sieving.

Before reducing the fruit to a purée spoon off and reserve some of the liquid if you want to thicken the soup.

Thickening the soup

In a medium-sized mixing bowl, blend 30 ml [2 tablespoons] cornflour into the reserved hot fruit juice. Stir the rest of the liquid into the cornflour mixture, then pour into the fruit purée. Add the wine, if used, at this stage. Bring to the boil over moderate heat, stirring, and simmer for 5 minutes.

Serving

Taste and adjust the seasoning. Enrich, as already described, if you wish. Serve cold in the same way as for vegetable purée soups.

TURNIP AND CUCUMBER SOUP

⧖⧖⧖ *This soup makes excellent and economical use of the part of a vegetable which is usually discarded. It is served cold, so the vegetables are not sweated.*

SERVES 4
225 g [½ lb] turnip tops
550 ml [1 pt] chicken stock
salt and pepper
1 medium-sized cucumber
250 ml [½ pt] sour cream
10 ml [2 teaspoons] freshly chopped dillweed

1 Wash turnip tops. Put into a saucepan, season and pour on the stock.

2 Bring to simmering point, cover and simmer for 20 minutes.

3 Reduce to a purée using a vegetable mill, sieve or liquidizer.

4 Peel and thinly slice cucumber. Stir into purée.

5 Allow to cool and then chill.

6 To serve, stir in sour cream and sprinkle with dillweed.

CREME DUBARRY

⧖ *Although it is made of modest ingredients this is a luxury soup named after the mistress of the French king, Louis XV.*

SERVES 4-6
65 g [2½ oz] butter
1 small cauliflower
1 celery stalk
1 medium-sized onion
salt and pepper
550 ml [1 pt] chicken stock
250 ml [½ pt] milk
pinch of ground nutmeg

1 Break cauliflower into florets. Slice onion and celery.

2 Melt 50 g [2 oz] butter in the saucepan and sweat vegetables in butter for 10 minutes, shaking pan occasionally.

3 Season and pour on stock and milk. Bring to simmering point, cover and simmer for 30 minutes or until vegetables are quite tender.

4 Reduce contents of pan to purée using vegetable mill, sieve or liquidizer.

5 Return soup to saucepan. Add nutmeg and reheat gently. Enrich the soup by stirring in the remaining butter cut into dice.

From Scandinavia, a deliciously cool fruit soup made from Morello cherries and white wine and flavoured with cinnamon.

CHILLED CHERRY SOUP

⧗⧗⧗ *The recipe gives the stoned weight of cherries, so you will need to buy about 1 kg [2 lb] altogether. Morello cherries add good colour and flavour to the soup which should be served as a refreshing dessert. A cheap, dry white wine is adequate to cook in the soup. Just before serving garnish each bowl with 15 ml [1 tablespoon] thin cream, small macaroons and a few whole cherries.*

SERVES 4-6
**450 g [1 lb] Morello cherries,
  stoned weight
225 g [½ lb] granulated sugar
half a cinnamon stick
1 lemon
30 ml [2 tablespoons] cornflour
400 ml [¾ pt] white wine**

1 Remove stalks and stone the cherries.

2 Place cherries in a medium-sized saucepan with the sugar, 550 ml [1 pt] water and the cinnamon.

3 Pare the zest from the lemon and add this to the pan.

4 Bring to simmering point, cover and simmer for 20 minutes.

5 Mix cornflour to a smooth paste with a little of the wine.

6 Stir the rest of the wine into the cornflour mixture and then pour into the soup.

7 Cook slowly, stirring until the soup comes to the boil and thickens slightly. Simmer for 5 minutes.

8 Remove and discard cinnamon and lemon rind.

9 Reduce contents of the pan to a purée using vegetable mill or liquidizer.

10 Allow to cool and then chill.

Variations
For chilled soups to start or finish a meal, use only 30 ml [2 tablespoons] sugar and replace the Morello cherries with any of the following flavours:
● 450 ml [1 lb] pears. Replace the cinnamon with 5 ml [1 teaspoon] ginger.
● Combine cherries with pears and replace white wine with red.
● Make a plum or apricot soup from 450 g [1 lb] plums or apricots and 50 g [2 oz] sugar. Replace the white wine with water and garnish with sour cream.
● Try a combination of melon and strawberry. Garnish with whole, small strawberries.

POTAGE CRECY

This is one of the most economical purée soups, both in terms of time and cost of ingredients. Old carrots will give the best flavour, especially if cooked with a pinch of sugar to bring out their sweetness.

SERVES 4
450 g [1 lb] carrots
1 large onion, weighing about
    225 g [½ lb]
40 g [1½ oz] butter
salt and pepper
550 ml [1 pt] stock
5 ml [1 teaspoon] freshly
    chopped thyme

1 Clean and thinly slice carrots. Finely chop onion.

2 Melt the butter in the saucepan and sweat vegetables in butter for 10 minutes, shaking the pan occasionally.

3 Season and pour on stock. Add chopped thyme. Bring to simmering point, cover and simmer for 20 minutes or until vegetables are quite tender.

4 Reduce contents of pan to a purée using a vegetable mill, sieve or liquidizer.

5 Return soup to the saucepan. Reheat gently. Enrich with a pat of butter, if liked.

PEA SOUP

Weigh the peas after shelling. Ham stock gives a good flavour to the soup. Halve the quantity of peas if you are using dried peas.

SERVES 4
700 g [1½ lb] peas
4 spring onions
25 g [1 oz] butter
salt and pepper
1.15 L [2 pt] stock
10 ml [2 teaspoons] freshly
    chopped mint

1 Chop the onions. Melt the butter in the saucepan, sweat peas and onions in butter for 10 minutes, shaking the pan occasionally.

2 Season and pour on stock. Bring to simmering point, cover and simmer for 20 minutes or until vegetables are quite tender.

3 Reduce contents of pan to a purée using a vegetable mill, sieve or liquidizer.

4 Return soup to pan. Stir in mint and reheat.

Variations
● Use drained, canned peas and only 550 ml [1 pt] liquid, including some of the liquid from the can for additional flavour.
● Substitute fresh broad beans for the peas.

CURRIED APPLE SOUP

This recipe includes onion which would normally be softened by sweating in butter but because the soup is served chilled this is not done. Choose a crisp type of apple such as Cox or Granny Smith. To garnish the soup reserve some paper-thin slices of unpeeled apple brushed with a little lemon juice.

SERVES 6
700 g [1½ lb] dessert apples
1 small onion
2.5 ml [½ teaspoon] lemon juice
2.5 ml [½ teaspoon] turmeric
2.5 ml [½ teaspoon] ground
    cumin
2.5 ml [½ teaspoon] ground
    coriander
pinch of chilli powder
salt
a pinch of ground cloves
850 ml [1½ pt] chicken stock
150 ml [¼ pt] thin cream
90 ml [6 tablespoons] natural
    yoghurt

1 Peel, core and chop the apples. Peel and finely chop the onion.

2 Put apples and onion in a saucepan, cover with half the stock and seasoning. Cover the pan and simmer for about 10 minutes or until tender.

3 Reduce contents of pan to a purée using vegetable mill, sieve or liquidizer. Stir in the remaining stock.

4 Allow to cool. When cold, stir in the cream and yoghurt, cover and chill.

5 Just before serving stir in 150 ml [¼ pt] cold water if the soup seems too thick. Check for seasoning and

add more salt and pepper if necessary.

6 Garnish with reserved apple slices.

GAZPACHO

This is a classic Spanish iced soup in which the vegetables are puréed raw. A liquidizer is best for the job – a sieve is totally unsuitable because of the raw, hard vegetables. Pass around small bowls each containing extra ingredients of cold croûtons, chopped olives, chopped cucumber, chopped onions and sliced hard-boiled eggs for each diner to sprinkle on top of his soup. This makes an excellent choice for a dinner party because it can be prepared well in advance but, as it is substantial, only serve small quantities of it.

SERVES 4
250 ml [½ pt] canned tomato
    juice
2 garlic cloves
half a cucumber
1 green pepper
1 red pepper
1 large onion
700 g [1½ lb] tomatoes
75 ml [3 fl oz] olive oil

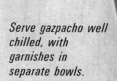

Serve gazpacho well chilled, with garnishes in separate bowls.

28

30 ml [2 tablespoons] red wine
  vinegar
salt
freshly ground black pepper
half a sprig of marjoram
half a sprig of basil

1 Peel and chop the cucumber.
   Remove white pith and seeds from
   green and red peppers and chop
   the flesh. Peel and chop the onion.

2 Blanch, peel, de-seed and chop
   the tomatoes. Chop the herbs.
   Peel and crush the garlic with a
   little salt.

3 Reduce all the ingredients to a
   purée using a liquidizer.

4 Add tomato juice. Increase
   quantity if the purée is very thick.

5 Chill for several hours in a refrigerator.

6 Stir well before serving.

Variation
If you don't have a liquidizer and are
using a vegetable mill, reserve the
tomato juice, oil, vinegar, salt and
pepper while you purée the vegetables. Then stir in reserved ingredients.

JERUSALEM ARTICHOKE AND TOMATO SOUP
*The subtle smoky taste of artichoke
is ideal for a purée soup, but the
colour is rather dull on its own so
tomatoes are added to cheer it up. As
you peel and slice the artichokes, keep a
bowl of acidulated water near by to drop
the artichokes into to prevent them
from discolouring. Garnish the soup
with crumbled grilled bacon or
croûtons or, for a special occasion,
with some fresh, pink prawns.*

SERVES 4
700 g [1½ lb] Jerusalem
  artichokes
1 large onion, weighing about
  225 g [½ lb]
25 g [1 oz] butter
225 g [½ lb] tomatoes
salt and pepper
1 garlic clove
850 ml [1½ pt] chicken or white
  stock

1 Peel and thinly slice Jerusalem
   artichokes. Chop the onion.

2 Melt the butter in a heavy-based
   saucepan over low heat. Add the
   onion and artichokes. Cover the
   pan and sweat, shaking the pan
   occasionally, for about 5 minutes.

3 Meanwhile, skin the tomatoes,
   halve and remove seeds.

4 Add tomato flesh to the pan, cover
   and sweat for a further 3 minutes.

Fennel vichyssoise is a rich summertime soup.

5 Crush garlic and add to pan with salt and pepper. Pour on stock.

6 Bring to simmering point, cover and simmer for 15 minutes.

7 Reduce contents of pan to a purée using a vegetable mill, sieve or liquidizer.

WALNUT SOUP

This soup is particularly delicious when made with 'wet' walnuts – the very early season walnuts where the skins slip off easily and the nuts are slightly moist. If using fresh walnuts, dip them in boiling water and then slip off the skins. Buy 450 g [1 lb] to allow for the weight of the shells. The garlic flavour is not overpowering, but is an essential part of the soup.

SERVES 6
**175 g [6 oz] walnuts, shelled
   weight
1 garlic clove
1.15 L [2 pt] chicken stock
150 ml [¼ pt] thick cream
salt and pepper**

1 Peel and crush garlic clove with a round-bladed knife or garlic crusher.

2 Put walnuts and garlic in a saucepan, cover with stock and season. Cover the pan and simmer for about 15 minutes or until tender.

3 Reduce contents of pan to a purée using a vegetable mill, sieve or liquidizer.

4 Return soup to the saucepan. Add cream and reheat gently. Check seasoning.

CHILLED MELON SOUP

This soup should definitely take its place at the beginning of a meal. The cool, fruity flavour is sharpened by the addition of lemon juice and mint. The soup requires no cooking but must be well chilled before serving.

SERVES 6-8
**2 large ripe honeydew
   melons
4 lemons
45 ml [1½ tablespoons]
   freshly chopped mint
pinch of ground cinnamon
125 ml [4 fl oz] natural
   yoghurt
150 ml [¼ pt] thin cream
sprigs of mint to garnish**

1 Cut the melons in half. Discard the seeds and scoop out flesh.

2 Reduce melon flesh to a purée using vegetable mill, sieve or liquidizer.

3 Squeeze the lemons and add the juice to the purée.

4 Stir in the chopped mint and cinnamon.

5 Cover and chill.

6 Just before serving, beat the yoghurt and cream together until smooth, then stir into the soup.

7 Garnish with sprigs of mint.

FENNEL VICHYSSOISE

The distinctive flavour of Florentine fennel makes an unusual and delicious iced soup to serve on a warm evening. If you plan to liquidize the soup be sure to discard all the outer, tough, stringy pieces from the fennel bulb before cooking or it will not purée satisfactorily.

SERVES 4
**350 g [¾ lb] Florentine fennel
550 ml [1 pt] water or chicken
   stock
salt and pepper
250 ml [½ pt] thick cream**

1 Clean the fennel bulbs, discarding tough stringy pieces. Reserve ferny fronds for garnish. Chop the fennel.

2 Put the fennel in a saucepan, cover with water or stock and then season. Cover the pan and simmer for about 15 minutes or until tender.

3 Reduce contents of the pan to a purée using vegetable mill, sieve or liquidizer.

4 Allow to cool. When cold, stir in cream, cover and chill.

5 Garnish with reserved fennel fronds.

Soups

cream soups

Velvety smooth cream soups have a stunningly superior taste. Usually made from fresh ingredients, combined with a delicately flavoured béchamel sauce and enriched with cream and flavoured with a hint of herbs, they have a magical elegance about them that belies their modest cost and simplicity of preparation.

Cream soups are really one step up from the simple purée soup. They take longer to make than the purée soup, but you will find that the mouth-wateringly good results are worth the extra effort. Velouté soups, which are more complicated to make, are really very special and probably the classiest of all soups. However, cream soups are not really everyday fare—they are for occasions when you want to pull out all the stops to impress your guests, and they provide a contrast in flavour, texture and colour to following courses.

Cream soups are, as their name suggests, rich and creamy. The cream both binds the ingredients together to produce a particularly smooth consistency and makes the soup taste very rich. Also butter is stirred into hot cream soups just before serving for glossy good looks.

Cream soups can be made from fish, poultry or vegetables. Red meat and fruit are never used. Usually the ingredients are cooked very gently in butter until tender (called sweating), then stirred into a thin béchamel sauce and reduced to a purée.

If root vegetables are used, thickening with béchamel is unnecessary. The starch content of the vegetable is a sufficient thickening so the ingredients are simmered in milk or stock and made into a purée. In all cases the soup is enriched with a final addition of cream or cream and butter just before serving.

Swirls of cream add to the eye appeal of this pale green lettuce soup, which can be served hot or cold.

THE INGREDIENTS
Vegetables

The vegetables that you use should be fresh but, as with purée soups, you can make good use of vegetable trimmings such as green leek tops or the outer leaves of a lettuce—even pea and bean pods make very good soups.

Almost any vegetable can be used to make a cream soup, apart from aubergine which is spongy in texture and doesn't give a good flavour. An unusual addition to the list is the stinging nettle which makes an excellent and really economical soup. Before you go out picking, equip yourself with thick gloves and a pair of kitchen scissors to cut through the rather woody stalk base. Once the nettles are cooked there is, of course, no sting left!

Nettles and all the green leaf family, including spinach, watercress and lettuce are suitable. Green beans, peas, tomatoes, mushrooms and leeks, as well as all root vegetables, such as Jersalem artichokes, make very good cream soups.

Very often a combination of two vegetables is used, one with a high starch content such as potato.

Poultry

The pale coloured flesh of chicken and turkey are ideal for making a cream soup. Any darker meat, such as beef or lamb, would ruin the colour of the soup and would also produce too strong a flavour. For the best results use the white meat from chicken or turkey, and discard the skin which does not have a particularly good flavour and does not purée well. The meat you use must always be cooked—and this provides an excellent way of using left-over chicken and turkey from a previous meal.

Fish and shellfish

The cooked flesh of cod or other white fish such as plaice, flounder, haddock, coley or whiting may form the basis of a fish cream soup. Be sure to remove all bones and skin before adding to the béchamel sauce. Of the shellfish, shrimps and prawns (which are supplied ready cooked) can be used to make a beautifully coloured cream soup. Carefully remove and reserve the shells before using—the shells may be used in a fish stock later.

The liquid

The liquid, either for the béchamel sauce or for cooking the vegetables themselves, may be milk, stock or water. Generally, milk is used for the green leafy vegetables so that the flavour of the vegetable is not overpoweringly strong and the colour is suitably delicate. Chicken or white stock is used for chicken cream soup and for other vegetables where its flavour will not overpower that of the main ingredient. A light vegetable stock may be used in the same way. Water may be used for tomato- and potato-based soups. Fish stock is used for fish soups.

Enriching

The extra rich flavour and smooth consistency of cream soups come from the final addition of cream and, in the case of hot soups, butter as well. The cream should be fresh and thick—thin cream would not give the same results. Measure the cream into a small bowl. Spoon in about 60 ml [4 tablespoons] of the hot soup and stir vigorously to mix thoroughly. The final addition of a little butter gives the soup an extra gloss.

EQUIPMENT

You will need the same equipment as described in the last chapter for puréeing. A vegetable mill with a fine grid is really better than a liquidizer for most soups with woody stringy matter that needs removing. Celery, for example, if liquidized needs sieving afterwards to remove any stringy matter.

You will also need a small bowl for mixing the cream, and a balloon whisk or spiral sauce whisk and sieve. A whisk is ideal for blending the creamy mixture from the bowl into the pan of hot soup and will do the job better than a wooden spoon. If lumps do occur when the creamy mixture has been added, a sieve can be used for straining. Conical sieves are specially shaped to speed up the process of straining liquids but an ordinary sieve could also be used.

BASIC METHOD
Using un-starchy vegetables

To make a cream soup with green leaf vegetables, or other un-starchy vegetables, such as tomatoes, make a béchamel sauce (see chapter on white roux sauces).

A heavy-based pan is needed for sweating vegetables. Purée soups with a liquidizer or vegetable mill. Whisk in cream with a beater. Strain with a conical strainer.

Always make a béchamel sauce and not a white sauce—the better quality of the béchamel is really worth the effort for these marvellous soups. The special flavour of the sauce is important in a cream soup which includes small quantities of vegetables.

Make the béchamel by infusing 550 ml [1 pt] milk with the flavourings. Then make a roux with 25 g [1 oz] each of butter and flour, add the strained milk, cover and simmer for 10 minutes. This gives a sauce of pouring consistency.

another vegetable, are made in the same way as for purée soups. Clean, peel and chop the vegetables and sweat them in a little butter for 5-10 minutes. Add stock or water according to the recipe and simmer until the vegetables are soft.

Reduce the contents of the pan to a purée using a vegetable mill, sieve or liquidizer. Reheat gently, season, thin and enrich.

Using chicken or turkey

A good cream soup can be made from chicken or turkey flesh. Cooked meat should always be used—preferably the white-coloured meat. Make a béchamel sauce from 550 ml [1 pt] well-flavoured chicken or turkey stock for every 175-225 g [6-8 oz] flesh. This is the weight required when the chicken or turkey is boned and skinned. Roughly chop the chicken or turkey meat (discarding the skin) and add this to the béchamel sauce. Simmer over gentle heat for 5 minutes to infuse the flavours. Reduce the contents of the pan to a purée using a vegetable mill or liquidizer—it is best to use a liquidizer here for really smooth results. A sieve would be impractical because of the difficulty of pushing the meat through, but the fine grid on a vegetable mill works satisfactorily. Reheat gently, season, thin and enrich as described overleaf.

Using fish and shellfish

For a cream soup using white fish such as cod, you will need 450 g [1 lb] white fish (including bones) to every 550 ml [1 pt] fish stock, which is made into a béchamel sauce.

Use fish which has been cooked by poaching, grilling or even boiled in the bag. Remove all the bones from the flesh with a fork.

If you are making a cream of shellfish soup you will need 225 g [$\frac{1}{2}$ lb] prawns or shrimps (in their shells) and 175 g [6 oz] cooked white fish.

Remove the prawns or shrimps from their shells and pound the flesh with a pestle in a mortar, or in a dish with the end of a rolling pin. Add this to the béchamel sauce. Simmer over gentle heat for 5 minutes to infuse the flavours. Reduce the contents of the pan to a purée using a vegetable mill or liquidizer. Sieving is impractical because of the bulk; it is best to use a liquidizer for puréeing fish soups. Reheat gently, season, thin and enrich as described overleaf.

Clean the vegetables and chop or slice them. Melt about 25 g [1 oz] butter in a thick heavy-based saucepan, add the vegetables, cover the pan and cook very gently for 5-10 minutes until most of the butter has been absorbed. This is called sweating. It is important to shake the saucepan or stir the ingredients occasionally to prevent them from burning and to ensure all the vegetables are evenly cooked.

Add the vegetables to the saucepan containing the béchamel sauce. Add complementary herbs, cover the pan and simmer gently over a low heat for 5-10 minutes to infuse the flavour of the vegetables and herbs in the sauce.

Reduce the contents of the pan to a purée using a vegetable mill, sieve or liquidizer, depending on ingredients used. If you are using a vegetable mill, it is best to use the finest grid to obtain a really smooth, well-blended soup.

Now check the soup for consistency. The final soup should be the consistency of thin cream so if it is too thick now, keeping in mind the final addition of cream will also thicken it slightly, thin the soup with a little stock or milk. Reheat gently, season, thin and enrich as described overleaf.

Using starchy vegetables

Cream soups that are made with a starchy vegetable such as potato, or with a combination of a starchy and

ADDING THE ENRICHMENT

A cream soup is enriched shortly before serving by the addition of thick cream, giving the soup its distinctive rich, smooth and creamy taste.

Place the thick cream in a mixing bowl and stir or whisk in about 60ml [4 tablespoons] of the hot soup. Pour this blended mixture back into the soup in the saucepan. Stir or whisk the soup, using a spiral sauce whisk or balloon whisk, until blended. If you poured the cream directly into the hot soup, the cream could curdle and disperse in small globules across the surface of the soup.

Once the cream is smoothly incorporated, the soup should be reheated before serving. Stir the soup occasionally over a moderate heat, but do not on any account allow it to boil. If the soup were allowed to boil, the cream would be irretrievably spoilt.

Hot cream soups can be given an extra gloss by the final addition of butter. To do this, cut butter into small pieces—allowing 25 g [1 oz] butter per 550 ml [1 pt] soup. Stir butter pieces one by one into the hot soup just before serving. If you are serving the soup cold do not add butter because it would rise to the surface of the soup.

SERVING

Cream soups are served as the first course of a meal—since they are too rich to serve large enough portions for a main course. Use a cream soup to provide a contrast in flavour and colour to the courses following it—for example, a well-balanced meal would be cream of mushroom soup, grilled lamb and mixed salad followed by orange sorbet or a selection of cheeses. The meal would be dull and the effect on guests probably depressing if you served cream of leek soup, chicken with tarragon and cream followed by syllabub!

Have the soup as hot as possible, or really well chilled, before serving. Never serve the soup lukewarm. Because cream soups are so rich you will only need about 150 ml [¼ pt] of soup per serving.

Chilling: all vegetable cream soups may be chilled, but a chicken, turkey or fish soup should be served hot. To chill a vegetable cream soup, allow the soup to cool at room temperature for 30-40 minutes before covering and placing in the refrigerator for 3 hours.

Step-by-step cream soup

⧖ *This method of making cream soups is suitable for unstarchy vegetables. The method is similar for poultry, fish and shellfish, where steps 4-6 are omitted. Make additions at step 7. For starchy vegetables, omit steps 1-3 and add liquid in step 7. To serve the soup chilled, omit the final addition of butter which would make the soup greasy.*

SERVES 4
1 large cucumber or 2 ridge cucumbers
1 medium-sized onion
salt
freshly ground black pepper
50 g [2 oz] butter
75 ml [3 fl oz] thick cream

For the béchamel sauce:
550 ml [1 pt] milk
half a small carrot
quarter of a celery stalk
1 bay leaf
salt and white pepper
pinch of nutmeg or mace
25 g [1 oz] butter
25 g [1 oz] flour

4 Meanwhile, wipe clean and chop the cucumber. Don't peel the cucumber as the skin will add colour. Peel and chop the onion.

5 Melt 25 g [1 oz] butter in a heavy-based saucepan over a gentle heat. As soon as the butter has melted add the vegetables.

9 Return the soup to the pan and place over a low heat. Taste and season lightly with salt and freshly ground black pepper.

10 Measure the cream into a small bowl. Spoon in about 60 ml [4 tablespoons] of the hot soup and stir vigorously to mix thoroughly.

1 Prepare vegetables and place them in milk with bay leaf. Bring slowly to the boil. Then cover and leave to cool for 30 minutes.

2 Make a roux with the butter and flour, remove from the heat and gradually stir in the strained re-warmed milk.

3 Return the pan to low heat and bring to the boil, stirring. Add salt, pepper, nutmeg or mace, cover and simmer for 10 minutes.

6 Cover pan and cook over gentle heat, shaking occasionally or stirring with a wooden spoon so vegetables cook evenly.

7 Add the softened vegetables to the béchamel sauce and simmer, covered, for 10 minutes to allow the flavours to infuse.

8 Reduce the contents of the pan to a purée using a vegetable mill, sieve or liquidizer. The liquidizer is probably the quickest to use.

11 Pour the cream and soup mixture back into the hot soup, whisking it in with a balloon or sauce whisk or stirring with a wooden spoon.

12 Reheat the soup carefully but do not allow it to boil or it will spoil. Meanwhile, cut the remaining butter into small pieces.

13 Stir or whisk the butter, one piece at a time, into the hot soup to give a final gloss. Adjust the seasoning and serve.

QUANTITIES FOR BECHAMEL-BASED CREAM SOUPS

Vegetable or meat	Béchamel sauce
artichoke, Jerusalem 350 g [¾lb] + 1 onion	550 ml [1 pt] milk based
asparagus 225 g [½ lb]	550 ml [1 pt] milk based
cauliflour 350 g [¾ lb] + 1 onion	550 ml [1 pt] milk based
celeriac 225 g [½ lb] + 1 onion	550 ml [1 pt] milk based
celery 450 g [1 lb]	550 ml [1 pt] milk based
chicken 175-225 g [6-8 oz] cooked meat	550 ml [1 pt] using chicken stock
chicory 225 g [½ lb]	550 ml [1 pt] milk based
cucumber 1 large or 2 ridge + 1 onion	550 ml [1 pt] milk based
fish 450 g [1 lb] white fish including bones	550 ml [1 pt] using fish stock
fish 175 g [6 oz] including bones + 225 g [½ lb] prawns including shells	550 ml [1 pt] using fish stock
leek 450 g [1 lb] + 1 onion and 1 carrot	550 ml [1 pt] milk based
lettuce 2 heads + 1 onion	550 ml [1 pt] milk based
mushroom 225 g [½ lb]	550 ml [1 pt] milk based
nettle 450 g [1 lb] + 1 onion	550 ml [1 pt] using white or vegetable stock
onion 450 g [1 lb]	550 ml [1 pt] using vegetable stock
pea 450 g [1 lb] shelled or frozen + 1 onion	550 ml [1 pt] using white stock
prawn or shrimp 225 g [½ lb] in shells + 1 onion and 1 carrot	550 ml [1 pt] using fish stock
tomato 450 g [1 lb] + 1 onion	550 ml [1 pt] using white or vegetable stock
turkey 175-225 g [6-8 oz] cooked meat	550 ml [1 pt] using chicken stock
turnip 450 g [1 lb]	550 ml [1 pt] milk based
watercress 225 g [½ lb] + 1 onion	550 ml [1 pt] milk based

Amounts of cream to use for enriching béchamel sauce based soups

275 ml [½ ml] soup—45 ml [3 tablespoons] cream
550 ml [1 pt] soup—75 ml [3 fl oz] cream
1.15 L [2 pt] soup—150 ml [¼pt] cream
1.7 L [3 pt] soup—250 ml [½ pt] cream

For vegetables soups based on stock, milk or water instead of béchamel, use double the quantity of cream.

Beautiful garnishes to float on well-chilled soup.

GARNISHES AND ACCOMPANIMENTS

The pale colour and smooth texture of cream soups lend themselves to crisp textures and strong colours of garnishes and accompaniments Decorate just before serving with julienne strips (matchstick-thin strips of vegetables such as raw carrot, celery, green or red peppers), paper-thin slices of cucumber or button mushrooms, chopped chives, sprigs of watercress, thinly sliced lemon, or extravagant swirls of thick cream. Alternatively, serve croûtons or crumbled crispy bacon or a few split almonds fried in butter until golden brown (particularly good with green bean soups). Whole peeled prawns add colour to fish soups, and chicken soup can be garnished with slivers of poultry breast. Serve garnishes (except for prawns and chicken slivers) in separate bowls so that guests may help themselves. In this way the garnishes remain crisp—floated in the soup too soon they would lose their texture and become soggy and unappetizing and may even sink.

STORING

The basic soup may be kept in a covered container in the refrigerator for a day or two but the cream should not be added until it is reheated for serving or the cream could go off. Any soup containing a large pro-

Choose appropriate decorations for each recipe.

portion of old potatoes may turn sour if kept any longer than this.

Freezing

Most soups freeze well although it is necessary to make some adjustments to the basic recipes. When making cream soups which are based on béchamel sauce for freezing, replace the flour in the sauce with cornflour. This is because soup which is thickened with ordinary flour tends to curdle on reheating. Don't freeze soups which have a large amount of potatoes in them because potatoes become slushy when frozen in a liquid.

If a soup recipe includes herbs and spices it is best to leave these out until the soup is defrosted for use. Cream is omitted because it is always added just before serving.

No soup should be kept in the freezer for longer than 2 months because it will develop a sour taste after this time.

Reheating

Allow the soup to defrost in the refrigerator or at room temperature. When liquid, place in a double saucepan and reheat it over gentle heat, stirring well. These precautions will stop the soup from separating. You may find that the soup has thickened with freezing and needs a little more stock or milk added to it on reheating. Adjust the seasoning, add the cream as described and serve.

CREAM OF LETTUCE SOUP

Instead of using 2 whole lettuces you could use the outer leaves of several lettuces and reserve hearts for salads. It is also a good way to use up lettuces which have gone rather too limp for a salad.

Serve hot or cold, depending on the weather. If serving cold do not enrich with butter. If serving hot accompany with croûtons.

The béchamel sauce is made with chicken stock to heighten the very delicate flavour of the lettuce.

SERVES 4
2 lettuces
1 small onion
salt
freshly ground black pepper
75 ml [3 fl oz] thick cream
50 g [2 oz] butter

For the béchamel sauce:
550 ml [1 pt] chicken stock
salt and white pepper
25 g [1 oz] butter
25 g [1 oz] flour

1 Make a roux with the butter and flour. Warm stock and stir in away from heat.

2 Return the pan to low heat and bring to the boil, stirring. Season with salt and pepper. Cover and simmer for 10 minutes.

3 Meanwhile, wash and dry the lettuces, peel and finely chop the onion.

4 Melt 25 g [1 oz] of the butter in the saucepan and sweat the onion and lettuce for about 10 minutes or until soft.

5 Add the onion and lettuce to the béchamel sauce and simmer, covered, for 10 minutes.

6 Reduce the contents of the pan to a purée using a vegetable mill, liquidizer or by passing through a sieve.

7 Return the soup to the pan, taste and season lightly with salt and freshly ground black pepper.

8 Measure the cream into a small bowl. Spoon in some of the hot soup and stir vigorously to mix thoroughly.

9 Pour the cream and soup mixture back into the hot soup, stirring all the time.

10 Reheat carefully but do not allow to boil. Meanwhile, cut the remaining butter into 5 or 6 pieces.

11 Stir the butter, one piece at a time, into the hot soup to give a final gloss. Adjust the seasoning and serve.

CREAM OF SPINACH SOUP

If you are using small young spinach leaves simply wash and cook them, stalks and all. Thick tough stalks of older spinach should be discarded. There is no need to chop the leaves but choose a pan large enough initially to fit them all in—they will soon decrease in size when cooked.

SERVES 4
450 g [1 lb] spinach
50 g [2 oz] butter
salt
freshly ground black pepper
75 ml [3 fl oz] thick cream

For the béchamel sauce:
550 ml [1 pt] milk
half a small carrot
quarter of a celery stalk
1 bay leaf
salt and white pepper
pinch of nutmeg or mace
25 g [1 oz] butter
25 g [1 oz] flour

1 Clean and chop the carrot and celery. Place them in the milk with the bay leaf. Bring slowly to the boil. Remove from heat, cover and leave to infuse for 30 minutes.

2 Make a roux with the butter and flour, remove from the heat and stir in the strained re-warmed milk.

3 Return the pan to low heat and bring to the boil, stirring. Season with salt, pepper and nutmeg or mace. Cover and simmer for 10 minutes'

4 Meanwhile, wash the spinach very thoroughly in a sinkful of cold, salted water. Drain, shake dry and discard any tough stalks.

5 Melt 25 g [1 oz] of the butter in a large saucepan over low heat.

6 Add the spinach, cover and sweat for about 10 minutes or until soft. Shake the pan or stir frequently so that the spinach cooks evenly and absorbs the butter without burning.

7 Add the spinach to the béchamel sauce and simmer, covered, for 10 minutes.

8 Reduce the contents of the pan to a purée using a vegetable mill, sieve or liquidizer.

9 Return the soup to the pan, taste and season lightly with salt and black pepper. Reheat gently.

10 Measure the cream into a small bowl. Spoon in some of the hot soup and stir vigorously to mix thoroughly.

11 Pour the cream and soup mixture back into the hot soup, stirring all the time.

12 Reheat carefully but do not allow to boil. Meanwhile, cut the remaining butter into 5 or 6 pieces.

13 Stir the butter, one piece at a time, into the hot soup to give a final gloss. Adjust the seasoning and serve.

Variations
●This soup can be made with frozen spinach. Use 275 g [10 oz] frozen spinach.
●For cream of mushroom soup, replace the spinach with 225 g [½ lb] mushrooms. Wipe clean and chop them, reserving a few slices for garnish. Use a vegetable mill for best results.
●For sorrel and spinach soup, replace half the fresh spinach with sorrell leaves. An all-sorrel soup would be to strongly flavoured.

Hot spinach soup is made even more delicious by scattering over crisp croûtons just before eating.

Add colour to cream of fish soup by garnishing with fresh prawns.

CREAM OF FISH SOUP

⧗⧗ *Any cooked white fish can be used in this extra fishy version; coley might replace the cod and thus offset the cost of buying the prawns. It is a marvellous way of using up left-over cooked fish, which has very few other uses, and yet the garnish of whole prawns makes the soup a luxuriously rich party dish. A crushed garlic clove adds good flavour to the soup which should be made with a good home-made fish stock.*

SERVES 4
450 g [1 lb] cooked cod
175 g [6 oz] prawns
1 garlic clove
salt and white pepper
75 ml [3 fl oz] thick cream
50 g [2 oz] butter

For the béchamel sauce:
550 ml [1 pt] fish stock
salt and white pepper
25 g [1 oz] butter
25 g [1 oz] flour

1 Make a roux with the butter and flour. Heat the stock and stir in away from the heat.

2 Return the pan to low heat and bring to the boil, stirring. Crush the garlic clove and add to the sauce with salt and pepper. Cover the pan and simmer for 10 minutes. Remove from the heat.

3 Meanwhile, remove skin and bones from the cod. Flake the flesh with a fork. Remove the shells from the prawns and pound in a mortar with a pestle, reserving a few whole prawns for the garnish.

4 Add the fish and prawns to the béchamel sauce and simmer, covered, for 10 minutes.

5 Reduce the contents of the pan to a purée using a vegetable mill or liquidizer.

6 Return the soup to the pan, taste and season lightly with salt and black pepper. Reheat gently.

7 Measure the cream into a small bowl. Spoon in some of the hot soup and stir vigorously to mix.

8 Pour the cream and soup mixture back into the hot soup, stirring all the time.

9 Reheat carefully but do not allow to boil. Meanwhile, cut the remaining butter into 5 or 6 pieces.

10 Stir the butter, one piece at a time, into the hot soup to give a final gloss. Adjust the seasoning and serve.

CREAM OF CHICKEN SOUP

This soup should be made with a well-flavoured chicken stock. The addition of lemon juice sharpens the soup to prevent it from tasting bland. Reserve a little of the chicken flesh, cut it into strips and garnish the soup with the strips just before serving.

SERVES 4
**225 g [½ lb] cooked, skinned
 and boned chicken meat
5 ml [1 teaspoon] lemon juice
salt
freshly ground black pepper
pinch of nutmeg
75 ml [3 fl oz] thick cream
50 g [2 oz] butter**

**For the béchamel sauce:
550 ml [1 pt] chicken stock
salt and white pepper
25 g [1 oz] butter
25 g [1 oz] flour**

1 Make a roux with the butter and flour. Warm the stock and stir in away from the heat.

2 Return the pan to low heat and bring to the boil, stirring. Season with salt and pepper. Cover and simmer for 10 minutes.

3 Meanwhile, chop the chicken meat into small pieces.

4 Add the chicken meat and lemon juice to the béchamel sauce and simmer, covered, for 10 minutes.

5 Reduce the contents of the pan to a purée using a vegetable mill or liquidizer.

6 Return the soup to the pan, taste and season lightly with salt, black pepper and nutmeg. Reheat.

7 Measure the cream into a small bowl. Spoon in some of the hot soup and stir vigorously to mix thoroughly.

8 Pour the cream and soup mixture back into the hot soup, stirring all the time.

9 Reheat carefully but do not allow to boil. Meanwhile, cut the butter into 5 or 6 pieces.

10 Stir the butter, one piece at a time, into the hot soup to give a final gloss. Adjust the seasoning and serve.

Variation
●A cream of turkey soup can be made with 225 g [½ lb] cooked turkey meat and 550 ml [1 pt] turkey or chicken stock.

VICHYSSOISE

This is an excellent example of how humble ingredients such as potato, onion and leeks can be turned into a spectacularly good soup. It is traditionally served chilled and tastes far better this way. Because of the addition of the starchy potato, this soup does not include a béchamel sauce.

SERVES 6
**225 g [½ lb] potatoes
1 large leek
2 large onions
850 ml [1½ pt] chicken stock
salt
freshly ground black pepper
250 ml [½ pt] cream
25 g [1 oz] butter**

**For the garnish:
1 small bunch of chives**

1 Peel and chop potatoes and onions. Wash the leek, remove most of the green part and discard. Chop.

2 Melt the butter in the saucepan and sweat the potato, onion and leek for about 10 minutes or until soft.

3 Pour over the stock and simmer, covered, for 25 minutes or until the vegetables are tender.

4 Reduce the contents of the pan to a purée using a vegetable mill, sieve or liquidizer.

5 Taste and season lightly with salt and freshly ground black pepper. Allow the soup to cool, then stir in the cream.

6 Chill the soup for about 3 hours. Just before serving, chop the chives and sprinkle over the soup.

Variation
●A really nourishing soup can be made of watercress (which contains vitamin A, vitamin C and iron) and potato. Wash one large bunch of watercress, remove tough stalks and chop. Reserve a few leaves for garnish. Peel and dice 450 g [1 lb] potatoes. Continue as for vichyssoise from step 2 and garnish with reserved watercress sprigs.

Velvety vichyssoise: many people think this the best of all chilled soups.

Sauces

white roux-based and sweet sauces

Smooth and subtly flavoured sauces are a cook's best friend. By following a few basic rules you hold the key to a whole repertoire of sauces which will add colour and variety to your meals, open up new avenues of cooking and quickly earn for you a reputation as an accomplished cook.

A simple, creamy well-flavoured sauce has countless uses in the kitchen. Everyday dishes such as

A smooth and creamy parsley sauce complements grilled fish

boiled or steamed cod, that sometimes look dull and unappetizing, can be turned into an eye-appealing dish by the simple addition of, say, a colourful parsley sauce—and every cook knows that good presentation of a dish means she is half-way to earning compliments and clean plates from all the family.

Savoury sauces can be used to complement a wide range of dishes—not only fish, but meat, poultry, egg, vegetable and pasta dishes. It may be part of the dish as in macaroni cheese, used to coat cooked foods such as chicken, or served in a sauce-boat as an accompaniment.

A sauce not only complements a dish but it also increases the food value of a meal by adding milk, eggs, cheese and other nutritious ingredients. It may also form the basis of other dishes—croquettes, for instance, are bound together by a thick white sauce (panada) and, by the simple addition of whisked egg whites, you have a soufflé.

Last but not least, sauces are really an economy. They can make a dish go further, and they are invaluable for reheating cold foods that might otherwise languish in the larder and eventually go to waste.

The vast number of different sauces in use in the kitchen come from a few basic methods. When you have mastered these, the variations follow quite simply and logically. For this reason these basic sauces are often called 'sauces mères' (mother sauces).

A roux-based sauce is one made by blending flour into melted fat and then adding a liquid. There are three main types of roux-based sauces: white, velouté and brown. The first of these is discussed in this course.

Starch may also be used to thicken sauces which don't contain any fat. Arrowroot or cornflour are blended to a paste with a little of the liquid to be used and then cooked in the same way as a roux-based sauce. This is not strictly a white sauce because when the liquid is fruit juice it clarifies with cooking to make a clear sauce.

Both white and cornflour-based sauces can be used for sweet and savoury dishes. However, a white roux-based sauce is more commonly used for savoury sauces.

Cornflour and more especially arrowroot are very suitable for thickening fruit sauces because they clarify when cooked, leaving a clear fruity colour. However, cornflour can be used for savoury dishes when a more 'gluey' consistency is required: an example is the Chinese sweet-and-sour sauce.

WHITE ROUX-BASED SAUCES

The white roux-based sauce is probably the most versatile and commonly used of all the sauces. It is quick to make and marries well with meat, poultry, fish, eggs, and vegetables. The finished dish is often named after the sauce that is served with it, for example, sole mornay (sole with cheese sauce).

General principles

White and brown roux-based sauces are made in basically the same way. Butter, margarine or oil is melted in a saucepan and flour or cornflour, in equal quantities, is added to it and cooked until the butter has incorporated all the flour. The resulting paste is known as a roux.

A liquid, usually stock or milk or a mixture of the two, is added to the roux, and they are cooked together to form a sauce.

The proportion of fat and flour to the liquid depends on the consistency of the sauce required. In other words, whether it is to be used to coat food, to be poured from a sauce-boat or to bind food together (see chart of consistencies of roux-based sauces, overleaf).

Choosing ingredients

Fat: butter and margarine are both suitable for white sauce.
Flour: never use self-raising flour which has a raising agent added to it. Plain flour is nearly always used in preference to cornflour, which gives a slightly different texture and can make the sauce too gluey, especially when a thick sauce is required.
Liquid: the liquid is usually milk, or, if the sauce is to be served with chicken, fish, veal or some vegetables, it can be made with equal quantities of milk and a suitably flavoured stock.

Equipment

Stainless steel or heavy-based aluminium saucepans are best, because sauces tend to burn easily and may be spoiled in thin aluminium pans. However, this can be remedied if you invest in an asbestos mat which can be placed underneath a thin-based saucepan. This will reduce the heat and help prevent burning. All pans should have close-fitting lids to prevent evaporation of the liquid during cooking.

Ideally, you should have two saucepans—one for making small amounts and one for larger amounts of sauce. Choose a pan that will be three-quarters filled by the finished sauce. Too large a pan increases the area in which the sauce could burn underneath and over which it could evaporate.

Use a wooden spatula or spoon for stirring sauces because a metal one would scratch your pans.

You will find either a spiral sauce whisk or a balloon whisk useful, and, for correcting a lumpy sauce, you will need a nylon mesh or stainless metal sieve of about 15 cm [6"] in diameter to fit over the pan or, alternatively, use a liquidizer.

Techniques explained

Every potential sauce cook has a nagging fear of her sauce going lumpy and looking nothing like the velvety smooth version which is mocking her from the open pages of her cookery book! But it really is unnecessary to panic. By keeping some simple points in mind you should be able to sail through like a true professional.

Always weigh the ingredients before you start cooking. Sift the flour so that it is really fine, and never try to skimp on the proportion of butter to flour—you will only get a dull and lumpy sauce. Stick strictly to the quantities and ingredients given in the consistency and derivative charts shown on the following pages.

Melt the fat so gently over a low heat that it simply runs over the bottom of the pan. Don't allow it to sizzle or it will quickly turn brown and ruin the delicate colour and flavour of the sauce. Draw the pan away from the heat when you add the flour and, later, the liquid, so that they can be worked in smoothly. After the flour has been added the pan is returned to the heat to allow the starch grains to burst and absorb the fat, giving a glossy finish to the finished sauce. Although professionals usually blend cold liquid into the hot roux, the beginner will find it easier to blend in a warm liquid. Heat the liquid until it is as hot as your finger can comfortably bear, take the roux off the heat, and pour in the liquid, a little at a time, stirring it constantly. This is done because it is easier to blend two foods together if they are approximately the same temperature.

Return the pan to the heat and bring to the boil stirring. Then reduce heat to very low, cover the pan and leave to simmer. Simmering enables the starch grains to expand and absorb the liquid thus thickening the sauce. Never be tempted to cut the cooking time (or the resulting sauce will have an unpleasantly overpowering floury taste), or to leave the sauce to boil—this would reduce the cooking time. It is important that the sauce just simmers, that is, when you can see a gentle agitation on the surface. Simmering temperature is from about 90° to 100°C [185° to 200°F].

It is worth remembering, too, that a little sauce goes a long way. Generally 250 ml [½ pt] of liquid will make a pouring sauce in a jug or cover portions for four people.

BECHAMEL SAUCE

This is not just a fancy French name for white sauce. The liquid is flavoured first, and it is always preferable to white sauce if you have the time to make it. The subtle flavour is especially good where there is either no further flavouring or where the additions are not dominant, for instance, hard-boiled eggs. Once the liquid has been infused with the flavourings, as shown here, the method is the same as for white sauce. Proportions given in this recipe make a coating sauce.

MAKES 250 ML [½ PT]
half a small onion
half a small carrot
a quarter of a celery stalk
250 ml [½ pt] milk
bay leaf
25 g [1 oz] butter
25 g [1 oz] flour
salt and white pepper
pinch of nutmeg or mace

KEEPING AND REHEATING

If you need to make a roux-based sauce an hour or so in advance, the surface of the sauce should be covered with a dampened circle of greaseproof paper when still hot. This will prevent a skin forming.

Never reheat the sauce over direct heat: it may easily burn or become lumpy. Remove the paper and place the pan containing your sauce on a trivet in another larger pan so that the bottom of the saucepan is not in direct contact with the heat. Half fill the pan with water—a roasting tin is ideal—and place it over the heat. This improvised version of a bain-marie or

Step-by-step to white roux-based sauce

1 Melt the fat slowly in a small saucepan. Never let it sizzle or it will become brown and change the colour and taste of the sauce.

2 Remove pan from heat, stir in plain flour. Return to low heat, stir gently for 1-2 minutes until smooth. Do not let it colour.

3 Put liquid in a separate pan. Heat through until it is as hot as your finger can comfortably bear. On no account let it boil.

4 Remove the roux pan from the heat. Add a little liquid, stirring vigorously. Add the remaining liquid gradually, still stirring.

5 When the mixture is smoothly blended, return the pan to the heat and bring the sauce to the boil, stirring continuously. Season.

6 Turn the heat to low, cover the pan and simmer for 5 minutes to complete the cooking of the starch.

Step-by-step to béchamel sauce

1 Cut the vegetables into small squares (called dicing) and put into a pan with the milk and seasonings.

2 Slowly bring the milk to simmering point. Remove from the heat, cover and leave for 30 minutes for the flavours to infuse.

3 Strain the milk through a sieve into a jug. Discard the vegetables in the sieve. Continue from step 1 for a white roux-based sauce.

water bath will allow the sauce to be heated more gently, although it should still be stirred or beaten with a sauce whisk from time to time.

Storing

You may find it more convenient to make your basic roux in larger quantities and to store this in the refrigerator. When the roux is cold, turn it out of the saucepan into a screw-top jar. The roux will keep for a week in the refrigerator.

To use, weigh 50 g [2 oz] of roux for coating sauce (or 25 g [1 oz] for a pouring sauce or 100 g [¼ lb] for a panada). Put in a pan, heat 250 ml [½ pt] of liquid and proceed from step 4 for a white sauce, whisking all the time.

Freezing

To freeze a roux, allow it to cool, then put about 50 g [2 oz] on pieces of kitchen foil. When cold, wrap each piece in the foil. Put in polythene bags, seal and freeze for 3-5 months.

To use, drop the frozen or thawed roux into hot liquid and whisk in.

To freeze a made-up white sauce (add flavourings when reheating) pour the cooled sauce into waxed containers, seal, label and freeze. This will keep for 2-3 months. To use, thaw for 1-2 hours at room temperature and reheat in a bain-marie.

CONSISTENCY OF ROUX-BASED SAUCES

Consistency	Flour and butter	Liquid	Uses
Pouring sauces Should be thick enough to glaze the back of a wooden spoon at boiling point.	15 g [½ oz] each	250 ml [½ pt]	Basis for soups and accompanying sauces.
Coating sauce Should be thick enough to coat the back of a wooden spoon.	25 g [1 oz] each	250 ml [½ pt]	For coating foods.
Panada sauce Should be very thick at boiling point.	50 g [2 oz] each	250 ml [½ pt]	Basis for soufflés and binding foods together, such as croquettes

Prawns, mushrooms, celery, cheese and other fresh ingredients add nourishment and flavour to white sauces.

DERIVATIVES OF THE BASIC WHITE & BECHAMEL SAUCES
After the basic sauce is made, stir in the additions away from the heat just before serving

Sauce	Additions	Method	Serve with
Anchovy 250 ml [½ pt] béchamel sauce	5 ml [1 teaspoon] anchovy essence		Poached or steamed fish.
Caper 250 ml [½ pt] béchamel sauce	15 ml [1 tablespoon] capers 15 ml [1 tablespoon] lemon juice	Liquid for béchamel equal quantities of milk and fish or white stock.	Boiled mutton, roast lamb or tripe. Boiled bacon.
Celery 250 ml [½ pt] béchamel sauce	2 celery stalks, 10 ml [2 teaspoons] lemon juice	Chop celery. Boil for 15 minutes. Purée.	Chicken or ham.
Cheese 250 ml [½ pt] white sauce	40-50 g [1½-2 oz] Cheddar cheese, 2.5 ml [½ teaspoon] dry English mustard	Finely grate the cheese. Stir cheese and mustard in just before serving.	Vegetables, pasta, egg or fish dishes.
Egg 250 ml [½ pt] béchamel sauce	1 egg	Hard boil the egg. Sieve yolk and chop white.	Steamed or poached white fish.
Mornay 250 ml [½ pt] béchamel sauce	50 g [2 oz] gruyère or Parmesan cheese 40 g [1½ oz] butter	Finely grate cheese.	Veal, chicken, eggs, vegetables and pasta.
Mushroom 250 ml [½ pt] béchamel sauce	50 g [2 oz] mushrooms 15 g [½ oz] butter	Thinly slice mushrooms. Sauté in butter. Liquid for béchamel: equal quantities of milk and chicken stock.	Roast or boiled chicken.
Mustard 250 ml [½ pt] white sauce	5 ml [1 teaspoon] English mustard, 5 ml [1 teaspoon] white wine vinegar, 5 ml [1 teaspoon] caster sugar	Liquid for sauce: equal quantities of milk and fish stock.	Fried or baked mackerel or herring.
Onion 250 ml [½ pt] white sauce	225 g [½ lb] onions, 25 g [1 oz] butter, 25 ml [1 fl oz] thin cream (optional)	Sauté onions until soft, but not brown. Purée with butter and cream.	Tripe, lamb or veal.
Parsley 250 ml [½ pt] béchamel sauce	15 ml [1 tablespoon] chopped parsley		Bacon, white fish or vegetables.
Prawn 250 mpl [½ pt] white sauce	75 g [3 oz] prawns or shrimps 10 ml [2 teaspoons] lemon juice 2.5 ml [½ teaspoon] anchovy essence, or 15 ml [1 tablespoon] tomato ketchup	Liquid for white sauce: equal quantities of milk and fish stock. Chop prawns or shrimps.	White fish
Tarragon 250 ml [½ pt] béchamel sauce	15 ml [1 tablespoon] freshly chopped tarragon		Chicken

What went wrong	Cause	CORRECTING MISTAKES Remedy
Lumpy sauce	Fat too hot when flour was added; or roux not cooked sufficiently; or liquid added too quickly without stirring enough. Lumps in sweet sauce indicate insufficient mixing of the starch and liquid, or insufficient stirring.	Push the hot sauce through a nylon or wire sieve into a clean pan. Or blend in a liquidizer for 1-2 minutes at high speed. Reheat carefully, stirring vigorously.
Raw flavour or dull sauce	Insufficient cooking of the starch.	Continue cooking.
Thin sauce	Wrong proportions of ingredients, over-cooking or undercooking of the roux.	Thicken by reducing the liquid. Place the saucepan over high heat and boil rapidly until the consistency is right. Stir continuously to prevent burning.
Thick sauce	Wrong proportions used or sauce allowed to evaporate during cooking.	Gradually beat in more hot milk or stock. Test again for seasoning.
Greasy sauce	Too much fat or overcooking of the roux, which causes the fat and flour to separate.	Remove pan from heat and use paper towels to soak up the surface fat.

SWEET SAUCES

There are plenty of sweet sauces in tubs and packets and tins sold today, but none is as good or as cheap as those you can so easily make yourself. Now that cream is so expensive it is well worth learning to make some of those tangy fruit and creamy sauces which were once the natural accompaniment to baked and steamed puddings, stewed and poached fruit, hot soufflés and pancakes.

Although sweet sauces are made from a starch base and not the roux of the savoury sauces, the method of cooking is very similar and the same rules apply to cooking the starch.

Basic sweet pouring sauce

This is the simple starch-thickened sauce which can be made with milk, fruit juice or water with other flavourings blended with cornflour or arrowroot. It is not strictly a white sauce except when the liquid is milk, or cream is added.

Arrowroot is generally used to thicken a fruit sauce because it gives a completely clear sauce and has the advantage of needing only a short cooking time. Never boil an arrowroot sauce for longer than specified in the recipe because it will lose its thickening qualities and the sauce will quickly become thin again. Starch-thickened sweet sauces may be made in advance and reheated in the same way as the roux-based sauces.

Sweet sauces are usually served from a sauce-boat at the table, although they may be poured over ice-cream before serving. Allow 250 ml [½ pt] of sweet sauce for four servings.

Flavouring sweet sauces

Simple milk sauces can be flavoured with 5 ml [1 teaspoon] of mixed spice or nutmeg, or 30 ml [2 tablespoons] of jam or marmalade—excellent with steamed puddings. The grated rind of half an orange or lemon adds a tangy taste to sauces made with fruit juice or water. For special occasions, turn your sauce into something special by flavouring with 30 ml [2 tablespoons] of rum, sherry, brandy or almost any liqueur. A richer sauce can be made by stirring in 30 ml [2 tablespoons] of thin cream.

Step-by-step to basic sweet sauce

▽▲ *This basic recipe can be adapted to make any number of delicious sweet sauces to serve with ice-cream or piping hot puddings. Granulated sugar is used as it dissolves easily and does not colour the sauce. This amount will feed four people generously.*

MAKES 250 ML [½ PT]

250 ml [½ pt] milk, fruit juice or water

15g [½ oz] cornflour or 7 g [¼ oz] arrowroot

25 g [1 oz] granulated sugar flavouring

15 g [½ oz] butter, optional

1 In a medium-sized mixing bowl, mix the starch with 30 ml [2 tablespoons] of the cold liquid, stirring continuously until thoroughly blended.

2 In a medium-sized saucepan, dissolve the sugar in the remaining liquid over medium heat, stirring until dissolved. Bring to the boil.

Pears in a hot chocolate sauce make an impressive dessert. Surround the pears with scoops of ice-cream just before serving.

3 Remove pan from the heat and pour the hot liquid in a gradual stream into the starch mixture, stirring continuously until blended.

4 Return the sauce to the pan and boil over medium heat for 3 minutes for cornflour or 1 minute for arrowroot, stirring all the time.

5 Add the flavouring. Just before serving, whisk in the butter with a balloon or sauce whisk to give a glossy finish.

Handy hints

- Keep a vanilla pod in a container of sugar and use this flavoured sugar in recipes where vanilla is required.
- Place a vanilla pod in the milk or other liquid used in the recipe when this is heated. The vanilla pod may then be removed, dried and stored for re-use until its flavour is too weak.
- Use vanilla essence—2-3 drops of essence is enough for 250-550 ml [½-1 pt] liquid. Always choose a good quality essence and test its strength before use.

Variations

- For chocolate sauce, melt 50 g [2 oz] plain chocolate in the sugared milk, or mix 15 ml [1 tablespoon] cocoa powder with the liquid.
- For a less sweet chocolate sauce, add 2.5 ml [½ teaspoon] instant coffee powder with the cocoa and starch to the sugared milk.
- For a coffee sauce, blend 15 ml [1 tablespoon] instant coffee powder with the starch and add to the sugared milk. Or use 50 ml [¼ pt] each of strong coffee and milk, add sugar and flavour with 2-3 drops of vanilla essence, or use vanilla-flavoured milk or sugar (for details see handy hints).
- For ginger syrup sauce, make the basic sauce with all water, or half water and half syrup from a jar of preserved ginger. Dissolve 100 g [¼ lb] Demerara sugar in the water or syrup mix, and add a small piece of lemon peel and 2-3 drops of lemon juice. Leave for 10 minutes, then remove the peel. For special occasions, add one or two pieces of preserved ginger cut into small pieces at the end of cooking time.
- For a butterscotch sauce using water, dissolve 125 g [¼ lb] Demerara sugar in half the water. Add 25 g [1 oz] butter and thinly pared rind of half a lemon. Bring to the boil and simmer for 5 minutes. Strain through a sieve into a clean saucepan and discard the peel. Blend the arrowroot with the remaining water and continue as for basic recipe. Add juice of half a lemon just before serving.
- For orange sauce, omit the sugar use 250 ml [½ pt] made-up frozen (or canned) orange juice and flavour with 5 ml [1 teaspoon] grated lemon zest.
- For a tangy lemon sauce, use the juice of 1 lemon and make up the rest of the liquid with water. Flavour with 5 ml [1 teaspoon] grated lemon zest.

CHICKEN VOL-AU-VENTS

This is a very economical way of spreading left-over cooked chicken among a number of people. These light vol-au-vents make an excellent lunch dish for 4 people. As a first course they will serve 8 people.

SERVES 4-8
175 g [6 oz] cooked, boned and skinned chicken
50 g [2 oz] mushrooms
8 individual vol-au-vent cases

For the sauce:
250 ml [½ pt] milk
half a small onion
half a small carrot
a quarter of a celery stalk
bay leaf
salt and white pepper
pinch of nutmeg or mace
25 g [1 oz] butter
25 g [1 oz] flour
5 ml [1 teaspoon] lemon juice

1 Prepare the vegetables for the béchamel sauce and infuse them in the liquid.

2 Heat the oven to 200°C [400°F] gas mark 6. Shred the chicken and thinly slice the mushrooms.

3 Sauté the mushrooms in a little butter until soft.

4 Meanwhile, make a roux in a small saucepan. Remove from heat.

5 Add the infused milk to the roux and stir. Season, cover and let it simmer for 5 minutes.

6 Stir mushrooms and chicken into the sauce. Season with lemon juice, salt and pepper.

7 Remove the tops and spoon in enough mixture to fill each vol-au-vent case, pressing well into the case with the handle of a spoon. Put the tops back in place.

8 Place vol-au-vents on a baking tray and heat for about 15 minutes.

HAM AND LEEKS AU GRATIN

Chicory may be substituted for the leeks.

SERVES 4
8 medium-sized leeks
8 slices of ham
4 slices of wholemeal bread
50 g [2 oz] butter

For the sauce:
50 g [2 oz] butter
50 g [2 oz] flour
550 ml [1 pt] milk
salt and pepper
5 ml [1 teaspoon] dry English mustard
100 g [¼ lb] Cheddar cheese

1 Trim and wash the leeks. Steam them for 20 minutes until tender.

2 Meanwhile, make a roux in a small saucepan. Remove from the heat.

3 Heat the milk, add to the roux and stir. Season, return to heat and

bring to boil stirring. Cover and let it simmer for 5 minutes.

4 Grate the cheese and add, with the mustard, to the white sauce.

5 Wrap each leek in a slice of ham and place in an ovenproof dish. Pour over the sauce.

6 Make breadcrumbs and heat grill to medium.

7 Top the dish with the breadcrumbs, dot with butter and brown under medium heat.

Variations

●For a simple cauliflower cheese, boil or steam a whole cauliflower and keep hot until needed. Pour over. 550 ml [1 pt] cheese sauce, sprinkle over 100 g [¼ lb] grated Cheddar cheese and grill under medium heat.

●Boil or steam cauliflower florets. Add 100 g [¼ lb] sliced spiced sausage to 550 ml [1 pt] cheese sauce and pour over the cauliflower. Sp-

rinkle over grated cheese and brown under medium heat.

●Arrange slices of hard boiled eggs and tomatoes in a buttered gratin dish and pour over 550 ml [1 pt] cheese sauce. Sprinkle over grated cheese and cook in the oven at 200°C [400°F] gas mark 6 for 15-20 minutes. Sprinkle over crisply fried smoked bacon and garnish with sliced tomatoes.

●Cook 225 g [½ lb] macaroni in plenty of boiling salted water for 8-10 minutes. Drain, mix with 550 ml [1 pt] cheese sauce and pour into dish. Top with 50 g [2 oz] grated cheese and brown under medium heat.

●For a more substantial dish, fold in 3 slices of chopped ham and 225 g [½ lb] skinned and chopped tomatoes to the macaroni mixture.

Serve creamy kedgeree or chicken vol-au-vents for a simple lunch or supper dish. Both are made with a delicately flavoured béchamel sauce which lightly binds the ingredients together.

CREAMY KEDGEREE

This is a creamy mixture of smoked fish, rice and an egg sauce. It is an ideal dish to prepare in advance. To reheat, cover with buttered greaseproof paper and place in a moderate oven for about 25 minutes.

SERVES 4
450 g [1 lb] boil-in-the-bag
  smoked haddock fillets
275 g [10 oz] long-grain rice
salt and black pepper
pinch of cayenne
  pepper
15 ml [1 tablespoon] freshly
  chopped parsley

For the sauce:
250 ml [½ pt] milk
half an onion
half a carrot
a quarter of a celery stalk
bay leaf
pinch of nutmeg or mace
25 g [1 oz] butter
25 g [1 oz] flour
1 medium-sized egg

1 Prepare vegetables and infuse in the milk with the bay leaf and nutmeg. Cover and set aside.

2 Put the rice, salt and 700 ml (1¼ pt) cold water into a large saucepan. Bring to the boil and stir once.

3 Immediately reduce the heat as low as possible. Cover the pan and simmer for 15 minutes without removing the lid or stirring.

4 Meanwhile, cook haddock according to manufacturer's instructions, and make the sauce.

5 Melt the butter slowly in a pan. Stir in the flour away from the heat. Return to the heat and cook stirring for 1-2 minutes.

6 Add the milk to the roux away from the heat, a little at a time, stirring vigorously.

7 Return the pan to the heat, bring to the boil, stirring. Cover and simmer for 10 minutes.

8 Hard boil the egg.

9 Turn the haddock out of its bag into a bowl, remove and discard the skin and flake the fish.

10 Test the rice by biting a few grains. If not quite tender, or if the liquid is not completely absorbed, replace the lid and cook for a few minutes longer.

11 Arrest cooking of egg by plunging in cold water. Shell the egg, chop the white and sieve the yolk.

12 Add flaked haddock, rice, egg and seasonings to the béchamel sauce. Stir well over moderate heat for 3 minutes or until it is hot.

13 Remove the pan from the heat and pile the mixture on to a warmed serving dish. Garnish with parsley.

CHOCOLATE PEARS

Here is a delicious combination: dessert pears poached in a flavoured syrup, served with ice-cream and hot chocolate sauce. The pears can be prepared an hour or two in advance ·if wished. The addition of butter gives the sauce a glossy finish.

SERVES 4
4 ripe dessert pears
350 g [¾ lb] caster sugar
1 vanilla pod
4 cloves
ice-cream

For the chocolate sauce:
250 ml [½ pt] milk
50 g [2 oz] dark chocolate
15 g [½ oz] cornflour
25 g [1 oz] granulated sugar
15 g [½ oz] butter

1 Peel the pears, leaving the stalks on. Remove the 'eye' from the base and level off to stand upright.

2 Choose a pan which is large enough to stand all the pears in. Put the sugar in the pan and add 550 ml [1 pt] water.

3 Bring to the boil, stirring, and then boil for 2 minutes.

4 Remove syrup from heat. Add vanilla and cloves, then carefully stand the pears in the pan.

5 Cover the pan and poach over low heat for 15-20 minutes until the pears are tender. Spoon the syrup over the fruit occasionally during cooking.

6 Lift the fruit out of the pan with a perforated spoon and place in a serving dish. Cool, cover and chill in a refrigerator for 30 minutes.

7 Put the cornflour in a small bowl and stir in a little cold milk to make a smooth paste.

8 Put the rest of the milk in a saucepan, add the broken chocolate and sugar, and stir over a moderate heat until the chocolate has completely melted.

9 Pour the hot chocolate liquid into the cornflour mixture and stir in.

Rødgrød and chocolate cream are two economical ways of using the sweet sauce method to make chilled creamy desserts.

10 Return the liquid to the pan and bring back to the boil. Cook for 3 minutes over a low heat, stirring continuously.

11 Add the butter in small pieces and beat with a balloon whisk until glossy. Cover and keep on a low heat.

12 Remove the pear dish from the refrigerator and uncover.

13 Surround the pears with scoops of ice-cream and pour the sauce over the pears, or serve separately in a sauce-boat.

RODGROD

Puréed fruit is used to make this smooth Scandinavian dessert which slips down your throat. It only takes a short time to prepare, but you should allow 2 hours chilling time. The amount of sugar to use varies according to the ripeness of the fruit. Fresh redcurrants are often tart.

SERVES 6
1 kg [2 lb] fresh or canned redcurrants
1 kg [2 lb] fresh or frozen raspberries
45 ml [3 tablespoons] arrowroot
100 g [¼ lb] caster sugar
50 g [2 oz] shredded almonds
150 ml [¼ pt] whipped cream

1 Purée the fruit (see chapter on purée soups) and mix together. Drain canned fruit first.

2 Mix the arrowroot with 30 ml [2 tablespoons] of the cold purée. Put the rest of the purée in a saucepan and bring to the boil over low heat, stirring continuously.

3 Remove pan from heat and gradually pour the hot liquid into the starch mixture, stirring continuously until blended.

4 Return the sauce to the pan and boil over medium heat for 1 minute, stirring all the time.

5 Sweeten to taste and allow to cool.

6 Meanwhile, put the almonds in the base of the grill pan and place close under medium heat to brown for 2 minutes. Reserve.

7 Pour the purée mixture into individual serving glasses and chill.

8 Before serving, decorate with whipped cream and sprinkle with toasted almonds.

CHOCOLATE CREAM

A simple chocolate sauce can be transformed into a rich dessert by the addition of whipped cream. This is still an economical chocolate pudding to serve to a family since it is based on cocoa and milk, rather than on real chocolate and eggs, as with some rich party sweets. You can, however, present it like a party sweet. Serve it in individual custard glasses or cocottes. Decorate with one of the following: 50 g [2 oz] chopped hazelnuts, 20 ml [4 teaspoons] chocolate-coloured sugar strands, or place a single crystallized violet in the centre of each pudding.

SERVES 4
250 ml [½ pt] milk
15 g [½ oz] cornflour
15 ml [1 tablespoon] cocoa powder
3 ml [½ teaspoon] instant coffee powder
25 g [1 oz] granulated sugar
150 ml [½ pt] whipped cream

1 In a medium-sized mixing bowl, mix together starch, cocoa and coffee powder with 30 ml [2 tablespoons] of the cold milk, stirring continuously until thoroughly blended.

2 Put the remaining milk into a medium-sized saucepan. Add the sugar and stir over medium heat until it is dissolved. Then bring the liquid to the boil.

3 Remove pan from the heat and gradually pour the hot liquid on to the starch mixture, stirring continuously until blended.

4 Return the sauce to the pan and boil over medium heat for 3 minutes, stirring all the time.

5 Allow to cool completely.

6 When cold, fold in the whipped cream and pour the mixture into individual serving dishes.

7 Decorate before serving.

Sauces

velouté sauces

Velouté sauces are a traditional part of classical French cookery but, unlike some classical recipes, velouté sauces are amazingly quick to make—and the results are stunningly good. Made with basic ingredients such as home-made stock, fresh eggs and cream, velouté sauces take you a step up the ladder from béchamel sauces to a most impressive style of cookery.

Velouté, as the name implies, means velvety and this is an aptly named sauce. The velouté sauce is really the rich relation of the basic béchamel sauce—richer both in colour and texture. A slightly cooked roux and the use of a well-flavoured stock instead of the rather bland milk gives a richer biscuity colour, and the final addition of egg yolks and cream makes it richer in texture.

Like the basic béchamel sauce, the véloute sauce is a sauce mère (mother sauce). Once you've mastered the technique of making it, you hold the key to many other classical French sauces, as you can see from the family tree chart.

Velouté sauces are perhaps the most useful of all the roux-based sauces; their creamy flavour and light texture can be used to coat poached chicken, veal, fish or plainly boiled or steamed vegetables. In fact, because the sauce is so rich, the food it complements should ideally be as simple as possible—the simpler the better. Velouté sauces also form the basis of a whole range of delicately flavoured soups, which are described in detail in a later course.

Velouté sauce, and sauces derived from it, is always made to a coating

consistency. Because it is so rich, a little goes a long way. A sauce made with 250 ml [½ pt] liquid and 25 g [1 oz] each of fat and flour is enough for 4 people when it accompanies a dish.

Small pieces of cooked chicken or turkey, poached in stock or left over heated in a velouté sauce, and this mixture can be used to make a complete dish (often called a blanquette), or to fill light puff pastry vol-au-vents, flan cases or pancakes to make mouth-watering starters, lunch or supper dishes.

Once you have mastered the simple white sauce, you will find that making velouté is simply a natural step up the ladder to a really impressive style of French cookery.

EQUIPMENT AND TIMING

To make a velouté sauce you will need the same equipment as that needed for the white roux-based sauces (see the previous chapter). You will also need a small measuring jug, a small mixing bowl, a fine sieve and a whisk. A conical sauce sieve is the best type of sieve to use as it is specifically designed to speed up the process of straining liquids. The use of a sauce whisk or balloon whisk gives a glossy look to the final sauce.

It takes less time to make a velouté sauce than to make a béchamel sauce. It should take you no more than 30 minutes including the preparation of flavourings.

INGREDIENTS

The ingredients used for a velouté sauce are similar to those for a béchamel or white sauce. It is important to use the very best ingredients—this is intended to be a really superb, classical sauce and it deserves all the attention and careful choice of ingredients to give the best results.

Fat

Choose either salted or unsalted butter for the fat. Butter gives the best flavour and colour to the sauce, and it is a pity to go to the trouble of making a velouté sauce and then economize on a few pence worth of fats. In emergencies margarine can be used instead of butter, but in this case do not attempt to colour the roux at all since this is almost impossible to do with margarine. Never use oil or

dripping—both would give the final sauce the wrong flavour, and oil will not colour.

Flour

Plain, sifted flour should be used except when you are making the sauce for freezing. In this case, use cornflour rather than flour and it will keep longer. Never use self-raising flour—your sauce does not need a raising agent.

Liquid

The liquid used for a velouté sauce should be a strong, well-flavoured stock. Chicken, veal or fish stock may be chosen according to the food with which the sauce is to be served. This stock may be taken from the pot in which the chicken or fish for the meal is cooking, or made separately.

Eggs and cream

The final addition of fresh thick cream and egg yolks gives all the velouté sauces their particular delicacy and richness. Cream and yolks are blended together (this is called a liaison) and added to the sauce towards the end of cooking time, thus thickening and binding the sauce. Use the yolks from medium-sized eggs and fresh thick cream. Don't try to economize by using thin cream because it will not give the same results.

BASIC METHOD

To make a basic velouté sauce, first prepare the mushrooms which are used to add taste—they are an optional extra, but they really do give the sauce a good flavour. Either whole mushrooms or mushroom trimmings can be used. Allow 3-4 small mushrooms (or the equivalent in peelings and stalks) to every 250 ml [½ pt] stock. Chop the mushrooms as finely as possible—the more cut surfaces there are the more the mushroom flavour will leak out into the sauce. Place the chopped mushrooms on one side.

Measure the stock that you will be using, pour it into a small, heavy-based saucepan and place over low heat to heat through gently.

Choose a small heavy-based pan in which to make the sauce. Put the butter into it and melt over low heat.

Remove the pan from the heat and stir in the flour to make a roux. You will need 25 g [1 oz] each of fat and

Step-by-step to velouté sauce

MAKES ABOUT 250 ML [½ PT]
25 g [1 oz] butter
25 g [1 oz] flour
250 ml [½ pt] hot chicken, veal or fish stock (depending on final dish)
3 or 4 small mushrooms or mushroom peelings or stalks finely chopped (optional)
1 egg yolk
30 ml [2 tablespoons] thick cream
salt
freshly ground black pepper
2-3 drops lemon juice

4 Add the chopped mushrooms or mushroom peelings and stalks if these are being used.

8 Add 75 ml [5 tablespoons] of the hot sauce to the liaison, a little at a time, stirring well.

1 Melt butter in a saucepan over gentle heat. Remove from heat and stir in the flour to make a roux.

2 Return pan to low heat and cook roux, stirring for about 4 minutes until it turns a pale fawn colour.

3 Quickly remove from heat. Gradually add hot stock, stirring to keep the mixture smooth.

5 Return to heat. Bring to boil stirring. Reduce heat, cover and simmer for 15 minutes.

6 Meanwhile place the egg yolk and cream in a small bowl and mix thoroughly with a fork or whisk.

7 Remove pan from heat and strain the sauce through a fine sieve into a clean heavy-based pan.

9 Pour the contents of the bowl into the pan in a steady stream, whisking or stirring as you do so.

10 Season to taste with salt and pepper and add 2-3 drops of lemon juice, but no more.

11 Return saucepan to low heat. Bring the sauce to boiling point, stirring continuously. Serve.

flour to every 250 ml [½ pt] stock.

Return the saucepan to low heat and cook the roux, stirring continuously, for about 4 minutes until it turns a very pale fawn colour. Watch carefully and take the pan away from the heat immediately the roux has changed colour. This point is very important because an essential characteristic of the sauce is the cooking of the roux to a straw or fawn colour (another name for velouté is fawn sauce). Never allow the roux to brown.

While the pan is away from the heat, add the hot stock, slowly at first, stirring all the time to incorporate it smoothly.

When all the hot stock has been stirred in, add the finely chopped mushrooms to the saucepan and return the pan to medium heat. Bring the sauce to the boil, stirring all the time.

Cover the pan, reduce to low heat and simmer the sauce for 15 minutes, stirring occasionally so that the full flavour of the mushrooms infuses with the sauce. Continue to stir the sauce from time to time.

While the sauce is simmering, place the egg yolk and cream in a small mixing bowl and blend them together with a fork or whisk to make the liaison. Allow 1 egg yolk and 30 ml [2 tablespoons] thick cream for every 250 ml [½ pt] of liquid used to make the sauce. Then remove the saucepan from the heat and strain the hot, well-flavoured sauce through a fine sieve into a clean heavy-based saucepan. This will remove the mushrooms and, conveniently, get rid of any lumps that might possibly have occurred! The mushrooms left in the sieve can be used for other dishes such as shepherds pie or a spaghetti sauce to provide bulk but will not, of course, give much flavour as most of this will have gone into the sauce.

Add egg yolk and cream liaison to the sauce. It is essential that this is done away from the heat. First add a few spoonfuls of the hot sauce to the liaison in the bowl and whisk or stir to mix thoroughly. Then pour the contents of the bowl in a steady stream into the hot sauce, beating all the time with a whisk or spoon until everything is incorporated. Never try to save time by adding the liaison directly to the hot sauce without the initial blending, because the sauce and liaison would not mix well and might curdle.

Lemon juice (2-3 drops for 250 ml [½ pt] sauce) is now added to the sauce to give it a subtle tangy taste. Do be frugal with the amount you use—if you add too much the flavour of the sauce will be overpowered by the acid taste and this cannot be rectified without spoiling the balance of ingredients.

Finally, return the pan to low heat and bring the sauce just to boiling point, stirring all the time, to allow the egg yolk to cook and thicken the sauce.

As soon as the sauce has reached boiling point remove the saucepan from the heat and use the sauce. Do not allow the sauce to continue boiling once boiling point has been reached.

SAUCES DERIVED FROM VELOUTE SAUCE

Basic velouté sauce is excellent in its own right, but like béchamel sauce it is a 'sauce mère' (mother sauce) and lends itself to a wide range of flavourings. Additional ingredients alter the flavour (but not the texture) of the basic velouté to produce 'daughter' sauces, many of which are as famous as velouté itself.

To make a sauce derived from velouté make the basic velouté as shown in the step-by-steps but omit the mushrooms in step 4 (because their flavour may conflict with the taste of the substitute ingredients). Unless otherwise specified, at step 10 add the extra ingredients specific to the particular sauce you are making. Always prepare the ingredients before you begin to make the sauce, so they are ready to use when you want them. All the derivative sauces given here are based on the use of 250 ml [½ pt] stock.

● For a velouté herb sauce, make a basic velouté sauce and flavour it with a few finely chopped sprigs of your favourite herb and pour over meat, fish or vegetables.

● For a rich garlic-flavoured sauce crush a garlic clove and add this with a bouquet garni and 4 whole peppercorns to the sauce. Strain the sauce just before serving and discard flavouring ingredients.

● For a velvety curry sauce, stir 5 ml [1 teaspoon] curry powder into the hot stock. This is added to the sauce early on as the curry spices need to be cooked for a while so that they develop properly.

● For a colourful paprika sauce stir 5 ml [1 teaspoon] ground paprika into the hot chicken stock.

● For a mushroom sauce, chop 50 g [2 oz] mushrooms. Place in a small saucepan, just cover with water and a squeeze of lemon juice. Bring to the boil, simmer for 1 minute, strain and pat dry. Add to a hot velouté sauce just before serving so that the colour of the sauce is not spoilt by dark mushroom juices. The flavour is improved when making this sauce if mushrooms are also used in step 4.

● For a Bercy sauce simmer 2 finely chopped shallots in 75 ml [3 fl oz] white wine in an uncovered pan until the wine is reduced by half. Stir wine and shallots into the velouté sauce, which has been made with fish stock, and just before serving stir in 25 g [1 oz] butter and 10 ml [2 teaspoons] finely chopped parsley.

● A spicy polonaise sauce can be made by stirring 76 ml [3 fl oz] sour cream or plain yoghurt, 5 ml [1 teaspoon] each of grated horseradish (or horseradish sauce), finely chopped fennel and lemon juice into a velouté sauce made with chicken stock. (The lemon juice used here is in addition to the basic velouté sauce lemon flavouring.)

● For poulette sauce make a basic velouté sauce with veal stock and stir in 10 ml [2 teaspoons] finely chopped parsley and 5 ml [1 teaspoon] lemon juice just before serving. Again, lemon juice is in addition to the basic velouté sauce lemon flavouring.

● For a suprême sauce, make a velouté sauce using strong chicken stock and replace the basic liaison with 3 egg yolks and 150 ml [¼ pt] thick cream.

● For a Chivry sauce boil altogether for 5 minutes a handful of spinach and 2-3 sprigs each of tarragon, chervil and chives. Drain and reduce to a purée by rubbing through a sieve.

This should give just under 15 ml [1 tablespoon] of purée. Stir this into the basic sauce made with chicken or fish stock so that it is coloured to a delicate green.

COOKING AHEAD

Ideally, a velouté sauce and any of the derivative sauces should be made just before serving, but you can make any of these sauces in advance and successfully store or freeze and reheat—providing you make the basic sauce only (up to step 5 in the step-by-step pictures). Liaisons and final flavourings must not be added until the sauce is reheated, just before serving.

Making in advance

If you make a velouté sauce an hour or two before it is needed, lay a circle of buttered greaseproof paper on the surface of the hot sauce to stop any skin forming. Set the sauce aside until it is required.

Storing

It is well worth making a larger quantity of basic velouté sauce than you need. Store some in the refrigerator in a covered container for use on another day as the basis of a soup or a sauce. It will keep for three or four days in this way.

Freezing

If you wish to freeze a velouté sauce, make the basic sauce but use cornflour rather than flour for the roux. Made in this way the sauce will keep for up to two months. Allow the sauce to defrost in the refrigerator before reheating.

Reheating

To reheat the basic sauce it is best to use a double boiler or bain-marie to be sure that the bottom of the pan is not in direct contact with the heat and that no lumps will form. Place the sauce in the top of a double boiler, or place the pan containing your sauce on a trivet in a pan half-filled with water, and reheat slowly over a gentle heat, stirring until the mixture is hot. If the sauce is at all lumpy strain it through a fine sieve into a clean pan. When the mixture is hot and smooth, gradually add the egg and cream liaison as described in the basic method.

Bercy
Add: white wine, shallots, butter and parsley.
Uses: this is a famous sauce which is traditionally served with poached fillets of sole, but you could also use plaice. Pour the sauce over the hot fish in a gratin dish and place under a hot grill to glaze the surface—it will only take 2 minutes.

Polonaise
Add: sour cream or yoghurt, horseradish, fennel and lemon juice.
Uses: a good spicy sauce to serve with grilled lamb cutlets and steaks. Serve in a sauce-boat.

Poulette
Add: freshly chopped parsley and lemon juice.
Uses: for coating chicken breasts or escalopes of veal, or pour over young broad beans, new potatoes or carrots before serving.

Suprême
Add: egg yolks and thick cream.
Uses: the ideal sauce to coat a suprême (breast) of chicken. Also excellent poured over hot sliced bacon or ham.

Garlic
Add: garlic, bouquet garni and black peppercorns.
Uses: for coating egg, vegetable and poultry dishes.

These dishes show some of the ways in which velouté-based sauces can be used. From left to right: new potatoes and mushroom velouté; sole with Bercy sauce; slivers of chicken breast and curry sauce; and paprika sauce in a sauce-boat.

RICH FISH VOL-AU-VENT
This delicately flavoured fish dish based on a Bercy sauce can be served in one large or eight small vol-au-vent cases. It is an excellent way of using up left-over cooked fish. Any white fish such as cod, plaice or coley can be used. Butter is whisked into the sauce at the end of cooking time to add an extra gloss and a rich flavour.

SERVES 4
275 g [10 oz] cooked white fish
100 g [¼ lb] shelled prawns
1 large or 8 small, cooked
   vol-au-vent cases

For the Bercy sauce:
2 shallots
75 ml [3 fl oz] white wine
50 g [2 oz] butter
25 g [1 oz] flour
250 ml [½ pt] hot fish stock
a sprig of parsley
salt
freshly ground black pepper
1 egg yolk
75 ml [3 fl oz] thick cream
half a lemon

1 Put the vol-au-vent on a baking sheet and place in the oven at 160°C [325°F] gas mark 3 to heat through while preparing the filling.

2 Remove and discard all skin and bones from the cooked white fish. Flake the fish with a fork.

3 Roughly chop the prawns using a mezzaluna or sharp knife.

4 Peel and finely chop the shallots. Place in a small saucepan, pour on the wine and simmer, uncovered, until the wine is reduced by half.

5 Melt 25 g [1 oz] of the butter in another saucepan over low heat.

FROM VELOUTÉ

Chivry (simple)
Add: tarragon, chervil and chives.
Uses: for fish or chicken breasts, this sauce contains chopped herbs.

Chivry (traditional)
Add: spinach, tarragon, chervil and chives.
Uses: this delicately green-coloured sauce looks superb poured over simple white fish such as sole or plaice, or poached chicken breasts.

Curry
Add: curry powder.
Uses: coat poached eggs, chicken or turkey breasts on a bed of rice.

Paprika
Add: paprika.
Uses: a delightful, delicately coloured sauce to coat poached or soft-boiled eggs, cooked chicken or turkey breasts.

Mushroom
Add: button mushrooms.
Uses: for coating escalope of veal, chicken breasts or new potatoes.

Remove from the heat and stir in the flour to make a roux.

6 Return the pan to low heat and cook the roux, stirring, for about 4 minutes or until it turns a very pale fawn colour.

7 Remove the pan from the heat and add the hot stock gradually, stirring continuously to keep the mixture smooth.

8 Stir in the shallots and wine. Return the pan to the heat and bring to the boil, stirring continuously.

9 Cover the pan and simmer for 10 minutes, stirring occasionally.

10 Stir in the chopped prawns and flaked white fish and continue simmering for a further 5 minutes.

11 Place the egg yolk and cream in a bowl and mix thoroughly with a fork or whisk. Add about 75 ml [5 tablespoons] of the hot sauce to the liaison, a little at a time and stirring well.

12 Pour the contents of the bowl into the saucepan, pouring in a steady stream and whisking or stirring the sauce all the time. Season to taste

and add 2–3 drops of lemon juice.

13 Cut the remaining butter into little pieces. Finely chop the parsley.

14 Return the sauce to the heat. Bring to boiling point, whisk in the butter and finely chopped parsley and remove immediately from the heat.

15 Pour the mixture into the hot vol-au-vent cases, cover with pastry lids and serve.

Variation
● This rich fishy filling can be used to fill a 20 cm [8"] cooked pastry case, or 8 pancakes.

ONIONS IN POULETTE SAUCE

This quickly made vegetable dish is an excellent accompaniment to simple roasts, boiled or grilled meat dishes. Choose onions of equal size so that they will be cooked at the same time. The mushroom flavouring is omitted when making the sauce as the onions have a strong enough flavour themselves. The sauce chart gives suggestions for other vegetables that can be served in this way.

SERVES 4
450 g [1 lb] small onions

For the poulette sauce:
25 g [1 oz] butter
25 g [1 oz] flour
250 ml [½ pt] hot chicken stock
1 egg yolk
30 ml [2 tablespoons] thick
cream
salt
freshly ground black pepper
2–3 parsley sprigs
half a lemon

1 Melt the butter in the saucepan over gentle heat. Remove from the heat and stir in the flour.

2 Return the pan to low heat and cook the roux, stirring for about 4 minutes until it turns a pale fawn colour.

Hungarian eggs are served on toast. Onions in poulette sauce should accompany simple meat dishes.

3 Remove from the heat and add the hot stock gradually, stirring continuously to keep the mixture smooth.

4 Return the pan to the heat, and bring to the boil, stirring continuously. Cover and simmer for 15 minutes, stirring occasionally.

5 Meanwhile, skin the onions but leave them whole. Place them in a saucepan of cold, salted water and bring to the boil. Cover and simmer for about 8 minutes or until just tender.

6 Wash and finely chop the parsley and squeeze the lemon.

7 Place the egg yolk and cream in a small bowl and mix thoroughly with a kitchen fork to make the liaison.

8 Remove the saucepan from the heat and add about 75 ml [5 tablespoons] of the sauce to the

liaison. Add it a little at a time, whisking or stirring well.

9 Pour the contents of the bowl into a saucepan. Pour it in a thin stream, stirring or whisking all the time.

10 Return the saucepan to the heat. Bring the sauce to boiling point and immediately remove the pan from the heat. Season.

11 Drain the onions, place in a warmed serving dish and pour over the sauce.

HUNGARIAN EGGS

This dish is quick to prepare and makes a nourishing start to a meal. The paprika flavouring is added with the stock when making the sauce to allow plenty of time for it to cook thoroughly and give its full flavour to the sauce. A base of crisp toast soaks up the egg yolk from the soft-boiled egg—you can use white or wholemeal bread.

SERVES 6
6 medium-sized eggs
6 slices bread
1 pimento, canned

For the paprika sauce:
25 g [1 oz] butter
25 g [1 oz] flour
250 ml [½ pt] hot chicken stock
5 ml [1 teaspoon] paprika
1 egg yolk
30 ml [2 tablespoons] thick cream

1   Cut the pimento lengthways into twelve thin strips.

2   Cut the bread into rounds with a large pastry cutter. Or place a large cup upside down on the bread and cut around the rim.

3   Toast the bread on both sides and keep warm.

4   Melt the butter in a small heavy-based saucepan over low heat.

5   Remove the pan from the heat and stir in the flour.

6   Return the pan to low heat and cook the roux for 4 minutes, until it is a pale fawn colour.

7   Remove the pan from the heat and stir in the hot stock, gradually at first, until it is thoroughly combined. Add the paprika.

8   Return the saucepan to low heat and bring to the boil, stirring.

9   Cover the pan, reduce heat and simmer for 15 minutes, stirring occasionally.

10 Meanwhile, soft boil the eggs. Arrest cooking by plunging them in cold water for 1 minute. Shell the eggs and put them in a bowl of warm water.

11 Place egg yolk and cream in a small bowl and blend together with a fork or whisk.

12 Remove the saucepan from the heat and add 75 ml [5 tablespoons] of the hot sauce to the egg and cream liaison.

13 Gradually pour the contents of the bowl into the saucepan, whisking or stirring all the time.

14 Return the saucepan to low heat and gradually bring to boiling point, stirring. As soon as the sauce reaches boiling point, remove the pan from the heat and cover.

15 Place the toast on warmed individual plates. Pat the eggs dry and place one on each piece of toast.

16 Carefully spoon some of the hot sauce over each egg.

17 Arrange 2 pimento strips in a cross over each egg and serve immediately.

Star recipe

BLANQUETTE DE VEAU

This delicious and classic party dish of tender veal and vegetables is lightly coated with a delicate and creamy velouté sauce flavoured with veal stock. Choose close-textured meat that is pale pink, soft and moist. Avoid flabby, wet meat. The meat is blanched (brought to the boil) and rinsed before cooking to remove the unattractive grey scum that initially rises to the surface of the pan. Serve garnished with triangles of fried bread. This provides a crisp contrast in textures. To add colour to the dish, these may be coated with chopped parsley. Hold the fried triangle by one corner and dip into melted butter and then into freshly chopped parsley, then arrange round the dish. Accompany the veal with hot fluffy rice or creamed potatoes and buttered green beans.

SERVES 6

1 kg [2–2½ lb] veal from the shoulder or knuckle, boned weight
1 medium-sized onion
24 baby onions
4 carrots
juice of half a lemon
1 bouquet garni
salt
freshly ground black pepper
100 g [¼ lb] butter
50 g [2 oz] flour
2 egg yolks
150 ml [¼ pt] thick cream
100 g [¼ lb] button mushrooms
5 ml [1 teaspoon] lemon juice

3 Place the veal in large pan three-quarters full of cold water. Bring to boil over medium heat.

4 Remove the saucepan from the heat and drain the veal into a colander.

5 Rinse the meat under cold running water. Drain and dry the meat on kitchen paper.

9 Return the meat and vegetables to the saucepan. Cover the pan and set aside.

10 In a pan, melt 50 g [2 oz] butter. Make roux away from heat. Stir over low heat until pale fawn.

11 Measure 850 ml [1½ pt] of reserved stock and stir into the roux away from the heat.

1 Peel carrots and onions. Chop carrots and finely chop medium onion. Leave baby onions whole.

2 Trim away and discard any veal fat. Cut meat into even-sized cubes, about 40 mm [1½"] square.

6 Rinse pan. Add meat, carrots, chopped onion, lemon juice, seasonings and bouquet garni.

7 Pour on just enough water to cover. Bring to boiling point, cover and simmer for 1½ hours.

8 Remove the saucepan from the heat and drain the liquid through a colander into a bowl. Reserve.

12 Bring to the boil, stirring, cover and simmer for 15 minutes. Meanwhile mix the liaison.

13 Away from the heat, stir a little sauce into the liaison. Whisk or stir liaison into saucepan.

14 Pour sauce into meat pan, cover and simmer for 10 minutes so meat absorbs sauce flavour.

15 Place the baby onions in a pan and just cover with cold water. Cover and simmer for 5–8 minutes.

16 Wipe mushroom caps clean with a damp cloth. Trim the stalks level with the caps.

17 Put the butter, mushrooms and lemon juice in a saucepan. Cover and simmer for 5 minutes.

Pile the hot veal on to a serving dish. Place the mushrooms and onions at each end and surround with fried bread triangles.

Sauces

brown sauces

A brown sauce, smoothly and carefully blended, enriched with herbs and simmered for a long time to develop its flavour, is the basis of many classic French dishes. The secrets of a successful brown sauce are in its seasoning and in the careful reduction of the liquid to achieve the right consistency and to concentrate the flavour.

Brown sauces are one of the glories of French cooking, and are exacting to make. There is, however, no mystery about them. The principles of their construction are the same as for white and velouté sauces covered in the previous two chapters.

Once you have mastered the basic techniques and practiced one or two of the classic sauces and gained confidence, the variety of sauces to be made is almost endless. The combinations and quantities can be varied according to what is available and your personal taste.

BASIC BROWN SAUCES

There are four basic brown sauces—simple brown sauce, jus lié, sauce espagnole and demi-glace.

Simple brown sauce: this is a modest household sauce suitable for everyday use. For this, a few vegetables are browned in fat, flour is added and cooked to form a brown roux, then brown stock is added and simmered. Good stock is desirable but the simple sauce is the only one of the four classic brown sauces that should be attempted with a bouillon cube or light vegetable stock in an emergency. This sauce takes about an hour to make.

Jus lié: the French name means juice with a binder or thickening agent. This is a much quicker alternative to simple brown sauce, taking about five minutes. Arrowroot or cornflour is used as an addition (liaison) to the basic stock and then cooked to thicken it. It is essential, therefore, to make this sauce with really good quality stock, because nothing is added in the way of vegetables or herbs and spices to give it extra flavour.

Sauce espagnole: this is a superior version of simple brown sauce. It is made by the same method, but is more time consuming and has more elaborate ingredients. Instead of a few simple vegetables as before, a variety of chopped vegetables is used. A flavoured fat such as bacon is included. The combination of the vegetables and the bacon is called a mirepoix in French. Flour is added and cooked to make a brown roux as with a simple brown sauce. The stock and herbs are added and cooked as before, but there are further additions in the form of tomatoes and further simmering takes place. The whole sauce takes about two hours to make.

Demi-glace: this is the 'crème de la crème' of brown sauces—its French name means a half-glazed sauce as it has a slightly shiny appearance. For this you should make an espagnole sauce (this need not be on the same day), then add more brown stock. This addition must be of the best quality brown stock (called a fond brun) made of meat bones. The sauce is then simmered again until reduced and refined to a half-glaze. (Half-glaze is the name given to sauces which are so reduced and refined that they will set to jelly when cold.) This sauce could take two and a half hours to make.

USES OF BROWN SAUCES
All the four basic sauces outlined above can be served with a variety of dishes. Indeed espagnole and demi-glace will make any dish special. However, they can also be used as the basis for a new creation, where additions are used to change and subtly enhance them. Espagnole and demi-glace are usually used for the richest and most luxurious sauces.

Jus lié and the simple brown sauce are the cheapest and quickest to make, which makes them the fastest practical way of lifting your daily cooking to a more accomplished level.

Espagnole is always preferable to the simple brown sauce and well worth making if time permits, and always worth preparing for a special occasion.

Demi-glace is for purists, people with plenty of time, for those odd occasions when fond brun (best quality brown stock) is plentifully available, and for when you are really trying to impress.

Dishes with brown sauces
Brown sauces are associated in most people's minds with meat and game, and it is true that they may be shown to best advantage when served in this way. There are many famous dishes which are named after the sauce which adorns them, for example clams à la diable, duck bigarade and tournedos chasseur. Recipes for many of the classic dishes follow in later courses.

However there are many more modest dishes, made from chicken, pork and veal with brown sauces, and even eggs are good served in this way. Vegetables, particularly if they have been cooked by boiling or steaming and then drained, are delicious served with one of the brown sauces. The sauce makes the vegetable into a subtle vegetarian meal with no hint of parsimony, rather the reverse!

These sauces may also be used as binders in dishes such as chicken and ham pie, or with fillings for vol-au-vents, or to bind rechauffés (reheated meat and vegetables).

EQUIPMENT
The equipment used for making brown sauces is the same as that needed for the white roux-based group. You must, however, take care not to leave the wooden spoon in the roux, because this reaches a high temperature and there is a risk that the spoon could burn.

A sieve is essential for finishing a brown sauce. One with a strong nylon mesh is best, particularly when wine or vinegar is being used, as a metal sieve could taint the flavour. It must be big enough to fit over a saucepan or bowl. The conical sauce sieve (called a chinois strainer) which fits inside the basin is traditional for the job. Its big advantage is that the sloping sides help the liquid to drip through quickly.

A double boiler or bain-marie is needed for reheating the made sauce. If you do not have one you can improvise with a pan or bowl on a trivet inside a larger pan containing boiling water.

INGREDIENTS
The ingredients and the method for three of the sauces brunes (brown sauces) are similar to those used for the white roux-based sauce given in

an earlier chapter. The fourth jus lié, is not a roux-based sauce at all, but is made in the same way as the sauces made with a starch liaison in that course.

Differences between brown and white roux
Like the white-roux sauce, the three principle brown sauces are based on a combination of fat and flour which is cooked; a liquid is then added and cooked to form a thickened sauce. Simple brown sauce, sauce espagnole and demi-glace, like white sauce and velouté, are all sauces mères (foundation sauces of French cookery).

The first difference between white and brown roux is that chopped vegetables are cooked in the fat before the roux is made. The fat used for the brown sauce may be strongly flavoured (for instance dripping or bacon fat) rather than mildly flavoured.

When flour is added, the roux of flour and fat is cooked until nut brown, before the addition of liquid. The liquid used will be richer in colour and more strongly flavoured; it may be stock from red meat or game, or jellied beef stock from meat bones.

Stock
A well-flavoured stock is essential for a good brown sauce. The better the stock, the better the flavour of the finished sauce. For a simple brown sauce, a light vegetable stock or a bouillon cube can be used in an emergency, but jus lié, sauce espagnole and a demi-glace all need high quality beef stock.

The meat juices strained from a

Some of the ingredients required to make simple brown sauces.

pot-au-feu (meat stewed in liquid for hours to provide a broth) can be used for the brown stock used to make a simple sauce or a sauce espagnole; this will give excellent results. However for the demi-glace, the addition should be jellied brown stock (called fond brun) made from meat bones and then carefully skimmed of fat as described in the stock chapter.

Fats

For a brown roux, the fat may be dripping, oil, clarified butter or a mixture of butter and oil. Butter gives a good flavour but burns easily unless clarified; you can add a small quantity of oil to the butter to counteract this.

To make clarified butter, melt it in a small heavy-based pan and cook gently without allowing it to colour. Skim off with a metal spoon any scum or impurities that rise to the surface. Strain through a small strainer lined with muslin into a small bowl with a lip. Let the butter settle, then pour it into a second bowl leaving impurities behind.

For a sauce espagnole bacon is used, which supplies a proportion of the fat as well as lending its individual flavour. Salt pork may also be used or a proportion of diced ham substituted to provide the meat flavour.

Flours

For a brown roux, plain white flour is used. However this would not give a smooth enough result for a jus lié.

For jus lié, cornflour or arrowroot are used to give a clear sauce when cooked. Plain flour cannot be used as cooking time is insufficient.

Vegetable additions

Chopped vegetables are cooked in the fat before the flour is added. In the case of simple sauce, these are normally onion and carrot.

For sauce espagnole a selection of vegetables includes onion, carrot and celery, in balanced quantities so that no one flavour predominates. When the chopped bacon (or salt pork) is added to these chopped vegetables the whole is known as a mirepoix.

Mushroom peelings may also be included at this point. Mushroom peelings are often mentioned in recipes; this dates from an age when mushrooms were regularly peeled, and their skins were a common by-product in kitchens. These were always used by the economical French housewife. Nowadays mushroom stalks are the best choice. As a rough guide use the stalks from 225 g [½ lb] open (not button) mushrooms to make 250 ml [½ pt] sauce.

Tomatoes are added to the sauce

espagnole in the second stage. The sieve may be used to remove the skins and seeds from the sauce after cooking.

All the vegetables strained from the sauce after simmering have lost most of their flavour; they can therefore add little in this respect to another dish. However they may be added for bulk to, for example, a shepherds pie or a bolognese sauce.

Seasonings

As the flavour of the stock plays an important part in the making of a brown sauce, the first step is tc taste the stock. Its flavour will influence any further choice of seasoning.

If you are preparing the stock especially with a view to making a brown sauce, omit the salt. The long simmering and reduction process concentrates the seasonings which can become excessive—indeed it is a good idea always to reduce or omit salt from stock, as this can be better added with the final seasonings.

In a sauce espagnole, a bouquet garni of herbs is used. This consists of parsley, thyme and a bay leaf.

67

Seasoning and herbs are generally added to the completed sauce to give it character and individuality, and so these additions may better be considered as part of the subject of derivative sauces. It is in your selection and judgement of quantities of herbs and seasoning that you can give individuality to your cooking, so that it is worth experimenting with their flavours.

Garlic is used too, in brown sauces, but it should be used with discretion.

BROWN-ROUX SAUCE

A brown roux is made by cooking a small amount of finely chopped vegetables in the fat until they are just coloured. The flour is then added and the mixture cooked until it is a rich nut brown.

When making the sauce, you must bear in mind the following points.

●Always measure the fat and flour accurately. Fat may exceed flour according to the recipe, but never the other way round.

●Do not allow the fat to become so hot that it fries the vegetables, but let them cook slowly over medium-low heat for 5-10 minutes, stirring now and again.

●Add the flour off the medium-low heat, then stir the roux steadily all the time with a wooden spoon over the heat, so that it cooks to an even nut-brown colour. This will take 5-10 minutes. Never use a high heat and do not allow the roux to burn because this gives a bitter taste to the sauce. It will also prevent the flour from thickening the sauce. If the roux burns by accident, throw it away and start again.

●The stock should be cold or warm but never very hot when added. Take the pan off the heat before stirring in the stock. Then stir over heat until thickened.

●Simmer the sauce half covered. The heat should be as low as possible, so that the surface of the sauce only shows a movement in one place. It is the gentle reduction of the sauce and concentration of the flavours that gives the sauce its consistency and excellent flavour.

●If the sauce evaporates and becomes too thick during cooking, it can be thinned with a little more stock. If there is no more stock available, you can use water as the flavours will have concentrated.

Step-by-step to making jus lié

⊠ *Unlike other brown sauces, jus lié does not have a roux as its base, but is a meat juice thickened by a liaison. A good quality brown stock is therefore essential. This is the quickest of all brown sauces to make.*

MAKES 250 ML [½ PT]
250 ml [½ pt] beef stock
15 g [½ oz] cornflour or 7 g
[¼ oz] arrowroot

1 In a medium-sized mixing bowl, mix the starch with 30 ml [2 tablespoons] of the cold stock, stirring until blended.

Step-by-step to making simple brown sauce

MAKES 250 ML [½ PT]
1 small carrot
1 small onion
20 g [¾ oz] dripping or 30 ml
[2 tablespoons] oil or 15 ml
[1 tablespoon] oil and 15 g
[½ oz] butter
20 g [¾ oz] flour
400 ml [¾ pt] beef stock
salt and black pepper

4 Remove pan from heat and stir in flour. Return to heat and stir for 5-10 minutes until nut brown.

5 Remove pan from heat and trickle in cool stock. Stir vigorously at first to blend evenly and smoothly.

2 Put the stock in a small heavy-based saucepan. Place over medium heat, and bring slowly to boiling point.

3 Remove pan from the heat and gradually pour the hot liquid into the starch mixture, stirring continuously until blended.

4 Return the sauce to the pan and boil, stirring, over medium heat for 3 minutes for cornflour or 1 minute for arrowroot. Season.

1 Wash and chop the carrot. Peel the onion and chop it finely. Measure the fat.

2 Melt or heat the fat over medium-low heat in a heavy-based pan about 15 cm [6"] diameter.

3 Add the vegetables and cook, stirring, for 5-10 minutes until they begin to brown.

6 Bring to the boil, stirring all the time. Half cover, reduce heat and simmer slowly for 45 minutes.

7 During simmering, periodically skim off fat. Add a little cold stock to help fat rise to the surface.

8 Strain, taste and season. Then reheat and serve, or use as the basis for another sauce.

●Never thicken a thin sauce by adding more flour at the last moment or it will taste of raw starch. To reduce it place the sauce in an uncovered pan over a high heat and boil until the consistency is right.

Degreasing

During the simmering process, you must skim off from time to time any scum or fat which rises to the surface of the sauce with a metal spoon. If the sauce still appears greasy, this may be corrected by adding a very small quantity of cold stock—about 45 ml [3 tablespoons] in two or three parts to the simmering sauce. This will encourage the grease to rise to the surface so that it may be easily skimmed off. This is called to 'dépouiller' a sauce—the French word meaning 'to skin'.

If the sauce is to be allowed to get cold, for storage or reheating later, any grease will set on top and can then be easily removed.

SERVING AND QUANTITIES

When planning to make a brown sauce, the first point to remember is that there should only be one rich sauce at a meal. You will be wasting your time, if you strive to create an effect by including more than one.

The amount of sauce should be small in proportion to the food. The meat (or dish) should not be swimming in so much sauce that it is necessary to take a spoon to it, but portions simply should be generously coated. When serving a sauce with grilled or sautéed meat, the meat is dished, coated with an average of 30 ml [2 tablespoons] per person. The remaining sauce is served in a sauce-boat.

For four people, 250 ml [½pt] is ample. Never be tempted to exceed this quantity; the result would be 'trop de richesse'.

Make a good quantity of sauce while you are at it. It takes no more time than a smaller quantity and can be stored to save you time on another day.

KEEPING AND REHEATING A BROWN SAUCE

A brown sauce may be kept hot and reheated in exactly the same way as a white sauce. If you intend to reheat the sauce, place a circle of buttered greaseproof paper over the surface when hot.

To reheat the sauce, place it in a double boiler or bain-marie. To prevent lumps forming, raise the temperature of the sauce gradually, by bringing the water in the outer pan slowly to the boil. Whisk the sauce while it is reheating with a sauce whisk. Strain the sauce after heating if this is necessary.

If you wish to make a derivative sauce proceed to make additions at this point.

STORING

All the basic brown sauces keep well, so it is worth always making them in larger quantities than will be eaten at one meal. And any of these four can be stored for at least a week in a covered jar in the refrigerator, but should be brought to the boil again after four days. Allow the sauce to cool, then replace it in its covered jar.

Brown sauces can also be frozen satisfactorily and stored for a month in the freezer. It is most convenient to freeze the prepared sauce in 150 or 275 ml [¼ or ½ pt] quantities. Freeze in measured containers then wrap individually in foil before placing in freezer bags or plastic containers for storage. You can then make instant use of the right amount, reheating the quantity you need for any particular dish.

ESPAGNOLE SAUCE

This is a sophisticated version of the simple brown sauce. More vegetables are used, while the mushroom stalks give the sauce a good colour and flavour. Bacon is added to the fat for extra flavour. Chopped ham may be substituted for the bacon as this makes the sauce less greasy without detracting from the flavour.

After the roux has been made, the sauce is simmered for an hour to concentrate its flavours. Chopped tomatoes are then added, and further simmering takes place. It is this long reduction, two hours cooking time in all, that clarifies the sauce and concentrates its flavours.

Espagnole sauce stores well, so it is advisable always to make double the quantity needed for one meal. This recipe will give you enough for two meals for four people, or one such meal plus enough to make demi-glace for four.

MAKES 550 ML [1 PT]
1 medium-sized carrot
1 stick celery
1 medium-sized onion
25 g [1 oz] mushroom stalks
50 g [2 oz] streaky bacon or ham
**40 g [1½ oz] dripping or 25 g [1oz] butter and 15 ml
[1 tablespoon] oil or 40 g
[1½ oz] clarified butter**
40 g [1½ oz] plain flour
675 ml [1¼ pt] good beef stock
1 bouquet garni
**225 g [½ lb] tomatoes or 10 ml
[2 teaspoons] tomato purée**
salt and pepper

1 Wash the carrot and celery, peel the onion, remove the earthy ends from the mushroom stalks and chop all the vegetables.

2 Rind and dice the bacon or ham. Melt the fat in a medium-sized heavy-based saucepan over medium heat and add the bacon, if using. Cook bacon for a minute.

3 Add the chopped vegetables and the ham, if using, to the fat. Cook gently until they begin to colour.

4 Add the flour off the heat, then cook for 5-10 minutes, stirring, until it is a rich nut brown.

Sauce chasseur turns simple lamb chops into a gourmet's delight.

5 Remove from the heat and gradually add the stock, stirring continually. Return to the heat and bring to the boil, stirring all the while.

6 Add the bouquet garni, half cover and simmer slowly for 1 hour.

7 During simmering, skim from time to time with a metal spoon. Three times add 15 ml [1 tablespoon] cold stock or water to precipitate the fat to the surface of the liquid, then skim the fat off.

8 Meanwhile, if using tomatoes, chop them and add them, or the tomato purée, to the hot sauce.

9 Half cover and simmer for a further ¾ hour. The tomatoes, if used, will reduce to a pulp and the sauce will further reduce.

10 Strain the sauce through a fine sieve into a bowl, pressing all the juices from the vegetables. Discard the vegetables.

11 If serving a proportion of the sauce immediately, rinse out the pan and pour back the quantity needed. Season to taste, reheat and serve.

12 For storing, season the sauce to taste in the bowl. Allow to become cold, cover and transfer to the refrigerator and subsequently to the freezer if wished.

DEMI-GLACE SAUCE

◩◩*Of the four basic brown sauces, this is the richest and the most flavourful—one of the glories of French cuisine. It is a good sauce to serve with sautéed tournedos, roast pheasant or partridge or, more often, with sautéed chicken. Sauces derived from it are also superb.*

Make the sauce espagnole following the previous recipe, steps 1-10.

MAKES 250 ml [½ pt]
250 ml [½ pt] espagnole sauce
150 ml [¼ pt] jellied beef stock

1 Put the sauce espagnole in a medium-sized heavy-based saucepan. Add the jellied beef stock and simmer until the sauce has reduced by one third to 250 ml [½ pt], about 30 minutes.

2 Adjust seasoning and serve. However, if you intend to use this sauce as the base for another, either allow to cool and reserve, or proceed immediately, as planned.

DERIVATIVE SAUCES

As well as being served to make dishes in their own right, the four basic brown sauces can be used to make other sauces. Basically the derivative sauces are made by adding extra ingredients to the mother sauce before serving.

Any one of the four sauces mères can be used. Examples of sauces derived from simple brown sauce are cider sauce and sauce lyonnaise.

However the majority of derivative sauces are made either from espagnole or demi-glace. Examples of the first are chasseur, bourguignonne and bigarade. Examples of the second are romaine, à la diable, fines herbes and rouennaise.

The best results are obtained from the two best quality sauces, espagnole and demi-glace. It would really be a waste of money to make an expensive addition to a simple sauce—to try, for example, to make a Périgueux sauce by addition truffles to a simple brown sauce.

Many of the sauces are double derivatives, setting aside for the moment the fact that demi-glace is itself made from espagnole.

A Périgueux sauce is made by adding truffles to a sauce madère, which is itself made by adding Madeira to an espagnole. A venaison is made by adding redcurrant jelly and cream to a poivrade, which is itself made by adding red wine and juniper berries to a simple brown roux.

Cider sauce, based on a simple brown sauce, is a tasty choice for gammon steaks.

Ingredients for derivative sauces

The choice of additions to make an individual sauce is extremely wide. This will depend on the dish of which it is to form part, the amount of time and sometimes money that you want to spend on it, available ingredients and lastly your own personal inspiration. Additions can be divided roughly into groups.

Vegetable or fruit additions: onions and other chopped vegetables may be added. These are invariably cooked before the addition is made. This may be by softening in butter or they may be simmered in liquid, usually wine. Oranges and frequently citrus zest are added to brown sauces.

Vinegars, alcohol and wines: red or white wine, cider, brandy or red- or white-wine vinegar all make successful additions. Alcoholic liquors and vinegar are invariably reduced before being added to the sauce mère.

Herbs and spices: fresh herbs are often added. These may be simmered in the sauce and then strained before serving or they may be added to the final dish. Cinnamon, nutmeg, mace, all peppers and Worcestershire sauce, all play a part.

Mustard, jelly and cream: mustard may be added to a finished sauce, or gooseberry or, more often, redcurrant jelly melted in it. Cream may be added to a brown sauce and heated through before serving.

Sugar: sugar may be cooked to a pale caramel and used as an addition.

Poultry livers: these may be cooked, pounded and then added.

Final garnishes: chopped items such as gherkins and capers may be added to a finished sauce.

Experimenting for yourself

The classic combinations are famous, but you will find there are several versions of the same sauce, giving different proportions of the same or similar ingredients. Most of the great French chefs have left their own version of a classic sauce. Try out some of the classic recipes and then experiment on your own. Think of the details and do not be afraid to improvise.

Planning forward

The prospect of making a sauce in order to make another sauce may seem daunting, but it is not really so, though it does require a little kitchen planning. You will soon come to regard it as an advantage to be 'half way there' to another delicious meal.

For example, you might find yourself making the brown stock given in the chapter on stocks, because you have bought meat bones. You might then plan to serve sauce espagnole and reserve part. Make the espagnole in the double quantity given in the recipe, serve half of it for a coming meal and reserve the rest.

You then have the two necessary elements to make a superb demi-glace in about half an hour, and almost as quickly, you can make sauces derived from the demi-glace such as sauce madère.

SERVING SUGGESTIONS

Sophisticated sauces make simple ingredients into memorable meals. Try some of the following ideas, using 250 ml [½ pt] sauce or substitute other sauce from the chart.

● Grilled chicken is a dish to remember with a sauce à la diable.

● Reheat cold bacon or ham slices in cider sauce, or pour cider sauce over grilled gammon steaks.

● Serve boiled Jerusalem artichokes with sauce italienne and garnish with grilled bacon slices for a main dish.

● Try soft-boiled eggs with a coating of sauce fines herbes. Serve a generous border of croûtons round the dish to provide a contrast in textures.

● Serve grilled kidneys with a sauce madère.

● Turn new potatoes into a main dish by covering them with a sauce chasseur; serve a green vegetable with them.

● Sauce lyonnaise, quicker to make than many other brown sauces, will make fried liver taste more exciting.

● Poached eggs are delicious served on canapés coated with sauce bourguignonne.

● For a single-crust pie, combine leftover mutton with a proportion of carrots and a mustard sauce.

● Try romaine sauce with steamed whole small onions as an impressive side dish to roast pork.

● Serve tongue hot with the slices coated with sauce piquante.

● Sauce bigarade, excellent with duck, can also be served with roast mutton as a change from mint sauce. With the addition of diced ham, bigarade is also suitable for pasta.

● Add port to a demi-glace instead of Madeira and use with chicken livers to fill vol-au-vent.

Classic sauces made by the brown-roux method (serves 6)

Sauce	Additions	Method	Serve with
A la diable 250 ml [½pt] demi-glace sauce	25 g [1 oz] chopped shallots, 15 g [½ oz] butter, 125 ml [4 fl oz] brandy or 175 ml [6 fl oz] white wine plus 15 ml [1 tablespoon] vinegar, 30 ml [2 tablespoons] tomato purée, 5 ml [1 teaspoon] each of chopped chervil, cayenne pepper, Worcestershire sauce.	Soften shallots in butter. Add brandy or wine plus vinegar. Reduce by boiling gently about 5-8 minutes to 50 ml [2 fl oz]. Add sauce and heat, then add tomato purée and chervil. Cook 5 min. Strain then add cayenne and Worcestershire sauce to taste.	Spicy sauce for grilled chicken and grilled meat.
Bigarade 250 ml [½ pt] espagnole sauce	50 g [2 oz] chopped shallots, 25 g [1 oz] butter, 2 Seville oranges, or 1 orange and 1 lemon, 175 ml [6 fl oz] red wine, 15 ml [1 tablespoon] redcurrant jelly.	Soften shallots in butter. Meanwhile pare zest from 1 orange, make julienne strips and blanch and refresh these twice. Squeeze citrus fruit and add juice, red wine and julienne strips to shallots. Reduce by boiling gently to 50 ml [2 fl oz] about 8 min. Heat the sauce and add wine mix and redcurrant jelly. Simmer 5 min. until jelly has melted and blended, strain if wished and serve.	Duck
Bourguignonne 250 ml [½ pt] espagnole sauce	25 g [1 oz] shallots, 15 g [½ oz] butter, 550 ml [1 pt] red wine, bouquet garni.	Sweat shallots in butter. Add red wine and herbs and boil gently for 25 minutes to reduce to 150 ml [4 fl oz]. Add sauce and boil gently to reduce to 350 ml [12 fl oz] about 5 min. Strain and serve.	Red meat, sautéed poultry (make in sauté pan), poached eggs.
Chasseur 250 ml [½ pt] espagnole sauce	50 g [2 oz] chopped shallots, 40 g [1½ oz] butter, 100 g [4 oz] mushrooms, 175 ml [6 fl oz] white wine, 100 g [4 oz] tomatoes or 15 ml [1 tablespoon] tomato purée, 15 ml [1 tablespoon] chopped parsley.	Soften shallots in butter and add finely sliced mushrooms. Cook 2 minutes. Add white wine and boil gently about 8 min. to reduce 50 ml [2 fl oz]. Add peeled, de-seeded, chopped tomatoes, cook 10 min. Add sauce then tomato purée if using. Add chopped parsley and serve.	Sautéed chicken, rabbit, grilled noisettes of lamb, noodles.
Cider 250 ml [½ pt] simple brown sauce.	150 ml [¼ pt] dry cider, ½ bay leaf, ½ clove.	Put cider, bay leaf and clove in pan. Boil gently until reduced to 50 ml [2 fl oz], about 5 min. Add sauce, simmer 5 minutes, strain and serve.	Sliced boiled bacon and ham.
Fines herbes 250 ml [½ pt] demi-glace sauce	175 ml [6 fl oz] white wine, 5 ml [1 teaspoon] each tarragon, chervil, chives, parsley, 5 ml [1 teaspoon] lemon juice.	Bring wine to boil, add herbs and boil 8 min. to reduce to 50 ml [2 fl oz]. Add sauce and lemon juice, simmer 5 min. then strain. Add extra chopped herbs if liked, then serve. For a tarragon sauce add 45 ml [3 tablespoons] tarragon.	Eggs, fish, a binding sauce.

Classic sauces made by the brown-roux method (serves 6)

Sauce	Additions	Method	Serve with
Italienne 250 ml [½ pt] demi-glace sauce	15 g [½ oz] butter, 50 g [2 oz] mushrooms, 50 g [2 oz] chopped ham, 25 g [1 oz] chopped onion, 150 ml [¼ pt] white wine, 15 ml [1 tablespoon] tomato purée, 10 ml [2 teaspoons] parsley.	Soften mushrooms in butter, add ham and onion. Cook gently 3-4 min. Add wine and boil gently for 5 min. to reduce to 50 ml [2 fl oz]. Add sauce and tomato purée and heat through. Add parsley.	Excellent with pasta, root vegetables such as celeriac.
Lyonnaise 250 ml [½ pt] simple brown sauce	50 g [2 oz] chopped onion, 15 g [½ oz] butter, 50 ml [2 fl oz] white wine, 50 ml [2 fl oz] white wine vinegar.	Soften onions in butter. Add wine and vinegar and boil gently 5 min. to reduce to 50 ml [2 fl oz]. Add sauce, simmer 15 min. Strain or serve with onions.	Liver, meat and vegetables.
Madère 250 ml [½ pt] demi-glace sauce	125 ml [4 fl oz] Madeira wine	Boil the Madeira gently until it has reduced by half, about 5 min. Add the sauce and simmer another 5 min.	Veal escalopes, meat and game.
Mustard 250 ml [½ pt] demi-glace sauce	50 g [2 oz] chopped onion, 25 g [1 oz] butter, 175 ml [6 oz] white wine, thyme, bay leaf, 10 ml [2 teaspoons] Dijon mustard, 5 ml [1 teaspoon] lemon juice.	Sweat onions in butter. Add wine and herbs. Boil about 8 min. to reduce to 50 ml [2 fl oz]. Add sauce and simmer 5 min. Strain then add mustard and lemon juice.	Grilled bacon, pork and ham.
Robert 250 ml [½ pt] demi-glace sauce	25 g [1 oz] onion, 25 g [1 oz] butter, 125 ml [4 fl oz] white wine, 20 ml [4 teaspoons] French mustard, 25 g [1 oz] gherkins, 5 ml [1 teaspoon] parsley.	Sweat the onion in the butter. Add the wine and boil gently for 5 min. until reduced to 50 ml [2 fl oz]. Add sauce and simmer 10 min. Strain if wished. Add mustard, gherkins and parsley.	Roast pork, grilled chops, kidneys.
Romaine 250 ml [½ pt] demi-glace sauce	30 ml [2 tablespoons] granulated sugar, 175 ml [6 fl oz] wine vinegar, 50 g [2 oz] sultanas.	Allow sugar to dissolve over gentle heat without stirring and to colour brown. Remove from heat and stir in vinegar. Reduce this by boiling gently until the sugar is on the point of caramelizing again, about 10 min. Add sauce and sultanas. Barely simmer until sultanas plump up.	Tongue, venison, beef, braised mutton.
Rouennaise 250 ml [½ pt] demi-glace sauce	25 g [1 oz] onions, 65 g [2½ oz] butter, 175 ml [6 fl oz] red wine, 175 g [6 oz] ducks' or chickens' livers.	Soften onions in 25 g [1 oz] butter. Add the wine and boil gently to reduce to 25 ml [1 fl oz], about 10 min. Dice the livers and cook them gently in the rest of the butter in another pan, this will take 6-8 min. Add a little of the demi-glace to the livers, then reduce them to a purée in a liquidizer or through a sieve. Add the rest of the demi-glace and the purée to the reduced wine, and heat.	Duck.

Loin chops
with sauce Robert

Star recipe

★

LOIN CHOPS WITH SAUCE ROBERT

⊠⊠ *These grilled pork chops are lifted from the ordinary and made dinner party fare by the sharp-tasting sauce, made from a demi-glace sauce. If you have sauce espagnole stored in the refrigerator, you can start at step 8 and the recipe will take you three-quarters of an hour. Serve with new potatoes.*

SERVES 4
4 loin pork chops
30 ml [2 tablespoons] oil

For the demi-glace sauce:
40 g [1½ oz] butter
1 small carrot

1 celery stick
1 small onion
25 g [1 oz] mushroom stalks
50 g [2 oz] streaky bacon
1 bouquet garni
675 ml [1¼ pt] good brown stock
10 ml [2 teaspoon] tomato purée
salt and black pepper
150 ml [¼ pt] jellied brown stock

For the sauce Robert:
1 small onion
25 g [1 oz] butter
125 ml [4 fl oz] white wine
25 g [1 oz] gherkins
20 ml [4 teaspoons]
  French mustard
5 ml [1 teaspoon] chopped
  parsley

1 Wash the carrot and celery, peel onion, chop with mushrooms. Remove bacon rind and chop.

5 Remove from the heat and trickle in the brown stock, stirring continuously. Bring to the boil.

6 Add the bouquet garni, cover and simmer for 1 hour. Skim off any fat that rises with a skimming spoon.

7 Add a spoonful of cold stock. Let the fat rise to surface and skim off. Do this again. Add tomato purée.

11 Turn grill to highest heat and arrange the chops in single layer in gratin dish.

12 Continue the sauce. Peel and chop onion. Melt butter in small heavy-based pan; cook onion till soft.

13 Add the wine and simmer to reduce by half. Add to demi-glace; simmer for 20 minutes.

2 Melt butter in a medium-sized heavy-based pan. Add the bacon and sweat for 2 minutes.

3 Add the vegetables and cook over low heat until onion softens. Stir occasionally.

4 Add flour off the heat, then cook, stirring all the time, until the roux is a rich nut brown.

8 Strain the sauce through a sieve, into a small saucepan, pressing all the juices from the vegetables.

9 Add the jellied stock. Simmer until the sauce has reduced to 250 ml [½ pt] about 30 minutes.

10 Brush the loin chops on both sides with a little of the oil. Set aside till ready to cook.

14 Grill chops 1 minute each side. Lower heat or dish and grill 5-7 minutes each side, basting.

15 Chop gherkins. When sauce is ready, stir in mustard, gherkins and parsley. Do not reheat.

16 Dish pork chops on to warmed serving dish. Spoon a little sauce over each portion of meat.

Sauces

mayonnaise and emulsion sauces

Creating a smooth, home-made mayonnaise by combining egg yolks and oil seems more like a conjuring trick than cookery. This course shows you just how to get the trick right and how to flavour and use mayonnaise in exciting ways.

Sauces made with egg yolks are rich and classic. There are two types of 'emulsion' sauce, as it is known. For the first type, egg yolks are combined with oil and seasonings, without cooking, and the result is a mayonnaise. The second type of emulsion sauce is based on egg yolks and butter, which are gently cooked together: the results are called fine butter sauces or hollandaise and these are described in detail in the next chapter.

MAYONNAISE AND ITS USES

Mayonnaise is the most famous and indispensable of cold sauces. Egg yolks and oil plus flavourings are blended together very carefully and gradually so the yolks hold in the other ingredients in creamy suspension. This glossy rich sauce has innumerable uses.

The basic mayonnaise acts as a spring-board for many other sauces, by the addition of fresh herbs and spices, tangy gherkins, anchovies and capers, colourful vegetable purées and refreshing fruit juices. Mixed with aspic jelly, mayonnaise becomes a mayonnaise collée for creating chaudfroids (which are used for coating cold meats).

A mayonnaise is one of the most adaptable of sauces. It is marvellous for dressing-up pieces of cold cooked chicken, salmon, turkey, ham or lobster—and can turn humbler foods such as simple poached cod or haddock into something special. It goes well with small amounts of left-over vegetables (that might otherwise be destined for the bin) which are diced and bound together by a creamy rich mayonnaise mixture to make the classic Russian and potato salads.

Hard-boiled eggs coated with a rich mayonnaise make one of the simplest, quickest and most attractive of all hors d'oeuvres. Mixed with prawns, shrimps or crab and a few seasonings, mayonnaise forms the basis of a seafood cocktail.

Even the very best commercially produced mayonnaises are an in-ferior copy of the real thing. On no account should the commercially marketed 'salad cream' be used in the place of mayonnaise—it is not the same thing.

A flawlessly smooth mayonnaise is the classic accompaniment to poached salmon steaks.

INGREDIENTS
The main ingredients are eggs and oil and it is important to use the correct proportions.

Eggs
It is important that the egg yolks used in mayonnaise are fresh—stale yolks may curdle the mixture. Large egg yolks are the best to use. The maximum amount of oil a large yolk will absorb is 175 ml [6 fl oz]. If you attempt to exceed this, it's a guaranteed failure, as the binding properties of the yolk will collapse, and the sauce will thin out or curdle. For beginners 125 ml [4 fl oz] is the sensible amount of oil to use, 150 ml [¼ pt] once you are confident.

A basic mayonnaise recipe usually gives 250 ml [½ pt] oil for 2 egg yolks, the addition of a third yolk makes a thicker sauce.

Some sauces in the mayonnaise family use cooked egg yolks. The hard-boiled yolks are pushed through a sieve and the mayonnaise made in the usual way. This gives the mayonnaise a different consistency and characteristic taste. This type of sauce cannot be made in a liquidizer. Cooked egg yolks will hold the oil in the same way as raw ones, but need a smaller quantity, about 50 ml [2 fl oz] per large egg yolk.

Flavourings
Ready-made French, dry or ready-made English mustard can be used according to taste, but usually 2.5 ml [½ teaspoon] each of mustard and salt are used to every 250 ml [½ pt] oil. Salt is essential, but pepper is a rarer addition. Season with 1.5 ml [¼ teaspoon] white pepper as black pepper will spoil the look of the mayonnaise.

Oil
The main flavouring of mayonnaise is oil and some recipes state that only olive oil should be used. In fact, olive oil used by itself is too strong for many palates, particularly if you are not accustomed to its fruity flavour. Olive oil is also very expensive, even when bought in bulk, so that a mixture of olive oil with one of the vegetable oils, such as corn oil, is more economical. The blander flavour of the resulting mayonnaise is preferred by many people. Use half olive oil, half corn oil for a less potent flavour, and 25 per cent olive oil, 75 per cent corn oil for economy.

Vinegar
Almost any vinegar can be used according to taste, except malt vinegar; the flavour of this is too strong for a mayonnaise. White-wine vinegar is the most frequently used, but try ringing the changes and find out what suits your palate by using a herb vinegar such as tarragon, or cider or garlic vinegar.

Lemon juice can replace vinegar in the same proportions—essential for a lemon-flavoured mayonnaise.

EQUIPMENT
The only equipment you need is an ordinary mixing bowl and a wooden spoon. However, you could use a wire balloon whisk or an electric whisk instead of a spoon—or even a liquidizer. This method is different (see liquidizer method).

It is important to be comfortable when making mayonnaise by hand, so choose a bowl which is large enough to move the spoon about in easily. Place the bowl on a damp tea-towel so it will stay put, leaving both your hands free to make the mayonnaise.

It's helpful, too, to have a measuring jug for the oil and a spoon for the lemon juice or vinegar, because it is important that the right quantities are used and that oil is added slowly. A method recommended for beginners which is even easier than pouring from a jug is to fill a bottle with the right amount of oil and then make two V-shaped notches in opposite sides of the cork stopper. The oil drops from the lower groove, while air enters the bottle from the upper groove, so that a slow measured pace is ensured.

THE BASIC METHOD
Many cooks (even experienced ones) are apprehensive of making mayonnaise, because they are afraid that it will curdle. It is undoubtedly a delicate job, but not very difficult once you understand the processes involved. Then, as long as you follow a few simple rules given here, the whole operation will go smoothly. After you have made mayonnaise a couple of times, you should confidently be able to make 550 ml [1 pt] mayonnaise in less than 10 minutes.

Incidentally, if you want to make larger quantities, it is probably better to make several batches, each using three or four yolks, rather than to make one huge batch using, for example, 12 yolks!

Principles and initial preparation
Basically, the process of making mayonnaise involves coaxing egg yolks into absorbing oil and, once absorbed, to hold it in suspension. This 'marriage' is achieved by having both oil and yolks at the same temperature or what might be described as 'in a receptive mood'.

Both eggs and oil should be allowed to stand at room temperature for one hour before making the mayonnaise. If you forget to allow time for this, cloudy and chilled olive oil can be made clear again by

Mayonnaise is created from egg yolks and oil, w

standing the bottle in a basin of warm water for a few minutes. Whole eggs in their shells can be immersed in tepid water, too, or gently warmed under a tap until room temperature is reached.

A warm mixing bowl will also help create the right atmosphere for the blending. Dip it in hot water, dry and place it firmly on a damp tea-towel.

Even after these precautions have been taken, the eggs need further encouragement to make them ready to welcome the oil. This is done by beating them for a minute or two to make them smooth, thick and sticky.

The next thing is to blend seasonings into the yolks—salt, mustard and vinegar or lemon juice (usually no more than 15 ml [1 tablespoon] of vinegar per two egg yolks at this stage). A little acid helps the oil to blend with the yolks. Blend the yolks in gently but firmly taking the wooden spoon or whisk round the sides and base of the bowl so they are well mixed. When the mixture is creamy, it is ready for the oil.

Incorporating the oil

Providing the preparations described above have been carried out, and the oil has been carefully measured, you should have no trouble in affecting the marriage. It is essential to introduce the oil to the yolks very slowly, particularly at first.

Hold the jug or bottle in your left hand and the spoon (or electric whisk) in your right—or vice versa if you are left handed. Rest the iip on the edge of the bowl and pour just one drop of oil on to the seasoned yolks beating it in with the spoon as you pour.

The beating should be fast but not furious (about two strokes per second) round the whole bowl to incorporate the oil evenly. After a few seconds, still beating, add a second drop of oil and blend it in. Continue beating in the oil, drop by drop, until the mixture starts to form a thick yellow paste. You can change hands, or change directions of beating, but you must not stop until the mixture has thickened.

It is very important not to rush the beginning; the yolks cannot absorb much oil at a time—and this is particularly true at the beginning. Never attempt to add another drop of oil until you are sure the previous one has been properly incorporated into the mixture. For the same reason, adding a fast trickle instead of a drop or two of oil before the oil is absorbed could cause curdling. So keep calm and do things slowly—in fact, you cannot add the oil too slowly.

Adding oil at the second stage

When the mixture is very thick and creamy and about one-third to one-half of the oil has been used up your success is assured. You can now rest a moment; the crisis point has passed.

It is now safe to start adding the remaining oil in a slow but steady trickle. Continue beating all the time as at the first stage. Every few moments stop trickling in the oil to double check that the oil is still being absorbed by the yolks and is not flowing too fast.

If the mayonnaise becomes so thick that beating is difficult and your wrists begin to ache, stop adding the oil. Beat in a little more lemon or vinegar before continuing. This will thin the mixture and make it easier to handle. Taste the mixture and if you think it is already sufficiently sharp use 15 ml [1 tablespoon] of water instead.

Finishing touches

When all the oil has been absorbed by the yolks, the mayonnaise should be the consistency of thick whipped cream. It will hold its shape when the spoon is lifted from the mixture and will drop with a slow plop back into the bowl.

e blended together with seasonings of mustard, salt and pepper to form a glossy rich sauce.

Step-by-step to making mayonnaise

2 large-sized egg yolks
2.5 ml [½ teaspoon] French or
  English mustard
2.5 ml [½ teaspoon] salt
15 ml [1 tablespoon] vinegar
  or lemon juice
250 ml [½ pt] olive oil or 50%
  olive, 50% corn oil

1 Assemble the equipment and the ingredients at least one hour before making the mayonnaise.

OR warm the eggs by immersing in warm water and the oil by standing in a jug of warm water.

3 Add mustard, salt, vinegar or lemon juice and beat with spoon or whisk for further ½ minute.

4 Rest lip of bottle with notched cork on edge of bowl and hold the whisk in your other hand.

5 Add the first drop of oil. Beat right round the sides and base until completely incorporated.

7 When mixture is thick, the crisis is over, so rest if necessary. Then start a steady trickle of oil.

8 Keep beating. If mayonnaise becomes too thick, thin with a little lemon juice, vinegar or water.

9 The finished mayonnaise should hold its shape, and drop from the spoon or beaters with a plop.

2 Warm bowl in hot water, dry, stand on cloth, add yolks and beat 1-2 minutes until thick and sticky.

6 When it is absorbed add the next drop. Never stop beating—change hands if necessary.

10 Beat in 15-30 ml [1-2 tablespoons] boiling water. Taste for seasonings, adding pepper if liked.

As a final insurance against separating, beat 15-30 ml [1-2 tablespoons] boiling water into the sauce. This is usually done if the mayonnaise is to be refrigerated before use. Taste to check seasonings and blend in more salt, vinegar or lemon juice if wished. Pepper is rarely used but can be added. Use freshly ground white pepper; black pepper would spoil the glossy smooth appearance.

CURING CURDLED MAYONNAISE
Curdling is usually the result of adding oil too rapidly in the initial stages, but it can be corrected. If the oil and egg show signs of separating try adding a few drops of cold water and beating very hard. This will only be successful if you catch the mayonnaise at the very first signs of curdling.

If the mayonnaise curdles completely, there are three methods of correction. They are all based on the principle of starting with a new emulsion and then adding to it the curdled mayonnaise, so that it emulsifies again.

Using a new egg yolk
Starting again with one fresh egg yolk is the most expensive method of curing curdled mayonnaise. Place the yolk in a clean bowl (which should be at room temperature) beat, then slowly pour the curdled mixture on to the egg, beating well between each addition. The mayonnaise will become very thick because of the extra yolk. To thin it down a little, beat a few drops of lemon juice or water into the final mayonnaise.

Using mustard
Warm a mixing bowl and put in 5 ml [1 teaspoon] of made mustard. Beat in 15 ml [1 tablespoon] mayonnaise, using a whisk. When the two are blended, gradually add the rest of the curdled mayonnaise, no more than 15 ml [1 teaspoon] at a time. This is a laborious method, but is sure to work and cheaper than adding an egg yolk.

Using a bread paste
The Italians soak a tiny bit of white crustless bread in water and pulp it down with a spoon until it looks like a thick cream (about 5 ml [1 teaspoon]). Then gradually blend in the sauce as previously described.

LIQUIDIZER METHOD
If you're nervous of failure when making a mayonnaise by hand, here is a foolproof method that is also quick and easy.

A mayonnaise can be made in a matter of minutes in a liquidizer. Even one-speed liquidizers will blend the mayonnaise without curdling. Ingredients are used in the same quantities—with one important exception. Most liquidizer blades are fixed too high above the base of the goblet to whip two egg yolks effectively. So (unless you plan to make large amounts of mayonnaise) use whole eggs, allowing one whole large egg per scant 250 ml [½ pt] of oil.

Made in this way, the mayonnaise does not have the same golden rich colour—it is much thinner and lighter, but it is certainly far better than the commercial type. An advantage of liquidizer mayonnaise is that it keeps successfully several days longer in the fridge than the traditional sort.

Place the whole eggs and seasonings in the liquidizer goblet. Cover and blend for four seconds. For liquidizers with speed control, reduce the speed to moderate and add the oil in a thin, steady stream through the opening in the cover, until it is completely blended with the eggs.

If you are using a liquidizer with one (high) speed, add the oil to the liquidizer in batches, stopping to rest the blades occasionally. Adjust the seasonings.

STORING AND FREEZING
You will probably find it convenient to make at least 250 ml [½ pt] mayonnaise at a time.

If you have any remaining after use, turn into a small bowl or jar just large enough to take it. Cover with cling film or foil to prevent a skin forming and store in a cold larder or in the bottom of the refrigerator. Hand-made mayonnaise will keep for up to a week. Liquidizer mayonnaise will keep for several days longer. Do not stir before bringing it back to room temperature or there is a danger of the mayonnaise thinning out.

Mayonnaise cannot be frozen because the ingredients freeze at different temperatures and the sauce would curdle on thawing making it most unappetizing.

Mayonnaise Variations

Unless otherwise stated these amounts are based on the basic mayonnaise using 250 ml [½ pt] oil, and the flavourings are in addition to those already in the basic mayonnaise.

Sauce	Additions	Method	Serving suggestions
Mousseline	2 egg whites	Whisk egg whites until standing in peaks and fold into the mayonnaise.	An economic, fluffy mayonnaise to serve with cold, lightly cooked vegetables.
Chantilly	½ lemon, 45 ml [3 tablespoons] whipped cream.	Season with lemon juice and fold in the whipped cream.	Serve with cold asparagus.
Rémoulade	15 ml [1 tablespoon] chopped parsley, tarragon, chervil or basil, 1 clove garlic, 5 ml [1 teaspoon] chopped capers, 5 ml [1 teaspoon] dry mustard, 2 small gherkins, finely chopped, 2.5 ml [½ teaspoon] anchovy essence.	Crush the garlic. Mix all the ingredients together and fold into the mayonnaise. Chill and serve.	Serve with grilled fish, cold pork, prawns or shrimps.
Aioli	3-4 garlic cloves	This mayonnaise is made without initial seasonings of mustard, vinegar or lemon juice. Crush garlic with a little salt to a very smooth paste. Work into the egg yolks before adding oil as for basic mayonnaise. When complete, add lemon juice, salt and pepper to taste.	A traditional dish from Provence consisting of a dish of the sauce surrounded with a mixture of lightly cooked vegetables such as broad beans, French beans, carrots, potatoes baked in their skins, hard-boiled eggs and boiled beef. Also good with hot fish soups and boiled fish.
Mayonnaise verte	30 ml [2 tablespoons] frozen spinach, ½ bunch watercress leaves, 15 ml [1 tablespoon] parsley, a little fresh tarragon.	Place additions together in a pan with a little water. Simmer for 5-6 minutes. Drain, squeeze dry and purée. Fold into basic mayonnaise.	This is the traditional sauce to serve with cold salmon or salmon trout.
Gribiche	Replace raw egg yolks with 3 hard-boiled egg yolks, 15 ml [1 tablespoon] French mustard, 1-2 hard-boiled egg whites.	Use only 150 ml [¼ pt] oil. Sieve egg yolks, add seasonings and mustard, then work in the oil as for basic mayonnaise. Chop egg white finely and fold into finished sauce.	Serve with shellfish and cold fish. Also good with cold cooked vegetables and for raw vegetables such as crudités.
Tartare	Use 2 hard-boiled egg yolks and 1 raw egg yolk, 5 ml [1 teaspoon] each of finely chopped chives, parsley and capers, 1 small gherkin.	Sieve the hard-boiled egg yolks. Make the mayonnaise with the hard-boiled egg yolks mixed with raw egg yolk. Finely chop the gherkin and fold the gherkin with the remaining additions into the finished sauce.	Serve with fried or grilled fish, cold beef and cold chicken.

VARIATIONS AND DERIVATIVE SAUCES

Derivative sauces are made by stirring or folding additional ingredients into the mayonnaise, after it has been made, to give extra flavour.

The chart of derivative sauces, opposite, shows mayonnaise variations, including those based on hard-boiled rather than raw egg yolks.

Hard-boiled egg mayonnaise

This type of mayonnaise has a slightly different taste and consistency. It is less rich, because less oil per yolk is used.

To make this type of mayonnaise the eggs are hard boiled and the whites reserved. The yolks are sieved to produce a fine texture. They are then mixed to a smooth paste with flavourings and the oil is gradually blended in exactly as described in the step-by-step method, the only difference being that no more than 50 ml [2 fl oz] is used per yolk.

If hard-boiled egg whites are very finely chopped and added to the resulting mayonnaise, they give a light flavour and good body—just right for spooning over cold foods.

Dry flavourings

Making mayonnaise gives an excellent opportunity for you to experiment and find your own favourite flavourings. All the quantities given here are based on a basic mayonnaise made with 250 ml [½ pt] oil.

●Fresh herbs such as parsley, tarragon, chervil, basil and chives are classic additions. The French call this type of mayonnaise aux fines herbes. Herbs should be finely chopped—use about 15 ml [1 tablespoon]. Try experimenting with one of your favourite herbs, or a judicious mixture of two or more. Dried herbs should never be used.

●Stronger flavourings are generally added in smaller proportions. For a garlic-flavoured mayonnaise use one crushed garlic clove (this is different from the classic aioli).

●Add a sharp, tangy taste to mayonnaise with approximately 5 ml [1 teaspoon] chopped gherkins, capers or anchovies (or anchovy essence).

●Curry can also be added to mayonnaise. Curry paste is preferable to powder because the flavours blend better than powder, and although it is not strictly 'dry' it does not alter the consistency of the mayonnaise. Use up to 15 ml [1 tablespoon] curry paste, according to taste—delicious with pasta, salads and cold chicken or turkey.

Liquid flavourings

Liquid flavourings added to a mayonnaise, unless in large amounts, will not alter the consistency radically. However, a liquidizer mayonnaise, which is naturally thinner, may become nearer to a pouring sauce. This type of mayonnaise is ideal for folding into foods (such as vegetables) which will glisten with a fine shiny coating.

●Orange or lemon juice (in addition to lemon or vinegar used in the basic mayonnaise) are both used to give a refreshingly tangy flavour. Use 15 ml [1 tablespoon] or more according to taste. The flavour of the fruit is barely perceptible, but the mayonnaise loses some of its richness. The grated zest of the fruit can also be used, which will make the flavour more pronounced. This is good with mixed vegetables, fruit and nut salads or cold white fish.

●Whipped cream folded into a mayonnaise is a creamy accompaniment to cold mixed vegetable selections or cold egg dishes. Use 45 ml [3 tablespoons] to 250 ml [½ pint].

Cold chicken pieces in a curry mayonnaise.

85

Substantial additions
●One small peeled and grated dessert apple and a little freshly grated horseradish folded into the mayonnaise is delicious with cold beef or smoked mackerel.

●Half a cucumber, seeded, peeled and grated plus 4-5 small tomatoes skinned, seeded and chopped plus a pinch of paprika with mayonnaise should be served with cold pork or bacon.

●To make an anchovy sauce to serve with cold white fish, pound 4-5 drained anchovy fillets, chop 2 hard-boiled eggs and fold into mayonnaise.

MANY WAYS WITH MAYONNAISE
Mayonnaise is one of the most adaptable sauces—it goes with fish, meat, rice, pasta and, in particular, with hot or cold vegetables. Here are just some suggestions for using mayonnaise.

●For a Russian salad, mix together 1 small raw cauliflower broken into florets, 45-60 ml [3-4 tablespoons] each of cooked diced potatoes, cooked beetroot and cooked peas. Add 4 chopped, stuffed olives and 3 chopped anchovy fillets and fold into equal quantities of basic mayonnaise and sour cream. Alternatively, put in the vegetables and the dressing in layers, with cooked beetroot at the bottom of the dish to prevent staining the rest of the ingredients.

●For a tuna salad, flake 175 g [6 oz] canned tuna fish. Dice 450 g [1 lb] unpeeled red-skinned apples and 4 celery sticks. Combine with a Chantilly sauce.

Ensaladilla is an hors d'oeuvre of summertime vegetables.

●For a broad bean hors d'oeuvre, serve hot broad beans with aioli.

●For a sandwich filling, mix grated cheese with mayonnaise and pile into crusty French bread (buttered if liked).

●When poaching fish such as turbot or brill, take out cooked fish and reduce the stock by boiling. Remove from the heat and stir in twice as much aioli as fish stock (fumet). Reheat carefully without boiling until it is piping hot. Pour the sauce over the fish and serve.

●Cut open baked potatoes and fill with a combination of sour cream, mayonnaise and chopped chives.

●For a Waldorf salad, finely dice 450 g [1 lb] apples, reserving one which should be sliced and sprinkled with lemon juice. Chop 5 celery sticks and 75 g [2 oz] shelled walnuts and fold into 150 ml [¼ pt] basic mayonnaise with the diced apples. Line a salad bowl with a washed and dried lettuce, pile the salad into the centre and surround with apple slices.

●For a continental salad, combine 225 g [½ lb] cold, cooked pasta shells with 75 g [3 oz] sliced frankfurter. Dress with 75 ml [3 fl oz] mayonnaise into which you have stirred 10 ml [2 teaspoons] curry paste.

●For winter special, chop 4 celery sticks, 50 g [2 oz] walnuts, 3 apples and fold in 45 ml [3 tablespoons] orange mayonnaise.

●For a summer dip, serve a dish of aioli with crudités—a selection of strips of carrot and celery, cauliflower florets, whole spring onions and strips of green pepper.

●Serve a rémoulade sauce with grilled sprats.

●For a sauce Riviera, mix 250 ml [½ pt] mayonnaise verte with 15 ml [1 tablespoon] each of finely chopped capers and anchovy fillets plus 50 g [2 oz] cream cheese. This makes an excellent sandwich spread or sauce for cold beef or chicken.

●For a delicious summer lunch dish make a mayonnaise aux fines herbes (with 15 ml [1 tablespoon] of two or more finely chopped fresh herbs). Then fold in cold, cooked and drained boil-in-the-bag smoked haddock. Surround the dish with sliced tomatoes, cucumber and hard-boiled eggs.

●A quick potato mayonnaise can be made by combining cold, cooked diced potatoes and home-made mayonnaise. For first-class results, dice steamed, peeled potatoes while still warm and mix with vinaigrette then, when potatoes are cold, cover them with mayonnaise to which you have added chopped chives. Chopped spring onions or chopped hard-boiled eggs and finely chopped anchovy fillets make superb additions.

●Serve orange-flavoured mayonnaise with cold grilled chicken and an undressed salad of orange and watercress.

ENSALADILLA
◪◪*This 'little salad' is a delicious Spanish hors d'oeuvre of fresh summer vegetables, steamed until just*

tender and served with a pungent aioli sauce. The method of making aioli differs from the basic mayonnaise in that the garlic is crushed and worked in with the egg yolk. The vegetables are prepared first to allow them to become cold. Steam the vegetables for best flavour, after first washing them le-carefully and paring and removing 3 any damaged parts.

This salad may be served plain or on a lettuce leaf or, for a party, it may be placed in a shallow bowl and un-moulded so that it retains the bowl shape. Decorate with strips of pimento.

SERVES 4
100 g [¼ lb] new potatoes
100 g [¼ lb] young carrots
100 g [¼ lb] broad beans
100 g [¼ lb] French beans
100 g [¼ lb] peas

For the mayonnaise:
1 large-sized egg yolk
1-2 garlic cloves
salt
150 ml [¼ pt] oil

1 Prepare the vegetables. Scrub the potatoes and young carrots, top and tail French beans and pod the peas and broad beans. Chop potatoes and carrots into quarters.

2 Place the potatoes in a steamer and steam for 10 minutes.

3 Add the broad beans, carrots and peas. Steam for a further 5 minutes.

4 Add the French beans and steam for 10 minutes until all the vegetables are tender.

5 Remove the vegetables from the steamer and allow to cool.

6 Bring the mayonnaise ingredients to room temperature, by removing from the refrigerator for about one hour before use. Warm the bowl by immersing in hot water.

7 Peel and chop the garlic and crush with a little salt.

8 Beat the egg yolk in the bowl for 1-2 minutes before adding the garlic. Beat again.

9 Beat in about half the oil, very carefully, drop by drop, until the mayonnaise takes on a thick, creamy consistency.

10 Rest the bottle on the edge of the bowl and trickle in the rest of the oil, beating all the time.

11 Dice all the vegetables until they are the same size as the broad beans.

13 Pour the aioli over the vegetables and stir gently so that all are coated.

BEETROOT MAYONNAISE

 This mayonnaise is based on the classic Gribiche sauce, which is made with cooked egg yolks. The 1.5 ml [¼ teaspoon] of mustard which usually goes into a mayonnaise is omitted here. Beetroot mayonnaise is particularly good with cold beef.

SERVES 4
450 g [1 lb] beetroot

For the mayonnaise:
3 eggs
salt
15 ml [1 tablespoon] French mustard
7-15 ml [½-1 tablespoon] lemon juice or vinegar
150 ml [¼ pt] oil
30 ml [2 tablespoons] whipped cream

1 Cut off the green tops of the beetroot taking care not to cut the flesh. Discard.

2 Place in a saucepan, pour over enough cold water to cover and bring to the boil. Cover and simmer for 2 hours for small beetroot, 3-4 hours for larger ones.

3 Meanwhile, for the mayonnaise warm the bowl to room temperature, by leaving it out for one hour or immersing in hot water.

4 Hard boil the eggs, drain and peel them. Halve the eggs, take out the yolks and push through a nylon sieve into the bowl. Chop the whites of two of the eggs and reserve.

5 Add salt, mustard and vinegar or lemon juice to the egg yolks and beat them well for half a minute.

6 Beat in about half the oil, very carefully, drop by drop, until it becomes a thick, creamy consistency.

7 Rest the bottle on the edge of the bowl and trickle in the rest of the oil, beating all the time.

8 Drain the beetroot. When cool enough, peel and slice or dice.

9 When the mayonnaise is finished, fold in the chopped egg whites and cream and spoon over the beetroot.

Serve sliced beetroot with Gribiche mayonnaise as an accompaniment to cold beef.

SEEAFOOD COCKTAIL

This classic favourite makes an attractive and easy-to-prepare first course for any meal. The piquant tomato-flavoured sauce is traditional for prawns but should not overpower them, so be frugal with the use of Tabasco. Save the outer leaves of the lettuce for use in another dish.

SERVES 4
1 lettuce
350 g [¾ lb] prawns or shrimps
paprika pepper
4 lemon wedges

For the mayonnaise:
1 large-sized egg yolk
salt
1.5 ml [¼ teaspoon] French or English mustard
7-15 ml [½-1 tablespoon] lemon juice or vinegar
150 ml [¼ pt] oil
few drops of Worcestershire sauce

dash of Tabasco sauce
30 ml [2 tablespoons] tomato ketchup
lemon juice

1 Wash and dry the lettuce leaves, then wrap in a clean towel. Finely shred the lettuce heart and crisp in the refrigerator.

2 Bring the mayonnaise ingredients to room temperature by removing them from the refrigerator for at least one hour before use. Warm the bowl by immersing in hot water.

3 Beat egg yolks in the bowl for 1-2 minutes before adding mustard and salt and vinegar or lemon juice. Beat again.

4 Beat in about half the oil, very carefully, drop by drop, until it becomes a thick, creamy consistency.

5 Rest the bottle on the edge of the bowl and trickle in the rest of the oil, beating all the time.

6 When the mayonnaise is finished, fold in the Worcestershire sauce, Tabasco and tomato ketchup. Season to taste with extra lemon juice and salt and white pepper.

7 Peel most of the prawns, reserving one or two unpeeled to garnish each serving. Fold the peeled prawns into the sauce.

8 Remove the lettuce from the refrigerator and line four round wine glasses with the shreds. Divide seafood mixture between them.

9 Finish with a pinch of paprika on top of each glass. Garnish with one or two prawns, set on the edge of each glass, and a wedge of lemon.

Variations

●For the prawns substitute the same weight of cooked crabmeat. Decorate the edge of the glasses with a thin slice of lemon.

●Use the prawn, shrimp or crabmeat mixture to stuff large tomatoes. Cut the top from each tomato and scoop out the seeds and most of the flesh, taking care not to pierce the walls of the shell. Fill with the seafood mixture and serve on a plate surrounded with lettuce and lemon wedges.

●Here's a more substantial dish. Replace mayonnaise seasonings with 5 ml [1 teaspoon] tomato purée. Hard boil 4 eggs, and halve them lengthways. Cook 125 g [¼ lb] rice and when cold toss in 45 ml [3 tablespoons] vinegar. Place the eggs cut side down on the rice. Spoon over prawns in mayonnaise sauce and garnish the edge of the dish with cucumber slices.

●For a mussel mayonnaise, omit the prawns and flavourings in the sauce. Grate 1 celeriac or chop 2 small celery sticks, 2 small red-skinned eating apples and 1 small gherkin. Thinly slice 1 apple and dip slices in lemon juice. Add the vegetables to the mayonnaise. Fold in 24 cooked mussels (if canned, make sure they are well drained) with 2.5 ml [½ teaspoon] ready-made mustard, a squeeze of lemon juice and 30-45 ml [2-3 tablespoons] whipped cream.

Sauces

egg and butter sauces

Hollandaise, béarnaise and their variations are the finest and most delicious sauces of classic French cookery. Luxuriously rich, they are the perfect accompaniment for grilled meats, poached fish, delicately steamed vegetables or soft-boiled eggs. Unfortunately, these sauces gained a reputation for being difficult to make and even the most experienced cooks have been known to quail before tackling them. However, once you understand the basic principles, fine butter sauces present no problems. Follow the step-by-step guide and you can't go wrong.

In French cookery, one of the first rules of sauce-making is to try to make the sauce from part of the main dish—the juice from the meat perhaps, or the water from the vegetables. Where no such base is present, as in the case of grilled meats, poached or steamed fish, steamed vegetables, rice, pasta and soft-boiled eggs, the resourceful French turn to fine butter sauces to add flavour and interest to the meal.

Fine butter sauces are a glorious emulsion of lemon juice, vinegar or wine, egg yolks and unsalted butter. The most famous of these sauces are hollandaise and béarnaise, classic names from the culinary lore of France.

Subtle and smooth, fine butter sauces enhance rather than drown the food they are served with. They are the classic accompaniment for salmon, plainly grilled steaks and lamb cutlets, steamed white fish, asparagus, artichokes, broccoli and other steamed or boiled green vegetables. Even humble soft-boiled eggs can be turned into a gourmet treat with a hollandaise or béarnaise accompaniment.

When making fine butter sauces, the aim is to produce a lukewarm, creamy smooth emulsion which barely holds its shape and is just thick enough to coat the back of the spoon. This might seem a complicated and hazardous business, but approach the sauce calmly, do everything carefully and little can go wrong.

The basic principle of making a fine butter sauce is to persuade egg yolks to hold fat in suspension. To help them do this and give the sauce flavour, a sharp base of lemon juice, wine or vinegar is used. The egg yolks are added to this, then the butter is beaten in, slowly and gently until a fine emulsion is formed. Add too much butter and the sauce will curdle. Let the sauce get too hot and the eggs will scramble. So, as you will see, the watchword is caution. Go carefully, follow the step-by-step guide and you will be delighted with the results of your efforts.

INGREDIENTS
Such delicately flavoured sauces deserve the finest ingredients.

The base
Purists say that hollandaise sauce should be made only from eggs, butter and lemon juice. The problem with this is that the end results are rather insipid, so modern versions of hollandaise use a reduction (boiled-down mixture) of dry white wine or white wine vinegar to give the sauce extra flavour. Allow 45 ml [3 tablespoons] dry white wine or white wine vinegar before reducing, for every 2 egg yolks.

Sauce béarnaise classically has a base of dry white wine, tarragon vinegar, shallots and a few leaves of fresh tarragon. Allow 45 ml [3 tablespoons] dry white wine, 30 ml [2 tablespoons] tarragon vinegar, 2 peeled and finely chopped shallots and four to five leaves of fresh tarragon for each 2 egg yolks. In the variations of hollandaise and béarnaise, the acid flavouring elements differ but the proportions remain the same.

The eggs
Large, fresh eggs should be used at room temperature. If you can get free-range eggs with deep yellow yolks, so much the better. The eggs must be separated, but don't waste the whites. Use them to make meringues, soufflé omelettes or whisk them until stiff and fold into scrambled egg to make it extra light.

The butter
Unsalted butter is best as the flavour is not so intrusive as that of the salted kind. Traditionally, 75 g [3 oz] butter is allowed per large egg yolk. These proportions are successful if you are an experienced and confident fine butter-sauce maker but for the beginner, it is much better to allow 50 g [2 oz] per egg yolk. This is the amount of butter the yolk will readily absorb; so it is wisest to use no more than this on your first attempt and so minimize the things that can go wrong and spoil the sauce.

Classic cookery books soften the butter, cut it into dice and add it, bit by bit, to the mixture of beaten egg yolks and acid reduction. Our method uses part cold butter and part melted butter which is added like oil to mayonnaise. The end result is exactly the same as if you follow the classic method, but you are much less likely to meet with disaster on the way.

Seasoning
When the sauce is thickened, it is seasoned with salt and pepper and lemon juice. Black pepper, although finest in flavour, is to be avoided, as it adds unpleasant black specks to the sauce. Fill your pepper grinder with white peppercorns instead. Do not however use the dust sold as white pepper. It will float rather nastily on the surface of your sauce. Lemon juice is stirred into the sauce just before serving—10 ml [2 teaspoons] gives the right amount of piquancy to the basic two-yolk sauce.

In hollandaise and béarnaise variations, freshly chopped herbs are sometimes added at this point.

EQUIPMENT
A double boiler or a basin whose rim will just fit over the top of the pan—so the base does not touch the water—is essential when making fine butter sauces. They are much too delicate to set directly over the heat.

To beat the sauce you need a balloon or sauce whisk. An electric mixer is not really suitable because fine butter sauces are not made in vast quantities and electric mixers do not cope well with small amounts. You also need a small pan for melting the butter and a second small pan for reducing the acid base of the sauce.

THE BASIC TECHNIQUE
The basic technique of making fine butter sauces can be divided into easy-to-follow stages. The amounts referred to here are the same as in the step-by-step recipe.

Fine butter sauces can be served with a wide variety of plainly cooked vegetables to add flavour and interest.

Making the reduction
When white wine or white wine vinegar is used for making hollandaise sauce, it must be reduced by rapid boiling so that the flavour is concentrated. The wine, vinegar, herb and shallot base for béarnaise is also reduced.

To make the reduction, put the ingredients in a small pan, chopping shallots and herbs, where used, as finely as possible. Set the pan over a fierce heat and allow to boil rapidly, until the liquid is reduced to about 30 ml [2 tablespoons]. Set this liquid aside to cool a little, straining it first if herbs and shallots have been added.

Preparing the double boiler
Prepare the double boiler by putting water in the lower half, making sure that the upper half does not reach the water level.

Alternatively, improvise with a basin that will fit snugly over the top of the rim of a pan. Never stand the basin on a trivet. Not only is this a rather unsteady arrangement when you are whisking, but you would only be able to get a very little water in the pan without it touching the basin.

When you have prepared the double boiler, place it over a low heat. At the same time, fill the sink with cold water. This may come in useful later should the sauce begin to curdle and require rapid cooling.

Preparing the butter
Cut off 25 g [1 oz] from the measured

butter and set it aside. Place the remaining butter in a saucepan with a lip and melt it gently over low heat. Pour it into a small jug and set aside in a warm but not hot place.

Preparing the eggs
Separate the eggs into a clean bowl, reserving the whites for use in other dishes. Remove the top part of the double boiler from the heat and put the egg yolks into the top part.

Adding the eggs
Whisk the eggs until they have thickened slightly. This will take about three minutes. Still away from the heat, add the cooled wine or vinegar reduction and beat for another half minute. Never, ever, add the reduction to the eggs while it is still hot. You will get a nasty scrambled effect.

Adding the butter
Divide the reserved cold butter in half. Cut both halves into dice and add half to the egg mixture. Place the top of the double boiler back over the bottom. The water underneath should be simmering gently. Beat slowly with a whisk for one to two minutes, making sure you scrape the mixture from the sides and bottom of the pan all the time. This is the most crucial part of the operation. It is essential that the water is not too hot. If it is, the mixture will thicken too fast

and become lumpy.

The mixture becomes smooth and forms a light cream on the wires of the whisk. When you begin to see the bottom of the pan between strokes, it is time to remove the pan from the heat.

Add the remaining half of the cold reserved diced butter. This will cool the yolks and stop them from over cooking. Whisk for about one minute, until the butter has been amalgamated with the sauce. Still away from the heat, start adding the melted butter, drop by drop at first, whisking all the time. Take care to incorporate the mixture from the sides and bottom of the pan or basin all the time.

The butter is added at this stage in the same way as oil in the early stages of making mayonnaise (see how in previous chapter). Never add more butter until the previous drop has been smoothly incorporated into the sauce and has slightly thickened it. If the butter is added too quickly, the egg yolks will reject it and that means the sauce will refuse to thicken.

When half the butter has been absorbed and the sauce is the consistency of thick cream, pour in the remaining butter in a slow, steady dribble, whisking all the time.

Seasoning
When all the butter has been added and the sauce is thick, season with

salt and white pepper. For extra flavour, you may also wish to add a squeeze of lemon juice at this stage.

COPING WITH EMERGENCIES
Should your sauce go wrong, there is no need to pour it down the drain. Quick action can usually save the day. Here is what to do.

Fast thickening
Should the sauce thicken too fast and begin to go lumpy before all the butter has been incorporated, plunge the base of the top part of the double boiler into cold water—a sink or bowl full, which you will have providently prepared in advance. Leave in the water for one minute, to allow the sauce to cool, then whisk hard to cool the yolks. When they are barely warm (test with a fingertip), return the double boiler to the heat, checking that the temperature of the water in the bottom part has fallen. Reduce the heat under the saucepan before continuing.

Sauce begins to curdle
If the mixture begins to show just a hint of curdling (dividing into blobs) it can be rescued by removing from the heat and beating in 5-10 ml [1-2 teaspoons] very cold water. Take the bottom pan off the heat to reduce the water temperature. Then slightly reduce the heat of the cooker before returning the pan to continue.

SERVES 4
45 ml [3 tablespoons] dry white wine or white wine vinegar
100 g [¼ lb] unsalted butter

2 large eggs
salt
freshly ground white pepper
10 ml [2 teaspoons] lemon juice

1 Place white wine or white wine vinegar in small pan over fierce heat. Boil rapidly until reduced to 30 ml [2 tablespoons]. Cool.

5 Place the remaining butter in a heavy-based saucepan over low heat. Allow to melt then pour it into a small jug. Set aside.

6 Separate yolks from whites. Place yolks in a clean bowl. Reserve the egg whites in the refrigerator for other dishes.

7 Remove the top of the double boiler from the heat and place the egg yolks in the top. Whisk with a balloon or sauce whisk.

11 When the mixture becomes smooth and forms a light cream on the whisk, and you can see the pan base, remove from heat.

12 Add the remaining half of the solid butter and whisk for about 1 minute until the butter has amalgamated with the sauce.

13 Still off the heat, start adding the melted butter, drop by drop at first. Whisk all the time and scrape from sides and bottom.

hollandaise sauce

2 To prepare a double boiler put water in the lower half. Water must not touch upper half of the boiler. Set over low heat.

3 Put some cold water in the sink, or large-sized bowl, in case you need to cool the sauce rapidly later on.

4 Cut off 25 g [1 oz] of the butter. Divide this in half and cut into small dice. Keep the dice separate and leave in a cool place.

8 When the egg yolks are creamy, stop whisking and, still away from the heat, add the wine or vinegar. Whisk for another half minute.

9 Add half of the diced butter to the eggs. Return the top to the boiler over heat, checking that the water is just simmering.

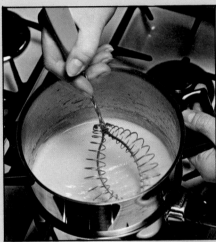

10 Begin whisking the sauce. Whisk slowly for 1-2 minutes, making sure you scrape the mixture from the sides and bottom of the pan.

14 When half the butter has been absorbed and the sauce is like thick cream, pour in the rest in a steady dribble, whisking well.

15 When all the butter has been added and the sauce is thick, season with salt and pepper. Stir in the lemon juice.

16 Transfer the sauce to a warmed (but not hot) sauce-boat and serve immediately. Hollandaise sauce is always served lukewarm.

Sauce separates

If the sauce separates into egg yolk and melted butter, remove it from the heat, empty into a bowl and wash out the top of the double boiler. Place a fresh egg yolk in the top of the double boiler, beat it then add the separated mixture a little at a time, beating well and keeping the heat low.

Sauce refuses to thicken

This is the result of adding butter too quickly. Rinse out a clean bowl with hot water, put 5 ml [1 teaspoon] lemon juice and 15 ml [1 tablespoon] of the thin sauce into this bowl. Whisk until it is creamy, then add the rest of the thin sauce a little at a time.

Sauce becomes too thick

If the sauce becomes too thick (remember, it should just hold its shape), remove it from the heat and beat in 15-30 ml [1-2 tablespoons] hot water, milk or cream.

Sauce turns to scrambled egg

This is the one occasion when nothing can be done to save the situation. Pour the mess down the drain and start again, working on a lower heat and with more caution this time.

PREPARING IN ADVANCE

Ideally, fine butter sauces should be prepared just before serving, but should you find yourself obliged to keep the sauce, for time reasons perhaps, it can be made an hour in advance. If you know you will have to keep the sauce warm, play safe by beating 5 ml [1 teaspoon] cornflour into the egg yolks at the beginning. This will stabilize the sauce.

When it is intended that the sauce should wait, stand the prepared sauce in a bain-marie (dish of warm water) allowing the water to come half way up the sides of the sauce container. Melt 25 g [1 oz] butter and whisk this in just before serving. Add seasoning and lemon juice.

Longer term storage

Hollandaise sauce may be stored in a screw-top jar in the refrigerator where it will keep for four days. This is a good idea if you want to serve cold meat later in the week. Make the sauce as described for advance preparation but do not add lemon juice and extra butter at the end. Allow the sauce to cool before placing it in a screw-top jar. It will set to a fairly solid butter in the refrigerator and will need to be re-heated before serving.

To reheat the sauce, stand a basin in a bain-marie containing warm water. Add the sauce 30 ml [2 tablespoons] at a time and beat well until melted. When all the sauce has been melted, add 25 g [1 oz] butter as described in advance preparation and add lemon juice in the usual way.

USING A LIQUIDIZER

Fine butter sauces can be made in a liquidizer but instead of the usual quantities, 100 g [¼ lb] butter is allowed for three egg yolks. Three egg yolks must be used as two is not sufficient to make a liquidizer sauce with this amount of butter. This means they do not have such a delicate flavour as sauces made in the classic manner. Fine butter sauce made using the usual ratio of butter to egg yolks would become so thick that the sauce would overheat the liquidizer motor.

One-speed liquidizers can be used to make fine butter sauces. If your liquidizer has several speeds, check with the instruction book. The speed for hollandaise and other fine butter sauces will be the same as for mayonnaise. For full details of making fine butter sauces in a liquidizer, see the step-by-step guide.

HOLLANDAISE VARIATIONS

There are several simple variations on the basic sauce hollandaise shown in the step-by-step guide. Their uses are given in the chart.
●For sauce mousseline, fold 50 ml [2 fl oz] whipped cream into the finished sauce.
●For sauce avec blanc d'oeufs, fold two stiffly beaten egg whites into the finished hollandaise.
●For sauce maltaise, use the juice and finely grated rind of a blood orange instead of the wine or vinegar base.
●For sauce divine, stir 15 ml [1 tablespoon] liquid made by reducing 30 ml [2 tablespoons] sherry, and 30 ml [2 tablespoons] whipped cream into hollandaise sauce.
●For sauce vin blanc, add 10 ml [2 teaspoons] reduced fish stock to the hollandaise sauce.

Step-by-step to hollandaise sauce in a liquidizer

1 First warm the goblet of your liquidizer. To do this, fill it with hot water, leave for 5 minutes, then rinse out and dry.

3 Place the butter in a heavy-based pan with a lip over low heat. Allow it to melt then pour into a small jug. Set aside.

5 While blending, add the melted butter in a very slow trickle. When the sauce is thick, stop adding butter if not all used.

SERVES 4
45 ml [3 tablespoons] dry white
wine or white wine vinegar
100 g [¼ lb] unsalted butter
3 large eggs
salt
freshly ground white pepper
10 ml [2 teaspoons] lemon juice

2 Meanwhile, place white wine or wine vinegar in a small pan over fierce heat. Boil until reduced to 30 ml [2 tablespoons]. Cool.

4 Separate the eggs and place the yolks in the liquidizer goblet. Add the reduction and blend for about 4 seconds until well mixed.

6 Season with salt, freshly ground white pepper and lemon juice. Blend for a further 10 seconds then turn into a warmed sauce-boat.

SERVING FINE BUTTER SAUCES

Sauce	Serving suggestions
HOLLANDAISE	Poached or grilled salmon steaks, asparagus, artichoke hearts, broccoli or calabrese.
Mousseline	With any of the above and with lamb cutlets.
Maltaise	With fried scampi, sole or plaice fillets. Also good with asparagus and broccoli.
Avec blanc d'oeufs	With poached and steamed white fish, broccoli and asparagus.
Divine	With chicken, sole, plaice.
BEARNAISE	With grilled steak, especially tournedos, shellfish and chicken.
Choron	With grilled fillet steaks, poached eggs and fish.
Foyot	Poached or soft-boiled eggs, veal sweetbreads.
Nivernaise	With grilled lamb cutlets, poached eggs, steaks, grilled chicken breasts.
Paloise	With grilled lamb cutlets.

SAUCE BEARNAISE

⊠⊠ *Sauce béarnaise is the sister of sauce hollandaise. It is very similar but thicker and stronger in flavour. It is used with grilled steaks and lamb chops, chicken and shellfish.*

SERVES 4
45 ml [3 tablespoons] dry white
wine
30 ml [2 tablespoons] tarragon
vinegar
2 shallots
4-5 leaves of fresh tarragon
100 g [¼ lb] unsalted butter
2 large eggs
salt
freshly ground white pepper
10 ml [2 teaspoons] lemon juice
4-5 leaves freshly chopped
tarragon (optional garnish)

1 Place the wine and vinegar in a small pan.

2 Peel the shallots, chop finely and add to the pan. Chop the tarragon leaves and add to the pan.

3 Boil over fierce heat until reduced

to 30 ml [2 tablespoons]. Strain, discard bits and pieces, and set liquid aside to cool.

4 Prepare the double boiler and set over low heat.

5 Cut off 25 g [1 oz] of the butter. Divide this in half and cut each half into dice.

6 Place the remaining butter in a heavy-based saucepan over low heat and melt.

7 Pour the melted butter into a small jug. Leave in a warm place.

8 Separate the egg yolks.

9 Remove the top of the double boiler from the bottom. Place the egg yolks in this.

10 Whisk the egg yolks until slightly creamy.

11 Add the reduction of wine and vinegar to the egg yolks and whisk for a further ½ minute.

12 Place the top of the double boiler back over the heat checking that the water is just simmering. Add half the diced butter.

13 Whisk the sauce for 1-2 minutes, making sure you scrape the mixture from the sides and bottom of the pan.

14 When the mixture becomes smooth and thick, and you can see the base of the pan between strokes, remove from the heat.

15 Now whisk in the rest of the cold butter. This will take about 1 minute.

16 Start adding the melted butter, drop by drop, whisking after each addition.

17 When the sauce is like thick cream, add the rest of the butter in a slow, steady dribble whisking all the time.

18 When all the butter has been added, season with salt and freshly ground white pepper.

19 Stir in the lemon juice. Chop the fresh tarragon leaves, if using and stir in.

Variations

There are many variations on sauce béarnaise. For their uses, see the chart.

●For sauce choron, stir 35 ml [1½ fl oz] tomato purée into the sauce just before serving.

●For sauce foyot, stir 30 ml [2 tablespoons] meat glaze or jelly from beneath good dripping into the sauce just before serving.

●For sauce nivernaise, work 1 clove of crushed garlic and 5 ml [1 teaspoon] finely chopped fresh parsley into the cold butter before adding to the eggs.

●For sauce paloise, replace the tarragon in sauce béarnaise with mint.

USING FINE BUTTER SAUCES

Although fine butter sauces may seem like a lot of trouble to make, they can be used in many ways.

●Mix cold sauce nivernaise with shredded florentine fennel or grated celeriac and serve as part of a cold hors d'oeuvre.

●For tournedos béarnaise, arrange grilled tournedos on a dish with small boiled new potatoes. Serve béarnaise sauce separately.

●For tournedos Henry IV, arrange grilled tournedos on fried croûtons. Place a cooked artichoke heart filled with thick béarnaise sauce on each. Garnish with grilled mushrooms and boiled baby new potatoes.

Tournedos Henri IV are classically served with béarnaise sauce.

●Fill the centre of globe artichokes with hollandaise sauce. As the leaves are pulled off, they are dipped into the sauce to be eaten.

●For a delicious salad, mix cold cooked sweetcorn and asparagus tips with sauce avec blanc d'oeufs.

●Make an economical meal more interesting! Serve lamb scrumpets with nivernaise sauce.

●For tournedos Helder, arrange grilled tournedos on croûtons. Place on each of the tournedos a ring of béarnaise sauce and in the middle of this, a spoonful of tomato purée. Garnish with baby new potatoes and grilled tomatoes.

●For eggs à la Beauharnais, soft boil eggs, arrest cooking, shell and place each egg on a warm, cooked artichoke heart. Mask with sauce divine.

●For a delicious yet economic first course, serve a mixture of boiled vegetables (such as broccoli, new potatoes, new carrots, young leeks) with hollandaise or mousseline sauce.

●Serve sauce divine with plain oeufs en cocotte.

●Use fine butter sauces to disguise and enhance cold meat. Paloise and nivernaise go with lamb; divine with chicken and turkey; maltaise with cold duck and game; choron goes especially well with beef.

Lamb

standard grilling

Lamb is ideally suited to grilling as the tenderness and fine flavour of the meat are preserved by quick cooking. It is a versatile meat too — both expensive and some cheaper cuts can be grilled successfully. This chapter discusses the ways you can use the more expensive cuts to make sophisticated dishes, including beautifully frilled cutlets, elegant noisettes and an impressive trimmed and decorated best end.

Lamb is grilled following the same basic method as pork (see relevant chapter), but there is one major difference. Unlike pork lamb does not have to be cooked through.

In fact lamb that is slightly underdone (called medium-rare) is a great treat: it has the rich flavour and moist tenderness usually associated with prime steak – at half the price.

Slightly underdone or medium-rare lamb has a crisp surface and is succulent and pink in the centre. In the grilling chart and recipes, times are given for both medium-rare and well-done. Never exceed the well-done timings: overcooked lamb tends to be dry and tough.

CHOOSING AND STORING LAMB

There are two types of lamb available in most countries – fresh home-produced and chilled or frozen imported. Home-produced lamb is usually the more expensive as it is considered superior in flavour and quality. Imported lamb is thawed by the butcher and sold ready to cook.

The younger the lamb, the more succulent the meat. Really young, fresh lamb has pale pink, finely grained flesh with firm creamy or white fat. Outer skin should be smooth and supple. The bones should have a slight bluish tinge and be moist and pink at the joints.

It is almost impossible to tell the quality of frozen lamb (even after thawing) as freezing reduces meat to a uniform colour and texture, so be sure to buy from a reputable supplier.

Cut your own noisettes of lamb from a best end of neck and serve topped with mouth-watering savoury butter.

Meat begins to dry out, losing freshness and flavour, once it is cut. A joint has a relatively small cut surface area and therefore keeps fresh longer than chops, cutlets or noisettes. So, when buying ahead, it is a good idea to get a meaty best end of neck and to cut it up yourself just before cooking.

When you get fresh or thawed lamb home, unwrap and stand it on a plate placing a sheet of greaseproof paper between small cuts to minimize the exposure of cut surfaces. Cover the plate loosely with kitchen foil or cling film. Store in the coldest part of the refrigerator (under the frozen food compartment) for a maximum of 3–4 days, or in a larder for 1 day.

A frozen cut of lamb should be put straight into the freezer or frozen food compartment of the refrigerator. It will keep for 4–6 months in a freezer and from 1–3 months in a frozen food compartment, depending on the star rating.

Cuts of lamb suitable for grilling

Cut	Description	Method (cooking times approximate)
Loin and chump chops 	Cuts most favoured for grilling: loin chops are small and lean with an eye of meat surrounded by fat. Chump chops look meatier but are bonier and usually cheaper as they come from further down the leg. Should be at least 2.5 cm [1″] thick. Sold ready-trimmed of fat.	Brush with oil or marinade. Grill under fierce heat for 1 minute or so on each side then under low heat for about 4 minutes on each side for medium-rare, or about 6 minutes on each side for well-done. Baste occasionally.
Best end of neck 	Also known as rack, this succulent, tender cut is made up of cutlets joined together by a bone running the length of the joint. Ask the butcher to chine ie. saw straight along the backbone, to trim the cutlet bones by 5 cm [2″] and to remove the skin. A small best end usually consists of 5–6 cutlets but a large one may have as many as 8. Allow 2 per person.	Brush with oil. Grill under fierce heat for 1 minute or so on each side, then under low heat for about 15–20 minutes on the bone side and 10 minutes on the fat side for medium-rare, or 25 minutes on the bone side and 10 minutes on the fat side for well-done. Always cook the fat side last so that the meat comes to the table golden and sizzling. Do not allow the fat side to over-brown.
Cutlets 	These are small lean chops cut from the best end of neck. They can be bought ready-prepared but it is better to buy chined, skinned and trimmed best end. Divide into cutlets just before cooking, allowing 2 per person.	Brush generously with oil or marinate. Grill under fierce heat for 1 minute or so on each side, then under low heat for about 3 minutes each side for medium rare, 4-5 minutes each side for well-done. Baste occasionally.
Noisettes 	Also called médaillons, these are made from best end of neck which has been boned, rolled, tied and cut into slices at least 2.5 cm [1″] thick. Noisettes can be bought ready-made from the butcher or prepared at home. Generally speaking, you get 1 noisette from every two cutlets in the best end.	Marinate or brush generously with oil and grill as for loin and chump chops, basting frequently.
Butterfly chops 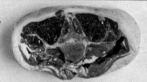	Also known as double chops, as the name implies, these are large chops. Taken from either the neck or the saddle, those from the saddle are larger and more expensive. Usually 2.5 cm [1″] thick with a narrow border of fat. Sold ready-trimmed.	Marinate or brush generously with oil and grill as for loin and chump chops, basting frequently.
Leg steaks 	Leg steak is a lean, very tender slice of meat from 1.25–2.5 cm [½–1″] thick taken from the top of the leg. Often sold completely trimmed of fat and with the small centre bone removed. Average weight of a leg steak is 225-350 g [½–¾ lb]. Allow 1 steak per person.	Brush with oil. Grill under fierce heat for 1 minute or so on each side then under low heat for 5–7 minutes on each side, depending on thickness and whether you want medium-rare or well-done. Baste frequently.

Dividing a best end into cutlets

Choose a meaty best end of neck. Ask the butcher to saw straight along the backbone which runs the length of the joint holding the cutlets together (this is called chining). Also ask him to remove skin and to shorten the cutlet bones, trimming them down by about 5 cm [2″].

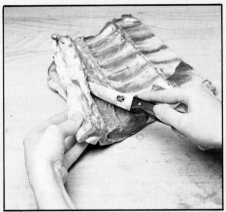

1 Using a small sharp knife, cut the chine bone away from flesh. Set aside for making stock.

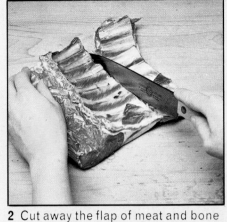

2 Cut away the flap of meat and bone remaining after trimming. Set aside for making stock.

3 Insert knife between 2 cutlet bones. Cut down to separate. Divide remaining cutlets.

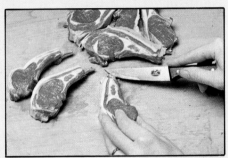

4 Scrape away and cut the thin covering of meat and fat from bone tops, leaving 2.5 cm [1″] bare.

5 Trim off any excess fat from around cutlets, leaving a narrow border of fat.

Making cutlet frills

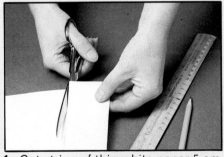

1 Cut strips of thin white paper 5 cm [2″] wide and about 10 cm [4″] long, one for each cutlet.

2 Fold each strip in half lengthwise so that one edge falls a little short of the other.

3 Bend the deep edge up over the narrow one and press in place along length with your finger.

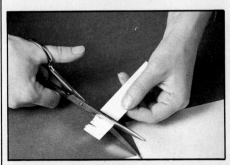

4 Holding the strip in your left hand, make close scissor cuts along the length of the folded edges.

5 Turn the strip around so the cut edge is away from you. Wrap strip around your little finger.

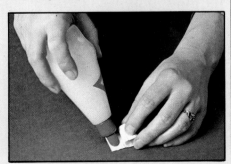

6 Put a dab of glue on the inside of the end of the strip. Press down firmly and leave to dry.

Step-by-step noisettes

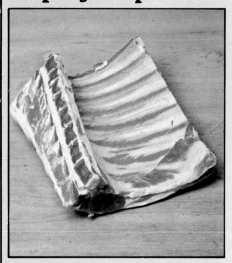

1 Lay skinned but unchined best end on a board, fat side down, chine bone end to your left.

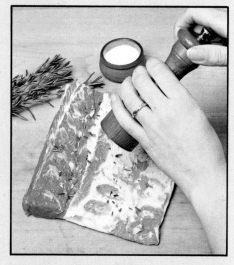

2 Insert a sharp knife between the top of the cutlet bones and the flesh.

3 Gradually work the knife down to the chine bone, freeing flesh from bones.

4 Remove the bones and reserve for making stock. Spread the meat on a flat surface, fat side down.

5 Season the cut surface of the meat with black pepper and rosemary (or thyme, coriander or garlic).

6 Starting at the thick end, roll up the meat into a firm, neat sausage shape.

7 Trim the flap (fat end) if there is more than enough to wrap once round the eye of meat.

8 Tie roll securely at 2.5–3.5 cm [1–1½″] intervals, using fine string and firm knots.

9 Using a sharp knife, cut the meat between each piece of string to make noisettes of equal thickness.

Making maître d'hôtel butter

MAKES 8 PATS

  100 g [¼ lb] unsalted butter
  45 ml [3 tablespoons] finely
    chopped parsley
  10 ml [2 teaspoons] lemon juice
  salt
  freshly ground black pepper

1 Cut butter (which must be at room temperature) into rough pieces and place in a bowl.

2 Add the chopped parsley and beat until the butter is evenly flecked with green.

3 Add lemon juice and seasonings. Beat until there are no droplets of lemon juice on the surface.

4 Turn the butter out of the bowl on to greaseproof paper. Pat into a rough roll shape using a knife.

5 Wet your hands with cold water and roll the butter to and fro until a smooth shape is formed.

6 Pat ends of roll into shape. Wrap in greaseproof paper and refrigerate for 3 hours or until firm.

7 Unwrap roll. Using a sharp knife, cut into slices about 6 mm [¼"] thick.

SIMPLE ACCOMPANIMENTS

Simple accompaniments add flavour and interest to grilled lamb and are an easy way to turn a plain dish into something more sophisticated. Both mint and redcurrant jelly are delicious and traditionally served with lamb. Here are two other suggestions.

● Give lamb a French flavour by rubbing the surface of the meat with a cut garlic clove just before cooking.

● For handsome looks and delicate aroma serve grilled lamb on a bed of fresh mint or rosemary.

SAVOURY BUTTERS

Requiring slightly more effort but well worth the trouble are savoury butters – pats of chilled unsalted butter flavoured with herbs, spices or other ingredients.

Place a pat of savoury butter on top of each portion just before serving so it gradually melts, mingling with the meat juices to make a mouthwatering instant 'sauce'.

The most famous and basic of all savoury butters is a mixture of butter (unsalted butter is best because of its beautiful pale colour), parsley and lemon juice, known as maitre d'hôtel butter. This is excellent with lamb and also suitable for serving with grilled red meats and fish.

All other savoury butters are made following this basic method. Simply replace parsley and lemon juice with alternative flavourings.

Each of the following is made using 100 g [4 oz] unsalted butter:

Mint Butter: 15 ml [1 tablespoon] finely chopped fresh mint.

Blue cheese butter: 50 g [2 oz] soft blue cheese, crumbled.

Coriander butter: 10 ml [2 teaspoons] ground coriander, plus a little grated orange zest (rind).

Rosemary butter: 10 ml [2 teaspoons] finely chopped rosemary.

Chive butter: 15 ml [1 tablespoon] finely chopped fresh chives.

Garlic butter: 2 garlic cloves, skinned and crushed, 10 ml [2 teaspoons] chopped fresh parsley and a squeeze of lemon juice.

Storing savoury butters

Savoury butters well wrapped in greaseproof paper will keep in the refrigerator for up to 2 weeks (those containing cheese will only keep for 1 week), and in a cold larder for 2 days. Freezing is not advised as the herbs and cheese go off quickly.

ISTANBUL CUTLETS

Refreshing yoghurt and cucumber sauce provides a delicious contrast to the rich, meaty taste of grilled cutlets. The sauce can be made in advance or while the cutlets are cooking. Serve it in a small bowl with a spoon so that diners can help themselves. Chops can be used instead of cutlets but remember to alter grilling time accordingly.

SERVES 4
8 trimmed lamb cutlets
15 ml [1 tablespoon] olive oil
150 ml [¼ pt] carton natural yoghurt
1 small cucumber
half a small onion
10 ml [2 teaspoons] finely chopped fresh mint
salt
freshly ground black pepper
2 bunches of mint to garnish (optional)

1 Heat grill, with pan and grid in position, until very hot. Brush the cutlets with oil and cook under fierce heat for 1 minute or so on each side to seal the surface.

2 Lower heat or move grill rack down and cook cutlets for a further 3 minutes on each side for medium-rare, 5 minutes on each side for well-done.

3 If wished, peel the cucumber using a potato peeler or sharp knife. Cut the cucumber in half lengthways and, if wished, scoop out and discard seeds with a teaspoon. Cut the flesh into dice.

4 Turn the yoghurt into a bowl and stir in cucumber.

5 Peel the onion and grate into the bowl, using the large holes on your cheese grater.

6 Add chopped mint and seasonings to taste to the bowl. Stir thoroughly to mix well.

7 Garnish the cooked cutlets with frills, arrange on a warm dish (on a bed of fresh mint if wished) and serve immediately.

FRENCH LAMB STEAKS

Leg steaks or fillet are very tender so there is no need for a marinade containing acid to break down tough fibres. But flavour can be rather bland so it is a good idea to impregnate the meat with herbs before cooking. Because the herbs cover the surface of the meat thickly they protect it from heat, so the initial cooking time under fierce heat is slightly longer than usual. Be sure to baste frequently as the herbs have a drying effect. Butterfly chops or noisettes can be used in place of leg steaks, but remember to alter cooking times accordingly and, because butterfly chops are larger, use a little more herbs.

SERVES 4
4 lamb steaks
olive oil
3 sprigs fresh rosemary or 15 ml [1 tablespoon] dried
3 sprigs fresh thyme or 15 ml [1 tablespoon] dried

1 Brush the lamb steaks with olive oil on each side.

2 If using fresh herbs, strip leaves off twigs. Discard twigs. Mix leaves and crush lightly with the back of a wooden spoon to release aromatic oils.

3 Sprinkle half the herbs over one side of the steaks and press down lightly with the back of a wooden spoon. Turn over and coat the other sides in the same way.

4 Place steaks on a plate or in a gratin dish. Cover with grease-proof paper or foil and leave in the refrigerator or a cool place for at least 3 hours.

5 Heat grill until very hot. Place steaks under grill (on the grid or in a heatproof gratin dish) and cook for 2 minutes on each side.

6 Lower heat or move the pan or dish further away from the heat and grill for a further 5 minutes on each side for medium-rare, 7 minutes each side for well-done, basting frequently. Serve immediately.

OXFORD JOHN

This is a simple version of an English recipe which dates from the 18th century. Spreading meat with a spicy paste before grilling is a process known as devilling. If you like highly spiced food, spread the paste over the chops about 1½ hours before you plan to cook them to allow time for the spices to soak right into the meat. For a milder flavour, spread on the paste half an hour before cooking.
Watercress goes well with Oxford John but parsley or fronds of Florentine fennel could be used instead.

SERVES 4
4 lamb loin or chump chops
50 g [2 oz] butter or margerine at room temperature
pinch cayenne pepper
freshly ground black pepper
5 ml [1 teaspoon] curry paste
2 shallots or 1 small onion
5 ml [1 teaspoon] Worcester-shire sauce
5 ml [1 teaspoon] English mustard
a few sprigs of watercress

1 Cut the butter roughly into pieces and place in a small bowl. Using a wooden spoon, beat (stir vigorously) until soft and creamy.

2 Add cayenne pepper, black pepper and curry paste. Mix well.

3 Peel shallots or onion. Put through a mincer, or grate, using the fine holes on your cheese grater.

4 Add the grated onion to the butter.

5 Add the mustard and Worcestershire sauce and mix well until flavours are thoroughly blended.

6 Using a round-bladed knife, spread the paste over both sides of the chops. Put the chops into a gratin dish, cover and leave in the refrigerator until needed.

7 Heat grill until very hot.

8 Cook the chops under fierce heat for 1 minute on each side then under low heat for 4 minutes each side for medium-rare, 6 minutes each side for well-done.

9 Garnish with watercress and serve immediately.

Variation

● For honey-glazed chops, mix together 50 g [2 oz] softened butter, 30 ml [2 tablespoons] clear honey and 10 ml [2 teaspoons] Meaux mustard (or any other mustard containing whole black mustard seeds). Spread over the chops at least 1½ hours before grilling as described above.

One of the joys of grilled lamb is that it blends well with other flavours. Reading from left, Oxford John has a spicy taste that is just right for cold days; elegant Istanbul cutlets with minty cucumber and yoghurt sauce pick up extra flavour from a bed of mint; succulent French lamb steaks have the aromatic tang of herbs.

Star recipe

NOISETTES JARDINIERE

The attraction of this party dish lies in the garnishes which must be prepared and arranged carefully to look really effective. Canned asparagus spears were used here but you can use fresh, steamed asparagus. Be sure to choose small spears with tight heads and a good colour.

Use very firm tomatoes and place them under the grill just long enough to warm through, not to cook them. The butter must be soft when used to fill the tomatoes so do not chill it.

Any of the savoury butters given on page 67 can be used.

SERVES 4
4 noisettes of lamb
2 large tomatoes
olive oil
50 g [2 oz] unsalted butter at room temperature
a sprig of fresh tarragon or 5 ml [1 teaspoon] dried
salt
freshly ground black pepper
1 × 425 g [15 oz] can asparagus spears.

1 Plunge the tomatoes into boiling water for 1 minute to loosen skins. Cool in cold water.

2 Using a sharp knife, nick the tomato skin near stalk base. Peel away and discard the skin.

6 Place the butter in a bowl. Beat (stir vigorously) with a wooden spoon to soften.

7 If using fresh tarragon, snip leaves and chop them finely, using small scissors in a mug or glass.

11 Meanwhile, heat the canned asparagus, following manufacturer's instructions.

12 Brush the tomatoes with oil and add them to the grill for the last minute of cooking time.

13 Remove the tomatoes from the grill and fill each half with 5 ml [1 teaspoon] tarragon butter.

14 Arrange the noisettes on a hot serving dish. Garnish with tomatoes and asparagus.

3 Using a sharp knife, make zig-zag cuts around the middle of each tomato.

4 Cut through the centre of the tomatoes and gently pull the halves apart.

5 Scoop out the seeds using a spoon. Discard. At this point, turn the grill to its highest setting.

8 Add the tarragon to the butter. Stir until well blended. Add salt and pepper to taste.

9 Brush the noisettes on both sides with olive oil. Grill under fierce heat for 1 minute each side.

10 Reduce heat. Grill for 4 minutes on each side for medium-rare 6 minutes for well-done.

A butterfly chop grilled then oven-cooked in foil with vegetables make a satisfying and succulent meal for one.

CHOPS IN A PARCEL

This is an ideal dish to serve when you have guests as it can be finished off in the oven while the first course is being eaten. It also has the advantage of not spoiling if left a little too long because the vegetables keep the chops moist.

To serve, unwrap the parcels carefully, lift chops on to a serving plate using a fish slice and spoon vegetables and juices over the top.

SERVES 4
4 butterfly lamb chops
100 g [$\frac{1}{4}$ lb] button mushrooms
2 small courgettes
1 small onion
2 ripe tomatoes
1 garlic clove
5 ml [1 teaspoon] dried oregano
30 ml [2 tablespoons] tomato purée
100 g [$\frac{1}{4}$ lb] butter
15 ml [1 tablespoon] olive oil

1 Heat oven to 200°C [400°F] gas mark 6.

2 Wipe mushrooms with a damp cloth and slice thinly into a bowl.

3 Cut knobbly ends off courgettes. Wipe skins clean and cut into thin oblique slices. Add to the bowl.

4 Peel the onion, chop finely and add to the bowl.

5 Put tomatoes in a separate bowl. Pour on boiling water to cover and leave for 1 minute. Drain and cool in cold water. Nick skins and peel

away using a sharp knife. Chop tomato flesh into rough pieces and add to the courgette mixture.

6 Skin and crush the garlic using either a garlic crusher or salt and a round-bladed knife. Add to the bowl.

7 Add oregano, tomato purée and 15 ml [1 tablespoon] hot water. Mix all ingredients together well.

8 Heat the grill, with pan and grid in position, until very hot.

9 Brush the chops with oil and cook under fierce heat for 1 minute or so on each side to seal.

10 Meanwhile, cut 4 rectangles of foil each measuring about 25 x 20 cm [10 x 8"].

11 Remove chops from under grill and place 1 chop on each rectangle of foil.

12 Spoon the vegetable mixture on top of the chops, dividing it equally between the 4 parcels. Dot each parcel with 25 g [1 oz] butter and any juice from the grill pan base.

13 Bring the long edges of foil together and crimp firmly. Twist the ends to make a cracker-shaped parcel.

14 Place the foil parcels on a baking sheet and cook in the centre of the

oven for 25 minutes for medium-rare, 30 minutes for well-done.

Variation

● For summer lamb parcels, cook 12 young carrots and 12 small new potatoes in boiling salted water for 3 minutes (this is called parboiling).

Meanwhile, brush 4 butterfly chops with oil and cook under fierce heat for 1 minute on each side. Place each chop on a piece of foil. Drain vegetables, slice and divide equally between the chops. Dot each chop with 25 g [1 oz] butter. Add a sprig of fresh mint to each, parcel up and cook in the oven at 200°C [400°F] gas mark 6 for 25 minutes if meat is required medium-rare, 30 minutes for well-done.

Handy hints

● Cutlet bones discarded from a best end of neck can be used to make spare ribs. Simply brush with honey and grill under fierce heat for 2 minutes each side. These are excellent for buffets, informal parties or just as a light snack.
● Remember to keep chine bones and other trimmings from lamb. They will come in useful for the stockpot.
● Brighten up a baked potato by serving it with savoury butter. Chive and blue cheese are particularly good.

Lamb

grilling kebabs

Leg, shoulder, fillet and breast of lamb are traditionally associated with roasting, casseroling and braising. In the East these are used for kebabs and other spicy, aromatic dishes grilled over a charcoal fire. This chapter shows you how to achieve the same delicious results using a conventional cooker. And, as a plus, how to make your own charcoal grill for outdoor cooking.

One of the best ways to grill the larger cuts of lamb is to make kebabs. Kebabs look impressive, taste delicious and are relatively economical because vegetables are usually added to make the meat go further. The basic essentials when making kebabs are tender meat, suitable skewers and a glowing fire.

Timing
Kebabs are quick work for the cook – involving you in a maximum total of about 45 minutes work – but overall time is considerable because the marinade must be left for several hours to do its work on the meat.

Cutting up the meat will only take you about 15 minutes. Preparing the other ingredients and threading the skewers will take about 15 minutes, and cooking takes up to 15 minutes, depending on the recipe.

Marinating
Marinades add flavour and moisture and break down tough meat fibres. It is preferable to marinate all meat for kebabs and particularly important for the cheaper cuts because cooking time is so short that it cannot tenderize the meat. If you tried to grill cheap meat without marinating, the results would be chewy.

More cuts of lamb for grilling

Cut	Description	Cooking method
Breast 	Breast is the most economical of all cuts of lamb. A long fatty strip with several rib bones, breast weights from 550 g-1 kg [1¼-2 lb]. When buying breast, choose a meaty one. If buying for riblets, ask the butcher to chop down between the rib bones.	Either divided into riblets and grilled in barbecue sauce or casseroled, cut into squares, crumbed and grilled. Breast requires lengthy cooking in order to extract excess fat and break down tough fibres.
Shoulder 	An oddly shaped, rather bony and quite fatty cut but very well flavoured and excellent for kebabs. Cuts of shoulder are sold in weights ranging from 1-2.30 kg [2-5½ lb]. A cut which weighs 1 kg [2 lb] will yield about 550 g (1¼ lb) boned meat. Ask the butcher to remove the awkward T-shaped bone as this is rather difficult to do at home.	Cut boned shoulder into 2.5 cm[1″] cubes or mince. Because it is fairly tough, shoulder must always be marinated for several hours before cooking. Always grill 7.50 cm [3″] away from fierce heat for 8-15 minutes. Turn and baste occasionally to moisten the meat.
Leg 	A very lean, quite expensive cut. Whole leg weighs from 1–2 kg [2–4½ lb]. Only the thick end (which can be bought separately) is suitable for kebabs. It will yield 550 g [1¼ lb] boned meat. It is cheaper to buy whole leg: use the thick end for kebabs and the shank end for roasting, braising or casseroling. Ask the butcher to saw thick end into 2.5 cm [1″] slices for kebabs.	Cut boned leg into 2.5 cm [1″] cubes. Because this is very lean meat it needs prolonged marinating to prevent drying out under the grill. Cook as for shoulder.
Fillet 	A long, very lean and rather expensive cut weighing from 550 g – 1 kg [1¼ – 2 lb]. This cut is the tenderloin muscle from the loin. As it is boneless, there is no waste. Fillet has a thin covering of fat which should not be removed before cooking as it helps to keep the meat moist.	Cut into cubes for kebabs. Because it is lean, fillet must be marinated then basted frequently during cooking. Cook as for shoulder kebabs, but baste frequently.

KEBAB SKEWERS

The length of the skewers you use depends on the position of the grill. If your grill is enclosed under the hotplate, you will have to make do with modest 25 cm [10″] or even smaller skewers. Oven gloves will be needed to turn them because the handles will get hot. If you have an open-ended eye level grill, you can be very impressive with 40 cm [16″] skewers. Skewers with fancy decorated handles are only suitable for outdoor grills as the handles will distort or char if used on a cooker.

LAMB FOR KEBABS

Lamb is first-class kebab meat as it has enough fat not to dry out under the grill and the less tender cuts, such as shoulder, respond well to marinating.

Choosing and storing

The basic guidelines for choosing and storing shoulder, leg, fillet and breast of lamb are the same as those given for the smaller lamb cuts given in the previous chapter but, because the cuts now under discussion are larger, storage times are slightly longer. If buying minced lamb, look for meat with a good pink colour, evenly flecked with fat. Avoid any mince which has a brownish tinge or seems dried up on the surface. Wrap and refrigerate mince as soon as you get home, and cook the same day.

How much meat to buy

To make kebabs for four people you will need 550 g [1¼ lb] of boned meat. This may seem like quite a small amount but remember that some kebabs are mixed with vegetables which make the meat go further, while those made from meat only are served with rice, pasta and other substantial accompaniments to make a complete meal.

When buying shoulder and leg of lamb to make kebabs, remember to allow for the weight of the bone – 1 kg [2 lb] thick end of leg or shoulder will yield about 550 g [1¼ lb] of meat after boning. Fillet contains no bone so gross and net weight are the same.

Preparation

Leg, fillet and shoulder of lamb must all be boned and divided into 2.5 cm [1″] cubes before being used for kebabs. Shoulder is also minced for certain Arabian kebabs. Breast is cut into riblets. The butcher will do all of these jobs for you but, as meat loses blood and therefore flavour as soon as it is cut, it is best to cut up the meat yourself as and when you need it. The step-by-step pictures show you the best way to prepare each cut. It is particularly advisable to mince meat yourself because mince is so finely chopped that it goes 'off' extremely quickly. Use a hand mincer or a liquidizer that minces, carefully following the manufacturer's instructions.

Unless you are very experienced and well equipped, however, there are some initial preparation stages (as indicated on the chart opposite) which it is sensible to ask the butcher to do, because he has the specialist tools.

Preparing leg of lamb for kebabs

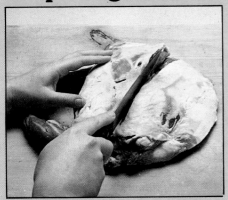

1 Cut the first slice of lamb into strips about 2.5 cm [1″] wide, avoiding the centre bone.

2 Cut across the strips at 2.5 cm [1″] intervals to divide the meat into cubes.

3 Free any meat left around the bone and reserve for stock. Cut other slices of meat in the same way.

Preparing shoulder of lamb for kebabs

1 Cut through the top of the piece of meat and spread it out flat on to a board.

2 Trim any ragged edges so that it forms a square. Keep trimmings for use in stock making.

3 Cut the meat into strips, then cut across the strips, to form 2.5 cm [1″] cubes.

Dividing breast of lamb into riblets

1 Spread the meat on a board. Trim away and discard skin and excess fat. Cut off the boneless end.

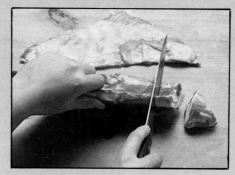

2 Using a sharp knife, cut down between the bones in the rib end to divide into riblets.

3 Using the point of the knife, remove the pieces of cartilage from the boneless (flap) end.

Other kebab ingredients

Chunks of vegetables or other ingredients are usually threaded on the skewers with the meat to add moisture, flavour and colour. These little extras also have the advantage of making the meat go further.

Onions: sharp, slightly crunchy onions provide an excellent foil to the rich taste of the meat in kebabs. You can use either large onions cut into pieces or button onions.

If you use button onions, they must be part-cooked first or else they will still be very raw when the rest of the kebab is cooked. Choose firm onions, peel them and put into a saucepan with enough cold water to cover them. Bring to the boil then reduce the heat and simmer for 5 minutes (this is called parboiling). Drain and refresh in cold water.

Peppers: choose firm shiny green, red or yellow peppers of any size. Cut in halves, remove stalks, pith and seeds and chop the flesh into 2.5 cm [1"] squares.

Tomatoes: really tiny tomatoes are ideal for making kebabs. Choose firm, slightly under-ripe tomatoes – very ripe ones may cook too fast and drop off the skewers. To prepare tomatoes for kebabs, wipe with a damp cloth but do not skin. Cut medium-sized tomatoes in half, leave baby ones whole. As an extra precaution against overcooking, it is a good idea to leave room on the ends of the kebab skewers and to slip on the tomatoes near the end of cooking time. Do not do this if a recipe specifically states that the tomatoes must go next to the meat: they may be needed to keep meat moist.

Mushrooms: choose firm cap or button mushrooms, ideally not more than 2.5 cm [1"] in diameter. Avoid very thin mushrooms because they are liable to break when skewered. Wipe clean with a damp cloth but do not peel – much of the flavour and goodness lies in the skins. Larger mushrooms can be cut into quarters or halves. Mushrooms tend to dry up under the grill. To preserve flavour and moisture, keep them well brushed with oil or marinade on both gill and skin side.

Miniature sausages: choose cocktail size fresh or canned pork sausages. If you are unable to get these improvise by using chipolatas. Twist each chipolata in two or three places and then cut between the twists to make several sausages.

Bacon rolls: those featured in the grilling pork chapter are ideal for kebabs as the fat from the bacon runs down the skewers and keeps the other ingredients moist.

Pineapple chunks: these add a fresh taste to kebabs. Choose the square rather than slightly triangular pieces as they stay on the skewers better.

Cutting an onion for kebabs

1 Peel away the outer, papery onion skin and cut off the root end.

2 Using a sharp knife, cut off a thick slice from one side of the onion.

3 Turn the onion and cut another slice. Continue until the core.

Lamb and Mutton

roasting

What can titillate the taste buds and stimulate the palate more than the distinctive smell of lamb roasting? Perhaps just the added touch of rosemary— which further enhances the smell. This chapter describes how to roast lamb and mutton on the bone, and how to carve the joints to make the most of the meat.

Roasting is one of the oldest ways of cooking meat—originally the word roasting implied cooking on a turning spit in front of an open fire. For those whose cookers include a modern spit-roasting device, something akin to the original method is again possible. However, in this book the method used for cooking lamb or mutton is in an enclosed oven—a method which, although correctly described as baking, is commonly known as roasting. The joints used here are straight roasts of lamb and mutton on the bone.

Saddle of lamb with the kidneys skewered to the fatty tail end.

LAMB

The quality of lamb is always at its very best in spring or early summer when the lamb is just a few months old. Imported frozen lamb brings 'spring' lamb to the shops out of season.

The natural flavour of young, top quality lamb is so delicate and delicious that it seems a sacrilege to do anything other than roast the prime cuts in the plainest way

possible to show off natural flavour to full advantage.

Lamb becomes mutton when the animal passes its first birthday—at this age joints become larger and

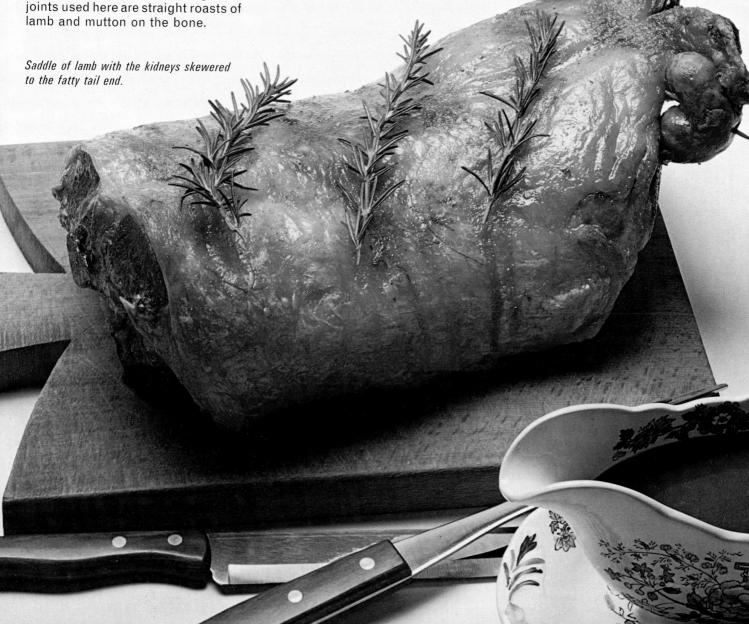

less succulent. Fresh (unfrozen) lamb is pale pink in colour and lightly marbled with fat whereas more mature meat is redder and fattier (this pinkness is not seen in meat which has been frozen).

MUTTON

In effect mutton is very mature lamb. The cuts are larger and heavier. The meat is darker in colour, firmer and fattier, and has a more pronounced flavour. Provided that the carcass has been well hung—and this is even more important ·with mutton than with lamb—the flavour of young mutton can be very good indeed.

For roasting, mutton should be between one and two years old. Older mutton is better cooked by a moist-heat method such as braising or boiling. Roast mutton in exactly the same manner as lamb but always use the low-temperature method.

CHOOSING AND STORING LAMB AND MUTTON

All lamb and young mutton are suitable for roasting with the exception of middle neck and scrag cuts. If stuffed with a succulent filling, and cooked at a moderate temperature, even breast can be roasted, and this is described in another course. ·

The visual signs which confirm that lamb is young and of prime quality are fine-grained pink flesh, and fat which is firm and white but not brittle. The outer layer of papery skin should be smooth and supple. When choosing legs and shoulders, pick those which are thick and well-rounded rather than scraggy. A thin covering of fat is essential for good flavour and even if you don't like to eat the fat, roast the joint complete and trim away the fat after cooking.

The same principles are used to select mutton although the meat will be darker in colour and possibly fatter. Avoid meat with a dry wrinkled skin or very yellow fat which looks crumbly—this indicates the meat is old.

To develop its full flavour and tenderness both lamb and mutton need ageing, that is, they must be hung in the butcher's cold store for about one week before being cooked. Ask the butcher about this when you buy a joint. If it has not been hung long enough you can improve the eating quality by keeping it in your

Cuts of lamb and mutton suitable

SADDLE weighing 2.7-4.5 kg [6-10 lb].
The saddle extends from the tail to the chump and loin. If a larger saddle is required sometimes the first rib of the best end is included too. The whole outer surface is covered with a thin layer of fat beneath the skin. There is a high proportion of bone in a saddle so you are likely to get a better meat yield from a larger rather than a smaller saddle. Choose a thick compact saddle. Allow 350 g [¾ lb] per serving, a little more if the saddle is small.
The butcher normally prepares a saddle so that it is ready for the oven when delivered. The whole joint is skinned and the fat is scored in a diamond pattern. The sides are folded under and the whole joint tied securely in shape. The tail, still attached to the joint is split in half and curled. Sometimes the kidneys are secured inside the curled tail and roasted with the joint. But the cooking time is really too long for kidneys and, ideally, they should be cooked separately and then skewered in place before serving.

LEG weighing 1.15-2.25 kg [2½-5 lb]. The leg is a prime, lean roasting joint covered with a thin layer of fat under the skin. Small legs of 1.4 kg [3 lb] and under are best roasted whole. The butcher will often divide larger legs into two smaller joints, namely the fillet end and the shank end, which is cheaper. A whole leg can be boned for stuffing. Allow about 225 g [½ lb] raw meat per serving.
The butcher normally chops the knuckle bone, leaving it attached by the skin only so that it can be removed easily after cooking. The thin skin covering the leg is usually left on and helps to retain all the juices within the meat. In the case of a whole leg basting is then un-necessary. When cooking the fillet end, which has two cut surfaces, basting is essential. The shank end tends to be muscular and, although it can be open roasted, it is best cooked by a moist-heat method such as pot roasting or braising.

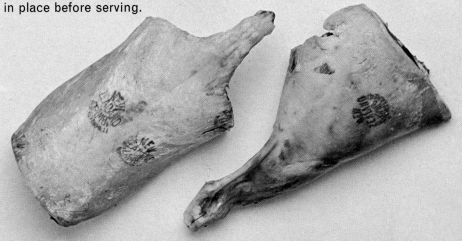

own refrigerator for several days before cooking it. This applies just as much to imported frozen meat (which the butcher has usually thawed) as to home-produced meat.

As soon as you get the joint home, remove the wrappings. Stand it on a plate, cover loosely with foil or polythene and keep it in a refrigerator or cold larder for up to three days. A cooked joint, lightly covered, can be kept safely in a cold larder for two days, or, loosely wrapped in foil to prevent drying, in a refrigerator for three days.

PREPARATION

The various cuts of lamb and mutton are described in the chart. Note the butchering and preparation they require. Jobs which involve sawing through bone are always done by the butcher because he has the right tools for each task. Other prepara-tions, such as skinning, can be carried out by either the butcher or the cook.

Chining: when the butcher prepares a best end of neck or a loin he saws along the whole length of the back-bone, freeing it from the rib bones.

LOIN AND CHUMP weighing 1.4-2 kg [3-4½ lb].

This is a prime roasting cut from one side of the back between the leg and shoulder. A whole loin includes the chump and, from a small carcass, they are cooked as a single joint. From larger carcasses they are divided into two smaller joints, namely the loin proper (next to the best end) and the bonier chump end next to the leg. The whole of the outer surface is covered with a thin layer of fat and skin. Allow 225-350 g [½-¾ lb] per serving.

The butcher normally cuts off about 5 cm [2″] of the belly flap and removes excess fat from inside the loin. Tell him whether you want the backbone chopped or chined to facilitate carving. The skin can be left on for a straight roast, or you can skin the joint and score the fat in a diamond pattern for a more decorative appearance. Always remove the skin if you plan to baste or glaze the joint. The loin can be boned for rolling and stuffing.

BEST END OF NECK weighing 700-900 g [1½-2 lb].

This is a small compact joint consisting of 6 or 7 joined cutlets from one side of the neck. The outside surface is covered with a thin layer of fat under the skin. Two best ends can be specially trimmed and tied to form a 'guard of honour' or a crown roast, both of which are described in detail in a later course. A small best end serves 3 portions and a large one 4 portions.

The butcher normally chops through the long rib bones shortening them by about 5 cm [2″] but leaves them attached to the joint so that they can be removed when you wish. This will be before roasting if you want to scrape the ends of the rib bones free of fat. Alternatively, they can be left in place and removed after roasting. Tell the butcher whether you want the backbone chined or chopped to facilitate carving. The outer fat layer makes further basting during cooking quite unnecessary. The meat is not usually skinned unless the joint is to be treated with a special baste or glaze which needs to penetrate the surface.

SHOULDER weighing 1.15-2 kg [2½-4½ lb].

The shoulder has a higher proportion of fat and bone than other roasting cuts but the meat is sweet and succulent. The outside surface is covered with a layer of skin with fat beneath. Small shoulders 1.4 kg [3 lb] and under are usually roasted whole, but larger shoulders can be cut into two smaller joints, namely the blade joint and knuckle joint. Shoulder is usually appreciably cheaper than leg or loin. Allow about 225-350 g [½-¾ lb] per serving to compensate for the high ratio of bone to meat.

The butcher normally chops the knuckle bone, leaving it attached by the skin only so that it can be removed after cooking. For a plain roast the skin is left on to help retain all the juices in the meat. The layer of fat beneath the skin keeps the meat basted naturally. If, however, the roast is to be spread with a special baste or a glaze then the joint should be skinned so that the flavours of the baste or glaze can penetrate. The blade bone which runs through the centre makes carving a little tricky.

After roasting, this bone can then be removed entirely, leaving the meat easy to carve.

Chopping: an alternative way of making it possible to carve the best end or loin is by chopping through the backbone between the ribs. This method is gaining popularity for a straight roast because the portions of meat with the bone attached look more generous on the plate.

Shortening the ribs: the long rib bones on best end of neck are shortened by about 5 cm [2″] by chopping through the ends of the

bones. This leaves a flap.

Chopping knuckle bones: without being asked, the butcher automatically chops through the bony knuckle end of a leg or shoulder so that this awkward end piece will fit into a roasting pan and can be removed after roasting.

Skinning: the meat is encased in a papery skin. For a plain roast this is left on to help retain all the juices in the meat. But when a joint is to be glazed, basted or crumb-coated the meat is skinned to allow the glaze or baste to penetrate and the coating to

adhere. To skin the meat, simply raise one corner of the skin with a sharp knife and pull firmly, drawing the skin back and away from the fat.

Wiping: avoid washing meat if possible. Simply wipe the unskinned surfaces with a clean thin cloth which has been wrung out in cold water.

Trimming: a thin layer of fat must be left on the meat; it can be trimmed after cooking but, if there are large chunks of fat present, these can be trimmed with a sharp knife. Also trim any stamp marks showing the country of origin or the grade.

Thawing frozen lamb

Unless you are certain that the meat has been aged before it was frozen it is advisable to allow time both for it to thaw thoroughly plus a little extra, before cooking. Ideally leave frozen joints in the refrigerator for a minimum of 48 hours and preferably four days.

Seasoning

The cut surfaces of a joint are not seasoned with salt because this will cause the juices to flow. Rub the skin or fat with salt and a cut clove of garlic, pepper and ground spices, or insert sprigs of herbs. If a joint has been skinned, lightly sprinkle the fat with plain flour to ensure a crisp, well-browned surface.

Garlic: for a positive flavour, cut peeled garlic cloves into thin slivers. Make tiny incisions through the skin and fat with the point of a knife and push the garlic slivers into the incisions. The amount of garlic depends on personal taste, but on average allow one clove to a best end, two cloves to a whole loin, and two or three cloves to a large leg or saddle.

For a milder flavour, tuck one or two peeled garlic cloves under the joint while roasting and remove them before carving. Alternatively, rub the whole surface of the joint with a cut garlic clove before roasting.

Spices: an aromatic French mustard or a mild green pepper mustard are excellent with lamb. Freshly ground coriander rubbed over the surface of the meat before roasting imparts a marvellously aromatic orangey flavour. Equally, the spiciness of freshly ground black pepper is a natural counterbalance to the fattiness of mutton.

Herbs: aromatic herbs impart deliciously subtle flavours to lamb and mutton but they need to be used with discrimination if they are to enhance rather than dominate. The type and degree of herb flavour used is a very personal choice.

Discard the remains of the cooked herbs before serving and garnish with fresh herbs if you wish.

Rosemary is a favourite in Italy where it is used alone or with garlic. Bear in mind that the new season's spikes of rosemary are tender and soft, but that late season or dried rosemary has sharp hard spikes which are unpleasant to find in one's mouth. If available, use whole sprigs of rosemary, fresh or dried, tucked

beneath the joint, under loose flaps of meat or around the bone—in fact anywhere, as long as they can be removed easily and entirely before the joint is served. Allow two to three small sprigs for a small joint, four to six for a large one. If using dried, powdered rosemary, sprinkle it sparingly over the surface of the meat.

Thyme is a strong herb. Use it in the same way as rosemary, but very sparingly. The milder lemon thyme is good with lamb and mutton as is lemon-scented balm (or melissa).

Mint can also be used under and around the lamb and removed before serving.

FOUR ROASTING METHODS

There are several different methods of roasting in an oven, each with certain advantages and disadvantages, but, on balance, low-temperature roasting up the meat is probably the most satisfactory for most people.

Searing method

The joint is roasted in a very hot oven 230°C [450°F] gas mark 8 for about 20 minutes to seal and brown the surface. Cooking is then finished in a moderately hot oven, about 190°C [375°F] gas mark 5. This method is not recommended except for fairly large roasts of prime quality meat. The sudden strong heat causes contraction of the muscles and loss of weight through shrinkage. It is a method that does nothing to encourage tenderness, but it does produce a good flavour because the meat juices are concentrated, especially near the surface of the roast.

High-temperature method

The joint is roasted at a constant heat in a fairly hot oven, 200°F [400°F] gas mark 6. This method produces a well-browned joint of good flavour but, again, it does nothing to improve tenderness, so it is suitable only for prime quality tender meat.

Low-temperature roasting

The joint is roasted at a constant heat in a moderate oven, 180°C [350°F] gas mark 4. Carefully conducted tests have shown that this method causes less shrinkage and improves the tenderness and succulence of the meat. The outside is acceptably brown and tasty, but naturally lacks

the more savoury finish of a faster roast. Because it causes a smaller loss of weight, this method is the most economical for the small joints which most people buy today.

Automatic oven roasting

The joint is put into a cold oven which has been set to switch itself on and cook for a predetermined time at a controlled temperature. It can be argued that this is not true roasting, but it is a very convenient method for anyone who has to be out all day. Although the joint may not be quite as brown as a conventional roast, the slow heating is an excellent way of tenderizing cheaper cuts of meat. When using this method follow the cooker manufacturer's instruction manual.

1 Rub entire surface of joint with black pepper but rub only the fat and skin with salt.

5 Tuck sprigs of fresh herbs under the joint and under flaps of meat so that they can be removed easily.

TIMING

It is impossible to lay down exact rules for timing roasts. Many variable factors determine the length of time needed for the heat to penetrate and cook the centre of the joint to the degree you like; these factors include the weight and thickness of the meat, the proportion of fat and the presence or absence of bone. Small joints take proportionately longer to cook than larger joints, and so do boneless and stuffed joints. If a joint is put into the oven straight from the refrigerator it will take a little longer to cook than one at room temperature. Finally, the individual performance of ovens can vary, so use the timing chart given here only as a general guide. In the long run it is experience that ensures success.

TIME CHART FOR LOW-TEMPERATURE ROASTING LAMB AND MUTTON ON THE BONE
Based on joints at room temperature and oven temperature of 180°C [350°F] gas mark 4

CUT	MEDIUM RARE meat thermometer 77°C [170°F] minutes per 450 g [1 lb]	WELL DONE meat thermometer 80°C [180°F] minutes per 450 g [1 lb]
Whole leg	25 minutes	35 minutes
Half leg	40 minutes	45 minutes
Whole shoulder	30 minutes	40 minutes
Half shoulder	40 minutes	45 minutes
Whole loin	25 minutes	35 minutes
Half loin or chump end	40 minutes	45 minutes
Saddle	20 minutes	25 minutes
Best end of neck	45 minutes	50 minutes

Step-by-step to low-temperature roasting

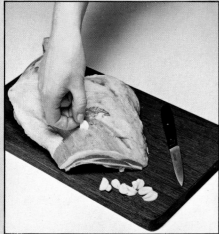

2 Make small incisions in the skin with a sharp knife and insert thin slivers of garlic.

3 Place the joint, fat side upwards, on a rack and put it into a roasting tin.

4 If the joint is skinned, sprinkle the fat with flour to aid browning and to give a crisp surface.

6 If using a meat thermometer, insert it but do not let it touch the bone. Roast the meat.

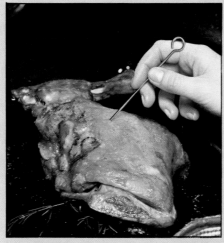

7 Baste if cut surface is very large or if joint is skinned. Check thermometer and test juices.

8 Rest the joint in a warm place for 10-15 minutes. This aids carving and allows time to make gravy.

The meat thermometer is inserted into the thickest part of the meat and positioned so that it can be read without removing the joint from the oven.

Basting is usually unnecessary, nor do you need to brush the joint with oil, or to add dripping before cooking, unless the skin has been removed or the meat has a large cut surface which needs to be kept moist by basting.

GRAVY

Although gravy is often thickened when served with roast lamb and mutton, and seldom when served with roast beef, there is no hard and fast rule about it and it is a matter of preference. Likewise, gravy can be strained or served without anything added to it. If the texture of the gravy is grainy or rough (due to herbs and spices) it would be sensible to strain it, but if the juices are smooth then there is no need to do so. The same thing applies to thick gravy. Lumps in thick gravy must be avoided; they are unsightly when the gravy is poured and are also unappetizing.

After you have transferred the joint to a serving dish and put it in a warm place to rest, discard herbs, remove rack and carefully pour the fat out of the roasting tin. Do this slowly to avoid pouring away the meat drippings which have collected in the pan during roasting. These have a strong savoury flavour and are valuable for making a tasty gravy.

Thin gravy

Pour off the fat from the juices. Put the pan over a medium heat and pour on 275 ml [½ pt] hot brown stock, vegetable water, wine or a combination of any of these. Stir to dissolve and incorporate the meat drippings from the base of pan.

Bring to the boil and continue stirring and cooking for about 3 minutes. Taste and season with salt and pepper if necessary, and pour into a warmed sauce-boat.

Thick gravy

Leave about 30 ml [2 tablespoons] fat in the roasting pan together with meat drippings. Away from heat stir into the fat 30 ml [2 tablespoons] of plain flour. Cook over a low heat stirring continuously for 2-3 minutes until the roux is coloured and free of

Lamb and mutton are probably best cooked until medium rare so the meat is very moist and tender and the centre still slightly pink, but some people prefer their roasts to be well done. The important thing is never to overcook because this dries out the meat and dulls the flavour.

With experience you will be able to judge just how long it takes to roast various joints to the right degree for your taste, but the use of a meat thermometer will simplify the matter (see below). Alternatively, check the meat juices of lamb or mutton before finally removing the joint from the oven.

Meat thermometers

A meat thermometer is a temperature gauge attached to a metal skewer which will show how well the inside of a piece of meat is cooked. Insert the skewer into the thickest part of the joint before it goes into the oven. Take care to avoid touching the bone which is a conductor of heat and can therefore influence the reading. Position the thermometer so that you can read it easily without having to remove the joint from the oven.

Lamb and mutton is medium rare when the inside of the meat reaches 77°F [170°F], and well done when the thermometer reads 82°C [180°F].

Testing the meat juices

The colour of the juices is a reliable indication of the degree of cooking. Insert a thin skewer into the centre of the thickest part of the meat, pull it out and check the colour of the juices which seep out. Do not pierce the meat more than twice. If the juices are reddish the meat is underdone and requires longer cooking; if they are slightly rosy the meat is medium rare; and, if colourless, the meat is well done.

LOW-TEMPERATURE ROASTING

Before starting to roast leave the meat in the kitchen for 2-3 hours to reach room temperature. Heat the oven to 180°C [350°F] gas mark 4. Weigh the joint and calculate its approximate cooking time.

Choose a roasting tin which is slightly larger than the joint. Allow room for vegetables if these are to be roasted around the joint, but never use too large a tin because uncovered areas encourage the fat to splash and mean extra oven cleaning. Some roasting tins come with fairly solid racks; these stand above the fat and lessen the splashing. The grid from some grill pans can be used in place of a rack.

116

lumps. Remove from heat and pour on 275 ml [½ pt] of brown stock or other liquid stirring all the while. Blend it into the roux, return to the heat and bring to the boil stirring continuously. Simmer for at least 5 minutes to cook the flour, stirring continuously. Season if necessary.

THE PRINCIPLES OF GOOD CARVING

Good carving is an economy. A skilled carver makes a joint go much further than one who merely hacks off the meat. If possible, always allow the meat to 'rest' in a warm place for 10-15 minutes before carving. This will make the meat firmer and easier to carve more evenly and economically.

1 The first essential is a long-bladed sharp carving knife. The blade should be sharpened to a keen edge each time before use, and then wiped with a clean cloth to remove any metal dust.

2 The second essential is a carving fork fitted with a guard. This protects the carver's hand should the knife slip accidentally.

3 Place the joint firmly on a large warmed dish. A wooden board can be used and spiked dishes are particularly good for holding the joint firmly in place and preventing it from slipping. Boards or dishes with gulleys to catch the meat juices also have advantages.

4 Use the knife with a gentle sawing movement so that it passes smoothly through the meat.

5 Whenever possible carve across the grain of the meat, thus shortening the fibres so the meat is more tender to eat.

CARVING LAMB ON THE BONE

A roast tastes best when the meat is carved in fairly thick, 6 mm [¼"] slices. When sliced too thinly much of the flavour and succulence is lost. One of the secrets of professional carving is knowing where and how the bones lie within the joint.

Leg and shoulder

The best methods of carving a leg and shoulder are shown in step-by-step pictures. You may also want to roast and carve a halved shoulder. Both the shank end and the blade end are carved in the same manner as a whole shoulder. If a leg is halved, the

Carving a loin

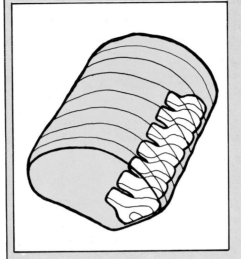 

Carving a leg fillet

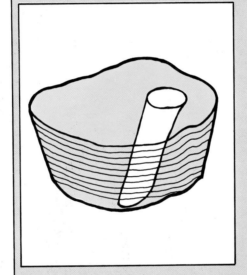 

Carving a best end

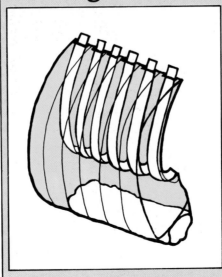 

117

Step-by-step carving a leg of lamb

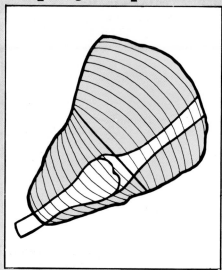

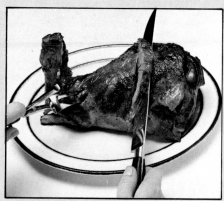

1 Set the leg firmly on the dish with the round side uppermost. Insert the carving fork near the knuckle and tilt the joint slightly towards you.

2 Make a cut in the centre, right through to the bone. Slant the knife a little and make a second cut down to the bone so that you remove a 6 mm [¼"] slice.

Carving a shoulder of lamb

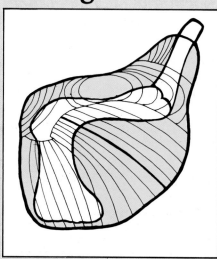

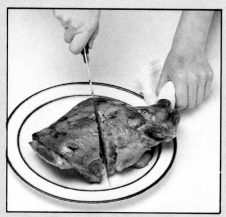

1 Carve a slice 6 mm [¼"] thick from the centre of the joint, cutting right through to the bone.

2 Continue carving slices from either side of the first cut until the bone gets in the way.

Carving a saddle of lamb

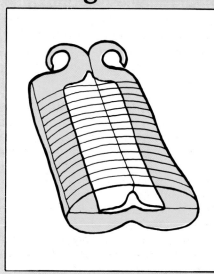

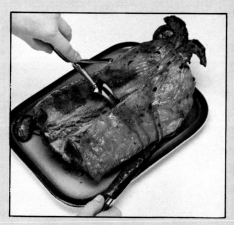

1 Make a cut the full length of the back, keeping the knife against the side of the backbone, cutting through to the bone beneath.

2 Slip the knife under the meat and free it from the bone. Make a cut parallel to the first to free the entire section of meat.

3 Continue slicing from either side of the first cut, angling the knife to obtain the longest slices you can, until all the meat has been cut from this side. Put down the fork.

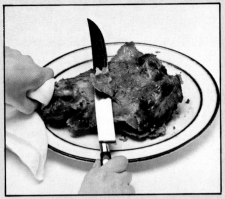

4 Turn the joint over. Cut off surplus fat, hold the joint firmly by the knuckle with your free hand and cut thin horizontal slices along the length of the leg.

3 Cut small horizontal slices from the shank bone until all the meat has been cut from the top.

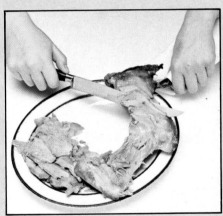

4 Turn the joint over and remove any surplus fat. Carve off the meat in thin slices as far as you can.

3 Carve this prime section in slices and repeat with the other side. Turn the joint over and make slanting cuts from the edges.

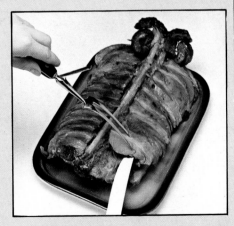

4 Reassemble the prime section on the bone. Serve these with a slice from the underside together with a slice of kidney.

shank end of the leg is carved as for a leg, but the fillet end is laid cut side upward (as shown) for carving.

Remember that legs and shoulders may be taken from either the right- or left-hand side of the animal and will differ accordingly.

Saddle
A saddle comprises two loins joined together but is carved in rather a different way, as shown in the step-by-step pictures. Meat is entirely freed from the backbone and ribs before being sliced.

Best end of neck
This joint is prepared by the butcher to aid carving. He may have chined it, so that after cooking you can remove the whole length of the backbone before carving. Alternatively, the butcher will have cut through the backbone between the ribs. In either case, carve by cutting between the rib bones to divide the meat into 12 mm [½"] thick cutlets.

Loin of lamb
The butcher will have chopped this joint through the backbone between the ribs. To carve, simply cut between the rib bones dividing the meat into 12 mm [½"] thick chops.

ACCOMPANIMENTS TO ROAST LAMB
Although lamb has a delicate flavour, it is rich and slightly fatty. It therefore responds to the contrast of fresh, clean and slightly piquant or sharp flavours.

Sauces, such as a distinctive, well flavoured onion or caper sauce, are suitable for serving with mature lamb or mutton and, being substantial, they will help the meat go further.

Jellies: redcurrant jelly is justly famous to eat with lamb, and easy enough to buy. If you are fortunate enough to have the ingredients to make your own jellies, the time spent in preparing redcurrant, apple and mint, gooseberry and mint, japonica or cranberry jelly will be amply rewarded. Any one of these jellies will make a simple roast lamb joint more delicious.

Mint: the Englishman's favourite herb flavour for lamb. Spearmint is the most popular variety used, but it is worth experimenting with others. For instance, apple mint has an equally fresh but more subtle flavour.

MINT SAUCE

If possible make this sauce an hour or two before it is needed so that the flavours develop and blend together. White wine vinegar and light soft brown sugar as used here give a better flavour than the harsh malt vinegar and white sugar often used.

SERVES 6
45 ml [3 tablespoons] freshly chopped mint
15 ml [1 tablespoon] soft brown sugar
60 ml [4 tablespoons] white wine vinegar

1 Put the mint and sugar in a small basin.

2 Add 30 ml [2 tablespoons] boiling water and stir until the sugar dissolves and the mint colours the water.

3 Stir in the vinegar and set aside until cold.

ROAST SADDLE OF LAMB

The saddle will serve at least eight people but, when ordering, tell the butcher specifically how many portions you require, especially if you want more than eight servings. The butcher will score the outer fat in a diamond pattern. Ask the butcher to supply the kidneys separately, still in their covering suet. These are not cooked for the full time but are added to the pan rack towards the end. Before serving they are stripped of suet and fixed to the tail end of the loin.

This large joint is covered for part of the time because it requires long cooking and would otherwise become too brown before the meat is cooked. The covering means that no basting is necessary until the kidneys are added 45 minutes before end of cooking.

SERVES 8
saddle of lamb, weighing about 2.7 kg [6 lb]
salt and black pepper
3 to 4 garlic cloves
sprigs of fresh rosemary

1 Heat oven to 180°C [350°F] gas mark 4.

2 Calculate the total cooking time according to the weight—in this case 2 hours for a pink roast and 2½ hours for a well-done roast.

3 Sprinkle the surface fat liberally with salt and pepper and rub in.

4 Peel the garlic cloves, cut in quarters and tuck in between the folds of skin underneath the joint.

5 Place the joint, fat side up, on a rack standing in a roasting tin.

6 Tuck 2 large sprigs of rosemary under the trussing string along the top of the saddle and 2 more underneath the joint.

7 Protect the curved fatty end from over-browning by covering with a piece of buttered foil. Then cover the entire joint with a piece of buttered foil or double grease-proof paper.

8 Cook in the centre of the oven.

9 For the last 45 minutes cook the kidneys in their suet on the rack beside the meat. Remove all the covering and baste the saddle to allow it to brown.

A glaze of redcurrant jelly and orange juice gives the fat round a best end of neck a special flavour.

10 Test that the meat is cooked and transfer to a warmed serving dish. Remove the trussing strings.

11 Remove the sprigs and loose spikes of rosemary and the garlic. Lay sprigs of fresh rosemary along the top of the joint as garnish.

12 Cut away and discard the fat from around the kidneys. Impale each kidney on one end of a cocktail stick and drive the other end into the meat beside the tail. Put the serving dish in the warmer to rest.

13 Pour off all fat from the dripping in the roasting tin and make a thin gravy.

5. Meanwhile, melt the redcurrant jelly in the orange juice by heating it gently in a small saucepan. (If the jelly doesn't melt smoothly you may need to press it through a strainer.)

6. Remove the rosting tin from the oven and spoon the jelly over the fat side of the meat. Then continue roasting for another 20 minutes for medium-rare, or 30 minutes for well-done. Baste occasionally.

7. Transfer the joint to a warmed serving dish and keep warm.

8. Remove the rack from the roasting tin. Gently tilt the tin so that the meat drippings collect in one corner and spoon off the fat that rises to the surface. Then stir in the lemon juice, bring to the boil, stirring, and cook over medium heat for 2-3 minutes. Season the gravy to taste and serve very hot.

MUSTARD BASTED SHOULDER OF LAMB

⬙⬙⬙ *A half shoulder of lamb is a useful small joint, reasonably inexpensive and enough for one meal without leftovers. A garlicky mustard baste adds interest to late-season lamb or young mutton. If possible apply the baste several hours before cooking to give the flavour time to penetrate the meat.*

SERVES 4
**half a shoulder, blade end, weighing about 1 kg [2 lb]
salt**

**For the baste:
1 large garlic clove
30 ml [2 tablespoons] yellow French mustard
2.5 ml [½ teaspoon] ground ginger
10 ml [2 teaspoons] soy sauce
15 ml [1 tablespoon] oil**

1. Skin the meat and wipe the unskinned surfaces with a damp cloth. Sprinkle the fat side lightly with salt and rub in, but avoid salting the cut surfaces.

2. For the baste, peel and crush the garlic and put it into a small basin with the mustard, ginger and soy sauce, then beat in the oil drop by drop.

BEST END OF NECK WITH REDCURRANT ORANGE GLAZE

⬙⬙ *A best end of neck makes a delicious small roast for three people and this simple glaze adds richness to the meat and a tang to the gravy. Ask the butcher to chop the backbone, so that the joint is easy to carve, and to remove the skin.*

When skimming the fat to make gravy, be careful to remove only the surface fat.

SERVES 3
**best end of neck of lamb weighing 700 g [1½ lb]
salt and pepper
30 ml [2 tablespoons] redcurrant jelly**

**15 ml [1 tablespoon] orange juice
10 ml [2 teaspoons] lemon juice**

1. Heat the oven to 180°C [350°F] gas mark 4.

2. Cut off the tops of the rib bones. Rub all surfaces of the meat (both the fat and the skin over the bone) with salt and pepper.

3. Place the meat, fat side uppermost, on a rack standing in a meat tin. Lay the tops of the rib bones in the tin to enrich the gravy.

4. Roast for 45 minutes.

3 Place the lamb on a rack in a roasting tin. Brush the baste all over the meat and leave in a cool place for 2-4 hours.

4 Heat the oven to 180°C [350°F] gas mark 4 and cook the lamb in the centre of the oven allowing 40 to 45 minutes per 450 g [1 lb].

5 Turn the lamb twice during cooking so that both sides brown evenly and neither over-browns. (If you do not turn it, the baste will form a brown crust over the top surface.)

6 Test the lamb and, when cooked, transfer to a warmed serving dish. Keep warm, remove the rack and pour off fat. Make the gravy.

Epaule d'agneau boulangère is a complete meal. A shoulder is roasted above a bed of potatoes, which is cooked in a little stock. The meat drips down on to the potatoes making them particularly appetizing.

EPAULE D'AGNEAU BOULANGERE

This French method of roasting a whole shoulder of lamb is particularly good because all the meat drippings are absorbed by the potatoes surrounding the joint— gravy is quite unnecessary.

Although liquid is included, this is only enough to be absorbed by the potatoes during cooking. The meat is placed on top of the vegetables, where it is above the liquid, and is therefore roasted and not braised. An ovenproof dish is used as this is smaller than a roasting pan and the potatoes will fit without space to spare.

The method is also suitable for a whole leg of lamb. A half leg or shoulder can also be used, but in this case the potatoes will need a longer cooking time than the meat, so cook them first and put small joints on top later.

SERVES 6
**shoulder of lean lamb
  weighing 1.5 kg [3½ lb]**
salt and pepper
2 or 3 garlic cloves
225 g [½ lb] onions
25 g [1 oz] butter
15 ml [1 tablespoon] oil
1 kg [2 lb] potatoes
275 ml [½ pt] brown stock

For the garnish:
**freshly chopped herbs, such
  as parsley or watercress**

1 Heat the oven to 180°C [350°F] gas mark 4.

2 Prepare the shoulder of lamb for cooking; do not skin it, but season fat side generously with salt and pepper.

3 Peel the garlic cloves and cut into slivers. Insert these into incisions in the meat and tuck them in around the bone and flaps of skin.

4 Peel and thinly slice the onions. Soften them in the butter and oil.

5 Peel and thinly slice the potatoes.

6 Lightly butter a large ovenproof dish, preferably one which can be used for serving. Arrange the potatoes and onions in layers, seasoning lightly between layers, and filling the base of the dish.

7 Pour in the stock which should reach almost to the top of the vegetables.

8 Arrange the meat on top of the vegetables.

9 Cook in the centre of the oven, allowing 30 minutes per 450 g [1 lb] for medium rare, 40 minutes for well done.

10 Sprinkle the potatoes with chopped herbs then serve in the roasting dish.

MUTTON TO TASTE LIKE VENISON

If you enjoy rich gamey flavours, this is an excellent way to cook a fine leg of mutton or mature lamb. Don't use a leg of young lamb because the robust marinade will be too forceful for the delicate flavour. Because the meat must remain in the marinade for several days, you need to use a cooked marinade (otherwise the vegetables in the marinade would go sour). Any left-over meat is excellent cold served with an orange, chicory and watercress salad.

SERVES 6-8
**1 leg of young mutton about
2.25 kg [5 lb]
45 ml [3 tablespoons] oil**

**For the marinade:
60 ml [4 tablespoons]
   olive oil
1 medium-sized onion
1 medium-sized carrot
1 celery stick
1 garlic clove
700 ml [1¼ pt] red wine
150 ml [¼ pt] red wine vinegar
10 ml [2 teaspoons] salt
2.5 ml [½ teaspoon] black
   peppercorns
1 bay leaf
sprig each of rosemary,
   thyme and parsley
4 crushed juniper berries**

**For the sauce:
400 ml [¾ pt] household stock
   or water
30 ml [2 tablespoons] plain
   flour
15 ml [1 tablespoon]
   redcurrant jelly
salt
freshly ground black pepper**

1 To prepare the marinade, peel and slice the onion, chop the carrot and celery and peel and halve the garlic.

2 Heat the oil in a saucepan over medium heat, then add all the

vegetables. Shake the pan to coat the vegetables with fat and cook gently for 5 minutes.

3 Add the wine, vinegar, salt, peppercorns, herbs and spices. Bring to the boil, cover and simmer gently for 15 minutes.

4 Remove from the heat and leave to become absolutely cold.

5 Skin the leg of mutton. Place in a deep glass or earthenware dish and then pour the cold marinade over it.

6 Leave to marinate for 4-5 days at room temperature—15°C [60°F]— or 6 days in a refrigerator. Turn the leg at least once a day.

7 When ready to cook, drain the leg (reserving the marinade) and pat dry with kitchen paper.

8 Heat the oven to 180°C [350°F] gas mark 4.

9 Put the leg on a rack over a roasting pan and pour the oil over. Roast, allowing 25 minutes per 450 g [1 lb] for a pink roast and 35 minutes for a well done.

10 Start preparing the sauce about 30 minutes before serving. Strain 150 ml [¼ pt] marinade into a saucepan, add the stock (or water), bring to the boil and leave to simmer gently. The liquid must be reduced to 275 ml [½ pt]. This should take about 5-10 minutes.

11 When the leg of lamb is cooked, transfer it to a warmed serving dish and leave to rest in a warm place while you make the gravy.

12 Carefully pour off all but 30 ml [2 tablespoons] fat from the roasting tin. Stir the flour into the fat remaining in the tin, then cook over moderate heat, stirring constantly, for 1-2 minutes to colour the roux.

13 Away from the heat, stir in the reduced marinade and stock mixture, and the redcurrant jelly. Bring to the boil, stirring, and season to taste. Simmer for 5 minutes, stirring occasionally. Transfer to a sauce-boat and serve with the lamb.

Pork and Bacon

grilling

Grilling is the easiest and quickest way to cook meat. But don't be deceived by the simplicity. Grilling is a method that demands the right choice of ingredients, the full attention of the cook and immaculate timing. Pork is a good meat for grilling and, happily, that goes for some economy cuts as well as the more expensive loin and chump chops usually associated with grilling.

THE BASIC PRINCIPLES
Grilling is a method of cooking by radiant heat, usually under a glowing gas or electric grill, or over the coals of a charcoal grill. The aim of grilling is to seal and brown the surface of the food whilst trapping the flavour and succulence inside. The cook's skill lies in positioning the food and timing the cooking to achieve just this effect.

Successful results depend on sealing the surface of the food very quickly so grilling always begins by cooking the meat under fierce, dry heat for a minute or so on each side.

By this time, very thin cuts such as bacon rashers are completely cooked. But other cuts need further grilling to cook the meat right through to the centre. This secondary stage of grilling is always done under reduced heat. How long and at what temperature varies according to cut but it is usually vital to brush the meat with fat every few minutes to preserve succulence and to prevent any possibility of burning. Cooking meat all the way through is particularly important with pork which, unlike other meats, should never be served when still pink and slightly raw in the centre.

CHOOSING AND STORING PORK AND BACON
Pork
The old British adage about buying pork only when there's an R in the month (i.e., not in the warm months between May and August) is completely out of date. With modern

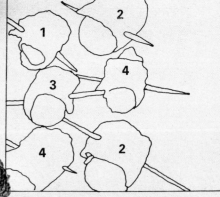

Serve savoury bacon rolls at buffets or (placed on rounds of hot buttered toast) at the end of a meal.
1 *Devils on horseback.*
2 *Banana-wrapped bacon rolls.*
3 *Pineapple-wrapped bacon rolls.*
4 *Piglets on horseback.*

Pork and bacon cuts suitable for grilling

Cut	Description	Method
 **Loin and chump chops**	Lean and tender cuts. Loin chops are most expensive and sometimes have a portion of kidney attached. The bonier chump chops come from the leg end of the loin. Depending on size, chops are usually 2-2.5 cm [¾"-1"] thick and already trimmed by the butcher.	If not already done, cut off rind and excess fat. Brush with oil or marinate before grilling. Grill under fierce heat for 1 minute or so on each side, then 5-7 minutes under low heat on each side, basting occasionally.
 **Spare rib chops**	Also called neck cutlets, these shoulder cuts consist of lean, well-flavoured meat. Economical but not as elegant as loin or chump chops, usually about 2.5 cm [1"] thick. Not to be confused with Chinese-type (sometimes called American) spare ribs—which are belly bones with little meat attached.	Brush with oil before cooking. Place in a gratin dish or on the base of the grill pan and grill under fierce heat for 1 minute or so on each side. Cover with sauce and grill under low heat for 7-8 minutes on each side, basting occasionally.
 **Belly**	Also known as streaky pork, this is one of the fattier and cheaper but very tasty cuts. Ask the butcher to cut it into thin slices—6 mm [¼"]. Thick slices are unsuitable for grilling.	No need to brush with oil or to baste. Grill under fierce heat for 1 minute or so on each side, then under moderate to low heat for 6-9 minutes on each side until crisp and golden. Save fat that drips into pan base for frying.
 **Fillet**	Also known as tenderloin, this is a long thin strip of lean meat found beneath the loin. It is fine-grained, tender meat with little or no fat. Cut into cubes and threaded on to skewers, fillet is ideal for kebabs.	Very lean meat so brush generously with oil, basting sauce or marinade. Grill under fierce heat for 1 minute or so on each side. Continue grilling under low heat for 7-8 minutes on each side, turning and basting frequently.
 **Gammon steaks** / **Bacon chops**	Gammon is available green (unsmoked) or smoked. Smoked slice of middle cut is best for grilling. An average portion weighs about 125-150 g [4-5 oz] and is about 6 mm [¼"] thick but it can be cut thicker if required. Bacon chops are back or shoulder cuts, usually sweet-cured and mildly flavoured. Usually trimmed and vacuum-packed. Available in 6 and 12 mm [¼ and ½"] thicknesses.	Trim away rind and snip deeply into fat. Because of the salt content, never use very high heat. Brush with melted butter and grill under moderate heat, turning once, for 5-8 minutes on each side, depending on thickness. Treat like gammon steaks. Brush with melted butter and grill under moderate heat, turning once, for 5-8 minutes on each side, depending on thickness.
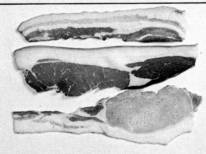 **Bacon rashers**	Streaky is the fattiest and cheapest cut. Middle, back and oyster are, in this order, leaner and more expensive. All available green, sweetcured or smoked, very thinly sliced-up to a maximum of about 3 mm [⅛"] thick.	If necessary, cut away rind and bones. No need to brush with oil but protect the lean of back rashers by overlapping the lean of one rasher with the fat of the next. Cooking time is too short to make bacon tough so, despite salt content, grill under high heat throughout, turning once, for 1-2 minutes each side until fat is crisp and lightly browned.

refrigeration it is safe to eat pork at any time of year—provided you remember it is the one meat that must always be cooked right through.

When buying, look for young pork which you can recognise by fine-grained, pale flesh and firm, creamy fat. The texture and colour of pork coarsens with age. Beware any meat that is sticky to touch, brownish in colour and with soft, greyish fat: it has probably been in the butcher's shop for some time.

Unwrap pork as soon as you get home. Put it on a plate and cover loosely with polythene or foil. Store in the coldest part of the refrigerator, (which is immediately under the frozen food compartment), where it will keep for up to three days. It is wise not to store pork in a larder for more than one day.

Bacon and gammon

Bacon is the brine-cured meat of a specially bred lean pig. Gammon comes from the hind leg; and bacon comes from the other parts.

● Unsmoked bacon or gammon (also known as green or pale) is milder in flavour and paler in colour than smoked.

● A modern sweet-brine cure results in an extra mild flavoured product.

● Smoked bacon (the smoking is done after the initial curing in brine) is dark in colour and has a much stronger flavour.

When buying, look for signs of freshness—a moist, fresh cut surface with firm white fat and deep pink meat. Avoid 'wet', dark or dried up looking meat or any that has soft oily fat. Fresh bacon and gammon smells mild and pleasant, never strong.

Store bacon and gammon in a refrigerator or cold larder for short periods only—up to about 5 days. Unless it is vacuum packed, protect bacon and gammon from dehydration by wrapping closely in foil or polythene or put it into an airtight plastic box. Once opened, treat vacuum packed bacon as fresh.

EQUIPMENT

The basic equipment is, of course, the grill with its pan and grid.

Knowing how the grill on your cooker works is very important—especially how quickly it heats up and cools down. The grill must be very hot when food is placed under it, so always heat the grill in advance, with

Trimming pork and bacon

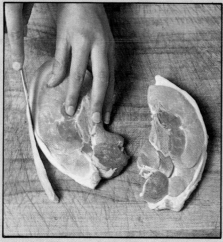

Loin and chump chops: are usually bought trimmed and ready to cook. If not, cut off rind and excess fat.

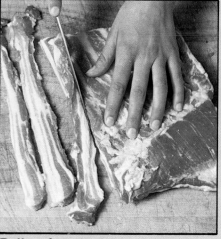

Belly of pork: (also called streaky pork) should be cut into thin slices—no more than 6 mm [$\frac{1}{4}$"] thick.

Gammon steaks: trim rind and snip deeply into the fat—or steaks will curl under heat of cooking.

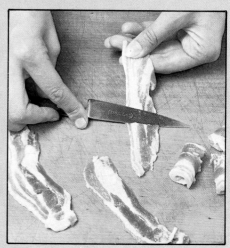

Bacon: cut away rind and gristle. For bacon rolls stretch with the back of a knife and cut into half lengths.

the pan and grid close to the heat, for as long as it takes to become glowing and hot.

Once the food has been sealed, however, the temperature needs to be reduced fairly rapidly so the food can continue cooking more gently. Either reduce the heat and keep the pan close to the source of heat, or keep the heat high and lower the pan right away from it. The first method is more economical on fuel but is only possible if your grill temperature adjusts evenly and fairly rapidly. If your grill cuts out in sections when the heat is turned down, or it takes a long time to cool down, you should use the second method.

You will also need a pastry brush to oil the grid, a spoon to baste fat or marinade over the food during grilling and a pair of tongs to turn the food

over. You can use a fish slice or palette knife in conjunction with a spoon instead but do avoid using forks as these may pierce the meat and allow juices to escape.

Fat will always melt during grilling and some juices drip down into the pan but you can save yourself a major cleaning job by lining the base of the pan with kitchen foil before you start grilling.

A shallow fireproof dish specifically designed to go under the grill (called a gratin dish) and pretty enough to take into the dining room is ideal for grilling foods which are cooked and served in a basting sauce or marinade. If you do not have a gratin dish, put the meat in the pan base (not on the grid) so the meat is surrounded by the liquid and keeps moist throughout cooking.

PROTECTING MEAT FROM DRYING

Naturally fatty cuts such as belly of pork and streaky bacon are moist enough to look after themselves but lean meats must be protected against drying out or sticking to the grid during grilling.

Oils and fats

The simplest protection involves brushing lean meats with oil or melted fat before cooking and repeating the process as necessary during grilling. As an extra precaution, brush the grid too to prevent sticking.

● Vegetable oils or olive oil (which also adds flavour) are ideal and easy to use. Simply brush some oil on both sides of the meat with a pastry brush.

● Melted dripping is an excellent alternative.

● Melted butter can also be used and adds distinctive flavour but it tends to burn easily.

● Melted lard is functional but has little or no flavour.

Basting sauces

Instead of spooning extra oil or melted fat over the meat during grilling, you can use a basting sauce to keep the meat succulent and add extra flavour.

Marinades

The third method involves marinating the meat for 2-8 hours before cooking, then basting the meat during grilling with the marinade mixture.

Marinating means steeping the meat in a mixture usually consisting of oil, acid (lemon juice, wine or wine vinegar) and seasonings.

The ingredients soak into the meat adding extra flavour and the acid content helps tenderize fibres, which is especially useful for less tender cuts of meat. Use herbs and spices of your choice but never include salt as this encourages the meat juices to leak out and is inclined to make the meat tough.

Marinade recipes

Preparing a lemon and herb marinade is shown in step-by-step pictures on this page. Alternative recipes, below, are enough for 8 chops each.

For Worcestershire marinade: mix together 125 ml [4 fl oz] each of olive oil and white wine vinegar. To this add 1 garlic clove, crushed or finely chopped, 5 ml [1 teaspoon] ground black pepper and 5 ml [1 teaspoon] each of Worcestershire sauce and paprika.

For Mexican marinade: mix together 125 ml [4 fl oz] of olive oil and 125 ml [4 fl oz] white wine vinegar. Add to this 45 ml [3 tablespoons] each of finely minced or chopped onion and green pepper, 125 ml [4 fl oz] fresh tomato juice, a sprig of fresh oregano or 5 ml [1 teaspoon] of dried oregano, 10 ml [2 teaspoons] chilli powder, 1 garlic clove crushed or finely chopped and salt and pepper to taste.

Marinating

ENOUGH FOR 4 LOIN OR CHUMP CHOPS

freshly ground black pepper
45 ml [3 tablespoons] lemon juice
45 ml [3 tablespoons] olive oil
1 bay leaf
small sprig fresh thyme or
½ x 2.5 ml [¼ teaspoon] dried thyme

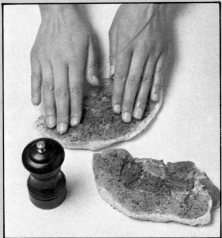

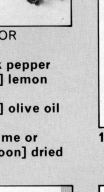

1 Use your hands to rub the surface of the trimmed pork chops with freshly ground pepper. No salt.

2 Pour the lemon juice into a large shallow dish. Stir in oil, mix well and add herbs.

3 Add the meat. Turn over to coat. Cover and leave in a cool place for 2-8 hours, turning occasionally.

Handy hints

MAKING THE MOST OF FUEL

Heat is an expensive commodity, so make the best use of your grill by following these penny-wise tips:

● Fill spaces with halved tomatoes or mushroom caps which have been brushed with oil or filled with savoury stuffings.

● When grilling bacon on the grid, first brush the base of the grill pan with a little oil or melted butter and break an egg into it. The egg will fry in (and be flavoured by) the fat that drips down from the bacon.

● If your grill is under the hotplate on the cooker or you have an eye-level gas grill, use the heat that rises from the grill to warm something—by placing bread rolls, plates, milk or water over the grill.

Step-by-step grilling pork chops

This is the classic way to grill chops. If you have marinated the chops there is, of course, no need to brush them with oil before cooking, and you can use the marinade mixture instead of oil in step 6.

1 Turn the grill to high. Brush grid with oil. Put grid and pan in position until red hot.

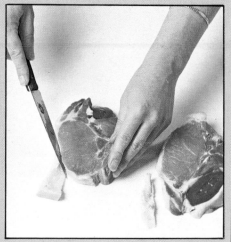

2 Meanwhile trim excess fat from the chops using a sharp knife. Brush generously with oil on each side.

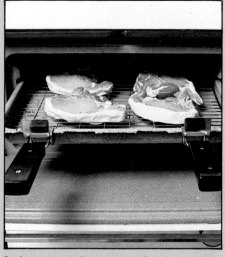

3 Lay the chops on the hot grid. Cook close to the heat for 1-2 minutes or until slightly brown.

4 Turn chops, using tongs to avoid piercing. Cook other side for 1-2 minutes under fierce heat.

5 Reduce heat to low or move grill pan to lowest position, depending on what type of grill you have.

6 Continue cooking for another 5-7 minutes on each side, turning and brushing with oil several times.

7 Season the chops with salt and pepper, garnish and serve.

BACON ROLLS

Plain or stuffed bacon rolls taste delicious and look very professional but they are, in fact, easy to make.

They make a lovely garnish for roast chicken or turkey: the flavours of bacon and poultry complement each other well and bacon rolls add a glamorous finishing touch to the serving dish.

Bacon rolls impaled on cocktail sticks or wooden tooth picks are easy to eat with your fingers without making a mess so they make ideal buffet or cocktail party food.

And don't forget that old-fashioned English favourite, the savoury—which makes a delectable change (and today an original one) from the inevitable dessert. Appetizingly filled bacon rolls served on fried bread or thick, soft buttery toast cut with pretty biscuit cutter shapes make elegant dinner party fare and, if the bread is omitted, bacon rolls make an acceptable treat for anyone trying to avoid the sugar-rich foods usually served for dessert.

DEVILS ON HORSEBACK

Streaky bacon is best for this classic savoury since the high fat content helps keep the filling succulent and moist. Steps 1-14 can be prepared well in advance if wished.

SERVES 4
8 large Californian prunes
850 ml [1½ pt] strong, hot tea
corn oil
8 blanched almonds
streaky bacon rashers
salt and cayenne pepper
4 slices white bread

1 Place the prunes in a small saucepan, pour on the tea, cover with a lid and cook over low heat for 30 minutes.

2 Remove the pan from the heat and set aside.

3 Heat 30 ml [2 tablespoons] oil in a heavy frying pan. Fry the almonds for 2-3 minutes, turning occasionally, until golden but not brown.

4 Lift the nuts out of the pan and roll them in a little salt and cayenne pepper.

5 Using biscuit cutters cut the bread into eight small decorative shapes.

6 Add more oil to the frying pan and allow to become very hot.

7 Fry the bread, turning as necessary, until golden and brown.

8 Drain the fried bread on absorbent kitchen paper towels. Place in a single layer on a baking sheet or serving dish and keep warm and crisp in a low oven.

9 Drain off and discard the prune liquid. Slit open the fruit with a sharp knife and remove the stones. Place an almond in each cavity.

10 Remove bacon rind and any gristle. Stretch each rasher by pressing flat with the back of a knife.

11 Cut each rasher in half and place a prepared prune in the centre of one half.

12 Wrap the bacon firmly round the filling. Place the bacon roll in a gratin dish—with the bacon overlap facing downwards so it cannot unroll during cooking. If necessary, secure with a cocktail stick.

13 Prepare the remaining devils in the same way.

14 Heat the grill until medium hot or, if preferred, heat the oven to 200°C

Neat bacon rolls look handsome and the flavour goes well with poultry.

[400°F] gas mark 6.

15 Cook the devils for 10-15 minutes until the bacon is golden brown. Turn occasionally if grilling.

16 Arrange the devils on the fried bread and serve.

Variations

● Instead of an almond the prune could be stuffed with any of the following: a rolled anchovy fillet, a small piece of pâté or a pimento-stuffed olive.

● For angels on horseback replace the stuffed prune with a fresh oyster. Dust with freshly ground pepper and a sprinkling of lemon juice.

● For mock angels on horseback use smoked oysters or smoked mussels, which are available in small cans from delicatessens and specialist food shops. Drain off oil and sprinkle with lemon juice.

● For ladies on horseback use chicken livers. Wash and dry the livers and cut away any white parts. Dust with cayenne pepper.

● For piglets on horseback use half-cooked cocktail sausages.

● Pieces of banana and pineapple cubes are other delicious fillings.

COUNTRY-STYLE CHOPS

Orange juice can be used instead of vinegar, lemon or wine in a marinade. Its relatively mild acidity complements the flavour of lean pork well, particularly when combined with rosemary. When you are entertaining or haven't time to watch the grill, prepare steps 1-6 and top the chops with orange slices. Then cover the dish with foil and transfer to the centre of an oven heated to 180°C [350°F] gas mark 4 for 30-35 minutes.

SERVES 4
4 loin or chump chops
1 small onion
2 juicy oranges
15 ml [1 tablespoon] olive oil
freshly ground black pepper
a sprig of fresh rosemary or
    5 ml [1 teaspoon] dried
    rosemary

1 Peel the onion and chop finely.

2 Grate the zest (rind) and squeeze the juice of one orange into a gratin dish.

3 Add the oil and mix well with a fork. Add the chopped onion, a good grinding of pepper and fresh or dried rosemary.

4 Place the chops in the dish and turn once or twice to coat all over. Cover the dish with foil and leave to marinate for 2-8 hours.

5 Heat the grill until very hot.

6 Place the gratin dish close to the grill and cook the chops under fierce heat for 1-2 minutes on each side until sealed and lightly browned.

7 Reduce heat to low or lower the dish and continue grilling for another 7 minutes on each side, brushing with the marinade from time to time.

8 Meanwhile, peel and thinly slice the remaining orange.

9 Cover the chops with orange slices and brush the orange slices with the marinade.

10 Grill for 4 minutes, until the orange is heated through.

SOMERSET GAMMON

Gammon is the exception to the rule that grilling always begins with fierce dry heat. This is because high salt content combined with high heat would produce tough meat. Use medium heat throughout cooking for succulent tender results and, because the temperature is not very high, you can use butter without danger of burning. Bacon chops could be used instead of gammon.

SERVES 4
4 gammon steaks each
    weighing about 175 g [6 oz]
25 g [1 oz] melted butter
2 eating apples
175 g [6 oz] mild cheese, such
    as Gruyere

1 Using kitchen scissors, trim the rind from the gammon and snip into the fat.

2 Brush the steaks on both sides with melted butter.

3 Brush the grid with melted butter and heat the grill, pan and grid until medium hot.

4 Put the gammon on the grid and grill for 4 minutes on each side, turning with tongs.

5 Meanwhile, core, peel and slice the apple into thin rings.

6 Lay the apples over the gammon and brush with a little butter. Grill for a further 4 minutes.

7 Grate the cheese and sprinkle it over the apple rings. Cook for a further 4-5 minutes or until the cheese is melted and bubbling. Serve immediately.

KENTISH BACON

Bacon chops are usually sweetcured and, therefore, mildly flavoured. They are usually sold ready-trimmed and vacuum-packed. As for gammon, bacon chops should be cooked under medium heat throughout. Gammon steaks are equally suitable for this recipe.

SERVES 4
4 bacon chops
25 g [1 oz] melted butter
2 large ripe peaches or a small
    can of apricot halves

1 Snip into the bacon fat to prevent curling during cooking.

2 Brush the bacon on both sides with melted butter.

3 Brush grid with melted butter and heat grill, pan and grid until medium hot.

4 Put the bacon on the grid and grill for about 5 minutes on each side, depending on thickness. Turn with tongs and brush with butter occasionally.

5 Meanwhile peel, halve and stone peaches and brush with melted butter. Or, drain canned apricots and brush with butter.

6 Place the fruit on top of the bacon and continue grilling for about 5 minutes.

LEMON AND PARSLEY PORK CRUMBLE

△ *A simple and inexpensive dish with a tangy fresh flavour—lemon zest admirably offsets the fatty texture of the meat. Because the meat is fatty, brushing it with oil before or during grilling is unnecessary.*

SERVES 4
8 slices belly of pork
25 g [1 oz] stale white bread
3-4 pimento-stuffed olives
1 lemon
15 ml [1 tablespoon] chopped fresh parsley
salt and pepper
3 tomatoes

In individual dishes : Gammon steaks topped with crisp apple and bubbling cheese make Somerset gammon a very appetizing dish.

Below left: Country-style chops with orange and rosemary make a pleasant change from plain grilled pork chops.

Below right: Lemon and parsley pork crumble is a luscious dish— and it proves that even a cheap cut of pork can make a tasty grill.

1 Heat the grill, with the pan and grid in position, until very hot.

2 Meanwhile, break the bread into pieces and rub against the fine holes of a cheese grater. Alternatively, make the crumbs in a liquidizer, following manufacturer's instructions.

3 Slice the olives and grate the zest (rind) from the lemon (taking care not to grate the bitter-tasting white pith).

4 Mix the crumbs, olives, lemon zest and parsley in a small bowl. Season with salt and pepper.

5 Lay the pork on the grid and grill under a fierce heat for 1 minute on each side, and then under moderate to low heat for 6-9 minutes on each side until crisp and golden.

6 Using tongs, remove the pork from the grid and transfer to a fireproof gratin dish. Reserve fat in the grill pan.

7 Slice the tomatoes and arrange them over the pork.

8 Sprinkle breadcrumb mixture on top and pour on a little fat from the grill pan.

9 Reduce the heat to low. Place the dish under it and grill until the crumb mixture turns golden brown.

Star recipe

ORIENTAL SPARE RIB CHOPS

Spare rib chops are lean but less tender than loin or chump chops. They grill best if liberally basted with a sauce. Do be sure to buy English cut or spare rib chops—American cut or Chinese spare ribs are not suitable.

SERVES 4
4 spare rib chops
45 ml [3 tablespoons] oil
1 small onion
1 x 225 g [½ lb] can peeled
  tomatoes
60 ml [4 tablespoons] wine
  vinegar
50 g [2 oz] soft brown sugar
30 ml [2 tablespoons] tomato
  sauce
10 ml [2 teaspoons] soy sauce

1 Brush the chops on both sides with a little of the oil. Set aside until ready to cook.

2 Chop onion finely: peel, cut in half, slice towards root, slice downwards then slice across.

6 Add the tomatoes, their juice, vinegar, sugar, tomato sauce and soy sauce to the saucepan.

7 Bring to the boil and simmer (cook below boiling point) for 10 minutes, stirring occasionally.

8 Meanwhile turn grill to highest heat and arrange the chops in a single layer in a gratin dish.

9 When heat is fierce, place dish under it. Cook chops for 1 minute on each side, turning with tongs.

10 Pour sauce over chops. Reduce heat to low or lower dish as far away from heat as possible.

11 Grill chops for 7-8 minutes on each side, turning and basting with sauce from time to time.

3 Pour the remaining oil into a small saucepan and set over low heat to warm gently.

4 Add the chopped onion and cook very gently for about 5 minutes until beginning to soften.

5 Turn tomatoes into a sieve over a bowl to reserve juice. Chop the tomatoes roughly.

Pork roasted without the rind, as in France, can be marinated first, or the fat rubbed with spices, and herbs added to the pan.

134

Pork

roasting

Roast pork with crisp brown crackling is a rich and succulent dish. It can also be roasted without the rind, in the French manner. Either way it is delicious properly cooked and with the right accompaniments. This chapter shows how to roast and carve pork and what to serve with it.

Pork is a relatively inexpensive meat, and can be roasted both on and off the bone. The meat is fat so one of its great virtues is that most of the main cuts can be roasted. Unlike lamb and beef, it is also practical to roast smaller weights of meat, because the outer layer of fat keeps it moist and shrinkage is kept to a minimum.

Pale meat, such as pork or veal, must be well cooked, never rare. Rare pork does not look attractive or taste very good and it can also be dangerous to your health.

Pork is very nutritious, but invalids, young children and elderly people sometimes find it is a little difficult to digest. Because it is rich in flavour it goes well with sharp refreshing accompaniments such as apples or cranberries.

CHOOSING PORK

Unlike beef, mutton and, to some extent, lamb, which need to be hung to tenderize the meat, pork is eaten fresh. It does not keep well, so you must be very careful where you store it and for how long. Thanks to modern cold storage, pork is no longer seasonal and can be bought safely at any time of the year. But in hot weather it should be bought only from a refrigerated display.

What to buy

Good quality meat from a young animal is firm and dry, fine grained and a pleasant pink colour. The fat should be creamy white and the rind smooth and supple. Freshly cut surfaces should be slightly moist. In older pork the colour gets darker, the fat becomes flabby and too thick and the rind is coarser and hairy.

If the pork is to be roasted by the English method (with crackling) you should buy it with the rind on. To encourage the rind to become crisper it must be closely and deeply scored. Check that the butcher cuts right through the rind into the fat underneath. Pork can also be roasted without the rind (by the French

Roast pork with sage and onion stuffing balls and apple sauce is a delicious meal for family or guests.

Cuts of pork suitable for roasting

Cut	Description	Butchering and preparation
Loin 4-6.3 kg [9-14 lb] 	The most expensive cut of prime lean roasting pork, cut from one side between the leg and shoulder. The loin is covered with a thin layer of fat, and the rind makes excellent crackling. The hind or chump end adjoining the leg has the kidney and the fillet attached. The neck or rib end is thinner. A middle cut is taken from between the two.	The loin is usually divided into 2, 3 or more cuts according to size (or into chops). All loin cuts need chining (removing the chine bone) to facilitate carving. The loin can be boned for stuffing.
Leg 3.6-5.5 kg [8-12 lb] knuckle end 	A prime, relatively lean roasting cut, which has a layer of fat, about 12 mm [$\frac{1}{2}$″] thick, beneath the rind. The fillet or middle cuts are leaner than the knuckle end, and both have two large cut surfaces which may need basting. Leg cuts are always expensive.	A small leg can be roasted whole, but is more often cut in half into fillet end and knuckle end. Larger legs can be cut in 3, giving fillet, middle and knuckle. The whole leg can also be boned for stuffing.
Fillet 350-500 g [12-18 oz] 	Also known as tenderloin, this is a lean tender strip of meat attached to the back loin. When sold separately it usually comes from a bacon carcass. There is very little or no fat and it needs to be basted frequently.	The fillet is sold in one piece and can be roasted whole. For open roasting it can be barded, with pork fat or streaky bacon, to keep it moist. It can also be cut open lengthways, through two-thirds of its thickness, and stuffed, rolled and tied.
Shoulder or neck end 2.2-3.6 kg [5-8 lb] 	This is the upper part of the shoulder, a versatile cut of fairly fat but very sweet eating meat. There are many different ways of cutting shoulder. It is usually fairly inexpensive.	Often cut into blade and spare rib. The blade makes a compact small roast. The spare rib is cut into a roasting joint and the remainder into spare rib chops. Alternatively, the whole shoulder is boned and tied and then cut into smaller pieces for roasting.
Hand and spring 1.8-3.6 kg [4-8 lb] 	A less expensive cut consisting of the lower part of the shoulder with the knuckle attached. The meat is lean but rather lacking in flavour.	The knuckle can be removed for salting and boiling, leaving a large cut for roasting. Sometimes boned for stuffing and rolling.
Belly 2-3.8 kg [4½-8½ lb] 	A relatively cheap and rather fat cut from the underside of the carcass. The thick end of the belly is thicker and leaner than the streaky end.	Usually divided into 2 or 3 pieces and sold on the bone for slow roasting. Can also be boned, stuffed and rolled, or salted.

method). If you intend to roast this way, ask the butcher to remove the rind for you but keep it to take home and cook it in the pan with the roast to enrich the gravy.

Pork has more flavour when roasted on the bone, but if you wish to roast off the bone, the butcher will bone and roll it for you.

CUTS OF MEAT

The cuts of pork suitable for roasting are described in the chart. As pork is a fat meat, most cuts can be roasted. However, the cheaper cuts may be more successfully cooked by covered methods such as pot roasting or casseroling, perhaps with the addition of wine or cider.

Sucking pig

An expensive roast, rarely seen in domestic kitchens, is sucking or suckling pig. This is a piglet aged between 3-8 weeks, weighing 5.4-9 kg [12-20 lb] and roasted whole. It is pork at its most delicate, but only suitable for formal parties, where it will serve up to 20 people.

A sucking pig is usually roasted on a rack with the front legs skewered pointing forwards and the back legs pointing backwards. The loin is stuffed with forcemeat or mild sage and onion stuffing, and tied. Check that the overall length will fit into your oven before buying.

The surfaces of the meat are seasoned and the rind rubbed with oil. The piglet is then cooked, covered with foil for half the time. Allow 15-20 minutes for each 450 g [1 lb] at 180°C [350°F] gas mark 4. Sucking pig is served complete with head and tail and with apple sauce or other appropriate garnishes, which may include an apple or lemon in the mouth.

It is carved by first detaching the head, carving the shoulder, then the leg and finally the loin. Unless the carver has had practice, it is perhaps best to carve it out of sight.

QUANTITIES

For average appetites allow 225-350 g [8-12 oz] of pork on the bone, and 150-175 g [5-6 oz] of boneless pork. You can cook quite a small roast successfully because the outer layer of fat will keep it moist, but a larger roast is more economical and can be eaten cold next day.

STORING AND REHEATING PORK

Pork must be absolutely fresh and of good quality when you buy it. As soon as you get the pork home, unwrap it, place it on a plate or tray and cover it loosely with foil or polythene to prevent the surface from drying. Do not store for longer than two to three days in a refrigerator, or one to two days in a cold larder. In warm or humid weather do not leave it in the larder longer than one day. Just before roasting, take the meat out and let it stand for 30 minutes at room temperature.

Cold cooked pork

Cooked pork should also be handled carefully, especially in warm weather. This is because bacteria multiply quickly and can cause serious food poisoning. Immediately the pork is cold, wrap it in foil to stop it drying out. The foil should be close to the meat, but not crimped to be airtight.

Store in the refrigerator for up to two days. Take it out of the refrigerator an hour before serving to bring the cold meat to room temperature.

Reheating cooked pork

Never reheat pork whole. If you use cold slices or cubes as a basis for another dish, it is essential that the pork is recooked right through (that is, the meat reaches boiling point) and is not just warmed up, in order to kill any bacteria that might have formed.

ROASTING PORK

Unlike beef and lamb, pork is not roasted by the high-temperature method. The low-temperature method is better suited to this meat because it ensures thorough cooking right through.

Pork cuts, except fillet, are self-basting, because they have an outer layer of fat. For the same reason no extra fat is needed in the roasting pan. The roasting pan should be just large enough to hold the meat, otherwise the fat disperses over a wide area and tends to scorch.

There are two methods of roasting pork: by the English manner with the rind or, by the French, without it.

To an Englishman, ever since Charles Lamb wrote his immortal essay on Roast Pig, the evocative words 'roast pork' are synonymous

with crisp crackling. For good crackling you need to roast in a dry atmosphere.

The French roast pork without the rind and add a little liquid, usually wine and water or stock, to the pan so that the meat cooks in a steamy atmosphere. The meat itself is not in the liquid but is raised up on a rack. This method produces an exceptionally moist and tender roast and is particularly recommended for eating cold.

The rind is known as the 'couenne' in France and is valued for its gelatinous qualities. French butchers remove the rind and supply it separately and it is cooked under the roast to give body to the gravy or used to enrich a casserole.

Crisping the crackling

The rind covering the leg, loin or shoulder, particularly from a young pig, gives the best crackling. The rind from the belly or hand and spring can be made into crackling but is less dependable—sometimes it crisps well but sometimes it does not.

For a good crisp crackling make sure the rind is closely and deeply scored, at intervals of 6 mm [$\frac{1}{4}$"], through into the fat below. If the butcher has not done this properly, you can finish the job yourself using a very sharp knife.

Before roasting, sprinkle the rind liberally with salt and some pepper. Rub this in and then rub the rind with oil or lard. Roast the meat on a rack so that the rind remains dry and is held clear of the drippings in the bottom of the tin. If allowed to fry in the drippings, the crackling becomes hard instead of crisp.

If the crackling is not quite crisp enough towards the end of cooking time, turn the oven up to 200°C [400°F] gas mark 6 for the last 10 to 15 minutes. An alternative method for crisping is to start the pork in an oven at 220°C [425°F] gas mark 7 and then to reduce the temperature after 15 minutes.

Other preparations

Pork to be roasted is rubbed all over the outside with salt. Salt is rubbed into the cut surfaces as well as into the rind, because this white meat does not give off juice when salted as red meat, such as beef, would.

If you are cooking crackling, the rind of the meat can be given a slightly herby flavour. Mix salt, dry mustard and powdered sage in equal quantities and rub these into the rind.

Pork may also be marinated to tenderize it or to flavour the meat or both.

The fillet, which has no outer fat layer, tends to dry out if open roasted without basting or barding. First remove the skin and any bits of fat. Then bard it with pork fat or streaky bacon in the same way as noisettes and tournedos (see grilling lamb and beef), or spread the meat with a little oil or butter before roasting and baste frequently.

Fillet can also be roasted covered for part of the time, and with the addition of a little wine and water or stock to the pan.

Stuffed pork
Pork may be boned, rolled and stuffed and this is described in a later course.

A fillet may also be stuffed to increase its bulk. This has the advantage that it does not dry out so quickly during cooking. To make a hole for the stuffing, cut the fillet two-thirds of the way through from one end to the other exactly along its centre, but so the meat is still in one piece (see star recipe).

Then make two further lengthways cuts to divide each side into two. Spread the stuffing over the fillet, working it down into the cracks between the length of meat. Re-form the fillet to make a roll and tie it along its length.

Roasting times
The times for low-temperature roasting given in the chart are only approximate. You also have to consider factors such as the thickness of the cut or variations in oven performances.

A meat thermometer, stuck firmly into the meat, takes the guessing out of how well the inside of the meat is cooked. Well-cooked pork should show a temperature of 85°C [185°F] at the end of cooking.

You can also test the meat by inserting a skewer into the thickest part of the meat. The juice, when you pull out the skewer, should be colourless.

Automatic oven roasting is not suitable for pork because the meat should not be taken out of the refrigerator or larder more than 30 minutes before cooking.

ACCOMPANIMENTS FOR ROAST PORK
The best accompaniments for pork are those which counteract its richness and offer a contrast in flavour. Tart fruit such as apples, goose-

Step-by-step roasting pork

1 Weigh the meat and calculate the roasting time. Leave at room temperature for 30 min. Heat oven.

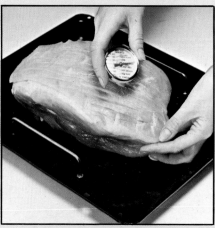

2 If not scored by butcher, score the rind at 6 mm [¼"] intervals cutting through into the fat below.

3 To encourage crisp crackling, rub rind generously with salt and pepper. Then rub with oil or lard.

OR for French method, cut rind away completely. Rub fat with salt, pepper and other seasoning.

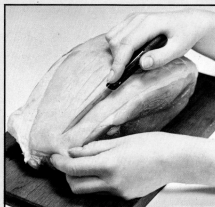

4 Insert thermometer if using. Place meat on rack in roasting pan. Put in oven. Add liquid if using.

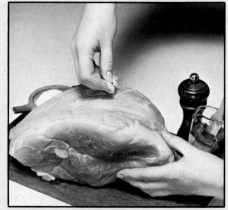

5 Roast for calculated time. Check thermometer or use skewer to see if done. Rest before carving.

Roasting times for pork at 180°C [350°F] gas mark 4	
Cuts on the bone*	**Minutes per 450 g [1 lb]**
Blade or small joints under 1.1 kg [2½ lb]	55
Belly	40
Leg, whole	40
part	45
Loin	40
Spare rib	45

*For boned and rolled or stuffed joints add 20-30 minutes to the given time.

berries, oranges, apricots, pineapples or cranberries are particularly good as accompanying sauce. So are piquant spicy and mustardy sauces.

Aromatic herbs such as sage, rosemary and thyme are successful cooked in the pan with the pork.

Spices such as juniper, coriander and peppercorns, all enhance the flavour of pork when cooked with it.

Traditional English accompaniments are apple sauce and sage and onion stuffing.

Gravy is made with fat from the roasting pan. This may be thickened with a little flour and stock or water. A little wine or cider can also be added to give flavour.

APPLE SAUCE

Sharp, early-season cooking apples are usually tart enough without additions, but late-season or bland varieties need added lemon or orange zest.

SERVES 6
450 g [1 lb] cooking apples
1 thin strip lemon or orange peel (optional)
25-50 g [1-2 oz] sugar
15 g [½ oz] butter

1 Peel, core and slice the apples into a saucepan. Work quickly to prevent apples from discolouring.

2 Add the peel (if used), 30 ml [2 tablespoons] of water and the

sugar. Cover, and stew gently for about 10 minutes or until tender.

3 Remove the peel. For a rough-textured sauce beat the apples with a wire whisk.

4 For a smooth sauce use a liquidizer or press the apples through a nylon sieve.

5 Return to the saucepan. Taste for tartness and add more sugar if necessary. If the sauce is a little thin, boil it uncovered until it reduces to a purée consistency. Stir in the butter. Serve hot or cold.

SAGE AND ONION STUFFING

This stuffing can also be used in the quantity given to stuff duck or a small goose. Put it inside boned pork (or a bird) or bake it separately in a dish under the roast as described here.

SERVES 4
225 g [8 oz] onions
25 g [1 oz] butter
100 g [¼ lb] white breadcrumbs
15 ml [1 tablespoon] finely chopped fresh sage or 10 ml [2 teaspoons] dried sage
5 ml [1 teaspoon] salt
freshly ground black pepper
30 ml [2 tablespoons] milk

1 Peel the onions, and cut into quarters. Put into a saucepan, cover with water and simmer gently, covered, for 10 to 15 minutes or until soft.

2 Drain, chop finely and return to pan.

3 Add 25 g [1 oz] of the butter and allow to melt. Then add the breadcrumbs, sage, salt and pepper and mix well.

4 Stir in enough milk to bind the ingredients together loosely.

5 If the stuffing is to be cooked separately, butter a gratin dish with the remaining butter. Put in the stuffing and smooth over the top, or form into balls.

6 Put the gratin dish in the oven, an hour before the meat is due to be ready. Place the dish on the shelf under the meat.

CARVING PORK
Make sure the carving knife is really sharp. It is easier to carve pork if you first remove part or all of the crackling by sliding the knife in horizontally through the layer of fat that separates crackling from the meat. Cut the crackling into strips and leave beside the roast. Carve the pork into moderately thick slices down to the bone. Arrange servings with a portion of crackling and any stuffing.

ROAST BLADE OF PORK AND SAGE AND ONION STUFFING

The blade is a compact cut for a small family. The meat, with the bone running through the centre, is deliciously sweet under a thin covering of fat and crisp crackling. Make the stuffing following the instructions given earlier in this course.

SERVES 4
.9-1.1 kg [2-2½ lb] blade of pork
salt
freshly ground black pepper
15 ml [1 tablespoon] oil
15 ml [1 tablespoon] flour
250 ml [½ pt] stock or vegetable water

For the accompaniment:
sage and onion stuffing

1 Heat the oven to 180°C [350°F] gas mark 4.

2 If the butcher has not scored the rind evenly and deeply, do it yourself with a sharp knife.

3 Check the weight and calculate the cooking time, allowing 55 minutes per 450 g [1 lb].

4 Wipe the meat with a clean damp cloth. Rub all the surfaces, particularly the scored rind, with salt and pepper. Then rub the rind with oil.

5 Place the meat, rind side up, on a rack standing in a roasting pan just large enough to hold it.

6 Roast the meat in the centre of the oven for 1 hour and 50 minutes to 2 hours and 15 minutes. There is no need to baste.

7 Meanwhile, prepare the stuffing, as described. Butter a small

Step-by-step carving the shoulder

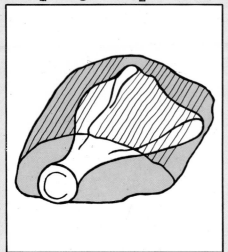

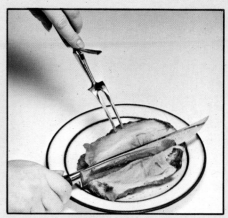

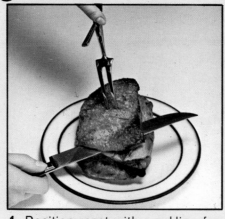

1 Position roast with crackling facing upwards. Remove a section of the crackling.

2 Carve slices until you reach the middle of the blade bone. Then carve the other side.

Step-by-step carving hand and spring

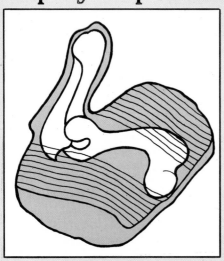

1 Remove some of the crackling from the top. Remove the rib bones from underneath the roast.

2 Carve slices from both ends to give portions a slice from the lean and fatty end. Slice crackling.

Step-by-step to carving a loin

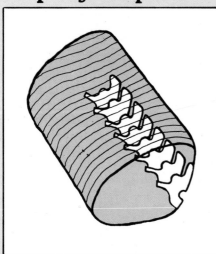

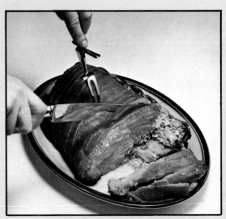

1 Use the point of a sharp knife to free the meat from chine bone.

2 Carve the meat downwards in slices including some crackling.

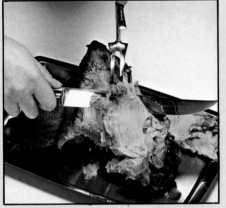

3 Turn the roast over and carve the meat in thin slices down towards the wide end of the bone.

Carving knuckle end of leg

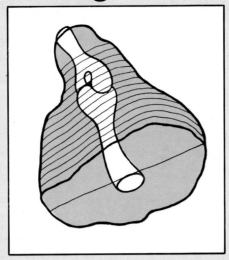

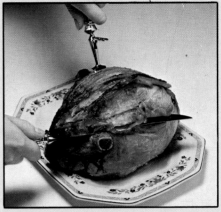

1 Starting from wide end, carve downwards, then cut across along bone to release slices.

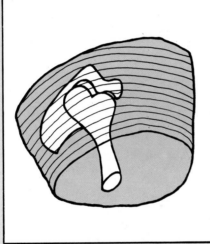

3 When the bone is reached, turn roast over and cut slices from either side of the bone.

Step-by-step carving fillet end of leg

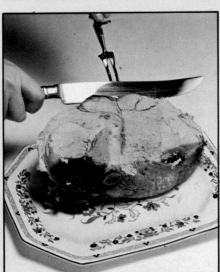

1 Remove a section of crackling from the narrow end and carve downwards at an angle across leg.

OR remove strips of crackling and then carve the meat into slices.

2 Work towards the thick end of the bone. Continue until you reach the big end of the bone.

3 Turn the roast round and start to cut from the other end cutting down to the bone.

ovenproof dish and spoon the stuffing into it, smoothing the surface, or form into balls.

8 An hour before the meat is due to finish roasting put the stuffing on the shelf below the roasting pan.

9 To check that the meat is cooked through, insert a skewer into its centre. The juices that flow out should be colourless, if not the meat is not ready.

10 Transfer to a hot serving dish and rest in a warm place while making the gravy.

11 Remove the rack from the roasting pan and pour off all but 15 ml [1 tablespoon] of the fat.

12 Sprinkle the flour into the fat and stir with a wooden spoon.

13 Put the roasting pan over a low heat, and cook the roux, stirring constantly, for 2–3 minutes until lightly browned.

14 Add the stock off the heat and stir in. Return to the heat and cook gently until the gravy thickens. Check the seasoning. Strain into a sauce-boat.

ROAST LOIN OF PORK WITH CRANBERRY APPLES

Crisp golden loin of pork surrounded by cranberry-stuffed apples makes an impressive main course for a dinner party and is comparatively easy to carve. Ask the butcher to chine the backbone to make carving easy. Freshly stewed fruit made from 225 g [½ lb] of cranberries and 75 g [3 oz] of sugar, simmered gently until tender can be used instead of the canned cranberry sauce.

SERVES 6
1.8 kg [4 lb] loin of pork
salt and pepper
15 ml [1 tablespoon] oil
6-8 medium-sized cooking apples
60 g [2½ oz] sugar
60 g [2½ oz] butter
225 g [8 oz] canned cranberry sauce
15 ml [1 tablespoon] flour
250 ml [½ pt] stock or vegetable water

1 Heat the oven to 180°C [350°F] gas mark 4.

2 Score the rind closely and deeply, if the butcher has not already done so.

3 Check the weight and calculate the cooking time, allowing 40 minutes per 450 g [1 lb].

4 Wipe the meat with a clean damp cloth. Rub all surfaces, and particularly the scored rind, with salt and pepper. Rub the rind thoroughly with oil.

5 Place on a rack in a roasting pan large enough to hold it. Roast the meat in the centre of the oven for 2 hours and 40 minutes.

6 Meanwhile wipe the apples, remove the cores with an apple corer, and run the tip of a pointed knife around the centre of the apples, just cutting through the skin. This allows the apples to cook without bursting.

7 Place the apples side by side in a baking dish. Put a spoonful of sugar and the same amount of butter in the core hole of each apple and pour the water into the dish around them.

8 An hour before the meat is due to finish roasting, put the dish of apples on shelf below the meat.

9 Five minutes before roasting time is due to end, warm the cranberry sauce in a small saucepan with 15 ml [1 tablespoon] of water.

10 Transfer the meat from the roasting pan on to a warm serving dish. Carefully drain the apples and arrange them round the meat.

11 Put a spoonful of cranberry sauce into each apple. Put the serving dish into the warmer.

12 Remove the rack from the roasting pan, pour off all but 15 ml [1 tablespoon] of fat.

13 Add the flour to the roasting pan and stir in.

14 Put pan over low heat and cook the roux, stirring constantly for 2-3 minutes.

15 Add the stock off the heat and stir in. Return to the heat and cook gently until the gravy has thickened. Check the seasoning and serve.

LOIN OF PORK ROASTED IN THE FRENCH MANNER

In traditional French cookery, the rind is removed and cooked under the roast to enrich the gravy

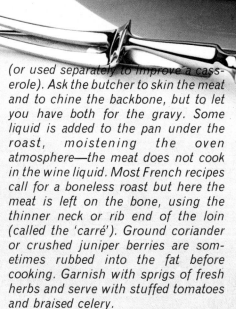

(or used separately to improve a casserole). Ask the butcher to skin the meat and to chine the backbone, but to let you have both for the gravy. Some liquid is added to the pan under the roast, moistening the oven atmosphere—the meat does not cook in the wine liquid. Most French recipes call for a boneless roast but here the meat is left on the bone, using the thinner neck or rib end of the loin (called the 'carré'). Ground coriander or crushed juniper berries are sometimes rubbed into the fat before cooking. Garnish with sprigs of fresh herbs and serve with stuffed tomatoes and braised celery.

SERVES 4
1.4 kg [3 lb] loin of pork from neck end
salt
freshly ground black pepper
2 large garlic cloves

Cranberry-stuffed apples are a deliciously tart accompaniment to roast loin of pork. If large apples are used they can be halved, as here, with cranberries in each half.

2 sprigs of fresh rosemary or
   3 sprigs of fresh thyme
150 ml [¼ pt] white wine
150 ml [¼ pt] stock

For the garnish:
sprigs of rosemary or thyme

1 Weigh the joint and calculate the cooking time, allowing 40 minutes per 450 g [1 lb].

2 Wipe the meat with a clean damp cloth, sprinkle all the surfaces generously with salt, and lightly with pepper, and rub in with your fingers.

3 Peel the garlic cloves, cut into slivers and tuck in between the bones.

4 Put the pork rind, chine bone and the rosemary or thyme in the bottom of the roasting pan.

5 Place the meat, fat side up, on the top and pour the wine with 150 ml [¼ pt] water over it. Leave in a cool place for up to 2 hours.

6 When ready to cook, heat the oven to 180°C [350°F] gas mark 4.

7 Pat the meat dry, and insert a meat thermometer. Put the meat on a rack in the roasting pan.

8 Roast the meat in the centre of the oven for 2 hours.

9 Check the meat is cooked. The meat thermometer should show a temperature of 85°C [185°F] if the meat is cooked.

10 Remove the bone and the rind from the pan. Dish the meat on to a warm serving plate.

11 Tilt the pan and spoon off the fat that rises to the surface.

12 Add the stock to the roasting pan, bring to the boil and simmer for 2-3 minutes. Check the seasoning.

13 Strain the gravy into a sauce-boat.

14 Garnish the top of the meat with sprigs of fresh herbs and serve.

HERB AND SPICE MARINADED SPARE RIB OF PORK

▨▨▨ *Spare rib is not a prime cut, but a good family roast and particularly tasty when treated with this dry marinade. Start preparations 24 hours before cooking. The spicy flavour of this roast calls for rather bland vegetable accompaniments such as creamed potatoes, braised red cabbage or macedoine of root vegetables.*

SERVES 4
1.4 kg [3 lb] spare rib of pork

For the marinade:
1 large bay leaf
15 ml [1 tablespoon] dried thyme or sage
7.5 ml [1½ teaspoon] ground nutmeg
1.5 ml [¼ teaspoon] ground cloves or allspice
15 ml [1 tablespoon] salt
2.5 ml [½ teaspoon] freshly ground black pepper
15 ml [1 tablespoon] flour
250 ml [½ pt] stock or vegetable water

1 Weigh the meat and calculate the cooking time, allowing 45 minutes per 450 g [1 lb].

2 Cut the rind off the pork and reserve. Wipe the cut surfaces of the meat with a damp cloth.

3 Crumble the bay leaf into a small bowl and add herbs, spices, salt and pepper. Mix well.

4 Sprinkle some of the marinade over one surface of the meat and rub in thoroughly with your fingers. Continue until all the surfaces have been covered and all the marinade is used.

5 Put the meat on a rack standing over a plate or tray. Cover loosely with foil or polythene and leave in the refrigerator or larder for 24 hours.

6 Take out 30 minutes before cooking and leave at room temperature. Heat the oven to 180°C [350°F] gas mark 4.

7 Put the pork rind in the bottom of a roasting pan and stand a rack over it. Place the meat, fat side up, on the rack.

8 Roast it in the centre of the oven for 2 hours and 15 minutes.

9 Check that the roast is cooked through by piercing with a skewer. If the juices are colourless the meat is done. Transfer to a hot serving dish and keep warm.

10 Remove the rack from the pan. Discard the rind and pour off all but a tablespoon of fat.

11 Add the flour to the pan and stir in.

12 Put the pan over low heat and cook the roux for 2-3 minutes.

13 Add the stock away from the heat and stir in. Return to the heat and cook gently until the gravy is thickened. Check the seasonings and serve.

MARINADED LEG OF PORK TO TASTE LIKE WILD BOAR

▨▨▨ *This is an excellent way to cook the shank end of a leg of older pork and is also delicious cold. Start to prepare the meat four days in advance to give the marinade time to penetrate and flavour the meat. The wine helps to preserve the pork so that it can be kept uncooked for a little longer than usual. The rind can be removed to help the marinade penetrate, or left on to cook to a rich colour and flavour. Though it doesn't crackle like a traditional English roast, score the rind the same way as for crackling.*

SERVES 5-6
1.4-1.8 kg [3-4 lb] leg of pork
15 ml [1 tablespoon] salt

For the marinade:
3 garlic cloves
1 medium-sized carrot
1 medium-sized onion
60 ml [4 tablespoons] olive oil
250 ml [½ pt] dry white wine
150 ml [¼ pt] wine vinegar
2 bay leaves
1 sprig fresh thyme
12 black peppercorns
5 juniper berries
5 coriander seeds

For the gravy:
15 ml [1 tablespoon] flour
250 ml [½ pt] stock

1 Wipe the meat with a clean damp cloth and rub it all over with salt.

2 Prepare the marinade. Peel and halve the garlic cloves, scrape and slice the carrot and peel and slice the onion.

3 Heat the oil and gently soften the vegetables in it for about 8 minutes, stirring frequently.

4 Put the wine and vinegar into a deep china or glass bowl. Add the cooked vegetables and oil, bay leaves and thyme.

5 Crush the peppercorns, juniper berries and coriander using a pestle and mortar or with the handle of a rolling pin in a small bowl. Add to the marinade.

6 When the marinade is cold put the pork into it and turn the pork over, so that all surfaces are wet.

7 Cover and leave for 4 days in the refrigerator or a cold larder, turning it at least twice a day.

8 When ready to cook, take out the meat, drain it thoroughly and scrape off all the marinade. Pat the meat dry with kitchen paper. Reserve 60 ml [4 tablespoons] of the marinade for the gravy.

9 Weigh the meat and calculate the cooking time, allowing 45 minutes per 450 g [1 lb].

10 Place the meat on a rack in the roasting pan and leave for 30 minutes at room temperature. Heat the oven to 180°C [350°F] gas mark 4.

11 Roast the pork in the centre of the oven for the calculated time.

12 Check the meat is cooked through, by inserting a skewer. The juices which run out should be colourless. Transfer to a hot serving dish and keep warm.

13 Pour off all but 15 ml [1 tablespoon] fat from the roasting tin. Add flour then stir over gentle heat until lightly brown.

14 Add stock away from the heat and the reserved marinade and stir in. Return to heat and bring to the boil. Simmer for at least 5 minutes, check seasoning and strain to serve.

Beef

grilling

Beef steaks are expensive, so here are the guidelines to help you get best value and flavour when choosing and grilling cuts ranging from large tasty T-bone steak to the smaller, elegant tournedos often favoured for formal parties. Steaks are a luxury and should be served as such, with the proper additions given here. Grill them on a ridged pan for a professional quadrilled appearance.

CUTS FOR GRILLING
Only certain cuts of beef are tender enough for grilling. You can be disappointed, even if you buy the right cut, because the eating quality of the meat depends also on the skill of the butcher. It must be taken from a prime quality carcass that has been aged—it must have been hung in a chill room for sufficiently long to develop its full flavour and tenderness. Beef which has not been hung for long enough is likely to be flavourless and tough. It is not always easy to tell the quality of frozen beef so buy fresh beef for grilling.

Good quality steak is expensive so, to get the best value, follow the guidelines given here when choosing a steak.

CHOOSING BEEF STEAKS
Prime quality beef steaks should always be cut across the grain of the meat. The cut surface should have a slightly moist look and smooth, velvety texture marbled with very fine threads of fat. The colour can vary but, if the beef has been well hung, it is likely to be a dull rather than a bright red. A bright colour means

that the meat is rather fresh, or it can be due to the transparent film sometimes used to cover pre-packed steaks on self-service counters. A moderate edging of fat makes for good flavour and succulence. If you don't like to eat fat, cut it off after cooking. Avoid buying steaks with obvious seams of gristle, and be very wary of meat which is very dark in colour or which has bright yellow fat: this could be cow beef, which is old and tough. Buy 150-225 g [5-8 oz] of steak for each person, depending on appetite and the cut — tournedos and entrecôte are usually served smaller,

Cuts of fillet of beef for grilling

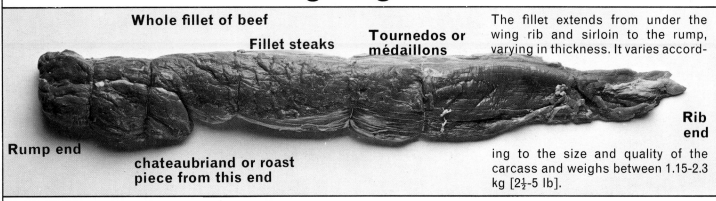

Whole fillet of beef

Fillet steaks

Tournedos or médaillons

Rump end

chateaubriand or roast piece from this end

Rib end

The fillet extends from under the wing rib and sirloin to the rump, varying in thickness. It varies according to the size and quality of the carcass and weighs between 1.15-2.3 kg [2½-5 lb].

Cut	Description	Method
 **Fillet steak**	The tenderest and most expensive steak of all, this is cut across the centre of the long strip of meat that lies beneath the sirloin and rump. Slightly oval in shape each steak is about 2.5-3.5 cm [1-1½"] thick and weighs 175-200 g [6-7 oz].	Brush with oil and grill close to fierce heat to seal the cut surfaces for about 1 minute each side. Lower the pan, or reduce heat to medium, and continue grilling for another 2 minutes each side for rare, 3 minutes each side for medium-rare and 4 minutes each side for well-done, basting occasionally during the grilling time. Season before serving.
 **Tournedos**	This is a chef's term describing slightly smaller, round fillet steaks. Also referred to as médaillons, these steaks weigh about 125-150 g [4-5 oz] each.	'Bard' with pork fat before cooking. Oil and grill as for fillet steaks.
 **Chateaubriand**	Another chef's term describing a double fillet steak, ie a long piece, weighing about 350 g [¾ lb]. Serves 2.	Prepare and grill as fillet steaks, but after sealing continue grilling under low heat for a total of 12-14 minutes for rare, 14-16 minutes for medium-rare and 16-18 minutes for well-done. Turn frequently to cook on all sides and season before serving. Carve into thick slices.

and don't forget to allow for the weight of the bone when buying T-bone steaks.

STORING STEAK

When you get home unwrap the steak, lay it on a flat plate and cover loosely with polythene or foil. Store in a cool place, preferably in the refrigerator under the frozen food compartment. The steaks can be kept there for three to four days, and both flavour and tenderness should benefit from this extra period of ageing. If you have no refrigerator do not keep for longer than 24 hours.

PREPARING STEAKS

For most steaks the only preparation needed is to brush them with oil about an hour before grilling. Then cover the meat loosely and keep in a cool place until you are ready to grill. **Rump steaks,** however, need a little more attention. Snip the edging of fat at intervals (right through to the meat but not into it) with scissors. This is because the fat contracts during cooking and snipping prevents the edges curling up. Lay the rump steak on a chopping board and beat it with a wooden rolling pin or meat bat. This helps tenderize the steak by breaking down connective tissue.

Beat the steak on both sides and in both directions. Beat vigorously to flatten the steak but not so hard that you reduce the steak to a pulp.
Garlic. The use of garlic is optional but, if you like it, you can wipe the steak, just before grilling, with a large, peeled clove of garlic, cut in half.

GRILLING STEAK

The five basic principles for grilling steak are the same as for other meats, excluding poultry.
1 The meat must be brushed with oil or a marinade to keep it moist; this

Cuts of beef steak for grilling

Cut	Description	Method
Rump steak	These are taken from across the rump in slices 2.5-3.5 cm [1-1½"] thick. The best steaks come from the middle cut of rump and the pointed end of the slice is considered the choice part. The flavour is excellent but it is apt to be tough unless the meat has been well hung. The slice of rump has a narrow edging of fat along one side. It is not necessary to remove this bit of fat.	Oil and grill close to fierce heat for about 1 minute each side to seal. Lower the pan (or reduce the heat to medium) and continue grilling for a further 2 minutes each side for rare, 3 minutes each side for medium-rare and 4 minutes each side for well-done. Season before serving.
Entrecôte	Originally the name given to a steak cut, literally, between two rib bones. Nowadays often used to describe a boneless sirloin steak.	Prepare and grill as for sirloin steak.
Minute steak	A chef's term for a very thin piece of boneless tender steak. It is often, but not necessarily, cut from the sirloin and is about 6-12 mm [¼-½"] thick.	These steaks cook quickly and are not thick enough to be served rare. They are best if pan fried, but can be grilled if you wish. Brush thoroughly with oil and cook under fierce heat for 1½ minutes each side for medium or 2 minutes each side for well-done. Season and serve immediately.
Sirloin steak	These are cut from a boned sirloin, and have a narrow edging of fat on one side. Because the surface area is larger than fillet steaks they are often cut thinner, 2-2.5 cm [¾-1"] thick. They can, of course, be cut thicker if required. This cut is also sometimes known as a porterhouse steak.	Oil and grill close to fierce heat for about 1 minute each side to seal. Lower the pan (or reduce the heat to medium) and, depending on the thickness, continue grilling for a further 2½-3 minutes each side for rare, 3-4 minutes each side for medium-rare and 4-5 minutes for well-done. Season before serving.
T-bone steak	Also sirloin steaks but including a small portion of bone as each steak is cut right across a sirloin on the bone. Often cut thicker than sirloin steaks, about 2.5 cm [1"] thick or sometimes more to serve two people in which case increase cooking time.	Prepare and grill as for sirloin steak.

should never include salt because this will encourage juices and flavour to leak out.

2 The grill must be very hot before the meat is put under it.

3 The meat must be seared for 1 minute on each side under fierce heat to seal and brown the surface. This is done whether it is to be rare or well done.

4 Turn the meat using tongs or a spoon and a fish slice to avoid piercing the surface.

5 Cooking continues at medium heat, with occasional basting, for the number of minutes of your choice.

People vary a great deal in the important matter of how they like their steaks cooked. Some people like them well-done, that is, cooked right through; others like them rare, that is, just seared on the surface and still quite raw inside (the French call this a 'blue steak'). But the majority of people choose medium-rare steaks — which are cooked and dark on the outside but pink in the centre when cut through.

Step-by-step to preparing tournedos

1 Put the fillet steak on a wooden board and, with a sharp knife, trim off all skin and fat.

2 Lay the sheet of fat flat on the board. Place the fillet in the centre of the fat.

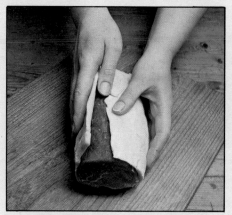

3 Wrap the fat around the fillet to cover. Trim excess fat to leave neat edges and avoid overlaps.

4 Tie with string in four places and pull slightly to keep the fillet in a good round shape.

5 With a sharp knife cut between the ties to divide the fillet into 4 tournedos.

6 Brush cut surfaces with oil, cover and leave in a cool place until required for grilling.

Timing the cooking is critical, and with experience you will know from the thickness of the steak just how long to cook it under your particular grill. As a guide, the chart gives the average grilling times to achieve the steak of your choice, but adjustments must be made according to the thickness of the steak.

The finger-press test
A useful test for 'doneness' is to press the surface of the meat with your index finger and note the resistance.
Rare meat feels soft and 'gives' readily when pressed.
Medium-rare meat feels firm when pressed but still has a little 'give'.
Well-done meat which is cooked right through but not overcooked, feels quite firm when pressed.
If you are still not sure, take a sharp knife and nick the steak in the thickest part so that you can see what stage

the cooking has reached. This is not an ideal way of testing as it allows some of the meat juices to escape. However, it is a useful check while you are gaining experience.

PREPARING TOURNEDOS
Although fillet steak is very expensive tournedos work out more reasonably priced than many other steaks because they are fairly small.

Tournedos belong to French haute cuisine, but are quite simple to prepare at home. They are cut from the smaller, rounder part of the fillet and become smaller as the fillet tapers towards the rib end.

Depending on the size of the fillet they should be cut from 2.5-3.5 cm [1-1½"] thick, across the grain of the meat. A piece of fillet weighing 700 g [1½ lb] is enough for four tournedos. You will also need a thin sheet of pork back fat (bard) to wrap around the

meat to protect it during cooking. This is called barding, and for 4 tournedos you should allow a piece of back fat no thicker than 6 mm [¼"] and weighing 175-225 g [6-8 oz].

PAN GRILLING
Pan grilling, or 'dry frying' as it is sometimes called, is familiar to all users of solid fuel cookers and can equally well be used on electric or gas cookers. To pan grill you need a very thick frying pan made of iron or cast aluminium. Better still is a special ridged iron pan which will give your steaks a really professional 'quadrilled' surface.

Grill according to the type of steak and its thickness, following the chart given on the previous page but decrease the cooking time slightly — by about 1 minute on each side. It is essential that the pan, like any other grill, is very hot before grilling starts.

Step-by-step pan grilling tournedos

1 Set the pan over high heat for several minutes until it is thoroughly hot.

2 Grease the pan with a piece of hard fat impaled on a fork, or by brushing it with oil.

3 When the greased pan is sizzling put in steak (if it does not sizzle the pan is not hot enough).

4 Cook over a fierce heat for 1 minute, pressing the steak firmly against the ridges of the pan.

5 Turn the steak over and seal and brown the second side in the same way as before.

6 Lower heat to medium. Turn steak over and cook at right angles to its previous position.

7 Turn the steak again and finish grilling for 1, 2 or 3 minutes for rare, medium or well-done.

8 Cut the string and remove it from around the tournedos. Repeat with the other tournedos.

9 Season the steak and serve it topped with a pat of savoury butter. Garnish with watercress.

TRADITIONAL ACCOMPANIMENTS

Steaks are luxury foods and deserve to be beautifully presented. It makes economic sense, too, to serve them with decorative edible garnishes and accompaniments because this means you can get away with slightly less meat per person.

Straw, chip or duchesse potatoes look good and taste delicious. Fried onion rings, sprigs of fresh watercress dipped in vinaigrette, a purée of chestnuts, grilled tomatoes and mushrooms are other optional extras.

Choose small firm tomatoes for grilling whole. Wash them and, with a sharp knife, cut a little cross just through the skin on the side opposite the stem. This allows the skin to shrink back during grilling without splitting. Grilling takes about 5 minutes but be careful not to let the tomatoes get too soft unless you like them like that. Larger tomatoes can be cut horizontally in half and grilled either side up, but do cook only one side — if you grill both sides the tomato tends to fall apart. Season the cut surface before serving.

Choose firm cap mushrooms. Minaret mushrooms look particularly pretty. Brush both sides generously with oil and grill with the steak, turning the mushrooms once. As mushrooms tend to dry out, baste them once or twice during grilling, which should not take more than 5 minutes in all.

Tournedos or médaillons are ideally suited for serving on artichoke bottoms or canapés. Crisply fried canapés, placed beneath tournedos, catch and absorb precious juices that run from the meat and make an attractive contrast in texture.

And don't forget that both savoury butters and mustard are, virtually speaking, a 'must' for steaks.

Make savoury butters as described in grilling lamb and use either in chilled pats to top steaks just before serving or spread generously over the nearly cooked grill. As the butter melts, spoon it over the meat as a baste. When serving, pour any remains from the grill pan base over the steak as a sauce. This second method is not suitable when using a ridged grill pan.

Here are a few more savoury butters particularly suited to serving with steak. For four steaks allow 50 g [2 oz] unsalted butter, salt and black

Making canapés

1 For each canapé take a slice of firm, one- or two-day-old white bread about 1 cm [⅓"] thick.

2 Cut out a circle, about the size of the tournedos, with a plain or fluted cutter.

OR place a coffee cup on the bread for a round shape and cut around it with a sharp knife.

3 For every 4 canapés heat 15 ml [1 tablespoon] oil and 50 g [2 oz] butter in a shallow pan.

4 When foaming, fry the canapés over medium heat for about 3 minutes each side until crisp.

5 Drain the canapés on absorbent kitchen paper and keep them hot until required.

pepper to taste plus any of the following:

● For mustard butter: 15 ml [1 tablespoon] French mustard and 15 ml [1 tablespoon] freshly chopped parsley. Suitable for steaks, chops, liver or fish.

● For green herb butter: 30 ml [2 tablespoons] finely chopped mixed fresh herbs, such as parsley, chives, tarragon and chervil, as available, and 10 ml [2 teaspoons] lemon juice. Suitable for steaks, fish and chops.

● For 'snail' butter: 15 ml [1 tablespoon] finely chopped or grated shallots or spring onions, 1-2 cloves of garlic, finely crushed, and 15 ml [1 tablespoon] freshly chopped parsley. Suitable for grilled meats or fish. This is the butter which is served in France with snails, which gives it its name. It does not, of course, contain snails.

KNOW YOUR MUSTARDS

Mustard is one of the most ancient condiments known to man and has always been a favourite accompaniment to meat, particularly steak. English and French households in the Middle Ages made their own mustard by pounding the seeds in a mortar and mixing the resulting rough 'meale' with vinegar, wine, honey and spices.

Nowadays, in the making of mustard, two distinct types of seed are used: brown mustard seeds containing important volatile oils, and white mustard seeds which are stronger and harsher. Both types are separately milled into flour and then blended in varying proportions, and with various additional ingredients, to produce the many different types of mustard available today.

English mustard. This is the only mustard available in powder as well as ready-prepared form. It is a pungent, smooth, yellow mustard made from a blend of white and brown mustard seeds plus spices and a little flour. Addicts like to mix their own mustard (from the powder plus water or milk) freshly for each meal. Mixed this way none of its pungency is lost, although ideally it should be prepared about 10 minutes before the meal to allow the flavour time to develop fully.

French mustards. These are usually more aromatic and less harsh than English mustard, and are blended with wine, wine vinegar or grape

juice. There are various types of French mustard, differing according to the blend of mustard seeds, spices and herbs. Meaux mustard is an interesting, rough-textured mustard containing pieces of mustard seed husk. It is of medium strength and light in colour. Dijon mustard is strongly flavoured and is smooth. Bordeaux mustard is relatively pale in colour, smooth and fairly bland.

German mustards are dark in colour and spicier than most mustards.

American mustard is smooth and similar in appearance to English, but milder.

Green pepper mustard. A relatively new invention, this is a subtle, smooth and delicious mustard flavoured with unripe green peppercorns from Madagascar. It blends particularly well with lamb and chicken as well as beef.

Using mustard in cooking

Mustards tend to lose their pungency so if possible add them to sauces shortly before serving. Brown-coloured mustards tend to 'muddy' the colour of a pale sauce so, where this matters, choose yellow mustard in preference to brown. Aromatic, herby mustards are delicious spread over rather fatty foods such as breast of lamb or pigs' trotters before breadcrumbing and grilling.

CHATEAUBRIAND STEAK

This is an expensive, impressive dish suitable for a small formal dinner party. Although traditionally served with château potatoes (explained in a later course), duchesse potatoes make an elegant alternative. Serve with grilled tomatoes and mushrooms and garnish with watercress. It is a complete main course, and a salad served separately is optional. Duchesse potatoes are made from a purée, piped into shape and baked.

SERVES 2

two 350 g [¾ lb] chateaubriand
   steaks
olive oil
225 g [½ lb] cap mushrooms
4 medium-sized tomatoes
salt and black pepper

For the duchesse potatoes:
450 g [1 lb] old potatoes
25 g [1 oz] butter
30 ml [2 tablespoons] milk
1 medium-sized egg
salt and black pepper
watercress

1 Heat the oven to 220°C [425°F] gas mark 7.

2 Peel and boil the potatoes. Purée them with hot milk, butter, lightly beaten egg and a good seasoning of salt and black pepper.

3 Pipe the purée on to a baking tray using a size 8 star nozzle.

4 Brown the potatoes in the oven for 30 minutes.

5 Heat the grill so that it is glowing. Brush the steaks liberally with oil.

6 Cook the steaks close to fierce heat and seal the surface — about 1 minute on each side.

7 Lower the grill pan and reduce the heat. Continue grilling for a total of 12-14 minutes for rare, 14-16 minutes for medium-rare and 16-18 minutes for well-done. Turn frequently to cook all over.

8 Meanwhile, clean and prepare the mushrooms, cutting away peel to decorate like minarets.

9 Brush the mushrooms on both sides with oil. Halve the tomatoes, brush with oil and season.

10 Add the mushrooms and tomatoes to grill pan for the last 5 minutes of cooking time.

11 Season the grilled steaks with salt and pepper and transfer to a warm serving dish.

12 Add the duchesse potatoes, tomatoes and mushrooms. Garnish with watercress and serve immediately.

Variation

●Instead of serving the fillet on a serving dish with duchesse potatoes, place the fillet on a serving plank with new potatoes, tomatoes and mushrooms. Garnish with finely chopped parsley or watercress and place a knob of savoury butter on the fillet.

SMOTHERED RUMP STEAK

This is a traditional English way of serving rump steak under a blanket of golden, melting onion rings. Start cooking the onions first so that both vegetables and meat are ready simultaneously and can be served as soon as cooked. Carve at the table.

SERVES 3
**450 g [1 lb] slice rump steak,
2.5 cm [1¾"] thick**
**30 ml [2 tablespoons] vegetable
oil**
3 medium-sized onions
**40 g [1½ oz] beef dripping or
25 g [1 oz] butter plus 15 ml
[1 tablespoon] oil**
salt and pepper
50 g [2 oz] maître d'hôtel butter
sprigs of watercress

1 Trim the steak and, with scissors, snip the edging of fat at intervals to prevent the steak curling.

2 Lay the steak on a chopping board and beat it vigorously on both sides and in both directions with a wooden rolling pin or meat bat.

3 Brush the steak with oil and cover loosely and keep cool until ready to cook.

4 Skin the onions under cold running water (to prevent tears) and if the outer layer of the onion is tough or discoloured remove this too. Slice thinly and push into rings.

5 Melt the dripping, or butter and oil, in a large, heavy shallow frying pan. When hot add the onions.

6 Cook over very low heat, turning frequently, until soft and golden. This will take about 20 minutes and cannot be hurried.

7 When the onions are half cooked, heat the grill until very hot.

8 Seal and brown the steak for 1 minute on each side.

9 Reduce heat and continue grilling for 2-4 minutes on each side, depending on whether you like steak rare, medium or well-done.

10 Lay the steak on a wooden or china platter and season with salt and freshly ground black pepper.

11 Spoon over the onions, dot with pats of maître d'hôtel butter and surround with sprigs of watercress.

TOURNEDOS WITH MUSHROOMS AND ARTICHOKES

Here the steaks are served on grilled mushrooms. They are garnished with deep-fried parsley sprigs and surrounded by artichoke bottoms filled with straw potatoes.

SERVES 4
4 prepared tournedos
paprika
olive oil
4 canned artichoke bottoms
1 packet straw potatoes
cooking oil
1 bunch of parsley
4 large flat mushrooms
salt and pepper

Chateaubriand steak served with maître d'hôtel butter and duchesse potatoes.

1 Dust the tournedos with paprika and brush with olive oil. Leave in a cool place until ready to cook.

2 Heat the artichoke bottoms according to manufacturer's instructions. Drain thoroughly on absorbent kitchen paper and keep warm.

3 Heat cooking oil in a small deep pan to 185°C [360°F] and heat the grill until very hot.

4 Wash, drain, dry and deep fry the parsley sprigs for 30 seconds. Drain on absorbent kitchen paper and keep warm.

5 Grill the tournedos under fierce heat for 1 minute on each side to seal.

6 Heat the potatoes in a hot oven or on the grill if possible.

7 Reduce heat or lower the pan and continue grilling for a further 1-3 minutes on each side, according to taste.

8 Brush the mushrooms generously with oil and add to the grill for the last 5 minutes of cooking time.

9 Place the mushrooms on a warm serving dish. Season with salt and pepper. Top with the tournedos and season again.

10 Surround the steaks with the artichoke bottoms, placing the cup side up, and fill with straw potatoes.

11 Garnish the tournedos with deep-fried parsley and serve immediately.

RUMP STEAK PRINCE ALBERT

This rich dish recaptures the glamour of Edwardian plushness. The mousse de foie gras gives a touch of luxury. If it seems too extravagant, a can of finely ground chicken liver pâté or a similar type of pâté can be used or you can use home-made pâté, which is described in a later course.

Ask the butcher to cut the steak in an even, thick slice trimmed of flaps or end pieces. It should have a thin border of fat along its edge. Carve this steak at the table.

SERVES 4
700 g [1½ lb] slice middle rump 3.5 cm [1½"] thick
salt and pepper
30 ml [2 tablespoons] vegetable oil
15 ml [1 tablespoon] finely chopped shallot or spring onion
100 g [¼ lb] mousse de foie gras or chicken liver pâté
10 ml [2 teaspoons] Madeira or medium-sweet sherry
50 g [2 oz] green herb butter

1 Prepare the steak by cutting through it horizontally with a sharp knife. Cut through the middle until you reach the fat so that the steak forms a pocket. Cut as near to the ends as you can without piercing the retaining wall of meat.

2 Brush the outside of the steak with oil and grind a little black pepper over it. Cover and set aside for an hour or until ready to be cooked.

3 Heat the oil in a small saucepan. Add the chopped shallot or spring onion and cook over gentle heat until softened.

4 Mash the pate in small bowl with a fork. Add the shallot and enough Madeira to mix to a spreading consistency. Check seasoning.

5 Heat the grill until very hot.

6 Open the steak pocket and spread the centre evenly with the pâté mixture, working it well into the corners. Lightly press the steak together again.

7 Seal the steak for 1 minute on each side under fierce heat.

8 Reduce heat or lower the pan and continue grilling for 2-4 minutes on each side according to whether you want it rare, medium rare or well done.

9 Spread the steak with green herb butter during the last few minutes of grilling time and baste with the butter as it melts.

10 Season the steak with salt and pepper when cooked. Place on a warm serving dish and pour the buttery pan juices on top of the steak. Serve immediately.

ENTRECOTE A LA BRETONNE

A simple, tasty dish that can be accompanied by a potato purée and mixed salad of French beans or broccoli.

SERVES 4
4 entrecôte steaks
30 ml [2 tablespoons] olive oil
salt and black pepper

For the sauce:
75 g [3 oz] butter
1 shallot or small mild onion
half small clove of garlic (optional)
5 ml [1 teaspoon] lemon juice
15 ml [1 tablespoon] freshly chopped parsley

For the garnish:
8 small tomatoes
watercress sprigs

1 Brush the steaks with oil and heat the grill.

2 Peel and chop the shallot and garlic.

3 Melt one third of the butter in a small pan over low heat.

4 Add the shallot and garlic and cook gently until they begin to soften.

5 Add remaining butter, lemon juice and parsley.

6 When melted and hot, pour the sauce into a heated serving dish and keep it warm.

7 Seal the steaks on both sides under fierce heat.

8 Reduce heat or lower the pan and continue grilling for 2½-5 minutes each side, according to choice.

9 Prepare the tomatoes and add them to the grill about 5 minutes before the steaks are ready.

10 Season the cooked steaks with salt and freshly ground black pepper. Transfer to the warm serving dish and turn the steak in the butter sauce.

11 Arrange the tomatoes on the dish, garnish the entrecôte steaks with watercress and serve immediately.

Beef

roasting

The earliest method of roasting beef was whole on the spit and consequently this catered for large numbers of diners. Roasts became associated with feasting in the baronial hall and this is how a baron of beef (the entire sirloin from both sides of beef) and a 'sir loin' (for a knight) got their modern names. Beef joints roasted in the oven are just as succulent. This chapter describes the various cuts of beef suited to roasting, suitable accompaniments and details on how to carve the joints.

Good quality joints of beef need nothing but correct roasting to make them perfect. Once roasted the joint must be carved in a way to make the most of the meat. Then, served with accompaniments such as the traditional Yorkshire pudding, roast potatoes and gravy, roast beef is still worthy of its traditions.

CHOOSING BEEF

Provided that you have a good butcher you can be sure that the quality of his meat is satisfactory. It is worth asking him how long he hangs his meat. Hanging about five days to a week in a cool room gives best flavour but many butchers do not have sufficient space, so this is not always possible. If you buy a joint that has been hung for less than five days, it will be improved by keeping it in your refrigerator for two or three days before cooking.

Prime beef is usually slaughtered between two and three years of age. Look for firm flesh, well-marbled with fat. The meat itself should be red and the fat may be white or slightly yellow according to the kind of animal—Jersey and Guernsey cattle always have yellow-tinted fat. Avoid beef that has a layer of gristle between the muscle and outer fat: it means the animal is old.

CUTS OF BEEF

The cuts of a carcass of beef are divided into three categories: prime, medium and coarse. Prime cuts are grilled or open roasted. Medium cuts can also be open roasted or may be cooked by slower methods such as pot roasting or braising. Coarse cuts are not included here as they should always be given long slow cooking to tenderize them and bring out their full flavour. In general, they are best used in stews and casseroles.

Beef, roasted to perfection, served with traditional accompaniments is an impressive and satisfying main course.

PRIME BEEF CUTS

Cut	Description and use
Fillet  Fillet is the most expensive prime cut. It is the undercut of the sirloin. Large pieces can be roasted: fillet is especially suited to high-temperature roasting and may be cooked in pastry (filet de boeuf en croûte). Small pieces are grilled and often appear on restaurant menus as tournedos or filet mignon (see MEAT & FISH 4).	
Rump 	Rump is considered by many people to have more flavour than other parts of the sirloin. Rump is usually sliced and sold as steaks but a large piece of rump can be roasted as a joint in its own right.
Sirloin 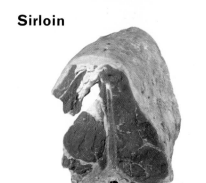	There is a sirloin on either side of the animal's back. The top side of it is often cut into steaks. These are then sold as porterhouse or entrecôte steaks. Sirloin, cut into suitable sizes, can be roasted on the bone with the fillet still attached underneath. For a smaller joint the fillet is removed entirely. The remaining meat is then taken off the bone and rolled and tied for roasting.
Wing rib 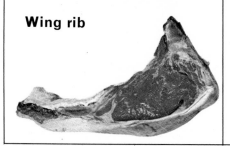	Wing rib is part of the sirloin nearest to the shoulder, without the fillet, and is good for roasting. It can be left on the bone or, off the bone, it is rolled and tied for roasting.

Prime cuts

Prime cuts are the most expensive cuts of beef. They all come from the loin or upper back of the animal and comprise the fillet, rump, sirloin and wing rib. They are the tenderest cuts and therefore are ideal for fast cooking methods—grilling or roasting. They tend to be lean and, if so, benefit by the addition of fat by larding or barding which keeps the meat moist during cooking.

These cuts are seldom seen whole but, even so, the smaller cuts that are purchased for an average family meal remain expensive. It is therefore worth making a feast out of a prime cut when you do have it.

Medium cuts

Medium cuts are less expensive than prime cuts. They comprise the fore rib, top and back ribs, top side and aitchbone. They are, however, less tender and therefore benefit by the slow cooking methods such as pot roasting and braising, where some liquid is also used. Nevertheless all the rib cuts are excellent for roasting though the results will not be so tender as a roasted prime cut. The cuts nearest the sirloin—fore ribs— are the most tender.

Coarse cuts

Coarse cuts of beef may on occasion be roasted; brisket and silverside are sometimes rolled and roasted by the low-temperature method. This is not however the best way of treating a coarse cut, as coarse meat needs long slow cooking to tenderize it. It is worth bearing in mind that fuel costs make them less economical.

QUANTITIES

As a general rule you will need between 125-225 g [4-8 oz] of boneless beef per person (depending on appetite) and about 175-275 g [6-10 oz] per person of cuts with an average amount of bone. Generally, joints weighing less than 1.4 kg [3 lb] are not suitable for roasting as they shrink too much, making them uneconomical. A barded or larded fillet, which is long and thin, is an exception to this.

Cuts which may be bought on the bone are sirloin, wing rib, fore rib, top and back rib and aitchbone. These cuts may also be bought from the butcher boned and rolled. Boneless cuts are fillet, rump and topside.

STORING BEEF
Fresh beef

Once you get it home, store fresh beef in the coldest part of the refrigerator or, failing this, in a cold, well-ventilated larder. Always unwrap meat before storing it. Place it on a plate or in a bowl and use a cloth or plastic film to cover it. Do not make the covering airtight, but allow a little air to enter and circulate. Some refrigerators have a special meat storage drawer into which you just place the unwrapped meat.

As a rough guide, large joints can be stored for about five days.

Cooked beef

For cold meat the cooked joint should ideally be uncarved, cooled and wrapped the moment it is cold. Wrapping prevents the beef from drying out. Use foil to wrap the beef closely but do not make the parcel airtight. Store immediately in the refrigerator. The meat must be used within two days.

ROASTING METHODS
There are two methods of roasting meat in fat: open and closed roasting, which, strictly speaking, is not true roasting, as a quantity of liquid is used. There are also three possible approaches for beef: searing it or high- or low-temperature roasting. High-temperature roasting is suitable only for prime cuts and low-temperature roasting is, in general, to be preferred.

Open roasting
For open roasting, put the baking tin with about 45 ml [3 tablespoons] fat into the oven when you switch it on to heat. When the right temperature is reached, remove the baking tin from the oven, place in it a rack and stand the meat on top. The rack raises the meat so that it does not sit in any juices that may leak from it. The rack does make basting more difficult.

Spoon hot fat over the joint then place it in the centre of the oven. The advantage of this method is that the hot fat helps to make an instant seal on the outside of the joint, keeping in the juices.

The meat must be basted regularly with hot fat from the roasting pan. For this job either use a heatproof spoon or a bulb baster, which sucks up the fat and squirts it where directed. Roasting is cooking by the direct heat method, which dries out the meat, so even larded meat needs some basting. For barded meat, basting may be reduced.

A choice of rare or well-done beef is largely a matter of taste, but it is customary to serve beef rare if it is to be carved and eaten cold. The chart gives the various cooking times for beef. The degree of rareness may be tested with a meat thermometer or by piercing with a skewer, but neither of these methods is really desirable, as the meat is pierced and releases its juices. Ultimately, experience is the best guide.

Some cookers have built-in rôtisserie facilities or you may own a separate spit roaster. When cooked on a spit, the joint will baste itself as it turns, because fat drips down the sides and is evenly distributed round the meat; thus a spit-roasted joint needs no basting.

MEDIUM BEEF CUTS	
Description and use	**Cut**
This joint adjoins the wing rib. It is fairly large and can be cooked on the bone or boned and rolled. It is also suited to slow cooking methods.	**Fore rib** 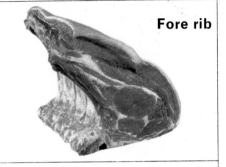
Also called middle rib, this joint adjoins the fore ribs at one end and the shoulder at the other. A joint with slightly less bone than the fore rib, it is well suited to low-temperature roasting.	**Top and back rib** 
This joint comes from the rear of the animal. It is lean and boneless. It is usually rolled by the butcher and sold ready for roasting. It is a good joint to roast at a low temperature.	**Topside** 
This is a large joint. Cuts from it are usually sold boneless. It is suited to low-temperature roasting and to slow cooking methods.	**Aitchbone** 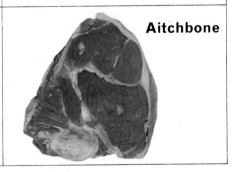

PREPARING BEEF FOR ROASTING
Fresh meat for roasting should always be removed from the refrigerator for long enough to allow it to reach room temperature before cooking. Two to three hours is usually long enough but this depends on the size of the particular joint you are roasting.

Frozen beef does not necessarily have to be thawed before it is roasted. However, large joints are better thawed as this improves the texture. Large joints are also difficult to roast successfully if they have not been thawed—the chances are that the outside will be cooked and the inside will still be half raw.

Some cuts of beef come with their natural coating of fat. Others are invariably sold by the butcher rolled and ready barded with an outer coating of fat. Some of the prime cuts of beef are very lean and may be barded or larded before cooking, or

157

Step-by-step to larding

1 Chill larding bacon. Then lay it on its rind. Cut through to the rind with warm knife, making 6 mm [¼"] thick pieces.

2 Rewarm the knife. Turn and cut the larding bacon lengthways at intervals of 6 mm [¼"] to release the strips of bacon.

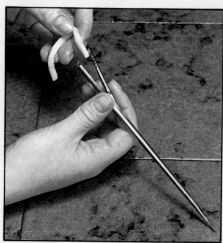

3 Insert a bacon strip in the needle by clamping the teeth of the larding needle on to the end of the lardon.

may be cooked en croûte to keep them moist.

Barding

Lean joints, removed from the bone and rolled, may be barded. This means a protective layer of fat is wrapped round the meat and tied at intervals with string. This is often done by the butcher, who will always bard a topside before it is sold.

You can also bard a lean joint at home. The advantage of this is that it keeps the joint moist with the minimum of basting and this is necessary if the meat is to be cooked by high-temperature methods.

The fat used is bacon, either back fat or streaky rashers. The method is the same for a whole joint as for noisettes of lamb as described in the grilling lamb chapter.

Larding

Larding is a rather fiddly and time-consuming method of attaching fat to the skin of a lean cut of meat. It is, however, decidedly worth the effort, as it improves the flavour, keeps the meat succulent and promotes even cooking. Larding is strongly recommended when roasting a fillet of beef, as this has no natural fat attached.

The fat used is called larding bacon. This is special fat cured without saltpetre. It is a solid block of fat bacon about 5-6 cm [2-2½"] wide. You will need 75-100 g [3-4 oz] including the rind for a 1.4 kg [3 lb] joint. Thin strips are cut from it called

lardons. On a special occasion the lardons may be cut and then marinated in brandy and herbs to give them extra flavour.

To cut the lardons, first chill the larding bacon for several hours; it will cut more neatly if cold. Place the bacon on a board with the rind side downward. Place a jug full of hot water beside you and warm in it a sharp cutting knife. Then carve across the bacon, down to the rind but not through it, making slices 6 mm [¼"] wide. Turn and then slice along the bacon, making slices of the same thickness.

You will need a larding needle (obtainable from kitchen shops). This is approximately 15 cm [6"] long with a spike at one end for piercing the meat. The other end has a hinged section with a row of teeth, which clamp down on the lardon.

The larding needle with the lardon in place is then inserted into the meat against the grain. This is so that when the meat is carved each slice will have a portion of lardon with it. The first lardon will lie on top of the joint and hang down on either side.

Start on top between the first pair of strings if the joint is tied. Take up a small portion of meat on the tip of the needle. Pull the needle through the meat with the lardon attached until an equal quantity of fat is hanging out on either side. The needle clamp is then released, a new lardon inserted and the process is repeated. Lard the joint in rows about 2.5 cm [1"] apart.

Position the rows so that the lardons lie alternately. On a fillet this will mean one across the top of the joint will be succeeded by a pair on either side, which may touch at the top. For a joint with a larger circumference, such as rolled topside, you could have three lardons in one row, followed by two in the next. The fat should give a chequer-board effect—each lardon bastes a surrounding area of lean meat during cooking.

Seasoning

Salt is rubbed into the fat or skin of the joint, but never into any cut surface, as this could draw the juices out and help to make the joint flavourless and dry. Pepper can be rubbed on all surfaces.

If you like the taste of garlic, rub the joint all over with the cut surface of a garlic clove before cooking for a mild flavour. For a more pronounced flavour make little slits in the joint with a sharp knife and insert tiny slivers into the meat.

Herbs which enhance the flavour of beef are lovage (which has a celery flavour), marjoram and thyme. These are cooked in the pan with the meat.

You can also affect the taste of the meat by your choice of fat. All fats are suitable, from dripping or lard to olive oil. If, however, you choose to roast one of the prime cuts by the high-temperature roasting method, you should avoid butter, as under these conditions it could burn.

4 Working across the meat grain, pick up 12 mm [½"] of meat on needle tip and pull the needle through.

5 Pull the lardon carefully through the meat until it hangs out an equal length on both sides. Release the needle clamp.

6 Make new rows of lardons at 2.5 cm [1"] intervals so that a chequerboard effect is created along the length of the meat.

TIMING AND TESTING

Beef may be roasted by the same method as lamb; it may be seared first at high temperature, then the temperature reduced for further cooking. It may be cooked fast at a high temperature, or more slowly at a moderate one.

Searing method of roasting

This method is only suitable for prime and medium cuts, as it does nothing to tenderize the meat, but it does seal in the flavour and gives a juicy joint. The joint is started in an oven heated to 220°C [425°F] gas mark 7 and roasted for 10 minutes. Then the temperature is turned down, and the oven temperature can be quickly reduced by leaving the door open while you baste the meat. Cook for the rest of the calculated time.

It is possible to cook the best quality and most tender beef by setting the oven at 260°C [500°F] gas mark 10 and then sealing the roast for 10 minutes. Then switch off the oven and, without opening the door, allow the joint to cook for the appropriate number of minutes for its weight, as the oven cools.

High-temperature roasting

This method is only suitable for prime joints, but medium cuts can be cooked by this method on occasion if they have been well hung and marinated to make them tenderer. Joints roasted at high temperatures have the best flavour, but the joint does shrink during cooking. The chart gives times for different cuts.

Low-temperature roasting

Low-temperature roasting makes meat fibres more tender and causes less shrinkage. Generally this is the best way to roast both prime and medium cuts of beef (the high-temperature method is best reserved as an emergency procedure when you are short of time). The chart gives the roasting times.

Meat thermometers

Meat thermometers are useful for indicating how well the inside of the meat is cooked. Some people prefer roast meat well done and others like it so that the blood runs along the knife blade when it is cut. With experience you will be able to judge just how long to roast for the kinds of joints you like. However, a meat thermometer checks rareness. Stick it in the thickest part of the joint before it goes in the oven. It indicates when the correct internal temperature has been reached and from this you can calculate how well cooked the meat is. Rare beef will show a temperature of around 60°C [140°F]; medium 75°C [160°F] and well done 77°C [170°F].

Meat skewers

Piercing the meat with a skewer and looking at the colour of the meat juices gives some indication of how well done the joint is though this method is not really desirable.

Insert then withdraw a thin skewer into the thickest part of the meat. If the juices are red the meat is underdone and requires longer cooking, if slightly rosy the meat is rare, if colourless the meat is well done. Don't be tempted to do a number of tests—each time the skewer is inserted into the meat, the juices flow from the incision.

Finger-tip test

Piercing the meat with a skewer loses some of the juice. For meats to be eaten rare, the finger-tip method is better, though it requires some practice. Press the cooked joint with your finger-tips. If it is soft and springy, it is underdone, and experience will teach you to recognize the response which indicates the degree of rareness you like best. If the meat is well done, the joint feels firm and resilient.

Using frozen meat

It is possible to roast small frozen joints but these will be rare inside.

When cooking frozen or defrosted meat, it is best to use a meat thermometer, so that you can be sure that the beef is cooked right through. Start off roasting a joint at 230°C [450°F] gas mark 8, for the first fifteen minutes to seal it. Insert meat thermometer and reduce heat to 180°C [350°F] gas mark 4. Allow 50 minutes per 450 g [1 lb]. Keep checking the thermometer until it is done to the degree you require.

Step-by-step roasting beef

A beef joint to be roasted should be at room temperature. A joint of about 1.4 kg [3 lb] should be removed from the refrigerator about two hours before cooking.

The low-temperature method is used here as this generally gives the most successful results and prevents the joint from shrinking.

Gravy is commonly made in the baking tin, using the meat drippings while the joint is resting before carving. This resting allows the meat to set making carving easier.

1 Weigh the meat, choose the temperature appropriate to the cut and calculate cooking time.

2 Heat the oven. Select the baking tin, measure fat and put tin and fat in the oven to heat.

3 Season, rubbing salt into the fat or skin of the meat, but never into cut surfaces. Rub in pepper.

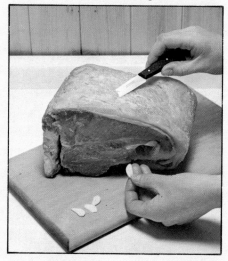

4 If wished, chop a garlic clove and make neat incisions in the meat with a knife point. Insert garlic.

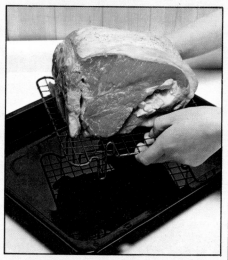

5 When oven is heated, remove hot tin. Put the joint on a rack and spoon the hot fat over. Roast.

6 If using frozen meat, insert meat thermometer after 15 minutes at a high heat. Reduce heat.

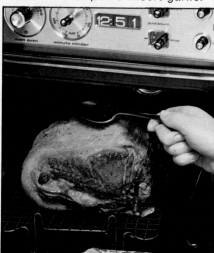

7 Baste every 15 minutes if meat has no fat and at half-hourly intervals for cut surfaces.

8 Test for rareness at the end of cooking time. Let the joint rest 15 minutes in a warm place.

ROASTING TEMPERATURES FOR BEEF

Cuts	Temperature	Off the bone			On the bone		
		Rare	Medium	Well done	Rare	Medium	Well done
Prime Cuts **Fillet**	*High temperature 220°C [425°F] gas mark 7	15 min per 450 g [1 lb] plus 15 min	20 min per 450 g [1 lb] plus 20 min	25 min per 450 g [1 lb] plus 25 min	not applicable		
Sirloin		as fillet	as fillet	as fillet	10 min per 450 g [1 lb] plus 10 min	15 min per 450 g [1 lb] plus 15 min	20 min per 450 g [1 lb] plus 20 min
Wing rib		as fillet	as fillet	as fillet	as sirloin	as sirloin	as sirloin
Medium Cuts **Topside**	Low temperature 190°C [375°F] gas mark 5	24 min per 450 g [1 lb] plus 24 min	28 min per 450 g [1 lb] plus 28 min	32 min per 450 g [1 lb] plus 32 min	not applicable		
Aitchbone		as topside	as topside	as topside	20 min per 450 g [1 lb] plus 20 min	25 min per 450 g [1 lb] plus 25 min	30 min per 450 g [1 lb] plus 30 min
Fore, top and back rib		as topside	as topside	as topside	as aitchbone	as aitchbone	as aitchbone
Coarse Cuts **Brisket**	Slow roasting 160°C [325°F] gas mark 3	not suitable	not suitable	40 min per 450 g [1 lb] plus 40 min	not suitable	not suitable	35 min per 450 g [1 lb] plus 35 min
Silverside		not suitable	not suitable	as brisket	not suitable	not suitable	as brisket

*Prime cuts may also be roasted by the low-temperature method. Follow the temperature and times in low-temperature section.

Roasting for cold beef

The best cuts for eating cold are the prime cuts, plus the ribs, topside, silverside and, among the coarse cuts, brisket.

While it is a sensible household practice to finish off the remnant of a cold joint the following day, this custom does not give you the best quality cold beef.

Roast a joint especially for eating cold. Cook it rare to medium rather than well done, as beef tends to dry out when cold. Then allow it to become cold before carving. This retains all the juices within the joint and it will also carve more economically. Keep the joint whole and refrigerate it if you don't intend eating it the same day.

ACCOMPANIMENTS

The classic accompaniments to English roast beef are Yorkshire pudding, roast potatoes and gravy, and either English mustard or horse-radish sauce.

However, these are not essential to the enjoyment of beef and it is worth experimenting with alternatives from time to time.

Roast potatoes

Potatoes roasted with the joint are both satisfying and economical. Only old potatoes are suitable for this method of cooking. It is important that they are all the same size, thus needing the same cooking time.

For a larger joint, cooked at high temperature, the potatoes may be roasted raw. To accompany a smaller joint to be roasted for less than one and a quarter hours, the potatoes should be parboiled (for five minutes for larger ones) and then dried by being shaken in a pan over low heat for a minute, before being added to the hot fat. To give them a crisp outside after roasting, scratch the surface with a fork before putting them in the pan.

The quantity of fat must be increased if potatoes are being cooked. For 1 kg [2 lb] potatoes, use 225 g [½ lb] dripping. It makes sense to use a smaller baking tin, so that the potatoes fit reasonably tightly. But be sure that the meat rack is smaller than the pan, so that you can get a spoon into the pan for basting.

Step-by-step to carving sirloin on the bone

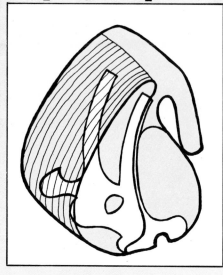

1 Work the knife along the backbone to just free the fillet, then turn it. Cut the meat clear of rib.

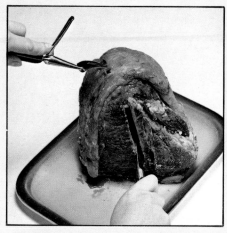

2 Stand the bone on end and free the uppercut from the rib bone on both sides.

Step-by-step to carving wing rib

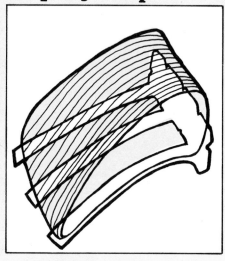

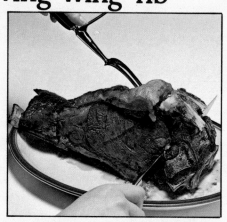

1 Cut down along the length of the backbone, along its entire length, to remove the chine bone.

2 Carve down in slices toward the ribs. Loosen the meat from the ribs and remove slices.

Put the potatoes in the hot fat in the tin and baste thoroughly. Then put in the rack and put the joint on it and baste the meat. Baste the potatoes every time you baste the meat. The potatoes must be turned half way through roasting time to brown the other side. To do this, remove the baking tin from the oven, then shut the oven door. Move the rack and the meat on to the serving dish. Turn the potatoes with tongs, baste then return the rack to the pan. Baste the meat and return the tin to the oven. When the meat is cooked, test the potatoes with a skewer. If the potatoes are insufficiently cooked or pallid in appearance, remove the roasting tin from the oven. Increase the oven heat to 200°C [400°F] gas mark 6. Transfer the potatoes to an ovenproof dish, together with a few spoonfuls of fat, and place them in the hottest part of the oven (at the top) and continue cooking for a further 10 minutes. Dish the joint on to a warm serving dish and let it rest in a warm place before carving. Meanwhile, make the gravy in the roasting tin.

Gravy

Beef tends to make more juice than lamb or mutton. For this reason it is traditional not to thicken the gravy, though this is a matter of preference (see roasting lamb for a good gravy thickening). Gravy is made with the meat dripping left in the roasting tin after the joint has been removed.

Let the juices settle for a minute so that the fat rises to the surface. Pour off the clear fat to the point that the pan juices begin to look muddy and a little of the meat juice begins to flow as well. You can then skim a little more with a metal spoon. If a dark gravy is wanted, this can be made by adding a slice of tomato sprinkled with sugar to the pan. The sugar will turn brown and lose its sweetness.

Add salt and pepper, about 150 ml [¼ pt] vegetable water, and the same quantity red wine or cider. Boil gently for about 10 minutes until the gravy has reduced. This quantity should serve four people. Taste and season then serve in a sauce-boat.

CARVING ROAST BEEF

Let the beef rest 15 minutes in a warm place to become set before carving.

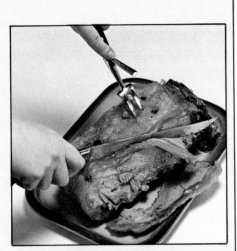

3 Carve each section of the freed meat in slices across the grain. Remove from bone to serve.

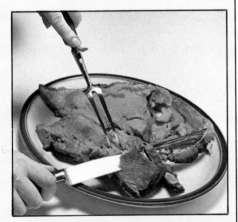

3 When nearly all the meat has been carved, lay the joint flat and carve the last slices horizontally.

This is even more important for beef than for lamb, as the slices are traditionally thin. Remove all strings before carving the meat. Once carved, the slices of beef cool quickly, so they should always be put on to very hot plates for serving.

Always carve across the grain of the meat using a very sharp knife and a fork with a guard. A carving dish studded with metal prongs will hold the joint steady. A small sunken area at one end of the dish is useful as the meat is very juicy. Spoon up these juices and add them to the gravy.

Boned, rolled meat can be carved by standing it lengthways on the dish and carving downward in slices. A smaller rolled joint is best standing upright in the dish and carved across horizontally.

ENGLISH ROAST BEEF

◪◪ *Wing rib is used for this recipe, but other prime or medium cuts are suitable. Extra weight is allowed here for the bones and the high-temperature method has been chosen to ensure that the potatoes are brown. Insert slivers of garlic into the fatty veins of the meat. If you prefer a milder taste, rub the meat surfaces over with the cut face of the garlic clove.*

Potatoes are cooked in the pan under the meat. The rack used must be smaller than the tin to permit basting with a spoon. Cooked with a joint of this size the potatoes will receive sufficient oven time to cook without parboiling. Extra fat is included to brown the potatoes.

A little extra roasting time must be allowed for that lost when taking the pan out to baste. The oven temperature is also reduced slightly each time the door is opened.

For a complete main course, only a green vegetable such as steamed cabbage, or a salad, is needed.

SERVES 6
2 kg [4½ lb] wing rib
225 g [½ lb] dripping
1 kg [2¼ lb] potatoes
salt and black pepper
1 clove of garlic

For the gravy:
1 slice tomato
5 ml [1 teaspoon] sugar
150 ml [¼ pt] vegetable water
150 ml [¼ pt] red wine
salt
black pepper

1 Heat the oven to 220°C [425°F] gas mark 7.

2 Measure the fat and put in baking tin in the oven.

3 Peel the potatoes. If the potatoes are too large to roast whole, cut them into halves or quarters.

4 Rub salt over the meat fat and pepper over all the surfaces.

5 Peel and chop the garlic finely. Pierce the fatty grain in the meat with the point of a knife and insert small slivers of garlic.

6 Take the tin out of the oven and put in the potatoes, spooning hot fat over them. Arrange a rack over the potatoes.

7 Arrange the meat on the rack, fat side uppermost. Baste the potatoes at the same time, dribbling fat through the wire rack on to their upper sides. If you are using a meat thermometer, insert it into the thickest part of the meat but do not let it touch the bone.

8 An hour after roasting has started, turn the potatoes. To do this, remove the tin from the oven and shut the oven door to conserve heat. Remove the rack and the meat to a serving dish and turn over all the potatoes with a pair of tongs. Baste the potatoes, then salt them lightly for a crisp finish. Replace rack and the meat and baste the meat. Return tin to the oven.

9 Roast for a total of 1 hour and 50 minutes. Try testing by the finger-tip method. Protect your fingers from the heat by a couple of layers of kitchen paper. Press the cut surface; if it depresses easily the beef is underdone. If it is firm and resilient the beef is already well done, so half way between the two is perfect.

10 Dish the meat on to a warm serving dish and surround by potatoes. Transfer them with the tongs, so that they do not drip fat into the serving dish.

11 Keep meat and potatoes in the warmer while you make gravy.

12 Pour off the fat until the meat juices start to flow out of the pan with the fat. Then skim off more fat with a spoon.

13 Add a slice of tomato with sugar on it to the drippings from the meat in the pan. Cook this over medium heat until the sugar colours dark brown.

14 Add the vegetable water and the wine. Boil over medium heat for 10 minutes until these reduce and the gravy thickens slightly.

15 Taste for seasoning. The gravy will probably not need salt, as that from the potatoes will be in the meat juices.

16 Strain into a sauce-boat and serve with the roast.

FILET DE BOEUF A LA MADERE

This is an expensive dish, but it is impressive and suitable for a formal dinner party. Its advantage is that, once larded, it is quick to cook and then easy to serve.

As fillets are long and thin, increasing their weight does not make them more substantial; weights under 1.4 kg [3 lb] may be roasted. If well larded, the fast high-temperature method can be used.

A little oil is included with the butter so that this will not burn before the pork lardons begin to melt and give off fat. Basting the beef with hot fat at the beginning helps to seal it.

Though fillet is the most expensive of beef cuts the weight needed per person is less than with some other prime cuts. Serve two slices, 12-18 mm [½-¾"] thick, per portion. The butcher will tie the fillet for you when you purchase it.

The sauce is made in the roasting tin to use the meat drippings. Skim the fat off then reduce the Madeira in the roasting tin and add the demi-glace, stirring all the time.

Accompany the fillet with new potatoes, tossed in butter and decorated handsomely on top with paprika.

SERVES 6
1 kg [2¼ lb] fillet of beef
45 ml [3 tablespoons] butter
5 ml [1 teaspoon] olive oil
salt
freshly ground black pepper
75 g [3 oz] larding bacon

For the sauce madère:
250 ml [½ pt] demi-glace
125 ml [4 fl oz] Madeira

1 Heat the oven to 190°C [375°F] gas mark 5. Put the butter into the baking tin with the oil. Put tin into the oven to heat.

2 Rub salt well into the skin of the fillet, but not into the cut sides. Rub pepper into the fillet all over.

3 Lard the fillet, following the step-by-step instructions.

4 Remove the tin from the oven. Put a rack in it and on this stand the beef. Baste the beef on all sides with the hot fat, then return tin to the oven.

5 Roast the beef for 45 minutes, basting it once halfway through cooking time.

6 At the end of roasting time, if you think that the meat might not be cooked, test it with a skewer. Pierce it from the side to a depth of 40 mm [1½"]. If the juices are rosy rather than bright red, the joint is rare, which is how you want it. If red, baste and return to the oven for a few more minutes, but on no account overcook it.

7 Dish the beef on to a warm serving

Filet de boeuf à la madère is a dish for special occasions and the wine sauce gives it a touch of luxury.

dish and allow it to rest in the warmer for 15 minutes before carving.

8 To make the sauce, skim off excess fat from the roasting tin with a spoon. Add Madeira and boil gently for about 5 minutes until it has reduced by half. Stir round the pan with a wooden spoon to release any scrapings.

9 Add the demi-glace to the pan and boil gently for a further 5 minutes stirring all the time.

10 Strain the sauce into sauce-boat.

11 Remove the strings from the beef fillet and serve accompanied by the sauce.

Variation
This fillet is excellent cold. Do not carve it until absolutely cold, then serve it sliced, accompanied by a béarnaise sauce.

ROAST BEEF WITH DEVILLED SAUCE

◪◪ *This juicy roast is well set off by a slightly sweeter version of the classic brown sauce à la diable, which is made in the roasting pan while the meat is resting.*

For a top quality sauce use 250 ml [½ pt] demi-glace. For simpler occasions, use leftover brown gravy, brown meat stock or stock from a good bouillon cube.

SERVES 6
1.4 kg [3 lb] topside
salt
freshly ground black pepper
45 ml [3 tablespoons] margarine

For the devilled sauce:
25 g [1 oz] shallot
175 ml [6 fl oz] red wine
15 ml [1 tablespoon] red wine vinegar
250 ml [½ pt] brown stock
30 ml [2 tablespoons] redcurrant jelly
10 ml [2 teaspoons] French mustard
10 ml [2 teaspoons] horseradish sauce
5 ml [1 teaspoon] Worcestershire sauce
salt
freshly ground black pepper

1 Heat the oven to 190°C [375°F] gas mark 5. Weigh the meat and calculate cooking time.

2 Put the fat in the baking tin and put this in the oven.

3 Rub salt into the meat fat and pepper into all surfaces.

4 Remove the tin from the oven. Put in a rack and place the meat on top. Baste thoroughly.

5 Put the tin in the oven and roast for 1 hour and 35 minutes. Baste the beef at half-hourly intervals.

6 Chop the shallot and assemble sauce ingredients.

7 At the end of roasting time, if you think that the meat might not be cooked, test it with a skewer. Pierce it from the side to the centre of the joint. If the juices are rosy it is ready. If they are bright red, baste and replace in the oven for a few more minutes.

8 Dish the beef on to a warm serving dish and place in the warmer to rest.

9 Pour off the fat until the meat juices start to flow out of the pan with it. Then skim off more fat with a spoon.

10 Add the shallot to the baking tin and put this over a medium heat. Cook until the shallot has softened, stirring occasionally with a wooden spoon.

11 Add the red wine and the wine vinegar and boil for 10 minutes until reduced to about 50 ml [2 fl oz].

12 Add the brown stock and the redcurrant jelly and continue gently boiling. Stir with a wooden spoon until the jelly has dissolved.

13 Add the mustard, horseradish sauce and Worcestershire sauce. Taste and season.

14 Strain the sauce into a sauce-boat and serve with the meat. Alternatively, the meat may be carved in the kitchen and some of the sauce used to coat the slices.

COLD ROAST ROLLS OF BEEF

◪◪◪ *Beef to be eaten cold is best cooked specially for this purpose; roast it by the low-temperature method for maximum tenderness and take it from the oven when rare. Allow the joint to become completely cold to seal in the juices before carving. Then cut very thin slices. This recipe is very economical as the slices are then stuffed.*

SERVES 10
1.4 kg [3 lb] rolled boned sirloin
45 ml [3 tablespoons] fat
salt and black pepper

For the celeriac stuffing:
small celeriac root
150 ml [5 fl oz] thick cream
10 ml [2 teaspoons] French mustard
30 ml [2 tablespoons] white wine vinegar
salt and black pepper

1 Heat the oven to 190°C [375°F] gas mark 5.

2 Put the fat into the roasting pan and put it in the oven to heat.

3 Salt the meat, rubbing it well into the fat but not into cut surfaces. Rub in black pepper.

4 Remove the hot tin from the oven, put in the rack and arrange meat on top of it, fat side uppermost. Baste well and return to the oven.

5 Roast for one hour and 35 minutes. Baste twice.

6 At the end of roasting time, if you are worried that the meat may not be cooked, test it with a skewer. Insert the skewer 40 mm [1½″] into the side of the meat. If the juices which run out are rosy, the meat is rare, which is correct. If the juices are bright red, baste the joint and return it to the oven for a few more minutes.

7 Remove from the rack and allow to become completely cold. Then wrap it in foil, but do not crimp the foil to make an airtight parcel. Reserve in the refrigerator until 20 minutes before serving.

8 For the stuffing, first prepare the celeriac. Peel the skin from the celeriac root and grate root on a coarse cheese grater or with an electric grater.

9 Put the cream into a medium-sized bowl and add the French mustard, vinegar and seasoning. Stir to mix.

10 Add the grated celeriac and turn it over in the bowl with a spoon until the shreds are thoroughly coated.

11 Remove the cold roast beef from the refrigerator and slice thinly. On this occasion there is no need to bring it to room temperature first as it will slice more finely when cold.

Cold roast rolls of beef filled with a celeriac stuffing.

12 Place a spoonful of celeriac mixture in the centre of each slice and roll it up. Arrange the rolls on a serving dish with the ends tucked underneath, so that the rolls remain neat. The individual slices should be so thin that they will warm to room temperature while you are stuffing and arranging them.

Variation
This can be served sliced and cold unstuffed and will serve 8 people. Accompany it with a tomato or potato salad dressed with a herb vinaigrette.

166

Chicken

grilling

Now that chicken is always available, pennywise cooks are constantly on the look out for new ways of cooking it. Grilling is often thought to be a rather dull way to cook chicken but if tangy herbs and spicy sauces are added it becomes deliciously interesting. Here you are shown how to choose for flavour, divide into portions and grill to perfection.

Thanks to agricultural progress chicken, once a luxury food reserved for high days and holidays, is now cheap enough to eat for everyday meals. There are sceptics who say that today's intensively reared birds taste just like cardboard but, cooked with flair, modern chickens are just as good and tasty as those of days gone by.

With suitable young birds, grilling is the simplest and most variable method of cooking. It enhances the flavour, retains the natural succulence of the bird and results in crisp, golden brown skin. Fresh birds can be grilled simply with herbs or a delicate basting sauce, while frozen birds can be given extra flavour with a robust sauce or topping.

Here we show how to divide both large and small birds. Small, young

The marinade used for Devilled chicken Delmonico is thickened with breadcrumbs and spooned over chicken before final cooking

birds are best for grilling. If serving, say, 8 people, it is better to buy two small birds and to cut each into 4 portions rather than to cut one large bird into 8 pieces.

CHOOSING CHICKEN

Chickens for cooking by methods other than boiling or long casseroling are all specially reared so that they will put on the maximum of tender flesh at minimum cost to the producer. Almost all chickens sold in poulterers, butchers and markets are reared indoors under controlled conditions. Outdoor or free-range chickens are rarely seen these days, partly because they are uneconomic, but mainly because their quality is difficult to control and it is hard to guarantee that the customer will always get a tender, tasty bird. It is in fact something of a myth that these free-range birds taste better. Because outdoor chickens run around and eat at will, they are prone to disease and liable to develop rather more muscle and sinew than is desirable for a tender grilling or roasting bird.

It is the processing method after killing, not the rearing, that most affects the quality of the chicken you buy and, for this reason, it is important to go to a butcher or poulterer if you want a really well-flavoured bird. There are several types and sizes of chicken available. These are described in the chart. Chickens are processed in four different ways: fresh, farm fresh, chilled and frozen.

Fresh chickens

Fresh chickens are seen in butchers' and poulterers' shops either feathered or plucked out with head and feet left on (known as New York dressed). These chickens come to the butcher with their feathers on. He then hangs them for about three days

Types of chicken suitable for grilling

Type	Description	Method
 **Poussins and double poussins**	Both available fresh, farm fresh, chilled or frozen. Poussins are killed when 4 weeks old and usually weigh about 450 g [1 lb], which means they will only serve 1 portion as the ratio of bone to meat is rather high. Double poussins are killed when about 6 weeks old and weigh about 1 kg [2 lb]. They can be cut in half or spatch-cocked to serve 2 portions. One double poussin between two is better value than a whole poussin each.	The most satisfactory way of cooking poussins is en cocotte or by pot roasting, although it is possible to spatchcock them, that is, opened out flat and skewered for grilling. Season, brush with butter or oil and grill for 10 minutes, skin side down, 12 cm [5"] away from medium heat. Turn and grill for another 8 minutes, basting occasionally. Double poussins are grilled as for a poussin but increase grilling time by 2-3 minutes on each side, depending on size.
 **Spring chicken**	Available fresh, farm fresh, chilled and sometimes frozen. Spring chickens are not reared in the spring as the name might suggest but are killed when 8 weeks old. They have an average weight of 1¼-1½ kg [2½-3 lb] and may be roasted or divided into portions for grilling.	Grill as for poussins, increasing the grilling time by 2-3 minutes each side, depending on the thickness of the pieces. Add the thinner breast portions to the grill 5 minutes after starting to cook the leg portions.
 **Roaster**	Sometimes also called a broiler (not to be confused with a boiler which is a much older bird), these chickens are available fresh, farm fresh, chilled, frozen or cut into portions. A roasting chicken is killed when it is between 8 and 10 weeks old and usually weighs from 1½-3 kg [3-6 lb], and is suitable for roasting whole or grilling divided into portions.	Season, brush with butter or oil and grill for 12 minutes, skin side down, 12 cm [5"] away from medium heat. Turn and grill for a further 10 minutes, basting occasionally. Increase grilling time for very thick pieces and add thinner breast pieces 5 minutes after the legs.
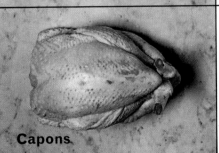 **Capons**	Available fresh, farm fresh, chilled and sometimes frozen, capons are male birds which have been treated with female hormones to make them put on a lot of weight in a short time. Capons are usually killed when 8 weeks old and weigh from 3-4 kg [6-8 lb]. Capons are suitable for roasting whole or dividing into portions and grilling.	Grill as for roaster portions. Cook as above, depending on size.

to allow the maximum flavour to develop before preparing for selling.

Look for chickens with smooth, unbroken flesh, a slightly pliable beak and breastbone and pale yellow legs with small scales. All these factors indicate a young, tender bird.

If you buy a New York dressed or feathered chicken, the butcher will charge you for the total weight of the bird before he has removed the head, feet, feathers and innards (called drawing or eviscerating). These 'extras' can add up to 1 kg [2 lb] to the weight of the bird, depending on its size, so always take this into account when buying. If you are unsure of how much to buy, ask the butcher. Make sure you take the giblets and feet with you to use for stock or giblet gravy.

Because selling chickens in this way is a fairly labour-intensive process they tend to be expensive but hanging does mean that the flavour is good.

Farm-fresh chickens
Farm-fresh chickens are hung and prepared for selling on the poultry farm. They are usually sold whole, oven ready with the giblets in a little bag inside. Once again, this is a labour-intensive process so the chickens cost more but taste good. You are not, however, paying for unusable parts as when buying a New York dressed chicken as the head, feet and innards have been removed before selling.

Chilled chickens

Chilled chickens are usually seen in chain stores. They are factory-produced birds, reared by intensive methods, killed when a certain weight (usually 1.4-1.7 kg [3-3½ lb]) is reached, plucked, eviscerated, then air-chilled immediately without hanging. Air-chilling is a dry method so the bird does not take in water as with a frozen chicken. For this reason, chilled chickens are slightly more expensive than frozen chickens. Chilled chickens are available oven ready, halved or as portions. They are always marked as chilled on the wrapping.

Frozen chickens

Frozen chickens are reared and killed in exactly the same way as chilled chickens and are usually sold in supermarkets and chain stores. The only difference is that in the freezing process the bird takes in quite a lot of water. The chicken is weighed after freezing and, in some cases, you may be paying for rather a high ratio of water to flesh. It also has a slight effect on flavour though expert opinion says that, if thawed correctly, frozen chicken is as good in flavour as chilled. Frozen chicken is available oven ready with the giblets in a little bag (usually placed in the cavity), halved or divided into portions.

How much to buy

Knowing how much to buy is always a problem with birds as their odd shape makes it hard to judge. Below is a quantity guideline for serving chicken plainly grilled. If the recipe you are using has several garnishes or a sauce, this amount can be decreased. All weights are for oven-ready birds (plucked and drawn, with head and feet removed) so, if buying fresh chicken, ask the butcher for a bird of whatever weight you require after drawing.

For two people you will need two poussins weighing 450 g [1 lb] each or one 700 g-1 kg [1½-2 lb] double poussin or spring chicken cut in half.

For four people choose a 1¼-1½ kg [2½-3½ lb] broiler and cut it into portions as shown in the step-by-step instructions.

For six people choose a 2.75-3.6 kg [6-8 lb] capon and cut it into joints as shown in the step-by-step instructions.

When serving chicken joints allow 1 large quarter or 1 breast or 2 drumsticks or 2 thighs per person. Wings are not really substantial enough to serve unless they are cut with a large portion of the breast attached, as shown in quartering chicken step-by-step.

STORING

Chicken, like all meat, is perishable and must be stored carefully to preserve goodness.

Fresh and farm-fresh chickens and portions

Remove butcher's wrapping and put the chicken on a plate. If the giblets are in a bag inside the bird, remove them. Cover the chicken lightly with greaseproof paper or kitchen foil to allow a little circulation of air and store in the coldest part of the refrigerator under the frozen food compartment. Whole birds will keep for 2-3 days, portions for a maximum of 36 hours. Alternatively, you can store whole birds in a cool larder for 1 day but never do this in warm weather as the flavour will go 'off' very quickly.

Chilled birds

Store the chicken in the polythene wrapping in which you bought it but loosen the wrapping a little to allow circulation of air and remove the giblets. Store in a refrigerator or larder, as for fresh or farm-fresh chickens.

Frozen birds

These must be placed in the freezer or the freezer compartment of a refrigerator as soon as you get them home. Store for up to 3 months, depending on the star rating of your refrigerator.

Cooked chicken

Cooked chicken joints are excellent picnic and packed lunch fare, but go 'off' very quickly so they must always be stored in a refrigerator and should be eaten within two days. If you plan to eat chicken cold, drain off any liquid immediately after cooking then cool the meat rapidly. As soon as the chicken is cold, wrap it loosely (in polythene, kitchen foil or shrink wrapping) to protect against drying out, to prevent infection and the transfer of food flavours. Refrigerate.

PREPARING

If you are planning to serve chicken joints, it is much cheaper to buy a whole bird and divide it up yourself. Although this might sound a daunting prospect, it is really very easy.

Equipment

To portion a chicken you will need a really sharp, large cook's knife. A good sharp knife will cut easily through bones and flesh. A blunt or serrated-edge knife should be avoided as it will tear the flesh.

If you find a knife awkward it may well be worth investing in a pair of poultry shears. These are large scissor-like implements with strong curved blades. A useful alternative to poultry shears, and especially good for cutting through chicken backbones, is a strong pair of kitchen scissors. The kind which are nicked at the bottom of the blades are best because they make cutting up poultry easier.

You will need a chopping board on which to stand the chicken.

Thawing

Before a frozen chicken can be cut into pieces, it must be thawed. For health reasons, it is most important to thaw chicken very thoroughly. Chickens contain tiny bacilli called salmonella. These are quite harmless when the chicken is cooked right through. If the chicken is not thawed

fully there will be a cold spot at the centre which will not cook quite as well as the rest of the bird. The bacilli remain active in this undercooked portion and, if eaten, can cause an attack of a particularly unpleasant and virulent form of food poisoning.

Frozen whole birds and portions sometimes come with thawing instructions and these should always be followed meticulously. When thawing chicken, leave it in the wrapping to avoid loss of juices.

The best place to thaw is in the refrigerator. When thawing a whole bird in the refrigerator, allow 5 hours per 450 g [1 lb] of chicken. This means a 1.4 kg [3 lb] chicken needs 15 hours to thaw properly. Portions will take about 6 hours. Chicken can be thawed at room temperature but this is a quicker process and is not quite so kind to the flavour of the bird as gradual thawing. When thawing at room temperature, allow 3 hours per 450 g [1 lb] of whole bird. Portions will need about 3 hours.

In an emergency, chicken thawing can be hastened by immersing the bird (still in its polythene wrapping) in cold water. This makes the flavour extremely bland and is not really advisable. Never immerse chicken in

hot water to speed thawing. It makes the flesh tough and does not thaw thoroughly.

Preparing for jointing
Before you start cutting up your chicken, make sure the giblets have been removed from inside.

To make cutting easier, it is a good idea to cut off the loose flap of skin at the neck end. Scissors are best for this job as the skin is rather awkward to cut with a knife.

You may also wish to remove the little oil sac situated above the parson's nose (the pointed end of the chicken where its tail feathers used to be). This little sac contains a rather strong oil which the chicken uses to lubricate its feathers. Some people feel it gives a fishy flavour. Removing the parson's nose itself is the subject of controversy. Some families have battles over who gets the parson's nose, while others regard it with horror, so this is very much a matter of personal taste.

There may be some little bits of feather left over after plucking. These are usually found on the legs and wings and are quite easily removed by pulling gently.

Removing the bony tips of the wings depends very much on what you are going to do with the chicken. If you are cutting large wing portions with a piece of breast attached, it is a good idea to leave the wing tips on as

Spatchcock chicken served with chips and garnished with lemon and watercress makes an appetizing main course.

they help to make a neat shape. Leave the tips on, too, if trussing a whole bird for spit roasting or grilling. The wing tips can always be cut off after cooking. Cutting off after cooking is quick to do as the bones become very soft.

On a fresh chicken, there may be a piece of yellow leg left on the end of the drumstick. Cut this off before starting preparation.

GRILLING CHICKEN
One of the joys of chicken is that, after cutting it into halves or portions, it needs very little else in the way of preparation before being grilled.

Advance preparation
Because chicken is a fairly dry meat, portions and halves must be brushed liberally inside and out with melted butter or olive oil before grilling. Cut surfaces of chicken are small and, unlike other meats, raw chicken does not bleed when salt is applied so seasoning can be done before cooking. This is in fact quite a good idea because salt crisps the skin.

Grilling
Because chicken is dry and delicately flavoured, grilling must be carried out under gentle heat throughout. This is achieved by positioning the grill pan 12-15 cm [5-6"] below the grill and setting the heat at about medium. There is no need to start grilling under fierce heat to seal the cut surfaces. This is because chicken is not red meat and, therefore, does not lose blood and juice as is the case in pork, lamb and beef. Also, cut surfaces with portions and halves are rather small.

Start grilling the chicken skin side down. Grill large portions and halves for 12-15 minutes, small portions for 8-12 minutes. Turn skin side up and grill large portions and halves for a further 10 minutes, small portions for 8 minutes. Baste with melted butter throughout cooking to prevent drying.

SPATCHCOCK CHICKEN
◰◰ *This is a very simple dish and, in order to ensure its success, be sure to use a fresh, plump double poussin.*

Although it is usual to start grilling the chicken skin side down, here the order is reversed and the chicken is

Step-by-step to chicken portions

1 Lay the chicken on a board. Cut off the oil sac and the parson's nose if wished. Then cut off the loose skin at the neck.

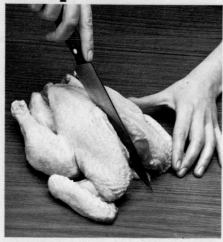

2 To halve the chicken, cut through and along the breastbone. The breastbone is very soft, so a sharp knife will do this easily.

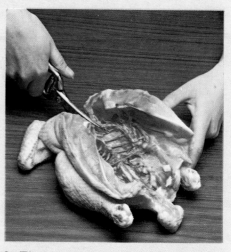

3 Then cut through the backbone. If the backbone is too hard to cut with a sharp knife, use poultry shears or kitchen scissors.

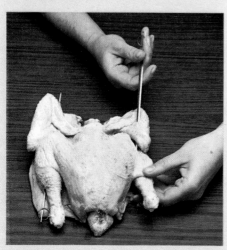

5 Now run a sharp, straight skewer through the leg and the fleshy part of the wing at one side. Repeat at other side.

6 To make chicken quarters, first cut the chicken in half. Lay the halves skin side up and cut diagonally between the leg and wing.

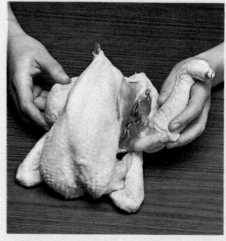

7 To joint a large chicken, first cut the leg away from the body. Pull the leg towards you so that the joint is exposed.

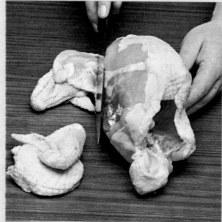

10 Cut through the joint to sever the wing and fold it into a neat shape with the attached breast meat tucked underneath.

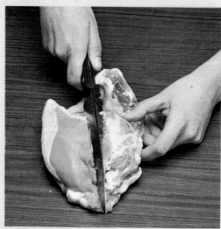

11 To remove the whole breast, first separate from the back by cutting through the rib bones along the side of the body.

12 Cut down the centre of the breastbone to divide the breast into 2. Large breasts may be divided again to make 4 portions.

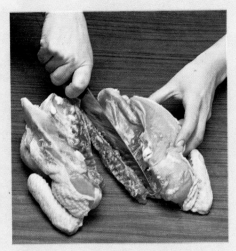

OR to remove the backbone completely, cut along each side of it with a sharp knife and then lift out. Save for stockmaking.

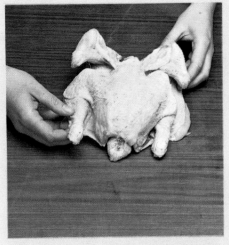

4 To spatchcock a chicken, first cut it in half through the backbone and open it out so that it lies flat on the board.

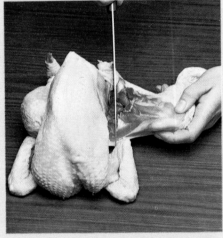

8 Now cut through the pink, moist part of this 'ball and socket' joint. Cut off the other leg. Set the two severed legs aside.

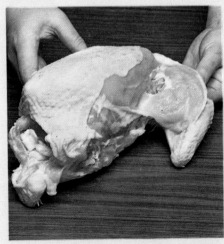

9 To remove the wing, first slice into the white breast meat to make a better portion. Pull the wings away to expose the joint.

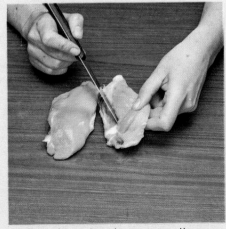

13 To skin the breast, pull away gently. To bone, insert a knife between rib bones and flesh and cut away gently. Save for stock.

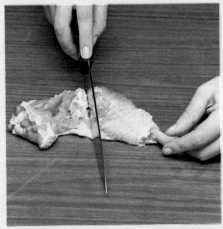

14 Large legs may be divided into thighs and drumsticks by cutting through the centre ball and socket joint.

grilled skin side up, turned skin side down and then, to finish, skin side up again. This last stage is to brown the breadcrumb mixture.

SERVES 2
1 double poussin, about 700 g [1½ lb] in weight
salt and pepper
half a lemon
50 g [2 oz] butter
25 g [1 oz] grated Parmesan cheese
1 thick slice two-day-old white bread

For the garnish:
2 lemon quarters
1 small packet straw potatoes
bunch of watercress

1 Cut off the leg shanks, parson's nose and loose neck skin.

2 Cut the chicken open right along the backbone.

3 Open the bird and press it flat.

4 Secure the bird by running a fine skewer through from the lower thigh to the wing on each side.

5 Rub the chicken with the cut lemon, season with salt and pepper and leave for 30 minutes in a cool place.

6 Heat the grill to medium. Melt the butter in a small pan.

7 Brush the chicken all over with melted butter.

8 Place the bird skin side up on the grid. Grill 12 cm [5"] below the heat for 8-10 minutes. Brush with more butter once during this time.

9 Turn the chicken over and grill the cut side for 10-12 minutes, basting it during this time.

10 Meanwhile, remove crust from bread and grate the bread on a grater over a plate (or use a liquidizer) to make 15 g [½ oz] fine crumbs.

11 Mix the breadcrumbs and the Parmesan cheese together.

12 Turn over the chicken again and sprinkle the skin evenly with the breadcrumb mixture.

Milanese chicken consists of boned chicken breasts topped with ham and tomatoes.

13 Dribble remaining melted butter from the saucepan (or spoon it from the grill pan base) over the crumbs, moistening them as evenly as possible.

14 Grill for a further 5-10 minutes until crisp and golden. Run a skewer into the thickest part of the chicken to see that juices run clear. If juices are clear the chicken is cooked. Pink juices indicate that further grilling is required.

15 Remove skewers and serve garnished with warm straw potatoes, wedges of lemon and watercress.

MILANESE CHICKEN

This is an excellent dish for a dinner party. Once the preliminary cooking is done the dish continues cooking in a very low oven until you are ready for it.

You can buy 2 chickens and cut the breasts off them (each chicken will give 2 portions) and save the rest of the meat for another dish. Alternatively, you can buy 4 portions of breast meat—the butcher will normally sell frozen portions.

SERVES 4
4 chicken breasts
4 slices cooked ham
salt
2 medium-sized tomatoes
40 g [1½ oz] grated Parmesan cheese

For the marinade:
30 ml [2 tablespoons] oil
30 ml [2 tablespoons] lemon juice
5 ml [1 teaspoon] salt
freshly ground black pepper

1 Work a sharp knife along the bones to loosen and then pull the meat away by hand so that the breasts are boneless. Remove all the skin and any attached fat.

2 Lay the breasts flat, in a single layer and a small space apart, between 2 sheets of greaseproof paper. Beat hard with a rolling pin to flatten the meat.

3 Mix all the ingredients for the marinade and pour into a shallow,

174

flame-proof dish large enough to hold the chicken pieces flat in a single layer.

4 Put in the chicken breasts, turn in the marinade, cover the dish and leave in a cool place for 2 hours.

5 One hour before serving time, heat the grill. Heat the oven to 150°C [300°F] gas mark 2.

6 Uncover the chicken and put the flame-proof dish 12 cm [5"] below the grill. Grill each side 5 minutes.

7 Meanwhile, plunge the tomatoes into boiling water for 1 minute, drain and refresh under cold water, then peel away the skins. Cut each tomato into 4 slices.

8 Remove chicken from under grill. Arrange a slice of ham on top of each of the chicken breasts. Top each with 2 tomato slices. Sprinkle on half of the Parmesan cheese and then cover the dish with foil.

9 Transfer to the oven and leave for 30-40 minutes. (They won't spoil at this low temperature if left a little longer.)

10 Five minutes before serving, heat the grill. Remove the dish from the oven, take off the foil, sprinkle the tops of the tomatoes with remaining Parmesan cheese and brown quickly under the grill.

11 Serve immediately.

DEVILLED CHICKEN DELMONICO

Frozen chicken quarters can be used for this dish as the spicy devilled sauce will keep the joints moist and enhance the flavour. The chicken must be completely thawed before cooking, of course, so allow adequate time for this if using frozen chicken quarters. Cooking is finished in the oven so it is a useful dish when you are entertaining. Served cold, it makes a piquant picnic meal.

SERVES 4
1 kg [2½ lb] chicken or 4 chicken portions
3 slices of two-day-old bread

For the devil spread:
65 g [2½ oz] butter
5 ml [1 teaspoon] mustard powder
10 ml [2 teaspoons] curry powder
10 ml [2 teaspoons] caster sugar
2.5 ml [½ teaspoon] salt
2.5 ml [½ teaspoon] paprika
5 ml [1 teaspoon] Worcestershire sauce

1 If using a whole chicken, halve it by cutting along the breastbone. Open the chicken and cut along the backbone. Remove the backbone and cut the chicken into quarters.

2 Turn the wing tips under and run a fine skewer through the leg and backbone to hold the joints flat while cooking.

3 Prepare the devil spread by melting the butter in a small pan over low heat. Stir in the remaining ingredients.

4 Heat the grill to medium heat and warm the oven to 180°C [350°F] gas mark 4.

5 Brush the chicken pieces on both sides with half the devil mixture. Lay the pieces skin side down and side by side in a shallow flame-proof dish.

6 Place the chicken dish 12 cm [5"] below the heat and grill for 5 minutes on each side.

7 Meanwhile, remove crusts from the bread and reduce to crumbs on a grater or in a liquidizer to make 50 g [2 oz] fine crumbs.

8 Re-heat the devilled mixture remaining in the saucepan. Add the crumbs, remove from heat and stir until crumbs have absorbed the liquid.

9 Spoon the crumbs evenly over the chicken pieces and transfer the dish to the centre of the oven.

10 Cook for 30 minutes. Serve hot or cold.

CHICKEN IN SPICY TOMATO SAUCE

This is the type of dish that soon becomes a family favourite. It is colourful, tasty and simple—suited to fresh or frozen chicken joints.

SERVES 4
4 chicken portions
50 g [2 oz] butter

For the sauce:
60 ml [4 tablespoons] tomato ketchup
15 ml [1 tablespoon] finely grated onion
30 ml [2 tablespoons] water
30 ml [2 tablespoons] wine vinegar
10 ml [2 teaspoons] soft brown sugar
2.5 ml [½ teaspoon] mustard powder
2.5 ml [½ teaspoon] salt

For the garnish:
bunch of watercress

1 Heat the grill to medium heat.

2 Melt the butter in a small sauce-pan. Brush the chicken joints all over with butter.

3 Remove the grid from the grill pan and arrange the chicken pieces, skin side down and side by side, in the bottom of the grill pan, or in a large flame-proof gratin dish.

4 Grill the chicken 12 cm [5"] away from the heat for 5 minutes. Turn the chicken over and grill for another 5 minutes.

5 Meanwhile, grate the onion over a plate to catch the juice.

6 Put the onion into the saucepan containing the remaining melted butter. Stir in the other sauce ingredients and simmer for 5 minutes.

7 Brush the chicken with the sauce and continue grilling under moderate heat, turning and brushing with more sauce every 5 minutes until the chicken is cooked right through, a total of 30 minutes.

8 If the grill pan was used, turn the chicken pieces on to a hot serving dish and spoon the sauce on top. Garnish with watercress.

COUNTRY-STYLE CHICKEN

This is a simple but attractive way of cooking chicken. Fresh chicken is recommended. Use a whole chicken and divide it into portions yourself (it's probably cheaper too) but if you are in a hurry you can buy chicken joints. If you buy fresh chicken joints on your way home you can have this dish ready to eat within 45 minutes of arriving in the kitchen. The skewers are run through the chicken to prevent the joints 'flying akimbo' during grilling, in which case some parts would be cooked before others as they would be closer to the heat.

SERVES 4
1 kg [2½ lb] chicken
1 large lemon
75 g [3 oz] butter
salt
freshly ground black pepper
4 large rashers of streaky bacon
225 g [½ lb] button mushrooms

For the garnish:
bunch of watercress

1 Heat the grill to medium heat.

2 Divide the chicken into halves by cutting along the breastbone. Open the chicken and cut along the backbone. Cut the chicken into quarters.

3 Run a small skewer through each leg and out by the backbone. Tuck the wing tips under.

4 Rub the chicken with the cut lemon, squeezing the lemon to release plenty of juice as you do so.

5 Melt the butter in a small pan and brush generously all over both sides of the chicken.

6 Sprinkle both sides of the chicken liberally with salt and lightly with pepper.

7 Lay the joints skin side down in the grill pan with the grid removed.

8 Place the chicken 12 cm [5"] below the grill and cook for 12-15 minutes.

9 Meanwhile, de-rind the bacon and cut each rasher in half crossways. Roll up and secure each piece with a cocktail stick.

10 Remove earthy ends, wipe but do not peel the mushrooms and brush over with some of the butter.

11 Turn the chicken skin side up, brush with remaining melted butter, or baste with the grill pan juices, and continue grilling for 5 minutes.

12 Add the bacon rolls and mushrooms around the chicken under the grill. Baste with the pan juices.

13 Continue grilling and lower the heat if the chicken shows signs of overbrowning. Turn the bacon and mushrooms to cook them on both sides, basting them as you do so.

14 Cook until the chicken's skin is brown and crisp and the bacon and mushrooms are ready.

15 Arrange the cooked chicken on a serving dish. Arrange the bacon and mushrooms around it and pour over any remaining lemon juice and the juices from the grill pan. Garnish with the watercress and serve immediately.

Variations

● For almond chicken, omit the bacon and mushrooms and instead fry 40 g [1½ oz] flaked almonds in a little butter for 1 minute until golden brown. Do this just before serving the chicken. Use medium heat and shake the pan to turn the nuts frequently to prevent burning. Add the lemon juice and pour over the grilled chicken. Serve immediately.

● For pineapple chipolata, omit the bacon and mushrooms. Brush 4 pineapple rings with butter and grill until golden. Grill 4 chipolata sausages at the same time and thread them through the pineapple rings for the garnish. Arrange on top of the grilled chicken in the serving dish.

BROILED CHICKEN WITH LEMON BARBECUE SAUCE

Here is an American recipe which gives the chicken an unusual flavour. You need to start preparations a couple of hours ahead to give the chicken time to marinate in the sauce. Fresh chicken is best for this recipe but you could use frozen chicken because the marinade will add flavour. (Broiled is the American word for grilled.)

SERVES 4
4 chicken portions

For the marinade:
1 garlic clove
5 ml [1 teaspoon] salt
2.5 ml [½ teaspoon] freshly ground black pepper
45 ml [3 tablespoons] oil
45 ml [3 tablespoons] lemon juice
bay leaf

For the garnish:
watercress sprigs
1 lemon

1 Peel and slice the garlic clove and crush with salt under the blade of a knife.

2 Put the garlic into an earthenware or glass dish, add all the other ingredients for the marinade and stir well.

3 Put the chicken pieces in the marinade and spoon the marinade over the chicken. Cover and leave in a cool place for at least 2 hours.

4 Heat the grill to medium heat.

5 Place the chicken pieces skin side down in the grill pan. Cook 12 cm [5"] away from the heat for 15 minutes, basting frequently with

1 *Chicken with lemon barbecue sauce.* **2** *Country-style chicken is served with bacon and mushrooms.* **3** *Substitute pineapple and chipolata sausages for the bacon and mushrooms for an attractive variation.*

the remaining lemon marinade.

6 Turn the chicken skin side up and grill for 10 minutes, basting fre-

quently with the lemon marinade.

7 Test the chicken by piercing it with a fine skewer to see that the juices run clear. If the chicken shows signs of overbrowning, turn the heat down. The skin should be crisp when the chicken is cooked.

8 Serve on a hot dish and garnish with lemon quarters and cress.

177

TANDOORI-STYLE CHICKEN

▨▨▨ *Frozen chicken can be used for this spicy chicken dish as it is marinated overnight in a yoghurt mixture which tenderizes and flavours the meat. A smaller chicken can be used if it is fresh—the weight given here allows for loss of weight due to thawing and skinning.*

If you like a hot dish add 5 ml [¼ teaspoon] chilli powder to the marinade. Powdered ginger is no sub-stitute for fresh root ginger and it is not suitable for this recipe. Fresh root ginger is sometimes available from vegetable markets and always from Indian food shops. Sesame, cumin and coriander seeds, rather than the powdered varieties, are used because the crushed seeds are far more aromatic than powders.

Traditionally, tandoori chicken is red so you can use a few drops of food colouring or spoonfuls of tomato purée to colour the chicken.

SERVES 4
1.6 kg [3½ lb] chicken or 4 chicken portions
salt and pepper
30 ml [2 tablespoons] butter
15 ml [1 tablespoon] lemon juice

For the marinade:
40 g [1½ oz] fresh ginger
2 garlic cloves
125 ml [4 fl oz] yoghurt
5 ml [1 teaspoon] sesame seeds

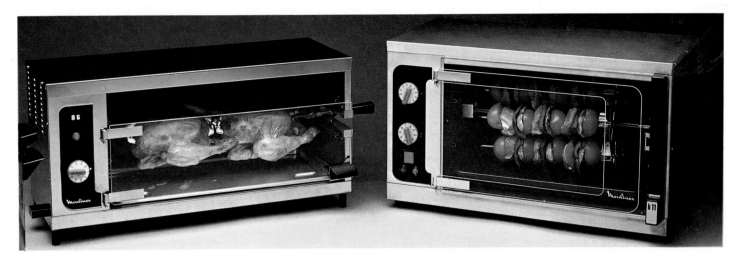

Rôtisseries are useful for controlled and even grilling whether for succulent whole chickens or exotic kebabs.

5 ml [1 teaspoon] coriander seeds
5 ml [1 teaspoon] cumin seeds
2.5 ml [½ teaspoon] red food colouring or 30 ml [2 tablespoons] tomato purée

For the garnish:
2 lemons
fresh coriander leaves or watercress

1 Peel and chop the ginger and garlic into very small pieces.

2 Crush the seeds in a mortar with a pestle or with a rolling pin in a small plastic bag.

3 Mix together the yoghurt, sesame, coriander and cumin seeds, ginger, garlic and red colouring or tomato purée.

4 If using a whole chicken, halve it by cutting along the breastbone. Open the chicken and cut along the backbone. Remove the backbone and cut the chicken into quarters.

5 Remove the skin and fat from the chicken portions and, using a sharp knife, make 3 or 4 incisions in the flesh of each portion.

6 Place the chicken pieces in a glass or earthenware dish and spoon the

If using frozen chicken for Tandoori-style chicken allow for weight loss due to defrosting and skinning.

marinade over. Cover and leave for 8 hours, turning occasionally and spooning over the marinade.

7 Heat the grill to medium heat.

8 Remove chicken from marinade and season with salt and pepper.

9 Remove grid and place chicken pieces in the grill pan with the bony side upwards. Pour over the lemon juice, dot with butter and grill 12 cm [5"] away from heat for 12 minutes, basting it two or three times during this time.

10 Turn over the pieces, baste with the pan juices and grill for 8 minutes, again basting the chicken two or three times. Test with a skewer to see that meat is cooked and tender.

11 Place on a warm serving dish. Garnish with coriander leaves and the lemons cut into wedges and serve. Use cress if no coriander.

ROTISSERIES

In rôtisserie cooking the meat is fixed to a spit which is either a long skewer-like pin which goes right through and out the other side or a pair of long 'forks' to grip the meat from either side. This spit is attached at both ends to a framework and is turned automatically. Heat may be from below or above according to the model used. The meat is then revolved slowly so that each side is in turn exposed directly for cooking. The big advantage of spit roasting or grilling is that all sides are quickly seared to seal in the natural juices. On a conventional grill you must hand-turn the meat several times to

just seal, and then cook it. The meat then continues to cook evenly without burning on any one side.

Lean meat should be lightly brushed with melted butter or oil, after fixing to the spit, to ensure that the outside does not brown too quickly. The meat needs no further basting because as it rolls the fat is distributed over the surface. Flavourings, such as herbs, in the cavity of a chicken are also distributed. It is an ideal method for cooking fatty meat if the heat is on top, as all excess fat drips away.

Most rôtisserie models come with a choice of spits. A single spit may be used with a chicken trussed as for roasting—or even two chickens with larger models. Several small game birds can be spit-roasted in a row, or boned and rolled roast meat. Some models have revolving baskets. Several spits can be used simultaneously to cook kebabs.

Barbecues burning both charcoal and gas are available with automatic spits fitted to them. Meat thus cooked is really grilled. Rôtisserie cooking is, in effect, a modern method of spit roasting—the ancient way of cooking meat over an open fire.

Electric models are available and these have heating elements at the top. Because there is a door which is shut, creating an enclosed, heated space, meat cooked in these is as much roasted as grilled. They have the advantage of a time switch, so there is no risk of the meat overcooking if you forget it. Without the spits they can also be used as small ovens—they heat quickly and are economical on electricity—or instead of a conventional grill for browning dishes finished off with cheese, breadcrumbs and other gratin toppings.

Chicken

roasting

A good cook will roast a chicken so that it has a golden crisp skin and juicy flesh—a simple but real treat. To get these perfect results requires time and care. Because chicken meat is dry thoughtless roasting can easily reduce it to a tasteless, sawdusty texture. This chapter describes the preparation, stuffing and roasting needed to produce a golden, succulent chicken and shows you how to carve economically.

CHOOSING CHICKEN FOR ROASTING

There's an old saying 'choose the bird that roosts next to the cockerel', and although it is no longer possible to follow this sage advice literally, we can still pick out the plumpest bird, which is the one the cockerel would have singled out! Other signs of youth, such as a pliable tip to the breastbone and a thin skin, are no longer relevant as all chickens sold for roasting are under three months old.

Since chicken meat is lean, it is worth looking for a bird with a thin layer of fat beneath the skin. This fat helps to keep the bird succulent when cooking. You will only find it on larger birds.

All types and sizes of chicken (as described in the previous chapter) are sufficiently young and tender to roast. The only bird you cannot roast is one labelled 'boiling fowl'. This is usually an old and fairly tough bird that has reached the end of its useful life as an egg producer.

Capon

This is a young cockerel treated by injection and then specially fattened for the table. Very few capons are reared nowadays so you may have difficulty finding one. Capons weigh between 2-3.6 kg [4½-8 lb] which is ideal when cooking for a large number of people. Prepare and cook the capon in the same way as a chicken, with the same stuffings and sauces.

INITIAL PREPARATION

Chicken is perishable and must therefore be stored carefully. Remove the butcher's wrapping and put the chicken on a plate. If the giblets are in a bag inside the bird, remove them and store separately. Cover the chicken only lightly with greaseproof

paper or kitchen foil, to allow a little circulation of air. Store it in the coldest part of the refrigerator at the top under the ice compartment.

It is most important to thaw frozen birds before cooking (see previous chapter), otherwise the centre may still be raw at the end of cooking time. Fresh or defrosted chickens should be removed from the refrigerator three quarters of an hour before cooking to bring the meat to room temperature. If the chicken is put into the oven straight from the refrigerator because of some emergency, allow an extra 20-30 minutes cooking time.

Most poultry is sold ready for cooking. But there are some preparations specific to roasting chicken which are as necessary to successful appearance and taste as actual roasting.

Look carefully at the bird's skin. If there are any unsightly stubbles where the bases of the feathers are still sticking in the skin remove them. Raise the skin at the point where the stubble occurs and grasp each stubble in turn between your thumb and a round-bladed knife, and tug sharply.

Rinse out the bird's body cavity by holding the tail end under a running tap. Lift the skin of the neck flap, so water runs through the bird. Drain the chicken thoroughly. Then pat dry inside and outside with kitchen paper. This is very important because if the chicken is left wet it will not acquire an attractively brown skin in the oven.

Season the inside of the bird. This is most important as flavours permeate more readily through the inner cavity walls than through the exterior skin.

Stand the bird up and grind salt and pepper into the body cavity through the tail end. You can use salt as well as pepper because there are no cut surfaces to bleed if salted. Chicken, being a white meat, can be salted before cooking.

It is a good idea to insert a moisture-creating ingredient, such as an apple, onion or lemon, inside the bird, as well as flavourings such as herbs or spices and garlic. A dessert apple, onion or lemon also adds a subtle flavour, and gives off juice as it cooks, which helps to keep this lean meat succulent and prevents it from drying out. Discard these additions before serving.

Step-by-step to stuffing a chicken

1 Stand bird up with its back to you. Open neck by holding skin back against the breast. Loosely pack the stuffing under the neck skin.

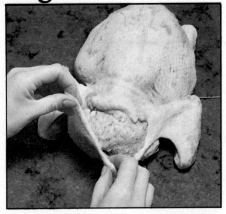

2 When the bird looks plump without being stretched, lay it breast side down. Fold neck skin over the back to enclose stuffing.

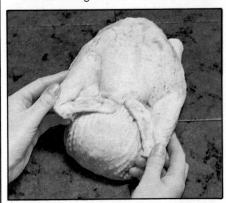

3 The neck skin is secured and held in position on the back of the bird by folding the wing tips over it on each side.

OR fasten the skin 'stitching' it to the back of the chicken with a small poultry skewer (which is removed when serving).

A walnut-sized piece of butter mashed together with salt, pepper and herbs is a valuable addition to the body cavity. The buttery juices can be used for the gravy at the end of cooking.

NON-STUFFY STUFFINGS

Stuffing the bird is another way of adding both moisture and flavour to the meat. A well-chosen stuffing can be the making of a simple roast chicken. It is also economical because it makes the meal more substantial.

Choose ingredients that will provide a stimulating contrast in flavour and texture. Stuffing can add the richness that lean poultry meat lacks. Mild bacon; bacon fat, butter, minced pork and pork sausage meat are all very suitable ingredients for stuffings.

Another important function of a stuffing is to help maintain the bird's moisture by generating steam during cooking. For this reason, stuffings themselves need to be fairly moist and should not be packed tightly but loosely into the neck end of the bird. Avoid stuffing the body cavity as this obstructs the circulation of heat (if you do increase the cooking time).

Although stuffings can be made the day before and refrigerated, they should not be put into the bird until shortly before cooking. The stuffing must be cold, or at least cool, when put into the bird. The quantities given in the recipes are sufficient for stuffing a 1.4-1.8 kg [3-4 lb] chicken. If there is too much stuffing for the neck cavity, the remainder can be cooked separately in a small covered dish on the shelf beneath the bird for the last 30-40 minutes of roasting time.

APRICOT AND HAZELNUT STUFFING

This is an unusual stuffing made with fruit and nuts. Allow the stuffing to cool before inserting it into the bird.

STUFFS 1.4-1.8 KG [3-4 LB]
CHICKEN
75 g [3 oz] dried apricots
50 g [2 oz] onion
1 celery stick
40 g [1½ oz] butter
25 g [1 oz] shelled hazelnuts
50 g [2 oz] white bread
2.5 ml [½ teaspoon] finely grated lemon zest
salt
freshly ground black pepper

1 Put the apricots in a bowl and pour over enough boiling water to just cover. Leave to stand while preparing the other ingredients.

2 Peel and finely chop the onion. Wash and chop the celery.

3 Melt the butter in a medium-sized saucepan. Gently fry the onion and celery until soft, but not brown.

4 Meanwhile roughly chop the hazelnuts. Drain and chop the apricots, reserving the liquid.

5 Make the breadcrumbs by grating on a coarse grater. With the pan off the heat add the crumbs to the pan. Add hazelnuts, apricots and lemon zest, with salt and pepper to taste.

6 Mix thoroughly. The apricots should provide enough moisture to bind the stuffing loosely. If the mixture seems too dry to bind, add a little of the water in which the apricots were soaked.

SAUSAGE MEAT AND APPLE STUFFING

This is a quick stuffing to make and must be used immediately before the apple has time to discolour.

STUFFS 1.4-1.8 KG [3-4 LB]
CHICKEN
1 cooking apple
225 g [8 oz] pork sausage meat
10 ml [2 teaspoons] dried herbs
salt and black pepper

1 Peel, core and chop the apple.

2 Put the sausage meat, herbs and seasoning into a bowl. Add the apple and mix thoroughly.

3 Use the stuffing for the neck cavity of a bird or cook in a dish underneath the roast for 30-40 minutes.

THREE HERBS STUFFING

This is a traditional parsley and lemon-flavoured stuffing with the addition of marjoram to give it an interesting new flavour. The stuffing should be crumbly in texture and very green.

STUFFS 1.4-1.8 KG [3-4 LB]
CHICKEN
45 ml [3 tablespoons] fresh parsley leaves
15 ml [1 tablespoon] fresh marjoram leaves or 5 ml [1 teaspoon] dried marjoram
5 ml [1 teaspoon] fresh lemon thyme leaves or 1.5 ml [¼ teaspoon] dried thyme
1.5 ml [¼ teaspoon] grated lemon zest.
50 g [2 oz] white bread
40 g [1½ oz] butter
salt and pepper

1 Finely chop all the fresh herbs.

2 Make the breadcrumbs by grating on a coarse grater.

3 Melt the butter in a small saucepan.

4 With the pan off the heat, stir the breadcrumbs and herbs into the butter and season to taste.

BACON AND CELERY STUFFING

This stuffing uses the chicken liver that comes with the bird. The stuffing is cooked first so allow it to cool before using it.

STUFFS 1.4-1.8 KG [3-4 LB]
CHICKEN
2 rashers smoked streaky bacon
2 small celery sticks
40 g [1½ oz] butter
1 chicken liver
50 g [2 oz] white bread
salt and pepper to taste

1 Remove the bacon rinds and cut the bacon rashers into pieces.

2 Wash the celery, split the sticks lengthways into 2 (or 3 pieces if broad). Cut into 1.2 cm [½"] dice.

3 Melt the butter in a small saucepan. Add the bacon and celery and fry, covered, for 5 minutes.

4 Wash and then blot the liver with kitchen paper. Remove any stringy parts. Chop and add to the pan.

5 Stir in the breadcrumbs and season to taste.

6 Allow the stuffing to cool then stuff into neck cavity of a chicken.

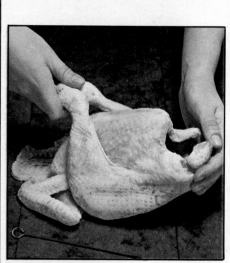

1 Laying the bird on its back lift the legs and pull them back towards the neck.

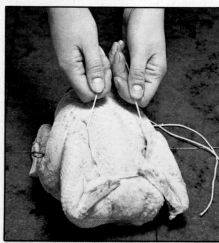

5 Cut a long piece of thin string and centre it, whilst placing it under the wings.

TRUSSING A CHICKEN

These days chickens and capons are usually sold drawn and trussed ready for the oven. Sometimes, however, you may need to truss a bird at home, or retruss one after stuffing it. The purpose of trussing is simply to hold the bird in a compact shape during cooking, so that it browns evenly and looks attractive when served. The joints of an untrussed bird would spread out in the oven and be very untidy. Parts like wing tips may also burn.

Trussing after stuffing is done either with a trussing needle, threaded with fine string, or very simply with a skewer and string as shown in detail in the step-by-step pictures below.

PRECAUTIONS AGAINST DRYING OUT

Chicken is a very lean meat and precautions both before and during roasting are essential to prevent it from drying out. The breast meat is especially susceptible to drying as it has no natural fat and, being at the top of the chicken, is more exposed to the heat.

The most usual precaution is to bard the breast. The breast is completely covered with thin rashers of mild fatty bacon, such as streaky, which are laid across it covering the top of the drumsticks as well. The barding bacon is removed just before the end of cooking to allow the breast to brown before serving. The bacon may be reserved and crumbled into

the gravy if you wish.

Another method is to cover the breast loosely with a double thickness of well-buttered greaseproof paper, a butter wrapper, or buttered foil. The paper is discarded 20 minutes before the cooking time is up. The chicken should be painted all over with a generous coating of oil or softened butter.

A method much practised in France, is to rub the bird all over with softened butter and to roast it breast downwards for the major part of cooking time. This method encourages the juices to run down into the breast meat and keeps it beautifully succulent. The bird is then reversed, breast upwards, for the last 20 minutes of cooking. Baste it

Step-by-step to trussing a chicken

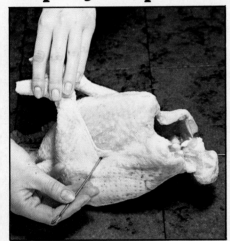

2 Pass a metal skewer through the body meat, inserting it in the angle of the thigh and drumstick.

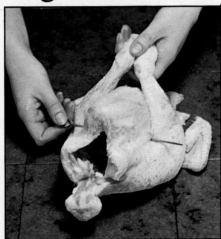

3 Push the skewer through the bird so that it emerges in the corresponding place on the other side.

4 Turn bird on to its breast. Fold the wing tips across the back to hold the neck skin in position.

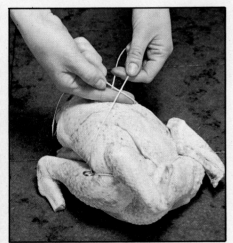

6 Draw the ends of string under, up and over the skewer ends then cross them over the bird's back.

7 Turn the bird on to its back. Twist the string around the leg ends then under the parson's nose.

8 Tie the two ends of the string securely so that the legs and tail are firmly held together.

thoroughly to allow the skin to brown. Baste again after 10 minutes and complete cooking time. The chicken should be succulent and tender.

CAREFUL ROASTING

The following simple rules will help you achieve a successful roast—crisp and golden outside, succulent within.

Always heat the oven so that it is at the required temperature when the bird is put into it. A fairly hot oven, 190°C[375°F] gas mark 5 is effective and economical for a small bird. A slightly lower temperature of 180°C [350°F] gas mark 4 is used for a larger bird to ensure that it is cooked all the way through. If the body cavity is stuffed, allow an extra 20-30 minutes.

For a crisp skin, rub salt all over with your fingers, working it well into the cracks. The oil or butter may then be painted on with a brush afterwards.

Unless roasting in the French way, place the chicken on a rack, breast side upwards. There is no need to put fat in the tin unless the giblets are used. If bacon is used for barding, this will make a certain amount of fat. The moisturizing ingredients inside the bird, whether butter or fruit or vegetable, will also make a certain amount of juice. This can be used for basting the bird in the last 20 minutes to ensure a crisp, golden skin.

If the breast is to be covered by foil or paper, this must be well-buttered with 15 g [½ oz] of butter or margarine. It is wise also to put a little butter inside the bird to create enough fat for basting. Baste two or three times during the last 20 minutes when the chicken is uncovered.

The French method

This method of roasting uses more fat and gives the chicken a crisp golden skin all over in much the same fashion as a rôtisserie-cooked chicken. It takes longer than the English method of roasting given above, because frequent basting and turning of the bird are necessary.

Butter is always inserted in the bird's cavity after seasoning. Herbs may also be added, the most common one being tarragon. The outside of the bird is rubbed over with salt and pepper and then generously brushed all over with a mixture of butter and oil or butter and lemon juice.

CHICKEN ROASTING TIMES
Times for cooking fully thawed, room-temperature birds, stuffed at the neck end only.*

oven-ready weight	number of servings	oven temperature	cooking time
1 kg [2 lb]	2-3	190°C [375°F] gas mark 5	1 hour
1.4 kg [3 lb]	4	190°C [375°F] gas mark 5	1 hr 20 mins
1.8 kg [4 lb]	5-6	190°C [375°F] gas mark 5	1 hr 40 mins
2.25 kg [5 lb]	7-8	190°C [375°F] gas mark 5	2 hours
2.7 kg [6 lb]	8-9	180°C [350°F] gas mark 4	2 hrs 15 mins
3.2 kg [7 lb]	10	180°C [350°F] gas mark 4	2 hrs 30 mins
3.6 kg [8 lb]	12	180°C [350°F] gas mark 4	2 hrs 45 mins

*If the body cavity contains stuffing, allow an extra 20-30 minutes cooking time.

THE GIBLETS

The giblets contribute a considerable amount of flavour to a chicken and should never be discarded. They consist of the neck, gizzard, heart and liver. When you buy an oven-ready bird the giblets are usually wrapped separately and tucked inside the body cavity. As soon as you get a fresh bird home or, if frozen, as soon as it has thawed, remove the giblets from their wrapping and wash them under the cold tap. Check that the liver is free of gall. Look for any area that is stained green and cut away and discard it as gall is very bitter. Remove any thick yellow skin remaining on the gizzard.

● Make stock from the giblets. Put all the washed giblets except the liver, into a small saucepan. Add a slice or two of onion, carrot and celery, a small bay leaf, 3 peppercorns, 1.5 ml [¼ teaspoon] salt, and 250 ml [½ pt] of water. Bring to the boil, cover, and simmer for 30 minutes. Cool, strain and use the stock for the gravy.

● Add the cooked heart, gizzard and neck meat, all finely chopped, to the stuffing.
● Cook the washed giblets, excepting the liver, in the roasting tin beneath the chicken. You will need to add 15 ml [1 tablespoon] of fat to the roasting tin. This is a simple way of ensuring that their flavour will enrich the gravy.
● The raw liver can be chopped and added to the stuffing or roasted beside the bird for the last 15 minutes of cooking time. Remember to baste it well. It can also be used to make liver and bacon rolls.
● If you can't use the giblets immediately, freeze them until you have collected enough to make a rich giblet soup.
● Cooked chicken carcasses can be frozen for making stock later, but be sure to freeze them promptly while they are still fresh.
● Freeze the livers separately so they can be used for a special omelette filling or for making a pâté.

The chicken is not placed upon a rack or trivet but laid in the pan on one side of its breast. Be sure that the thigh in the highest position is well buttered. After 25 minutes the chicken is turned on to the other breast. Baste all the upper surface thoroughly with the pan juices. Finally after 25 minutes, the chicken is turned on to its back and the breast is thoroughly basted for browning.

To test when a chicken is cooked

Undercooked chicken is slimy and unpleasant to eat, pink at the thickest part round the thigh joints and it gives off a pink juice when pierced. It can also be a health hazard. It is important to cook chicken thoroughly, until a meat thermometer inserted into the fleshiest part of the thigh registers 80-82°C [175-180°F].

Step-by-step to roasting chicken

1 Remove the bird from refrigerator to reach room temperature. Weigh and calculate the cooking time.

2 Sprinkle cavity liberally with salt and black pepper. Insert stuffing or moisturizing ingredients.

3 Place chicken, breast upwards, on a rack or trivet in a roasting tin. The juices drain into the tin.

4 Bard or cover the chicken breast and thigh tops with thin rashers of bacon. Roast the chicken.

5 Remove and discard bacon 20 minutes before cooking ends, so that the skin can crisp.

6 Baste the chicken with the pan juices two or three times to moisten and help crisp the skin.

7 Test the chicken by piercing it with a skewer. If the juices run clear the chicken is ready.

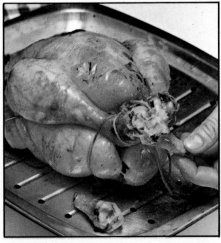

8 Twist the leg shanks to remove them. Remove any trussing string and the skewers if present.

9 As you lift the bird to transfer it, tilt it so that the juices run from the tail end into the pan.

An alternative reliable test is to pierce the chicken deeply in the thigh with a skewer and note the colour of the juices that run from it. When fully cooked the juices will be colourless or yellowish. If they are pink, return the roast to the oven and continue cooking a little longer before testing again.

Dishing up

Choose a serving dish large enough to accommodate the chicken and any garnishes such as bacon rolls, chipolatas or watercress. There should also be plenty of room for the chicken joints as the carver separates them from the carcass. It makes carving more difficult if the plate is crowded.

As you lift the bird to place it on the warmed serving dish, tilt the tail end (the end with the parson's nose) downward for a few seconds. The juices in the body of the bird will then drain into the roasting pan and improve the gravy.

Always leave the chicken to rest for ten minutes before carving, to allow the meat to set. This also gives you time to make the gravy.

Cut the trussing string and pull away from the bird. Remove the skewer if there is one. Using a piece of kitchen paper to keep your fingers clean, twist off the leg shanks, which are inedible and unsightly. Before serving, if you wish, you can use a cutlet frill to cover the ends of the legs, but this is not essential.

Cooked garnishes are then arranged round the dish. Salad garnishes must be added at the very last moment before serving.

CARVING A CHICKEN OR CAPON

It is easy to make a professional job of carving a chicken or capon. The flesh is very tender, and, once you have mastered the art of finding and severing the ball and socket thigh joint, there are no real problems.

Step-by-step to carving a large chicken

1 Drive the fork into the bird to hold it firmly and carve off the right leg and thigh.

2 Holding the knuckle joint, sever the thigh from the drumstick through the ball and socket joint.

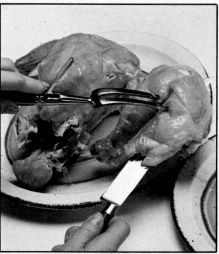

3 Turn the dish and carve the left side. Each of the four leg pieces with breast meat makes a portion.

5 Again turn the dish, so that the wishbone is to your right. Insert knife in front of breastbone.

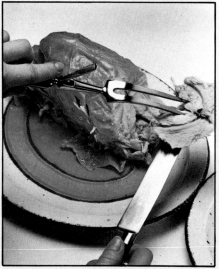

6 Cut down following curve of wishbone. With breast meat this makes one portion.

7 With front end facing you, carve the breast into thin slices using downward strokes of the knife.

The method of carving a large chicken or a capon is an extension of that used for a small bird, so if possible practise on a small bird first. As well as a sharp knife, and a carving fork with a finger guard, you will need a spoon for serving a crumbly stuffing. A napkin is also used for holding the leg tip when the thigh and drumstick needs to be divided.

CLASSIC ACCOMPANIMENTS

Classic accompaniments are chicken liver and bacon rolls, pork chipolatas and, of course, bread sauce.

Step-by-step to carving a small chicken

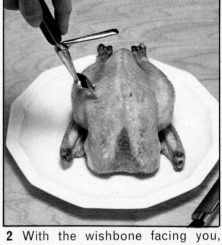

1 The chicken should be allowed to rest before carving in order that the meat can firm up.

2 With the wishbone facing you, hold the bird firmly in place by driving the fork into left side.

3 Cut through the skin and around the right leg joint to free the leg from the body of the chicken.

4 Starting at the wishbone end of the breastbone, hold the knife close against the carcass.

4 Carve each of the wing joints. (Serve with some of the breast meat to make two more portions.)

5 Carve away the whole breast and wing in one piece so that you have the second portion.

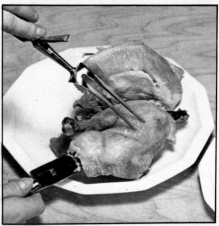

6 Repeat the carving on the other side until the bird is divided into four portions.

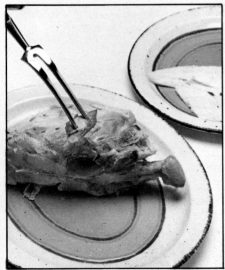

8 Portions can be made up of breast meat and any remaining meat such as the oyster pieces on the back.

BREAD SAUCE

This essentially English sauce adds both piquant flavour and contrast to the texture of the chicken. The secret of well-flavoured bread sauce depends on a long enough infusion of the onion and spices in the milk to impart a really distinctive flavour. The consistency should be that of thick cream, neither thin nor stiff.

SERVES 6
1 small onion
2 cloves
250 ml [½ pt] milk
4 peppercorns
1 small blade mace
1 bay leaf
50 g [2 oz] stale white bread
salt
25 g [1 oz] butter or 15 ml
[1 tablespoon] cream

1 Peel and slice the onion, stud it with the cloves.

2 Put the milk into a small saucepan and add the studded onion, peppercorns, mace and bay leaf.

3 Bring slowly to boiling point. Remove the pan from the heat, cover it and leave in a warm place to infuse for at least 30 minutes, preferably longer.

4 Make the breadcrumbs by grating the bread on a coarse grater.

5 Strain the milk and discard the onion, herbs and spices. Return the milk to the saucepan and stir in the breadcrumbs.

6 Leave to stand for 15 minutes while the crumbs absorb the milk.

7 Reheat gently before serving, add salt to taste and stir in the butter or cream.

FRENCH ROAST CHICKEN

The French method of open roasting a small chicken differs from the English in that the bird is cooked initially on its side and needs turning and basting. It is usually cooked without a stuffing, and is invariably served with a crisp green salad. Traditionally the quantity of gravy is very small, but is very well flavoured. Potato crisps can be warmed through in the oven and used as a garnish.

SERVES 4
1.4 kg [3 lb] chicken
salt and pepper
50 g [2 oz] butter
sprigs of fresh or dried herbs,
such as rosemary, lemon
thyme or tarragon
10 ml [2 teaspoons] oil
giblet stock

1 Heat the oven to 190°C [375°F] gas mark 5.

2 Wash, drain and dry the chicken.

3 Mash the salt and pepper into 15 g [½ oz] butter. If you are using dried herbs, these may be added to the butter. Put the butter and any fresh herbs into the body cavity. Retruss the bird if necessary.

4 Rub salt and pepper over the chicken skin. Melt the remaining butter with the oil and brush the bird liberally all over.

5 Rest the bird on one side of its breast in a roasting tin just large enough to hold it comfortably. Roast in the centre of the oven for 25 minutes.

6 Turn the bird on the other side, baste with the butter and oil, and roast for another 25 minutes.

7 Meanwhile prepare the giblet stock and leave to simmer.

8 Turn the chicken breast upwards and baste with the remaining butter and oil or drippings in tin.

9 Fifteen minutes before the end of cooking time, baste the chicken with the juices that have collected in the roasting tin.

10 Test if the chicken is cooked by piercing the thigh with a skewer. The juices should be colourless.

11 Tilt the bird to drain the juices from the body cavity into the roasting tin.

12 Transfer the chicken to a large warm serving dish. Remove the trussings, skewers and leg shanks and keep warm.

13 Tilt the roasting tin and pour off any surplus fat, leaving the drippings behind. Strain the giblet stock into the tin.

14 Bring to the boil over medium heat. Stir and scrape round the pan to release the scrapings from the bottom of the tin.

15 Simmer for 5 minutes until stock has reduced. Check the seasoning. Serve in a warm sauce-boat.

TRADITIONAL ROAST CHICKEN

A large chicken, or a capon, is the bird to choose when you plan to spend time preparing all the delicious trimmings. Instead of expensive bacon for barding, cover the bird with foil, and reserve the bacon for rolls to eat with the bird. It helps to prepare the breadcrumbs for stuffing and sauce in advance.

SERVES 7-8
2.25 kg [5 lb] roasting chicken
25 g [1 oz] butter
three herb stuffing (or any other
stuffing)
salt and pepper
small dessert apple
giblet stock
the chicken liver
bread sauce
4 rashers streaky bacon
225 g [½ lb] pork chipolatas

For the garnish:
a few sprigs of watercress

The French roast a chicken by placing it on its side initially, turning and basting it and then completing roasting time in the usual position.

1 Remove the butter from the refrigerator. Uncover and leave to come to room temperature.

2 Prepare the stuffing and leave to cool.

3 Heat the oven to 190°C [375°F] gas mark 5.

4 Prepare, wash, drain and thoroughly dry the chicken. Sprinkle the body cavity and the skin with salt and pepper.

5 Peel the dessert apple and put it into the body cavity.

6 Fill the neck end of the bird with the stuffing, fold the skin over the back and secure with wing tips or poultry skewer. Retruss the bird if necessary.

7 Spread some of the butter on a piece of foil to cover the breast, then spread the rest all over the chicken.

8 Stand the chicken on a rack in a roasting tin and cover the breast loosely with the buttered foil. Roast in the centre of the oven for a total of 2 hours.

9 Meanwhile prepare the giblet stock (reserving the liver). Infuse the milk for the bread sauce.

10 Cut the rinds off the bacon, stretch the rashers with a knife, and cut in half. Place a portion of chicken liver on each piece of bacon, roll up and impale on a small skewer.

11 Separate the chipolatas and put in a lightly greased ovenproof dish.

12 Half an hour before the end of roasting time discard the foil and baste the chicken with the pan juices. Put the dish of chipolatas, uncovered, on the shelf beneath the bird.

13 Quarter of an hour before roasting time is up, baste the bird again and put the liver and bacon rolls on roasting tin base.

14 Finish making the bread sauce. Put it into a sauce-boat or serving bowl and keep warm.

15 Test if the bird is cooked by piercing the thigh with a skewer. If the juices are colourless remove the chicken from the oven.

16 Tilt the chicken to drain the juices from the body cavity into the roasting tin.

17 Place the bird on a heated serving dish. Remove the trussing strings and the skewer. Break off the leg shanks.

18 Arrange the chipolatas and bacon rolls round the chicken and keep warm.

19 Tilt the roasting tin and skim off the surface fat. Strain the giblet stock into the roasting tin. Put the tin over a medium heat and bring to the boil, stirring. Simmer for 5 minutes until the quantity of liquid has reduced. Check seasoning and transfer to a sauce-boat.

20 Just before serving, garnish the tail end of the bird with watercress.

ROAST TARRAGON CHICKEN

⊠⊠ *Chicken, cream and fresh tarragon are one of the great flavour combinations for the summer months. This chicken is roasted by the French method. Dried tarragon has its uses for flavouring but for this simple recipe fresh tarragon is essential.*

New potatoes, French beans and buttered baby carrots would make a perfect accompaniment.

SERVES 4
**1 oven ready chicken weighing
   1.4 kg [3 lb]
50 g [2 oz] butter at room
   temperature
salt and ground black pepper
3 tablespoons fresh tarragon
   leaves
1 small clove garlic
150 ml [¼ pt] thin cream
5 ml [1 teaspoon] flour
15 ml [1 tablespoon] cold
   chicken stock**

1 Remove the butter from the refrigerator to bring it to room temperature.

2 Heat the oven to 190°C [375°F] gas mark 5.

3 Wash and dry the chicken. Sprinkle the body cavity with salt and pepper and rub salt over the skin.

4 Chop the tarragon leaves roughly. Peel and crush the garlic. Reserve half the butter then cream 25 g [1 oz] with the garlic. Add half the tarragon leaves. Put this mixture into the body cavity of the bird.

5 Truss the chicken if necessary, then spread it all over with the remaining softened butter.

The pineapple rings left over from the stuffing are used as a garnish.

6 Place the bird on one side of its breast in a roasting tin just large enough to hold it comfortably. Roast in the centre of the oven for 25 minutes.

7 Turn the chicken on to its other breast and baste it thoroughly. Roast for 25 minutes.

8 Finally turn the chicken breast upwards. Baste it with the pan drippings and roast for another 25 minutes basting it two or three times.

9 Test the chicken, by piercing with a skewer. The juices should be colourless.

10 Tilt the chicken so that the juices run into the pan, then transfer the bird to a warmed serving dish. Remove the trussing strings, skewer and the leg shanks. Keep warm.

11 Add the cream and the rest of the chopped tarragon to the buttery juices in the roasting tin. Heat gently over a low heat. Stir round the pan with a wooden spoon to release the scrapings.

12 Put the flour in a small bowl and add the cold stock. Stir to a smooth paste.

13 Spoon a little of the hot cream on to the flour paste and incorporate it.

14 Transfer the flour paste back to the roasting tin off the heat. Stir to incorporate.

15 Return the baking tin to a gentle heat and bring to the boil, whisking continually with a small wire whisk. Simmer gently for 2-3 minutes to cook the flour. Check the seasonings.

16 Joint the chicken and pour a little of the sauce over it. Serve the rest in a sauce-boat.

ROAST CHICKEN WITH PINEAPPLE WALNUT STUFFING

◻◻ *Trying a new stuffing is a good way of ringing the changes on roast chicken. The flavours and textures of both pineapple and walnuts are in pleasant contrast with chicken, but it is essential to use top quality canned pineapple. The stock can be made with half a bouillon cube as the giblets are roasted in the tin with the chicken and will add their flavour at the end.*

SERVES 4
1.4 kg [3 lb] chicken with giblets
salt and pepper
25 g [1 oz] butter
250 ml [½ pt] stock

For the stuffing:
350 g [12 oz] canned pineapple
   rings
50 g [2 oz] walnuts, chopped
40 g [1½ oz] butter
50 g [2 oz] dry white
   breadcrumbs

1 level teaspoon salt
half a lemon

For the garnish:
a few walnut halves
watercress

1 To make the stuffing, drain the pineapple rings, weigh out 100 g [4 oz] and chop them, reserving the rest for the garnish.

2 Chop the walnuts and grate the zest from the half lemon.

3 Melt the butter for the stuffing in a small saucepan, add the breadcrumbs and stir and cook for a minute or so.

4 Stir the chopped pineapple, chopped walnuts, salt, lemon zest and add enough pineapple juice to give the stuffing a fairly moist consistency.

5 Heat the oven to 190°C [375°F] gas mark 5.

6 Wash, drain and dry the chicken.

7 Sprinkle the body cavity with salt and pepper, and rub well into the skin. Insert 12 g [½ oz] of butter into the cavity.

8 Fill the neck end of the bird with the stuffing and retruss the bird.

9 Soften the remaining 12 g [½ oz] butter. Use some of it to grease a piece of kitchen foil. Spread the rest of the butter all over the bird. Cover the breast with foil.

10 Put the giblets, but not the liver, in the bottom of the roasting tin, and stand the chicken, breast up, on a rack, over them.

11 Cook in the centre of the oven for 1 hour.

12 Remove the foil, baste the bird with the pan drippings, and put the liver in the tin beside the bird and baste it. Cook for another 20 minutes.

13 Test the chicken by piercing the thigh with a skewer. The juices should be colourless.

14 Tilt the chicken to drain the juices into the roasting tin and transfer the chicken to a warmed serving dish. Remove the trussing strings and break off the leg shanks.

15 Add the stock to the roasting tin and bring to the boil, stirring and scraping to release the sediment from the bottom of the tin. Simmer for 2-3 minutes until slightly reduced.

16 Check the seasonings then strain the sauce into a sauce-boat and discard the giblets.

17 Halve the remaining pineapple rings, arrange them around the chicken, topping each half with a walnut. Tuck a few sprigs of watercress between the chicken legs.

CHICKEN BRICKS

A chicken brick is a clay pot with a lid. The pot is shaped to hold a trussed chicken leaving a minimum of spare space. No liquid is added to the pot and very little fat. Although the chicken is cooked covered, it nevertheless emerges golden and succulent.

Before use the brick is soaked in cold water for ten minutes. The clay absorbs water, which gradually evaporates during cooking, helping to keep the chicken moist.

Wipe the inside of the brick with the cut side of a garlic clove before cooking. The chicken is then brushed with a little olive oil and seasoned with salt and pepper. If you wish, vegetable additions may be included in the brick to add flavour.

The brick is put into the cold oven at the same time as the oven is set and gradually heats up with the oven. A high temperature setting of 260°C [500°F] gas mark 10 is used. A chicken of 1.4 kg [3 lb] will need one and a half hours. The juices that form during cooking can be used for gravy once the chicken is cooked.

CHICKEN WITH LEMON AND MUSHROOMS

This recipe for chicken roasted in a brick is quick and trouble free to cook as it does not require any basting. The vegetable additions are included to add flavour and are not for eating.

SERVES 4
1.4 kg [3 lb] chicken
garlic clove
salt and pepper
50 g [2 oz] mushrooms
half a lemon
fresh basil or a sprig of
**   rosemary**
15 ml [1 tablespoon] olive oil

1 Soak the brick in water for 10 minutes then wipe it to remove surface moisture. Rub the inside with the cut side of a garlic clove.

2 Season the body cavity of the chicken with salt and pepper.

3 Remove the earthy ends of the mushroom stalks and chop the mushrooms. Chop the lemon roughly and add mushrooms, lemon, lemon juice and the herbs to the body cavity.

4 Season the chicken liver. Chop roughly and add it to the body cavity.

5 Rub the chicken over with salt and pepper and then brush with olive oil.

6 Place the chicken in the brick and put on the lid.

7 Put the brick in a cold oven. Set the temperature to 260°C [500°F] gas mark 10. Cook for 1½ hours.

8 Remove the bird from the brick and spoon the stuffing out of the bird. Press the stuffing with the back of the spoon to make it release the juice then discard the pieces.

9 Tilt the bird so that the juices flow out from the inside and reserve.

10 Transfer the bird to a warm serving dish. Joint it and serve with the chicken juices poured over.

Green Salads

preparation and dressings

To many people the word 'salad' is synonymous with 'lettuce' and, because lettuce is seasonal, salads are often associated only with summer eating. Learn how to make best use of all sorts of leafy green vegetables — how to choose them, wash and keep them crisp, make interesting combinations of texture and flavour, and how to mix salad dressings — so you can enjoy refreshing green salads all the year round.

All sorts of leafy green vegetables are delicious raw and, with their nutritional values undiminished by cooking, they make for very healthy eating. Salads are cheap, quick and simple to make. But (and this golden rule applies to all cooking) the simpler the dish, the more important it is to choose and prepare your ingredients with care if the results are to prove excellent.

Few things are more unappetizing than a salad bowl containing limp and gritty saladstuffs, with leaves that are yellowing at the edges or bruised and sodden with an over generous or too early dose of dressing.

The essential characteristic of a good salad is freshness. This means vegetables must be in peak condition, cool and crisp, and gently tossed in a little well-flavoured dressing just before serving.

Leafy green salad vegetables

Look for fresh green colours and firm hearts when choosing lettuces. Round or cabbage types have soft leaves. Cos are long-leaved and crisp. Webb's are round and very crisp, and Iceberg are like the heart of a Webb's lettuce.

Slice or pull apart Chinese cabbage. Leaves are firmer than lettuce but more tender than cabbage.

Red, white and green cabbages (but not Savoys) can all be used to make crunchy salads. Discard outer leaves, core and cut into quarters. Slice across very finely (called shredding). Dress 30 minutes before serving.

Lambs lettuce is sometimes called corn salad. Use like lettuce, treating gently as the leaves are tender.

American cress is similar in appearance to watercress but more peppery in flavour. Mustard and cress is milder. Clean American and watercress and keep fresh by immersing in cold water. Discard tough stalks before serving.

Chicory has white leaves with yellow tips. Green tips indicate bitterness. Remove core and separate leaves.

Escarole, or batavia, is similar to endive but has broader, less curly leaves. Use pale centre for salads.

Sorrel and nasturtium leaves can be chopped finely and used sparingly to add piquancy to salads.

Dandelions are pleasantly sharp in flavour—and free. Always choose very young, very pale leaves.

Use young Brussels sprouts. Trim outer leaves and stalks. Shred finely. Dress 30 minutes before serving.

Endive makes a useful winter substitute for lettuce and the crisp, curly leaves look very attractive.

Young spinach is excellent for salads. Remove tough stalks and wash very thoroughly in salty cold water.

CHOOSING GREEN SALADSTUFFS

The best way to ensure both freshness and variety is to use ingredients in season, experimenting with different vegetables as the year goes round. Leafy vegetables are very perishable and, ideally, should be eaten within hours of picking—but this is only practicable for gardeners

Obtaining quality and value for money is more difficult for the shopper. The natural seasonal cycle of availability has been distorted by the advent of international refrigerated transport: many vegetables are now on sale all year round—and, unless you know your seasons really well, it is difficult to know what is hothouse cultivated, imported or really good fresh, home-grown produce. Moreover, additional confusion is created by the fact that many vegetables are now sold ready trimmed and packaged—and this can disguise telltale signs of ageing and staleness.

The wise shopper makes friends with a good greengrocer. Asking his advice makes good sense: he is an expert and it is in his interest to take trouble over regular customers (the modest but regular buyer is more important to him than the one-off big spender). As a general rule, you are likely to get best value by buying what you see to be most plentiful: produce that is abundant and reasonably priced is almost certainly home-grown and in season, whereas produce that is scarce and costly is liable to be hothouse cultivated or imported.

Try to buy vegetables sold loose so you can check freshness. The basic signs to look for are firm, crisp leaves of good colour. Avoid cabbages and lettuces with hard, dry stalks and by-pass any leafy vegetable that looks bruised or wilting at the edges. A little dirt, however, is nothing to worry about. And it is, in fact, an advantage to buy vegetables complete with the stalk and tough outer leaves, which you may wish to discard before eating, because these act as a natural protective wrapper conserving freshness and moisture within.

KEEPING VEGETABLES FRESH

Once in the kitchen, your vegetables must be stored in such a way as to preserve maximum freshness until you are ready to eat them. It is important to keep leafy greens cool and to exclude air. Storing salad vegetables unwashed and untrimmed takes up a bit more room but helps to keep them fresher. Most leafy green vegetables keep well for 2-4 days if wrapped in polythene bags and stored in the crisper compartment of a refrigerator. Use a rigid container instead of a polythene bag for vegetables (such as chicory and lambs lettuce) which bruise easily.

Hard cabbages, however, need no wrapping and will store well for 4-7 days on a ventilated larder shelf.

CLEANING AND CRISPING SALADSTUFFS

An hour or so before eating, salad vegetables should be trimmed and washed.

After this, if wished, leaves can be broken up into bite-sized pieces. Hands are gentler than a knife and cause less bruising so use them to tear tender leaves. Chicory and dandelion leaves are best left whole as cut edges release bitter juices and they tend to brown unattractively. Cabbages and Brussels sprouts are hard so they should be cut up very finely (called shredding) with a sharp stainless steel knife or equipment specially designed for shredding vegetables, such as a mandolin.

Drying and chilling

Once washed, the leaves must be dried. This is important because wet salads are tasteless and uninviting. Drying tender leaves is a delicate job if you are to avoid bruising. Using a salad spinner is the ideal answer. Simply place the washed salad into the plastic colander provided, place it in the bowl, cover with the lid and turn the handle. As the vegetables spin round gently the water is drawn off them and into the bowl leaving you with a colander full of cool just-damp leaves. Or shake the salad in a wire salad basket. Alternatively (and this involves no special equipment) enclose the leaves lightly in a clean towel, hold the corners and shake gently to absorb moisture.

Whenever possible, the salad-stuffs should then be gently wrapped in a clean, dry towel, put into a polythene bag and placed in the crisper compartment of the refrigerator for 30-60 minutes. This will refresh the leaves, making them crisp and even more appetizing than if they were served immediately. But remember that long-term storage of damp vegetables will make the leaves turn yellow, so wash and refrigerate them only an hour or so before your meal.

Step-by-step preparing saladstuffs

1 Trim off stalk end and discard any wilting outer leaves.

2 Separate leaves, removing tough stalks or core if necessary.

3 Wash leaves thoroughly in a sink or large bowl of cold water.

4 Wash again in fresh water it necessary. Shake lightly to drain.

5 Spin (or shake gently in a tea towel) until leaves are just damp.

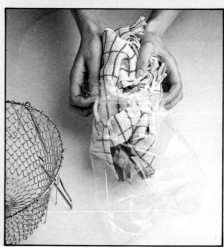

6 Wrap in a fresh towel. Cover with polythene. Chill for ½-1 hour.

SALAD DRESSINGS

A good dressing is an essential part of a salad (the word salad derives from the Latin 'sal' meaning salt). A dressing usually contains fat, acid and flavourings, and this not only makes a salad taste more interesting, but it also makes the best of the goodness of the vegetables. The fats, eggs and oils used in dressings act as carriers for the fat soluble vitamins which are found in large quantities in salad vegetables and fruit, and the acid used protects the ascorbic acid (vitamin C) in the vegetables. Dressings also add to the food value of salads, as they themselves contain many essential oils, vitamins and mineral trace elements.

Choosing fats

Oil is the most popular and frequently used fat in salad dressings. You can use one of the cheaper oils, sold under the label of cooking or salad oils. Sunflower oil has a slightly nutty flavour; groundnut oil and corn oil are both tasteless, but the delicate flavour of olives is characteristic of simple salad dressings, such as vinaigrette, so use a good olive oil whenever possible.

Olive oil is easy to buy and it works out less expensive if you buy a large [one gallon] can rather than several smaller bottles.

The cheaper kinds of oil are best kept for making the more highly spiced dressings, in which strong flavours would mask the delicate olive taste.

If you like experimenting in the kitchen, you could also try using other oils. The following are excellent but extravagent alternatives and their distinctive flavours may not be to everyone's liking, so buy a small amount at first. Walnut oil, sesame seed oil, coconut oil, apricot oil and oil of almonds are all available from health shops, delicatessens and some supermarkets.

Creams, cheeses and milks can all be used in place of oil in some dressings with particularly delicious results. Choose, according to the vegetables involved, thick [double], thin [single] or sour cream; or cream, curd or cottage cheese; or, very popular with slimmers, buttermilk or natural unsweetened yoghurt.

Butter is another alternative to oil. Melted and seasoned just before pouring over a salad, it makes a delicious and unusual hot salad dressing. The fat that collects in the pan base when grilling bacon can also be used—its smoky flavour goes particularly well with sharp-flavoured leafy vegetables such as dandelion and spinach.

Eggs are sometimes combined with oil (as in mayonnaise) or butter (eg sauce Béarnaise) to make thick and very rich dressings. The making of these delicious but rather complicated sauces is described in detail in a later lesson on emulsified sauces. Here we describe the simpler uses of eggs in salad dressings—pounding hard-boiled eggs for an old-fashioned salad cream and stirring soft-boiled eggs into a basic vinaigrette.

Choosing acids

Vinegar is the type of acid used in most salad dressings but it is usually omitted if the dressing is hot or the salad contains citrus fruit (the fruit itself provides all the acidity needed). There are several types of vinegar to choose from. Wine vinegars (red and white) are less harshly flavoured than the malt and cider vinegars and are, therefore, preferable for most salad dressings, although the piquancy of malt suits some vegetables particularly well and cider vinegar goes well with salads that include apples.

Some malt vinegars are more delicate than others and those which are instilled with herbs (tarragon-flavoured malt vinegar is widely available and particularly good) make aromatic and delicious substitutes for wine vinegar if the latter is unavailable.

Lemon, lime and orange juice can also be used for salad dressings. They should always be freshly squeezed and it is sometimes a nice idea to include a little grated zest too.

SALAD BOWLS

Deep bowls are better than shallow platters or dishes because the depth allows plenty of room for mixing the ingredients without losing any over the sides.

Wooden bowls are most popular, usually turned or hand carved in a wood such as teak. They are often sold with long-handled salad servers to match. Never leave wooden bowls to soak in hot water or they may crack or become distorted. They can be immersed briefly in water to wash but they are best cleaned by wiping with a damp cloth. If the wood appears very dry, occasionally rub the inside all over with olive or another type of salad oil.

Glass bowls are also ideal and a mixture of green leafy vegetables looks pretty and refreshing showing through the transparent sides.

Pottery bowls are suitable too but some designs are a little 'heavy' for the crisp and light nature of most salads. Plain white bowls look good for green salads.

Making your own salad dressings is fun—and there are lots of tasty ingredients to choose from.

197

Using garlic

The flavour of garlic is strong and it should never be allowed to pre-dominate either salad or dressing, but it can be used in various ways to add subtle aroma or distinctive flavour. If you decide to use garlic, first separate one clove from the garlic bulb, and peel away the clove's papery thin skin with a knife.

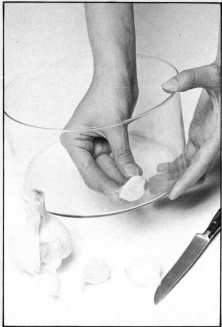

For mild flavour, cut a garlic clove in half, rub the cut side round the inside of the salad bowl and discard.

Or quarter a garlic clove and place it in a dressing for 1 hour to flavour. Strain off before serving.

For stronger flavour, slice garlic, sprinkle with salt and crush with knife blade. Add to dressing.

Alternatively use a garlic press to squeeze juice from the clove directly into the salad dressing.

VINAIGRETTE OR FRENCH DRESSING

This is the classic and most widely used of all salad dressings. The traditional proportions are 3 parts oil to 1 part vinegar but many people prefer a blander taste (just add more oil) and some prefer a sharper flavour (increase the vinegar). As shown below, endless variations on this basic recipe can be made by adding herbs or extra flavourings.

This basic recipe makes enough vinaigrette for one small salad.

Disposable screw-top jars and soft-drink bottles are useful for mixing and storing vinaigrette (but use only those which have vinegar resistant lids because vinegar will corrode metal and the metal will, in turn, spoil the flavour of the dressing). The basic mixture will keep in a larder or larder-cupboard for about 5 days. So, if you eat a lot of salads, it's worth making a fairly large quantity of vinaigrette at a time. Make the basic recipe only as fresh herbs and other additional flavourings should be added just before serving: they will lose colour and taste during storage. Never refrigerate the dressing or it may thicken and solidify.

VARIATIONS ON VINAIGRETTE

Make the basic recipe as described then stir in any of the following:
- 5 ml [1 teaspoon] mustard, tomato purée or anchovy essence.
- 15 ml [1 tablespoon] chopped chives, capers or gherkins.
- 10 ml [2 teaspoons] grated horse-radish or Worcestershire sauce or soy sauce.
- A few drops of chilli pepper sauce.
- 15 ml [1 tablespoon] crumbled Roquefort, Danish blue or Stilton.
- 10 ml [2 teaspoons] fresh chopped herbs such as parsley, chervil, dill, tarragon or mint.
- 5 ml [1 teaspoon] dried herbs: dill weed, basil and marjoram are about the only ones that can be used successfully in salads.
- Half a small garlic clove for a double quantity of basic dressing.
- For vinaigrette à l'oeuf, make a double quantity of basic vinaigrette and add 1 egg that has been soft-boiled for $3\frac{1}{2}$ minutes. Stir the yolk into the dressing, then add the chopped white plus 15 ml [1 tablespoon] chopped fresh parsley or chives.

Making basic vinaigrette

15 ml [1 tablespoon] wine
  vinegar
salt
freshly ground black pepper
45 ml [3 tablespoons] olive oil

1 Measure the wine vinegar into a small bowl, jug or cup.

2 Add salt and pepper and stir with a fork to dissolve the salt.

3 Pour on the oil and beat vigorously to mix and thicken.

ENGLISH SALAD CREAM
This is a light, almost fluffy-textured dressing which makes an excellent and less rich alternative to mayonnaise.

2 hard-boiled egg yolks
a pinch of salt
a pinch of cayenne pepper
5 ml [1 teaspoon] English
  mustard
5 ml [1 teaspoon] caster sugar
30 ml [2 tablespoons] white
  wine vinegar
150 ml [$\frac{1}{4}$ pt] thick cream

1 Rub the cold egg yolks through a sieve into a small bowl.

2 Using a wooden spoon mix the salt, cayenne, mustard and sugar into the yolks.

3 Add 5 ml [1 teaspoon] of the vinegar and mix well.

4 Gradually add the cream, stirring lightly all the time.

5 Blend in remaining vinegar.

YOGHURT AND HONEY DRESSING
Here is a refreshing dressing which is particularly good with cucumber, grated root vegetables and tomato salads (described in detail in FRUIT & VEGETABLES 2).

juice of half a lemon
5 ml [1 teaspoon] clear honey
150 ml [$\frac{1}{4}$ pt] natural yoghurt
1 garlic clove
salt and pepper
15 ml [1 tablespoon] fresh
  chopped mint

1 Mix the lemon juice and honey together in a small bowl.

2 Gradually blend the yoghurt into the lemon-honey mixture.

3 Slice the garlic and crush it with a little salt.

4 Stir the garlic into the dressing and season with pepper. Add mint.

MARMALADE DRESSING
This is excellent with an orange, olive and watercress salad. Although the dressings for salads containing citrus fruit are usually made without acid, a little is used here to counteract the sweetness of the marmalade.

15 ml [1 tablespoon] orange
  juice
5 ml [1 teaspoon] grated
  orange zest
30 ml [2 tablespoons] marmalade
a pinch of sea salt
freshly ground black pepper
60 ml [4 tablespoons] olive oil

1 Stir the orange juice and zest into the marmalade in a small bowl.

2 Add salt and pepper and mix well.

3 Using a fork, blend in the olive oil and adjust seasoning to taste.

TOMATO SOUR CREAM
This dressing is excellent with shellfish as well as vegetables. The slight acidity of tomatoes and sour cream make the inclusion of lemon or vinegar unnecessary.

125 g [$\frac{1}{4}$ lb] tomatoes
150 ml [$\frac{1}{4}$ pt] sour cream
5 ml [1 teaspoon] paprika
15 ml [1 tablespoon] fresh
  chopped basil or marjoram

1 Put the tomatoes in a bowl, cover with boiling water and leave for

Watercress, orange and olive salad is very refreshing.

199

2 minutes to loosen skins.

2 Drain and peel tomatoes. Chop roughly and rub through a sieve.

3 Gradually stir in the sour cream.

4 Then blend in the paprika and the fresh chopped herbs.

SWEET AND SOUR DRESSING
As this dressing is spicy the delicate flavour of olives would be lost. Use nutty or flavourless oil instead.

30 ml [2 tablespoons] sesame seeds
15 ml [1 tablespoon] soft brown sugar
45 ml [3 tablespoons] cider vinegar
30 ml [2 tablespoons] soy sauce
freshly ground black pepper
30 ml [2 tablespoons] sunflower or corn oil

1 Pound the sesame seeds in a mortar and pestle or put them in a polythene bag and crush with a rolling pin.

2 Stir the vinegar into the sugar.

3 Add the sesame seeds, soy sauce and pepper and mix well before stirring in the oil.

TARRAGON CREAM
Here is a very delicately flavoured dressing, which is delicious with cucumber and cabbage lettuce.

a pinch of salt
5 ml [1 teaspoon] caster sugar
freshly ground black pepper
30 ml [2 tablespoons] tarragon vinegar
150 ml [¼ pt] thin cream

1 Put the salt, sugar and plenty of pepper into a small mixing bowl.

2 Pour on the vinegar and mix well with a fork.

3 Add the cream gradually, stirring with light movements of the fork, so it thickens slightly.

4 Taste for seasoning and blend in a little more vinegar if wished.

MIXED GREEN SALADS
After the crisping process, assemble the salad. Ideally this should be done immediately before eating or certainly not long before.

If you do have to prepare a salad in advance, cover the bowl with a damp tea towel and keep in a cool place: it will lose its freshness in a warm room.

Add the dressing at the last moment, just before serving, and this may be done at table. If the dressing is poured over too soon the leaves will wilt and become floppy. The exceptions to this rule are hard cabbage and sprouts. After shredding, soften these vegetables a little by pouring on the dressing and leaving for half an hour or so. In this case add other ingredients to the salad bowl just before serving.

The size of the salad depends on when you are serving it—as a main vegetable you will need more generous helpings than for a side salad or a salad to serve between courses, alone or with cheese. Different ingredients will also affect quantity—less will be needed if the salad is based on strongly flavoured ingredients such as spinach or dandelion, or on chewier ingredients such as cabbage or endive.

GREEN SALAD IDEAS
● Dandelion leaves are delicious simply seasoned with freshly ground pepper and coarse sea salt. Add snippets of crisply grilled bacon and pour on the melted bacon fat just before serving (no vinegar or lemon).
● Sprigs of watercress, slices of orange and black olives go well together, particularly with a marmalade dressing.
● Watercress or American cress and oranges are also good with strips of drained, canned red peppers and a little raw onion.
● A crisp-leaved Webb's lettuce is lovely simply sprinkled with chopped fresh herbs. Add anchovy essence to the vinaigrette dressing.
● For a really crunchy salad mix finely shredded cabbage with slices of unpeeled green apple, walnut pieces and spring onions. Dress with English salad cream.
● Young spinach leaves combine well with tiny cubes of cheese (choose a mild Edam or Gruyère) and slivers of pear. Dress with vinaigrette to which crumbled blue cheese has been added.
● A cabbage lettuce with a few tender young peas (raw) and piquant sorrel is excellent with tarragon cream.
● Crisp Chinese cabbage with sliced spring onions, cubes of ripe avocado pear and a few stoneless dates add up to a delicious oriental salad, particularly if tossed in a sweet and sour dressing.
● Endive or escarole combine well with mustard and cress. Serve with vinaigrette à l'oeuf or basic vinaigrette made using lemon juice instead of wine vinegar.

Making a green salad

1 If you like mild garlic flavour, rub the cut side of half a garlic clove round the inside of the bowl.

2 Put salad vegetables (according to season) into the bowl—not too many strongly-flavoured leaves.

3 Scatter mustard and cress or fresh herbs evenly over the other ingredients.

4 Make viniagrette or any other dressing of your choice and beat well to emulsify.

5 Pour over the salad. Don't use too much—just enough to coat lightly. Never swamp the salad.

6 Use your hands or salad servers to toss ingredients and coat evenly. Serve the salad immediately.

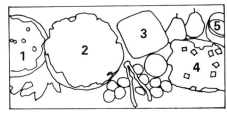

Here are just some of the salads described 'in Green salad ideas':
1 Tarragon cream dressing perfectly complements a summery salad: buttery cabbage lettuce with young peas and finely chopped sorrel leaves.
2 The same salad, without dressing.
3 A crunchy, vitamin-packed winter salad made from shredded white cabbage, sliced apple, walnuts and spring onions.
4 An ideal way to end a meal: raw spinach salad with cubes of cheese and slivers of pear.
5 Vinaigrette à l'oeuf is just one of many delicious variations on basic vinaigrette dressing.

Surprise green salad

The surprising thing about this salad is that the delicious butter and sesame seed dressing is warm. Don't pour on the dressing until you are ready to serve the salad—if added too soon the butter will solidify. To keep the dressing warm until needed, pour into a jug, stand in a bowl of hot water and cover the bowl and jug with foil.

SERVES 4
4 medium-sized heads of chicory or 1 endive
3 spring onions
15 ml [1 tablespoon] sesame seeds
50 g [2 oz] butter
salt and freshly ground black pepper

1 Using a sharp knife, cut a thin slice from the base of each head of chicory. Remove the core using a sharp knife or apple corer and discard. Pull away any bruised or brown outer leaves and discard. Gently separate the leaves and wash in cold water. Shake lightly and dry carefully in a tea towel, salad spinner or basket. Wrap leaves gently in a fresh, dry tea towel and put the towel into a polythene bag in the crisper drawer of the refrigerator for 30–60 minutes. If using endive, remove the stalk and separate the leaves, discarding any that are bruised or brown. Wash and crisp as for chicory.

2 Put the leaves of chicory or endive into the salad bowl.

3 Cut the bottom (root end) off the spring onions and trim away about 10 cm [4″] of the green tops. Remove transparent outer skin and slice thinly.

4 Drop the onions into the centre of the salad bowl.

5 Toast the sesame seeds. To do this, put the sesame seeds in a small frying pan (add no fat) and cook, stirring over medium heat until lightly browned.

6 Add the butter to the pan, allow to melt then cook over medium heat until foaming and browned.

7 Add salt and pepper to the salad and toss lightly. Pour over the warm dressing and toss lightly using salad servers. Serve immediately.

The aroma of honey-mustard basting sauce is enough to rouse most appetites—and the succulent, tenderness of kebabs is well-balanced by nutty-textured rice and a crisp salad.

Mixed Salads

choice and preparation

Expand your salad repertoire. Excite the palate and please the eye with colourful and crunchy textures. Use less conventional salad ingredients such as crispy beansprouts, green peppers, celeriac and Florentine fennel as well as buttery-soft avocado pears, fresh fruit, olives and nuts.

SALADS FOR ALL OCCASIONS

Learning how to make the most of health-giving raw vegetables is time well spent. An imaginative medley of contrasting tastes and textures enhanced by the right dressing is a delight to look at as well as to eat. And – bonuses for the time and budget-conscious cook – salads are quick and easy to prepare and relatively cheap. They are very versatile too and not, as some people seem to think, merely an accompaniment to cheer up leftover cold meats.

Salads can be served as a separate course at the beginning of a meal, as a side dish to accompany a hot main course, as an integral part of the main dish, or at the end of the meal.

Continental Europeans particularly like to serve salads and cheese on the same plate, to eat with a knife and fork. A fresh green salad goes best with hard cheeses, while root vegetables (especially if combined

Layered Oriental salad both looks and tastes fresh and colourful.

with fruit) offset soft and cream cheeses.

Mixed salads can look striking when decoratively arranged – a pretty table centrepiece and the perfect appetizer to impress your guests and get your party off to a good start.

Simply add slices of cooked meat, flaked fish, chopped hard-boiled eggs, nuts, cheese or cold cooked rice to turn your salad into a satisfying main course dish – and this is an excellent way of using up small quantities of leftover foods.

Several small bowls (each containing a different one-vegetable salad and coated with an appropriate dressing) make a handsome addition to a buffet table and enable guests to pick and choose. Several individual salads, plus perhaps a dish of sardines or freshly peeled prawns, are also ideal to serve as hors d'oeuvres.

CHOOSING AND STORING SALAD VEGETABLES

A salad is as good as its ingredients, and crisp vegetables, such as leafy green ones, lose their freshness easily. Buy little and often and stick to seasonal vegetables: this will ensure freshness and help you cut housekeeping costs.

Never use size alone as a guide to quality – a large vegetable is not necessarily a good one. In fact, small is beautiful more often than not, because large vegetables tend to be tougher and less delicately flavoured. In particular, courgettes, beetroot, radishes, peas and beans must be young for use in salads.

In general, avoid vegetables which are soft or wilting and those with bruises and a wrinkled or broken skin. Look for firm flesh, glossy skins and crisp leaves.

Most root vegetables store well if kept loose, unwashed and untrimmed on a ventilated rack in a cold larder. Soft vegetables that bruise easily need to be carefully wrapped to protect against damage.

Avocado pear: strictly speaking an avocado is a fruit, not a vegetable. Ripen in kitchen or larder cupboard and 'hold' in the refrigerator for up to 4 days. Leave the stone in a cut avocado half; sprinkle the surface with lemon juice to prevent discolouration, wrap tightly in cling film and refrigerate for up to 24 hours.

Beansprouts: refrigerate washed and dried beansprouts in an airtight plastic container for up to 4 days.

Beetroot: store in a cool larder for up to 4 days or in the crisper compartment of a refrigerator for up to 1 week. Never wrap in polythene or cling film because they will turn mouldy if they are unable to breathe.

Carrots: keep loose, unwashed and unwrapped in a larder for up to 1 week. Parsnips, swedes and turnips (a little of which make a well-flavoured addition to a salad) can be stored the same way.

Cauliflower: store whole, unwashed and untrimmed in an airtight container with a tightly fitting lid, in a cool dark larder or the crisper compartment for 24 hours only.

Celeriac: store whole, unwrapped in a larder for up to 2 weeks.

Celery: darkness is essential. Wrap an unwashed, unbroken head and store in a larder or crisper compartment for up to 5 days; or washed, dried and wrapped for 2-3 days.

Cucumber: store whole, tightly wrapped in foil, in the crisper compartment for up to 5 days. Store halves in a larder for up to 3 days, standing stems in water and covering cut ends with cling film.

Courgettes: keep up to 5 days individually wrapped in foil or in rigid containers in a larder or refrigerator.

Florentine fennel: store for up to 1 week in a polythene bag in the bottom of the refrigerator or up to 5 days in the larder.

Mushrooms: must be protected from losing their moisture. Put into a rigid airtight container and keep in the refrigerator for up to 3 days.

Onions: whole onions keep for several weeks if stored loose in a ventilated rack in a larder. Always wrap peeled segments tightly in cling film and keep in a crisper compartment for a few days only. Unwashed spring onions keep for 3-4 days in the crisper compartment.

Peppers: store peppers in the crisper compartment of a refrigerator for up to 1 week. Place whole peppers loosely in a polythene bag and wrap cut portions tightly in cling film.

Radishes: store unwashed radishes in an airtight plastic container in the crisper compartment or larder for 3-4 days.

Tomatoes: keep slightly unripe tomatoes loose in the crisper compartment making sure they don't touch each other. Use within 3–4 days when ripe but still very firm.

Avocado pears add delicate colour and creamy texture to salads. When ripe, they yield slightly if pressed.

1 Crisp celery has bright green, upright leaves. **2** Crunchy celeriac is firm and has a sweet celery flavour.

Look for brightly coloured peppers with firm, glossy skins. Red peppers are mature and sweeter than green.

Raw vegetables to include in your salads

Beansprouts (from oriental stores and some supermarkets) are crisp and fresh. Discard brown shoots.

Firm, juicy carrots are colourful and tasty. Old ones are best for salads. Scrape skins and grate.

Fresh cauliflower has a crisp white head of closely packed, firm florets and clear green outer leaves.

Delicately flavoured raw courgettes are soft and chewy. Choose small courgettes with bright silky skins.

A little aniseed-flavoured Florentine fennel bulb and feathery leaves add piquancy to salads.

Use tiny raw mushrooms whole, but thinly slice the larger ones. Never dress tomatoes until meal time.

Choose small plump radishes for crispness and firm-skinned cucumbers for a cool, refreshing taste.

1 English and Dutch onions are sharp and strong. **2** Large Spanish onions are sweeter and milder. **3** Spring onions are crisp and pungent. **4** Shallots are the most delicately flavoured of all.

Preparing salad vegetables

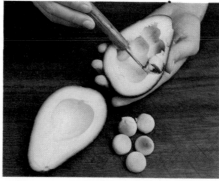

Avocado pears: using a stainless steel knife to prevent discolouration, cut in half and remove stone. Prepare just before serving and sprinkle cut surfaces with lemon juice to prevent discolouration. Fill the cavities, or peel and dice or scoop into balls and add to salads.

Carrots: old carrots have the best flavour and are easier to grate. Scrape or scrub skins first. They are very bulky and filling so a surprisingly small quantity is needed to make a large salad.

Peppers: the red are moister, sweeter versions of the green variety. Strongly flavoured, so use sparingly. Halve, remove stalk, pith and seeds, then slice finely.

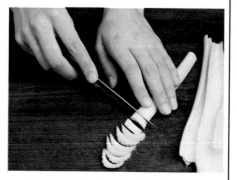

Celery: cut off root and top leaves. Separate sticks and scrub under cold water to remove grit. Remove any stringy or brown parts and chop.

PREPARING SALAD VEGETABLES

Salads should be easy to eat, so cut the ingredients into bite-sized pieces, or even smaller if the vegetables are very hard.

Remember that vitamins are quickly lost, especially from cut surfaces, so prepare your ingredients as you need them, handling as little as possible.

Wash or scrub them under cold running water (never leave them to soak as this destroys their texture and food value) then scrape, peel, slice or chop according to type.

A heavy, wooden, chopping board which does not slip is invaluable. (Keep one side for chopping pungent vegetables such as garlic and onions and the other for fruit.) A good sharp knife will make the jobs of scraping and chopping root and other hard vegetables quick and easy. A stainless steel knife is essential for some vegetables as carbon steel stains and taints their flavours. Use a potato peeler for vegetables which need peeling, and a strong box grater or mandolin for grating. A mandolin is also excellent for shredding (fine slicing) vegetables quickly and efficiently. A Parisienne cutter is useful for cutting soft fruit such as melon or avocado pear into decorative ball shapes.

Beansprouts: rinse, drain and dry. Discard any bitter brown shoots.

Beetroot: although usually cooked, they are excellent raw. Peel, grate and

*These are the basic tools you'll need for making crunchy salads: **1** Lancashire peeler **2** Parisienne cutter or melon baller **3** sharp vegetable knife **4** mandolin slicer **5** box or conical grater.*

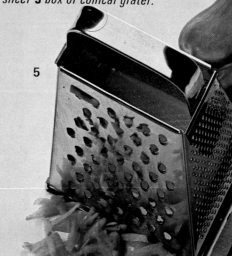

use in small quantities to add crunch and colour to salads.

Cauliflower: trim off leaves and rinse under cold water. Break into tiny florets.

Celeriac: as for beetroot, but sprinkle with lemon juice after grating and leave for 1 hour.

Courgettes: treat in the same way as cucumbers, but never peel.

Mange-tout or sugar peas: top and tail, slice or use whole.

Mushrooms: trim off earthy ends (not the whole stalk). Use tiny button mushrooms whole, but caps are best very thinly sliced. Do not peel, wipe skins with a damp cloth.

Parsnips, swedes and turnips: as for beetroot.

Peas and broad beans: pod and be sure to use only very young and tender varieties.

Radishes: trim away leaves and 'tail' of root.

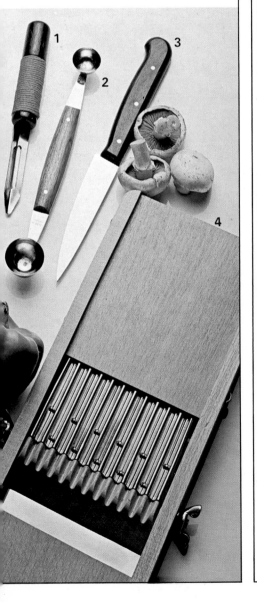

Cucumbers: trim ends, peel if wished, slice very thinly (a mandolin is best) or dice. Only add dressing just before serving or their high water content will dilute the dressing unattractively and weaken its flavour. Alternatively, remove seeds or salt before serving to extract some of the moisture.

Florentine fennel: trim away bulb base, leaves and any browning outer layers. Halve and shred or slice very finely. Use sparingly unless you are addicted to the taste of aniseed. Use fronds for garnishes.

Tomatoes: quarter or slice and peel if wished. Plunge in boiling water for 1 minute. Drain and cool under cold running water. Nick skin near stalk with a sharp, pointed knife and gently pull away skin.

Onions: peel and chop finely or slice across thinly and push into rings. Use sparingly in salads as raw onions are very pungent.

SALAD IDEAS

What goes with what? One-vegetable salads can be delicious but a mixture of textures, colours and flavours can be very appetizing too. Some very successful mixed salads are described here, or you can have fun creating your own salad recipes. Be careful to choose ingredients that complement each other or you could end up with a meaningless hotch-potch of a salad.

Remember that, as a general rule, it is best to add your dressing just before serving – and this is vitally important for tomatoes and cucumber which quickly become floppy and watery. But some of the harder vegetables such as peas, beans, cauliflower, celery, Florentine fennel and also mushrooms, benefit from being dressed before they are served. This often softens them slightly and gives their flavours a chance to penetrate. You will need about 150 ml [$\frac{1}{4}$ pt] of dressing for one large salad.

● Cauliflower makes an excellent base for a winter salad. Mix florets with a little grated carrot, parsnip or celeriac. Add plenty of unpeeled sliced green apple and coat with lemon-flavoured vinaigrette.

● To make a main course dish to follow a hearty soup, add cubes of cold pork or ham and a handful of peanuts to the salad described above. Dress with English salad cream.

● Finely slice button mushrooms, sprinkle with lemon juice, salt and black pepper and leave for 30 minutes. Then toss in olive oil and mix with seedless white grapes for a delicious American-style first course.

● For a really healthy salad, surround a mound of grated carrots with slices of avocado pear. Top with walnut pieces and sprigs of watercress and dress with freshly squeezed orange juice.

● For a salad to serve at the end of a meal with cheese, mix paper-thin slivers of Florentine fennel with sprigs of watercress. Sprinkle on some olive oil and a little sea salt and top with toasted almonds just before serving.

● Greek salad makes a good appetizer or, served with crusty hot French bread, a summery lunch dish. Mix strips of red pepper, sliced tomatoes and black olives with a little shredded white cabbage and rings of onion.

1 Almond-topped fennel and watercress salad served with cheese 2 First-course grape and mushroom salad 3 Hearty Greek salad with feta cheese 4 Winter cauliflower, carrot and apple salad.

Dress with a garlicky vinaigrette to which several lightly crushed coriander seeds have been added, and top the salad with a scattering of cubed feta cheese or white Stilton.

● Sprinkle a little fresh chopped basil on thinly sliced tomatoes and serve as part of an hors d'oeuvres or as a side salad.

● For a dinner party first course or a cool lunch dish, combine balls of avocado pear and melon with peeled prawns or bite-sized pieces of cooked chicken. Toss in freshly squeezed lemon juice and add a scattering of cashew nuts and chopped fresh mint just before serving.

● Make a tasty and attractive appetizer by halving and stoning an avocado pear. Fill the cavities with grated celeriac moistened in sour cream dressing. Top with the feathery fronds of Florentine fennel or sprigs of mint. Allow 1 avocado pear per person and serve with wholemeal rolls for a nutritious meal.

● Make an unusual and refreshing oriental salad by mixing beansprouts with a few spring onions and chopped celery. Topped with a layer of sliced mange-tout, tomatoes and watercress, this looks beautiful too.

● Green peppers, sliced orange and fronds of feathery Florentine fennel make an excellent and attractive alternative topping for this salad.

● Marinate tiny button mushrooms in vinaigrette and drain; add peanuts and watercress to make an excellent side salad to accompany roast chicken or duck.

● Make an exotic Middle East salad with strips of pepper, finely chopped onion, quarters of tomato and a few crushed coriander seeds. Moisten with a little freshly squeezed lemon juice and serve with tahini dressing and warmed pita bread.

SOUR CREAM DRESSING

This is excellent with grated root vegetables, particularly if you garnish it with freshly topped mint, dill or Florentine fennel.

ENOUGH FOR 1 SALAD
    small garlic clove
    juice of 1 lemon
    5 ml [1 teaspoon] sugar
    pinch of salt
    freshly ground pepper
    150 ml [¼ pt] sour cream
    fresh herbs

1 Slice the garlic clove and crush.

2 Mix in lemon juice, sugar, salt and pepper.

3 Stir in the sour cream and fresh herbs.

HOT SWEET AND SOUR SAUCE

Serve this richly flavoured sauce hot with crunchy vegetables.

ENOUGH FOR 1 LARGE SALAD
    15 ml [1 tablespoon] cornflour
    45 ml [3 tablespoons] vinegar
    60 ml [4 tablespoons] tomato ketchup
    45 ml [3 tablespoons] sugar
    175 ml [6 fl oz] water
    15 ml [1 tablespoon] oil

1 Put the cornflour into a bowl and add the vinegar to make a smooth paste.

2 Add the tomato ketchup, sugar and water and stir to mix.

3 Heat the oil in a saucepan and add the sauce mixture to it, stirring continuously until it comes to the boil. Boil for 1 minute.

AVOCADO DRESSING

Serve this rich smooth dressing with a plain one-vegetable salad.

ENOUGH FOR 1 LARGE SALAD

1 ripe avocado pear
30 ml [2 tablespoons] lemon juice
1 small onion finely chopped
salt
dash of chilli pepper sauce or chilli powder
150 ml [¼ pt] thick cream

1 Peel, stone and chop the avocado into dice. Sprinkle with lemon juice.

2 Reduce to a purée in a liquidizer or mash with a stainless steel fork until quite smooth.

3 Stir salt and chilli into the cream.

4 Then mix into the avocado mixture, stirring gently until flavours are well blended.

BUTTERMILK CUCUMBER SAUCE

Peel the cucumber if you wish but the peel adds colour to this pale, cool dressing. Either way, this is a good dressing for slimmers.

ENOUGH FOR 1 LARGE SALAD
    half a cucumber
    125 g [¼ lb] curd or **Philadelphia** cheese
    150 ml [¼ pt] buttermilk
    salt
    freshly ground black pepper
    10 ml [2 teaspoons] lemon juice

1 Cut the cucumber in half lengthways, scoop out and discard seeds using a teaspoon.

2 Chop the cucumber roughly and put it into a liquidizer together with the cheese and buttermilk.

3 Blend until smooth and stir in salt, freshly ground black pepper and lemon juice.

4 Cover and chill for 30 minutes before serving.

TAHINI DRESSING

A thick paste made from sesame seeds, tahini is similar to peanut butter and packed full of protein. It is available from specialist food stores and health shops. If you prefer a thinner dressing, increase the amount of water.

ENOUGH FOR ONE LARGE SALAD
    45 ml [3 tablespoons] tahini

Two cool appetizers: a halved melon shell is filled with melon and avocado balls, shrimps and cashew nuts while a tasty mixture of grated celeriac in sour cream dressing fills an avocado pear.

1 garlic clove
freshly squeezed lemon juice
5 ml [1 teaspoon] freshly
   chopped parsley
paprika

1 Put the tahini in a bowl. Gradually add 90 ml (6 tablespoons) cold water, stirring well with a fork until blended.

2 Chop the garlic clove and crush. Stir into the tahini.

3 Add lemon juice to taste.

4 Stir in the chopped parsley and season lightly with paprika.

BLUE CHEESE DRESSING
This thick, rich dressing is particularly good with leafy green salads as well as vegetable salads containing fruit.

ENOUGH FOR ONE LARGE SALAD
100 g [$\frac{1}{4}$ lb] cottage cheese
60 ml [4 tablespoons] buttermilk
30 ml [2 tablespoons] wine
   vinegar

50 g [2 oz] blue cheese
freshly ground black pepper

1 Push the cottage cheese through a fine sieve with the back of a wooden spoon to remove any lumps.

2 Stir in the buttermilk and then the wine vinegar.

3 Mash the blue cheese until very soft, then add to the other ingredients and mix until well-blended.

4 Season lightly with freshly ground black pepper.

SPICY TOMATO SAUCE
This sauce is easy to make and excellent with salads made from soft, chewy vegetables such as cauliflower and courgettes.

ENOUGH FOR ONE LARGE SALAD
60 ml [4 tablespoons] tomato
   ketchup
60 ml [4 tablespoons] olive oil
30 ml [2 tablespoons] thin
   cream
dash of chilli sauce
salt
freshly ground pepper
caster sugar

1 Put the tomato ketchup, olive oil, cream and chilli sauce into a glass

jar with a screw-top lid.

2 Screw lid firmly and shake the jar vigorously until all the ingredients are well-blended.

3 Season with salt, freshly ground black pepper and sugar to taste.

BITTER-SWEET DRESSING
This dressing is excellent with a grated carrot or coleslaw salad. The sweetness of the marmalade is offset by the sharpness of the lemon juice and spring onions.

ENOUGH FOR ONE LARGE SALAD
100 g [$\frac{1}{4}$ lb] cottage cheese
30 ml [2 tablespoons] fine-cut
   marmalade
30 ml [2 tablespoons] buttermilk
45 ml [3 tablespoons] freshly
   squeezed lemon juice
2 spring onions

1 Push the cottage cheese through a fine sieve, using the back of a wooden spoon, to remove any lumps.

2 Add the marmalade and mix well.

3 Stir in the buttermilk and then the lemon juice.

4 Chop the spring onions very finely and stir into the dressing.

Tomato and Mozzarella salad

Mozzarella is a white cheese of elastic consistency made from buffalo milk. Served with ripe juicy tomatoes and fresh basil it gives you a real taste of southern Italy where this unusual cheese originates. It slices easily but must be very fresh. If you cannot buy fresh basil use half the quantity of dried basil, or substitute fresh or dried oregano. No vinegar is used in the dressing as this encourages the tomatoes to 'bleed'. The dressing is added only shortly before serving so that it can be absorbed by the tomatoes without seeping into the cheese.

SERVES 4
450 g [1 lb] tomatoes
225 g [½ lb] Mozzarella cheese
10 ml [2 teaspoons] fresh basil
60–75 ml [4–5 tablespoons] olive oil
salt
freshly ground black pepper

1 Cut the Mozzarella into 3–6 mm [⅛–¼"] thick slices and arrange in the centre of a large serving dish.

2 Slice the tomatoes thinly and arrange around the Mozzarella. Cover with cling film and set aside in a cool place.

3 Chop the basil finely.

4 Measure the oil into a small bowl, add the basil and season to taste with salt and freshly ground black pepper.

5 Five minutes before serving pour the dressing over the tomatoes.

Green Vegetables

boiling and steaming

Cooked leafy green and podded vegetables are so often relegated to the role of plate fillers that many cooks don't appreciate just how delicious vegetables can be. Cooked with care and served with imagination, they are worthy of a dish in their own right and can form the basis of an excellent meal.

Few things are more unappetizing than the stale smell and soggy sight of over-cooked vegetables. They are distasteful to eat, and to say 'they are good for you' is nonsense.

It is true, of course, that leafy green and podded vegetables are important sources of vitamins and minerals; and they are also particularly good sources of roughage (fibrous matter which stimulates the digestive system). But all this goodness is only present in fresh, raw vegetables: vitamin and mineral content are destroyed almost entirely by too much cooking.

Most vitamins and minerals are heat soluble, or water soluble, or both. This means some goodness is inevitably lost as soon as vegetables go into the cooking pot (which is one of the reasons why nutritionists are always urging us to eat more un-cooked vegetables) but loss can be minimized by brief and careful cooking. Two of the quickest and best methods are boiling and steaming: follow the basic rules given here and you will enjoy vegetables that look and taste really delicious and are genuinely good for you !

THE PRINCIPLES OF BOILING

Boiling is an excellent way to cook vegetables. It is so quick that few nutrients are lost, and this means

maximum flavour and colour are also retained. But to call this cooking process boiling is slightly misleading because, for best results, vegetables should in fact be cooked at a gentle simmer.

The saucepan. A pan with a well-fitting lid is essential. Not only does it save fuel and prevent cooking smells escaping, it also prevents valuable vitamins, which rise in the form of steam, from being condensed into the atmosphere. Stainless steel, non-stick finish, hard enamel or aluminium pans are all suitable. Copper pans should not be used – they destroy vitamin C on contact. Poor quality, soft enamel pans should also be avoided. They are inclined to chip and wear at the seams which can release harmful salts of antimony into food. The size of pan depends on the amount of vegetables you plan to cook. Choose the smallest pan possible – this means there will be less water to dissolve valuable vitamins.

There's no need to use lots of water; in fact it is preferable to use only enough to just cover the vegetables. Add salt: just a pinch, too much will encourage vegetable juices to leak out. Never add baking soda: it may help to preserve green colours but it destroys vitamins and makes vegetables go limp.

It is important that the water is at boiling point when you add vegetables because the water at this temperature retains the vitamin C as much as possible and also slightly intensifies green colours.

Keep heat high, cover pan with the lid and bring back to the boil as quickly as possible. Then reduce the heat and simmer the vegetables gently. Keep the pan covered throughout cooking.

Simmering will cook vegetables just as fast as boiling; it saves fuel and, because it causes less bumping around in the pan, vegetables keep their shapes better.

PRINCIPLES OF STEAMING

Steaming (a method of cooking vegetables over rather than in water) is a lesser known but excellent alternative way to ensure that your vegetables are properly cooked and retain their shape and texture: because they are not immersed in water, they never become waterlogged.

Steaming takes slightly longer than boiling and some special equipment is needed. This does not have to be expensive or elaborate and you will get plenty of use out of it – in fact, many people find that once they have steamed vegetables they never want to boil them again.

There are two ways of steaming: open steaming and closed steaming. Open steaming means that the vegetables are placed in a perforated container over a pan of bubbling hot water so that they are cooked by the steam penetrating the holes in the container. Closed steaming means that the vegetables are placed in a solid container over a pan of bubbling water, and the steam does not touch the vegetables at all. The container is heated by the rising steam from the pan and the heat of the container cooks the vegetables.

The open method cooks vegetables more quickly than the closed, but the closed method preserves even more of the original flavour. Any juices that seep out of the vegetables during cooking are trapped in the container rather than escaping into the cooking water.

A whole boiled or steamed cauliflower can be served with vinaigrette and freshly chopped parsley for everyday salads or dressed up for a special occasion with stoned black olives and strips of pimento arranged in a lattice pattern.

213

Types of steamer

Flower steamer: this is the cheapest type of steamer to buy and is first-rate providing you use a saucepan with a well-fitting lid. The sides are perforated petals hinged to a perforated base which stands on three or four legs to raise it clear of the water so that only the steam penetrates the holes and cooks the vegetables. You can open the petals wide like a full-blown flower or close them tight like a bud, depending on how many vegetables and what size pan you are using.

Lidded steamer: this has solid sides, a perforated bottom and its own lid. It is designed to sit on top of a saucepan which is half full of water. This steamer has graduated ridges underneath so it can fit snugly on to saucepans of varying sizes. Some models are divided into compartments so you can cook two or three vegetables simultaneously yet keep each type separate. More expensive models are available with their own base pan.

Chinese steamers: these are little basketwork containers with solid sides, open-weave bases and their own lids. They are designed to fit on top of a small saucepan. You can build a 'tower block' of several containers with a lid on the top one, which is ideal for steaming small portions of several different vegetables. Chinese steamers can be bought from most Chinese supermarkets and stores.

Double boiler or porringer: this is a set of two saucepans (one fitting on top or just inside the other) with one lid. You three-quarters fill the larger, bottom saucepan with water, putting your vegetables in the upper pan, so that the vegetables are cooked by the closed method of steaming.

Improvised steamers

If you don't possess a steamer of any kind and are eager to start steaming straight away, you can improvise in the following ways.

A stainless steel or enamel colander which fits snugly inside a saucepan can be used for open or closed steaming. For open steaming, place the vegetables directly in the colander; for closed steaming wrap them loosely but firmly in a foil parcel. In both cases cover the top of the colander carefully with a double layer of kitchen foil to prevent steam escaping.

You can also close steam by putting vegetables into a basin: cover the basin with foil, stand the basin on a trivet or scone cutter in a pan half full of water and cover the pan with a well-fitting lid or foil.

Alternatively, put your vegetables between two heatproof soup plates (one inverted to act as a lid) and place over a saucepan half full of bubbling hot water.

The amount of water placed in the pan depends on which steaming method you are using. If you are using the open method, use very little water: it must never be able to bubble up through the holes and touch the vegetables. If using the closed method, the water should come about half way up the vegetable container.

Always wait until the water is boiling and the steam is rising before you put the vegetables in the steamer.

Once the vegetables are in the steamer, cover immediately or steam will escape into the air and your vegetables will take unnecessarily long to cook.

A fast boil is not necessary, so save fuel by keeping the water bubbling gently – just as much steam will rise.

COMMON PRINCIPLES

Vegetables really do taste best if they are washed, prepared, cooked and served in quick succession. The whole process does not take long so do everything as near as possible to mealtime and try to avoid preparing vegetables in advance, or cooking ahead and reheating them.

Length of cooking

Vegetables are cooked as soon as they are tender, and it takes less time to reach this stage than many people imagine. It is a good idea to stand by the stove while vegetables cook so you can catch them at the exact minute they are done. Test with a skewer or fork or lift a piece from the pan to taste. Never leave vegetables to cook until soft: they will lose flavour and vitamins and, if boiling, are liable to become a nasty, soggy, waterlogged mess.

Draining

Drain boiled vegetables thoroughly as soon as cooked (saving the liquid for gravies, health drinks or stocks). Many cooks claim they can drain vegetables by lifting the lid a little,

Steamers come in all shapes and sizes: **1** *Two heatproof soup plates make a quick improvisation.* **2** *Lidded steamers have a perforated base.* **3** *A colander becomes an efficient steamer if covered with foil.* **4** *A foil-covered basin can be used as a closed-steamer.* **5** *Pretty basketwork Chinese steamers build up into a 'tower block'.* **6** *A double boiler can be used for sauce making as well as steaming.* **7** *The cheapest, custom-made steamer of all is the flower steamer which can be adjusted to fit various pan sizes.*

tilting the pan and letting the liquid pour out, but this is far from satisfactory. For quicker and more effective results always tip the vegetables into a colander or a sieve (metal colanders are strongest and last longer than plastic ones) and drain away liquid. Leafy vegetables, such as spinach and shredded cabbage, which absorb water easily, benefit from being lightly squeezed with a vegetable press or the back of a wooden spoon to release surplus liquid.

Return the drained vegetables to the cleaned-out pan and place over very low heat for a few seconds to drive off any remaining excess moisture. Then add butter, season to taste with salt and pepper, turn into a warm vegetable dish and serve as soon as possible.

Keeping vegetables warm
Vitamins and minerals will be lost from vegetables if they are kept hot for any length of time. Green vegetables will start to smell unpleasantly as well.

If, through some unforeseen circumstance, you do have to keep cooked vegetables waiting, the best way to do it is to drain the vegetables as soon as they are cooked, refresh them by pouring cold water over them and drain again. Cover and set them aside until needed. To reheat, put the vegetables into a shallow pan without any water and heat gently until the steam stops rising.

VEGETABLES TO BOIL OR STEAM
So many vegetables boil and steam successfully that it is simpler to list those which are unsuitable for either of these cooking methods.

Vegetables with a very high water content, such as cucumber, tomatoes, aubergines and mushrooms, are better cooked by other methods. Also, red cabbage and peppers lose their firmness and flavour if boiled or steamed.

Hard root vegetables, such as celeriac, turnips, parsnips and carrots can be steamed but will take a very long time unless chopped into little pieces, so boiling is the method more often used for these.

Delicate vegetables that lose their shape or become waterlogged easily, such as asparagus, cauliflower, broccoli, chicory, leeks and marrow, are better steamed than boiled.

vegetables to boil and steam

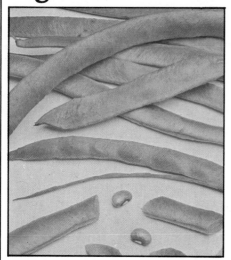

Runner beans should have their coarse 'strings' removed before being cut into slices for cooking.

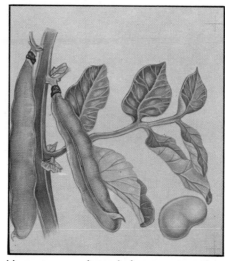

Very young broad beans can be cooked in the pod. Large ones are shelled before cooking.

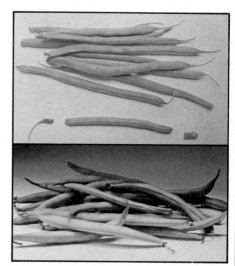

French beans (above) are topped and tailed and then cooked whole. Green or bobby beans (below) are sliced.

There are three types of broccoli – white, purple and calabrese. Look for firm, tightly packed heads.

Kale should have dark green, close curly leaves and strong thick stalks. Kale is a type of cabbage.

Spring or Cornish greens come in various sizes. Choose firm, green, tightly packed heads.

Tiny mange-tout are a delicate green and have the best flavour. Simply top and tail. The name means 'eat all'.

Pea pods should be firm and plump. Save the pods after shelling – they can be used for soup.

Swiss chard is two vegetables in one because the ribs and leaves are used separately in different ways.

Shown on the left are a number of leafy green and podded vegetables which are suitable for boiling and steaming (excluding those illustrated in the MIXED SALADS chapter) and a chart (overleaf) gives boiling and steaming times. Root and other vegetables which can be cooked by these methods are described in the following chapter.

PREPARING FOR COOKING

All vegetables need to be washed before cooking. Do this thoroughly but quickly. Remember that water reduces vitamins B and C, so never leave vegetables to soak. Rinse them under a running cold tap or, if very gritty, plunge into a sink of cold water, swirl them around quickly then drain.

Further preparation depends on the type of vegetable. A good sharp vegetable knife will speed the preparation of many vegetables, and a mandolin is useful for shredding (slicing very finely) cabbage and other vegetables. You can also buy various other gadgets for specialist jobs, such as stringing beans, but most of these are gimmicky and can also be expensive.

Broad beans: pod or, if very small and tender, cook in their pods – 700 g [1½ lb] beans in the pod gives about 450 g [1 lb] podded beans.

Broccoli: cut away the tough stalk ends. Divide very large heads into florets.

Curly kale: cut off tough stalk ends and discard. Shred the leaves as for cabbage.

French beans: cut off the ends of the pods (called topping and tailing) then leave whole.

Greens: pull leaves away from the tough stalk, discard stalk and shred leaves as for cabbage.

Mange-tout: top and tail as for French beans.

Peas: split open shells, remove peas and discard shells – 700 g [1½ lb] peas in the shell gives about 575 g [1¼ lb] shelled peas.

Runner beans and bobby beans: top and tail, cut away the tough ridges along the edges of the pod (called stringing), then slice obliquely.

Swiss chard: trim the mid-ribs free of all green leaf. Scrape mid-ribs to remove the stringy parts and cut into pieces. Chop the leafy parts as for cabbage.

Step-by-step to steaming vegetables

1 Put water in the pan and position steamer basket. Water must not come through the holes.

OR if using a closed steamer, check there is enough water to come half way up the sides of the inner pan.

2 Bring water to the boil. Put vegetables in the steamer, cover and return to boil.

3 Lower the heat immediately so that the water simmers gently but the steam is still rising.

4 Check the water level from time to time and top up with boiling water if necessary.

5 If cooking a large amount of vegetables, turn them occasionally to ensure even cooking.

6 Test the vegetables with a skewer or fork to see if they are tender in the centre.

7 Turn the vegetables (and their liquid if closed steaming) into a serving dish. Add butter and season to taste.

217

Step-by-step to boiling vegetables

1 Salt the water and bring to the boil. It need not be boiling furiously, just moving gently.

2 Add the prepared vegetables. The water will now go off the boil and become still.

3 Allow the water to come back to the boil. Cover the pan with a well-fitting lid.

4 Reduce heat so that the water is simmering gently, rather than boiling which serves no purpose.

5 Near the end of cooking time, test the vegetables with a skewer or kitchen fork.

6 Remove from heat and drain the vegetables in a colander, reserving the liquid.

7 If cooking a leafy vegetable, such as cabbage, extract excess water with a vegetable press.

8 Return vegetables to the cleaned-out pan and put briefly over low heat to drive off moisture.

9 Stir in butter, pepper and other seasonings. Turn into a warm dish and serve immediately.

BOILING AND STEAMING TIMES

(All times for open steaming. Add a few minutes for closed steaming)

Vegetable	Boiling time	Steaming time	Vegetable	Boiling time	Steaming time
Beans			Cauliflower		
broad	15 minutes	20 minutes	whole	20 minutes depending on size	25–30 minutes
French, bobby and runner	8–10 minutes	10–12 minutes	florets	10 minutes	12–15 minutes
Broccoli	10 minutes	15 minutes	Chicory	10 minutes	12–15 minutes
Brussels sprouts			Kale	5–8 minutes	10–12 minutes
(small whole)	8 minutes	12 minutes	Mange-tout	5 minutes	8 minutes
Cabbage			Peas	10–15 minutes	15–20 minutes
white, summer,			Spinach	8 minutes	12–15 minutes
Savoy	5–8 minutes	10–12 minutes	Swiss chard		
greens	10–12 minutes	12–15 minutes	ribs	20–25 minutes	—
Celery	10 minutes	12 minutes	leaves	5–8 minutes	10–12 minutes

WHEN TO SERVE VEGETABLES

Properly cooked vegetables can be such a treat that you are liable to find your family wanting to eat more of them, and more often (steamed, buttery cabbage is a very far cry from the nightmarish soggy mess so often served at school and canteen lunches). Instead of 'meat and two veg' – an anonymous and shameful role if ever there was one – vegetables can be a worthy dish in their own right. Make the main course more interesting by serving small quantities of several different vegetables; use beautifully cooked vegetables as the central ingredient for a main course; copy the French cooks and serve vegetables as a separate course before the main dish. This makes good gastronomic sense, and economic sense too. Vegetables make an excellent, refreshing start to a meal, and, as they take the edge off appetites as well, you can serve less of the more expensive meat or fish dish that follows.

Cold cooked salads

Cooked vegetables make delicious salads to serve as a first course or as a side dish with meat or fish. After boiling or steaming, simply toss in a vinaigrette dressing and allow the vegetables to cool before serving. Brussels sprouts, chicory, broccoli, French beans and cauliflower are all suitable. Vinaigrette with added hard-boiled egg or blue cheese is excellent for this purpose. Here are some suggestions:

● For French bean salad, toss cooked French beans while still warm in vinaigrette. Allow to cool, then add thinly sliced onion rings, chopped fresh savory and parsley.
● For crunchy sprout salad, toss whole baby Brussels sprouts while still warm in vinaigrette. Allow to cool, then add chopped hazelnuts.
● For rose cauliflower, toss cooked cauliflower florets while warm in vinaigrette. When cold, garnish with skinned and seeded tomatoes, which have been mashed to a pulp, and a sprinkling of chopped parsley.
● For apple and bean salad, fill shell-shaped leaves from the heart of a Webb's lettuce with cooked French beans, a sliced red eating apple and chopped walnuts stirred into a little mayonnaise.

New ways to serve hot vegetables

Plain, correctly boiled or steamed vegetables tossed in butter and seasoned with salt and pepper can be very good but simple sauces and toppings add variety and flavour. Try the following ideas:
● Use stock instead of water when boiling vegetables.
● Add herbs or spices to the cooking liquid when boiling. Savory goes well with cabbage. A bouquet garni complements all vegetables.
● When closed steaming, cook herbs with the vegetables. Add a knob of butter or a dash of wine. The natural vegetable juices will mingle with these to produce a delicious instant sauce.

● Buttered crumbs add crunch and texture. To make, melt 50 g [2 oz] butter in a heavy-based saucepan over low heat. Add 50 g [2 oz] fresh white breadcrumbs. Stir until golden brown. Sprinkle over vegetables just before serving.
● Noisette butter gives vegetables a 'lift'. To make, melt 25 g [1 oz] butter in a heavy-based pan over low heat. Add a squeeze of lemon juice and allow to brown gently. Pour over vegetables just before serving.
● Add a crushed garlic clove to noisette butter for beans and peas; chopped stuffed olives, capers and parsley for cauliflower; toasted sesame seeds or poppy seeds for kale and Brussels sprouts; grated nutmeg for cabbage and cauliflower.
● Crumble crisply grilled smoked bacon over cabbage, cauliflower, kale, greens or peas. Use the melted fat from the bacon instead of butter.
● Sprinkle cooked vegetables with toasted crumbs and a little grated Parmesan cheese.
● For quick cauliflower cheese, grate Gruyère or Cheddar cheese over the top of a cooked cauliflower. Brown under a hot grill. Sprinkle with crisply-fried smoked bacon and sliced hard-boiled egg just before bringing to the table.

Simple additions can transform everyday vegetables. Rose cauliflower gets extra flavour from a tasty tomato topping while vinaigrette and chopped nuts add flavour and crunch to Brussels sprout salad.

CAULIFLOWER VINAIGRETTE

The cauliflower can be divided into florets but looks much more effective if left whole. It is served on a bed of cabbage leaves which are blanched (plunged into boiling water) first to give them a better colour and make them more edible. If you are unable to obtain canned pimento, decorate the cauliflower using thin strips of ham.

SERVES 4
1 large cauliflower
6 large cabbage leaves
2 large garlic cloves
60 ml [4 tablespoons] chopped parsley
225 ml [8 fl oz] vinaigrette
200 g [7 oz] canned pimento
12 black olives, stoned

1 Wash the cauliflower and trim it carefully, removing any tough outer leaves and the end of the coarse stalk.

2 Boil or steam the cauliflower until it is firm but tender, then drain thoroughly.

3 Meanwhile, plunge the cabbage leaves into boiling water for 3 minutes. Drain and arrange on a serving plate.

4 Skin and crush the garlic cloves using either a garlic crusher or sprinkle with salt and crush with the back of a knife.

5 Stir the garlic and parsley into the vinaigrette.

6 Place the cooked cauliflower on the cabbage leaves and, while the cauliflower is still warm, pour on the vinaigrette. Set aside to cool for 15 minutes.

7 Drain the canned pimento and cut into narrow strips.

8 Decorate the cauliflower in a lattice pattern using the strips of pimento. Place an olive in each square. If the olives seem rather unsteady, cut a slice off the base of each one.

Variations
● For a more filling dish, decorate cauliflower vinaigrette with sieved hard-boiled egg yolk and chopped egg white.

A traditional dish from France, salade Niçoise can be served as a first course or made into more substantial fare by adding drained canned tuna fish.

SALADE NICOISE

This classic French dish makes an excellent first course but can be varied to make a main lunch dish by adding a can of drained tuna fish. Crisp leaves from the heart of a Webb's or Iceberg lettuce are best as they provide a crunchy base.

SERVES 4
250 g [10 oz] cold cooked French beans
1 lettuce heart
6 medium-sized cold cooked potatoes or drained canned potatoes
6 tomatoes
125 ml [4 fl oz] vinaigrette
6 anchovy fillets, halved
10 black olives
30 ml [2 tablespoons] capers

1 Pull the lettuce heart apart and arrange the leaves decoratively on a large shallow serving plate.

2 Cut the cooked French beans into 2.5 cm [1"] lengths and place in a large mixing bowl.

3 Cut the potatoes into dice (small squares) and add to the bowl.

4 Skin and quarter the tomatoes and add to the bowl.

5 Add the vinaigrette and toss until all the ingredients are well coated.

6 Pile the dressed ingredients on top of the lettuce leaves. Garnish with anchovy fillets, olives and capers in a decorative pattern.

QUEEN'S CHICORY

Chicory may be either boiled or steamed. If you boil it, wrap each head in a piece of clean cloth and squeeze gently to extract the water before browning in butter. This is essential: if boiled chicory is merely drained in a colander, it tends to be rather soggy.

SERVES 4
4 heads of chicory
1 thick slice of white bread
100 g [¼ lb] butter
1 slice of lean ham
juice of half a lemon
salt and pepper

1 Remove any ragged or brown outer leaves from the chicory. Cut off base and remove centre core.

2 Boil the chicory for 10 minutes or steam for 12-15 minutes.

3 Meanwhile, cut the crusts off the bread and reduce to breadcrumbs using a grater or a liquidizer.

4 Melt 25 g [1 oz] of the butter in a heavy-based pan over low heat.

5 Add the crumbs and stir until browned. Set aside.

6 Cut the slice of ham into small thin strips.

7 Drain and squeeze the chicory if it has been boiled.

8 Melt the remaining butter in a heavy-based saucepan over low heat. Add the lemon juice and salt and pepper to taste.

9 Add the ham and chicory. Increase heat a little and cook, turning frequently, until well browned.

10 Turn the contents of the pan on to a serving dish and sprinkle the crumbs on top.

TOMATO CABBAGE

Dutch or summer cabbage can be used to make this dish. Savoy cabbage is not suitable as it is rather loose and tends to fall apart when cooked in quarters.

SERVES 4
1 medium-sized cabbage
250 ml [½ pt] well-flavoured chicken stock
6 large ripe tomatoes
salt and pepper
20 ml [1½ tablespoons] tomato purée
150 ml [¼ pt] sour cream
10 ml [2 teaspoons] caraway seeds

1 Remove any ragged outer leaves from the cabbage and cut off the end of the coarse stalk.

2 Cut the cabbage into quarters.

3 Boil the cabbage in the chicken stock for 5–8 minutes.

4 Meanwhile, skin 4 of the tomatoes. Cut the flesh into pieces. Place in a bowl and mash to a pulp with a fork.

5 Add the tomato purée to the pulped tomatoes and season very generously with salt and pepper.

6 Add the sour cream and stir to mix well.

7 Turn the sauce into a heavy-based pan, place over low heat and stir until well blended and heated through.

8 Drain the cabbage thoroughly and arrange in a serving dish.

9 Slice remaining tomatoes and place them between the wedges of cabbage.

10 Pour on the sauce and garnish with a sprinkling of caraway seeds.

Tomato cabbage with its piquant sour cream, tomato and caraway seed topping gives this usually scorned vegetable exciting colour and flavour.

Root Vegetables

boiling and steaming

Roots, tubers and other commonplace vegetables can easily be made into delicious and inviting-looking dishes. You don't need to indulge in sophisticated cooking methods: choose really fresh ingredients, boil or steam them with care, and add imaginative finishing touches – the chances are that even self-confessed vegetable haters ask for second helpings!

The principles of boiling and steaming vegetables (as detailed in the previous chapter) are really quite simple. Most vegetables are largely composed of water, so incorrect temperature and prolonged cooking will produce soggy and tasteless results. Accurate temperature and careful timing are crucial to success. Choosing the freshest possible ingredients, preparing them properly, and presenting the cooked vegetables attractively are also important. Do all these things and your dish (whether humble carrots or luxury asparagus) will be fit for a king.

CHOOSING AND STORING HARD VEGETABLES

It is almost impossible to overstress the importance of freshness. Although roots, tubers and other hard vegetables keep longer than the leafy green and podded vegetables described in the last chapter, the sooner they are eaten after picking the better their flavour, texture, colour and nutrients will be.

As a general rule, look for firm skins, and choose vegetables that feel heavy for their size. Avoid specimens with wrinkled skins, bruises or yellowing leaves. Whenever possible buy loose vegetables that are unwashed and untrimmed, and store them like that: earth, roots and leaves all act as protectors, keeping in the moisture and vitamins. Remove them at the last minute, just before cooking.

Refrigeration is the best form of storage for all vegetables (with the exception of potatoes) but few people have refrigerators large enough to hold everything, and root vegetables and tubers are low on the priority list. The more delicate vegetables described here (asparagus, sweetcorn, globe artichoke, marrow and courg-

ettes) should be stored if possible in the crisper compartment of a refrigerator. Give them plenty of room to prevent bruising or protect them by placing in rigid containers. A cool, dark, well-ventilated larder shelf is perfectly adequate for the less perishable roots and tubers, but try to avoid storing them in a vegetable basket in the kitchen: the light and warmth of an ordinary room (and particularly a busy, sometimes steamy kitchen) will quickly make them deteriorate.

The identification chart shows vegetables in peak condition – how you should buy them – and the cooking chart gives boiling and steaming times for each vegetable.

PREPARING FOR BOILING AND STEAMING

In addition to the chopping board, knives, peelers and shredders described within the previous chapter, there are two extra pieces of equipment which you may find useful: a tough scrubbing brush for cleaning vegetables and a 'comb' holder to firmly grip onions and other hard vegetables while slicing or chopping.

Because goodness leaks out through cut surfaces, it is best to chop vegetables as little as possible. Cook them whole whenever practicable. This is essential for beetroot, sweetcorn and globe artichokes, and is usually possible when boiling potatoes, carrots, turnips, parsnips, courgettes and sweet potatoes. Larger vegetables, such as marrow, will of course have to be cut up in order to fit into a pan, but it is unnecessary to chop any vegetable finely – except when using the closed method of steaming. If you are using the latter method then always chop hard vegetables into small pieces because the cut surfaces will not matter: the nutrients and flavour that leak from the vegetables cannot escape into the water or steam but are trapped in the closed container and act as a natural sauce to serve with the cooked vegetables.

Whether you cut up your vegetables or leave them whole, do make sure they are all of similar size – or some will be perfectly cooked while others are still half raw.

Carrots, celeriac, kohlrabi, parsnips, potatoes, salsify, swedes, sweet potatoes, turnips. Remove the leaves and root base where

Preparing Jerusalem artichokes

1 Scrub Jerusalem artichokes and cook whole in their skins. Then cut off the thin woody ends and, if wished, peel away skins.

OR peel before cooking: place in acidulated water. Cut off long ends and peel (and slice if wished) under water.

Preparing leeks

1 Cut off leek roots and remove green tops to within 7.5 – 10 cm [3–4″] of the white stem.

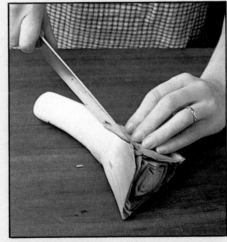

2 Use a sharp knife to split leeks lengthways to within 7.5 cm [3″] of root base.

3 Hold at an angle in clean cold water. Fan layers gently and wash away grit.

4 If leeks are still gritty, stand upside-down for 2 minutes in a jug of water.

Step-by-step preparing asparagus

1 Wash the stalks carefully under cold running water or in a basin, to remove any sand or grit.

2 Trim off woody ends and scrape the stems with a sharp knife to remove scaly leaf points.

3 Tie in bundles. Keeping tips level, tie with string just below tips and further down stalks.

necessary and thoroughly scrub skins clean. Rather than plunging all vegetables into a sink full of water, scrub them one at a time to reduce their contact with water (remember that many vitamins are water-soluble).

With the exception of celeriac and swedes, which have tough rather inedible skins, these vegetables can either be cooked in their skins or peeled, as you wish. Flavour and nutrients lie close to the skin so it is preferable to leave them unpeeled. Moreover, peeling inevitably involves some wastage, and takes up more of your time. But if you do decide to peel vegetables, scrape them as finely as possible. In the case of potatoes and sweet potatoes, for minimum wastage and maximum flavour, peel them after cooking, when skins slip off quite easily.

Celeriac, parsnips and salsify all have flesh which darkens rapidly on exposure to air (called oxidization), so you will need to protect each chunk, immediately after cutting, by putting it into a bowl of acidulated water (water with lemon juice or vinegar added).

Marrow. Remove stalk and cut the marrow in half lengthways. Use a sharp spoon to scoop out seeds and membrane, then peel away skin and cut the flesh into chunks. Alternatively, cut the marrow across into rings, then remove the seeds and peel from each ring. Steaming is preferable to boiling because marrow is a very soft and watery vegetable and can easily become mushy if immersed in water. This is also true of courgettes and pumpkin.

Courgettes (also called zucchini). Removing seed is unnecessary unless courgettes are overgrown to the size of a marrow – in which case treat them as marrow. If very small, wipe clean and cook whole. Their skin is tender so there is no need to peel. Cut medium-sized courgettes into thick slices.

Pumpkin. Cut in half from stalk to base. Cut each half into four segments. Discard stalk and peel away skin with a sharp knife. Scrape away seeds and membrane, and dice the flesh.

Beetroot. It is very important not to puncture beetroot skins until after cooking or they will 'bleed'. Wash them carefully, twist off foliage and cook whole. Steaming is unsuitable as the cooking time would be unbearably long. Beetroot is cooked when

More vegetables

Fresh sweetcorn has a bright green husk and plump, creamy-coloured (not dark yellow) kernels.

Parsnips are long rooted and slightly sweet in flavour. Turnips are round and white, some having greenish tops.

Swedes are roundish with golden flesh. All varieties have brown skin, some vary to greenish bronze.

to boil and steam

Jerusalem artichokes are knobbly white or purple tubers – unattractive looks belie a subtle smokey flavour.

Kohlrabi – a swelling of stem base above ground – is white or purple with white, turnip-flavoured flesh.

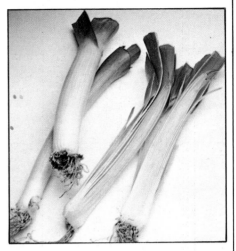

Leeks should have straight white stems and crisp green tops – usually only the white part is eaten.

Potatoes should have smooth, blemish-free skins. New potatoes are small and floury in texture.

Pumpkin is bought in large slices. Look for firm skin and close-textured orange-yellow flesh.

Salsify (also called vegetable oyster) is a white root with soft flesh. It has a faint sea flavour.

Choose globe artichokes with well-packed dark green leaves. Avoid any with purplish, splitting leaves.

Sweet potatoes are floury in texture and taste sweet. Their skins range from pale pink to deep purple.

Asparagus should be a fresh green colour with firm, tightly packed heads. Avoid large spears.

COOKING CHART

	Boiling		Steaming*	
	Whole	**Chopped**	**Whole**	**Chopped**
Beetroot	small 2 hours large 3–4 hours	unsuitable	unsuitable	unsuitable
Carrots	young 10 mins old 20 mins	15 mins	young 20 mins unsuitable	20 mins
Celeriac	unsuitable	20 mins	unsuitable	20 mins
Courgette	10–15 mins, depending on size	4–5 mins	20–30 mins, depending on size	15 mins
Jerusalem artichoke	unpeeled 10 mins peeled 7 mins	5 mins	15 mins	5 mins
Kohlrabi	20–40 mins, depending on size	20 mins	45 mins	25 mins
Leeks	15–20 mins, depending on size	5–10 mins, depending on size	20 mins	10 mins
Onion	small 15–20 mins, depending on size large 30–40 mins, depending on size	5–10 mins, depending on size	unsuitable	20 mins
Parsnip	20 mins	10–15 mins, depending on size	50 mins	20 mins
Potato	new 15–20 mins, depending on size old 20–25 mins, depending on size	15 mins	new 30 mins old unsuitable	30 mins
Pumpkin	unsuitable	unsuitable	unsuitable	10 mins
Salsify	unsuitable	10–15 mins, depending on size	25 mins	15 mins
Marrow	unsuitable	unsuitable	20 mins	15 mins
Swede	45 mins	20–30 mins, depending on size	1 hour	30 mins
Turnip	10–30 mins, depending on size	10 mins	45 mins	30 mins
Sweet potato	20–30 mins	15–20 mins, depending on size	unsuitable	30 mins
Asparagus	unsuitable	unsuitable	10–15 mins depending on size	unsuitable

Unless otherwise stated, all vegetables are medium-sized.

* These times are for open steaming. Closed steaming will take longer.

Globe artichokes, corn-on-the-cob, and asparagus are eaten with fingers.

skins feel loose. Drain, then rub off skins.

Sweetcorn. Remove the husk gently, peeling off each leaf separately. Trim away the stalk end with a sharp knife. Pull off the silks and rinse the cob under cold running water. Always boil in unsalted water. If you want to remove kernels from the cob after cooking, hold the hot cob with a cloth and pull away kernels with a fork, or cut them off with a knife.

Leeks. Dirt and grit has a tendency to get trapped between skin layers so always wash leeks very carefully under cold running water or in a basin. Gritty leeks are very unpleasant to eat. Cook whole or slice. Thin slices are essential for closed steaming. Leeks are better steamed than boiled because they easily lose shape if they are immersed in water.

Jerusalem artichokes. The flesh discolours (oxidizes) when exposed to air, so, if peeling before cooking, do it under water. Jerusalem artichokes change rapidly from just tender to mushy, so careful timing is vital. It is best to check their progress frequently during cooking.

Asparagus. Steam this delicate vegetable: boiling water can make the stalks floppy. Allow 6–8 stalks per person. Wash carefully, then tie in bundles of no more than 8–10 stalks, depending on size. Steam the bundles standing upright if using a special asparagus pan, or laid flat for alternative methods. Never squash the stalks or bend them. To open steam, use a flower steamer – completely opened out to enable the bundles to lie flat. To close steam, lay bundles between two large, heatproof plates.

SERVING SWEETCORN, GLOBE ARTICHOKES AND ASPARAGUS

Corn-on-the-cob, globe artichokes and asparagus are three vegetables which are always eaten in the fingers, so they are fun food as well as being delicious.

Each person has his or her own small dish of sauce. You pick up the cob, an artichoke leaf or asparagus spear, dip the tip in the sauce and eat. Re-dip in sauce after each mouthful.

This can be a messy business so it is best to serve these vegetables at fairly informal occasions rather than run the risk of ruining smart clothes. It is a good idea to supply each person with a finger bowl filled with warm water and a slice of lemon. Or give everyone an extra napkin.

It is possible to buy special artichoke plates with a central hollow for the whole artichoke and separate compartments for the accompanying sauce, and for discarded leaves. To buy these plates would be an unnecessary extravagance unless you grow your own artichokes or eat them very often. Ordinary plates are perfectly suitable, you merely put a teaspoon under one side of each plate so that the sauce collects in one area and is easy to dip into. Also provide a large dish in the centre of the table for the discarded leaves.

You can also buy special dishes and holders for corn-on-the-cob. Dishes are cob-shaped, and holders are like miniature two-pronged forks, usually with wooden handles, which pierce the cob, one at each end. Cob holders are not expensive and it is certainly far more comfortable to use them instead of holding a piping hot cob in your fingers.

Corn-on-the-cob is always served hot. Asparagus and globe artichokes can be served either hot or cold.

Hot melted butter is the simplest and perhaps best sauce to accompany all three of these vegetables when served hot. Cold or just lukewarm artichokes and asparagus are delicious served with vinaigrette, mayonnaise, hollandaise or mousseline sauce. Globe artichokes can be served with a stuffing instead of a sauce (see STAR RECIPE).

SERVING IDEAS FOR OTHER VEGETABLES

● Toss cooked, chopped kohlrabi in melted butter. Sprinkle with fresh chopped basil or chives and a little finely grated lemon zest.
● Stir a little Dijon mustard into thin cream and pour over cooked celeriac.
● For sweet and sour swede, melt a little butter and brown sugar together until sugar is dissolved. Remove from heat. Add freshly squeezed lemon juice and a little grated nutmeg. Toss hot, boiled or steamed swede in the sauce and serve.
● Toss cooked, chopped turnips in seasoned thin cream and sprinkle with crumbled, crisply grilled bacon.
● Peel, chop and lightly fry an onion in a little butter. Add diced hot beetroot and a carton of seasoned sour cream. Stir to mix well and re-heat very gently. Sprinkle with fresh chopped dill or parsley and serve.
● Pour melted butter over cooked, hot parsnips and sprinkle with caraway seeds.
● Put cooked salsify into a heatproof dish. Sprinkle with a mixture of grated Cheddar cheese, grated Parmesan

cheese and breadcrumbs. Brown under a hot grill until cheese is bubbling.

● Melt some butter and stir in a spoonful or two of sherry. Season and pour over cooked carrot sticks. Sprinkle with chopped parsley.

● Cook sweet potatoes and remove skin. Mash with butter, a little fresh orange juice, ground cinnamon, sugar and salt.

● Beat together olive oil and wine vinegar. Stir in a little lemon juice, tomato purée, oregano and salt and pepper. Pour over steamed slices of marrow while still warm. Serve cold as a salad.

● Toss cooked, cubed Jerusalem artichokes in melted butter and sprinkle liberally with lemon juice and paprika.

● Put cooked, hot whole onions into a warm dish. Sprinkle with grated Cheddar cheese and flaked almonds. Dot with butter and brown under a hot grill until cheese is bubbling.

● Dot hot, cooked potatoes with cream cheese and sprinkle with fresh chopped chives.

● Shape softened butter, oregano and a little chilli sauce into balls, chill, then serve with sweetcorn kernels.

● Coat equal quantities of cooked leeks and carrots with melted butter, Worcestershire sauce, salt and pepper and sprinkle with lots of fresh chopped parsley.

● Coat cooked courgette slices in melted butter, then sprinkle with coarsely chopped unsalted peanuts and ground sea salt.

● Melt butter and brown sugar together until sugar has dissolved. Stir in ground cinnamon and grated nutmeg and salt. Toss cooked chopped pumpkin in this mixture and sprinkle with lemon juice and toasted coconut shreds.

RED FLANNEL HASH

Always use freshly cooked beetroot – never pickled ones – for this traditional American dish.

SERVES 4
450 g [1 lb] potatoes
450 g [1 lb] cooked beetroot
450 g [1 lb] corned beef
45 ml [3 tablespoons] thick cream
salt and pepper
1 onion, weighing about 225 g [½ lb]
15 g [½ oz] butter

1 Scrub the potatoes and cut into even-sized pieces. Boil or steam until tender.

2 Allow to cool slightly, then peel away skins and cut into dice.

3 Skin and dice the beetroot. Chop the corned beef.

4 Mix potatoes, beetroot and corned beef together. Add the cream and season with salt and pepper.

5 Chop the onion finely.

6 Melt the butter in a large frying pan over low heat. Add the onion and cook, stirring it for 3 minutes.

7 Stir in the corned beef mixture.

8 Increase heat to medium and cook, without stirring, for 5–8 minutes until underside is crusty.

9 Using a fish slice and palette knife, turn the hash over and cook the other side.

SAVOURY CHARLOTTE

Here is a good way to turn leftovers into a tasty dish. Use one vegetable

or a mixture. Potatoes, sweetcorn kernels, carrots, celeriac and swede are all suitable.

SERVES 4
225 g [½ lb] cooked vegetables
4 hard-boiled eggs
125 g [¼ lb] cooked ham
3 small onions
200 ml [7 fl oz] condensed mushroom soup, and 75 ml [3 fl oz] milk OR 275 ml [½ pt] thick white sauce
5 ml [1 teaspoon] Dijon mustard
salt and pepper
75 g [3 oz] fresh white breadcrumbs
25 g [1 oz] shredded suet
50 g [2 oz] grated Cheddar cheese
25 g [1 oz] butter

1 Dice the cooked vegetables. Chop the eggs and ham.

2 Heat the oven to 180°C [350°F] gas mark 4.

3 Peel and blanch the onions: put them in boiling water and cook for for 5 minutes. Drain and refresh under cold running water, then chop finely.

Leeks Provençàle and courgettes a la Grecque are excellent served as appetizers or to accompany a plainly cooked main course.

6 Using a draining spoon, transfer courgettes to a shallow serving dish.

7 If much liquid remains in the saucepan, boil over high heat to reduce it.

8 Pour the sauce over the courgettes, remove bay leaf, and allow to cool.

9 When cold, cover and chill in the refrigerator for at least 30 minutes (and not more than 24 hours) before serving.

LEEKS PROVENCALE

Leeks in a tomato and garlic sauce make a delicious hot vegetable, and they are equally good served as a cold salad. Twelve small leeks will weigh about 1 kg [2-2½ lb]. Always steam rather than boil leeks to retain shape and maximum flavour.

SERVES 4
12 small, young leeks
4 large tomatoes
2 garlic cloves
30 ml [2 tablespoons] olive oil
30 ml [2 tablespoons] chopped parsley
pinch of caster sugar
juice of half a lemon
salt and pepper

1 Trim, thoroughly wash and drain the leeks. Steam until tender but still firm.

2 Meanwhile, prepare the sauce. Skin the tomatoes and chop the flesh.

3 Crush the garlic into a small saucepan.

4 Add oil, tomatoes and parsley and cook over fairly high heat for 2–3 minutes, stirring constantly, until the tomatoes are pulped.

5 Remove the pan from the heat. Stir in the sugar and lemon juice, and season to taste with salt and pepper.

6 Lay the leeks on a serving dish and pour the sauce on top.

4 If using canned soup, mix it with cold milk in a large bowl.

5 Stir the prepared vegetables, eggs and ham into the soup mix or white sauce, and season with mustard, salt and pepper.

6 In a separate bowl, mix the breadcrumbs, shredded suet and cheese.

7 Grease a heatproof dish of 1.15 L [2 pt] capacity with a little of the butter which should be at room temperature.

8 Spoon half the breadcrumb mixture into the base of the dish. Pour vegetable mixture on top and cover with the remaining breadcrumb mixture.

9 Dot with the remaining butter and bake for 30–40 minutes or until top has browned.

COURGETTES A LA GRECQUE

This delicious salad can be completely prepared a day ahead. Serve it as an appetizer or to accompany a plainly cooked main course. If you feel extravagant, use 60 ml [4 tablespoons] dry white wine instead of lemon juice.

SERVES 4
450 g [1 lb] courgettes
1 small onion
6–8 coriander seeds
juice of 1 lemon
60 ml [4 tablespoons] olive oil
1 bay leaf
1 large pinch dried thyme
salt and pepper

1 Slice the courgettes, discard the knobbly ends, and finely chop the onion.

2 Lightly crush the coriander with the back of a spoon to release oils and aroma.

3 Put the vegetables and all remaining ingredients into a saucepan with 250 ml [½ pt] water.

4 Bring to the boil, cover the pan and reduce the heat. Simmer for 15 minutes.

5 Remove the lid and simmer for a further 10–15 minutes until vegetables are tender and most of the liquid has been absorbed.

Star recipe

GLOBE ARTICHOKES WITH FISH STUFFING

▨▨ *Any left over cooked fish can be used or, alternatively, buy skinned frozen white fish fillets and steam them. For a special occasion you could use half fish and half prawns.*

SERVES 6
6 globe artichokes
half a lemon
400 ml [14 fl oz] mayonnaise
chives
parsley
6 canned anchovy fillets
5 ml [1 teaspoon] capers
large pinch paprika
salt and black pepper
450 g [1 lb] white fish, cooked

1 Cut off artichoke stalks and tough outer leaves. Rinse, shake dry and rub cut parts with lemon.

2 Trim tips of leaves. Fan open outer leaves, pull out inner leaves and scrape away hairy choke.

6 Chop 30 ml [2 tablespoons] each of chives and parsley. Drain and chop anchovies and capers.

7 Turn the fish into a bowl and flake (break up) with a fork. Add peeled prawns if used.

8 Add herbs, capers and anchovies. Mix 5 ml [1 teaspoon] lemon juice with mayonnaise and stir into fish.

9 Open artichokes a little and carefully spoon some of the stuffing into the centre of each.

To eat, use fingers to pull off a leaf. Dip in the stuffing and scrape fleshy base between teeth.

When all outer leaves are eaten, use knife and fork to cut artichoke bottom into chunks.

3 Plunge upside-down in a large pan of boiling water. Add a little lemon juice (or vinegar) and salt.

4 Cook for 15-40 minutes, depending on size. Leaves pull away easily when the artichoke is cooked.

5 Squeeze cooked artichokes gently to extract water. Drain upside-down and leave until cold.

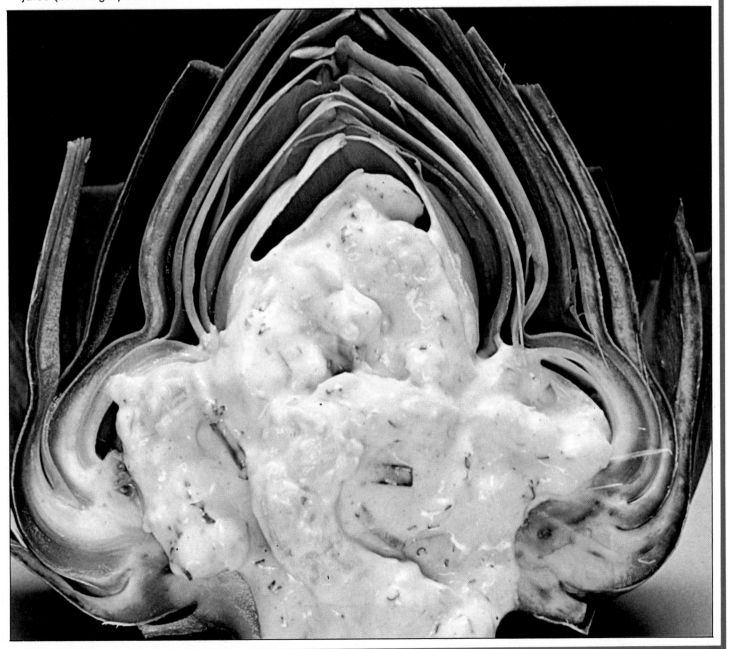

JERUSALEM ARTICHOKES IN MILK

An old-fashioned way of cooking Jerusalem artichokes is to simmer them in milk. The milk will increase their bulk to produce a creamy rich dish.

SERVES 4
700 g [1½ lb] Jerusalem artichokes
juice of 1 large lemon
1 onion, weighing about 225 g [½ lb]
125 g [¼ lb] lean bacon
25 g [1 oz] butter
150 ml [¼ pt] milk
5 ml [1 teaspoon] dried sage
freshly ground black pepper

1 Peel the Jerusalem artichokes under acidulated water. Cut off long ends. Dice and put into fresh acidulated water.

2 Thinly slice the onion and dice the bacon.

3 Melt the butter in a saucepan over low heat. Add onion and bacon and cook for 5 minutes, stirring from time to time.

4 Drain the artichokes thoroughly. Add them to the pan and, with a wooden spoon, turn to coat all over with the butter.

5 Stir in the milk, sage and pepper.

6 Increase heat a little and bring to simmering point. Lower heat and simmer, uncovered, for 10 minutes or so until artichokes are tender but not broken up, and most of the milk has been absorbed.

SWEETCORN SALAD

An average cob of corn will yield about 100 g [¼ lb] of kernels. If you can't get fresh, frozen sweetcorn kernels can be used instead. Use home-made mayonnaise if possible.

SERVES 4
450 g [1 lb] cooked sweetcorn kernels
2 celery stalks
1 green pepper
4 spring onions
45 ml [3 tablespoons] mayonnaise
45 ml [3 tablespoons] sour cream
15 ml [1 tablespoon] lemon juice
2.5 ml [½ teaspoon] dried basil
salt and pepper

Four colourful ways to serve plainly cooked vegetables. 1 Sherried carrots with parsley. 2 Potatoes with butter and chives. 3 Baby beets with sour cream. 4 Sweetcorn kernels with chilli butter.

1 Spoon mayonnaise, sour cream, lemon juice, basil, salt and pepper into a screw-top jar.

2 Shake vigorously until the dressing is well blended. Set aside for 15 minutes.

3 Meanwhile, chop the celery, de-seed and chop pepper and slice spring onions finely.

4 Put the sweetcorn and other vegetables into a salad bowl and mix together.

5 Add the dressing and toss well.

6 Cover and chill for 15–20 minutes before serving.

Variation
● For Frankfurter sweetcorn salad, a hearty lunch dish, add 225 g [½ lb] Frankfurter sausages cut into slices and use 2.5 ml [½ teaspoon] Worcestershire sauce instead of basil in the dressing.

Vegetables

puréeing

Velvety, delicious and with lots of uses, vegetable purées are an asset to any cook's repertoire. Simple and economical to make, they can be served as an imaginative accompaniment to a main course, used as a topping to eke out expensive meat and fish, made into hearty meals in their own right or piped to put a party face on a plain dish.

A purée is the smooth, creamy mixture which is produced when cooked vegetables are either mashed, sieved, passed through a food mill or liquidized. Often butter, milk, eggs, cream, herbs, cheese and other ingredients are added for extra flavour and richness.

Despite their air of luxury, vegetable purées are economical to make. Old, tough, misshapen or blemished root vegetables which are unsuitable for serving whole become smooth and delicious when puréed; end of season beans and peas lose their stringiness and, by mixing complementary purées together (such as potato and spinach, swede and parsnip), you can use up small amounts of vegetables which are left over at the end of the week.

Purées are a life-saver, too, when there are not quite enough vegetables to go round, and they can bring a touch of inspiration to even the plainest meal. Favourites, such as potatoes, go further when mashed with butter and milk. They can be used to top meat or fish pies, to eke out the expensive main ingredient, or to make savoury meals in their own right.

Making vegetables into a purée does mean a little extra work for the busy cook but the results are well worth the effort. And, if there's a baby in the house, making purées for the whole family can actually save time because it eliminates the need to make a separate special dish for the baby. Purées are also an excellent way of serving vegetables to anyone suffering from a stomach ulcer or any other complaint requiring a low-fibre diet.

Purées can be piped, and this is an ideal way to serve vegetables when you are out to impress your guests. Even a homely shepherds pie is elevated to dinner party status when topped with whirls of beautifully piped potato.

Duchesse potatoes are a simple way to give a plain dish a glamorous look.

Timing

The length of time it takes to make a vegetable purée depends very much on the cooking time of the vegetable you have chosen and the puréeing method. Drying will take 1 minute, mashing takes about 8 minutes, sieving about 10 minutes, milling about 8 minutes and liquidizing about 4 minutes. Piping will take about 10 minutes and browning piped purées takes a further 30 minutes. These timings are based on quantities to serve 4.

COOKING FOR PUREEING

Boiling is the best way to cook vegetables for puréeing (with the exception of very watery vegetables such as mushrooms, which are simmered in butter). Purées of steamed vegetables do not have quite such good flavour and root vegetables tend to develop a slightly sticky texture.

Boil vegetables in the normal way, as described in previous chapters, but cook them a few minutes longer than you would if the vegetables were to be served whole. This is because they must be quite soft to purée successfully. Always use vegetables of the same size, or cut them into even-sized pieces, so they will be cooked simultaneously.

You can add extra flavour to purées by adding herbs to the cooking water or boiling them in well-flavoured chicken, white or household stock instead of water.

Drying

Before being puréed, vegetables must be dried to get rid of excess moisture which would make the purée sloppy. To dry vegetables, drain them thoroughly in a colander after boiling, return them to the saucepan and shake over low heat for 1 minute. Then purée immediately while the vegetables are hot: they are softer and easier to pulp at this stage.

FOUR WAYS TO PUREE

There are four different ways in which vegetables can be puréed. Each method suits some vegetables better than others, as shown in the chart. The only exceptions are marrow and pumpkin which naturally reduce to a purée during cooking.

Peel marrow and pumpkin, cut into chunks and cook over a low heat in the minimum of stock or water, about 30 ml [2 tablespoons] per 425 g [1 lb] of vegetables. Mash down the vegetables from time to time during cooking. The end result will be a pulp which needs no further treatment.

Mashing

This is the simplest method. All parts of the vegetable are amalgamated into the purée, so it is important to use young, tender vegetables and to peel them before mashing. Mashing is only suitable for the smoother-textured root vegetables, such as potatoes, swede and turnips. Parsnips and other vegetables with woody fibres should not be mashed.

To mash vegetables you will need a strong potato masher. A metal masher made up of thin bars is easier to work with than the kind which has a metal disc with perforated holes because the vegetables do not stick to bars so easily. A masher with bars is also easier to clean. If you do not have a masher, a strong four-pronged fork can be used but it is more difficult and time-consuming to achieve really smooth results with a fork.

As the masher or fork presses down on the cooked vegetables, it breaks them up and gradually reduces them to a smooth pulp. Don't skimp the mashing, and make sure your masher reaches every corner of the pan or you may end up with a purée that is perfect in parts and lumpy in others. Mashing is quite hard work and it takes considerable muscle and stamina to achieve really velvety results.

Sieving

This is a more thorough method and it produces a finer-textured purée which is excellent for soups, sauces, soufflés and baby foods, as well as for simple purées and making into savoury cakes. There is no need for peeling and you can safely use slightly older, tougher vegetables because the coarse parts of the vegetable are left behind in the sieve. When calculating quantities, bear in mind that the net weight of a sieved purée is lighter than one which is mashed because tough fibres are extracted.

To sieve vegetables, you need a strong wood- or metal-framed nylon sieve. Plastic-framed sieves are not suitable as they tend to buckle as you press down on the vegetables.

You will also need a heavy wooden spoon or, better still, a vegetable press. A vegetable press is a mushroom-shaped wooden implement and is very effective for pushing things through a sieve as it enables you to exert pressure over a wider area and, therefore, to do the job more quickly. You will also need a bowl or a second saucepan which fits neatly under the sieve to catch the purée.

To sieve vegetables, first chop them coarsely. Then put them into the sieve, a few at a time, and either push them through with the back of the spoon using a stirring motion, or rub them through with the vegetable press. Move the press round in half circles for the maximum effect. Remove and discard skins and stringy fibres from the sieve after each batch of vegetables has been processed, and scrape the purée from the underside of the sieve into the bowl, using a round-bladed knife.

Milling

Putting vegetables through a food mill has the same effect as sieving but it is quicker and has the advantage that the texture of the purée can be varied by changing the discs in the mill.

As for sieving, you can use older vegetables and there is no need to peel them because the coarse parts are left behind.

Food mills are usually sold with a choice of three discs; with small holes for a very fine purée, with medium holes for a medium purée and with large holes for a coarse purée.

The boiled and drained vegetables are cut into rough pieces and fed into the mill in small quantities. As you turn the handle of the mill the vegetables are pushed out through the holes in the disc. Discard skins and scrape the base between batches, as for sieving.

Always follow manufacturer's instructions when using a food mill and clean the mill thoroughly and as soon as possible after use or vegetable scraps will harden and clog up the mechanism.

Liquidizing

This is the most effortless, quickest way to reduce vegetables to a purée but it does have certain disadvantages.

Liquidizing, like mashing, means

every part of the vegetable is puréed, so vegetables must be young, tender and peeled. Fibrous vegetables can be liquidized but the final texture of the purée can be somewhat uneven, so milling or sieving are preferable. Many models will only process vegetables if liquid is also added to the goblet and, even with this addition (see FINISHING TOUCHES), you may have to stop and start the machine and push the mixture down with a spatula from time to time.

The final important factor is timing. Do follow manufacturer's instructions very carefully: whizz vegetables for just a few seconds too long and your purée will be more like a soup.

FINISHING TOUCHES

After puréeing, the vegetables will have cooled down considerably and will need re-heating before they can be served. Turn them into a clean saucepan with additional ingredients to enrich them and add extra flavour. Stir over very low heat for about 3-4 minutes, depending on quantity.

These extra ingredients fall into two categories: enrichments and flavourings. Enrichments are important because they give purées a smoother texture as well as improving taste; flavourings are optional.

Enrichments

Butter is the most popular and frequently used additive – and it really is preferable to margarine. Use butter alone for green vegetables, allowing 50-75 g [2-3 oz] per 450 g [1 lb] of vegetables, depending on how velvety you wish the purée to be.

Equipment for puréeing and piping. 1 a heavy colander. 2 Grids for a food mill. 3 A food mill. 4 Wood-framed nylon sieves. 5 Glass bowls to collect the purée and wooden spoons to press it through the sieve. 6 A nylon piping bag and selection of vegetable nozzles. 7 Wooden vegetable presses.

For starchy vegetables (such as potatoes, parsnips, swedes, celeriac, turnips, and Jerusalem artichokes) or potatoes mixed with another vegetable, either use butter alone or help to keep costs down by using a combination of milk and butter. Allow 30 ml [2 tablespoons milk] and 25 g [1 oz] butter for 450 g [1 lb] vegetables. Cold milk will give tacky results. Always heat it for smooth, fluffy results.

Cream and yoghurt are other enrichments which turn a plain purée into a luxury dish. You can use thick or thin or sour cream or natural yoghurt, allowing 30 ml [2 tablespoons] per 450 g [1 lb] of vegetables if used to replace milk, more cream or yoghurt if used alone. Only use alone with strongly-flavoured vegetables such as roots, spinach, sorrel and cauliflower because cream is bland and tends to diminish flavours.

For a real luxury treat you can also include a lightly beaten raw egg, allowing 1 medium-sized egg per 450 g [1 lb] vegetables. This addition makes for richer flavour and a stiffer consistency so it is always included when the purée is made for piping.

The combination of milk and butter is usually used for so-called mashed or everyday vegetable purées, while butter alone or with cream is usually reserved for the finer quality, special occasion purées. The term 'creamed' refers to purées containing egg.

Flavourings

In addition to salt and freshly ground black pepper, the flavour of many vegetable purées is improved by the inclusion of herbs or spices.

● Freshly grated nutmeg adds piquancy to swede, cauliflower, celeriac and potatoe purées. Add 2.5 ml [½ teaspoon] per 450 g [1 lb] of vegetables.

● Garlic goes well with potato and all leafy green purées. Allow 1 crushed clove per 450 g [1 lb] of vegetables.

● Chopped fresh savory goes well with broad bean purée. Allow 5 ml [1 teaspoon] per 450 g [1 lb] of purée.

● Mint and peas have always been great friends. Add 5 ml [1 teaspoon] of freshly chopped mint to each 450 g [1 lb] of purée.

● Freshly chopped chives and parsley add colour and flavour to pale, bland potato, parsnip and celeriac purées. Allow 10 ml [2 teaspoons] per 450 [1 lb] of vegetables.

● Orange is a surprising but delicious addition to beetroot purée. Add the juice and finely grated rind (zest) of one medium-sized orange to each 450 g [1 lb] purée.

● Chopped hazelnuts, peanuts or almonds are good sprinkled over all purées.

● Crisp, deep-fried cubes of white bread (called croûtons) provide a crunchy contrast to purées. Sprinkle over purée just before serving.

Step-by-step to perfect creamed potatoes

SERVES 4
450 g [1 lb] old potatoes
25 g [1 oz] butter
30 ml [2 tablespoons] milk
1 medium-sized egg
salt
freshly ground black pepper
chives, parsley or garlic
(optional)

1 Choose small potatoes, or cut large ones into even-sized pieces. Boil in salted water until tender.

2 Drain the potatoes. Return to the pan and shake dry over low heat for 1 minute.

3 Holding the potatoes with a cloth, remove skins. Then cut the potatoes into fairly small pieces.

4 Rub the potatoes through a sieve, using a vegetable press or the back of a wooden spoon.

5 Heat the milk and butter together until melted and hot but not boiling. (Never use cold milk.)

6 Add the potatoes to the pan and beat the mixture with a spoon over low heat until fluffy.

7 Remove the saucepan from the heat. Beat the egg, add to the potatoes and mix until blended.

8 Stir in freshly ground pepper plus chopped chives, parsley or crushed garlic, if wished.

Puréeing leafy green vegetables

1 Prepare the vegetables and cook them in boiling salted water until very tender.

2 Place the medium-sized disc in the food mill and stand it over a large bowl.

3 Drain the vegetables, return to the pan and dry over low heat for 1 minute, shaking occasionally.

4 Place a small quantity of vegetables in the hopper of the mill. Turn the handle to purée them.

5 Continue in this way until all the vegetables have been puréed, then season with pepper.

6 Return the vegetables to the pan, add the butter (and flavourings, if wished). Re-heat gently.

PIPING VEGETABLES

Vegetable purées can be piped to make decorative whirls, borders, rosettes, nests and fancy toppings for savoury dishes. Creamed potatoes are frequently used in this way (the most famous piped vegetable dish of all is duchesse potatoes) but creamed swede, turnip, parsnip and carrot can also be piped successfully, either alone or mixed half-and-half with potato. Leafy green vegetables alone are not suitable for piping. The vegetables must be creamed – a purée without egg is not stiff enough to stand up after piping. The vegetables should also be cool. There are two reasons for this: first, they hold their shape better when cool and, second, a piping bag full of hot vegetables would be most uncomfortable to hold. You can make about 10 whirls, 15 rosettes or 4 nests from 450 g [1 lb] potato purée.

Equipment

There is no need to own a battery of complicated icing equipment in order to pipe vegetables. All you need is an icing bag (nylon is easier to clean than cotton) and a rope or star meringue nozzle (size 6 or 8 for rosettes, nests and whirls, size 12 for covering pies and casseroles). You will also need a baking tray if you are piping whirls, rosettes or nests.

How it's done

Although many cooks are afraid of piping, there are no great mysteries involved in doing it successfully. Just remember the basic rules given here and follow the step-by-step guides and you'll be piping perfectly in no time.

● Never over-fill the bag. About half full is enough.

● Never allow the bag to become empty. Refill when you have used half the purée.

● When piping on to a baking tray, do not grease it or the vegetables will fry rather than brown.

● Never lift the nozzle until you have finished the whirl, nest, rosette or line. To look effective, piping must be done with a smooth, flowing motion. If you stop and start, you will not get a good effect.

● Lift the nozzle off cleanly when you have finished.

● Keep a steady pressure with the squeezing hand. If you vary the pressure, the line of piped vegetables will vary too and you will end up with a mish-mash of thick and thin lines.

● If you make a mistake, don't panic. Just scrape the vegetables back into the bag and start again.

Step-by-step to duchesse potatoes

1 Place a size 8 star nozzle inside a nylon piping bag so that the decorative end protrudes from the hole at the bottom.

2 Stand the bag in a clean jam jar or glass, nozzle end down. Half fill the piping bag with cool, creamed potato.

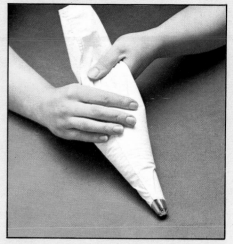

3 Lift the piping bag out of the jar. Smooth the empty part of the bag to expel air then twist it firmly.

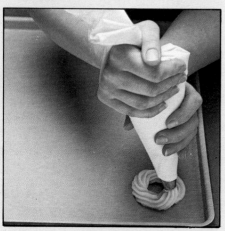

4 Squeezing steadily with your right hand, and guiding the nozzle with the left, make a 5 cm [2″] circle on a baking tray.

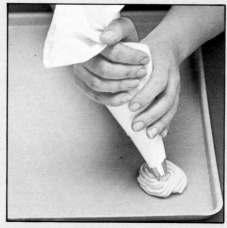

5 Without lifting the nozzle, now pipe a 2.5 cm [1″] circle resting on the inside edge of the first large circle.

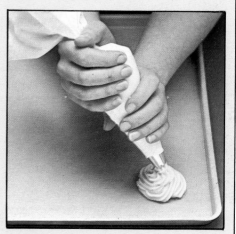

6 Still without lifting the nozzle, make a very small circle over the inside edge of the second. Lift off the nozzle when half way round.

7 Continue piping in this way, leaving 2.5 cm [1″] spaces between each whirl. Refill the bag when half the potato has been used.

8 Brown the whirls in the oven at 220°C [425°F] gas mark 7 for **30** minutes or until pale golden in colour.

Re-heating

Before you can serve piped vegetables they must be re-heated. The best way to do this is to place them in an oven heated to 220°C [425° F] gas mark 7 for 30 minutes. The high heat encourages the shapes to set and gives them an attractive browned look.

Do not grease the baking tray as this will make the vegetables fry – non-stick trays are best. Remove the vegetables from the tray using a fish slice.

When using any piped vegetables as a topping for a savoury pie, remember that this extra cooking time will affect the main part of the pie, so adjust the total cooking time accordingly.

More ways to pipe vegetables

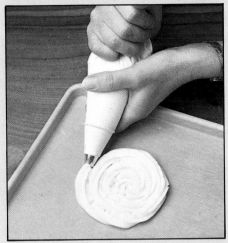

1 For potato nests, make a 10 cm [4"] solid circle using a size 6 rope nozzle.

2 Using a size 8 rope nozzle, make a larger, deeper circle on top of the outer edge of the first.

3 Brown in a hot oven. Lift the nest off tray using a fish slice and fill with any savoury mixture.

1 For a fancy topping for a savoury pie, pipe a line around the outside of the pie using a size 12 rope nozzle.

2 Continue piping lines in decreasing circles until all of the pie is covered.

OR cover the pie with rosettes using a size 6 star nozzle. Squeeze, lift and repeat. Try to make all the rosettes the same size and shape.

Handy hints

● Small amounts of left-over vegetable purée can be frozen in ice-cube trays, and are very useful if you have a baby to feed. To use, simply place the frozen purée in a saucepan with a little butter and heat gently.

● Potato purée can be used in place of flour to thicken soups and casseroles. Put a few table-spoons of purée in a cup, add a little of the hot liquid from the casserole or soup, stir briskly, then pour the contents of the cup into the dish and stir for 1–2 minutes until well blended.

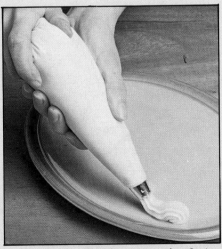

1 For a fancy border use a size 8 star nozzle. Hold the bag away from you and squeeze out 2.5 cm [1"] of purée.

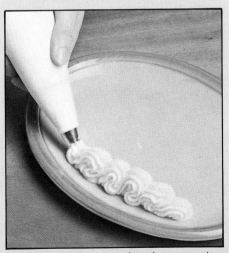

2 Keeping the nozzle close to the dish, squeeze again, then lift so that a scallop shape is formed by the purée.

QUICK AND TASTY WAYS WITH PUREES

There are so many delicious things that you can do with vegetable purées which will add an original touch to any meal. Here are a few of the simplest, quickest ones to try.

● For green duchesse potatoes, strip the leaves from 2 bunches of watercress. Plunge in boiling water for 1 minute, drain thoroughly, then reduce to a purée with 450 g [1 lb] cooked potatoes and pipe as described.

● A tasty idea from Germany is to mix 350 g [¾ lb] creamed potato with 50 ml [2 oz] unsweetened apple purée. Serve with roast pork, duck or any spiced or smoked continental sausage.

● Bubble and squeak is an old favourite. Mix together equal quantities of creamed potato and cooked, finely chopped cabbage or broccoli, spinach or Brussels sprouts. Fry in a little dripping, stirring occasionally, until lightly browned.

● Rumbledethumps are small bubble and squeak patties. Make the bubble and squeak as above. Using floured hands, form the bubble and squeak into small balls. Flatten, dust with wholemeal flour and fry in dripping until golden brown.

● For interesting flavours combine two vegetables in one purée using equal quantities of potato and celeriac or peas.

● Puréed beetroot and apple (75% beetroot 25% apple) makes an excellent accompaniment to roasted game.

● For leek and potato patties, mix 225 g [½ lb] potato purée with 225 g [½ lb] steamed and chopped leeks. Form into patties, brush with beaten egg and cook in an oven heated to 200°C [400°F] gas mark 6 for 30 minutes or until golden and puffy.

● For oeufs soubise make a purée of onion with plenty of cream. Pour over hot soft-boiled eggs and garnish with parsley and triangles of fried bread.

Vegetables to purée

VEGETABLES	METHOD	SUGGESTED ADDITIONS
Artichoke (Jerusalem)	Sieve or mill	Milk or cream, butter and a pinch of nutmeg
Beetroot	Sieve or mill	Grated rind (zest) and juice of an orange
Broad beans	Sieve or mill	A little cream and chopped fresh savory
Carrots	Sieve or mill	Butter and sour cream or yoghurt, chopped fresh parsley or chives
Cauliflower	Mill or liquidizer	Butter, cream and a crushed garlic clove or nutmeg
Celeriac	Sieve or mill	Milk or cream, butter and a pinch of nutmeg
Leeks	Sieve or mill	Butter and cream
Marrow	Mash occasionally during cooking. No further treatment needed	Cream and a little cinamon
Mushrooms	Liquidizer	Cooked in butter so there is no need for additions. Add a crushed garlic clove during cooking for extra flavour.
Onions	Mill or liquidizer	Butter, fresh or sour cream or yoghurt
Parsnip	Mill or liquidizer	Butter, cream and a little nutmeg
Peas	Sieve, mill or liquidizer	Cream and chopped fresh mint
Pumpkin	As marrow	Cream and cinnamon or stem ginger
Potatoes	Masher, sieve, mill or liquidizer	Milk or cream, butter, eggs plus a crushed garlic clove or chopped fresh chives
Sorrel	Mill or liquidizer	Cream and butter
Spinach	Mill or liquidizer	Cream and butter plus a crushed garlic clove
Swede	Masher, sieve or mill	Butter and a little grated nutmeg
Turnip	Masher, sieve or mill	Butter and a little grated nutmeg

CARROT AND CREAM CHEESE PATE

When mixing the cream cheese and carrot purée, add the cheese a little at a time, otherwise it will not blend evenly.

If you do not have a pâté dish or a loaf tin, use an 18 cm [7"] sandwich tin instead. Line the tin with greaseproof paper to prevent sticking.

SERVES 4
800 g [1¾ lb] carrots
350 g [¾ lb] full fat cream cheese
10 ml [2 teaspoons] freshly chopped parsley
salt and pepper
a few chopped chives
a few sprigs of watercress and cucumber slices for garnish

1 Scrub the carrots, cut off the tops and root ends and cut into pieces. Cook in boiling salted water for 7 minutes.

2 Drain the carrots, return them to the cleaned-out saucepan and dry over low heat for 1 minute, shaking the pan occasionally.

3 Mash the carrots with a strong fork or vegetable masher or put through coarse grid of a food mill to give a tough-textured purée.

4 Allow the purée to become cold then beat in the cream cheese a little at a time using a fork. The cream cheese binds the mixture.

5 Add the chopped parsley and chives, season with salt and pepper and mix until well blended.

6 Place a sheet of greaseproof paper in a 12.5 cm [5"] loaf tin to line. Press the mixture firmly into the tin and level the top with a palette knife.

7 Cover the tin with foil and refrigerate for 3 hours.

8 Run a knife between the pâté and the loaf tin to loosen it. Place a plate on the top and invert, lifting the dish away from the plate.

9 Decorate the top of the pâté with the cucumber slices and watercress sprigs. Cut into slices and serve immediately.

Carrot and cream cheese pâté is a good way to use up old or blemished carrots. It is excellent spread on toast.

Variation

● Instead of carrots use mushroom, pea or broad bean purée. Garnish with sliced tomatoes.

MUSHROOM SUPPER

A purée of open-type mushrooms is really delicious but their greyish colour can deter some people. You can use white button mushrooms instead but their flavour is less good and they are often more expensive.

SERVES 4
450 g [1 lb] mushrooms
75 g [3 oz] butter
45 ml [3 tablespoons] sour cream
4 slices wholemeal bread
4 slices cooked ham
20 ml [4 teaspoons] chopped parsley

1 Wipe the mushrooms with a damp cloth but do not peel. Remove earthy stalk ends.

2 Slice the mushrooms in half.

3 Melt the butter in a heavy-based saucepan. Add the mushrooms, cover and simmer gently for about 10 minutes or until tender.

4 Remove the saucepan from the heat. Allow the mushrooms to cool a little, then stir in the cream.

5 Pour the mushroom mixture into a liquidizer and blend at medium speed for 40 seconds.

6 Toast the wholemeal bread on both sides. Butter the toast if wished.

7 Place a slice of ham on each slice of toast. Top with mushroom purée.

8 Re-heat under a hot grill for 1 minute. Sprinkle with chopped parsley and serve immediately.

Variation

● For pea and bacon supper make a purée using 350 g [¾ lb] peas mixed with 30 ml [2 tablespoons] cream. Make the purée either using a food mill or a liquidizer. Pile on wholemeal toast and top with crisp crumbled bacon.

SPRING TERRINE

This hot savoury loaf makes an economical and imaginative meal and is delicious served with sauce tartare or a garlic-flavoured tomato sauce. After cooking the terrine, leave the loaf to stand for a few minutes so that it shrinks away from the sides of the dish and comes out cleanly.

SERVES 4

1 small cauliflower
1 medium-sized onion
1 bunch watercress
6 rashers streaky bacon
2 thick slices wholemeal bread
2 medium-sized eggs
150 ml [¼ pt] sour cream
30 ml [2 tablespoons] freshly chopped parsley
pinch of grated nutmeg
freshly ground black pepper
15 g [½ oz] butter

1 Heat the oven to 190°C [375°F] gas mark 5, and heat the grill.

2 Peel the onion and cook in boiling salted water for 15 minutes, or until tender.

3 Remove the outer leaves and coarse stalk end from cauliflower and discard. Divide into florets.

4 Add the cauliflower to the onion for the last 10 minutes of cooking time.

5 Meanwhile, remove the rind from the bacon rashers and grill two of them for 1 minute on each side.

6 Remove the crusts from the bread and reduce to crumbs using a cheese grater or a liquidizer.

7 Remove the coarse stalk ends and any blemished leaves from the watercress. Set a few sprigs aside.

8 Plunge remaining watercress in boiling water for 1 minute.

Vegetable purees can be used to make substantial dishes. Shown left is cheesy Gipsy Pie and right, tasty cauliflower Spring Terrine.

9 Drain the vegetables and dry over low heat for 1 minute, shaking the pan occasionally.

10 Chop the onion into rough pieces with knife and fork and add to the cauliflower and watercress.

11 Pass the mixture through the fine grid of a food mill. Or reduce to a purée in a liquidizer for about 40 seconds at medium speed.

12 Break the eggs into the purée and mix with a fork until well blended.

13 Cut the two cooked bacon rashers into small strips; add to purée.

14 Add the sour cream, breadcrumbs and seasonings. Stir with a fork until well blended.

15 Butter the base and sides of a 1 kg [2 lb] loaf tin or pâté dish.

16 Lay the whole bacon rashers along the bottom of the dish. Pile the purée on top and level with a palette knife.

17 Cover with a piece of greased kitchen foil and cook in the centre of the oven for 1 hour.

18 When cooked, remove the foil and leave to stand for about 3 minutes. Run a knife around the inside of the dish. Invert a plate over the top, turn the dish upside down and lift the dish away from the terrine.

19 Garnish with the reserved sprigs of watercress and serve.

GIPSY PIE

◢◣*Use a deep dish to cook this pie. Do not grease it – the potato contains enough butter to prevent it from sticking. Any extra grease would make the pie fry.*

SERVES 4
675 g [1½ lb] potatoes
1 medium-sized onion
a little oil
40 g [1½ oz] butter
45 ml [3 tablespoons] milk
1 medium-sized egg
175 g [6 oz] Cheddar cheese
6 ripe tomatoes
freshly ground black pepper
sprigs of parsley to garnish

1 Heat the oven to 200°C [400°F] gas mark 6.

2 Peel the potatoes, cut into chunks and cook in boiling salted water until tender.

3 Meanwhile, peel and chop the onion and fry in oil until golden and transparent.

4 Drain the potatoes and dry over low heat for 1 minute, shaking the pan occasionally.

5 Mash the potatoes until quite smooth.

6 Put the milk and butter in a saucepan and heat until the butter is melted and the milk is hot.

7 Add the potatoes and beat over low heat until fluffy.

8 Remove from the heat. Beat the egg and add to the potatoes. Stir until well blended.

9 Grate the cheese and stir 150 g [5 oz] into the potatoes.

10 Slice the tomatoes thinly.

11 Place one third of the potato in a deep 18 cm [7"] oven proof dish. Level potato with a palette knife.

12 Place half of the onions and a third of the tomatoes over the layer of potato. Season with freshly ground black pepper.

13 Make another layer of potatoes, onions and tomatoes.

14 Add a final layer of potato. Arrange the remaining sliced tomatoes in a pattern on top and sprinkle with remaining cheese.

15 Cook in the centre of the oven for 30 minutes until golden and bubbling.

16 Garnish with parsley and serve immediately.

Variations
● For half the potato substitute either leek or spinach. If using leeks, omit the onion and use 4 rashers of crisply fried crumbled bacon instead.
● For a slimmer's pie, use cauliflower instead of potato.

JERUSALEM SAVOURY

◢◣*As Jerusalem artichokes have a short season and are sometimes difficult to obtain, mixing them with another purée is a good idea.*
Cloves give the onions an unusual and interesting flavour but they can be omitted if wished.

SERVES 4
350 g [¾ lb] Jerusalem artichokes
2 medium-sized onions
2 cloves
40 g [1½ oz] butter
45 ml [3 tablespoons] thick cream
freshly ground black pepper
salt
2 slices stale wholemeal bread

1 Scrub the artichokes but do not peel them.

2 Peel the onions and stick a clove in each one.

3 Cook the artichokes in a pan of boiling salted water for 15 minutes, or until tender. Add onions after 5 minutes.

4 Meanwhile, make breadcrumbs using a liquidizer or a grater.

5 Drain the vegetables, cut them into pieces and return to the cleaned-out pan.

6 Dry for 1 minute over low heat, shaking occasionally.

7 Pass the vegetables a few at a time through a food mill, using the medium blade.

8 Add the cream and a good seasoning of black pepper to the purée and stir well to thoroughly blend all the ingredients.

9 Melt 25 g [1 oz] of the butter in a heavy-based pan over low heat.

10 Add the crumbs and cook until browned (this will take about 1 minute). Shake the pan occasionally to prevent sticking.

11 Add the remaining butter to the purée and re-heat gently, stirring occasionally.

12 Turn the purée into a serving dish and top with the browned crumbs.

POTATO SOUFFLÉ

In this soufflé the potato supplies the starch element and forms the panada without the addition of white sauce. The potatoes are puréed and mixed with thick cream. Extra egg whites are included (and slightly fewer yolks) to help the heavy mixture rise.

SERVES 4
**30 ml [2 tablespoons]
  breadcrumbs
450 g [1 lb] potatoes
3 eggs
2 egg whites
75 ml [3 fl oz] thick cream
75 g [3 oz] grated Parmesan
  cheese
salt and pepper
pinch each of nutmeg and
  cayenne**

1 Butter a 1.15 L [2 pt] soufflé dish then coat with breadcrumbs. Tip out excess. Put it in the refrigerator to chill.

2 Set the oven to 190°C [375°F] gas mark 5. Put a baking tray on the centre shelf and remove upper shelves.

3 Peel the potatoes and simmer in salted water for 20 minutes.

4 Drain and purée the potatoes by putting through a sieve or vegetable mill. Allow to cool.

5 Separate the eggs. Add the two extra whites to the other whites in the largest bowl. Beat the yolks with a wooden spoon.

6 Mix the cream, cheese and mixed egg yolks into the warm potato purée. Add seasoning.

7 When the oven has reached the required temperature, add a pinch of salt to the egg whites. Whisk until stiff—until they stand in peaks on an upturned whisk.

8 Put two spoonfuls of egg white into the potato purée and stir in, to reduce the stiffness of the panada.

9 Fold the potato mixture into the egg whites, using a rubber spatula or metal spoon.

10 Pour into the soufflé dish. Put dish on heated baking tray and bake for 25 minutes.

244

Vegetables

shallow frying

Shallow-fried vegetables are a family favourite. They are soft, golden and melting, crisp on the outside and tender within. Learn the simple technique of how to prepare different types of vegetable for successful frying.

The principle of shallow frying is to cook vegetables in fat over direct heat—to produce a crisp outside and tender centre within, not, as is sometimes the case, burnt offerings!

It is very important to prepare the vegetables correctly, use the right fat and equipment and gauge timing and temperature exactly.

There are four types of shallow frying: softening, sweating, browning and sautéing. Softening, sweating and browning are usually preliminaries to other cooking methods, such as soups, casseroles or stews. Sautéed vegetables are served without further cooking.

Vegetables (usually sliced or diced) are softened in fat over a low heat. Stir or shake the pan occasionally until they are quite tender. Sweating vegetables is done by covering the vegetables and fat with a lid and cooking them over a low heat until they are soft but not brown. The browning technique is done by softening the vegetables first, then increasing the heat so that they are coloured. This gives the final dish a good colour, and is especially suitable for meat dishes.

Sautéing is true shallow frying. The vegetables are cooked in a sauté pan (described under Equipment) with a little fat. During cooking, the vegetables are moved around and turned over constantly in the pan so that they are evenly browned. This moving about has led to the term sauté, from the French 'sauter', to jump, because the vegetables are jumped or shaken around as they cook.

This chapter shows you how to sauté perfectly, to make complete vegetable dishes.

A whole range of fresh vegetables can be shallow fried, either on their own or in tasty combinations.

TYPES OF VEGETABLE TO SAUTE

Firm vegetables (such as root vegetables) are perhaps the most suitable for shallow frying because they retain their shape and absorb the fat well. Softer vegetables, such as marrow and aubergines, need a little initial preparation before cooking. Only leafy green vegetables, such as spinach and lettuce are not suitable for shallow frying.

Aubergines, courgettes, cucumber and marrow

These rather watery vegetables should be sprinkled with salt before cooking to extract excess moisture (the French call this process dégorgé). First wipe the skins clean with a damp cloth and trim off the ends of the vegetables. Leave on the skins, which help hold the shape of the vegetables. Cut aubergines, courgettes and marrow into 12 mm [½"] slices and cucumber into 6 mm [¼"] slices. Remove the marrow seeds.

Salting: prepare the vegetables at least 40 minutes before you intend to fry them. Place the sliced vegetables in a colander, sprinkling generously with salt between layers; sea salt or another coarse salt is best for this purpose. Cover the vegetables with a plate that just fits snugly inside the colander, and press it down heavily by putting a weight such as a kitchen jar on top. It is best to stand the colander on a draining-board before you start so that the water can drain away. Leave for at least 30 minutes so that the juices (in the case of aubergines, unpalatable bitter juices) are drawn out. Thoroughly rinse each slice under a cold running tap and pat dry with kitchen paper.

Celery and florentine fennel

Cut off the green tops from the celery and fennel and trim the bases (reserve the feathery fronds of fennel which can be chopped and used in a salad). Cut celery into 3.75 cm [1½"] lengths, chop the fennel to roughly the same size as the celery.

Mushrooms

For frying whole, use dark, open mushrooms. Wipe the mushroom caps clean with a damp cloth and trim the stalks level with the caps. The more delicately flavoured button mushrooms should be thinly sliced.

Onions and leeks

Peel onions and chop them. Baby onions may be left whole. Trim and wash leeks and slice into 6 mm [¼"] rounds. Alternatively, cut leeks in half lengthways and then into matchstick-sized pieces.

Peppers

Cut off the tops of the peppers and remove and discard the pithy core and seeds. Cut the peppers into 25 · 6 mm [1 · ¼"] strips or into 12 mm [½"] dice. Because they have a very strong taste, peppers are best fried in a mixture of vegetables.

Potatoes, turnips, parsnips and Jerusalem artichokes

Scrub the vegetables. You can leave the skins on to get a rich earthy flavour. Slice old potatoes into 6 mm [¼"] slices. Leave new potatoes whole. Peel and slice artichokes, turnips and parsnips at 6 mm [¼"] intervals. Parsnips should not be more than 2.5 cm [1"] across.

Tomatoes

Although you can buy so-called 'frying tomatoes' in many greengrocers' shops, tomatoes are not really very suitable for frying because they are so juicy. To prepare tomatoes for frying, scald them by placing them in a bowl of boiling hot water for 15 seconds and then remove and skin them. For frying, either leave them whole or cut them in half lengthways.

EQUIPMENT

It is very important to choose the correct pan for each different type of frying. For softening, sweating and browning, use a medium-sized frying-pan with a good thick base and relatively low sides—5 cm [2"] high. In this type of pan the sides rise straight from the base at a slight angle sloping outwards. Omelette pans are not really suitable for frying as they have gradually curving sides. The vegetables in this shape of pan are inclined to 'creep' up the sides and as a result do not cook evenly.

A special frying-pan is sold for sautéing vegetables. This is called a sauté pan or 'sautoir'. It has a heavy base and straight sides to contain the vegetables as they move round inside the pan. The sides of the pan, however, are not as high as those of a saucepan. They should not be more than 5 cm [2"] high, otherwise they would tend to trap moisture in the pan and this would prevent the vegetables from becoming properly crisp. A family-size sauté pan should measure 20 cm [8"] across the base.

Cast iron, stainless steel and heavy enamel are ideal materials for both types of pan. For softening, sweating and browning, the large two-handled skillets or paella pans, made of cast iron or steel, are suitable. However, it is very important that your sauté pan has a long handle, so that your hand will not get splattered with hot fat as you are frying. If possible, choose a pan with a handle made of heatproof material, such as wood or plastic, because you handle a sauté pan more frequently than a saucepan. If you are buying a cast-iron pan check that the handle is suitably long, as it may get very hot close to the frying-pan.

Apart from the sauté pan you will need a metal fish slice to turn the vegetables over, and to remove them from the pan. Although you can use a spatula for this job, a fish slice is best because excess fat can drip through the holes as the vegetables are lifted from the pan.

TYPES OF FAT

Different types of fats and oils have different qualities and flavours, so choose one which complements the vegetables to be fried. Fried vegetables absorb a good deal of fat as they cook and so pick up the flavour.

Butter can be used for frying all raw vegetables. It is particularly appropriate for the more delicate tasting ones, such as courgettes and button mushrooms. However, butter has a fairly low smoke point, that is, it burns fairly easily. If you are going to fry cooked or parboiled vegetables which are usually fried at a high temperature, it is a good idea to mix the butter in equal quantities with a good quality oil. The oil can stand higher temperatures and prevents sticking and burning.

Oils suitable for mixing with butter are groundnut oil or sunflower oil. Olive oil gives a distinctive flavour to vegetables and it can be effectively used alone.

Dripping or bacon fat can be used to give a meaty flavour to root vegetables and onions. Choose dripping or bacon to complement the flavours of your main dish.

Speck, the smoked fat, gives a smoky, salty taste to vegetables. It is usually supplied in one large piece. Chop it up into small pieces and put it in a frying-pan over a low heat to let it sweat out liquid fat, which is the fat used for frying. This process, called rendering down solid fat, is continued until the fat has all been exuded. Either discard the pieces that are left in the pan or keep them in the pan to make crisp, tasty additions to the final dish.

Lard and commercial shortenings are colourless and flavourless and do not contribute any quality to the final dish. However, they can be used for gently softening onions, for example, as the first stage in the preparation of a main dish.

Step-by-step to salting vegetables

1 Wipe the vegetables clean with a damp cloth, but do not remove the skin.

2 Trim off the stalk end and the tip, then cut the vegetables into thin slices across.

3 Place some slices in a colander. Sprinkle generously with salt and repeat after each layer of slices.

4 Cover the vegetables with a plate that just fits snugly inside the colander and weigh down.

5 Leave for at least 30 minutes on the draining-board so that all the excess juices are drawn out.

6 Rinse each slice thoroughly under a cold running tap, and pat dry with kitchen paper.

FLAVOURINGS

Single, or mixed dishes of hot, sautéed vegetables invite the use of imaginative flavourings. Use freshly chopped herbs such as sage, thyme, parsley, savory or finely chopped garlic, or a little grated orange or lemon rind added to the pan during the last few minutes of cooking. Choose the herbs to suit the vegetables.

Grated cheese such as Cheddar, Gruyère or Parmesan can be sprinkled liberally over the final dish. This will melt slightly over the vegetables and add extra flavour.

TIMINGS

Shallow frying vegetables takes a relatively short time because the vegetables are generally either sliced or chopped before cooking. The timings for raw vegetables are given here.

Root vegetables, such as potatoes, artichokes, parsnips, swedes and turnips, fried sliced or chopped, need the longest cooking time. To soften and then brown, they need about 20 minutes. Whole new potatoes, if they are small, should take no longer.

Sliced or chopped celery, fennel, courgettes and whole button onions cook in 15 minutes. Sliced onions take a little less time. Leeks and marrow take 10 minutes—green peppers a couple of minutes longer.

Watery vegetables, such as cucumber and aubergines, take only five minutes to shallow fry. Whole or sliced mushrooms take three minutes and tomatoes only need to be 'shown the pan' for about one to one and a half minutes.

Vegetables which have been partially cooked will take less time to fry because they are already soft and the pan is put over a higher heat than with raw vegetables. The vegetables are then finished off by browning nicely all over. This should take no more than 5-10 minutes.

THE BASIC METHOD

Shallow frying or sautéing vegetables may seem misleadingly simple to do, but there is, in fact, quite a knack to it. There are some vital points to remember if you are to get it right every time. The most important things to keep in mind are to prepare the vegetables correctly, to use the right pan, to get the correct depth and heat for the fat in the pan, and to fry the correct quantity of vegetables at a time.

Size
Whether you are frying a single vegetable or a mixture of different vegetables, make sure that they are small and all the same size. Large pieces of raw vegetable would take a long time to soften (and may consequently burn) while unevenly sized pieces will be ready at different times.

Blotting vegetables
The vegetables should be as dry as possible. Pat raw vegetables, such as potatoes, and dry with kitchen paper on the cut sides after chopping. Any drops of water that come into contact with the hot fat in the pan will cause spitting and the vegetables will be soggy rather than crisp.

Parboiling
The hard root vegetables such as potatoes, parsnips, Jerusalem artichokes, swedes and turnips have the longest cooking times. To shorten this they can be parboiled before frying. This reduces subsequent frying time and, because the vegetables are soft on the outside, they go deliciously crisp when fried.

Parboil the vegetables whole, until they are soft on the outside but still firm inside, then drain them very thoroughly. When they are cool enough to handle, chop or slice as required.

Blanching
The slightly bitter taste of green peppers can be eliminated by blanching. Slice the peppers, place them in a pan of cold water and bring to the boil. Drain the peppers into a sieve and then dry the pieces thoroughly on kitchen paper.

Quantity of fat
Have enough fat in the frying-pan to give you around 6 mm [¼"] in the bottom. The amount you use depends on the size of the pan, but a rough guide is 25-40 g [1-1½ oz] fat or 60-90 ml [4-6 tablespoons] oil for each 450 g [1 lb] of vegetables in a 20 cm [8"] pan base. This gives enough fat for the vegetables to crisp well, without burning or becoming soggy.

Heating the fat
Place the fat or oil in the frying-pan (if you are using a mixture of oil and

butter, add them together) over a low heat until completely melted and hot—it will take about 30 seconds.

Temperatures
Different vegetables are cooked over different heats. The following guide is for raw vegetables—parboiled vegetables should be cooked on a rather higher heat.

Celery, fennel and whole or sliced onions should be cooked on a low heat, so that they are completely softened without crisping.

Vegetables best cooked on a medium heat are potatoes, artichokes, parsnips, swedes, turnips, courgettes, leeks, marrow, cucumber and aubergines. Increase the heat under the frying-pan to medium before frying. For crisp rather than just softened onions, use a medium heat instead of a low one.

Smaller, watery vegetables such as whole or sliced mushrooms and tomatoes should be cooked over a medium to high heat to prevent them breaking down and all the juices leaking out into the pan.

249

Step-by-step to sauté potatoes

450 g [1 lb] waxy potatoes
15-20 g [½-¾ oz] butter and 30-45
ml [2-3 tablespoons] oil

1 Parboil the potatoes, drain and dry them thoroughly. Cut each potato across into 6 mm [¼"] slices.

2 Put enough fat in a sauté pan to cover the base to 6 mm [¼"] depth. Place over low heat.

3 Increase heat to medium, add enough potatoes to just fill pan. Cook a few seconds.

4 Start to turn the potatoes with a fish slice, and keep turning them regularly.

5 As the potatoes begin to absorb the fat, shake the pan over the heat to prevent sticking.

6 When the potatoes are cooked, lift them out with a fish slice allowing excess fat to drain away.

7 Place the potatoes on 2-3 layers of paper towels which will absorb any extra grease.

8 Slide the potatoes from the paper towels on to a warmed serving dish. Sprinkle herbs if wished.

Vegetable quantities

Slide the vegetables from the chopping-board into the pan over the correct heat. Don't put too many vegetables into the pan at once. If the vegetables are piled up in several layers, moisture will not be allowed to escape from underneath and they will become slightly limp and soggy before they brown.

If you have a large quantity of vegetables to cook you can either use two frying-pans at once, or fry in batches. Keep the first batch of cooked vegetables warm, until the others are ready, in a dish lined with paper towels to mop up excess grease. Do not cover the dish because the vegetables may go soggy. Turn them into a serving dish when all the vegetables are ready and serve immediately.

Turning the vegetables

Once the vegetables are in the pan, allow them to fry for about 15 seconds on one side, then turn them frequently during the rest of their cooking time, to ensure that they are evenly browned. As the vegetables begin to absorb the fat from the pan, shake the pan frequently so that they do not stick to the base.

Vegetables with a very short cooking time, such as mushrooms, tomatoes and aubergines, need to be turned only once during cooking. This seals in the juices and the outside becomes crisp. Both mushrooms and halved tomatoes should be fried on the cap, or rounded, side first.

Draining off fat

As soon as the vegetables are ready—crisp and golden on the outside, with a soft centre—lift them out of the frying-pan with a fish slice. Hold them over the pan for a moment to allow excess fat to drain away.

To be absolutely sure that you get beautifully crisp results, have ready two to three thicknesses of kitchen paper towels laid out on a flat surface (a draining-board is ideal). Slide the vegetables on to the paper and allow about half a minute for any grease to be absorbed. Then, if you are only frying one batch, tip the vegetables into a hot serving dish.

Batch frying

If you are frying a second batch of vegetables in the same pan, you will find that the first vegetables to be cooked absorb most of the fat or oil. Add enough fat to give you a depth of about 6 mm [¼"] again in the bottom of the pan. Heat the fat and fry the vegetables as before.

TASTY IDEAS FOR SAUTE DISHES

● For a simple party dish, fry chopped celery in butter over a low heat for 15 minutes. Add some chopped walnuts to the pan for the last few minutes of cooking and serve them scattered with the grated zest of one orange.

● Fry sliced onions and sliced potatoes together over moderate heat for 20 minutes in half butter and half oil. Alternatively, add chopped spring onions to the pan five minutes before the end of cooking time. Transfer to a serving dish and gently toss in chopped fresh herbs such as parsley or chives.

● For lemony mushrooms, fry mushrooms quickly, cap side first, in dripping or bacon fat for three minutes, turning once. Mix in grated lemon zest or some chopped lemon thyme, or freshly chopped parsley just before serving.

● Sauté parboiled parsnips in butter over a high heat. Then toss them with grated cheese or finely chopped fresh parsley.

● Toss sliced marrow in seasoned flour before frying; there is no need to salt the marrow first. The flour may be seasoned with a little paprika or curry powder as well as salt and pepper. Use bacon fat, speck or butter and add sliced onion to the pan when the fat melts. Then add the marrow slices. Cook over a medium heat for 10 minutes. Toss the vegetables in chopped sage before serving. As an alternative to sage, dill or caraway seeds can be added to the pan with the onions.

● Fry a mixture of sliced parsnips and sliced potatoes together in half butter and half oil.

● For glazed onions, fry button onions in butter or dripping over low heat. Sprinkle over a little soft brown sugar a few minutes before the end of cooking time and shake the pan well to coat the onions. Just before serving, toss in finely chopped parsley or thyme. Serve sprinkled with grated Cheddar, Parmesan or Gruyère cheese.

● For a fennel hors d'oeuvre, fry chopped fennel in butter over low heat for 15 minutes. Add chopped shelled walnuts to the pan for the last few minutes of cooking. Just before serving, pour in the juice of a lemon and let it bubble. Serve the fennel with lemony juices poured over.

● Fry sliced leek rings over a medium heat in butter for 10 minutes. Add freshly chopped parsley or savory just before removing the leeks from the pan. A little Dijon or Meaux mustard can also be added. Mustard-flavoured leeks are a good accompaniment to pork.

● Fry sliced swedes in dripping over a medium heat for 20 minutes. Add a little chopped rosemary or thyme to the pan for the last few minutes of cooking.

● Crispy onion rings make a substantial vegetable dish. Dip onion rings in beaten egg and then in seasoned flour until they are coated. Fry in dripping over a medium heat until the rings brown. The flour takes on the meaty flavour of the fat. Drain on paper and serve hot with grilled meat or cold as an accompaniment to drinks—a change from nuts and crisps.

● For a garlic-flavoured vegetable medley, fry salted and drained sliced aubergines and courgettes together with sliced onions and mushrooms. Use butter and add chopped garlic to the pan. Tomatoes can be added at the last minute after skinning and chopping.

● Bring out the smoky flavour of Jerusalem artichokes by frying them in bacon fat or speck. Cook a little bacon in the fat first. Remove, dice and reserve. Fry the artichokes for 20 minutes over a medium heat, then return the bacon to the pan for long enough to reheat it. Add some finely chopped fresh sage and sprinkle grated strong cheese on the top before serving.

● Fry turnip slices in a mixture of butter and oil. For the last few minutes of cooking time, scatter in a little mustard powder or add chopped sage or lemon thyme.

● Combine sliced Jerusalem artichokes and leeks and fry in bacon fat or dripping.

● Fry sliced celery, onions, mushrooms and green peppers in olive oil with a little chopped garlic. Tomatoes can be added to this dish at the last minute after skinning and chopping. To make a complete dish, turn this mixture into a pie dish, top with pastry and bake in the oven.

ROSTI

A famous Swiss dish, the success of rösti depends on using waxy potatoes to get the right texture. It is traditionally served with veal in a creamy sauce but is excellent with creamy chicken and plain grills and roasts. A 22.5 cm [9"] sauté pan is best for this quantity of potatoes.

SERVES 4
700 g [1½ lb] potatoes
75 g [3 oz] streaky bacon
1 onion
60 ml [4 tablespoons] lard
salt
freshly ground black pepper

1 Parboil the potatoes in their skins and allow them to become quite cold. They are easiest to handle when refrigerated overnight.

2 Peel away the potato skins and grate the flesh on the coarse grater.

3 Remove the bacon rind and cut the bacon into matchstick pieces. Peel and finely chop the onion.

4 Melt the fat in a heavy-based sauté pan over low heat. Add the bacon and onion and cook over low heat until softened. Then increase heat a little and allow them to brown.

5 Add the potatoes, season with salt and freshly ground black pepper and fry over medium heat. Loosen the mixture occasionally round the base of the pan, turning over with a fish slice or spatula. Cook for 30 minutes.

6 Press the potatoes down into the pan to form a firm cake, cover with the sauté pan lid and continue frying over medium heat until a golden crust has formed underneath. This will take about 15 minutes.

7 To serve, invert the mixture on to a warmed dish, so that the crusty golden surface is uppermost.

Variations
Ring the changes in the following ways, using the same weight of vegetables, bacon and oil as the basic recipe.
● For a parsnip cake, cook then mash parsnips and continue from step 3.

● Mix cooked mashed swedes or turnips with equal amounts of potato. Add grated nutmeg when using swedes. Add a little mustard powder when using turnips, cook as for potatoes.

CAULIFLOWER SAUTE

Parboiled sautéed cauliflower makes a special dinner party vegetable. The garlic may be omitted if you think your guests will dislike it. The breadcrumbs may be replaced with almonds, which are browned in the same way before adding lemon juice.

SERVES 4
1 cauliflower
1 bay leaf or bouquet garni
1 garlic clove
1 lemon
50 g [2 oz] butter
50 g [2 oz] dried breadcrumbs

1 Parboil the cauliflower in lightly salted water with the bay leaf or bouquet garni. Drain well.

2 Peel, crush or finely chop the garlic and squeeze the lemon.

3 Melt the butter in a heavy-based sauté pan over low heat. Increase the heat to medium, add the garlic and brown the cauliflower quickly, turning all the time.

4 Remove the cauliflower from the pan to a warm serving dish and keep hot.

5 Brown the dried breadcrumbs in the fat, then pour in the lemon juice.

6 Pour the lemony crumbs over the cauliflower and serve.

AUBERGINE CACIK

This recipe calls for the aubergines to be lightly dusted with flour. This will keep them deliciously crisp, but care must be taken during frying as they brown easily. Aubergine cacik is a Turkish hors d'oeuvre but it makes a good side dish with a grill. The amount of oil used depends on the size of the pan as you need a depth of 6 mm [¼"] in the base.

SERVES 4
450 g [1 lb] aubergines
40 g [1½ oz] flour
salt and pepper
90-150 ml [6-10 tablespoons] olive oil

For the sauce:
1 garlic clove
150 ml [¼ pt] sour cream or yoghurt
salt
freshly ground black pepper

1 Peel and crush the garlic, stir into the sour cream or yoghurt with plenty of salt and freshly ground black pepper. Chill in the refrigerator.

Serve rösti with veal or on its own for a simple lunch. Potatoes sautéed with parsnips or onions go well with hot or cold meats.

2 Clean the aubergines and trim off the ends. Cut across each aubergine into 6 m [¼"] slices.

3 Place the aubergine slices in a colander over a draining-board, sprinkling generously with salt between layers.

4 Cover with a plate that fits snugly inside the colander and weigh it down heavily. Leave the colander on the draining board to drip for 1 hour, so that the bitter brown juices are drawn out.

5 Thoroughly rinse each slice under a cold running tap and pat dry with kitchen paper.

6 Season the flour with salt and pepper. Dip the aubergine slices in the flour, till all sides are dusted. Shake off the excess flour.

7 Pour enough olive oil into the bottom of a sauté pan to a depth of 6 mm [¼"] and place over low heat.

8 Increase the heat to medium and place a few aubergine slices at a time into the pan. Fry for 2 minutes. Carefully turn the slices over with a fish slice or kitchen tongs, and cook for a further 3 minutes.

9 Remove the cooked aubergines from the pan and keep hot in a kitchen paper-lined dish while you fry the rest.

10 Fry further batches of aubergine slices, topping up the pan with olive oil as necessary.

11 Drain the final batch on kitchen paper and turn all the aubergines into a warmed serving dish. Serve with the chilled sauce in a separate bowl.

Variation

● For a cheaper version, use half aubergines and half courgettes. Cut the courgettes in thin diagonal slices and salt in the same way as for aubergines (there is no need to dust the courgettes with flour). Proceed as before by frying them together in batches.

Vegetables

roasting

Roast potatoes are a universal favourite but did you know that leeks, swede, turnips, carrots and parsnips can be roasted too? Try serving roast vegetables for a change. They are full of flavour and, very filling.

Everyone loves potatoes roasted around the meat but, for most cooks, that is where vegetable roasting ends. This is a pity because many root vegetables can be roasted—with delicious results. Roast vegetables make excellent accompaniments to meat and fish dishes and if a little cheese or bacon is added, they make a meal in themselves.

With rising fuel costs, it is a good idea to make the best use possible of oven heat. If the oven is already heated to cook a joint, casserole or a savoury pie, you can utilize the valuable heat and space by serving roast rather then boiled or steamed vegetables as an accompaniment.

Roasting vegetables does not commit you to having just one vegetable with your meal. Roast different kinds together, adding those which need the least cooking heat last. Here you will find lots of good and tasty ideas to make your cooking more economical and interesting.

SUITABLE VEGETABLES AND THEIR PREPARATION

Many people think that potatoes are the only vegetable which can be roasted but there are many others which can be cooked in this way with good results.

Beetroot taste much better roasted than they do boiled. Choose small round beets. Parboil them for 30 minutes, as they are very hard. Cut in half lengthways and slip off the skins before roasting.

Carrots can be roasted whole, in butter if new, around a joint of meat if old. Simply scrub new carrots and halve or quarter lengthways if very large.

Celeriac looks like a tough customer but takes well to roasting. Peel and cut into slices 2 cm [¾"] thick. Brush with lemon juice to prevent discolouration.

Jerusalem artichokes develop a melting texture and an earthy flavour when roasted. Peel and cut in half lengthways. Rub with lemon juice to prevent discolouration.

Leeks can be roasted alone in butter or around a joint of meat. Prepare the leeks just as you would for boiling.

Marrow makes a good, filling dish when roasted. Peel the marrow, cut into rings about 5 cm [2"] thick and remove the seed section if wished.

Mushrooms are not usually thought of as vegetables to roast but this is a tasty and unusual way to cook them. Choose large flat mushrooms. Trim off the stalks level with the caps. Save the stalks for use in stock, soup or sauce. Wipe the caps.

Onions can be roasted whole in butter or around a joint of meat if small, halved or quartered if large. Spanish onions have the best flavour.

Potatoes are the vegetables everyone thinks of when roasting is mentioned. Old potatoes are best for roasting though new potatoes can be roasted if wished, but they don't produce the same floury results. Peel the potatoes. Leave whole if small, halve or quarter if large.

If wished, the potatoes may be parboiled before roasting though many people say this does not give such good results as starting roasting with the potatoes in a raw state.

Parsnips are delicious roasted around a joint of meat or in butter. Prepare as for old carrots.

Pumpkin is a much-loved vegetable in the United States and South Africa but rather neglected in other countries. Cut the pumpkin into slices about 5 cm [2"] thick. Remove the peel and seeds. Cut into 2.5 cm [1"] chunks before roasting.

Swede keeps all its flavour but loses any trace of stringiness if roasted. Peel and cut into 2.5 cm [1"] dice.

Turnip can also be roasted and is prepared in the same way as swede.

EQUIPMENT

The only equipment needed for roasting vegetables is an ovenproof dish or roasting tin. Metal dishes are best because they conduct the heat well and encourage the vegetables to cook evenly. A shallow cast iron gratin dish is perfect for roasting vegetables. Failing this a meat roasting tin can be used.

Ovenproof glass dishes can be used for roasting vegetables but you may find that cooking time is slightly increased because glass does not conduct the heat so well as metal.

FATS

The fat is very important when roasting vegetables as this is what helps the vegetables to cook and gives flavour.

When roasting vegetables around meat, there is no need to add extra fat as the meat provides sufficient to cook the vegetables and add flavour.

You will need about 75 g [3 oz] of fat per 450 g [1 lb] of root vegetables, pumpkin, marrow and leeks and about 100 g [¼ lb] fat per 450 g [1 lb] mushrooms. Never use more fat than this or the end result will be soggy and swimming in grease.

Salted butter is best for mushrooms, swede, turnips, beetroot,

A selection of roast vegetable, from left to right: roast leeks with chopped parsley, whole roast onions, roast diced swede; roast carrots sprinkled with fresh rosemary, roast parsnips with parsley. All are beautifully simple to cook and delicious served alone or as an accompaniment to roast meat, poultry or fish dishes.

celeriac, carrots, Jerusalem artichokes and marrow.

Well-flavoured beef or pork dripping is excellent with all root vegetables, including potatoes, giving beautiful crisp results. It also goes well with onions, leeks, pumpkin and marrow.

Bacon fat adds flavour and can be used with root vegetables, marrow, pumpkin and leeks. To give the required amount of fat, you will need about three large rashers of streaky bacon. Cut the bacon into small pieces and heat gently in a heavy-based pan over low heat until the fat runs freely. Speck can be used in the same way.

Lard can be used for root vegetables and potatoes but it does not add any flavour so should be reserved for days when there is nothing else available.

HERBS FOR FLAVOUR

To give roast vegetables more flavour, try placing a fresh herb sprig in the bottom of the dish. If the vegetables are roasted in butter, chop the herbs and combine them with the butter. Dried herbs are not suitable for roasting vegetables as they simply fry and don't give off any of their flavour.

Sage goes well with potatoes, carrots, onions and leeks. Thyme goes well with carrots, swede, turnips and parsnips. Dillweed and basil

both go well with mushrooms. Bay goes well with all vegetables. If you can't find fresh bay, a dried bay leaf may be used instead as it will not fry in quite the same way as other dried herbs.

THE BASIC PRINCIPLES

When vegetables are roasted, they are cooked in the oven in fat. This has the effect of making the outside of the vegetable slightly crisp and brown, while the inside remains tender and floury.

Parboiling

To speed cooking, some people like to parboil root vegetables for about 5 minutes before starting roasting. This does reduce roasting time but the vegetables are more inclined to absorb fat than if roasted from raw as the surface is softer.

The only time when it is essential to parboil, is if you are cooking the vegetables around meat and they take longer to cook than the meat. Parboiling means that the vegetables and the joint will be ready at the same time. Parboiling is also essential when roasting beetroot as they are very hard. Parboiling, except in the case of beetroot, is normally for 5 minutes. Drain the vegetables, re-fresh in cold water, drain again and pat dry with kitchen paper.

If potatoes are parboiled a good way to ensure they have a crisp surface is to roll them in plain flour before placing in the fat. You can also give parboiled vegetables a decorative and crisp finish by marking with a fork.

Heating the fat

The fat is placed in an ovenproof dish in the oven which is heated to 180°C [350°F] gas mark 4, and allowed to melt and become hot until it is sizzling but not smoking. This is the ideal temperature for roasting vegetables but if you are roasting around the joint and the temperature is higher, the vegetables will not spoil though the outsides may be rather crisp. Cooking time will also be slightly shorter.

Alternatively, roast the vegetables in a separate dish on the floor of the oven where the temperature is lower. The vegetables must not be added until the fat reaches the right temperature. If you put the vegetables in the fat before it is hot enough the outer surface will not be sealed.

If cooking around the meat wait until the fat is flowing freely and is sizzling.

Adding the vegetables

Place the prepared vegetables in the fat (on the pan base not the grid if cooking with meat) and turn them so that all sides are coated. This ensures even cooking.

Oven position

Most vegetables should be roasted in the centre of the oven where the heat is even. Potatoes however, should be roasted at the top of the oven where the temperature is slightly higher than given in the chart. This will ensure that they are crispy and golden brown.

Basting

During cooking, baste the vegetables from time to time with fat from the dish and turn them once. This ensures even cooking and prevents the part of the vegetables in contact with the dish being further cooked than the rest.

For crisp results, drain the vegetables on kitchen paper before serving. If the vegetables have to be kept waiting, drain on kitchen paper and keep in the bottom of the oven in an uncovered dish. Don't cover the dish or the vegetables will be steamy and unpleasant when served.

TASTY IDEAS

●Try roasting different vegetables together, adding those which need the shortest cooking time last. Potatoes and parsnips, carrots and swedes, turnips and carrots go well together. Cut into dice and roast in dripping.

●To make a meal from roast vegetables, lay a few rashers of streaky bacon across the top of the vegetables about 10 minutes before the end of cooking time. The bacon will be beautifully crisp.

●To give roast onions a beautiful glaze, brush them with honey allowing 30 ml [2 tablespoons] per 450 g [1 lb] about 10 minutes before the end of cooking time. You can also do this with carrots and swede. If you find the honey a little hard to spread, sprinkle with 25 g [1 oz] per 450 g [1 lb] brown sugar instead.

●Give the roast vegetables a tang by mixing mustard with the fat. Meaux, Dijon, French and German mustards are all good. Swede turnip and potatoes are particularly good with mustard.

●After roasting parsnips, remove the woody core and fill the cavity with grated cheese. Place under the grill until the cheese is golden and bubbling.

ROASTING TIMES FOR VEGETABLES

All times are for 450 g [1 lb] of vegetables cooked at 180°C [350°F] gas mark 4.

Vegetable	Time
Beetroot parboiled	60 minutes
Carrots whole, new	75 minutes
old, halved or quartered	45-60 minutes
diced	35 minutes
Celeriac	45 minutes
Jerusalem artichokes	45 minutes
Leeks	60 minutes
Marrow	45 minutes
Mushrooms	15 minutes
Onions baby	45 minutes
large, halved	50 minutes
quartered	45 minutes
Parsnips	as old carrots
Pumpkin	45 minutes
Potatoes small, whole, raw	70 minutes
parboiled	50 minutes
halved raw	60 minutes
halved, parboiled	45 minutes
large, quartered, raw	60 minutes
quartered, parboiled	40 minutes
diced, raw	35 minutes
Swede in chunks	75 minutes
diced	50 minutes
Turnip	as swede

Step-by-step to perfect roast potatoes

1 Measure fat and put in ovenproof dish. Place in oven heated to 180°C [350°F] gas mark 4.

2 Prepare the potatoes, cutting larger ones into halves or into quarters.

3 If wished, parboil the potatoes in salted water for 5 minutes. Drain well, dry and roll in flour.

OR for a decorative, crisp finish, scratch the surface of the potatoes with a fork.

4 When the fat is sizzling but not smoking, remove from the oven. Place the potatoes in the fat.

5 Turn the potatoes using two spoons so that all sides are well coated with fat. Add any herbs.

OR place the potatoes around the meat in pan base when the fat has started to run. Turn in fat.

AND baste the potatoes from time to time during cooking and turn them once using two spoons.

6 When the potatoes are brown on the outside, remove from the dish and serve. Discard herbs.

MUSHROOM ROAST

Because mushrooms are naturally tender vegetables, they need only a short cooking time. They need to be well coated with butter, so the butter is melted and poured over. Mixing the mustard with the butter means all the mushrooms are flavoured. Mushrooms cooked in this way make an unusual accompaniment to meat and poached fish.

SERVES 4
450 g [1 lb] open mushrooms
100 g [¼ lb] butter
15 ml [1 tablespoon] French or German mustard

1 Heat the oven to 180°C [350°F] gas mark 4.

2 Trim the mushroom stalks level with the caps. Wipe the caps.

3 Melt the butter in a heavy-based pan over a low heat.

4 Using a pastry brush, spread an ovenproof dish with butter.

5 Place the mushrooms, cap side down, in the dish.

6 Stir the mustard into the remaining butter. Pour over the mushrooms.

7 Roast for 15 minutes on the centre of the oven or until the mushrooms are tender.

CARAWAY BEETS

Beetroot must be parboiled before it can be roasted as it is a very hard vegetable. Parboiling for 30 minutes is enough to soften the beetroot without making it so soft that the fat will soak in. After the beetroot has been cut in half, it is essential to place it cut side down in the butter so the cut surface will be sealed and will not bleed.

SERVES 4
450 g [1 lb] small round beetroot
75 g [3 oz] butter
10 ml [2 teaspoons] caraway seeds

1 Wash the beetroot to remove the earth but do not break the skin or cut off any root or top.

2 Place the beetroot in boiling salted water and cook for 30 minutes.

3 Meanwhile, heat the oven to 180°C [350°F] gas mark 4.

4 Place the butter in an ovenproof dish and put in the oven.

5 Drain the beetroot and pat dry on kitchen towel.

6 Slip off the skins and cut the beetroot in half lengthways and cut off root and tops.

7 Place in the sizzling butter, cut side down. Turn the beetroot in the butter so they are well coated, making sure the cut side remains down.

9 Scatter the caraway seeds on top. Roast the beetroot for 1 hour in the centre of the oven basting from time to time but do not turn. Serve with the caraway butter spooned over.

POTATO AND HERB ROAST

New potatoes are so good it seems a pity to roast them but if you get some which are rather large for boiling, roasting gives a good flavour. Roasting new potatoes with their skins on gives a tasty compromise between roast and baked potatoes. The potatoes are not turned so that they can absorb the herb flavour through the cut side.

SERVES 4
450 g [1 lb] new potatoes
6-8 dried fennel stalks or sprigs of fresh thyme

1 Heat the oven to 180°C [350°F] gas mark 4.

2 Place the butter in an ovenproof dish. Put in the oven.

3 Scrub the potatoes and cut in half lengthways.

4 Remove the dish from the oven when the butter is sizzling. Lay the herbs in the dish.

5 Place the potatoes cut side down on the herbs. Spoon the butter over the potatoes.

6 Roast in the top of the oven for 1 hour without turning or basting.

7 Serve immediately, discarding the herbs.

JERUSALEM SANDWICHES

Sandwiched together with cheese and cooked ham, roast Jerusalem artichokes make a main course. Choose large well-shaped artichokes. You will not be able to sandwich smaller ones. Artichokes discolour quickly when exposed to air so peel them in water which contains a little vinegar or lemon juice.

SERVES 4
900 g [2 lb] Jerusalem artichokes
150 g [5 oz] speck
100 g [¼ lb] Edam cheese
100 g [¼ lb] cooked ham

1 Heat the oven to 180°C [350°F] gas mark 4.

2 Place the speck in an ovenproof

dish. Put in the oven until the fat runs. This will take about 10 minutes.

3 Peel the artichokes under water, in a bowl of acidulated water and leave in the bowl until the butter is ready.

4 Drain and dry the artichokes. Place in the sizzling butter turning so that all sides are well coated.

5 Roast for 45 minutes in the centre

of the oven basting from time to time and turning once.

6 Meanwhile, cut the cheese into as many slices as there are artichokes.

7 Remove the artichokes from the oven and increase oven temperature to 200°C [400°F] gas mark 6.

8 Lift out of the butter. Split each artichoke lengthways without cutting right through but leaving a hinge.

9 Place a piece of cheese and a piece of ham (cut the ham to size with scissors) down the centre of the split artichokes.

10 Reassemble the artichokes.

11 Place back in the ovenproof dish. Return to oven for about 5 minutes until the cheese is bubbling. Serve immediately.

ROAST POTATOES WITH ONION RINGS

⊠⊠ *Because the onions and potatoes are cut into small pieces, they must be well coated with fat. A high temperature is needed to give the potatoes and onions a crisp surface and to make sure they are cooked through.*

SERVES 4
700 g [1½ lb] old potatoes
2 medium-sized onions
100 g [¼ lb] beef dripping
freshly ground black pepper
1 slice wholemeal bread
25 g [1 oz] butter

1 Heat the oven to 200°C [400°F] gas mark 6.

2 Place 25 g [1 oz] of the dripping in the bottom of an ovenproof dish. Place in the oven.

3 Peel the potatoes and cut into 6 mm [¼"] thick slices.

4 Peel the onions and cut into rings.

5 Lay half the onions in the bottom of the dish. Cover with all the potatoes, seasoning well with black pepper between each layer of potatoes.

6 Melt the remaining dripping in a heavy-based pan over low heat. Mix the remaining onions into the fat and pour over the potatoes.

7 Roast in top of the oven for 1 hour. No basting is needed.

8 Just before the end of cooking time, melt the butter in a heavy-based pan over low heat.

9 Using a cheese grater or liquidizer, reduce bread to crumbs.

10 Add the crumbs and fry gently until brown and crisp.

11 Scatter over the dish of potatoes and onions.

Three tasty ways with roasted vegetables, from left to right: mushroom roast has a tangy mustard flavour, Jerusalem sandwiches are Jerusalem artichokes roasted and then sandwiched with ham and cheese to make a filling supper dish, caraway beets have the tangy flavour of caraway seeds.

259

Vegetables

grilling

Crisp and golden on the outside, soft and succulent within, grilled vegetables are easy to do and make a perfect accompaniment to main meat and fish dishes. With the addition of cheese or other savoury flavourings they can be turned into light lunch or supper dishes—and tangy appetizers too.

Grilling is a quick, efficient and delicious way of cooking vegetables. The vegetables are prepared, brushed with oil or clarified butter and cooked under a hot grill just long enough to make them succulent and tender inside, with a crisp, golden finish on top.

Grilling brings out the flavour of the vegetables by subjecting them to heat, without destroying or masking their freshness.

Grilled vegetables are also immensely adaptable. Brushed with oil or butter and grilled, they make ideal accompaniments to grills and roasts—try grilled mushrooms with steak, tomatoes with roast lamb.

They can be dressed up in lots of different ways. With the simple addition of freshly chopped herbs, garlic or cheese they can be served as attractive, yet economical first courses—just the sort of thing that can be created in minutes to help stretch out a meal when unexpected guests arrive.

The techniques of grilling vegetables are basically very easy. The most important factor to bear in mind is that the grill must be heated beforehand. There are several additional points to note which are given here.

WHICH VEGETABLES TO USE

Vegetables most suitable for grilling are those which only take a short time to cook, such as tomatoes, mushrooms, green and red peppers and aubergines. Longer-cooking vegetables such as cauliflower, carrot and all root vegetables need to be par-cooked first or they would become dry and unpalatable before being cooked through—no matter how much they were basted with fat. Similarly, leafy green vegetables are unsuitable because they would shrivel up under the intense direct heat.

Vegetables which need longer cooking are first parboiled, or steamed. Place them in a gratin dish, and top with a sauce or cheesy mixture. As well as preventing them drying up under the grill, this will also give them a delicious crunchy top.

PREPARATION
For quick-cooking vegetables:
Remove stalks from tomatoes and wipe the skin clean with a damp cloth, leaving the skin on. Cut in half horizontally.

Both button and flat mushrooms are suitable for grilling. Wipe the skins clean and trim the stalks level with the cap. Always leave mushrooms whole, even large ones, since the juices may leak out through cut surfaces.

For green and red peppers, cut off the stalk end, scrape out the white pith and seeds and cut into even-sized pieces.

Wipe the skin of aubergines clean, trim off both ends and cut into 12 mm [½"] rings, or into cubes. Salt (dé-gorgé) the aubergines as described in detail in the chapter on shallow-frying vegetables.

For longer-cooking vegetables:
Prepare in the usual way, then boil or steam for half to three-quarters normal cooking time so that they are tender on the outside, but still firm in the centre.

Courgettes and very young marrows should be wiped clean, the ends trimmed, and cut into 6 mm [¼"] slices. If you intend to use a more mature marrow, peel and remove the 'woolly' centre and seeds.

Moistening
As with fruit, vegetables to be grilled should be moistened to prevent them drying out under the grill. Brush the vegetables with oil or clarified butter just before grilling. It is best to use butter which has been clarified as this process prevents the butter burning under the intense heat of the grill (clarify butter by melting butter and skimming off the scum). You can, however, use melted butter if you wish.

Mushrooms with clarified butter give the best flavour, tomatoes and peppers can be brushed with oil or clarified butter, while aubergines are best brushed with oil only.

Flavouring
Although moistened, seasoned grilled vegetables taste delicious, their flavour can also be enhanced by adding complementary flavourings. Extra flavouring is particularly recommended when they are to be served with a plain grill or roast or as a first course.

All flavourings (except cheese) are best added half way through grilling time. This is especially necessary when fresh herbs are used as these should not be allowed to brown.

Herbs are a natural partner for vegetables. Basil goes particularly well with tomatoes, and any herb of your choice can be sprinkled over mushrooms and aubergines. Liberally sprinkle fresh, chopped herbs over the vegetable. If using dried herbs halve the quantity.

Crushed coriander seeds give a deliciously spicy flavour, especially good with mushrooms. Crushed garlic is also good. As a rough guide, use one garlic clove to every 225g [½ lb] vegetable. For a milder flavour use chopped onion or spring onions. Make sure they are very finely chopped or they will still be unpleasantly raw tasting when the vegetables themselves are perfectly cooked. Use one small onion or several spring onions for every 450 g [1 lb] vegetables.

Strong cheese such as Gruyère, Mozzarella, Parmesan and Cheddar give a deliciously melted, crispy coating to tomatoes, mushrooms and aubergines and parboiled vegetables. The cheese can be grated and sprinkled, or sliced and placed on top before grilling. You will need 75–100 g [3–4 oz] of cheese for 450 g [1 lb] vegetables.

Colourful, delicious and quickly cooked, grilled vegetables can be served as a first course or as an accompaniment to a main course.

COOKING
There are two ways of grilling vegetables—either on the grill grid or in a gratin dish placed on top of the grill grid. The former method is really only suitable for plainly grilled tomatoes and mushrooms, or vegetable kebabs threaded on skewers. Any drippings from the pan under the grill can be spooned over the vegetables when these are served.

Vegetables that are grilled with flavourings such as cheese are best grilled in a gratin dish. Flavourings drip into the dish, keeping maximum flavour, and also the vegetables can be served straight from it. The great advantage of using a gratin dish is that there is no heat loss and no time wasted in transferring vegetables from pan to serving dish. Nor is there a danger of vegetables collapsing or breaking and becoming misshapen during the transfer. It also minimizes washing-up!

The grill is heated to the correct temperature with the grid and grill pan in place, about 5 cm [2"] below the heat.

If you are using a gratin dish, brush the dish with a little fat to prevent the vegetables sticking. It is also a good idea to brush the grid of the grill pan with fat just before placing the vegetables on top.

Basting
To prevent vegetables drying up during cooking they should be basted. This generally applies to vegetables which need a shorter cooking time.

Vegetables which need a longer cooking time are parboiled and usually covered by a sauce or cheesy topping which keeps them moist and prevents them from drying out.

Baste two to three times during cooking if vegetables are being grilled plain in a gratin dish. Baste by tipping the dish and spooning over the oil and any natural juices that may have leaked out. Brush vegetables on the grill grid with a little extra butter or oil.

TEMPERATURE AND TIMING
The two important things about grilling vegetables are temperature and timing. Do stay by the grill and keep a careful eye on progress. You want juicy tender insides and crisp outsides to your vegetables.

Too long under a fierce heat, or lack of basting will produce burnt offerings, with a black charred outside and raw centre. It is equally easy to get mushy soggy results if the heat is too low and there is too much basting. This makes the vegetables tender all through but lacking in crispness; they taste a bit dull too and may also collapse and thus look uninviting.

The grill should be set at a moderate heat for soft vegetables. Harder vegetables should be started at a slightly lower heat initially to give them time to soften without burning, but increase the heat towards the end of cooking to ensure crisp results.

Tomatoes are grilled cut side up for 10–15 minutes without turning. Mushrooms are grilled gill side up for about six minutes without turning. Peppers, aubergines, courgettes and marrows take two to three minutes each side, turning once.

If the vegetables are par-cooked, finishing them off under the grill takes only about five minutes.

IDEAS FOR GRILLED VEGETABLES

Grilled vegetables are very versatile. They may be served as accompaniments to grills and roasts, or as delicious but not too filling first courses. Sometimes they can even be a light meal in themselves. They also give a good contrast of texture if served with boiled or steamed meat or fish dishes. Try some of the following ideas.

●Halve six large tomatoes. Brush the cut sides with clarified butter or oil, sprinkle with salt and a good grating of black pepper. Grill under moderate heat, sprinkling lightly with chopped fresh or dried oregano half way though cooking time.

●For grilled garlic aubergines, halve the aubergines lengthways. Do not peel. With a sharp knife, score the flesh of each half several times. Rub generously with salt and place cut side down on a draining board for at least 30 minutes to allow excess liquid to drain out.

Squeeze lightly, rinse and dry with kitchen paper. Skin three cloves of garlic and cut into slivers. Push the slivers into the cut surface of the aubergines. Brush with oil and sprinkle each aubergine half with 15 ml [1 tablespoon] freshly grated Gruyère.

Although aubergines are a soft vegetable, the pieces are thick so they require a low heat until soft and cooked through. Grill under low heat for 15–20 minutes. Increase the heat to moderate for the last three minutes to turn them golden brown and crisp on top. Serve as a vegetable accompaniment to a meat dish or as an appetizer.

●For Italian mushrooms, choose large flat-capped mushrooms. Brush the gills only with clarified butter and sprinkle each with 5 ml [1 teaspoon] of grated Parmesan cheese. Grill under moderate heat until golden brown and bubbling.

●For caramelized cabbage, shred a small green cabbage and simmer in a little water until nearly tender. Drain thoroughly and toss in butter. Put into a buttered gratin dish and sprinkle with 50 g [2 oz] Demerara-type sugar. Cook under a hot grill until the sugar caramelizes. Remove and serve immediately. This is excellent with boiled bacon.

●For Mozzarella tomatoes, cut the tomatoes into very thick slices (about 4 cm [1½"]) and cover with a little chopped fresh or dried basil and thin slices of Mozzarella cheese. Season with salt and freshly ground black pepper after cooking under a hot grill. This is delicious as a first course.

GRILLED PEPPER SALAD

This is a piquant appetizer to be served cold before a rich or creamy main course. Instead of grilling the peppers until tender, their skin side is deliberately seared to blacken it and it is then rubbed off.

SERVES 6
8 green or red peppers
6–8 anchovy fillets
3 garlic cloves
45 ml [3 tablespoons] freshly chopped parsley
60 ml [4 tablespoons] olive oil
10 ml [2 teaspoons] lemon juice
salt (optional)
freshly ground black pepper (optional)

1 Heat the grill to moderate with the grill pan and grid in place.

2 Cut off the stalk ends of the peppers, halve lengthways and scrape out the white pith and seeds.

3 Place the peppers under the grill, skin side up, and then grill until their skins blister and blacken all over.
This takes only a few minutes so be careful not to overdo it.

4 Meanwhile, fill a large bowl with cold water. When the peppers are ready, plunge them into the cold water and leave for 2 minutes.

5 Drain the peppers and rub off the skins—they should slip off easily.

6 Cut each pepper in four across the width.

7 Cut the anchovy fillets into 6 mm [¼"] lengths. Peel and finely chop the garlic.

8 Combine the peppers with anchovies, garlic and chopped parsley.

9 Place the olive oil and lemon juice in a small pan over a high heat.

10 When the mixture is very hot, pour over the peppers and mix lightly. Allow to cool.

11 When the mixture is cold, taste for seasoning and add salt or pepper if necessary. Refrigerate until required.

Variations

Aubergines can be grilled in the same way. In the variation below they are mashed with the flavourings (but no anchovies) to produce a deliciously smoky flavoured hors d'oeuvre to be served with toast. There's no need to heat the oil and lemon juice for this version.

●For mock caviare, choose four small aubergines. Wipe clean, leave whole and grill under moderate heat, turning as necessary, until the skins blister. Plunge in cold water, rub off the skins and trim off the ends. Mash the flesh with the olive oil, lemon juice, parsley and garlic and season to taste. Pile into a small serving dish and serve chilled accompanied with melba toast.

MIXED VEGETABLE KEBABS

Choose good-sized, firm tomatoes and medium-sized aubergines for the kebabs. For best flavour, moisten the kebabs with olive oil.

SERVES 6
1 aubergine
6 tomatoes
2 green peppers
225 g [½ lb] button mushrooms
1 garlic clove
45 ml [3 tablespoons] oil
2.5 ml [½ teaspoon] salt
freshly ground black pepper

1 Heat the grill to moderate with the grill pan and grid in place.

2 Wipe the aubergine clean, trim the ends and cut into 12 mm [½"] dice.

3 Wipe tomato skins and cut into quarters.

4 Cut off the stalk end from the green peppers, halve lengthways and scrape out the white pith and seeds. Cut into large, even-sized pieces.

5 Wipe the mushrooms clean and trim stalks level with the caps.

6 Crush the garlic and mix together with the oil, salt and pepper.

7 Thread the vegetables on to six skewers and brush liberally with the oil mixture.

8 Place the skewers on the grid of the grill pan and grill until vegetables are tender, turning and brushing with oil mixture two to three times. Serve immediately.

ANCHOVY AND TOMATO TOASTS

The sweetness of the tomatoes and the tangy flavour of the anchovies provide a delicious contrast in flavour. The anchovy paste is spread on the untoasted side of bread rounds while still warm so that the bread absorbs the flavour. Serve before a rich main course, or as a snack at any time of the day. Use olive oil for the best flavour.

SERVES 6
6 large tomatoes
2 garlic cloves
40 g [1½ oz] canned anchovy fillets
30 ml [2 tablespoons] oil
half a lemon
salt
freshly ground black pepper
6 thick slices of bread
75 g [3 oz] cream cheese

1 Heat the grill to moderate with the grill pan and grid in place.

2 Peel and crush the garlic. Drain and chop the anchovy fillets.

3 Pound them together in a mortar with a pestle until they form a smooth paste. Stir in 15 ml [1 tablespoon] oil.

4 Squeeze juice from the lemon and add it to the paste with salt and black pepper to taste.

5 Cut or stamp the bread with a cutter into large rounds. Toast on one side only under the grill.

6 Remove from the grill, and immediately spread the anchovy and garlic paste on the untoasted side.

7 Halve the tomatoes and arrange, cut side upward, on top of the paste. Brush the tomatoes with the remaining oil.

8 Place on the grid of the grill pan and grill for 15 minutes or until the tomatoes are tender.

9 Remove from the heat and serve topped with knobs of cream cheese.

Variation
● Replace the anchovy fillets with 50 g [2 oz] smoked cod's roe.

Grilled pepper salad is a piquant combination of peppers, anchovy fillets garlic and parsley.

CRISPY CHICORY

In this recipe, grilling is used to finish off and give texture to the vegetable; it also brings out the flavour beautifully. The basic cooking is, of course, boiling or steaming.

SERVES 4
4 heads of chicory
100 g [¼ lb] butter
15 ml [1 tablespoon] lemon juice
salt
freshly ground black pepper

1 Heat the grill to high with the grill pan and grid in place.

2 Prepare the chicory by trimming the root end and discarding any limp outer leaves.

3 Boil the chicory for 10 minutes or steam for 12–15 minutes until tender.

4 As soon as they are cool enough to handle, squeeze the chicory as dry as possible with your hands.

5 Meanwhile, place the butter in a small saucepan and melt over a low heat. Remove from the heat.

6 Place the chicory in a gratin dish and pour over the melted butter and lemon juice. Turn the chicory to coat them all over. Season with salt and plenty of black pepper.

7 Place the gratin dish under the grill until the chicory is slightly crisp all over, turning as necessary. Serve immediately.

CAULIFLOWER GRATINEE

This is a cauliflower cheese with a difference. It makes a good lunch or supper dish, and can be made entirely from leftovers if you wish, by replacing the salami with slices of cold, cooked sausage or tiny rolls of ham.

SERVES 4
1 cauliflower
50 g [2 oz] butter
25 g [1 oz] finely sliced salami
freshly ground black pepper
225 g [½ lb] tomatoes
50 g [2 oz] cheese
50 g [2 oz] brown breadcrumbs

Beneath the crisp, golden cheese and breadcrumb topping is a tasty combination of tomatoes, salami and cauliflower. It makes a good lunch or supper dish.

1 Heat the grill to moderate with the grill pan and grid in place.

2 Prepare the cauliflower, divide into florets and boil for 8–10 minutes until nearly tender.

3 Grease a gratin dish with 25 g [1 oz] butter, and arrange the drained cauliflower florets in it.

4 Remove loose skins from salami and tuck the slices in between the florets. Season with black pepper.

5 Slice the tomatoes and arrange on top of the cauliflower.

6 Finely grate the cheese, combine with the breadcrumbs and sprinkle on top of the tomatoes.

7 Dot the top with the remaining butter and grill until hot, bubbling and crisp on top.

Vegetables

simmering

For mouth-watering vegetable dishes packed with flavour, simmering is a method worth learning about. It's a gentle way to cook vegetables and add other flavours to them without destroying their natural freshness, and it also has the undoubted advantage of being simple—as you will see from these recipes and step-by-step guide.

Simmering is a little known but absolutely delicious method of pan-cooking vegetables which produces exceptionally tender and tasty results. Delicate, watery vegetables, such as cucumber and lettuce lose none of their superb flavour when simmered. Root vegetables become mouth-wateringly tender. Green leafy vegetables retain their colour and freshness. Basically, the vegetables are cooked slowly and gently in their own juices. A little fat is used to prevent them from sticking to the pan and to enrich the finished dish. Herbs, spices and other flavourings may also be added and usually a little

liquid, but most of the latter will be absorbed by the vegetables during cooking.

Mastering the art of simmering is really quite simple and once you have grasped the basic rules given here you will find a whole new world of vegetable cookery is open to you. Have fun creating your own à la maison variations by mixing two or more vegetables, adding different flavourings to produce a succession of unusual and tasty dishes. Simmered vegetables can even be made into a one-pot meal with the addition

of smoked sausage, belly pork or bacon—a really economical and tasty way to feed your family.

WHEN TO SERVE
Simmered vegetables can, of course, be served as an accompaniment to meat or fish dishes but they are so appetizing that they are worth serving as meals in their own right. Simmered potato dishes, such as the recipes for potatoes and bacon, are quite substantial enough to be served alone, or with something simple, such as poached eggs. Others, particularly the less familiar

vegetables, such as celeriac, and especially tiny sweet courgettes make imaginative first courses. Not only are these vegetables worthy of being served alone, they have the decided advantage of blunting the appetite before the more expensive main course comes along.

Simmered vegetables can be made into warming one-pot meals which are cheap to prepare. Add belly pork, smoked German or Dutch sausage, frankfurters or viennas to cabbage, potatoes or any of the root vegetables and you have a tasty fuel-saving meal for the family. For a hearty one-pot idea, see the Star Recipe.

WHICH VEGETABLES TO USE AND HOW TO PREPARE THEM

Many different kinds of vegetable can be simmered and it is an especially good cooking method for watery types, such as cucumber and lettuce which can be neither boiled nor steamed. All root vegetables can be simmered.

Cabbages of all types are excellent simmered because there is no risk of waterlogging. Cut them into quarters, remove the tough stalk and then shred or cut into small squares.

Spring greens, curly kale and Brussels sprout tops lose all trace of bitterness when simmered. Remove the leaves from the stalks and shred as for cabbage.

Spinach and sorrel are ideally suited to simmering because this gentle cooking method preserves their delicate flavour. Prepare as for boiling or steaming.

Brussels sprouts which are over-large or past their best can be rescued by gently simmering. Remove any yellowed or damaged outer leaves. Do not cut a cross in the base, or the sprouts would overcook.

Cauliflower, broccoli, including calabrese can all be simmered and should be broken into florets, having first cut off any really coarse stalks and leaves.

Cabbage lettuce develops excellent flavour when simmered and this is an exciting and different way to serve this often maligned vegetable. Cut off the stalk end and any damaged outer leaves. Separate the leaves, wash and shred. Lettuce hearts can be simmered whole, halved or quartered.

Runner beans and French beans have a high moisture content so are well suited to simmering. Trim the strings from runner beans and either leave the beans whole if small or cut them into pieces if large. French beans need only to be topped and tailed. Break them in half if they are very large. Broad beans can be simmered in their pods if young, or shelled if very large.

Mange-tout need only topping and tailing.

Peas are shelled in the normal way.

Baby carrots are scrubbed and left whole. Larger carrots are scrubbed and cut into thin slices or rings.

Swede, turnip and celeriac are peeled and cut into dice.

Parsnips are best if the woody core is removed. Peel, cut into quarters, cut out the core and slice.

Baby new potatoes need only scrubbing—cook and serve them with the skins on. Scrub old potatoes and cut into chunks or slices. Remove the skin after cooking.

Jerusalem artichokes are best peeled before cooking—this can be difficult to do afterwards. Cut into slices about 2.5 cm [1"] thick.

Whole small courgettes make an attractive and unusual dish. Simply cut off the knobbly end. Larger courgettes are sliced.

Cucumbers are cut into 2.5 cm [1"] thick slices.

Marrows are cut into 2.5 cm [1"] thick slices.

Mushrooms are really delicious simmered. The open type are best but the colour of the cooked dish can be rather unappealing. Button mushrooms do not have such fine flavour but keep their colour better. Wipe the mushrooms and remove the stalks. Chop the latter and cook them with the mushrooms. Leave the mushrooms whole or slice if large.

Button onions are skinned and simmered whole.

The white part of leeks can be simmered whole or cut into slices. Prepare the leeks as shown in the chapter on boiling vegetables.

Celery and fennel are both good simmered because their distinctive flavour is preserved and all traces of stringiness are removed. Cut off the green tops from celery and scrub the stalks. Cut into 2.5 cm [1"] pieces. Celery hearts can be simmered whole, halved or cut into quarters. To prepare fennel for simmering, remove the feathery green fronds. Scrub the bulb then cut in half or in four if very large. Cut into slices 6 mm [¼"] thick.

FATS

Fat is an essential ingredient when simmering. It prevents the vegetables

from sticking to the pan, helps to soften them, encourages them to release their juices and can enrich the flavour of the final dish.

Butter may be used for all vegetables and is excellent for leafy greens, celery and potatoes, baby carrots and courgettes.

Margarine can be used in place of butter: it provides the necessary lubricant but it is no match for flavour, so avoid it if you want really first class results.

Dripping: meaty beef dripping gives a hearty flavour to robust root vegetables such as swede and turnip. If the dripping includes a little jellified meat juice at the bottom, so much the better.

Bacon: for a smoky, slightly salty flavour, use smoked streaky rinded

bacon. Chop it into small pieces and place over low heat until the fat runs freely. Extra fat in the form of butter or dripping is usually added when bacon is used to prevent the flavour from being too salty.

Speck: this smoked continental fat is suitable for root vegetables and cabbage. Cut the speck into small pieces, place in a pan over low heat and cook until the fat flows freely and the little pieces of speck have turned brown. Leave the little brown bits in the pan: they add extra flavour and bite to the vegetables.

Olive, sunflower and walnut oil can be lavished on leeks and courgettes.

LIQUIDS

When most vegetables are simmered, liquid is added. This helps to tenderize the vegetables and it encourages them to give up their juices. The exceptions are spinach, sorrel, cucumber, lettuce, courgettes, mushrooms and baby new potatoes which are naturally juicy and have no need of extra liquid to assist in cooking. However, only a very small amount of liquid is used; by the time the vegetables are tender all of the liquid should have evaporated or been absorbed by the vegetables.

The liquid can be plain water but for the sake of flavour it is better to use brown or white stock, cider, white or red wine, or milk. Alternatively, use equal quantities of water with any of the other liquids mentioned.

FLAVOURINGS AND ADDITIONS

Variety can easily be given to simmered vegetables by using different herbs, spices or other additions to create new flavours.

Salt is nearly always used (a generous pinch is usually plenty for 450 g [1 lb] vegetables) but is unnecessary if you are using other highly-flavoured additions and is also

Butter, bacon, lard, olive or sunflower oil can all be used as the fat element when vegetables are simmered. Wine or cider vinegar can be added to give a piquant flavour to the finished dish. Vinegars go especially well with red cabbage, button onions and leeks but should be added in moderation or the vegetables will be too sharp in flavour.

omitted when bacon provides the fat element.

Freshly ground black pepper is another favourite flavouring. But where other seasonings are added as soon as simmering point is reached, pepper is usually best stirred into the dish after the vegetables are cooked.

Freshly chopped herbs go well with almost all simmered vegetables. Parsley, chives, savory and bay leaf are all good choices.

Spices add flavour to the blander root vegetables. Nutmeg, cayenne pepper, paprika, made German or French or Meaux mustard and mace are all good vegetable flavourings. Cloves and aniseed are good but use with discretion.

Sauces such as Worcestershire, soy or tamari are good for the blander flavoured vegetables, as are pounded anchovies or anchovy essence.

Tomato purée is excellent with leeks and courgettes.

Garlic is a great giver of flavour and can be used freely with all vegetables. Chopped spring or Spanish onions make milder flavoured alternatives.

Chopped nuts: a handful added to simmered vegetables gives extra flavour. Unsalted peanuts or cashews, hazelnuts, walnuts and almonds are all good.

Dried fruit: try a handful with cabbage or carrots—the flavours combine surprisingly well.

Brown sugar added to onions, carrots or potatoes gives a beautifully caramelled effect. It also takes

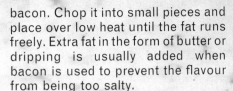

Handy hints

● If you want to give simmered vegetables the flavour of wine but have no wine available, try this clever and economical French trick. Instead of white wine use three-quarters white stock and one-quarter white wine vinegar. Instead of red wine, substitute three-quarters of the quantity with brown stock and one-quarter with red wine vinegar.

● If you want to simmer a mixture of vegetables, some of which take longer to cook than others, simply start simmering the hard vegetables first and add the softer ones to the pan a little later so that they will all be cooked at the same time.

Vichy carrots have a golden glaze of brown sugar and butter. This is a tasty way to cook old carrots.

away the slightly sharp flavour sometimes found in red cabbage.

Grated orange or lemon zest go well with green vegetables, such as broccoli and Brussels sprouts.

Chopped eating apples go well with red cabbage.

EQUIPMENT
Apart from the usual utensils necessary for preparing vegetables, the only piece of equipment you will need for simmering, is a heavy-based pan with a tight-fitting lid.

It is essential that the lid fits really well so that the vegetables and their juices are properly sealed in and can cook gently. If your pan lids are a little loose, first cover with foil—this will give a tighter fit. A heavy base is essential for even distribution of heat and to prevent sticking. A sandwich-based aluminium pan is ideal and so is a vitreous-enamelled cast-iron casserole (which has the added advantage of being so good looking that you can serve as well as cook the vegetables in it). If you have no really heavy-based pan, take the precaution of using an asbestos mat suitable for use on modern gas and electric cookers.

HOW TO SIMMER
Melt the fat in a heavy-based pan over medium heat. Add the vegetables and cook, stirring or shaking the pan for a minute or two so that they are well coated with fat. This will also help to soften the vegetables a little and give them their distinctive fresh flavour. Then pour on the liquid. As soon as it reaches boiling point, reduce the heat to low.

Add salt and other flavourings and additions if used (but not pepper unless specifically mentioned in a recipe), cover the pan and leave to simmer gently until the vegetables are tender. Stir or shake the pan from time to time to prevent sticking and to ensure even cooking. Check the vegetables for tenderness by testing with a fine skewer or the point of a knife. Season the cooked vegetables with freshly ground black pepper and serve with any juices which remain in the pan. If there is a lot of liquid left, you can continue simmering for a few minutes, uncovered, to reduce and thicken the 'sauce'. Stir in a spoonful or two of thick cream (exact quantities depend on the vegetable) if you want a particularly rich dish.

QUICK AND TASTY IDEAS
There is no need to go in for complicated recipes when simmering vegetables. Try the following deliciously simple ideas. All are for 450 g [1 lb] vegetables.

●For Dijon sprouts, simmer equal quantities of Brussels sprout tops and leeks with 60 ml [4 tablespoons] olive oil, 150 ml [¼ pt] white stock and 10 ml [2 teaspoons] Dijon mustard.

●For herby cabbage and celery, simmer equal quantities of green cabbage and celery with 25 g [1 oz] butter, 150 ml [¼ pt] white wine and flavour with 5 ml [1 teaspoon] freshly chopped thyme.

●For Savoy savoury, simmer Savoy cabbage with 60 ml [4 tablespoons] olive oil, 150 ml [¼ pt] white wine and flavour with 10 ml [2 teaspoons] tomato purée, 10 ml [2 teaspoons] pounded anchovies and 5 ml [1 teaspoon] freshly chopped thyme.

●For farmhouse leeks, simmer leeks with 60 ml [4 tablespoons] olive oil and 150 ml [¼ pt] white wine. Flavour with 10 ml [2 teaspoons] Meaux mustard.

●For German celery, simmer celery with 25 g [1 oz] butter, 150 ml [¼ pt] white stock or milk and flavour with 1 large crushed garlic clove.

●For spring beans, simmer whole young broad beans with 25 g [1 oz] butter, 150 ml [¼ pt] water and 6 finely chopped shallots.

●For Vichy carrots, simmer carrots with 25 g [1 oz] butter and 150 ml [¼ pt] water. Add 50 g [2 oz] brown sugar. Cook until all the liquid has evaporated and the carrots have a shiny brown glaze. Button onions may also be treated in this way.

●For glazed turnip, simmer diced turnip in 25 ml [1 fl oz] water. When tender, add more butter and 50 g [2 oz] brown sugar. Shake over low heat until glazed and golden in colour.

●For French potatoes, simmer baby new potatoes in 25 g [1 oz] butter and no liquid. Add finely chopped sage, parsley, chives or a crushed garlic clove.

●For mushrooms à la crème, simmer 450 g [1 lb] cap mushrooms in butter with 1 large crushed garlic clove. Stir in 30 ml [2 tablespoons] thick cream after cooking. Serve on toast.

Guide to simmering (all quantities for 450 g [1 lb] vegetables)

Where alternative liquids, fats or flavourings are given, each one is equally good.

Vegetable	Fat	Quantity	Liquid	Quantity	Additions	Quantity	Timing
artichokes Jerusalem	butter	25 g [1 oz]	white stock water milk	200 ml [7 fl oz]	nutmeg paprika mustard	5 ml [1 tsp] 5 ml [1 tsp] 10 ml [2 tsp]	20-25 mins
beans, broad	olive oil	60 ml [4 tsp]	white stock water white wine	150 ml [¼ pt]	savory chopped bacon tomato purée	10 ml [2 tsp] 2 rashers 30 ml [2 tbsp]	12-15 mins
French		(as broad beans)			(as broad beans) plus garlic	1 clove	12-15 mins
runner		(as broad beans)					12-15 mins
broccoli calabrese	butter	25 g [1 oz]	white stock water	150 ml [¼ pt]	grated lemon zest chopped hazel nuts or walnuts	5 ml [1 tsp] 25 g [1 oz]	15 mins
Brussels sprouts		(as broccoli)					15 mins
cabbage white and green	butter bacon speck	25 g [1 oz] 2 rashers plus 15 g [½ oz] butter 25 g [1 oz]	white stock water cider white wine	150 ml [¼ pt]	chopped onion nutmeg paprika	1 medium 5 ml [1 tsp] 5 ml [1 tsp]	15-20 mins
red		(as white and green)	cider red wine red wine vinegar	150 ml [¼ pt]	chopped onion chopped apple brown sugar raisins cloves	1 medium 1 medium 50 g [2 oz] 50 g [2 oz] 2-3 medium	25-30 mins
carrots old	butter	25 g [1 oz]	white stock water cider	200 ml [7 fl oz]	thyme brown sugar mustard aniseeds	5 ml [1 tsp] 50 g [2 oz] 10 ml [2 tsp] 5 ml [1 tsp]	20-25 mins
new		(as old)					30 mins
cauliflower	butter	25 g [1 oz]	white stock water white wine milk	150 ml [¼ pt]	nutmeg paprika chilli sauce mustard Worcestershire sauce tomato purée pounded anchovies	5 ml [1 tsp] 5 ml [1 tsp] 15 ml [1 tsp] 10 ml [2 tsp] 10 ml [2 tsp] 30 ml [2 tsp] 15 ml [1 tbsp]	15 mins
celeriac	butter	25 g [1 oz]	cider milk white stock water	200 ml [7 fl oz]	nutmeg mustard	5 ml [1 tsp] 10 ml [2 tsp]	20-25 mins
celery	butter	25 g [1 oz]	white stock water milk white wine	150 ml [¼ pt]	none needed		25 mins
cucumber	butter	25 g [1 oz]	none		chopped spring onions	1-2	10 mins

Vegetable	Fat	Quantity	Liquid	Quantity	Additions	Quantity	Time
courgettes	butter	25 g [1 oz]	none required		finely chopped onion	1 medium	15 mins
marrow	olive oil	60 ml [4 tbsp]			crushed garlic	1 clove	
					tomato purée	30 ml [2 tbsp]	
fennel	(as celery)						10 mins
greens (inc. Brussels sprouts tops and curly kale)	butter bacon butter dripping	25 g [1 oz] 2 rashers plus 15 g [½ oz] 25 g [1 oz]	cider water white stock	150 ml [¼ pt]	nutmeg crushed garlic	5 ml [1 tsp] 1 clove	15-20 mins
leeks	olive oil	60 ml [4 tbsp]	white stock white wine water cider	150 ml [¼ pt]	crushed garlic tomato purée pounded anchovies mustard	1 clove 30 ml [2 tbsp] 15 ml [1tbsp] 10 ml [2 tsp]	15-20 mins
lettuce	(as cucumber)						10 mins
mange-tout	butter	25 g [1 oz]	white stock water	150 ml [¼ pt]	savory parsley	10 ml [2 tsp] 10 ml [2 tsp]	10 mins
mushrooms	butter	25 g [1 oz]	white stock white wine milk	150 ml [¼ pt]	crushed garlic tomato purée chopped parsley chopped chives mustard	1 clove 30 ml [2 tbsp] 10 ml [2 tsp] 10 ml [2 tsp] 10 ml [2 tsp]	15 mins
parsnips	butter dripping bacon + butter speck	25 g [1 oz] 25 g [1 oz] 2 rashers 15 g [½ oz] 25 g [1 oz]	cider water white stock brown stock	200 ml [7 fl oz]	nutmeg paprika mustard chilli sauce	5 ml [1 tsp] 5 ml [1 tsp] 10 ml [2 tsp] 10 ml [2 tsp]	20-25 mins
potatoes new	butter	25 g [1 oz]	none needed		chopped sage chopped parsley chopped chives crushed garlic	10 ml [2 tsp] 10 ml [2 tsp] 10 ml [2 tsp] 1 clove	30 mins
old	butter bacon + butter dripping speck	25 g [1 oz] 2 rashers 15 g [½ oz] 25 g [1 oz] 25 g [1 oz]	water white stock brown stock cider	200 ml [7 fl oz]	(as new potatoes)		30-40 mins
sorrel	(as spinach)						10 mins
spinach	butter	25 g [1 oz]	none needed		chopped spring onions thick cream chopped bacon savory crushed garlic	4-5 30 ml [2 tbsp] 4 rashers 10 ml [2 tsp] 1 clove	10 mins
swedes	(as parsnips)						20-25 mins
turnips	(as parsnips)						20-25 mins

270

Step-by-step simmering vegetables

1 If using butter or dripping, place the fat in a heavy-based pan and melt over medium heat.

2 If using bacon fat, chop roughly and cook in a little butter until coloured.

3 If using speck, dice and cook until the fat runs and the speck is brown.

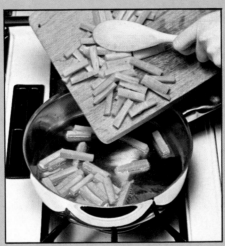

4 If using oil, measure it into the pan and allow to warm through gently over moderate heat.

5 Add prepared vegetables and turn to coat with fat. Pour on liquid (if used) and bring to the boil.

6 Reduce heat. Add salt, spices, herbs and any extras such as nuts or dried fruit, onions or sugar.

7 Cover the pan tightly and simmer gently until vegetables are tender. Stir once or twice during cooking.

8 If much liquid remains, continue simmering uncovered for 2-3 minutes to evaporate excess.

9 Season cooked vegetables to taste with pepper. Stir in cream, if wished, and serve immediately.

THYME AND MUSTARD CARROTS

This is a superb way to cook large winter carrots. There is a little more liquid than usual in this dish in order to make the carrots really tender and full of flavour.

SERVES 4
450 g [1 lb] carrots
25 g [1 oz] butter
150 ml [¼ pt] white stock
75 ml [3 fl oz] dry white wine
15 ml [1 tablespoon]
   chopped fresh thyme or 10 ml
   [2 teaspoons] dried
5 ml [1 teaspoon] Meaux
   or other seeded mustard
salt
freshly ground black pepper

1 Scrub the carrots, remove the root end and top, and cut into slices 6 mm [¼"] thick.

2 Melt the butter in a heavy-based pan over moderate heat.

3 Add the carrots, and stir to mix well.

4 When the carrots are coated with fat, add the wine and stock. Bring to the boil.

5 Reduce heat so that the carrots are just simmering, then add the thyme, mustard and salt.

6 Cover and cook for 20 minutes. If there is any liquid left after cooking, uncover and continue to cook until the liquid is reduced and the carrots are slightly glazed and speckled with pieces of thyme and mustard seed.

7 Away from the heat, season to taste with freshly ground pepper and serve.

SPRINGTIME SPINACH

If spinach is cooked in liquid, it becomes waterlogged. The only liquid used here is the water which still clings to the leaves after washing. It is essential to turn the spinach several times during cooking, so that every leaf is cooked. If you can't obtain fresh marjoram use dried but this is much poorer in flavour.

SERVES 4
700 g [1½ lb] spinach

1 bunch spring onions
40 g [1½ oz] butter
10 ml [2 teaspoons]
   chopped fresh marjoram or
   5 ml [1 teaspoon] dried
salt
freshly ground black pepper

1 Break off the stalks from the spinach, rinse thoroughly in several changes of cold salted water and shake dry.

2 Cut off the root end and any ragged green parts from the spring onions, remove the transparent skin and chop finely.

3 Melt the butter in a large heavy-based saucepan over medium heat.

4 Stir in the spinach and the onions.

5 When the vegetables are coated, reduce heat to low, add the herbs and salt.

6 Cover the pan and simmer for 10 minutes, turning the spinach frequently.

7 Cook uncovered for a minute or two to evaporate any excess liquid.

8 Season with freshly ground black pepper, stir to mix and serve.

POTATOES AND BACON

This is a really hearty dish which is filling enough to be eaten alone. No salt is added because of the salt in the bacon. Freshly ground black pepper is added during rather than after cooking to increase flavour.

SERVES 4
700 g [1½ lb] potatoes
3 rashers streaky bacon
15 g [½ oz] butter
400 ml [¾ pt] white stock
1 bay leaf
8 fresh sage leaves chopped or
   5 ml [1 teaspoon] dried sage
freshly ground black pepper

1 Peel and thickly slice the potatoes.

2 Rind the bacon, cut into pieces and put in heavy-based pan over medium heat with the butter. Cook until the bacon is just coloured.

3 Add the sliced potatoes.

4 Cover and cook for 5 minutes, shaking the pan occasionally, until the potatoes are slightly softened and coated with fat.

5 Pour on the stock and bring to the boil.

6 Reduce heat, add herbs and freshly ground black pepper. Cover and simmer gently for 40 minutes. Shake the pan from time to time (this is better than stirring which might break up the potatoes).

7 Remove bay leaf before serving.

MUSHROOMS PERSILLADE

No liquid is used in this dish as this quantity of mushrooms naturally yields plenty of juices. Large cap mushrooms are best as they have the finest flavour.

SERVES 4
1 kg [2 lb] cap mushrooms
50 g [2 oz] butter
4 rashers middle-cut smoked
   bacon
1 large garlic clove
30 ml [2 tablespoons] finely
   chopped parsley
salt
freshly ground black pepper
4 thick slices wholemeal bread

1 Cut away the earthy end of the mushroom stems, cut off the stalks and chop. Wipe the mushroom caps.

2 Melt the butter in a heavy-based pan over moderate heat.

3 Rind the bacon, cut into pieces, add to the pan. Cook until just coloured.

4 Meanwhile, peel and crush the garlic clove.

5 Add mushrooms to the pan and reduce heat. Stir to coat with fat. Season with salt and add the garlic and parsley.

6 Cover the pan and simmer for 10 minutes.

7 Meanwhile cut off the crusts from the bread and toast the bread on both sides.

8 Pile the cooked mushrooms on to the slices of wholemeal toast. If wished, decorate each with a parsley sprig.

9 Season with plenty of pepper and serve very hot.

ONIONS AGRODOLCE

Because of the high quantity of sugar in this dish (both dried fruit and onions are high in sugar) you must shake the pan frequently during cooking to prevent the onions from sticking to the bottom. There is no need to season with black pepper after cooking because cayenne pepper provides all the spice that is needed.

SERVES 4
25 button onions
45 ml [3 tablespoons] olive oil
75 ml [3 fl oz] port
75 ml [3 fl oz] red wine vinegar
30 ml [2 tablespoons] soft brown sugar
25 g [1 oz] raisins
salt
cayenne pepper

1 Peel the onions.

Left: onions Agrodolce are a classic dish from the Mediterranean and have a rich syrupy sauce. Right: French potatoes are cooked in butter and delicately flavoured with herbs and garlic. Baby new potatoes are best for this dish.

2 Place the olive oil in a heavy-based pan over low heat. Allow to warm.

3 Place the onions in the pan. Cook until they begin to brown, shaking the pan so that the onions are browned on all sides.

4 Add the port and vinegar and bring to the boil.

5 As soon as boiling point is reached, reduce the heat to simmer and stir in the brown sugar, raisins, salt and cayenne pepper.

6 Cover and simmer for 15-20 minutes until the onions are tender and the liquid has reduced to a thick syrup. Spoon the syrup over the onions when serving.

ROTKOHL MIT APFELN

This *meal-in-a-pot* from Germany uses rather more liquid than do most simmered vegetable dishes because the cooking time is unusually long in order to cook the pork. Pork is included both to provide fat and to make the dish more substantial. Do not use salt belly of pork— the flavour is too pronounced.

If you do not wish to use belly of pork, use 50 g [2 oz] speck instead in step 3 to provide the fat element and add smoked boiling sausage or frankfurters to provide the meat. These should be added to the cabbage 20 minutes before the end of cooking time to heat through.

SERVES 4
700 g [1½ lb] red cabbage
75 ml [3 fl oz] red wine vinegar

50 g [2 oz] soft brown sugar
225 g [½ lb] belly pork cut into 6 mm [¼"] thick rashers
2 medium-sized cooking apples
2 medium-sized onions
2 whole cloves
1 bay leaf
50 g [2 oz] raisins
30 ml [2 tablespoons] dry red wine

1 Remove tough outer leaves from the cabbage. Cut into quarters, remove stalk, and shred finely using a mandolin or sharp knife.

2 Place the cabbage in a large mixing bowl. Add the red wine vinegar and sugar. Toss with your hands to coat the cabbage.

3 Remove the rind and bone the pork. Cut into 3.7 cm [1½"] cubes. Place in a heavy-based pan over low heat. Cook until just browned.

4 Meanwhile, peel, core and roughly chop the apples. Peel and chop one onion and add it to the pan and cook 5-10 minutes.

5 Add the cabbage, bay leaf and raisins to the pan. Stir well, turning all the ingredients so they are well mixed and coated with fat.

6 Peel the remaining onion and stick with the two cloves. Bury in the centre of the cabbage mixture, add apples. Reduce the heat to low.

7 Bring 550 ml [1 pt] water to the boil and add to the pan. Bring to simmering point, stir once then cover with a well-fitting lid.

8 Simmer for 2 hours, checking the liquid level and stirring from time to time. Add more liquid if the cabbage seems dry.

9 When the cabbage is cooked, there should be no liquid remaining. Stir in the red wine. Remove and discard bay leaf and onion.

SURPRISE BAKED TOMATOES

These tomatoes, with their 'surprise' filling make a delicious first course. They can also make a light lunch or supper dish accompanied by hot buttered toast or egg noodles. Choose the largest, best-shaped tomatoes you can find, and use the scooped out pulp in soups, sauces or stocks. There is no need to score around the middle of the tomatoes, because the tops are taken off instead which obviously prevents the tomatoes from splitting.

SERVES 4
4 large tomatoes
salt
freshly ground black pepper
4 medium-sized eggs
15 ml [1 tablespoon] freshly chopped chervil or parsley

1 Position oven shelf in centre and heat to 180°C [350°F] gas mark 4.

2 Cut a small slice off the top of each tomato and scoop out the pulp. Sprinkle the inside of the tomatoes with salt and pepper.

3 Place the tomatoes in a lightly greased, shallow, gratin dish.

4 Break a whole egg into each tomato 'cup', season with salt and pepper and sprinkle with chopped herbs.

5 Place the tops back on the tomatoes.

6 Bake tomatoes in oven for 20 minutes, until the eggs are set and the tomatoes cooked. Serve immediately.

Vegetables

baking

Baking is a no-fuss way of cooking vegetables. They need the minimum of preparation and the maximum flavour is conserved. They can be served as accompaniments to a main course or, with the addition of herbs, cheese or other flavourings, as a tasty first course or light lunch or supper dish.

Baking is one of the simplest and easiest ways of cooking vegetables: little is needed in the way of equipment or additional ingredients. The full flavour and nourishment of the vegetables are conserved by this means of cooking.

When the oven is on to cook a dish of any kind, it makes good sense and takes little extra time to pop a few vegetables in the oven to bake alongside it. The result is delicious and the cooking is economical.

Baked vegetables are less rich than vegetables that are roasted; they also require less preparation and attention. They are therefore a good choice when the rest of the meal is rather rich, for slimmers or, simply when you have little time to give to the preparation and cooking.

CHOOSING VEGETABLES FOR BAKING

When choosing vegetables for baking, make sure that they are of a good size and quality. Small vegetables are unsuitable because you need a good proportion of tender, melting flesh to skin; small vegetables are 'all skin' when baked.

The vegetables must be of good quality because tough cores and bad pieces, apart from superficial blemishes, cannot be removed before baking. Choose even-sized vegetables so that they take the same length of time to bake or, if some are smaller, add these to the oven later during the cooking time.

SUITABLE VEGETABLES AND THEIR PREPARATION

Before baking vegetables they can be pricked by stabbing once or twice with a fork. This is done as a precaution against the skins bursting during cooking due to the pressure of steam building up inside the vegetable.

Aubergines can be baked; choose ones of medium size, wipe clean with a damp cloth and remove the stem. When cooked they can be split or cut into slices and served with garlic or herb butter. Baked aubergine can also form the basis of a delicious cold relish.

Jerusalem artichokes are excellent when baked—and cooking them by

this method saves all that fiddly peeling! Simply scrub large Jerusalem artichokes, being careful to get into all the little crevices, and prick once or twice with a fork.

Onions are delicious when baked. Choose large onions, leave the skins on and carefully trim off the root and stalk end and cut a cross in the top to make them easier to open and eat.

Parsnips bake well but choose them carefully—they must be of good size but without any sign of woodiness. Scrub, trim and prick.

Peppers can be baked whole—the seeds and stem are removed after they are baked, when the papery outermost skin can also easily be removed. There is no need to prick the skins before baking. Baked peppers can be sliced and served with butter, or chopped up and mixed with oil and vinegar, then chilled as part of a salad or relish.

Potatoes need no introduction! A jacket-potato is one of the delights of autumn and winter. Choose medium to large potatoes, scrub well and either score the skin lightly with a knife or prick several times with a fork. To get a really delicious crispy skin, you can roll the potatoes lightly in oil and sprinkle all over with salt before baking.

Squashes, although not often obtainable in Britain, are well known in most other countries. If you can buy (or grow) the tiny round butter or custard squashes they are an exquisite vegetable when baked. Just wash them and prick lightly. When they are done, cut a slice off the top, scoop out the seeds and replace with butter or garlic butter, salt and freshly ground black pepper.

Swedes can be baked in the same way as potatoes. Choose swedes no bigger than large potatoes, scrub, prick and bake whole. If only larger swedes are available, cut in half and place cut-side down on a greased baking sheet.

Tomatoes bake well. Wash them first and score round their middles with a sharp knife (as for baked apples). This prevents them bursting and makes it easier to remove the skins when eating them.

Turnips are baked like swedes and potatoes. Choose them carefully, avoiding any which have been damaged by maggots (to which turnips are very prone). Scrub and prick or score lightly two or three times with a knife.

ADDITIONAL INGREDIENTS

Vegetables can be baked without any additions, but a little oil or butter rubbed over the skins gives them a softer texture when baked. This also gives a juicy crispness instead of a dry finish—and a grey appearance in the case of potatoes!

Be careful not to add too much fat or the vegetables will roast instead of bake. If the skins are to be eaten, they can be sprinkled with table or sea salt and freshly ground black pepper, and seeds such as dill, caraway or fennel before baking, for extra flavour.

EQUIPMENT

Little special equipment is needed— just a baking sheet or shallow casserole, preferably metal as this conducts the heat best. This must be large enough for the vegetables to be spread out in one layer.

A potato spike is useful too— four, six or eight metal spikes are joined together on which the potatoes (or other root vegetables) can be stuck before baking. It conducts the heat up through the vegetable and helps it bake more quickly. Oil the spikes to prevent sticking before pushing them into the vegetables. If you haven't a potato spike, skewers can be used instead. However, although a potato spike or skewers are useful in helping to cut down cooking time, they are by no means essential and the vegetables will cook perfectly well on their own.

TEMPERATURES AND TIMING
Temperatures
The temperature at which vegetables are baked is not crucial, which is a blessing since they can be popped in the oven at the same time as other dishes. A heat of 180–200°C [350–400°F] gas mark 4-6 is usual. But vegetables can be baked for longer at a lower temperature, say 160°C [325°F] gas mark 3, if this is more convenient, for example when they are being cooked alongside a milk pudding, fruit cake or stew.

The oven position can vary too, depending on temperature and conditions. Vegetables can be placed near the centre of a hot oven but towards the top of a cooler one. If possible turn the vegetables once during cooking, to make sure they cook evenly. To test if they are done, squeeze gently in a clean cloth or insert the point of a skewer or knife into the centre—they should feel completely soft.

Timing
The time a vegetable takes to bake depends very much on the size, as well as the type. However, a rough guide can be given, based on the more usual temperature of 180-200°C [350-400°F] gas mark 4-6, and for medium-sized vegetables. If you are baking at a lower temperature, and/or the vegetables are very large you must, of course, allow more time. Smaller vegetables (which are not very suitable anyway) will take a shorter time to cook.

Onions, parsnips and swedes will take about 1¼ hours and turnips 1 hour. Allow ¾ hour for squash; Jerusalem artichokes, aubergines and peppers will take between ½ and ¾ hour. Tomatoes will have the shortest cooking time of 10-15 minutes—potatoes take the longest time of between ¾ hour and 1¼ hours.

SERVING IDEAS
●Split Jerusalem artichokes after baking and serve with a dollop of chilled sour cream into which a few dill seeds have been stirred.
●Halve baked aubergines and scoop out most of the flesh. Mash the flesh into a pulp, mix with a little tomato purée, salt, pepper and chopped parsley and pile back into the skins. Serve the aubergines as a course on their own or as an attractive accompaniment to a plain meat dish.
●Halve baked swedes lengthwise. Scoop out the centres, mash with butter, salt, pepper and top of the milk or cream. Pile the mixture back into the skins, pop back into the oven for a few minutes to reheat.
●Baked turnips are good served split, with mustard butter or grated cheese.

Baked vegetables can be stuffed to make hearty supper dishes, or served plain as a nutritious accompaniment to roast or grilled meat dishes.

Tasty fillings for baked potatoes

How to fill baked potatoes

You can add variety to baked potatoes by serving with savoury fillings, some of which are substantial enough to serve as a light lunch or supper dish. Allow one potato per person. To prepare (unless otherwise indicated), slice off 1.2 cm [½"] from the long side of the baked potato, remove the pulp carefully with a teaspoon, taking care not to break the skin. Place the pulp in a mixing bowl and combine with the prepared filling. Pile back into the shell and put back in the oven for 10-12 minutes. Unless otherwise stated, these recipes serve 4.

1 Make a cross in side of potato, squeeze. Use 150 ml [¼ pt] sour cream or yoghurt and plenty of chopped fresh chives as a topping.

2 Combine 225 g [½ lb] canned sweet corn with 30 ml [2 tablespoons] finely chopped walnuts, and butter. Season lightly before baking.

3 Sauté 4 slices of diced streaky bacon, 100 g [¼ lb] sliced mushrooms, and one small chopped onion together, until the onion is soft. Bake.

4 Halve a baked potato. Mash pulp with butter and seasoning. Pile back, break an egg into each half. Bake for 10 minutes or until egg white is set.

5 For soufflé potatoes, mix 2 egg yolks, 8 chopped anchovy fillets, butter and seasonings with potato pulp. Fold in two stiffly whipped egg whites. Bake.

6 Combine pulp with 100 g [¼ lb] flaked, smoked haddock, 30 ml [2 tablespoons] finely chopped parsley, pinch of cayenne pepper, and butter. Bake.

7 Combine the potato pulp with 100 g [¼ lb] grated Cheddar cheese, 15 ml [1 tablespoon] chutney, 1 finely chopped celery stick. Bake.

8 Make use of left-over cooked mince mixture. Combine with pulp and seasoning, top with grated Cheddar cheese and grill under high heat for 6-8 minutes.

Vegetables

stuffing

Stuffing is a well-known way of making things go further—and it doesn't just apply to meat or poultry. Stuffed vegetables make wonderful and economical dishes. In this course you will find out how to stuff vegetables to make interesting hors d'oeuvres and tasty savoury dishes.

Stuffed vegetables are an excellent way of making both leftovers or cheap ingredients, such as cooked vegetables or rice, look special. The method also makes more expensive ingredients, such as crabmeat or avocado, go a long way. Although stuffed vegetables look as though a lot of trouble has gone into the preparation, they are in fact not complicated to prepare.

Many vegetables can be stuffed. Vegetables with leaves, such as cabbage, can be opened, stuffed and then re-formed for cooking. Individual leaves, such as vine leaves, can be stuffed, rolled and cooked. Larger vegetables, such as aubergines and marrows can be scooped and refilled with some of the flesh combined with other ingredients, before cooking. These methods are covered in later courses on stuffed vegetables. In this course the method is given for stuffing tomatoes, for eating hot and cold, stuffed mushroom caps, which are treated in the same way, and also stuffing celery and cucumber.

Stuffed vegetables are versatile and can be served at any meal from breakfast to late-night supper. They make tasty but light dishes—and they can look highly decorative too. Attractive as a garnish for grills and roasts, they are also good on their own as an unusual starter. If made fairly substantial by the accompaniment of a tasty sauce, French bread, rice or noodles and salad, they become a complete light lunch or supper dish in their own right.

Stuffed tomatoes and mushrooms can be served hot or cold (mushrooms are marinated before serving as a cold starter). Cucumber and celery are usually raw and therefore served cold. However, cucumber can also be stuffed and baked to make a deliciously unusual hot vegetable dish.

CHOOSING THE VEGETABLES

It is important that the vegetables you choose should be of the right shape. They should also be in first class condition, with no blemishes to be removed as the shell must be firm to provide an edible and non-porous container for the filling. Anything too small cannot be stuffed satisfactorily. A small vegetable is fiddly to prepare and, if baked, may fall apart during cooking, leaving a horrible soggy mess instead of a neat and decorative parcel.

Tomatoes which are evenly shaped and medium- to large-sized are best. Medium-sized tomatoes can be stuffed whole, larger ones can be halved and stuffed. You can also use very large, unevenly shaped tomatoes which do not look quite so attractive but are good for informal, family meals. They are a good choice for the mince or rice-type fillings so popular in the Mediterranean. One of these will probably give two servings for a first course, depending on size.

Mushrooms for stuffing should be large and flat and 5–7.5cm [2–3″] across. If you can get the large mushrooms which are slightly cup shaped, these are even better as they hold the filling well. Allow 3–4 mushrooms per person, depending on size and the course of the meal at which they are to be served.

Cucumbers for stuffing should be plumpish—small ones will not hollow out satisfactorily—and there will not be enough room inside for the stuffing. A plump, large-sized cucumber will serve 5–6 people if stuffed and served raw as hors d'oeuvre. Stuffed and cooked it will serve three for a more substantial dish.

Celery sticks should be as fresh and crisp as possible when they are to be

Cold stuffed tomatoes make an unusual and elegant start to a meal, or they can be turned into a meal if served with a salad.

stuffed. An average-sized stick will give two servings, either as a light first course or to nibble with drinks before eating. Stuffed celery is not really substantial enough to serve as a main course.

PREPARATION AND COOKING

The preparation of vegetables for stuffing may seem rather fiddly, but in fact it takes only a short time to do.

Celery and cap mushrooms are easy to prepare, as they have natural hollows to fill with stuffing. Care must be taken with cucumber and tomatoes to scoop out enough flesh to leave room for the stuffing but not to break the 'walls' or 'base' of the vegetable.

Celery: trim off the top leaves, separate the stalks and trim off the flat end near the base (save this for stuffing other vegetables or for stews etc). Tear off and discard any tough fibres from the outside sticks, and cut into 7.5–9 cm [3–3½"] lengths. Put in the stuffing and serve raw.

Cucumber: if you are making cucumber 'cups' to serve raw, wipe the cucumber clean but leave on the skin. If you like, you can flute the skin for added decorative effect. Trim off the ends and cut the remaining cucumber into 4 cm [1½"] lengths. Stand the cucumber lengths up to form a 'cup' and hollow out the seeds with a teaspoon. Leave about 6 mm [¼"] round the sides and base.

A cucumber for stuffing and baking is prepared in a different way and will look like a stuffed celery stick when done. The cucumber is peeled and the skin is removed in this case because it is inclined to become bitter when cooked. Cut the lengths in half lengthways and carefully scoop out all the seeds, using a small spoon. Discard the scooped-out seeds. Once this is done the cucumber is then stuffed. Place cucumbers to be baked in a greased, shallow gratin dish in a moderate oven at 180–190°C [350–375°F] gas marks 4–5, for 15–20 minutes until tender.

Whether you plan to serve the cucumber raw or cooked, the cucumber cups or halves should first be salted. Turn them upside down to drain for 30 minutes to draw out excess moisture. If you do not do this, you may find that the moisture will seep into the filling making it soggy and wet instead of just moist. Rinse and pat dry before stuffing.

Mushrooms: wipe, but do not peel the mushrooms. If you are serving them raw but marinated, you can flute the skin, using an extremely sharp knife but this really does not look attractive on cooked mushrooms. Cut off the stems level with the black gills. Often the stems are chopped up and added to the stuffing mixture, or they can be saved and added to sauces and casseroles. Marinate the mushrooms if you are serving them cold and raw. Before cooking the mushrooms moisten both sides and place them, gill side up, in a shallow, greased gratin dish. If you are cooking them to serve hot, brush them with butter. But if you are cooking them to serve cold, brush them with oil because this looks and tastes less fatty when cold.

Place a heap of stuffing on top of each mushroom, piling it up in the centre but not too close to the sides, or it may leak out during cooking. Pour any liquid round the mushrooms in the gratin dish. Cook at 180–190°C [350–375°F] gas mark 4–5 for 15–20 minutes until the stuffing is lightly browned and cooked. If cooking the mushrooms in liquid, baste the edges two or three times during cooking so that they do not dry out.

Tomatoes: wash and remove the calyx. If stuffing tomatoes whole, use a small sharp knife to cut a small slice off the top of each. This slice may be used as a lid on top of the stuffed tomatoes. If stuffing them in halves, cut in half horizontally. If they are going to be eaten cold and raw, you can make the cuts straight across or in a zig-zag for a more decorative design. If, however, a particular tomato is very misshapen or lopsided you may have to take a thin slice off the base to enable it to stand up properly. Use a small sharp knife so that there is no danger of cutting completely through the shell. This is however, only recommended for tomatoes to be eaten raw. It is not desirable to pierce the skin if the tomato is to be cooked as moisture will leak out.

Using a small teaspoon, scoop out the centres of the tomatoes, the pips and pulp, leaving a cavity for the stuffing. Do this carefully, making sure you do not break the skin, if the tomato is to be cooked. The pips and pulp can be sieved and added to the stuffing or used in soups or sauces. If you are serving the tomatoes without 'lids' you can chop the fleshy part (discarding the skin) and add to the stuffing for use for flavouring soups etc. Alternatively the 'lid' can be used to cover the stuffing.

Sprinkle a little salt into the tomato cavities and turn them upside down on a plate. Leave for 30 minutes to draw out excess moisture. Rinse to get rid of the salt and pat dry with kitchen paper. Fill the cavities with stuffing and, if they are to be cooked, place in a greased gratin dish and cook at 180–190°C [350–375°F] gas mark 4–5 for 15–20 minutes.

INGREDIENTS FOR STUFFINGS

The stuffing for vegetables should always be moist, but not so moist as to become wet and therefore leak out of the vegetable 'case'. Many different types of filling can be used, and it makes an excellent way for you to make imaginative use of small amounts of leftovers. The stuffing must be firmer and drier when celery is to be served as finger food, to avoid any embarrassing spills!

Uncooked stuffings

For tomatoes, the stuffing usually consists of cooked fish, poultry or vegetables, mixed with a little mayonnaise or mayonnaise plus whipped cream or yoghurt, to bind and moisten the dry ingredients.

Garlic, herbs and spices can be added; paprika and curry paste are particularly good if a spicy mixture is required.

For cucumber, celery and marinated mushrooms, curd, cottage or cream cheese makes an excellent base for uncooked stuffings. Any of these can be mixed with chopped nuts, mashed avocado, and finely chopped fresh herbs.

Other adaptable stuffings that can be used to stuff vegetables without too much advance preparation are cooked shellfish, tinned tuna fish, taramasalata or any other smooth fish pâté, such as smoked mackerel or kipper. Spoon the stuffing in or pipe for pretty looks—but only pipe if the stuffing is smooth. Top with olives or other attractive garnishes.

Cooked stuffings

Making a cooked stuffing gives plenty of scope for imagination. As long as the stuffing is moist (but never wet), light and tasty, and complements the flavour of the vegetable to be stuffed, there are no hard and fast rules.

With the exception of cheese and finely diced raw vegetables and nuts, the stuffings are cooked in advance because baking time is too short for say, mince, to cook thoroughly.

Cooked stuffings usually include a base of either soft, fresh breadcrumbs, cooked Patna or brown rice or thick béchamel sauce. Other ingredients are then added to the base for flavour.

These other ingredients can be flaked cooked fish, chopped fried bacon, lightly sautéed chopped chicken livers, minced ham or other meat or finely grated cheese, or a mixture of these. The portions vary, but one part of meat or fish etc to one part breadcrumbs, cooked rice or sauce is the usual balance.

Additional flavourings such as chopped parsley or other herbs, finely chopped fried onion, crushed garlic, grated lemon zest, salt, pepper, nutmeg and other spices can be added as required.

Crunchy ingredients, such as nuts, add texture and flavour as well as food value. Additional vegetables, such as finely chopped cooked celery, tiny diced raw carrot and cooked peas can be added to the mixture. Sometimes, particularly for a garnish, tomatoes or mushrooms are stuffed entirely with other vegetables.

The finished mixture should be moist but firm enough to hold its shape; it can be moistened with melted butter, single cream, a little stock or, for a special occasion, a few drops of wine.

Moistening
A little vegetable oil is needed for brushing over mushrooms if they are to be served cold. This keeps them moist during cooking. You only need a small amount, just enough to keep them from drying out. The dish in which stuffed vegetables are cooked may be greased with butter, or with vegetable oil if the vegetables are to be served cold.

Sometimes a small quantity of liquid—wine, stock or a mixture of stock and wine—is poured round tomatoes, cucumber or mushrooms in the dish to a depth of about 3 mm [$\frac{1}{8}$″]. This adds moisture and provides a sauce to serve with the vegetables but, as long as the casserole is well buttered, extra liquid is not essential.

When creating your own variations, if you are in doubt about adding liquid, it is best to omit it to avoid the danger of the dish being too moist.

SERVING SUGGESTIONS
When and how to serve stuffed vegetables depends largely on the vegtable used and what you have chosen to stuff it with. But raw stuffed celery, cucumber, tomato and marinated mushrooms all make a

Cucumber cups with a stuffing of vegetables bound in mayonnaise make an attractive garnish to cold fish.

good start to a meal. The crisper vegetables make good finger food for a buffet or to serve with drinks.

Hot stuffed tomatoes and mushrooms can be served straight from the dish, or on a bed of buttered noodles or cooked rice. They make an unusual vegetable accompaniment to hot grilled or roast meat or baked fish. Baked cucumber is particularly good for the latter. Stuffed tomatoes and mushrooms are delicious served on fluted rounds of toast or crisp fried bread as a light first course or savoury.

You can also make these hot dishes into a more substantial and nourishing meal by serving with a rich, well-flavoured cheese sauce. Here are some ideas for different fillings and ways of serving stuffed vegetables.

●Try stuffed tomatoes with chopped mushrooms which have been fried in butter with garlic and chopped parsley; cook, and serve on buttered noodles as a light supper dish.

●For a delicious hot hors d'oeuvre, top mushrooms with a mixture of 225 g [$\frac{1}{2}$ lb] crabmeat and 150 ml [$\frac{1}{4}$ pt] béchamel sauce, flavoured with lemon juice and chopped parsley.

●Left-over macaroni cheese or cauliflower cheese combined with finely chopped anchovy fillets make good stuffings for both tomatoes and mushrooms. These make a good mid-week supper dish.

●Celery is delicious with a piped taramasalata filling topped with pimento stuffed olives—an ideal mixture of piquant flavours to serve with drinks before dinner.

●Mix cold cooked peas with chopped fresh basil or mint and use to stuff halved raw tomatoes. Serve with a nutty rice salad as a healthy vegetarian lunch.

●Stuff mushrooms with a mixture of cooked, stoned and chopped prunes and crisply fried bacon, bound lightly together with a little béchamel sauce and serve on rounds of toast for a savoury snack.

●Stuff tomatoes with chopped, sautéed chicken livers before baking. Serve on fluted rounds of toast. These make excellent dinner party savouries.

●For an excellent vegetable garnish for roast or grilled lamb serve stuffed tomatoes, provençal-style. Fill the tomatoes with a mixture of fresh white breadcrumbs, crushed garlic, chopped parsley and seasoning moistened with oil before baking.

CHEESY STUFFED MUSHROOMS

This is an example of a stuffing that is partially cooked in advance. It is

Making stuffed cucumber and celery

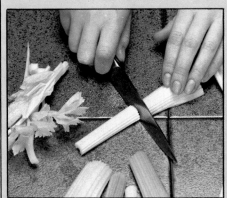

1 Trim ends of celery sticks. Strip away and discard any tough outer fibres and cut the celery into 7.5–9 cm [3–3$\frac{1}{2}$"] lengths.

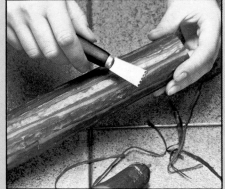

2 For raw cucumber cups, wipe but do not peel the cucumber. Trim off and discard the ends. Flute the skin if liked.

3 Cut cucumber into 4 cm [1$\frac{1}{2}$"] slices. Stand cucumber upright and scoop out seeds leaving 6 mm [$\frac{1}{4}$"] round sides and base.

5 Sprinkle the cucumber cups and boats with salt. Turn upside down to drain for 30 minutes. Carefully blot dry with kitchen paper.

6 While the cucumber is draining prepare the ingredients for the stuffing and cook if necessary.

7 Spoon the filling into the prepared celery or cucumber, piling up fairly high in the centre. If serving raw, garnish.

very important that the onion be sweated until quite tender before being used to stuff the mushrooms, otherwise it will still be somewhat raw when the mushrooms and other ingredients are cooked to perfection.

With its mixture of cheese and lemon this hot dish is light and refreshing, but nourishing enough to serve for supper or lunch. Cauliflower in béchamel sauce and grilled tomatoes go well with it.

SERVES 4
12 large-sized flat mushrooms
100 g [¼ lb] butter
1 large onion
4 thick slices of white bread
1 lemon
175 g [6 oz] Cheddar cheese
45 g [3 tablespoons] chopped parsley
salt
freshly ground black pepper

4 For cucumber boats to be cooked, wipe the cucumber, trim off ends, and cut lengthwyas into 9 cm [3½"] lengths. Scoop out seeds.

8 For cucumber boats to be cooked, place in a greased gratin dish and bake in a moderate oven for 15 minutes.

Step-by-step to stuffing tomatoes

1 Slice off tops of tomatoes at stalk end and cut in half horizontally, straight across or zig-zag.

2 Scoop out flesh and seeds with teaspoon, taking care not to break the skin.

3 Sprinkle cavities with salt. Turn tomatoes upside down to drain for 30 minutes. Rinse and pat dry.

4 While the tomatoes are draining, prepare the ingredients for the stuffing and cook if necessary.

5 Fill the tomatoes with prepared stuffing. Replace lids if wished. To serve raw, add a suitable garnish and serve.

6 To cook, place in greased gratin dish; pour liquid round if wished. Bake in moderate oven for 15 minutes.

285

1 Heat the oven to 180°C [350°C] gas mark 4.

2 Wipe the mushrooms and cut off stalks level with gills. Finely chop the stalks.

3 Melt the butter in a medium-sized saucepan over low heat. Remove from the heat and brush the mushrooms on both sides with melted butter. Place them, gill side up, in a buttered shallow oven-proof dish.

4 Peel and finely chop the onion and add, with the chopped mushroom stalks, to the remaining butter in the pan. Cover and sweat over low heat for about 10 minutes or until the onion is tender.

5 Meanwhile, reduce the bread slices to crumbs. Grate 15 ml [1 tablespoon] zest from the lemon and squeeze 45 ml [3 tablespoons] juice. Grate the cheese.

6 Remove the pan from the heat and add breadcrumbs, lemon zest and juice, chopped parsley and grated cheese to the onions. Season with salt and pepper and mix well.

7 Divide the mixture between the mushrooms, mounding it in the centre of each. Press the mixture lightly with your fingers to make a neat shape if necessary.

8 Bake, uncovered, for about 20 minutes, until the mushrooms are tender and the stuffing is golden brown and lightly crisped.

TOMATOES STUFFED WITH AVOCADO

These cold stuffed tomatoes make an elegant first course, with buttered thin brown bread. Alternatively, for a light summer lunch, serve them with a crisp lettuce salad with plenty of chopped fresh herbs and a well-flavoured vinaigrette sweetened with a pinch of sugar.

SERVES 4
**8 medium-sized tomatoes
salt
1 large ripe avocado
15 ml [1 tablespoon] lemon
    juice
225 g [½ lb] curd cheese or
    cottage cheese**

**15 ml [1 tablespoon] chopped
    chives
freshly ground black pepper
3 drops Tabasco sauce
paprika pepper**

1 Remove tomato calyxes and cut tomatoes in half horizontally in either a plain or zig-zag edge.

2 Carefully scoop out tomato pulp. Sprinkle inside of tomatoes with salt, turn upside down and leave to drain for 30 minutes.

3 Peel, halve and stone the avocado. Sprinkle with lemon juice and mash with a fork until smooth.

4 Place the curd cheese into a medium-sized mixing bowl and mix together with the avocado and chives. Season with salt, pepper and Tabasco.

5 Rinse and carefully dry the tomatoes. Pipe the mixture into each half, sprinkle with paprika and serve.

TOMATOES WITH RICE STUFFING

This is a Grecian recipe for cooking stuffed tomatoes and in Greece would probably be served chilled or at room temperature as a meze or hors d'oeuvre. The tomato lids are used to seal in the moisture of the stuffing and a little liquid surrounds them during cooking to provide a 'natural' sauce. Left-over cold cooked rice could be used instead of the brown rice. Vegetable or chicken stock are both suitable as cooking liquids for the rice.

SERVES 4–6
**100 g [¼ lb] brown rice
275 ml [½ pt] stock
6 large tomatoes
30 ml [2 tablespoons] oil
1 medium-sized onion
2 garlic cloves
90 ml [6 tablespoons] tomato
    purée
90 ml [6 tablespoons] chopped
    parsley
30 ml [2 tablespoons] chopped
    mint
2.5 ml [½ teaspoon] dried
    oregano
salt
freshly ground black pepper**

1 Wash and pick over the rice. Put it

Flat-capped mushrooms make an ideal container for a stuffing of onion, herbs and cheese flavoured with lemon and baked until golden on top and piping hot.

in a medium-sized pan with the stock. Bring to the boil. Stir once. Cover the pan, reduce heat and simmer for 45 minutes or until the rice is tender and all the water is absorbed.

2 Meanwhile, cut off and reserve the top of each tomato. Carefully hollow out the centres. Discard the seeds but reserve the pulp.

3 Sprinkle the tomato cavities with salt and leave upside down to drain for 30 minutes.

4 Heat the oven to 180°C [350°F] gas mark 4.

5 Peel and firmly chop the onion and crush the garlic cloves.

6 Heat the oil in a fairly large frying-pan. Sweat the onion, uncovered, until quite tender.

7 Drain off any remaining water and fluff the rice.

8 Add the cooked rice, tomato pulp, half the tomato purée, the herbs, garlic and seasoning to the onion in the pan. Cook briskly over medium heat until mixture is fairly stiff. This helps to flavour the rice. Stir continuously both to help the liquid to evaporate and also to prevent sticking.

9 Rinse and dry the tomatoes carefully. Arrange them in a greased ovenproof dish. Fill them with the stuffing and put the top slices back on as 'lids'.

10 Mix the remaining purée with about 30 ml [2 tablespoons] water, salt and pepper and pour it round the tomatoes.

11 Bake for about 20 minutes or until the tomatoes are tender.

CELERY WITH CREAM CHEESE AND WALNUT STUFFING

These are savoury titbits to serve with cocktails or as part of a buffet.

They are filled with a really stiff stuffing that is essential for finger food.

SERVES 4
8 celery sticks
100 g [¼ lb] cream cheese
50 g [2 oz] shelled walnut halves
half an eating apple
25 g [1 oz] sultanas
salt
freshly ground black pepper

1 Trim the celery and cut off the large flat end. Reserve for use in soups and sauces. Cut the rest of the celery into 7.5–9 cm [3–3½"] lengths.

2 Place the cream cheese in a medium-sized mixing bowl. Roughly chop the walnuts.

3 Wipe the skin of the apple clean. Do not peel. Core and finely chop.

4 Beat the rest of the ingredients into the cream cheese.

5 Pile the filling into the celery boats.

STUFFED MARINATED MOUSHROOMS
*This light dish makes an excellent starter for a summer meal and is quick to prepare once the mushrooms have been marinated.*

SERVES 3
6 large mushrooms
pinch of mustard powder
pinch of caster sugar
salt and pepper
30 ml [2 tablespoons] wine vinegar
60 ml [4 tablespoons] corn or olive oil
75 ml [3 fl oz] thick or whipping cream
15 ml [1 tablespoon] lemon juice
1 celery stick
30 ml [2 tablespoons] chopped fresh chives
30 ml [2 tablespoons] chopped fresh parsley
50 g [2 oz] ham
parsley sprigs

1 Wipe mushrooms and trim off stalks level with caps. Wrap stalks and reserve.

2 Place mushrooms in a single layer, gills facing upwards, in a shallow dish.

3 Put mustard, sugar and seasoning in a bowl. Add vinegar and oil and stir with a fork to blend.

4 Pour marinade over the mushrooms. Cover the dish with foil and leave in a cold place for 4–8 hours. Spoon marinade over mushrooms occasionally.

5 Whip cream until it stands in stiff peaks. Stir in the lemon juice.

6 Wash and chop the celery. Finely chop the ham. Stir them into the cream with the chopped herbs and season to taste.

7 Transfer mushrooms from the marinade into a serving dish. Stir any left-over marinade into the cream mixture.

8 Using a teaspoon, divide the stuffing between the mushrooms, mounding it in the centre of each cap. Garnish with parsley sprigs.

CUCUMBER WITH SHRIMP STUFFING

⊠⊠ *Serve this delicately flavoured dish as an unusual hot start to a meal, or with cooked vegetables as a light luncheon dish. It is also good cold, cut into 2.5 cm [1"] pieces as a buffet nibble. It will make three servings as an hors d'oeuvre, two as a light main course.*

SERVES 2–3
1 medium-sized cucumber
salt
50 g [2 oz] butter
1 lemon
25 g [1 oz] flour
150 ml [¼ pt] milk
100 g [¼ lb] peeled shrimps
15 ml [1 tablespoon] freshly chopped parsley
freshly ground black pepper

1 Peel cucumber thinly. Cut into three equal-sized pieces, then slice these lengthwise and, using a teaspoon, scoop out the seeds.

2 Sprinkle cucumber with salt and leave upside down on a plate for 30 minutes to draw out excess liquid.

3 Meanwhile, position shelf in the centre and set the oven to 180°C [350°F] gas mark 4. Grease a shallow ovenproof dish using 15 g [½ oz] of the butter. From the lemon grate 5 ml [1 teaspoon] zest and squeeze 30 ml [2 tablespoons] juice.

4 Melt 25 g [1 oz] of the butter in a small pan. Remove from the heat and add the flour. Return pan to a moderate heat for 2–3 minutes, stirring, then remove from heat and gradually add the milk. Return to heat and simmer gently, stirring all the time for 3–4 minutes, until smooth and thick.

5 Remove pan from heat and gently stir in the shrimps, lemon zest and 15 ml [1 tablespoon] of the juice, the parsley and black pepper.

Taste and add the remaining juice if necessary.

6 Rinse and dry cucumber pieces and arrange in the greased dish.

7 Divide the shrimp mixture between the cucumber pieces, spooning it neatly into the cavities.

8 Dot with remaining butter, put into the centre of oven and bake for about 40 minutes, until filling is puffed up and lightly browned and cucumber is tender when pierced with the point of a knife.

Variations

● For an egg stuffing, omit shrimps and use two hard-boiled eggs, finely chopped, and add 5 ml [1 teaspoon] chopped fresh dill weed to the sauce.
● For a mushroom stuffing use 175 g [6 oz] cleaned, sliced button mushrooms. Fry gently in the melted butter before adding the flour. Season the sauce with grated nutmeg.

Desserts

hot and cold fruit purées

Small amounts of fresh fruit purées provide the ideal answer to summertime desserts when combined with frothy whisked egg whites. This course shows you how to create light and lovely hot soufflé-like whips, and cool and refreshing snows.

Frothy, light-as-air desserts are just the thing to finish off a summer meal. They provide a taste of sweetness without being too rich or heavy.

The desserts described here are the most economical of the fruit purée desserts, being made from small amounts of fruit purée and whisked egg whites. This is an excellent way of using up the inevitable spare egg whites you have when making mayonnaise or hollandaise for summer meals.

Served cold, they are known as snows. Served hot, they are baked in the oven, to emerge as delicious hot soufflé-like mixtures, known as whips, risen and trembling majestically high above the sides of the dish.

Apart from making a refreshing end to the meal for all the family, these types of dessert are ideal for diners on a special diet (such as low cholesterol) who are often unable to eat rich foods, such as cream, butter and egg yolks.

Cold snows are sometimes enriched by the addition of whipped cream or evaporated milk. These are known as snow-creams and obviously are not suitable for dieters!

THE BASIC ELEMENTS

Whips and snows are made up of two basic parts. The fruit purée base which gives the flavour, and the egg whites which add bulk to the snows and make the whips rise. Egg whites tend to mute and tone down the flavours, so it is important that the fruity base has a fairly pronounced taste—otherwise the resulting dish will be almost too delicate to enjoy.

For this reason dried fruit such as prunes and apricots, which have a strong flavour, make good bases, as do strongly flavoured fresh fruit such as black or redcurrants and raspberries. More delicate fruits are best if their natural flavour is boosted by the addition of orange or lemon zest, spices or a touch of liqueur.

It is also important that the fruit purée is on the dry side otherwise the whisked egg whites won't be able to hold it in suspension properly and the mixture may separate. So drain off most of the liquid before reducing the fruit to a purée. If the resulting

purée seems too stiff you can always blend in a little more liquid—but it is difficult to remove excess liquid from a purée, unless you cook it again to evaporate the liquid.

EQUIPMENT
Only a few pieces of equipment are required to make these desserts.

You will need a sieve for seedy fruit or a liquidizer for puréeing the fruit. A food mill will not give completely smooth results. A large mixing bowl and whisk are needed for whisking the egg whites.

For the whips, choose a soufflé dish which will allow the mixture to come two-thirds up the sides of the dish. If the dish is only half full, the mixture will not rise satisfactorily above the rim. Overfilling the dish may produce disastrous results—with the mixture rising high and falling down the sides of the dish!

If you don't have a suitably sized soufflé dish you can use a cake tin instead, although it won't look so pretty on the dining table.

In either case there is no need to grease the dish—the mixture rises without sticking to the sides.

Glass or plain white pottery bowls or individual glasses all make attractive containers for snows.

SNOWS AND SNOW-CREAMS
These are basically an uncooked version of whips, but they use less egg white in proportion to fruit purée. Probably the most well known of these is apple snow.

Snows
The quantities for a snow are 250 ml [½ pt] thick purée (for which you will need approximately 450 g [1 lb] fruit) and two medium-sized egg whites. Again, the fruit can be fresh or cooked.

The purée is folded into the egg whites with soft, light motions. The uncooked mixture is then turned into a serving dish or individual glasses or bowls and served on its own or with accompanying biscuits, such as langues-de-chat or shortbread fingers, and pouring cream if wished.

Unlike whips, snows can be prepared in advance—but no more than an hour, otherwise the egg whites will collapse and the ingredients separate. Do not refrigerate if preparing

in advance (chilling mutes flavours) but keep in a cool place.

Snow-creams
Snow-creams are snows which are enriched with whipped cream or evaporated milk. Because they include cream as well as egg whites, it is particularly important that the purée is thick and very flavoursome, or the results will be bland. Evaporated milk, although more economical, is only suitable with really strongly flavoured fruit. The pronounced taste of the milk would overpower and mask delicate flavours. Remember to boil and chill evaporated milk before whisking. To do this, boil the unopened can in water for 15 minutes, refrigerate overnight, then whisk until thick.

For a cream snow you will need 150 ml [¼ pt] cream and two egg whites to every 250 ml [½ pt] purée. Fold the fruit purée into the cream, then fold the resulting mixture into the whisked egg whites. Turn into a serving dish or glasses and serve as for snows—although accompanying cream is quite unnecessary.

WHIPS
These are basically the simplest form of soufflé—but there are no egg yolks, no gelatine and much less fuss altogether! The method is considerably easier than for traditional soufflés so it is a good stepping stone for the less experienced cook towards the classic and more complicated hot soufflés which require more skill and nerve for success.

Since a hot whip cannot be kept waiting, timing is very important. It should, in fact, take no more than 45-50 minutes from start to finish. (This does not include time for stewing or poaching fruit bases, since this must be done in advance and allowed to cool.)

This includes 10 minutes for puréeing the fruit in a sieve (a liquidizer takes a matter of seconds), six to seven minutes for whisking the egg whites, two to three minutes for folding the purée in and 20-25 minutes cooking time.

Work out how long the meal will take to eat and plan accordingly. Have the purée ready, then whisk the egg whites and fold the purée into them and place in the oven. This should be done 35-40 minutes before you wish to eat the dessert. There is

no harm in keeping guests waiting a few minutes at the end of the meal—it gives them time to digest the main course, and to fully appreciate the magically risen dish when it arrives hot from the oven.

Preparation of the fruit
The fruit can be raw or cooked. It should be sweetened or given extra flavourings where necessary, then reduced to a thick, smooth purée.

This preparation of the fruit should always be done first. In the case of cooked fruit, it should be done well ahead as the purée must be quite cold when added to the egg whites—otherwise the mixture is liable to collapse. On average you will need 450 g [1 lb] fruit or 250 ml [½ pt] purée for four medium-sized egg whites.

Once the cold purée is ready, heat the oven to the required temperature. It will take longer for the oven to heat up than it will take you to prepare the mixture, so prepare your equipment and ingredients, but do not start mixing for a few minutes.

Adding the egg whites
When the oven is nearing the right temperature, turn the egg whites into a large dry mixing bowl. Add a pinch of salt or cream of tartar if specified in the recipe (these are sometimes used to help stabilize the egg whites and the acidic content of the fruit). Whisk until the eggs stand in stiff upright peaks when the whisk is held upside down.

Add the purée to the egg whites, scraping the purée dish clean with a rubber-bladed spatula to avoid wastage. Fold the purée into the egg whites using a metal spoon and swift but light cutting and folding movements.

Cooking the whip
Scrape the mixture with the spatula into a soufflé dish and immediately place in the centre of the oven. Do not on any account open the oven door during the first 10 minutes or so of cooking time—the draught would make the whip sink—and, preferably, don't open it until cooking time is up.

Bring the dessert to table immediately it is ready, when it will have risen above the sides of the dish in a dramatic manner. If you stop to admire it in the kitchen, the chances are that it will have sunk sadly by the time it reaches the dining table.

RHUBARB SNOW

⬛⬛ *Rhubarb stewed with redcurrant jelly gives this dish a good flavour and colour.*

SERVES 4
450 g [1 lb] rhubarb
60 ml [4 tablespoons] redcurrant jelly
2 medium-sized egg whites
salt

1 Heat the oven to 180°C [350°F] gas mark 4.

2 Clean and trim the rhubarb and cut into 5 cm [2"] sticks. Spread half the jelly over the bottom of a small casserole. Put in the rhubarb and spread the rest of the jelly on top.

3 Cover the dish and bake in the oven for 45 minutes.

4 Drain off excess liquid, purée the fruit and allow to go cold.

5 Put the egg whites in a large mixing bowl. Add a pinch of salt and whisk to firm peaks.

6 Fold the purée into the egg whites, using light cutting and folding movements.

7 Turn the mixture into a serving dish or four dessert glasses and serve.

SUMMER FOAM

⬛⬛ *This recipe differs from the usual hot whip. The fruit should always be puréed through a sieve—the results would be far too pippy in a liquidizer. Because the purée is no thicker than a thin juice, the amount of egg white is halved. The rather unorthodox method of whipping up the mixture in a saucepan gives marvellously quick results—but care must be taken not to brown the mixture. A hand-held (or electric) rotary whisk is best for the job.*

SERVES 4
225 g [½ lb] redcurrants
225 g [½ lb] raspberries
100 g [¼ lb] icing sugar
2 medium-sized egg whites
pinch of salt

1 Wash then purée the raspberries and redcurrants together through a sieve. Add the sugar and mix.

2 Put the egg whites in a large mixing bowl. Add a pinch of salt and whisk to firm peaks.

3 Tip the purée into the egg whites, and incorporate it with light cut-

Fold a fruit purée into whisked egg whites, using light movements.

ting and folding movements.

4 Turn this mixture into a saucepan. Place the pan over a low heat and whisk continuously for about 3 minutes until the mixture starts to thicken and rise like a soufflé.

5 To serve hot, pour into wine glasses and accompany with cream.

6 To serve cold, pour into a deep serving dish which is just large enough to hold the foam, and leave to cool.

7 When cold some of the juice will separate and sink to the bottom. Just before serving stir briskly with a fork.

Variation
● For an autumn foam, replace the redcurrants and raspberries with blackberries and blackcurrants.

APRICOT SNOW-CREAM

XXX *This is a rich-tasting yet economical version of a snow-cream, using evaporated milk in place of fresh cream. A strong tasting fruit is used to counter-balance the distinctive caramel flavour of evaporated milk.*

SERVES 4-6
225 g [$\frac{1}{2}$lb] dried apricots
150 ml [$\frac{1}{4}$ pt] evaporated milk
2 medium-sized egg whites
pinch of salt

1 Soak the apricots in plenty of hot water for 8 hours or overnight.

2 Boil an unopened can of evaporated milk in water for 15 minutes. Refrigerate overnight.

3 Drain the fruit and purée.

4 Stiffly whip the evaporated milk and fold the purée into it.

5 Put the egg whites in a large mixing bowl. Add a pinch of salt and whisk to firm peaks.

6 Tip the purée and cream into the bowl and fold it into the egg whites, using light cutting and folding movements.

7 Turn the mixture into a serving dish or individual dessert glasses and serve.

Variations

Using 450 g [1 lb] fresh fruit to 2 medium-sized egg whites, try making other delicious snow-creams with 150 ml [$\frac{1}{4}$ pt] fresh, thick cream rather than evaporated milk.

●For a strawberry snow-cream, purée fresh strawberries with about 15 ml [1 tablespoon] Cointreau. Flavour the purée with the grated zest of an orange and sweeten to taste with icing sugar.

●For a fresh apricot snow-cream, poach the apricots with a vanilla pod. Remove the pod before puréeing the apricots with a little of their liquid.

●For a punchy peach snow-cream, stone the peaches (and skin if puréeing with a liquidizer) and purée with 15 ml [1 tablespoon] cooking-grade brandy. Sweeten to taste with sifted icing sugar.

●For a raspberry and peach snow-cream purée together 225 g [$\frac{1}{2}$ lb] each of raspberries and peaches. Sweeten to taste with sifted icing sugar.

●Use up an overripe melon, by puréeing 450 g [1 lb] of the flesh with a little ginger syrup. Top the snow-cream with chopped preserved ginger.

GOOSEBERRY SNOW

X *There's no need to top and tail the gooseberries if you are sieving them, but if you are using a liquidizer this must be done. You will get more purée in a liquidizer, but it will include seeds and skin. Use different quantities of egg white depending on which version you do—one large egg white is sufficient for a sieved purée, two medium-sized egg whites for a liquidized purée.*

Two contrasting ways of serving fruit purée: hot banana whip and a cool gooseberry snow decorated with chopped, crystallized angelica.

SERVES 4
450 g [1 lb] gooseberries
75 g [3 oz] sugar or 15 ml
[1 tablespoon] honey
1 elderflower head or 2 scented
geranium leaves
2 medium-sized egg whites
pinch of salt

1 Top and tail berries if necessary.

2 Put the fruit in a heavy-based saucepan. Add half the sweetener, not more than 60 ml [4 tablespoons] water and the geranium leaves or elderflower.

3 Cover the pan and cook over low heat for 15-20 minutes, shaking the pan or stirring occasionally.

4 Half-way through cooking time taste the fruit and add remaining sweetener if the fruit is still too tart for your taste.

5 Turn into a sieve to strain off all the liquid and the geranium or elderflower, then reduce the fruit to a thick purée and set aside until quite cold. Sieve again to remove pips, if wished.

6 Put the egg whites in a large mixing bowl. Add a pinch of salt and whisk to firm peaks.

7 Tip the purée into the bowl and fold it into the egg whites using cutting and folding movements.

8 Turn the mixture into a serving dish or four dessert glass dishes and serve.

Variations
Use the same quantities of fruit and egg white to create many different snows. Stew or poach the fruit according to type and add complementary flavourings in place of the geranium or elderflower. Try some of the following ideas.

●For a plum snow, flavour the purée with 15 ml [1 tablespoon] syrup from preserved ginger, making sure that the fruit is well drained before puréeing.

●For a bramble snow, purée equal quantities of apple and blackberries stewed together. When combined with the egg whites the snow has a delicate rosy hue.

●For a quince and apple snow, stew equal quantities of peeled, cored and quartered apples and quinces with the sugar and 2 strips of lemon zest.

CALIFORNIAN WHIP
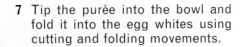*Delicious though they are, it is sometimes difficult to persuade the family to eat prunes 'au naturel'. Under the guise of a hot, soufflé-type dessert you will find that they go down a treat. Hot tea and lemon rind give the prunes a delicious, tangy flavour.*

SERVES 6
225 g [½ lb] prunes
400 ml [¾ pt] hot tea
1 lemon
100 g [¼ lb] caster sugar
4 egg whites
1.5 ml [¼ teaspoon] cream of tartar
salt

1 Peel the zest from the lemon. Soak the prunes for 8 hours or overnight in the hot tea with the lemon zest and sugar.

2 Strain the prunes and discard the lemon zest. Stone and purée the prunes with 30 ml [2 tablespoons] of their liquid.

3 Position oven shelf in the centre and heat the oven to 180°C [350°F] gas mark 4.

4 Put the egg whites in a large mixing bowl. Add a pinch of salt and whisk to firm peaks.

5 Tip the purée into the bowl and fold it into the egg whites using light cutting and folding movements.

6 Turn the mixture into a 15 cm [6"] 1.15 L [2 pt] soufflé dish and bake for about 25 minutes. Serve immediately.

BANANA WHIP
The crunchy taste of nuts adds a deliciously unusual element to the smooth, hot mixture of bananas.

SERVES 6
6 medium-sized bananas
1 orange
100 g [4 oz] caster sugar
40 g [1½ oz] flaked almonds or shelled walnut halves
4 egg whites
salt

1 Position oven shelf in the centre and heat the oven to 180°C [350°F] gas mark 4.

2 Place the nuts in a frying-pan over medium heat and, shaking continuously, toast them for 2 minutes.

3 If using walnuts, place them in a plastic bag and rub to remove the skins.

4 Turn the nuts on to a board and roughly chop.

5 Peel the bananas and thoroughly mash with a fork. Grate the zest and squeeze the juice from the orange. Add the zest and juice to the bananas with the sugar and nuts. Mix well.

6 Put the egg whites in a large mixing bowl. Add a pinch of salt and whisk to firm peaks.

7 Tip the banana mixture into the bowl and fold it into the egg white using light cutting and folding movements.

8 Turn the mixture into a 16.25 cm [6½"] 1.4 L [2½ pt] soufflé dish and bake for about 30 minutes. Serve immediately.

293

Desserts

trifles and charlottes

Rich and delicious, these beautiful desserts are rarely seen these days, although they were great favourites in the days when dining was a grander affair than it is now. English trifles and French charlottes are rich, creamy and sinful puddings that will prove to be an irresistible finale to your dinner parties.

Gorgeous desserts from days gone by, trifles and rich, cold charlottes are a much neglected culinary delight these days. Trifles might see the light of day at Christmas, but charlottes rarely make an appearance, even in restaurants.

This is a great pity because these can be truly magnificent desserts—and trifles are really very easy to make. These are not everyday puddings, perhaps, but certainly for the times when you want to serve something a little special.

Both trifles and charlottes have to be completely prepared in advance. Trifles positively benefit from being prepared well in advance, so this means you can have a splendid dessert all ready to serve on the day of your party. Last minute fuss is eliminated, leaving you time to concentrate on the rest of the food.

A trifle, tipsy cake or whim-wham as it used to be called, is a layered creation of sherry-soaked sponge, fresh fruit, rich egg custard and whipped cream, decorated on top with fruit and nuts.

A charlotte is moulded and turned out before serving. The mould is lined with sponge fingers and then a rich filling of crème Chantilly flavoured with fruit, chocolate or coffee, or a rich bavarois is poured in. Gelatine is sometimes added to the filling, so the charlotte is left to set for several hours and then turned out. The combination of biscuity outside and rich, creamy inside is irresistible.

Both desserts are not worth making unless top quality ingredients are used. This means that they are definitely not cheap to make. But take heart—they are very rich, so a little goes a long way!

EQUIPMENT FOR TRIFLES

Because a trifle is made in layers you need a glass dish to show it off. A traditional trifle dish is quite deep—about 15 cm [6"]—and has slightly sloping sides. It is about 2.5 cm [1"] narrower in diameter at the bottom than at the top.

Victorian trifle dishes came on little legs and were always made of cut glass. Today, glass dishes are less ornate but it is still possible to find attractive examples at a reasonable price.

Trifles may also be made in individual servings. For these, use fairly deep glass fruit dishes.

For the actual making of the trifle, very little is needed in the way of special equipment. You will need a sharp knife for cutting the sponge, and a double boiler or a basin and pan improvisation for making the custard. You will also need a bowl in which to whip the cream for the topping and if you are making fancy decorations, a piping bag and 1.2 cm [½"] star nozzle.

INGREDIENTS FOR TRIFLES

Trifles are rather like the 'little girl with the little curl' in that when they are good they are very very good, and when they are bad they are horrid! The quality of a trifle depends very much on the right ingredients being used without any stinginess.

Never try to economize by cutting down on fruit, using jelly in place of custard or a commercial topping instead of cream. A trifle made the commercial way with soggy sponge, canned fruit, jelly, packet custard and artificial cream is distasteful. A good trifle should have four distinct layers—sponge, fresh fruit, egg-rich custard and cream. Decorating is the only really optional feature.

Sponge

The first thing that goes into a trifle dish is the sponge base. The sponge is soaked in alcohol, and so that the liquid will really sink in and not remain on the top, very dry sponge must be used.

Special trifle sponges with a sugar coating can be bought but a stale plain sponge cake or a plain, jam-filled Swiss roll is just as good. Cut it into thickish slices about 4 cm [1½"] across.

Jam

For extra flavour, the sponges are split and sandwiched together with jam. Traditionally, raspberry, strawberry or apricot jam is used, but there is no need to stick to these. Be sure though that the chosen jam suits the layer of fruit which follows. If you are using a Swiss roll there is no need to spread with jam.

Alcohol

Whether they are left plain, or are sandwiched together with jam, the sponges are generously soaked in alcohol.

Traditionally, this was a mixture of sherry and brandy, but today it is more usual to use sherry alone or Marsala. Don't be mean with whatever alcohol you choose, or the trifle won't have the traditional tipsy flavour. If you allow about 30 ml [2 tablespoons] per person the trifle should be well flavoured.

Omitting the alcohol would not have the same effect, but for teetotallers or children you could substitute fruit juice. Canned pineapple or orange juice, or a combination of

Step-by-step to traditional trifle

SERVES 6
6 trifle sponges or 1 stale
   sponge cake about 17.5 cm
   [7"] diameter
jam
150 ml [¼ pt] sweet sherry

4 medium-sized eggs
15 ml [1 tablespoon] caster
   sugar
10 ml [2 teaspoons] cornflour
   (optional)
550 ml [1 pt] milk

1 vanilla pod
6 large or 12 small
   peaches
250 ml [½ pt] thick or whipping
   cream
24 blanched, toasted almonds

1 Trim the sponges or sponge cake to fit snugly into the base of a glass trifle dish 20 cm [8"] diameter at the widest part.

2 Split the sponges and sandwich liberally with jam. Place in the dish. Pour on the sherry and leave to soak for at least 3 hours.

3 Meanwhile, make the custard with the egg yolks, sugar, cornflour, milk and vanilla. Strain, cover and set aside to cool slightly.

4 Skin and stone peaches and cut each one into 6 slices on a plate. Place on top of the trifle sponge and pour on juice from plate.

5 Uncover the cooled custard, stir, and pour on top of the fruit. Whip the cream until it reaches the soft peak stage.

6 Spread the whipped cream over the custard with a spatula. Spike the cream with the blanched, toasted almonds.

freshly squeezed orange and lemon juice with grated orange and lemon zest, makes a pleasant, though not traditional, pudding.

Fruit
The next layer in the trifle is of fresh or cooked fruit. If you are using raw fruit, such as peaches, apricots or nectarines, make sure that they are very ripe. Orange, pineapple and banana in particular all taste good

with the sherry-soaked base of a trifle. Strawberries and raspberries are wonderful for a summer trifle. Very ripe pears can also be used.

If apples, gooseberries and blackberries are used they must be cooked. Apples can be gently stewed and then puréed. Gooseberries and blackberries are stewed and left whole. Drain the fruit from the cooking liquor, or the extra juice will make the sponge too soggy. Fresh

currants are not really suitable as they produce a lot of juice and not much flesh when cooked.

Custard
Next comes the custard. The custard used is a thick crème anglaise made with four whole eggs per 550 ml [1 pt] of milk, cooked slowly over water. Traditionally, vanilla-flavoured custard is used, but there is no reason why other flavours should not be

introduced, providing they are used with discretion.

Orange or lemon custard go well with all fruit. Simply add the juice and zest of two oranges or two lemons to the custard when it is cool. Reduce the cream or milk accordingly. Chocolate-flavoured custard, made by grating 75 g [3 oz] plain chocolate into every 550 ml [1 pt] of milk before it is heated, goes well with raspberries and pears.

For extra lightness, you can combine whisked egg white with the custard. Fold the cold custard into one or two stiffly whisked egg whites, according to preference.

Cream
Last but not least comes the topping of whipped cream. Using either thick or whipping cream, it should be lightly whipped before being spread on top of the custard. If you wish you may flavour the cream with orange or lemon zest, a drop or two of almond essence or a little sherry, but this is rather gilding the lily as the trifle is already well flavoured with alcohol and fruit.

MAKING A TRIFLE
If your trifle is to taste as good as it should, the assembly must be done correctly. It is a good idea to start your trifle two days in advance, soaking the sponge one day and completing the assembly on the evening of the next.

Keep the trifle covered in the refrigerator and remove about an hour before serving to decorate. In hot weather, it may be wise to leave the cream layer until just before serving, though the trifle is better if all the layers can be put together and left.

The sponge base
First of all, prepare the sponge base. Choose your trifle dish and select enough trifle sponges to fit snugly in the base and provide a layer about 4 cm [1½"] thick, or a sponge cake which fits snugly into the dish. You will find it easiest to have a trial run, fitting the sponge first before spreading it with jam.

Halve the sponges or cake and spread liberally with jam. Re-assemble and place in the dish. Now pour the chosen alcohol over the sponges, cover and set aside in a cool place for at least three hours to allow the alcohol to soak in and mingle with the jam.

Custard
Now make the custard with 4 whole eggs, 5 ml [1 teaspoon] cornflour (optional) and 550 ml [1 pt] milk. Cover the custard and set aside to cool. If left uncovered an unattractive skin will form.

The fruit
Once the soaking interval for the sponge base is up, prepare the fruit. Unless the fruit is cooked, do not actually start preparation until you are going to put the fruit in the dish or juice will be lost.

This layer should be about 4 cm [1½"] thick. The amount of fruit you use will depend on the type you are using. A rough guide is given here.

Peaches, apricots and nectarines should be skinned, halved, stoned and then each fruit sliced into about six before putting on the sponge. Prepare the fruit on a plate so that the juice is saved, then pour the juice from the plate on to the trifle. Allow one fruit per person, two if small.

Allow one orange per person, making sure you remove all the pith and membrane before putting into the dish, either in slices or preferably segments. Bananas are easy to prepare. Allow one to two bananas per person, depending on the size; cut each one into rings. A pineapple can be cut into slices and the centre core removed. Allow one pineapple for a trifle for 6, cut the slices 2.5 cm [1"] thick and you will have a layer of the correct depth. Once again be sure to save the juice and pour it over.

Strawberries should be hulled and halved if small, sliced if larger. When halving, put the fruit cut side down on the sponge so that it absorbs some of the sherry. Pears should be peeled, halved, cored and sliced into six as for peaches. Raspberries are left whole. For a trifle to serve six you will need about 700 g [1½ lb] berries.

If your are using cooked fruit, be sure to drain it well otherwise the trifle will be too sloppy.

Adding the custard
As soon as the fruit layer has been added, uncover the custard and stir once.

The custard can be folded into whisked egg white at this stage. The custard is then poured over the fruit. Cover the trifle bowl again and set it aside in a cool place while the cream is prepared.

Cream
The cream should form a layer about 1.2–2 cm [½–¾"] thick. Turn it into a bowl and lightly whip until it will just hold its shape in soft peaks, but do not continue until it is stiff. Add the flavourings by carefully stirring in, if you are using them, and spread over the top of the trifle with a palette knife.

Alternatively, whip the cream until it reaches the firm peak stage and pipe over the trifle using a 1.2 cm [½"] star nozzle.

Timing
You need to start a trifle a considerable amount of time before you intend to eat it. However, by no means do you have to spend all that time in the kitchen, because there are considerable time lags between each process.

The trifle base takes the longest. It should be left to soak up the alcohol for a minimum of three hours. During this period the custard is made; this takes about 30 minutes. Preparing the fruit should take about 20 minutes at the most if raw, a little longer in some cases, if cooked. Whipping the cream takes no more than 10 minutes. So, in all, the process takes about 3 hours and 30 minutes, although you will be in the kitchen for not much more than an hour.

Once assembled, the trifle should be left in a cool place for at least four hours. Leave it longer than this if possible, to allow the flavours to amalgamate.

CHARLOTTES
Charlottes are more difficult to make than trifles because the moulds are lined with biscuits (sometimes jelly too), filled with creamy filling and then unmoulded. They can, however, also be covered with biscuits after unmoulding.

There are two types of cold charlotte. A Chantilly charlotte has a filling of crème Chantilly which is easily made. A charlotte Russe has a filling of bavarois, a flavoured custard which take a bit longer to prepare. The skill lies in the assembly, so charlottes are not so daunting to make as they may appear. A charlotte does make a spectacular party centrepiece and the result is as good to eat as it is to look at.

EQUIPMENT FOR CHARLOTTES

Like trifles, the most important piece of equipment needed for a charlotte is the dish. In this case it is a mould, as the charlotte is turned out. Special charlotte moulds with slightly sloping sides and little 'ears' on the sides, which aid turning out, can be bought and are fairly inexpensive.

If you don't want to buy a charlotte mould, you can use a deep sponge cake tin, metal ice-bucket or soufflé dish instead. Charlotte moulds come in millilitre [pint] sizes. If you are not sure of the capacity, before lining the mould fill it with water to check how much it will hold. This will give you some guide to the amount of filling needed, though this will be slightly less than the mould capacity because the mould will also include biscuits and/or jelly.

To line the base of the charlotte mould, you will need greaseproof paper. If you plan to soak the sponge fingers for the charlotte in alcohol, you will need a shallow bowl or soup plate in which to put the alcohol and a wire tray on which to drain the fingers afterwards.

If you are making a charlotte russe, you will need a double boiler to make custard, as for trifles. You will also need a large bowl in which to whip the cream.

INGREDIENTS FOR CHARLOTTES

Like trifles, there can be no stinting on the ingredients for a charlotte. Both types of charlotte, Chantilly and russe, use sponge fingers and may use jelly but they are made distinctive by their fillings.

Sponge fingers

Sponge fingers are used to line the sides and sometimes the base of the mould. They should be rounded on one side and flat on the other and of a light dryish sponge that won't soak up the filling. If not dry enough the sponges will turn soggy and the charlotte can be very difficult to get out of the mould and the sponge fingers could break.

Special sponge fingers called cuillers may be bought. Alternatively, use langues-de-chat or boudoir biscuits. The number of fingers you need depends on the size of the mould. It's a good idea to buy extra to allow for breakages.

You may, if you wish, flavour the biscuits with sherry, brandy or a liqueur or a mixture of equal quantities of any of these and a fruit juice. Only a little liquid is needed as the biscuits should be dampened rather than saturated. About 30–45 ml [2–3 tablespoons] should be sufficient for even the largest number of biscuits. After using for the biscuits, any leftover liquid can be added to the charlotte filling.

Jelly

Some charlottes have jelly instead of biscuits in the base. The jelly must be home-made (remember, no inferior ingredients)—lemon jelly coloured with a little edible colouring is best. Only a very small amount is needed—enough to make a layer about 6 mm [¼"] deep in the base of the mould—so the best thing to do is make a family-sized jelly in your largest suitable container and use some of this, reserving the rest for dessert on another day.

If you wish to make patterns in the jelly, you will need some angelica which can be cut to leaf shapes, or flaked or halved blanched almonds both of which, used separately or together, are equally attractive.

Charlotte Chantilly filling

This charlotte has a flavoured whipped cream filling sweetened subtly and carefully. All of the quantities given here are based on using 550 ml [1 pt] cream. For a Chantilly filling you will need slightly less lightly whipped cream than the capacity of the mould. This is because you must allow for the amount of space taken up by the biscuits.

To sweeten the Chantilly cream, you need 50 g [2 oz] caster sugar per 550 ml [1 pt] cream. The vanilla flavouring that is usually added is omitted here, since the cream is always flavoured with another ingredient.

The cream may be flavoured with grated lemon or orange zest, or 30 ml [2 tablespoons] of alcohol of your choice per 550 ml [1 pt] cream.

Flavourings for Chantilly.
If you wish to make a fruit-flavoured Chantilly, you must adjust the quantity of the basic mixture given above. Calculate the quantity of filling needed (allowing for the biscuits) for the mould. Then make up this amount from half Chantilly cream

and half fruit purée. The purée must be fairly dry to prevent the cream from being too sloppy.

Strawberry, raspberry, nectarine, peach and apricot purées are all good as these fruit can be pushed through a sieve raw. There is no need to sweeten the fruit as the cream is already sweetened. If you use strawberry purée, you may also like to add a few drops of edible pink food dye to boost the colour—but this is optional. You will need 450 g [1 lb] fruit to make 250 ml [½ pt] purée.

If using grated orange or lemon zest, you will need the usual amount of crème Chantilly. Allow the zest of three oranges or lemons to every 550

Step-by-step to

1 Choose mould (preferably metal) at least 10 cm [4"] deep for impressive results—a traditional charlotte or straight-sided one.

3 If using a liqueur, dip the biscuits into the liqueur. Transfer biscuits to a wire tray and leave to drain for 5 minutes.

ml [1 pt] cream.

For chocolate Chantilly, you need 100 g [¼ lb] plain chocolate. Flavour the chocolate cream with orange zest and alcohol but do not include sugar, as the chocolate is already sweet.

For coffee Chantilly, allow 45 ml [3 tablespoons] strong ground or 30 ml [2 tablespoons] instant coffee. Add this to the sweetened cream. To infuse the coffee, you will need about 45 ml [3 tablespoons] boiling water.

Gelatine. Although the whipped cream (plus a stiff purée if used) should be sufficiently firm to turn out without any trouble, the Chantilly may be set with a small amount of gelatine. Only 6 g [¼ oz] is needed and

gelatine is dissolved in 45 ml [3 tablespoons] water, except where coffee is used when it is dissolved in the coffee liquid. Purists may not do this, but it is an optional extra as a precaution against collapsing when unmoulding.

Charlotte russe filling

Charlotte russe is filled with a bavarois mixture—rich custard which is flavoured, set with gelatine and enriched with cream.

Flavourings. For vanilla or chocolate fillings, make up the bavarois in the same way as for a trifle using the custard method, allowing four whole eggs per 550 ml [1 pt] of milk.

preparing and lining charlotte moulds

2 To biscuit line base, lay in one biscuit and cut to a point at centre. Cut other biscuits to cover entire base in a wheel shape. Remove.

OR for a jelly base, rinse mould in cold water. Carefully pour in thin layer of home-made jelly in a flavour to match filling. Half set.

AND if wished, when half set, decorate by carefully placing fruit and/or nuts in jelly. Press down lightly. Leave to set quite firmly.

4 Meanwhile, oil base and sides lightly with tasteless oil. Line base with greaseproof paper and grease again.

5 Shake excess liquid off base biscuits and carefully arrange in the mould, rounded sides facing the bottom.

6 Stand side biscuits round inside edge of mould, rounded sides outwards. Do this for jelly and for biscuit-based charlottes.

Step-by-step to Chantilly filling

1 Prepare flavouring—purée fruit, squeeze juice and grate zest, melt chocolate or infuse coffee.

2 Soak the gelatine in water (or fruit juice or coffee if used) and dissolve over low heat for 3 mins.

3 Whip cream to soft peaks. Fold in sugar (except for chocolate) and flavouring, gently but thoroughly.

4 Using light movements incorporate cooled gelatine into cream. Do not deflate air bubbles.

5 Stir occasionally until cold and almost setting. Speed up process by doing this over ice.

6 Spoon filling carefully into prepared mould. Level top with palette knife, cover and chill to set.

Calculate the capacity of the mould, remembering to deduct a little to allow for biscuit space. Three-quarters of the filling consists of custard. The remaining quarter is made up with whipped cream.

If making a fruit-flavoured filling, make half as much custard as you need for the mould. Flavour this with the same quantity of apricot, peach, nectarine, raspberry or strawberry purée. Do not sweeten the purée as the custard is sweet enough. Once again, the remainder is made up with cream.

If making orange or lemon custard, proceed in the same way as for a trifle. Make custard to fill three-quarters of the capacity needed and

Step-by-step to

1 Prepare flavourings as shown in charlotte Chantilly instructions. Melt chocolate directly in milk.

5 Place the custard in its container in a bowl of water and ice to cool. Stir occasionally.

enrich with one-quarter of cream.

If making a coffee-flavoured custard, make three-quarters as much custard as needed. Flavour with coffee as given for Chantilly and then make up the amount with whipped cream.

Gelatine. The custard is set with a small amount of gelatine to make it firm enough to turn out. You need 15 g [½ oz] which is dissolved in 60 ml [4 tablespoons] water.

MAKING A CHARLOTTE

Assembling a charlotte may seem like a fearsome task but if you take it slowly and calmly it is quite simple.

If you don't have the correct mould you may find the idea of making a charlotte the correct way a little daunting. An easier way of making a charlotte that looks authentic is to mould the filling first and turn it out. Spread the filling with whipped cream and then stick the biscuits in position. In this case the flat sides of the biscuits face the cream. This is the only type of charlotte where the quantity of filling made should be the same as the actual capacity of the mould, because there are no biscuits taking up space.

The classic method is described here.

Lining the base

There are two ways to line the base of a charlotte mould—with jelly and with biscuits.

Jelly. If you are lining the base of the mould with jelly, first rinse it out with cold water. This will prevent the jelly sticking. Never oil the mould if jelly is to be used—the oil makes the jelly cloudy.

The jelly should be prepared well in advance. You could make a jelly for the family and just use a little of it to line the bottom of the mould. Make the jelly of the same fruit as is used to flavour the Chantilly or bavarois creams. Plain jellies may be of the packet or home-made type.

Pour enough jelly into the base of the mould to make a layer about 6 mm [¼"] deep. Place in the refrigerator or

bavarois filling for charlotte russe

2 Make thick bavarois custard as 22. Use cornflour to stabilize it.

3 Remove from the heat and cool slightly before gently stirring in any other flavouring.

4 Soak the gelatine for 5 minutes. Dissolve over low heat and incorporate into custard when cool.

6 Whip the cream to soft peak stage and fold in the cold custard when it is on the point of setting.

OR for a less rich version, whisk egg whites and carefully fold in the cool custard and whipped cream.

7 Carefully spoon mixture into prepared mould, cover top with biscuits if wished, cover and chill.

freezer or in a bowl of iced water to speed setting. If you wish, decorations can be embedded in the jelly. Do this when the jelly is half set, positioning the decorations with an eye for their effect in terms of colour and size.

Biscuits. If you are dipping the biscuits in liqueur, do this and drain on a wire rack with a saucer below to catch the drips, for five minutes. However, if you are lining the base of the mould it is easiest to cut the biscuits to shape first and then soak them, so set aside about one-third of the biscuits for the base.

To line the base of the mould with biscuits, first oil the whole mould with flavourless cooking oil and then cut a circle of greaseproof paper to fit the base. The easiest way to do this is to draw round the base. Put the paper circle in the base of the mould and oil again.

Cut the biscuits to fit; place one of the biscuits in the base of the mould, rounded side down, with one end against the wall of the mould, and the other pointing to the centre. Using a sharp knife, cut the end which is to the centre into a point. The apex of the point should come exactly halfway across the base of the mould. Use this biscuit as a pattern to cut the others. Fit the biscuits together in a circle in the base of the mould. These biscuits may then be dipped in liqueur before being replaced in the base of the mould.

Lining the sides

Regardless of whether the base is biscuit or jelly lined, the sides of a charlotte are always lined with sponge fingers.

Stand the fingers upright around the edge of the mould. Keep them as close together as possible, otherwise the filling may leak out between them. Do not worry if the biscuits protrude over the top of the mould—these can be trimmed but it is safer to do it when the filling has set and will hold them securely ensuring a level cut.

If you have coated the bottom of the mould in jelly, remove it from the refrigerator when it is half set. Arrange biscuits along the side walls of the mould, pushing them down into the jelly. When they are all in position refrigerate until the jelly is completely set before adding the filling.

Step-by-step to unmoulding and decorating charlottes

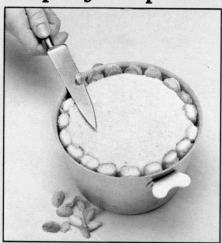

1 Trim biscuits protruding beyond the mould rim with a sharp knife, to make a flat base.

2 Turn out when set firm and near eating time. Invert on to chilled plate, tap sharply, ease off gently.

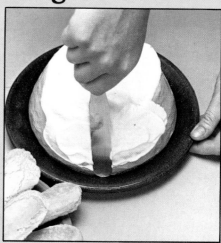

3 If moulded without biscuits, mask top and sides with cream and stick biscuits around sides.

5 Piped cream or a combination of cream and fruit can be used on a jelly topping.

6 It is traditional to tie ribbon around waist of charlotte. Secure with pin and make bow if wished.

7 Pipe cream around the base of russe if wished. A Chantilly is too rich for this decoration.

The filling
The mould is now ready to fill with either a Chantilly or a bavarois filling.

Chantilly. For a plain Chantilly filling, lightly whip the thick cream. You will need sufficient to fill the space inside the biscuits to the level of the edge of the mould (remember that whipping will increase the volume). Sweeten the cream with 50 g [2 oz] caster sugar, but do not include the vanilla extract flavouring. To flavour the cream you need 30 ml [2 tablespoons] of alcohol.

If making a fruit-flavoured Chantilly reduce the quantity of cream. You will need half the quantity of unsweetened fruit purée to half sweetened crème Chantilly—with or without alcohol. Fold the fruit purée carefully into the whipped cream and

4 Garnish top with simple fruit decoration if biscuit topping and fruit filling are used.

8 Leave in a cool place for 30 minutes—not the refrigerator as the cold numbs flavour.

sweeten to taste.

If using oranges or lemons, grate the zest from the fruit and squeeze out the juice—you need one fruit. Carefully stir the juice into sufficient cream to fill the mould inside the biscuits.

For chocolate Chantilly, melt the chocolate in a double boiler. Allow the chocolate to cool slightly. Meanwhile whip the cream, but do not sweeten it, and stir in the flavouring of sherry, brandy or a liqueur. Then add the slightly cooled chocolate to the cream and stir in.

For coffee Chantilly, infuse the coffee in 45 ml [3 tablespoons] hot water. Leave until cold. Strain if ground coffee was used, then use this coffee liquid to dissolve the gelatine and so combine the operations of flavouring and setting.

Setting a Chantilly filling. To set other Chantilly fillings than coffee, soak the gelatine in 45 ml [3 tablespoons] of water in a small pan and heat it for 3 minutes to dissolve. Allow the liquid to become cool before pouring into the whipped, flavoured, sweetened cream in a thin stream. Add the gelatine carefully, stirring all the time. If the gelatine is too hot it will curdle the mixture.

Once the gelatine has been added, leave the cream in a cool place, stirring from time to time until on the point of setting. When this point is reached, pour into the lined mould, cover and leave to set for about three hours.

Charlotte russe. First make the custard for the bavarois, following instructions for trifles and allow it to cool. Flavour the custard using any of the flavourings in the amounts suggested in ingredients.

When the flavouring has been added, the gelatine is added. Soak 15 g [½ oz] gelatine in 60 ml [4 tablespoons] water per 550 ml [1 pt] of custard and heat gently to dissolve. Allow to cool and then pour into the custard in a thin stream, stirring all the time.

Place the bowl containing the custard in another bowl of iced water or ice cubes and stir until just setting. When this point is reached, lightly whip the cream and fold this into the custard, incorporating as much air as possible. Pour the custard into the prepared mould. At this stage, you may cover the top of the filling (which will become the base when turned out) with biscuits in the same way as

the base, but this is an optional extra. Cover the mould and set aside for about 4 hours—longer for larger charlottes.

Trimming the biscuits
When the filling has set, trim off the biscuits. This is easy to do by running a sharp knife along the edge of the mould, removing everything above it. The base of the pudding will then be flat and will stand up securely.

Turning out
After setting comes the turning out. Do this as near serving time as possible, bearing in mind that you must allow time to decorate. Once decorated, if cream is used, the biscuits may start to go soggy, so eat the dessert if possible, within one hour of decorating, no more than two. Do not refrigerate again as the cream may pick up other flavours but leave the dessert in a very cool place.

Invert a plate over the top of the mould. Invert the whole so that the plate is the right way up again. Give a sharp tap before lifting off the mould—this will help dislodge the pudding. You will now see why it is so important to use a mould of the right size—the filling must come right to the top, otherwise it will have to fall as it drops on to the plate in unmoulding and could break.

Gently ease the mould away from the charlotte—this is where the ears come in handy.

It is also a good idea to have some spare biscuits. If you break one you can carefully lift this off and replace it with a new one after unmoulding, using a little whipped cream as 'cement'.

Decorating
To decorate a charlotte, arrange complementary fresh fruit around the base or pipe a border of cream around. Cream may also be piped around the top. Don't go mad with the decorations or the charlotte will look unpleasantly fussy.

Traditionally a charlotte is served with a band or ribbon around the middle. Wide florists ribbon is best. Cut a slightly longer length of ribbon than will go around the charlotte. Place around the charlotte and get someone to hold it while you secure it with stainless steel pins. Push the pins into the biscuits. Then make an attractive bow.

Sophisticated decorations make trifles even more appealing. **1** Pipe a lattice in cream across the top of the trifle. Fill alternate squares with halved cherries and grated chocolate.

1

2

2 Pipe swirls of S-shaped cream in lines across the pudding. Arrange halved strawberries in alternate rows and place diamonds of angelica along each cream row.

NURSERY TRIFLE

⊠⊠⊠ *This trifle contains no alcohol and is especially good for children or when you want to serve a fairly special but economical dessert. Stale chocolate-flavoured Swiss roll (not covered in chocolate) makes the perfect base for this trifle but stale chocolate cake could be used instead.*

SERVES 6
1 chocolate Swiss roll
2 oranges
6 large bananas
4 medium-sized eggs
50 g [2 oz] caster sugar
550 ml [1 pt] milk
1 vanilla pod
150 ml [¼ pt] thick cream
100 g [¼ lb] green grapes
50 g [2 oz] shelled walnut
halves

1 Cut the Swiss roll into slices 4 cm [1½"] thick and place in the base of a glass dish 20 cm [8"] diameter and about 15 cm [6"] deep. The slices must fit neatly and cover the entire base.

2 Grate zest from the oranges and squeeze the juice. Sprinkle zest over Swiss roll and pour on juice. Cover and leave in a cool place to soak for 3 hours.

3 Scald the milk with the vanilla pod in a small pan. Cover and leave to infuse for 20 minutes.

4 Slice the bananas and place in an even layer on the sponge. Arrange in a decorative pattern.

5 Prepare a double boiler. Whisk the eggs and sugar together in the top pan off the heat, until the mixture is light and thick.

6 Remove the vanilla pod from the milk. Pour the milk on to the eggs and sugar, stirring the mixture all the time.

7 Place the pan containing the custard on the double boiler and cook over low heat for 20 minutes, until the custard will coat the back of a spoon.

8 Cover the custard and allow to cool. Stir once before pouring over the bananas.

9 Lightly whip the cream and carefully spread over the top of the custard. Cover and refrigerate for at least 5 hours.

10 Move the trifle to a cool place at least 30 minutes before eating. Prepare the grapes by peeling, halving and deseeding.

11 Decorate with grapes and walnut halves.

3 *To make a posy of flowers, make crystallized rose petals into flowers and place candied violets and angelica cut to the shape of leaves in between. Pipe cream to make a lacy pattern round the outside to look like a doily.*

BOODLE'S ORANGE TRIFLE

⊠⊠⊠ *This trifle is very simple to make as it has only two layers—sponge and orange-flavoured cream. The dish comes from Boodle's gentlemen's club in St James's Street, London, and is still very popular. The orange flavouring soaks into the sponges and the result is irresistible.*

SERVES 4

4 trifle sponges or a sponge
    cake 18 cm [7"] diameter
60 ml [4 tablespoons] orange
    marmalade
120 ml [8 tablespoons] Grand
    Marnier or sweet sherry
4 oranges
2 lemons
30 ml [2 tablespoons] caster
    sugar
550 ml [1 pt] whipping or
    thick cream

1 Select a dish about 20 cm [8"] diameter and 10 cm [4"] deep.

2 Split the sponges and sandwich together with orange marmalade. Place in the base of the dish.

3 Pour the Grand Marnier or sherry over the sponges. Cover and leave to soak for at least three hours in a cool place.

4 Grate the zest of 2 of the oranges and one of the lemons and place in a separate bowl.

5 Squeeze the juice from all the fruit. Add to the zest together with the sugar. Stir to dissolve sugar.

6 Whip the cream until it reaches the soft peak stage. Add to the fruit juice and sugar and carefully fold in.

7 Pour the cream and fruit juice mixture over the sponges. Cover and chill for at least 10 hours to allow flavours to amalgamate, but remove to fairly cool room temperature 30 minutes before serving.

ZUPPA INGLESE

⊠⊠⊠ *Although the Italians regard their zuppa inglese as a cake, it is like an English trifle except that it has more than one layer of sponge and the whole thing is liberally soaked in rum for at least a whole day for the flavours to amalgamate. Here is a chocolate and pear version of this rich pudding. Less sugar than usual is added to the custard because of the amount of sugar which is in the chocolate.*

CHARLOTTE RUSSE AUX FRAISES

⬚⬚⬚ *A bavarois custard is flavoured with strawberries and enriched with cream to make this deliciously fruity charlotte russe. A thin layer of home-made strawberry jelly makes an attractive topping when the dessert is unmoulded.*

SERVES 6
about 24 sponge fingers
30 ml [2 tablespoons]
  strawberry jelly
4 medium-sized eggs
25 g [1 oz] caster sugar
250 ml [½ pt] milk
15 g [½ oz] gelatine
150 ml [¼ pt] thick cream
225 g [½ lb] strawberries

For the decoration:
150 ml [¼ pt] thick cream
100 g [¼ lb] strawberries

1 Estimate how many sponge fingers you need. Rinse a 850 ml [1½ pt] mould with cold water.

2 Pour the strawberry jelly into the bottom of the mould.

3 When the jelly is half set, line the sides of the mould with the sponge fingers.

4 Prepare a double boiler. Cream the eggs and sugar together until light and creamy. Fill a large bowl half full of iced water.

5 Scald the milk and pour it on to the egg mixture. Put the custard mixture in the top of the double boiler and cook over low heat for 20 minutes, stirring all the time, until the mixture will coat the back of a spoon.

6 Strain the custard into a bowl and stand this in the bowl of iced water to cool, being careful that no water gets into the custard.

7 Soak the gelatine in 60 ml [4 tablespoons] water. Dissolve over low heat for 3 minutes. Meanwhile purée the strawberries.

8 Pour the gelatine into the custard in a thin stream, stirring all the time. Allow to cool.

9 Fold strawberry purée into custard. Stir until it begins to set.

Charlotte russe aux fraises and Charlotte turinoise are good examples of the two different types of charlotte that can be made. One is custard-based and the other cream-based.

SERVES 6
1 sponge cake, 20 cm [8"]
  diameter
250 ml [½ pt] dark rum
6 large ripe pears
4 medium-sized eggs
50 g [2 oz] sugar
550 ml [1 pt] milk
75 g [3 oz] plain cooking
  chocolate

For the decoration:
150 ml [¼ pt] thick or
  whipping cream
angelica

1 Cut the sponge cake in half horizontally. Trim one half to fit the base of a trifle dish which is 20 cm [8"] diameter and about 15 cm [6"] deep.

2 Line the dish with the trimmed sponge half and pour half the rum over the cake. Set aside for at least 3 hours.

3 Peel, halve, core and slice two of the pears. Place on top of the rum-soaked sponge.

4 Prepare a double boiler. Whisk the eggs and sugar together in the top pan, off the heat, until light and thick.

5 Grate the chocolate. Add it to the milk in a pan and scald, stirring occasionally to incorporate the chocolate.

6 Pour the scalded milk on to the eggs and sugar. Transfer to the double boiler and cook over medium heat, stirring for 20 minutes until the custard will coat the back of a spoon. Allow to cool.

7 Pour half the custard over the pears. Place the remaining sponge half on top and pour over the rest of the rum. Cover and set aside for at least 3 hours for the flavours to amalgamate. Cover the remaining custard and set aside.

8 Prepare the remaining pears. Place on top of the sponge. Top with the remaining custard.

9 Whip the cream until it will stand in stiff peaks. Spread or pipe the whipped cream over the top of the custard and decorate with angelica.

10 Leave the zuppa inglese for at least one day before eating so that flavours will amalgamate.

10 Lightly whip the cream. Fold in the setting custard.

11 When on the point of setting, pour the mixture into the lined mould. Cover with cling film or kitchen foil, or a plate if there are no protruding side biscuits.

12 Leave to set for 4 hours or more.

13 When set trim any protruding side biscuits by running a knife along the rim of the mould. Invert a plate over the charlotte, tap and turn out.

14 Whip the cream and pipe around the base and top to decorate. Arrange whole strawberries on top.

15 Place a wide ribbon around the charlotte, fixing in place with stainless steel pins. Make an attractive bow.

Variation
●For charlotte russe aux framboises, line the base with a home-made raspberry jelly and set a few whole raspberries in the jelly. Substitute the same weight of strawberries for raspberries in the recipe and garnish in the same way.

CHARLOTTE TURINOISE
▧▧▧ *This chestnut-flavoured char-lotte is an example of a charlotte Chantilly and is a really special-day dish. Because chestnut purée is very strongly flavoured, only half the usual amount of purée to cream is used. Canned chestnut purée can be bought both sweetened and unsweetened. If you use the sweetened kind, do not sweeten the cream.*

SERVES 6
about 24 sponge fingers
30 ml [2 tablespoons] dark rum
550 ml [1 pt] thick cream
50 g [2 oz] caster sugar
250 ml [½ pt] unsweetened
    chestnut purée
6 g [¼ oz] gelatine

For the decoration:
150 ml [¼ pt] thick or
    whipping cream
100 g [¼ lb] marrons glacés
    or chocolate flakes

1 Oil a 850 ml [1½ pt] charlotte mould

or sponge cake tin and line the base with greaseproof paper. Oil again.

2 Cut the biscuits to size to fit the base and calculate how many will be needed for the sides.

3 Dip the biscuits one by one into the rum and drain for 5 minutes on a cake rack over a plate.

4 Line the base and sides of the mould with the biscuits.

5 Lightly whip the cream. Fold in the sugar and the rum left over from the biscuits.

6 Fold the chestnut purée into the cream.

7 Soak the gelatine in 30 ml [2 tablespoons] water, then dissolve over low heat. Allow to cool a little.

8 Pour the gelatine into the cream mixture in a thin stream, stirring very lightly.

9 Leave until on the point of setting, stirring gently from time to time. This will take about 10 minutes.

10 Put the cream mixture into the biscuit-lined mould. Cover with cling film or foil, or with a plate if there are no protruding biscuits. Put in the refrigerator for 4 hours to set.

11 When set trim any protruding biscuits by cutting with a knife.

12 Turn out the charlotte. Whip the cream to stiff peaks. Decorate with marrons glacé halved widthways or chocolate flakes and piped rosettes of cream.

Variations
●For apricot charlotte Chantilly, dip the biscuits in apricot brandy. For the filling, purée 700 g [1½ lb] fresh ripe apricots, stir into about 400 ml [¾ pt] Chantilly cream flavoured with left-over apricot brandy. After unmould-ing, decorate with angelica and sliced apricots.
●For raspberry or strawberry Chan-tilly, make the filling from half and half cream and fruit purée (using 450 g [1 lb] fruit to make the purée). Flavour biscuits and cream with sweet sherry or Marsala.

Desserts

cold soufflés

Like most cold puddings, cold soufflés can be prepared in advance, so that whatever else happens at your dinner party, the dessert is ready to eat.

EQUIPMENT

The most important piece of equipment in making cold soufflés is the dish. If the dish is the wrong size for the amount of mixture used, the soufflé will not have the correct 'risen' effect. Traditionally, soufflé dishes with straight sides are used for making cold soufflés. The chart gives the correct dish sizes for various amounts of mixture.

To make the all-important collar for the dish you will need greaseproof paper. Do not use kitchen foil as it tends to crease and this will spoil the edge of the soufflé. To secure the paper, you will need adhesive tape, freezer tape is good as it remains adhesive under most conditions. To brush the paper, you will need flavourless cooking oil.

To cook the eggs and sugar, you will need a double boiler. This can be either a proper double boiler or a basin and pan improvisation. Whichever you use, the water should be warm when you start and it must not touch the base of the egg and sugar container.

To whisk the eggs and sugar and later the egg whites and cream, you will need either a balloon or electric whisk. A balloon whisk gives the most bulk and the lightest results but also takes the longest time. You must wash and dry the whisk in between whisking cream and egg whites otherwise the egg white will not stand up.

To cover the soufflé while it is in the refrigerator and prevent the absorption of other food flavours, you will need some kitchen foil or cling film. This rests loosely over the dish.

If you wish to decorate the finished soufflé with cream, you will need a piping bag and a small star vegetable nozzle.

INGREDIENTS

The ingredients for cold soufflés must be used in the correct proportions as given here.

Eggs

Large eggs are always used. For an 850 ml [1½ pt] soufflé which will serve 6 people, you will need 4 eggs. The eggs are always separated and the yolks beaten in a double boiler over heat with sugar until creamy. The whites are whisked and folded into the soufflé at a later stage. The quantity of whites to yolks is always the same so there are no problems with left-over whites or yolks.

Sugar

When making cold soufflés caster sugar is always used and 25 g [1 oz] is allowed for every egg used.

Flavouring

The flavouring for a cold soufflé may be either chocolate, coffee, liqueur or fruit.

Chocolate: If using chocolate, allow 15 g [½ oz] plain dark chocolate to every egg yolk. Where chocolate is used, it is broken into pieces and melted in the double boiler before the egg yolks and sugar are added.

Coffee: If coffee is used, allow 5 ml [1 teaspoon] instant coffee or 10 ml [2 teaspoons] coarsely ground coffee for every egg.

The same water is used for infusing the coffee and for melting the gelatine. The water should be boiling when poured on to the coffee but quite cold by the time it is needed to melt the gelatine. So always prepare coffee early and remember to strain if ground coffee is used.

Liqueurs: Some classic soufflés are flavoured only with liqueur. Suitable liqueurs are Grand Marnier, Tia Maria, crème de menthe, green Chartreuse, crème de cassis and framboise. Allow 10 ml [2 teaspoons] liqueur per yolk. Place in double boiler with the eggs and sugar.

Citrus fruit: Citrus fruits have the zest grated and the juice extracted. The amount of fruit and how much zest or juice is added to the soufflé depends on the recipe.

Soft fruits: Soft fruits such as raspberries, strawberries, ripe apricots, peaches and nectarines can all be puréed raw. Peaches, apricots and nectarines should be skinned and stoned. All these fruits may be either pushed through a sieve or puréed in a

As you ease the paper collar away, you will see that the set soufflé supports itself. After the paper has been removed, the soufflé is ready for decorating. Whipped cream and angelica look attractive.

liquidizer. When pippy fruits are liquidized, they will have to be sieved afterwards to remove pips. The amount of fruit used depends on the recipe. Currants, gooseberries and blackberries will require gentle poaching before being sieved.

Gelatine

Cold soufflés are meant to have a soft, melting texture so only a little gelatine is used. Usually 15 ml [1 tablespoon] of gelatine is allowed for every 4 eggs. This amount of gelatine is usually dissolved in 45 ml [3 tablespoons] liquid.

Cream

Lightly whipped cream gives body to the texture of a soufflé, helping it to stand up, and adds richness to the flavour. The cream must be lightly whipped otherwise it will crush all the characteristic lightness out of the soufflé. The usual amount of cream to use with 4 eggs is 175 ml [6 fl oz]. Use either thick or whipping cream.

of hands is useful here to hold the paper while you stick the tape. Secure the overlap with a paper clip to prevent the soufflé mixture leaking in between the layers of paper at the join.

To prevent the soufflé sticking to the paper, brush the inside lightly with flavourless cooking oil.

Preparing the base

First prepare your chosen flavouring. If using chocolate, break into small pieces. Prepare a double boiler, place the chocolate in the top and melt over low heat. If using coffee, infuse it in hot water and leave. It is wise to do this before you start preparing the dish to allow it time to infuse. Citrus fruits should have zest removed and juice extracted. Other fruits are puréed either raw or cooked, depending on type.

Separate the eggs and place the yolks in the top of the prepared double boiler with the sugar. Add the sugar and citrus juice and zest or liqueur if using. Adding citrus at this stage brings out the flavour and cooks the zest. Adding liqueur removes any harsh 'spirit' flavour. Keeping the heat low, whisk until creamy and thick. This will take about 10 minutes with a balloon whisk or 5 minutes with an electric whisk. The mixture has reached the correct stage when it will leave ribbon-like trails.

As soon as the mixture has thickened (when it will leave a coating on the whisk), remove the top of the boiler from the base and set aside to cool, stirring from time to time.

Adding flavouring and gelatine

Sprinkle the gelatine powder on the amount of water given in the recipe or in cold, strained coffee if used. Soak for 5 minutes then dissolve over low heat for 3 minutes. While you are

MAKING A COLD SOUFFLE

Making a successful cold soufflé may be divided into six stages.

Preparing the dish

The amount of gelatine needed to give a cold sweet soufflé the correct texture is not sufficient in the early stages of setting to support the mixture above the rim of the dish, so aid must be given in the form of a paper collar. This collar must be positioned around the dish before the soufflé mixture is poured in and must remain in place until the soufflé is completely set. If a collar is not used or if it is removed too soon, the soufflé will not have the spectacular 'risen' look for which these dishes are famous.

To make the collar, you will need a double thickness of greaseproof paper long enough to go around your chosen soufflé dish with a 2.5 cm [1"]

overlap for a secure join. The paper must be wide enough to project 7.5 cm [3"] above the rim of the dish. Double thickness paper is essential as a single thickness does not have the strength to support the mixture. Wrap the collar around the dish, pull tightly and secure with freezer tape. (Ordinary adhesive tape tends to lose its stickiness in the refrigerator.)

Alternatively, use a rubber band or tie securely with string. Another pair

SIZE GUIDE TO DISHES* FOR COLD SWEET SOUFFLES

Diameter	Quantity	Number of eggs required	Number of servings
12.5 cm [5"]	550 ml [1 pt]	3	4
13.3 cm [5¼"]	850 ml [1½ pt]	4	6
15 cm [6"]	1.15 L [2 pt]	6	8
18 cm [7"]	1.4L [2½ pt]	9	10

*For individual servings, each amount will divide equally into the number of dishes given in servings.

waiting for this to happen, whip the cream until it will just hold its shape (but not until it is stiff) and set aside.

If using fruit purée, stir into the egg and sugar base. Pour in the gelatine in a thin stream from a height to encourage cooling, stirring all the time. Leave the mixture until the edges show signs of setting, stirring from time to time. This will take about 15 minutes.

Adding cream and egg whites

Whisk the egg whites until they will stand in soft peaks but not until they are stiff and dry.

First fold the flavoured base through the cream using a metal spoon and a figure-of-eight movement. When all the flavoured base has been incorporated, fold the cream and flavoured base mixture into the egg white in the same way. It is essential to keep movement light and avoid vigorous stirring or the air in the mixture will be destroyed.

Setting

Turn the soufflé mixture into the prepared dish, scraping out the bowl with a spatula. This ensures none of the mixture is wasted—important as these are quite expensive dishes to make. Level off the top if necessary. If the mixture is properly aerated and the correct size dish is used, the mixture will come within 2.5 cm [1″] of the top of the paper collar. Cover the soufflé dish loosely with foil or cling film and place in the refrigerator for 3 hours, until set. The soufflé is set when it offers a slight resistance if you press the surface with your fingertips and has a soft spongy texture.

Unwrapping and decorating

When the soufflé has set, remove the adhesive tape from round the dish. Gently insert a round-bladed knife between the soufflé and the paper. Pressing gently against the soufflé and moving the knife round, peel off the paper.

Remove your soufflé from the refrigerator at least 30 minutes before serving, but not longer than 2 hours before serving. This removes the coldness and brings out the flavour. Decorate as wished. Do not place the decorated soufflé in the refrigerator but keep in a cool place. A decorated soufflé is impossible to cover and would absorb food flavours in the refrigerator.

Step-by-step to cold soufflé

Lemon soufflé or soufflé Milanaise, as it is sometimes called, is the nicest of all cold soufflés. Whatever flavour you use, be it fruity, chocolate or coffee, make your soufflé following the basic method shown and you will have a success every time. Cold lemon soufflé should be removed from the refrigerator at least 30 minutes before serving to allow the flavour to develop.

SERVES 6
3 lemons
100 g [¼ lb] caster sugar
4 large eggs
15 ml [1 tablespoon]
  gelatine powder
175 ml [6 fl oz] thick cream

1 Prepare collar for a 13.3 cm [5¼″] soufflé dish and attach with adhesive tape and a paper clip. Prepare a double boiler.

5 Beat the eggs, sugar and lemon flavouring until thick. This will take 10 minutes with a balloon whisk, 5 minutes with an electric whisk.

6 As soon as the mixture will coat the whisk, remove from the heat. Set aside to cool, stirring from time to time.

10 Leave until just setting, stirring occasionally. Fold into the cream using a metal spoon in a figure-of-eight movement.

11 Whisk the egg whites until they will stand in soft peaks and then fold in the mixture using the same movement as before.

2 Paint the inside of the paper collar with flavourless cooking oil to prevent the finished soufflé sticking to the paper.

3 Grate the zest from one of the lemons and extract the juice from all three. Place in a double boiler top. Set boiler over low heat.

4 Separate the eggs and place the yolks in the top of the double boiler. Add the caster sugar to the double boiler.

7 Place the gelatine in 45 ml [3 tablespoons] cold water. Soak for 5 minutes then dissolve over very low heat for 3 minutes.

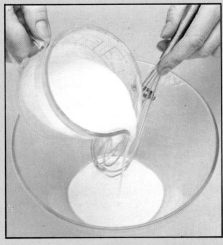

8 Whip the cream lightly so that it is thick but not so that it is stiff. Cover and set aside in a cool place until required.

9 Pour the gelatine into the soufflé mixture in a thin stream, stirring all the time to prevent threads forming.

12 Turn the mixture into the prepared soufflé dish. Cover loosely with foil and leave to set in the refrigerator for 3 hours.

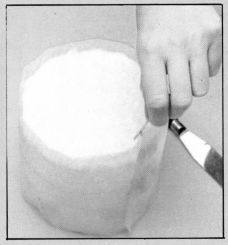

13 Gently remove the adhesive tape and the paper clip. Insert a round bladed knife between the soufflé and the paper.

14 Slowly move the knife around the soufflé, pressing gently, and easing away the paper as you go. Decorate as wished.

Decorative ideas

When decorating cold soufflés, decorate only the exposed edge with cream, not the middle. Using heavy decoration in the middle spoils the elegant appearance of the soufflé. Chopped nuts or grated chocolate may be pressed into the sides of the soufflé with a knife (or with your fingers if you have cool hands and a light touch). Where berry fruit is used, it should always be hulled, as it is awkward to remove the hulls from strawberries later on. Do not decorate the soufflé more than about 1 hour before needed.

1 To coat the sides of a soufflé with nuts, first chop the nuts finely using a mezzaluna.

2 Hold the plate level with soufflé and scoop the nuts up on to the soufflé sides, pressing gently.

3 A soufflé may be coated with finely grated chocolate, in the same way.

4 To make a pretty edging, pipe a shell border with a small vegetable nozzle.

5 Decorate the border with strips of blanched orange or lemon zest, or candied citron.

6 For a fruity soufflé, decorate with halved strawberries and cream rosettes.

7 Slivers of toasted almond can be used to decorate a whipped cream border.

8 To make angelica leaves, cut angelica stalks at angles to make leaf shape.

Star recipe

★

SOUFFLE MONTE CRISTO

This is a truly splendid vanilla and chocolate layer soufflé which is surprisingly simple to make. It is very rich, so serve after a light main course or for a buffet. A jam jar is placed in the centre of the soufflé dish while it sets so the finished soufflé has a hollow in the middle which is filled up with fruit. Do not try to improvise by using a ring mould and turning it out— there is not enough gelatine in this mixture for the soufflé to stand firm. If you place a few ice cubes in the jam jar, it will speed setting.

SERVES 8
6 large eggs
175 g [6 oz] caster sugar
2-3 drops vanilla extract
20 ml [4 teaspoons] gelatine
   powder
200 ml [7 fl oz] thick cream
2 chocolate flake bars
225 g [½ lb] canned pineapple
   cubes or fresh pineapple
100 g [¼ lb] ratafias or
   macaroons
90 ml [6 tablespoons] sweet
   sherry

For the decoration:
whipped cream

1 Prepare a 1.15 L [2 pt] soufflé dish. Also prepare a double boiler, using tepid water.

2 Separate eggs and place yolks in boiler top. Add sugar, vanilla and half the sherry.

3 Place boiler over low heat. Whisk eggs and sugar until light and creamy in texture.

7 Set the mixture aside in a cool place. Leave until just setting, stirring from time to time.

8 Select a jam jar that will come level with top of paper collar. Stand this in centre of soufflé dish.

9 Whisk egg whites until they will stand in soft peaks. Lightly whip the cream. Fold in egg mixture.

13 Continue in this way until all chocolate flake and egg mixture are used, ending with mixture.

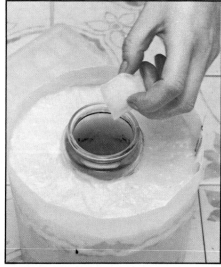

14 Place a few ice cubes in the jam jar, cover soufflé and refrigerate for 2 hours to set.

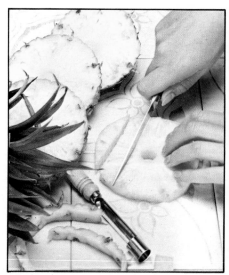

15 If using canned pineapple, drain reserving a little juice. If using fresh, cut into cubes.

4 Remove from heat and set aside to cool. Place gelatine in a pan with 60 ml [4 tablespoons] water.

5 Soak gelatine for 5 minutes then dissolve over low heat, without stirring, for 3 minutes.

6 Pour the gelatine into the egg and sugar mixture in a thin stream, stirring all the time.

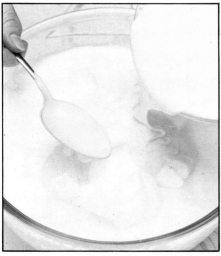

10 When all base has been folded into the cream, fold into the whisked egg whites.

11 Break up the chocolate flake bars into pieces using the point of a sharp knife.

12 Pour a quarter of the soufflé mixture into the dish. Cover with a layer of chocolate flakes.

16 Place pineapple pieces in a bowl. Add biscuits and sherry and leave to soak for 1 hour.

17 Remove soufflé from refrigerator. Fill jam jar with hot water, leave for 3 seconds then lift out.

18 Remove collar. Pile fruit and biscuit filling into the middle. Decorate with whipped cream.

Desserts

biscuit crust flans

It isn't necessary to be a super pastry cook in order to make a stunning flan. Tasty biscuit crust 'pastry' is ideal for cheesecake and many other sweet and savoury flans and it is very easy to make. It's quick too – which means you can devote more time to the fun of creating delectable and decorative fillings.

Flans, custard or fruit filled, are always popular. They taste delicious and, if carefully decorated, provide the perfect party centrepiece. But the idea of making the flan case terrifies some people. If you have problems with pastry, the answer is to make your flan using trouble-free biscuit crust 'pastry'. This isn't, in fact, a pastry at all but is made from dry ingredients (crushed biscuits or cereal) bound together with a liquid element which hardens on setting— either by refrigerating or by very brief cooking.

DRY INGREDIENTS
Biscuits: plain, crumbly, slightly porous biscuits are best as they make good crumbs and readily absorb the liquid element used to stick them together. Digestives, gingersnaps, shortbread, crispbreads and plain fruited biscuits are all good choices.

Avoid plain, very close textured biscuits, such as arrowroot, as these do not crumb well—they reduce to a fine powder instead. And do not use biscuits coated with chocolate or sandwiched together with cream as these are too sticky to crush successfully into crumbs.

Cereals: cornflakes, puffed rice, rolled oats, muesli (provided it does

You don't need to be a pastry cook to make this mouthwatering dessert—a variation on midsummer flan.

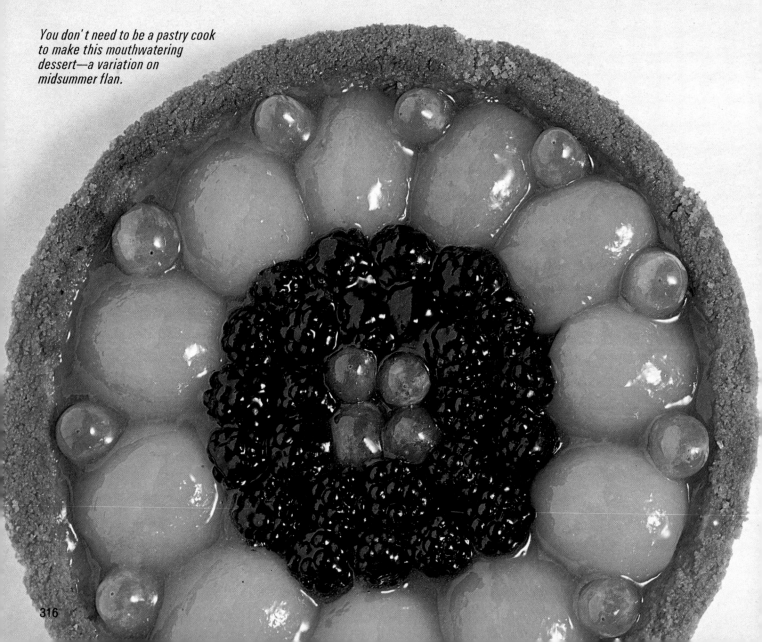

316

not contain whole nuts or lumps of dried fruit) and bran flakes can all be used without crushing. Pressed wheat breakfast biscuits can also be used but they must be crushed. Sugar or honey-coated cereals are not suitable as they will not stick together.

FLAVOURINGS

Although not essential, it is a nice idea to introduce extra ingredients to flavour your 'pastry'. So little herbs or spices are needed that they can be used in addition to the full quantity of biscuit or cereal. But you will need more of other flavourings so these must be used in place of some of the biscuits or cereal – or the balance of dry to liquid ingredients will be upset.

To give variety, sometimes reduce your chosen cereal or biscuit by 25g [1 oz] and replace with 25g [1 oz] of any of the following: finely chopped dried fruit or nuts, mixed peel, dessicated coconut, ground almonds or chopped fresh strawberries (delicious with shortbread). Or add flavour by using 5ml [1 teaspoon] cinnamon, ginger, mixed spice, nutmeg, finely chopped angelica or finely grated orange, lemon or grapefruit zest.

THE LIQUID ELEMENT

In order to make the biscuit crumbs or cereal and flavourings stick together (called binding) and form a crust, they are mixed with a liquid element which hardens on setting.
Melted butter is most commonly used and is far and away the best fat for all flan cases. Dice the butter roughly, place it in a heavy-based pan and stir over low heat. As soon as the butter is melted, remove it from the heat. Don't be tempted to

go away and leave the butter to melt by itself – it burns very quickly.

For a sweet flan, stir sugar into the melted butter as soon as the pan has been removed from the heat.
Butter and syrup or black treacle: these are good mixtures for use with gingersnaps or cereal. Use one part butter to two parts syrup or treacle. Put both ingredients in a heavy-based pan and cook gently, stirring all the time. Remove pan from heat as soon as ingredients are melted and well blended.
Chocolate: plain dessert or cooking chocolate makes a good binding for sweet biscuits, gingersnaps, puffed rice or cornflakes. Break the chocolate into pieces and put in a bowl. Stand the bowl on a trivet (a metal scone cutter or an inverted saucer will do) in a heavy-based pan half full of simmering (not boiling) water. Cook over low heat stirring the chocolate occasionally. Top up the pan with more hot water as needed. Don't use cold water: this would lower the temperature and the chocolate would take longer to melt. Use melted chocolate as soon as possible once prepared.

PROPORTIONS

If biscuit crust is to be crisp and crunchy, the ingredients must be in correct proportion to one another. As a general rule you should use half as much binding ingredient as crumbs or cereal. If making a sweet flan

bound with butter, the amount of sugar should be just about one sixth of the amount of biscuits.
The only exceptions to this rule are as follows:
1 If using biscuits which include a lot of butter (such as shortcake), reduce the butter used for binding by one third.
2 If using biscuits which have a sugar coating (such as shortcake) reduce sugar by half.

GUIDE TO BISCUIT CRUST QUANTITIES

Flan ring diameter	Dry ingredients (including flavourings)	Binding ingredients (butter, or butter with syrup or treacle, or chocolate)	Sugar (omit when using syrup or chocolate)	No. of servings
18 cm [7″]	175 g [6 oz]	75 g [3 oz]	25 g [1 oz]	4-5
20 cm [8″]	225 g [½ lb]	125 g [¼ oz]	40 g [1½ oz]	5-6
23 cm [9″]	350 g [12 oz]	175 g [6 oz]	50 g [2 oz]	6-7
25 cm [10″]	450 g [1 lb]	225 g [½ lb]	65 g [2½ oz]	8-9

1   *Heavy-based saucepans minimize the chances of burning food.*
2   *Trivet: use when melting chocolate (see page 20).*
3   *Rotary whisk: for whisking quickly.*
4   *A flan ring with straight sides and a removable base is essential.*
5   *Mezzaluna or hachinette: useful for chopping herbs and nuts.*
6   *Spoons: metal for binding, wooden for stirring; pastry brush for glazes.*
7   *Glass jug: for measuring liquids.*

8   *Balloon whisk: traditional and best but you need a strong wrist.*
9   *Sieving ensures crumbs are of even size. Choose a coarse mesh.*
10   *Rolling pin: the heavier the better.*
11   *Mixing bowls: for a variety of jobs.*
12   *Crumbs can be made in a liquidizer but be careful not to grind too fine.*
13   *Box grater: sturdy and easy to use.*
14   *Use measuring spoons for accuracy.*
15   *Roll of polythene bags: use when crushing biscuits and storing 'pastry'.*

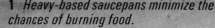

EQUIPMENT

To make biscuit crust you will need:
● plastic bag with wire twist tie
● rolling pin (or milk bottle)
● coarse sieve
● heavy-based saucepan
● mixing bowl
● large spoon
● flan ring

The plastic bag: simply crushing the crumbs on a flat surface can be a messy business as they tend to jump off the table on to the floor. Life is made much easier if you put the biscuits into a plastic bag first. Use either a heavy-duty bag or two bags, one inside the other, to avoid the danger of splitting during crushing. Exclude air by smoothing the bag with your fingers, then seal firmly.

The rolling pin should be fairly heavy in order to crush the crumbs effectively. If you do not have a rolling pin, a milk bottle will do.

A liquidizer: alternatively, you can crumb the biscuits in a liquidizer but don't allow them to become too fine or they will not stick together.

The coarse sieve: a coarse sieve is essential in order to separate any over-large crumbs from the rest because, unless the crumbs are of fairly even size and texture, the biscuit crust will not stick together.

The heavy-based pan: this is used to melt the butter or other binding ingredient. It must be heavy based otherwise the binding may burn.

The mixing bowl: this must be fairly large. If the bowl is too small, and the mixture not well stirred, the biscuit crust will fall apart.

The spoon used for mixing should be a large metal tablespoon as this cuts through the crumbs better than a wooden spoon.

The flan ring: always use a plain-sided flan ring with a removable base. A plain-sided ring is important because biscuit crust is rather brittle and does not mould well to crinkled edges. A removable base is important because it is almost impossible to get biscuit crust out of a rigid-bottomed flan dish without breaking the 'pastry'.

In theory you could use a bottomless flan ring placed on a baking sheet but, in practice, this proves somewhat difficult: it slips when you try to press the crumb mixture into

position, and a flan ring on a tray may be too large for the refrigerator.

COOKING AND REFRIGERATING

To save time, biscuit crust flans made with biscuits and butter (plus sugar for sweet flans) can be refrigerated or baked to set the 'pastry'. Baking takes only 10 minutes and produces particularly crisp and delicious results: because the 'pastry' is hardened, there is less chance of the filling soaking into it.

All flans made with cereals and flans made from biscuits bound with chocolate or syrup must be refrigerated—they cannot be baked. Refrigeration takes a minimum of 5 hours and it is preferable to refrigerate overnight for crisp results.

FILLINGS

Once your biscuit crust flan case has set, it can be filled with a wide choice of sweet and delicious fillings. Choosing tasty mixtures and adding final decorative touches is fun to do but do remember that, even when set firm, biscuit crust is fairly porous and liable to soak up liquid: it will become unpleasantly soggy unless your filling is fairly dry and firm in texture. Wherever practicable, only fill the flan case shortly before serving.

Fresh or cooked fruit and cream or chopped walnuts in a custard can all be used. Fruit can be used alone and looks highly decorative if carefully arranged, but most other ingredients are best incorporated into a basic filling mixture with a firm,

creamy texture—such as whipped cream, whisked evaporated milk, sweetened cottage, curd or cream cheeses, jelly or a thick custard such as crème patissière.

TIMING
Making the flan case:

1 If using crushed biscuits or cereals and butter, allow a total of 35 minutes: 10 minutes for crushing and binding, 15 minutes for moulding the 'pastry' into the flan tin, and 10 minutes for baking.

2 If using biscuits with another binding ingredient such as chocolate or syrup, allow an extra 5 hours as the flan case needs a long period of refrigeration in order to set.

3 If using cereals which do not need crushing, allow a total of about $5\frac{1}{2}$ hours: 5 minutes for binding, 15 minutes for moulding and 5 hours for refrigeration.

For types 2 and 3 it is best to make the flan case the day before and to refrigerate it overnight.

Filling: the time needed to fill and decorate the flan case depends on what you choose as filling. Something instant, such as whipped cream simply studded with nuts, angelica and glacé cherries, is so quick to do that you need not start filling the flan until about 15 minutes before the meal. More complicated fillings will take longer, and longest of all is a filling which has to set (such as jelly)—in which case the flan filling must be prepared and placed in the

flan case at least 3 hours before serving. But, as a general rule, the nearer mealtime you fill the flan case the better the results will taste—because there is less chance for the filling to soak into the 'pastry' and make it soggy.

STORING BISCUIT AND CEREAL CRUST FLANS

Unfilled biscuit and cereal crust flan cases will store well in an air tight tin, the refrigerator or freezer.

In an airtight tin: if well wrapped in foil, a biscuit crust case will keep for up to a week. Cereal crust cases however, will keep for only 2 days as they tend to turn stale and chewy if kept longer than this.

In the refrigerator: well wrapped in foil or polythene so that they do not absorb moisture and smells, biscuit and cereal crust cases will keep in the refrigerator for 2 days.

In the freezer: biscuit crust cases freeze well. If making cases for freezing, it is a good idea to make them in a foil dish as this avoids putting a flan tin out of use. You can freeze a flan case which has been taken out of the tin but it must be well wrapped and placed in a rigid box to avoid damage from the weight of other foods. Biscuit crust cases keep for up to 6 months in the freezer. Cereal crust cases cannot be frozen as they do not thaw well.

Filled biscuit crust cases can be kept in an airtight tin or the refrigerator for one day. If kept longer than this, the filling begins to soak in. Filled flans cannot be frozen as they do not thaw well.

Step-by-step making biscuit crust 'pastry'

1 Using your fingers and butter at room temperature (or the wrapping from the packet of butter) grease the sides and base of a plain sided flan tin with removable base.

2 Break the biscuits into pieces. Put in a heavy-duty polythene bag. Exclude air by smoothing the sides of the bag with your hands and seal the bag top.

3 Place the rolling pin at one end of the bag of biscuits and roll across it, pressing down firmly. Continue until all the biscuits are crushed.

6 Add sugar, if used, to the butter. Add any flavourings to the crumbs. Pour on butter and mix with a spoon until crumbs cling together.

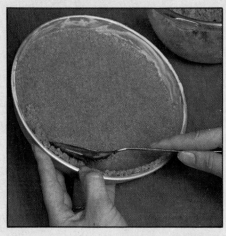

7 Scatter a 6 mm [¼"] layer of crumbs evenly over flan ring base. Press evenly and lightly in place with the back of a spoon.

8 To coat the ring sides, first tilt the flan ring towards you. Place two spoonfuls of crumbs on the section of ring nearest to you.

11 Cook in centre of oven heated to 180°[350°F] gas mark 4 for 10 minutes. Check towards the end of cooking time to ensure the flan case does not burn. Allow to cool.

12 When cold, gently run a round-bladed knife around the inside edge of the flan ring to loosen the crumb case from the sides.

13 Stand flan tin on an inverted cake tin or bowl which is slightly smaller in size. Slide flan ring sides down, away from case.

4 Tip the crushed biscuits into a coarse sieve (not a fine sieve) over a mixing bowl. Sieve, rubbing any large pieces through the mesh with the back of a spoon.

5 Put the butter in a heavy-based saucepan over very low heat. Remove from heat as soon as the butter has melted.

9 Using the back of a spoon, press crumbs into a layer 6 mm [¼"] thick. Continue in this way until all of the flan ring side is covered.

10 Work a smooth-sided jar around sides and over base of flan case to press the crumbs in place and flatten any uneven sections.

14 Put flan tin base on a flat surface. Insert a round-bladed knife between base and biscuit crust and ease 'pastry' gently off base.

15 Tilt crumb case away from you and, pushing gently, slide the crumb case off the flan tin base and on to a flat serving plate.

BANANA CRUNCH

◣◣◣ *Overripe bananas which have turned slightly black are ideal for making this flan as they mash well and have a delicious flavour. And of course they are cheaper than bananas in prime condition. Steps 6-8 take only a few minutes to do and are best left until just before mealtime because the banana mixture will discolour if exposed to air for long.*

SERVES 4-5
  40 g [1½ oz] butter
  45 ml [3 tablespoons] golden
    syrup
  150 g [5 oz] rolled oats
  25 g [1 oz] chopped dates,
    sultanas or raisins
  125 g [¼ lb] peanut brittle
  5 large bananas
  30 ml [2 tablespoons] double
    cream

1 Melt 25 g [1 oz] butter and the syrup over very low heat.

2 Place the oats and dried fruit in a large mixing bowl. Pour on the butter and syrup and mix together well with a metal spoon.

3 Use remaining 15 g [½ oz] butter to grease an 18 cm [7"] flan tin.

4 Press the cereal crust mixture into the prepared flan tin. Place in a plastic bag, seal and refrigerate for at least 5 hours, or overnight.

5 Break the peanut brittle into fairly small pieces (an easy way to do this is to follow the method described for crushing biscuits).

6 Peel 4 bananas. Slice into a bowl and mash with a fork. Add cream and half the crushed peanut brittle. Mix well with a fork.

7 Remove flan case from ring. Pile the banana mixture into the 'pastry' case. Level the top with a round-bladed knife.

8 Decorate flan with remaining peanut brittle and sliced banana.

Variation
● For chocolate banana crunch, use bran flakes or puffed rice in place of rolled oats. Reduce peanut brittle by half, using it to fill the flan only, and decorate with 50 g [2 oz] grated milk or plain chocolate.

Preparing basic fillings

1 For simple cheesecake filling, push cottage cheese through a nylon sieve into a mixing bowl.

2 Add cream cheese and stir vigorously until both cheeses are well blended and smooth.

1 To make a glaze, sieve jam into a heavy-based pan. Add liquid. Stir over low heat until blended.

2 Pour glaze, a little at a time, on to flan. Spread evenly over fruit, using a pastry brush.

1 For jelly cream, boil an unopened can of evaporated milk in water for 15 minutes. Refrigerate overnight then whisk until thick.

2 Make jelly using half normal quantity of liquid. When half set (quivers if shaken), stir jelly into whisked evaporated milk.

1 To melt chocolate, break into a basin. Stand on a trivet in a pan of simmering water.

2 Stir the chocolate gently to break up lumps and speed the melting process. Use as soon as smooth.

MIDSUMMER FLAN

⧗⧗ *Fresh fruit makes the best filling but canned or frozen can be used.* If using canned, be sure to drain it first. Save some of the juice for making the glaze.

SERVES 4-5

**175 g [6 oz] digestive biscuits
grated zest of 1 orange
90 g [3½ oz] butter
25 g [1 oz] caster sugar
275 g [¾ lb] mixed strawberries,
raspberries and blackberries
45 ml [3 tablespoons] redcurrant
jelly**

1 Crush biscuits and sieve into a bowl. Add orange zest.

2 Melt 75 g [3 oz] butter over very low heat. Add sugar, pour over biscuits and mix until crumbs will cling together when squeezed.

3 Use remaining 15 g [½ oz] butter to grease an 18 cm [7″] flan tin.

4 Line flan tin with biscuit crust. Bake in an oven heated to 180°C [350°F] gas mark 4 for about 10 minutes. Allow to become cold.

5 Meanwhile, hull the strawberries, raspberries and blackberries if using fresh and rinse in cold water. Cut strawberries in half. If using frozen or canned fruit, drain and leave whole.

6 Remove cold flan from tin.

7 Arrange fruit decoratively in base of flan, making alternating circles of red and black.

8 Place redcurrant jelly in a heavy-based pan with 30 ml [2 tablespoons] fruit juice or water. Stir over low heat until melted and blended.

9 Carefully brush the glaze over the fruit to coat evenly. Leave to set for 15–30 minutes.

Variations

Instead of strawberries, raspberries and blackberries with redcurrant glaze, use any of the following:
● Apricots, blackberries and grapes with sieved apricot jam glaze.
● Sliced bananas dipped in lemon juice with a glaze made from lemon or grapefruit jelly marmalade.

Desserts

rich shortcrust flans

Sweet rich shortcrust is simply an enriched variation on ordinary shortcrust pastry. This means the proportion of fat to flour is higher than for ordinary shortcrust and egg yolk replaces most of the water used to bind the rubbed-in mixture. The preparation and handling of sweet shortcrusts need a little more care than ordinary shortcrust but the results—a sweetened, extra-crisp and biscuit-like pastry—are well worth while.

WHAT IS ENRICHED SHORTCRUST PASTRY?

Enriched shortcrust pastry is known by a number of names including flan pastry, richcrust, rich shortcrust and sweet rich shortcrust. This can be confusing, but don't worry; the various names all refer to shortcrust pastry which is enriched by the addition of extra fat—usually butter—and egg yolk. The enrichment gives it a 'shorter' (crisper) texture and also improves the flavour of the pastry.

This classic design of glazed apple slices conceals a thick apple purée which perfectly complements the crisp pastry.

Enriched shortcrust is usually flavoured and, because its biscuit-like texture combines well with a sweet filling, it has become common practice to sweeten the pastry. The addition of sugar also enhances the texture of the pastry and its buttery flavour. Other flavours can be used to produce more unusual results and suit individual tastes.

USING SWEET RICH SHORTCRUST

Sweet rich shortcrust is always used to line bakeware for large and small open sweet tarts. (It is not, of course, suitable for savoury fillings.) It is especially good for dishes which are to be served cold, as it retains the crispiness far better than ordinary shortcrust and its superior flavour is more noticeable when cold.

Sweet rich shortcrust pastry is also better suited to small individual moulds, such as tartlettes and bateaux, than ordinary shortcrust because it can be rolled more thinly and is easier to mould to shape.

Unlike ordinary shortcrust, sweet rich shortcrust is never used as a 'lid' or covering for a filling. There are two sound reasons for this. The first is purely practical: its delicate, crumbly texture means the pastry has a tendency to crack, making it difficult to transfer to the baking dish without breaking. This doesn't matter when used for lining, but does make it unsuitable for covering a filling as it is difficult to keep toppings in a smooth, presentable shape.

The second reason boils down to the chemistry of cooking—how sweet rich shortcrust behaves when cooked. Because of the balance of the ingredients there is not enough water to completely moisten the starch granules contained in the flour. So, when the dough is heated the fat, which melts, is not readily absorbed and literally runs out. When used as a lining, the baking dish or mould helps to hold the pastry together and to keep it in shape. The heat of the metal fries the melted fat and this gives the pastry its characteristic crisp texture.

As the pastry cools after baking, the fat solidifies and sets while the mould ensures the pastry stays in the right shape.

If sweet rich shortcrust were used as a covering it would not have enough support to stay in shape and so would fall into the filling as the fat melts. The result would be a crust with an unappetizing crazed appearance—extremely crumbly and difficult to serve.

EQUIPMENT

Sweet rich shortcrust is made by the rubbing-in method, so you will need all the usual equipment for pastry-making, such as scales. In addition you will need:
● a small mixing bowl and a teaspoon for blending the yolk and water
● a metal spoon for stirring in the sugar
● a plastic or rubber-bladed spatula for scraping the yolk and water mix out of the bowl
● a metal kitchen knife for incorporating the liquid into the rubbed-in mixture.

You will also need bakeware. If your tins are at all new, it is advisable to grease them lightly for the first few times when using sweet rich shortcrust, as the sugar contained in the pastry may cause it to stick slightly.

Large open tarts are generally baked in French flan tins, fluted English flan rings or porcelain flan dishes, but you can use a plain-sided English flan ring or a cake sandwich tin with a loose-bottomed base instead. But do remember that the different tins vary slightly in the amount of filling they will hold and so you will have to adjust the quantity of ingredients and cooking time accordingly. Also, porcelain is not such an efficient conductor of heat as metal, so you should allow a slightly longer cooking time for both pastry and filling when using a porcelain dish.

Small open tartlettes are best baked in individual moulds. You can use a tartlet tin instead, but these are really meant for sweets such as jam tarts and are shallower than individual moulds. This means they do not provide much room for the bulky kind of filling normally used with sweet shortcrust pastry.

French tartlette tins are individual, deep, round moulds made of metal. They come in a number of sizes, with either plain or fluted sides, and some have a loose base. The most commonly used type has plain sides, a fixed base and is medium-sized: the tin measures about 6 cm [2½"] in diameter and 1.2 cm [½"] in depth. Because the moulds are unstable, they are always placed on a metal baking tray or sheet before they are baked in the oven.

Because they are quite large, individual tarts made in French tartlette tins make good dessert portions but are rather too big to be served as dainty tea pastries.

Step-by-step to sweet rich shortcrust

225 g [½ lb] plain flour
pinch of salt
10 ml [2 teaspoons] caster sugar
175 g [6 oz] butter
1 medium-sized egg yolk
10 ml [2 teaspoons] cold water

2 Use a metal spoon to lightly stir in the sugar. Cut the fat into the flour and rub in lightly and quickly until the mixture resembles fine breadcrumbs.

4 Use a chilled metal kitchen knife to incorporate the liquid into the mixture by lightly and swiftly drawing the dry ingredients from the sides into the centre.

In addition to French tartlette moulds, a number of other individual moulds are used for small tarts and flans (both sweet and savoury) made with enriched shortcrust. These other moulds come in a wide variety of shapes and sizes.

1 Sieve the flour and salt into a large, cool, mixing bowl. (If using brown flour, tip in the bran which remains in the sieve and stir in lightly.)

3 Blend the egg yolk and water together with a teaspoon. Pour this liquid into the centre of the rubbed-in mixture, scraping out the bowl with a plastic spatula.

5 When the mixture sticks together to form a ball of dough, turn on to a lightly floured board and knead briefly until smooth. Wrap the dough and chill for 30 minutes.

INGREDIENTS

Flour: for sweet rich shortcrust plain flour is always used because self-raising flour would give too soft and spongy a texture. Many cooks recommend using the finest white flour available as this makes a very delicate pastry. However, if you are a health-food addict, there's no reason why you shouldn't use brown flour instead—but don't expect the same results. Pastry made with brown flour tends to be more crumbly and therefore more difficult to handle. It has a slightly heavier texture and an attractive, nutty flavour.

Salt: a pinch of salt is always added to bring out the flavour of the other ingredients.

Fat: butter is normally used as it gives the best flavour, but you may use margarine instead. Because of the high proportion of fat, lard or cooking fat is not suitable because it makes a very sticky pastry which is not only crumbly but also extremely difficult to handle.

The standard proportion for enriched shortcrust is four parts flour to three parts fat. So for 225 g [½ lb] flour you will need 175 g [6 oz] fat. This proportion gives a good 'short' (light and crisp) pastry.

Sugar: generally 10 ml [2 teaspoons] sugar are added to every 225 g [½ lb] flour, although you can increase the quantity of sugar up to half that of flour. The more sugar you use, the sweeter and crisper the pastry, but do bear in mind the sweetness of your filling; a very sweet pastry is not needed for the sweeter fillings as the end result will be too rich.

Either caster or icing sugar may be used. Icing sugar gives a shorter texture, but it tends to make the edges of the pastry spread a little when baked. Caster sugar is best where good shaping is important, for example, when you are making cases for individual moulds such as tartlettes and bateaux.

Granulated sugar is not suitable as its large crystals will not dissolve or blend in satisfactorily. This results in a pastry which, when cooked, is spotted with overbrowned sugar grains.

Liquid to bind: this may be egg yolk alone, egg yolk mixed with a little cold water or whole beaten egg. Whole eggs do not give such a successful result as yolks. The yolk provides the liquid element needed to bind the rubbed-in mixture and it also gives an appetizing golden colour. Because it contains fat, it also helps to enrich the pastry and contributes to the crumbly texture.

Recipes normally call for one medium-sized egg yolk plus 10 ml [2 teaspoons] of cold water to every 225 g [½ lb] flour.

MAKING SWEET RICH SHORTCRUST PASTRY

All the rules you observe for ordinary shortcrust apply to sweet shortcrust—but it is even more important to abide by them. Because of the high proportion of fat there is an even greater risk of the mix becoming oily and sticky. A dough that has been allowed to become warm and oily will produce a tough pastry which has lost its melt-in-the-mouth texture. So be sure to have your equipment, ingredients and hands as cool as possible. If at any stage you fear things are becoming too warm, place the bowl in the refrigerator for a few minutes.

Before you start to make the dough, pop a metal knife (to incorporate the liquid into the rubbed-in mixture) into the refrigerator to chill or stand it in iced water.

To make the pastry, first weigh and sieve the flour together with the salt into a large, cool mixing bowl. (If you are using brown flour, tip the bran which remains in the sieve into the rest of the flour and lightly mix it in.) Then mix the caster sugar together with flour and salt. Cut the fat into the sugar and flour and, using your fingertips, rub it in as quickly and lightly as possible. Stop rubbing in as soon as the mixture resembles fine breadcrumbs.

If you are using icing sugar, then this is best added after you have rubbed the fat into the flour. You may, if you prefer, stir caster sugar in after, rather than before, rubbing in, but the method of adding caster sugar first has certain advantages. The presence of the small, sharp crystals of sugar helps to break down the fat and so speeds up the rubbing-in process. This is important as anything which reduces the handling of the dough is an asset. Also, it means that you can use fat which is colder and harder than that used for ordinary pastry.

Blend the egg yolk with the water in a small mixing bowl. This breaks down the outer film of the yolk and reduces the fat globules to smaller particles, which means they can be incorporated in the mix more easily and more thoroughly.

Pour the blended yolk and water into the rubbed-in mixture. (Use a plastic spatula to scrape the bowl clean.) Then, using the chilled kitchen knife, incorporate the liquid into the rubbed-in mixture. To do this, draw the dry ingredients from the sides of the bowl into the centre with a light, swift action, until the mixture sticks together as a firm ball of dough.

Turn the dough on to a very lightly floured surface and knead until smooth. The kneading should be done as lightly and swiftly as possible. Wrap the dough as is done for ordinary shortcrust to prevent it drying out and place it in the bottom of the refrigerator to cool and relax for a good 30 minutes. Don't be tempted to skimp on the time— sweet rich shortcrust is much more fragile than ordinary shortcrust and does not respond well to rolling. It has a tendency to crack and stick and the longer it has to relax in the refrigerator, the easier it will be to handle.

Rolling out

If you have chilled the dough for longer than 30 minutes, allow it to stand for a few minutes at room temperature to soften slightly. Otherwise you can use the dough straight from the refrigerator. Remove the wrapping and place on a lightly floured working surface. To minimize the amount of rolling, gently pat out and flatten the dough to the shape you want with the palm of your hand. Then roll out with light, gentle strokes, frequently running the blade of a chilled palette knife between the working surface and the pastry to prevent sticking.

If any cracks or tears appear it is better to leave them rather than trying to repair them with your hands—the more you try to overcome any faults the worse they will become and the quality of the pastry will suffer.

If you find the dough sticking too much and becoming unmanageable, don't try and get round this by sprinkling the surface of the dough liberally with flour. The flour will be worked into the surface of the pastry forming an outer coating which will harden during baking, giving a tough, unappetizing pastry with a flat taste. Instead, using the rolling pin, lift the dough carefully on to a sheet of greaseproof paper, cover it with cling film or another sheet of greaseproof paper and place it in the refrigerator for about ten minutes to recover. This might delay the baking, but the time lost is not a waste as the pastry will remain in good condition.

LINING TINS WITH SWEET SHORTCRUST

The quantity of pastry needed to line different-sized French flan tins is partly dependent on the depth. English flan rings require the same amount of pastry as French flan tins, but as they are deeper, there will be slightly less excess pastry to trim away.

Remember that new tins should be lightly greased to prevent sticking. How to line French flan tins and English flan rings with shortcrust is the same for all pastry types. The only additional point to note when using sweet shortcrust is as follows: when you have pricked the base of the pastry with a fork, pop the lined dish in the refrigerator for 10 minutes. (There is no need to cover the dough.) This brief chilling is important because it helps to keep the dough in shape and to prevent the pastry running down the sides of the tin during baking.

Lining French tartlette tins

As a rule-of-thumb guide, just under 25 g [1 oz] pastry is sufficient to line one medium-sized tartlette tin so, if you are making six tartlettes you will need 150 g [5 oz] sweet shortcrust. This, as you will remember, means pastry made with 150 g [5 oz] flour.

First of all, cut off a small piece of dough and roll it into a marble-sized ball and reserve. Then cut the remaining pastry into six equal-sized pieces. Roll out each piece of pastry to a round, about 2.5–4 cm [1–1½″] wider than the diameter of the tops of the tins. This should be 3 mm [⅛″] thick. (Because sweet shortcrust doesn't take too kindly to rolling out, this method is easier than rolling out one large piece of dough and then stamping out rounds with a cutter.)

Place a round of pastry loosely in each tin. Lightly flour the small ball of pastry and use this to ease the dough into place. Gently pat and press the dough into the shape of each mould, working from the centre of the base outwards and up the sides of the tin.

Make sure there are no air pockets trapped between the pastry and the sides of the tin. The reason for using a ball of pastry to mould the dough into shape, rather than your fingers, is that there is no risk of your nails tearing the pastry.

The traditional way of removing the excess pastry is to roll the rolling pin across the rim of the moulds. However, this can be a bit tricky as the moulds are not particularly stable and if you are a beginner, you will probably find it easier to trim the pastry with a sharp knife. Use short, swift strokes to get a clean edge.

If you do want to try the traditional method, place three or four moulds close together (about 1.2 cm [½″] apart) on the working surface. Then roll the rolling pin firmly across the rims in several directions until the pastry is firmly cleaned off. Trim the remaining moulds in the same way.

Place the lined moulds on a metal baking tray then, using your fingers, lightly press the sides of each lined tin to make sure the pastry still fits snugly. Prick the base and sides of each lined mould with a fork to release any trapped air and to help prevent the pastry rising during cooking. Chill (uncovered) in the refrigerator for 10 minutes before baking.

BAKING BLIND

Sweet rich shortcrust is always completely baked blind unless the filling you choose requires further cooking when added to the pastry case. In this instance, the pastry is only partially baked blind, as it undergoes further cooking with the filling.

The pastry is normally baked in an oven heated to 200°C [400°F] gas mark 6. It is baked for 10 minutes covered with beans and then for a further three to five minutes without the lining or beans, to set the pastry, for partially blind-baked cases. For fully blind-baked cases, bake for a further five to 10 minutes until the pastry is dry and browned.

In recipes where the amount of sugar is half the weight of flour, however, the pastry is cooked at a slightly lower temperature—190°C [375°F] gas mark 5—to prevent over browning. Large pastry cases of 25 cm [10″] or more, baked at the lower temperature, require a slightly longer cooking time, but for small tartlettes the cooking time remains the same.

To bake blind French flan tins and English flan rings lined with sweet rich shortcrust, first line the pastry with foil then fill it with beans or rice to weigh it down.

The method of baking blind French flans is very similar to that for tartlette tins. Because the French moulds are bigger and deeper than tartlette tins, they are baked at a higher temperature. The cases should be left until completely cold before being removed from the mould as hot pastry is very fragile and breaks easily.

FILLINGS

The melting, yet biscuity, texture of sweet shortcrust provides an excellent foil for soft or semi-soft fillings. To preserve the texture of the pastry, add your filling as close to serving time as possible.

Soft fresh fruit is one of the most popular fillings. Small, perfect fruit are best as they can be used whole and look most attractive. Large or misshapen fruit should be sliced. The prepared fruit is decoratively arranged in the pastry case and then generously brushed with a warm jam glaze. The glaze gives a good finish

to the dish and also keeps the fruit moist. When the glaze has set the flan is ready for serving.

Poached fruit also makes an excellent and attractive filling. Take care, however, to cook the fruit until just tender—mushy overcooked fruit not only looks unappetizing but will also make the pastry soggy.

Poached fruit must always be very well drained and, as an extra precaution to prevent the juices sinking into the pastry, the pastry case is brushed with jam glaze before the fruit is added.

Canned or bottled fruit can be used in place of poached fruit.

Fruit purées make a good filling in their own right, but are even better when combined with another ingredient such as lightly whipped thick cream. Always use a thick, well-flavoured purée.

Jelly is often used as the basis for a filling. Used on its own, flavoured jelly does not provide a particularly good contrast with the pastry; when set, it has a rather 'dry' texture. However, it is delicious when combined with other ingredients which give a softer texture, such as thick fruit purée, fresh fruit, whipped cream or whisked egg white.

A jelly filling is always added to the pastry case when partially set. If added while still liquid the pastry will be soaked and will lose its crispness; on the other hand, if you wait until the jelly has set, it will not fall into the shape of the pastry case.

Filling ideas

● A creamy filling for tartlettes is made from equal quantities of petits suisse and sour cream mixed together. Add caster sugar to taste, fill the completely blind-baked tartlettes and scatter toasted almonds on top.

● Summer medley is easy to make in a fully baked flan case. Spread whipped, thick cream, sweetened to taste, over the flan base. Cover with a ring of strawberries and then a ring of raspberries, alternating the fruit until the flan is full.

● For banana and grape tart, spread mashed banana mixed with 5 ml [1 teaspoon] lemon juice in a fully baked flan case. On top arrange green and black grapes in alternating rings.

An attractive, yet simple, decoration of alternate rings of black and white grapes add a professional touch to this tart.

STORING AND FREEZING

The uncooked dough will keep well in a refrigerator for up to five days, as long as it is carefully wrapped to prevent drying out (cling film is best). To freeze, wrap in freezer cling film or heavy-duty foil and store for up to three months. Allow it to thaw at room temperature still in the wrapping.

Sweet rich shortcrust is best eaten on the day it is baked, but you can prepare and bake blind the (unfilled) pastry case in advance. It can be stored in a clean, airtight tin or, wrapped, in the refrigerator for about eight hours or overnight.

To freeze a blind-baked and unfilled pastry case, place in a rigid plastic freezer container to protect the delicate sides and store for up to six months.

FRESH STRAWBERRY TARTLETTES

There's no need to coat the inside of the pastry cases with glaze, because the rich cream cheese filling hidden beneath the fruit protects the pastry from becoming soggy. The glaze is brushed over the surface of the fruit, as this keeps the strawberries in good condition and gives an attractive, shiny appearance. The quantity of sugar given in the recipe is only a guide and you can alter it to suit your own taste.

When fresh strawberries are not in season, thawed frozen strawberries may be used instead.

MAKES 6 TARTLETTES
150 g [5 oz] sweet shortcrust pastry
75-100 g [3-4 oz] cream cheese
60-75 ml [4-5 tablespoons] thick cream
25 g [1 oz] caster sugar
225 g [½ lb] fresh strawberries

For the glaze:
45 ml [3 tablespoons] redcurrant jelly

1 Position the oven shelf above centre and heat the oven to 200°C [400°F] gas mark 6.

2 Line 6 French tartlette tins with the pastry and chill for 10 minutes, then completely bake blind.

3 Set the baked tartlettes aside and leave them to cool in their tins. When completely cold remove the pastry cases from the tins and arrange on a serving plate.

4 Whip the cream until it forms soft peaks then mix with the cream cheese and caster sugar, divide it between the six cases.

5 Rinse, drain and hull the strawberries. Leave small berries whole, slice or halve the larger fruit. Arrange the strawberries decoratively in the tartlettes, making sure they cover the cream cheese mixture. Set the tartlettes aside while you make the glaze.

6 Press the redcurrant jelly through a sieve into a small saucepan. Heat gently until melted, but do not allow to boil.

7 Brush the warm glaze generously over the fruit and allow to set.

Variations
Lots of other fresh fruit can be used in place of the strawberries over the cream cheese filling. Try some of the following ideas:
● For special raspberry tartlettes, use fresh or frozen raspberries and stir 10 ml [2 teaspoons] framboise liqueur or kirsch into cream cheese filling.
● Make grape tartlettes. Use a mixture of black and green grapes and de-seed before arranging over the cream cheese filling.
● For cherry tartlettes, choose ripe dessert cherries and stone before arranging in the tartlettes.
● For berry tartlettes, use a combination of blackberries, raspberries and strawberries.

FRENCH APPLE TART

Dessert apples are used for the slices in this tart because they hold their shape better, but cooking apples are used to make the purée.

SERVES 6
175 g [6 oz] sweet shortcrust pastry
275 ml [10 fl oz] thick, sweet apple purée
450 g [1 lb] dessert apples
60 ml [4 tablespoons] golden syrup
1 lemon
60 ml [4 tablespoons] redcurrant or apple jelly
30 ml [2 tablespoons] calvados (optional)

1 Position the oven shelf above centre and heat the oven to 200°C [400°F] gas mark 6. If you are using a fluted flan dish, put a baking sheet in the oven to warm.

2 Line a 20–23 cm [8–9"] French flan tin, English flan ring or fluted flan dish with the pastry. Chill briefly then partially bake blind, by baking 10 minutes filled with beans and a further 3 minutes without the beans. If you are using a flan dish, stand this on the baking sheet.

3 Remove the pastry from the oven and allow to cool, still in the tin.

4 When the flan case is completely cold, add the cold apple purée.

APRICOT AND ORANGE TART

⧖⧖ *Prepare the poached fruit in advance, by simmering it gently in a sugar syrup until it is tender but still firm, and leave to cool in the syrup. Canned apricots may be substituted when fresh apricots are not available. Reserve the syrup.*

SERVES 6
150 g [5 oz] sweet shortcrust pastry
2 oranges
450 g [1 lb] poached apricots
90 ml [6 tablespoons] apricot jam

1 Position the oven shelf above centre and heat the oven to 200°C [400°F] gas mark 6.

2 Line a 20 cm [8"] French flan tin or English flan ring with the pastry. Chill briefly then completely bake blind, by baking 10 minutes blind and then a further 10 minutes without the lining and beans. Remove the pastry case from tin and cool on a wire rack.

3 Finely grate the zest from one of the oranges and reserve. Peel both oranges, making sure you remove all the pith. Slice the flesh into very thin rounds and set aside.

4 Drain the apricots thoroughly (reserving the syrup) and set aside.

5 Gently heat the apricot jam with 60 ml [4 tablespoons] of the reserved syrup in a heavy-based saucepan. When melted, press through a sieve. Add the orange zest to the glaze.

6 Coat the inside of the cold pastry case with half of the warm glaze.

7 Arrange the orange slices in circles over the base of the flan case. Then place the apricots decoratively over the oranges.

8 If the glaze has become cool, reheat it gently. Brush the fruit generously with the warm glaze and allow to set.

Variation
● For plum and orange tart, simply substitute poached cooking plums for the apricots..

5 Grate the zest from the lemon with a citrus zester and squeeze the juice from half the lemon.

6 Put the syrup in a small heavy-based pan and add the lemon zest and juice. Warm until the syrup melts slightly and then stir to mix.

7 Peel and core the apples and cut into very thin slices.

8 Cover the purée with concentric rings of overlapping apple slices, starting with the outside ring and working towards the middle. Pour the lemon syrup evenly all over the apple slices.

9 Bake the tart for 20 minutes to cook

Juicy strawberries top a creamy cheese filling for tartlettes. Apricots and orange slices fill the tea-time tart.

the apple slices. If using a porcelain dish, stand it on the baking tray.

10 Remove from the oven and allow to cool.

11 In a small heavy-based pan warm the jelly with the calvados, if using, or use 30 ml [2 tablespoons] water. Stir until the jelly has melted. Brush over the cold apple slices.

12 Serve the tart cold or warmed through.

329

Desserts

fruit dumplings

Cooking apples are traditionally used for dumplings because they are easy to core and will sit firmly, leaving you both hands free to shape the pastry.

Fruit dumplings are so called because the pastry is moulded around the enclosed fruit. Cooking apples are the traditional and the most suitable fruit to use.

Classic dumplings are made with suet pastry, whereas fruit dumplings use shortcrust pastry. As the seams tend to open and the filling leak out, the parcel is usually placed upside down on a greased baking tray.

Peel and core each apple before putting it on a pastry square and then fill the cavity. As a rough guide, a medium-sized apple will take about 15 ml [3 teaspoons] filling, but this will vary with the size of the core cavity.

The best fillings are thick and tightly packed; have fun experimenting with your own recipes or try some of the following:
● Chopped dates, grated lemon zest and black treacle.
● Marmalade and chopped almonds.
● Honey, whole hazelnuts and a little ground cinnamon, allspice or cloves.
● Dried mixed fruit, walnut pieces and golden syrup or soft brown sugar.
● Fresh or frozen raspberries, blackberries or blackcurrants plus a little caster sugar to sweeten and a sprinkling of ground spice.

BRAMBLE AND APPLE DUMPLINGS

Fresh or frozen blackberries can be used for this recipe. Grease the baking tray to prevent sticking because the filling does tend to leak.

The dumplings are put into a hot oven to crisp the pastry and then the heat is lowered so that the pastry does not burn while the apples are cooking.

SERVES 4
225 g [$\frac{1}{2}$ lb] shortcrust pastry
4 small cooking apples

20 ml [4 teaspoons] caster sugar
125 g [$\frac{1}{4}$ lb] blackberries
beaten egg to glaze
4 cloves

1 Heat oven to 220°C [425°F] gas mark 7.

2 Divide the pastry into four equal pieces and on a lightly floured board roll into squares approximately 20 × 20 cm [8 × 8″].

3 Peel and core the apples.

4 Stand each apple on a square of pastry and fill each core cavity with 5 ml [1 teaspoon] caster sugar and then as many blackberries as you can push in.

5 Cut two corners off each pastry square and set these aside.

6 Damp the edges of one pastry square with cold water then gather up the edges neatly to the top of the apple, moulding the pastry round the fruit. Press edges firmly together to seal. Repeat for the other 3 dumplings.

7 Turn the dumplings, sealed edge down, on to a lightly greased baking sheet. Prick a hole in the top of each one to allow steam to escape.

8 Mark a leaf pattern on the triangle trimmings and use a little beaten egg to seal them on top of the dumplings. Pierce a clove in the centre to look like the stalk.

9 Transfer the dumplings on to a lightly greased baking tray and brush them with beaten egg.

10 Place in the oven on the shelf above the centre and bake at 220°C [425°F] gas mark 7 for 15 minutes. Then reduce the heat to 180°C [350°F] gas mark 4 and continue to bake for a further 30 minutes or until cooked.

11 Serve hot or cold with sugar to sprinkle.

1 For 4 dumplings cut 225 g [$\frac{1}{2}$ lb] pastry into 4 equal pieces. Roll out to squares 20 × 20 cm [8 × 8″].

5 Place dumplings on a lightly greased baking tray, sealed side down, to keep seams closed.

Making apple dumplings step-by-step

2 Cut 2 corners off each square and set aside. Place a prepared apple in centre of each square and fill.

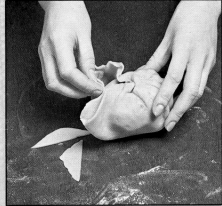

3 Damp the edges of each pastry square then gather up the edges neatly to the top of the apple.

4 Mould the pastry round the fruit, then press the seams firmly together to seal.

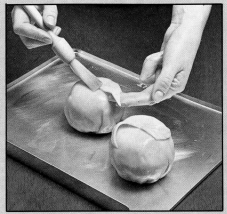

6 Mark a leaf pattern on triangular trimmings. Seal on to dumpling with a little beaten egg.

7 Prick the top of each dumpling with a fork to make holes for the steam to escape.

8 Brush with beaten egg and sprinkle with sugar to give the pastry a sweet glaze when cooked.

Star recipe

FROSTED PLUM TRICORNS

▱ *Crisp pastry encasing a surprise*
◪ *filling of plums and cream makes these decorative parcels an impressive dessert. Yet they are economical to make as only one plum is needed for each parcel and not a scrap of pastry is wasted because the shapes are cut from the main body of the pastry. Choose firm, good-sized plums for the filling.*

SERVES 4
175 g [6 oz] shortcrust pastry
8 plums
40 ml [8 teaspoons] caster sugar
150 ml [¼ pt] cream

For the glaze:
milk
caster sugar

TRICORNS

Tricorns are pyramid-shaped pastry parcels with a fruit filling.

Tricorns are extremely decorative, but rather tricky to make so the fruit must be able to sit firm, leaving you both hands free to shape the pastry. Suitable fruit include fresh plums, apricots, greengages and bananas. Canned or soft fruit is not firm enough.

To prepare stoned fruit, wash, halve and stone the fruit. Peel and quarter bananas. Fill cavities of stoned fruit with caster sugar (and some spice if liked) before sandwiching the two halves together.

1 Heat oven to 200°C [400°F] gas mark 6. Then prepare the fruit. Cut right round each plum, split in half and remove the stones.

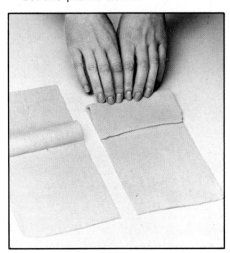

2 Fill the cavity of each plum with 5 ml [1 teaspoon] caster sugar. Sandwich the halves together and set the plums aside.

3 Roll the pastry out on a lightly floured board to a rectangle 30 × 26 cm [12 × 10″]. Cut in half lengthways.

4 Fold each strip in half and unfold. Then fold both ends of each strip to the centre crease and unfold back to original position.

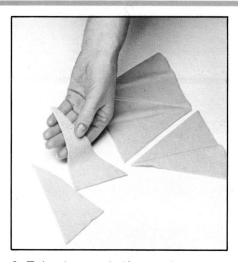

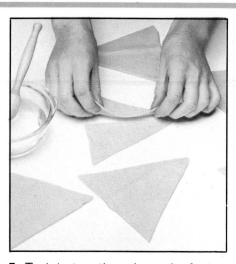

5 Cut each strip into 3 equal tri-angles by cutting diagonally up and down, using the crease mark as your guide.

6 Take the two half triangles at the end of each strip and put them together to make another 2 equal triangles.

7 To join together, damp the facing edges, overlap them slightly and press seam firmly to seal. Repeat for second triangle.

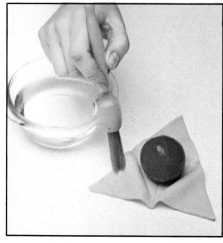

8 Make the guidelines for shaping the tricorns. Take each triangle, fold each point to its opposite side and unfold after each fold.

9 Brush the edges of the triangles with cold water. Stand a prepared plum upright in the centre of each pastry triangle.

10 Bring each corner of pastry up to meet at the top of the plum to make a pyramid shape. Seal the seams firmly together.

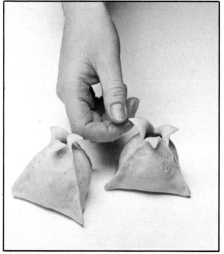

11 Fold back the tips of the pastry, making a hole for the steam to escape. Carefully transfer tricorns on to an ungreased baking tray.

12 Brush sides with milk and sprinkle with sugar to give the pastry a sweet glaze. Bake above centre of oven for 30 minutes.

13 Just before serving, dribble a little cream into the steam vent to fill the tricorns and sprinkle lavishly with caster sugar.

Desserts

mousses and creams

Sweet mousses and creams are rich and truly splendid desserts. Smooth and creamy, they look spectacular and taste delicious. Care is needed for success but the results are more than worth the effort.

Sumptuously laced with cream and rich with eggs, sweet mousses and creams are puddings for the times when you want to put on the ritz, rather than for everyday.

These luscious desserts are comparatively expensive to make but have the advantage that their very richness means a little goes a long way. This, combined with the fact that preparation can be done well in advance, makes these sweets perfect fare for serving large numbers. Served either in a mould or turned out, tastefully decorated with whirls of whipped cream, chocolate, nuts or fruit, these splendid sweets make a glorious centrepiece at a special dinner party, or a wedding or christening buffet.

What are sweet mousses and creams?

Traditionally flavoured with coffee, chocolate or fruit, mousses and creams need care if they are to succeed, so be prepared to spend some time in the kitchen.

Mousses are made with eggs, sometimes with extra egg yolks added, which are beaten together with sugar over heat until thick and creamy. The mixture is then flavoured, set with gelatine and enriched with lightly whipped cream. Sometimes whisked egg white is folded in just before moulding to give extra light results. Some mousses are made without eggs—with cream, sugar, gelatine and flavouring only—but these are rarely seen.

Creams have a rich custard base. The custard is flavoured, cooled over ice and set with gelatine. It is then stirred over ice again until just setting, when whipped cream is added. A classic example of a cream is the famous bavarois, a rich dessert made with more eggs than usual, which was created for King Ludwig of Bavaria.

INGREDIENTS

The basic ingredients for mousses and creams differ slightly so they are listed separately. All amounts given below are for 550 ml [1 pt] mousses and creams, which will serve four to six people.

Mousses

Mousses are easier to make than creams and have fewer ingredients.

Eggs form the basis of a mousse. The usual number of eggs is 3 whole eggs and 2 egg yolks for a 550 ml [1 pt] mousse. The eggs should be large and at room temperature.

Sugar. To every whole egg 25g [1 oz] sugar is usually used, though this may differ from recipe to recipe. Caster sugar is best, because it dissolves easily when beaten with the eggs over heat. Caster sugar is very receptive to damp and can be lumpy, so sieve it first.

Gelatine. Despite the number of eggs used, these alone are not sufficient to bind the mousse, and gelatine is still needed to make the mousse stand up. Never use more than 15 g [½ oz] gelatine for a 550 ml [1 pt] mousse. Using more will make the mousse unpleasantly rubbery and destroy the characteristic light texture. The gelatine is usually dissolved in 45 ml [3 tablespoons] water but this varies from recipe to recipe.

Cream. Lightly whipped cream is folded into the mousse mixture just after the gelatine, rather than when the mousse is about to set. This gives sweet mousses their characteristic smooth texture. For a 550 ml [1 pt] mousse using 3 whole eggs and 2 egg yolks, you will usually need 150 ml [¼ pt] thick whipped cream.

Egg whites. Occasionally, egg whites are folded into sweet mousses when on the point of setting. For a 550 ml [1 pt] mousse, the whites from the 2 separated eggs used to make the mousse base are used. Whisk the egg whites lightly until they stand in soft peaks.

Creams

Creams are richer than mousses and have more ingredients. The custard base is a richer version of the crème anglaise used in the construction of trifles.

Milk. Milk is used to make the rich custard base. For a 550 ml [1 pt] cream, use 250 ml [½ pt] milk. Always use whole milk, never reconstituted skimmed milk. Only whole milk can give the correct rich flavour, and the creamier the milk, the better.

Eggs. For most sweet creams, 3 egg yolks are used for every 250 ml [½ pt] milk. This is sufficient to make a custard which will coat the back of a spoon. Where a richer custard is required (as in bavarois), you may find up to 5 egg yolks, or sometimes 3 egg yolks and 2 whole eggs being used for 250 ml [½ pt] milk.

Sugar. Caster sugar is beaten with the eggs to make the custard. Usually, 15 g [½ oz] of sugar per egg yolk or whole egg is allowed. This means that for a normal 3-egg cream, you would use 40 g [1½ oz] sugar.

Cornflour. To help stabilize the custard 5 ml [1 teaspoon] cornflour can be whisked with the eggs and sugar.

Gelatine. Gelatine is used in creams in the same proportion as in mousses, 15 g [½ oz] per 550 ml [1 pt].

Cream. More cream is added which makes creams richer than mousses. Thick cream is lightly whipped and folded into the cream when it is on the point of setting. The usual amount of cream for a 550 ml [1 pt] mousse is between 150 ml [¼ pt] and 250 ml [½ pt], depending on the recipe.

Flavourings for mousses and creams

The same flavourings can be used for both mousses and creams—both coffee and chocolate make elegant, traditional mousses and creams.

Coffee can be either instant or ground. Both instant and ground must be infused in water to bring out the flavour and if ground is used it must be strained before being added to the mousse or cream mixture. For a 550 ml [1 pt] mousse or cream, you will need 30 ml [2 tablespoons] instant coffee, or 45 ml [3 tablespoons] coarsely ground coffee, infused in 60 ml [4 tablespoons] boiling water. If coffee is used, the gelatine is sometimes dissolved in the cold coffee but this varies from recipe to recipe.

Chocolate for mousses and creams should be the dark, bitter, dessert kind. For a 550 ml [1 pt] mousse or cream you will usually need 100 g [¼ lb] chocolate. For a mousse, the chocolate is usually melted over water and then the egg yolks and sugar are added. For a cream, it is melted in the milk used for the custard.

Fruit. Fruit makes pretty and refreshing mousses and creams. Suitable fruits are those which make a fairly liquid, smooth purée or which simply reduce to juice, as with citrus fruit. Oranges, lemons and limes are all suitable as are raspberries, strawberries, loganberries, blackberries, gooseberries, apricots, peaches, nectarines and black and redcurrants.

When using citrus fruit, the zest and juice are both used. The amount depends on how strongly flavoured you want the mousse or cream to be and on the recipe being used. Canned concentrated orange juice, reconstituted with water, may be used instead of fruit juice.

Raspberries, loganberries and strawberries can be puréed raw. Hull and wash, then either purée by pushing through a nylon sieve or blending in a liquidizer. If you use a liquidizer, the resulting purée will have to be sieved to get rid of any pips. You will need 150 ml [¼ pt] of purée for a 550 ml [1 pt] mousse or cream. At least 225 g [½ lb] of fruit will be needed if using peaches, apricots, nectarines, gooseberries or strawberries. If using raspberries, blackberries or currants where there is little flesh, allow 350 g [¾ lb] fruit. Apricots, peaches and nectarines should be skinned and stoned before being puréed in a liquidizer. Soaked dried apricots may be used if wished.

Blackberries, gooseberries and currants should be poached gently in a little water (but not sugar) until tender before being puréed.

Liqueurs. Mousses and creams can be given extra flavour with the addition of liqueurs. Only a little must be used or the true flavour of the mousse or cream will be masked. About 15 ml [1 tablespoon] is sufficient for a 550 ml [1 pt] mousse.

Grand Marnier goes well with orange or chocolate, Tia Maria goes well with chocolate and coffee, cointreau goes well with peaches, apricots and nectarines, crème de cassis with blackcurrants and framboise with raspberries and strawberries. Brandy or rum may also be used with any of these ingredients but as spirits can taste rather raw when uncooked use only 5 ml [1 teaspoon].

EQUIPMENT

To make both mousses and creams, you will need a double boiler as very gentle cooking is essential. If you don't own a double boiler, improvise with a bowl which will fit inside a pan without actually touching the water. If your pans are the shallow kind and this is difficult, the bowl can stand inside a flat-bottomed steamer.

A whisk is another essential, both to whisk eggs and sugar together and to whip the cream. A balloon whisk is best but if you are in a hurry, an electric whisk may be used. Rotary whisks tend to be difficult to handle in a bowl over heat.

Creams require rapid cooling once the custard has been made so you will need a large bowl, such as a washing-up bowl, half full of cold water and ice cubes. If your refrigerator won't make this much ice at one time, enquire at a local liquor shop or bar where ice is often sold in large quantities for parties etc. Ice cubes may be made in advance and stored in the freezing compartment in plastic bags. If you have room, place the water in jugs in your refrigerator to chill.

Because they are set with gelatine, both mousses and creams require moulding. If you don't want to turn out the mousse or cream, make it in a soufflé dish or any other pretty serving dish you may have. If you are turning out the mousse or cream, choose metal or plastic rather than pottery moulds. Mousses are traditionally made in simple moulds while rich creams, especially a bavarois,

are made in elaborate castellated moulds. Beware though of very fancy moulds. It is difficult to get the mousse or cream out cleanly. To enable the mousse or cream to be turned out, the mould must be brushed lightly with flavourless cooking oil.

Mousses and creams must be covered while setting otherwise they will absorb other food flavours from the refrigerator. Kitchen foil or cling film may be used.

Mousses and creams look beautiful decorated with piped cream so, if you wish to do this, you will need a piping bag and a selection of large nozzles. One star, one rope and one shell nozzle will meet most requirements.

MAKING MOUSSES

Making mousses can be divided into five stages and if you follow recipes stage-by-stage, little can go wrong.

The base

First prepare the flavouring (unless using chocolate) and set aside. The base of a mousse is a mixture of eggs and sugar beaten together over heat until thick and creamy.

Prepare a double boiler. Put tepid water in the bottom and make sure it does not touch the base of the top of the boiler. Place over low heat. Break the eggs and place extra yolks with them in the top of the double boiler. Add the sugar. Now whisk the eggs and sugar. After about 5 minutes' whisking (less if you are using an electric whisk), the mixture will turn thick and pale lemon in colour. When the mixture leaves a faint trail when the whisk is lifted, stop whisking and remove from heat. If chocolate is

used, it is melted first over the hot water. Then add the eggs and sugar before whisking.

Whisking over heat is essential to cook the eggs so don't be tempted to avoid this step by whisking the eggs and sugar together cold.

Adding the flavouring

The prepared flavouring is now stirred into the mixture away from the heat except if coffee or chocolate is being used. If coffee is used, it is infused in water, left until cold and, if ground, strained. The gelatine is dissolved in the coffee before it is added to the eggs and sugar. If chocolate is used, it is melted in the double boiler first, then the eggs and sugar are added and the whole is whisked together.

Adding gelatine

First soak the gelatine for 5 minutes in the amount of liquid specified in the recipe you are using, then dissolve for 3 minutes over low heat without stirring. Cool the mixture.

As soon as the gelatine has cooled add it to the mousse base in a thin stream, stirring all the time. Stirring is essential otherwise 'ropes' of set gelatine will form.

Adding cream

Place the cream in a large bowl and

lightly whip it. Now fold the mousse mixture into the cream a little at a time, folding lightly but thoroughly. Scrape out the top of the double boiler with a plastic spatula to avoid waste. The mousse mixture should now be left in a cool place until it is on the point of setting. Stir it gently from time to time—but not too vigorously or bubbles will form. When on the carefully using a suitable oiled container—see below.

Moulding
When the mousse is beginning to set but will not hold a clean edge, it is ready for moulding. If whisked egg white is added, it should be lightly whisked and folded in at this point. Turn the mousse into your chosen serving dish or mould, previously brushed with flavourless cooking oil. Level off with a spatula, cover with cling film or foil and put in the refrigerator for the time stated in the recipe used.

Remove the mousse from the refrigerator or turn it out, taking time to do it very carefully, 30 minutes before required. This takes the chill off the mousse and brings out the flavour.

MAKING CREAMS
There are nine stages in making perfectly smooth, delicious creams.

Preparing flavouring
If you are using a fruit or coffee flavouring, it must be prepared first as there will be no time to do this later.

Beating eggs
Place the egg yolks and whole eggs, if used, in a large bowl with the sugar. Whisk with a balloon or electric whisk until pale lemon in colour and creamy in texture. Beat in 5 ml [1 teaspoon] cornflour if wished. This will take about 5 minutes using an electric whisk at high speed. Set aside. At this stage, half fill a washing-up bowl with ice cubes and iced water as there will be no time to do this later. If you can, keep the bowl in the refrigerator.

Scalding the milk
In order to speed the cooking of the eggs and reduce the risk of the custard curdling, the milk must be scalded. If the cream is to be

chocolate flavoured, the chocolate is grated and added to the milk at this point. The milk is then gently heated until bubbles appear at the edges. As soon as this happens, remove from the heat. If you are using chocolate, stir until it is all melted.

Cooking the custard
Pour the scalded milk on to the egg and sugar mixture, stirring all the time. Turn into the top of a double boiler set over low heat and cook for 20 minutes, stirring all the time. It is essential that you keep stirring otherwise the custard may curdle. Continue until the custard will coat the back of a spoon lightly. Remove from the heat.

Cooling
As soon as the custard is thick enough, strain it into a large bowl and place the bowl in the bowl of ice cubes to cool. This will take about 10 minutes. While you are waiting for the custard to cool, soak and dissolve the gelatine and lightly whip the cream. It's important that gelatine be ready when wanted. After dissolving, the gelatine must be allowed to cool for 5 minutes as hot gelatine curdles milky mixtures.

Adding gelatine
Pour the gelatine into the custard in a thin stream, stirring all the time. As soon as the gelatine has been added, stir in the flavouring (unless liquid, in which case the gelatine may have been dissolved in it).

Thickening
Now stir the custard over the ice until it begins to thicken to a cream. This will take about 20 minutes and although it is time consuming, it is essential to keep stirring otherwise the custard will set unevenly and the cream will be ruined.

Adding the cream
As soon as the custard has thickened, the whipped cream must be folded in. It is actually easier to fold the custard into the cream, little by little, than vice versa. Use a spatula to scrape out the custard bowl so that there is no waste.

Moulding
Mould the cream in the same way as given for mousses. Like mousses, creams may be either turned out or left in the mould.

Step-by-step to ric

In this example, it is shown how egg white may be folded into a mousse. If you include the egg whites, you will need an 850 ml [1½ pt] mould, otherwise use a 550 ml [1 pt] mould.

SERVES 6–8
4 oranges
5 large eggs
75 g [3 oz] caster sugar
15 g [½ oz] gelatine
150 ml [¼ pt] thick cream
**15 ml [1 tablespoon]
   flavourless cooking oil**

4 The mixture is ready when the whisk leaves a faint trail when it is lifted. Remove from heat.

8 Leave in a cool place until almost setting, stirring from time to time so setting is even.

veet mousse

1 Grate the zest from three of the oranges and set aside. Squeeze the juice from all the oranges.

2 Prepare a double boiler. Break 3 whole eggs into the top. Separate other eggs and add yolks to boiler.

3 Add the sugar. Place boiler over low heat and whisk eggs and sugar until light and creamy.

5 Place the gelatine in the orange juice and soak for 5 minutes. Dissolve over low heat. Cool.

6 Stir the gelatine into the egg mixture in a thin stream. Stir in the orange zest.

7 Lightly whip the cream in a large bowl. Stir in the egg mixture a little at a time.

AND if egg white is used, whisk until it will stand in soft peaks and fold into the mousse mixture.

9 Turn the mixture into an oiled 550 ml [1 pt] mould or serving dish, cover and leave 1½–2 hours to set.

10 Turn out the mousse 30 minutes before needed. Mop up any liquid with a paper towel and decorate.

Step-by-step to sweet cream

SERVES 6–8
225 g [½ lb] strawberries
3 egg yolks
40 g [1½ oz] caster sugar
250 ml [½ pt] milk
15 g [½ oz] gelatine
200 ml [7 fl oz] thick cream
15 ml [1 tablespoon]
    flavourless cooking oil

1 Wash and hull the strawberries. Push through a sieve or liquidize and sieve. Set aside in a cool place.

2 Fill a bowl with ice cubes and leave in a cool place. Prepare a double boiler making sure the water in the bottom does not touch the top.

5 Pour the milk on to the eggs, stirring all the time. Replace the top of the double boiler over the bottom.

6 Set the double boiler over low heat and cook the custard for 20 minutes, stirring all the time with a wooden spoon.

7 When the custard will coat the back of a spoon, remove from heat. Strain into a large bowl and place on ice to cool.

10 Allow the gelatine to cool then pour into the custard in a thin stream, stirring all the time with a spoon.

11 Fold the prepared strawberry purée into the custard and start stirring. Stir until the mixture is thick and will coat the spoon.

12 When the mixture is on the point of setting, fold it into the cream using a figure of eight movement adding a little at a time.

3 Put the egg yolks into the top of the double boiler or a bowl. Add all of the sugar. Whisk, off the heat, until light and pale.

4 Place the milk in a heavy-based pan over moderate heat. As soon as bubbles appear at the edges, remove the pan from the heat.

8 Measure 45 ml [3 tablespoons] cold water into a small heavy-based pan. Add gelatine and soak for 5 minutes.

9 Dissolve the gelatine over low heat without stirring until liquid is clear. Lightly whip the cream in a large bowl.

13 Lightly brush an 850 ml [1½ pt] mould with flavourless oil. Pour in the mixture, cover and leave 1½–2 hours to set.

14 Turn out on to a serving plate 30 minutes before required. Mop up moisture with kitchen paper and decorate as wished.

BROWN BREAD CREAM

This Victorian dessert has a delicious nutty flavour. Traditionally, it was served with cold chocolate sauce but perhaps it appeals more to modern tastes if served alone, garnished with whirls of cream and chocolate curls. Brown bread cream is similar to a bavarois but not quite so rich. Bought chocolate flake lightly crumbled makes a good decoration.

SERVES 6–8
250 ml [½ pt] milk
1 vanilla pod
3 large egg yolks
40 g [1½ oz] caster sugar
5 ml [1 teaspoon] cornflour
4 thick slices brown bread
15 ml [1 tablespoon] flavourless oil
15 g [½ oz] gelatine
250 ml [½ pt] thick cream

For the garnish:
whipped cream
flaky chocolate

1 Place the milk and the vanilla pod in a heavy-based pan over low heat. Remove from heat as soon as bubbles begin to appear at the edge of the milk. Cover and set aside for 20 minutes to allow the vanilla pod to infuse.

2 Place the egg yolks in the top of a double boiler or bowl. Add the sugar and cornflour to the yolks and whisk until light and creamy.

3 Cut the crusts off the bread and reduce to crumbs. Fill a washing-up bowl with ice cubes and leave in a cold place.

4 Brush inside of an 850 ml [1½ pt] mould with oil.

5 Remove the vanilla pod from the milk, dry and set aside to use again. Pour the milk gradually on to the eggs, stirring the mixture all the time.

6 Replace the double boiler top and stand the boiler over low heat. Cook for 20 minutes, stirring all the time, until the custard will coat the back of the spoon.

7 As soon as the custard is ready, plunge the base of the top of the boiler into the ice. Stir in the breadcrumbs.

8 While the custard is cooling, soak the gelatine in 45 ml [3 tablespoons] cold water in a small heavy-based pan for 5 minutes. After soaking, put over low heat for 3 minutes to dissolve. Cool.

9 Pour the dissolved gelatine into the custard in a thin stream, stirring all the time. Stir until on the point of setting (about 15–20 minutes).

10 Lightly whip the cream. Fold the custard into the cream, a little at a time. Turn the cream mixture into the mould.

11 Cover the mould and place in the coldest part of the refrigerator. Leave to set for 1½ hours.

12 Turn out the mould on to a serving plate 30 minutes before needed.

13 Pipe a border of cream rosettes around the bottom of the cream on the plate. Top each rosette with a flake of chocolate. If you have used a flat-topped mould, you may also pipe around the top in the same way.

BLACKCURRANT MOUSSE

This is a delicious mousse to serve when summer fruit is plentiful. Before being added to the mousse, the blackcurrants must be poached in a little water until tender and then sieved. They are not sweetened, as all the sugar is needed to make the creamy base with the eggs. As an alternative to turning this mousse out, serve it in tall glasses topped with a whirl of cream decorated with whole blackcurrants or slivers of citrus peel.

SERVES 4–6
450 g [1 lb] blackcurrants
5 large eggs
75 g [3 oz] sugar
15 g [½ oz] gelatine
150 ml [¼ pt] thick cream

For the garnish:
whipped cream
citrus peel
blackcurrants, poached and drained
15 ml [1 tablespoon] crème de cassis (optional)

1 Wash and strip off the blackcurrants. Place in a heavy-based pan

with 125 ml [4 fl oz] cold water. Cover and simmer gently over low heat for 10 minutes until tender.

2 Drain the blackcurrants and reserve the liquid. Push fruit through a sieve. Mix the purée with the drain-off liquid and set aside.

3 Prepare a double boiler. Break 3 of the eggs into the top of the boiler. Separate the remaining eggs and add the yolks to the boiler top.

4 Add the sugar. Set the boiler over low heat and whisk eggs and sugar until pale in colour and creamy. Remove from heat.

5 Add the gelatine to 45 ml [3 tablespoons] of the blackcurrant juice in a small heavy-based saucepan and leave to soak for 5 minutes. Dissolve over low heat for 3 minutes without stirring.

6 Lightly whip the cream in a large bowl while gelatine cools.

7 Stir the remaining blackcurrant purée into the egg mixture. Pour in the gelatine in a thin stream, stirring all the time.

8 Stir the mixture into the cream a little at a time. Leave in a cool place until almost setting, stirring from time to time.

9 Divide the mousse mixture evenly between 6 tall glasses. Cover each glass and set in the refrigerator for 1½ hours. Remove 30 minutes before needed.

10 Top each glass with a whirl of whipped cream. Decorate the cream whirl with thinly pared strips of citrus rind or with a few poached blackcurrants. Spoon a little crème de cassis over each mousse, if wished, and serve.

Variations
●For strawberry mousse, replace blackcurrants with strawberries (do not cook). Dissolve the gelatine in 45 ml [3 tablespoons] water. Raspberries, peaches, nectarines and apricots may be used in the same way.
●For chocolate and orange mousse, melt 100 g [¼ lb] dessert chocolate in a double boiler. Add eggs and sugar as given in blackcurrant mousse then flavour with the grated zest of an orange. Set with 15 g [½ oz] gelatine dissolved in the juice of 1 orange. If wished, add 15 ml [1 tablespoon] Grand Marnier for extra flavour. Decorate with mandarin orange sections and whipped cream.

MOUSSE CHINOIS
◰◰◰ This is a favourite recipe of Mrs Beeton who called it ginger cream. Based on preserved ginger, this rich sweet is rather expensive to make, so is only for really special meals. This mousse is not turned out but served as Mrs Beeton would have said, 'in your best glass dish'. Less sugar is used than usual because of the sweet ginger syrup.

SERVES 6
4 large egg yolks
15 ml [1 tablespoon] caster sugar
75 g [3 oz] preserved ginger plus 22 ml [1½ tablespoons] of the syrup
15 g [½ oz] gelatine
250 ml [1¼ pt] thick cream
whipped cream
citrus peel

1 Prepare a double boiler. Place the egg yolks in the top of the boiler. Chop the ginger.

2 Add the sugar. Place the top on the bottom of the double boiler and whisk over low heat until light and creamy and the whisk will leave a trail.

3 Remove from the heat and stir in the ginger and syrup.

4 Soak the gelatine in 45 ml [3 tablespoons] cold water for 5 minutes. Place over low heat to dissolve for 3 minutes. Cool.

5 Pour the gelatine into the mousse mixture, stirring all the time to blend in the gelatine.

6 Lightly whip the cream in a large bowl and fold the mousse mixture into it a little at a time.

7 Leave the mousse until just setting, stirring from time to time so that it sets evenly.

8 Turn into a glass serving dish, cover and leave to set in the refrigerator for 1½ hours.

9 Remove from the refrigerator 30 minutes before needed. Garnish with whirls of whipped cream and top with slivers of citrus peel.

MOCHA BAVAROIS
◰◰◰ A combination of coffee and chocolate make this traditional bavarois rich and delicious. Bavarois is always turned out, so choose a pretty mould.

SERVES 8–10
400 ml [¾ pt] milk
50 g [2 oz] dessert chocolate
6 large egg yolks
75 g [3 oz] caster sugar
5 ml [1 teaspoon] cornflour
30 ml [2 tablespoons] instant coffee powder
15 ml [1 tablespoon] Grand Marnier (optional)
15 g [½ oz] gelatine
250 ml [½ pt] thick cream
15 ml [1 tablespoon] flavourless cooking oil

For the garnish:
whipped cream
coffee beans or hazelnuts

1 Prepare a washing-up bowl full of ice cubes and leave in a cool place. Prepare a double boiler.

2 Pour the milk into a heavy-based pan. Grate the chocolate into the milk.

3 Dissolve the coffee in 45 ml [3 tablespoons] boiling water. Stir into the milk mixture.

4 Place egg yolks in the top of a double boiler and add the sugar and cornflour. Beat until light and fluffy.

5 Heat the milk until bubbles appear at the edges, stirring to dissolve the chocolate. Remove from heat.

6 Pour milk on to the eggs, stirring all the time. Place the double boiler over low heat.

7 Cook for 20 minutes, stirring all the time, until the custard will coat the back of a spoon. As soon as this point is reached, place in the ice to cool.

8 Stir in the liqueur if using. Put 45 ml [3 tablespoons] cold water into

a small heavy-based pan and add the gelatine. Let it soak for 5 minutes. Then dissolve over low heat for 3 minutes. Allow to cool.

9 While waiting for the gelatine to cool, whisk the cream lightly.

10 Pour the gelatine into the custard in a thin stream, stirring all the time. Stir for 15–20 minutes, until on the point of setting.

11 Fold the custard mixture into the cream a little at a time.

12 Brush a 1.15 L [2 pt] mould with oil. Pour in the custard. Cover and leave to set for 2 hours.

13 Turn out the bavarois 30 minutes before needed. Pipe a border of cream rosettes around the base on the plate and top each rosette with a coffee bean or hazelnut.

Variations

●For raspberry bavarois, make a plain custard without coffee and chocolate flavouring. At step 8, stir in 250 ml [½ pt] raspberry purée then continue as for mocha bavarois. Any other puréed sharp fruit (strawberries, blackcurrants, redcurrants, blackberries) may be used in place of raspberries.

●For chocolate bavarois, omit coffee from the above recipe.

ENGLISH GOOSEBERRY MOUSSE

⊠⊠ This is a traditional mousse made without eggs. Simple and quick to make, it looks beautiful decorated with whipped cream and angelica. Be sure to use tart green gooseberries, rather than the yellow dessert variety. A high proportion of fruit and cream is used to give body.

SERVES 8
450 g [1 lb] gooseberries
45 ml [3 tablespoons] caster sugar
40 g [1½ oz] gelatine
25 g [1 oz] finely chopped hazelnuts

250 ml [½ pt] thick cream
2-3 drops green food colouring
15 ml [1 tablespoon] oil

For the garnish:
whipped cream
angelica

1 Top, tail and wash the gooseberries. Place in a pan with 250 ml [½ pt] water and sugar and cook over low heat for 10–15 minutes, until the gooseberries are tender. Purée in a liquidizer and sieve.

2 Place 60 ml [4 tablespoons] water in a small heavy-based pan. Add the gelatine and leave to soak for 5 minutes. Dissolve over low heat for 3 minutes. Cool.

3 Whip the cream. Fold the purée and hazelnuts into the cream.

4 Pour in the gelatine in a thin stream stirring all the time. Stir in the food colouring.

5 Leave until just setting (about 15 minutes) stirring from time to time.

6 Brush an 850 ml [1½ pt] mould with oil. Pour in the mixture. Cover and leave in the refrigerator for 1½ hours to set.

7 Remove from the refrigerator 30 minutes before needed. Turn out and garnish with rosettes of whipped cream topped with angelica cut into leaves.

Desserts

meringue suisse

Being able to make meringue well is a great asset to any cook, opening up a whole new world of delicious cakes and puddings. Meringue suisse is the easiest and most versatile meringue to make and can be used for a large number of dishes, ranging from traditional lemon meringue pie to mouthwateringly unusual chocolate chinchilla pudding.

Just how meringues work has always had the aura of a particularly successful and intriguing conjuring trick. Simply by beating air into egg whites, adding sugar and cooking you can make an attractive topping for pies and fruit, or a deliciously crisp shell to fill with cream or ice-cream and fruit.

When air is beaten into egg whites, their volume is dramatically increased. If sugar is then added, a marshmallowy mixture is created which can either be briefly cooked so that it remains soft inside, or cooked for a long time in a low oven, driving all the moisture out, leaving crisp shells.

Although many cooks are afraid of meringue, having had dreadfully sticky or dry-as-dust failures, making it successfully is really very easy. As long as you use the egg whites and sugar in the correct proportions and scrupulously clean equipment, nothing should go wrong. So, if the perfect lemon meringue pie has always eluded you, read on and become an expert!

INGREDIENTS
In order to make the meringue 'magic' work, you must use the correct ingredients in the correct proportions.

Eggs
Eggs are obviously the most important ingredient of meringue as their whites form its basis. Large eggs are always used and it is better if they are a few days old, as the white will then have thickened and will be easier to whisk than the thinner white of very fresh eggs. The eggs should always be at room temperature as they will then whisk quicker and to a larger volume.

To make meringue the eggs are separated. The yolks can be used to enrich creamed vegetables, make

mayonnaise, make crème anglaise (either to eat alone or to be used as an ice-cream base), to enrich scrambled eggs or for baking (for example, rich shortcrust). To store cover the yolks with water. Cover the container and keep in the refrigerator where they will last for four days. To use, simply drain off the water.

Stabilizer
To stabilize the egg whites and make them hold their shape when whisked, cream of tartar or salt is added. A pinch of either is enough and should be added to the egg whites before whisking.

Sugar
Sugar is added to egg whites to give flavour and to enable them to be cooked without collapsing. Caster sugar, never granulated, is used. Granulated is coarse and would give a 'weepy' meringue with little bubbles of caramel on the surface. Granulated sugar also destroys the albumen in the egg white and can cause the meringue to sink. Usually, 50 g [2 oz] sugar is used for every two egg whites. It is important to good meringue suisse that the correct amount is used. If too little sugar is used, the meringue may collapse, if too much is used, it will be 'weepy'.

EQUIPMENT
Very little equipment is needed for making meringues.

Bowl
A large bowl in which to whisk the egg whites is the most important thing. The classic bowl for whisking egg whites is an unlined copper bowl. A chemical reaction takes place when the moist egg whites come in contact with the copper—this stabilizes the egg whites. Unlined copper bowls are, however, mainly found in professional kitchens.

For the ordinary domestic kitchen, a large, wide pottery or glass bowl will be fine. The bowl must be scrupulously clean. Any trace of grease and the egg whites will refuse to whisk into a snow. One way to ensure that there is no grease in the bowl is to wipe it round with a clean cloth dipped in a little vinegar or lemon juice before use.

The whisk
Classically a balloon whisk is used to beat whites for meringues. Its structure is such that it allows the maximum amount of air to be beaten into the egg whites, giving the greatest volume and lightest texture of meringue mixture. The whisk you use to make meringues must be clean, grease free and dry. Like the bowl, it is a good idea to wipe the whisk with a cloth which has been dipped in lemon juice or vinegar before use. Dry very thoroughly.

An electric whisk speeds the job of making meringue but gives a denser texture and less volume than the traditional balloon whisk. Be careful when using an electric whisk. There is a danger of overbeating which causes the egg whites to collapse. Only hand-held whisks are suitable. The bowl must be tilted when whisking the egg whites and this is impossible when using a heavy, table model mixer.

Rotary whisks are not suitable for making meringues as it is impossible to tilt the bowl while whisking.

Baking trays
If you are baking meringue shells, you will need a baking tray. Non-stick trays are best. Failing this, use a baking tray lined with oiled grease-proof paper or silicone paper.

THE BASIC PRINCIPLES
Making meringues can be divided into various stages.

Separating the eggs
It is very important to separate yolks and whites correctly, avoiding breaking the yolks. If any trace of yolk gets into the white when separated, the white will not whisk. This is because the yolk contains fat which prevents aeration. If you should accidentally get a speck of yolk in with the white, fish it out with a piece of egg shell or with a spoon.

If you know separating eggs is not your strong point, it might be a good idea to buy a patent egg separator before making meringues. These are very cheap and ensure no unwanted yolk will sneak into the white.

After you have separated the eggs, add a pinch of cream of tartar or salt to the whites. This will help them hold their shape when whisked. Store the yolks under water.

Whisking
The next stage is to start whisking the egg whites with either a balloon whisk or a hand-held electric whisk. Start whisking slowly at first, tilting the bowl to allow the maximum incorporation of air. The whites will first turn foamy and then begin to thicken. At this point, increase the whisking speed. The whites will soon turn thick and close in texture. To test if you have whisked far enough, lift the whisk away from the whites. If the whisked white hangs in stiff peaks from the whisk and stands up in stiff peaks in the bowl, it is time to add the sugar.

Adding the sugar
At first only half the total amount of sugar is added. It is whisked into the meringue. This usually takes 3–4 minutes. When the sugar has been dissolved, the meringue will have a

4 large eggs
pinch of salt or cream of tartar
225 g [½ lb] caster sugar

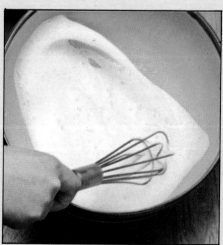

4 As the whites begin to turn foamy, increase beating speed until the mixture is thick and white.

glossy appearance. The reason for whisking in only half the sugar is that meringue collapses if you whisk a lot in at once, so whisking in a little makes it smooth without the possibility of disaster.

The remaining sugar is then folded in, half at a time. The best instrument for this is a metal spoon as it cuts easily through the meringue, enabling the sugar to be distributed evenly. To fold in, place the sugar in the bowl with the meringue. Using the spoon, fold the meringue over the sugar. Continue to do this until the sugar has been evenly distributed throughout the meringue.

As soon as this stage has been completed, the meringue must be used. If you leave it to stand, it will begin to separate and collapse.

COOKING

The way meringue is cooked depends on how it is to be used. The oven must be preheated to the correct temperature.

Toppings

If the meringue is to be used as a topping for a pie or stewed fruit, first pile it on to the base, spreading it all over with a palette knife. Using the handle of a spoon, rough up the meringue so it stands in peaks. Alternatively pipe the meringue on to the pie or fruit using a star or rope vegetable nozzle. If you want a soft meringue, brown on the outside but of a marshmallow consistency inside, cook for 5 minutes at 220°C [425°F] gas mark 7. For a crisper meringue topping, cook at 180°C [350°F] gas mark 4 for 30 minutes.

'Dry' meringues

Meringue shells and bases for meringue cakes are dried out in a very low oven rather than cooked. The aim is to make the meringue dry and crisp without colouring it. The meringues are placed on the lowest shelf in the oven and dried for 2–3 hours at 110°C [225°F] gas mark ¼ leaving the door slightly ajar. If you have a solid fuel cooker, the tray of meringues can be placed on the hot-plate cover for several hours or overnight.

Another successful method of cooking meringues is to heat the oven to 260°C [500°F] gas mark 10. Put the meringues on the oven floor and turn off the oven. Do not open the door for at least five hours. Alternatively, leave the meringues in a warm airing cupboard or warming drawer overnight.

Step-by-step to meringue

1 First separate the eggs, placing the whites in a large, grease- and moisture-free bowl.

2 Add a pinch of salt or cream of tartar to the bowl and stir in with a fork.

3 Tilt the bowl away from you and start whisking the whites with a balloon or electric whisk.

5 To test if the whites are ready, lift the whisk away. They should stand in stiff peaks.

6 Add 100 g [¼ lb] of the sugar. Whisk slowly for 3 minutes or until the sugar is amalgamated.

7 Now fold in half of the remaining sugar using a metal spoon. Fold in the rest in the same way.

Making a meringue topping

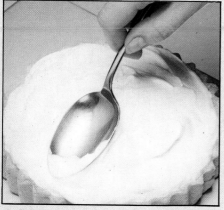

1 Spread meringue over the prepared pie. Make sure meringue touches the edges. Shape top with spoon.

OR pipe the prepared meringue on to the pie through a nozzle in rings, starting with the outside ring.

OR Scatter caster sugar over the meringue for a sweeter topping, or scatter flaked almonds.

2 Bake at 220°C [425°F] gas mark 7 for 10 minutes, until the meringue top is golden.

Making and using meringue shells

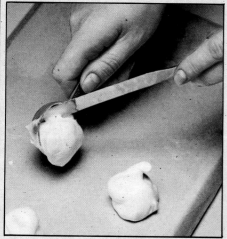

1 For meringue shells, take 15 ml [1 tablespoon] of meringue mixture and place on a baking tray.

2 Round each meringue with a wet knife. Bake in a low oven until the shells are crisp and dry.

3 Sandwich the meringue shells in pairs with fruit, cream or ice-cream, alone or mixed together.

4 To decorate, dip a skewer in melted chocolate and dribble a trail of chocolate across each meringue.

SERVING IDEAS

Meringue can be served in many different ways. Here are some quick and easy ones to try.

●For snowy apples, top baked apples with meringue mixture. Sprinkle with almond slivers and cook in an oven heated to 200°C [400°F] gas mark 6 for 10 minutes, until the meringue is golden and puffy. Make snowy pears in the same way.

●Give plain stewed fruit a special look by topping with meringue. If wished, the meringue can be decorated with angelica and glacé cherries.

●Crush dry meringues and stir them into ice-cream while it is still soft. Freeze and top with a further layer of crushed meringue.

●Sandwich meringue shells with a mixture of cream and chopped stem ginger, strawberries, raspberries, peaches, nectarines or apricots.

●For meringue and strawberry gâteau, make three flat meringue bases. Sandwich together with strawberry ice-cream into which you have mixed sliced strawberries. Decorate the top with more strawberries. Any soft fruit may be used in place of strawberries.

●Top a plain jam tart or individual jam tarts with meringue to give a special look.

●For an unusual contrast of textures, stir crushed crisp meringue into coffee- or chocolate-flavoured custard. Sprinkle with a topping of crushed meringue.

Making and using meringue stars

1 As a topping for fresh fruit, pipe rosettes of meringue on to a baking tray using a star nozzle.

2 Bake in a low oven until dry and crisp. Use to top fresh fruit or a fruit compote.

3 Alternatively, sandwich meringue stars with cream or fruit and cream. Serve with coffee.

Making meringue cakes

1 For large meringue cakes, pipe a circle of meringue on to a baking tray, using a medium rope nozzle.

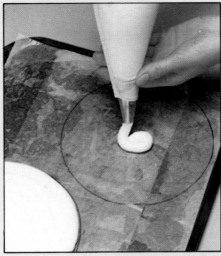

2 Pipe two other circles in the same way. Cook as for meringue shells until crisp and dry.

3 Lift the meringues and place one on a serving plate. Spread with fruit and cream or ice-cream.

4 Place the other meringue on top of the filling. Cover with filling and top with final meringue.

5 Alternatively, spread a baked meringue base with cream and top with a crown of meringue stars.

6 Fill the centre of the cake with fruit and cream and decorate with more cream if wished.

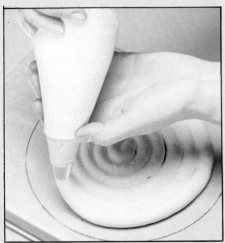

7 To make a meringue layer, first pipe one large circle using a large plain nozzle.

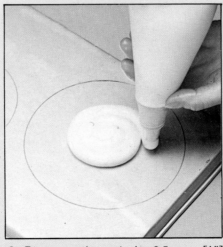

8 Pipe another circle 2.5 cm [1"] smaller than the first and a final circle 2.5cm [1"] smaller than the second.

9 Bake, cool, then, with the largest circle at the bottom, sandwich together with cream and fruit.

351

FLOATING ISLANDS

Floating islands or oeufs à la neige need care to be successful but are so delicious that this dish is well worth the effort. The egg whites are poached rather than oven cooked, so less sugar than usual is used and it is all whisked in, to enable it to dissolve in the egg whites.

SERVES 4–6
400 ml [¾ pt] milk
250 ml [½ pt] thin cream
30 ml [2 tablespoons] caster sugar
1 vanilla pod
10 ml [2 teaspoons] cornflour
4 eggs
pinch of salt
100 g [¼ lb] caster sugar

1 Place 250 ml [½ pt] milk, the cream, 30 ml [2 tablespoons] sugar and the vanilla pod, which you must split lengthwise, in a heavy-based pan over medium heat.

2 Heat until bubbles appear at edge. Remove from heat, cover and leave to infuse for 10 minutes.

3 Remove the vanilla pod. Take out 15 ml [1 tablespoon] of the liquid and blend with the cornflour in a small bowl. Stir this cornflour paste into the liquid in the pan.

4 Replace the pan over medium heat and bring to the boil slowly, stirring all the time. Lower the heat and simmer for 2–3 minutes to cook and to take away the raw taste from the cornflour.

5 Separate the eggs. Put the yolks into the top pan of a double boiler and beat until just frothy. Add the cream mixture in a thin stream, beating all the time.

6 Put the pan over the bottom half of the double boiler, containing hot, but not boiling, water. Cook for about 15 minutes, stirring all the time until the sauce will coat the back of a spoon. Do not let the sauce boil or the egg yolks will curdle. Remove from heat and leave to cool.

7 Mix the remaining milk with 550 ml [1 pt] water in a wide, deep frying-pan.

8 Add salt to the egg whites and whisk until stiff. Add 100 g [¼ lb] caster sugar a little at a time, whisking between each addition until the sugar dissolves in the white and no longer feels grainy.

9 Bring the milky water to the boil then reduce the heat so that it is just simmering.

10 Shape 15 ml [1 tablespoon] of the meringue mixture into a mound with a knife and drop it into the milky water. Repeat three more times.

11 Poach the 'islands' for 4 minutes, turning half-way through cooking time with a palette knife so that all sides are cooked. Do not cook for any longer than 4 minutes or they will fall apart.

12 Lift out the islands with a slotted spoon and lay on a wire rack or kitchen paper to drain.

13 Cook the rest of the meringue mixture in the same way.

14 Pour the sauce into a serving dish. Arrange the islands on top. Chill for 30 minutes before serving.

Variations
●For caramel floating islands, prepare as above. Combine 50 g [2 oz] caster sugar with 15 ml [1 tablespoon] cold water and cook over low heat until the sugar has melted. Increase the heat so the liquid browns and bubbles and turns to caramel. Spoon a little caramel over each island and allow to set before serving.
●For chocolate floating islands, add 75 g [3 oz] grated dessert chocolate to the milk at step 1 of the recipe. Allow the chocolate to melt into the milk, stirring all the time, then proceed as usual.
●For orange floating islands, substitute the thinly pared rind of an orange for the vanilla pod. When still warm, flavour the sauce with the juice of the orange and 10 ml [2 teaspoons] Grand Marnier.

●For coffee floating islands, flavour the milk with 15 ml [1 tablespoon] instant coffee dissolved in 5 ml [1 teaspoon] boiling water. Stir 5 ml [1 teaspoon] Tia Maria into the sauce while it is still warm.

LEMON MERINGUE PIE

Lemon meringue pie is a traditional favourite that is deceptively easy and inexpensive to make. It traditionally has a crisp meringue topping which is sprinkled with a little caster sugar before cooking to give it a golden glaze.
Make the sweet rich-crust pastry following the instructions given in the chapter on shortcrust pastry flans, and then blind bake, again referring to the same chapter.

SERVES 4
175 g [6 oz] sweet rich-crust pastry
1 large lemon
30 ml [2 tablespoons] granulated sugar

**30 ml [2 tablespoons]
   cornflour
2 eggs
15 g [½ oz] unsalted butter
pinch of salt
100 g [¼ lb] caster sugar**

1 Heat the oven to 200°C [400°F] gas mark 6.

2 Roll out the pastry and line a 18 cm [7″] flan ring. Bake blind in the centre of the oven for 10 minutes. Remove the beans and lining and bake for a further 5 minutes. Remove from oven when cooked.

3 Meanwhile, peel the rind from the lemon using a swivel-type potato peeler. Squeeze the juice from the lemon.

4 Put the lemon rind, granulated sugar and 250 ml [½ pt] cold water in a pan. Place over low heat and stir until the sugar has dissolved, then bring to the boil. Boil for 1 minute.

5 Remove the pan from the heat.

Blend the cornflour in a bowl with the lemon juice until smooth.

6 Pour the syrup through a strainer on to the blended cornflour, stirring well.

7 Separate the eggs. Add the egg yolks and the butter to the lemon and cornflour mixture. Beat until the butter has melted and the mixture has turned thick. If the mixture seems a little thin, return it to the pan and heat gently, stirring constantly, until it thickens.

8 Reduce the oven heat to 150°C [300°F] gas mark 2.

9 Remove the cooked pastry case from the flan ring and pile in the lemon mixture.

10 Add salt to the egg whites and whisk until stiff. Whisk in half the caster sugar then fold in the rest in two batches, reserving 5 ml [1 teaspoon].

11 Pile the meringue mixture on top of the lemon filling. Spread from the edge to the centre, making sure the meringue joins the pastry edge. Fluff the meringue into peaks with the handle of a spoon. Alternatively, the meringue may be piped over the filling using a large star or rope nozzle.

12 Sprinkle the remaining caster sugar over the meringue mixture and cook in the centre of the oven for 20–30 minutes until the meringue is crisp and golden. Serve warm.

Variations
● For orange meringue pie, substitute a large orange for the lemon.
● For lime meringue pie, substitute 3 limes for the lemon.

Lemon meringue pie is one of the best loved of all dishes using meringue.

353

QUEEN OF PUDDINGS

A Victorian nursery dessert, Queen of puddings is a tasty way to use leftovers. Either stale white bread or sponge cake may be used for the filling. Sponge cake has been used here as it makes a richer pudding than bread-crumbs.

SERVES 6
550 ml [1 pt] milk
50 g [2 oz] butter
1 lemon
150 g [5 oz] caster sugar
2 eggs
100 g [¼ lb] stale sponge cake
pinch of salt
45 ml [3 tablespoons] strawberry or apricot jam

1 Heat the oven to 180°C [350°F] gas mark 4.

2 Place the milk and butter in a pan. Remove the zest from the lemon with a swivel potato peeler and add to the pan. Bring to the boil and remove from the heat.

3 Add 25 g [1 oz] sugar to the boiled milk. Stir for 2 minutes to dissolve. Squeeze the juice from the lemon and add to the milk. Leave, covered, to infuse for 10 minutes.

4 Meanwhile, separate the eggs. Butter a 850 ml [1½ pt] dish, reduce the cake to crumbs and put these in the dish.

5 Beat the egg yolks and stir into the milk. Strain the liquid on to the crumbs. Stir well, so that all the crumbs are saturated.

6 Place in the centre of the oven and cook for 20 minutes or until set.

7 Meanwhile, add salt to the egg whites and beat until they will stand in stiff peaks. Add half the remaining sugar and beat in.

8 Fold the rest of the sugar into the egg whites. Remove the pudding from the oven and increase the heat to 200°C [400°F] gas mark 6.

9 Spread the jam over the top of the pudding. Cover with meringue, spreading from the middle. Cook in the centre of the oven for 10 minutes until the meringue is puffy and golden.

SALZBURGER NOCKERLIN

This meringue pudding is quick to make and can be served either alone or with jam, or caramel or chocolate sauce.

SERVES 4
4 eggs
5 ml [1 teaspoon] vanilla extract
5 ml [1 teaspoon] finely grated lemon zest
15 ml [1 tablespoon] plain flour
pinch of salt
225 g [½ lb] caster sugar
15 g [½ oz] butter
15 ml [1 tablespoon] icing sugar

1 Heat the oven to 180°C [350°F] gas mark 4.

2 Separate the eggs. You will only need two of the yolks, so reserve the others for another use.

3 Using a fork, beat the vanilla extract and lemon zest into the egg yolks. Sift in the flour and beat in with the fork.

4 Add the salt to the egg whites. Whisk with a balloon or electric whisk until the whites will stand in stiff peaks.

5 Whisk in half the caster sugar. Fold in the remaining sugar, half at a time.

6 Using a spatula or metal spoon, stir about 30 ml [2 tablespoons] of the whites into the egg yolks.

7 Now fold the yolk mixture into the whites, using a metal spoon.

8 Butter an oval ovenproof dish. Pile the egg whites into the dish in four mounds which should not touch each other.

9 Place in the centre of the oven and cook for 10–12 minutes until brown on the outside but still soft on the inside. Sift icing sugar over and serve immediately.

Two very different but delicious ways of using meringue. Top, queen of puddings, a favourite Victorian dessert. Below, Salzburger nockerlin, a vanilla-flavoured meringue cake from Austria.

CHOCOLATE CHINCHILLA

This is another inexpensive and easy egg meringue pudding. Chocolate chinchilla rises to great heights in the oven but will collapse as it cools. It is eaten cold so, to prevent too dramatic a collapse, leave in a draught-free atmosphere—for example in a warming drawer or airing cupboard. It will still shrink but the crinkly crisp texture and spongy centre are quite delicious. You can eat this pudding straight from the oven but, be warned, it is extremely rich and sweet when hot. To serve, turn on to a serving dish and accompany with rum-flavoured cream. Because drinking chocolate which contains sugar is used, slightly less sugar than usual is needed to make the mixture for the meringue.

SERVES 6
50 g [2 oz] powdered drinking chocolate
5 ml [1 teaspoon] powdered cinnamon
6 eggs
pinch of salt
225 g [½ lb] caster sugar
15 g [½ oz] butter

1 Heat the oven to 180°C [350°F] gas mark 4 and butter a 1.15 L [2 pt] ovenproof dish.

2 Sift the chocolate and cinnamon powders into a bowl. Separate the egg whites from the yolks. Reserve the six egg yolks under water in a tightly covered container in the refrigerator, until needed for another dish or sauce.

3 Add the salt to the egg whites. Whisk until they will stand in stiff peaks.

4 Whisk half the sugar into the egg whites. Fold in the remainder, half at a time.

5 Add the dry chocolate and cinnamon mixture to the egg whites, folding in with a metal spoon until evenly distributed.

6 Pile the meringue mixture into the ovenproof dish and cook in the centre of the oven for 45 minutes or until well risen.

7 Leave in a draught-free place to cool. Serve with rum-flavoured cream or with thin pouring cream if wished.

355

Coffee meringues with hazelnut cream

◪◪◪ *Meringue shells once made will keep crisp and fresh for up to two weeks provided they are stored in an airtight tin or container. Do not, however, put in the hazelnut cream filling until the day on which the meringues are to be served.*

MAKES 16 SHELLS
3 large eggs
175 g [6 oz] caster sugar
250 ml [½ pt] thick cream
125 g [¼ lb] hazelnuts
15 ml [1 tablespoon] coffee essence or instant coffee

1 Heat the oven to 110°C [225°F] gas mark ¼.

2 Separate the eggs putting the whites into a large, clean, grease-free bowl. Do not let any yolk fall into the whites. Reserve the yolks, covered with water, in an airtight container.

3 Using a balloon whisk, whisk the egg whites until they stand in stiff peaks.

4 Add half the sugar and whisk again until the whites regain their stiffness.

5 Gently fold in the remaining sugar with a metal spoon. Add the coffee essence or instant coffee which you have mixed with 15 ml [1 tablespoon] water and stir in with light movements.

6 Lay a sheet of greaseproof paper on a baking tray and brush lightly with oil.

7 Take a generous tablespoonful of the meringue and place on the tray. Smooth each heap of meringue with a wet palette knife to give a good rounded shape.

8 Continue until all the meringue has been used. Smooth each heap with the wet palette knife.

9 Place in the bottom of the oven for 2½ hours until the shells are firm and dry. If the meringues seem to be getting much darker than a pale coffee colour leave the oven door ajar and turn off the heat.

10 Cool the meringue shells on a baking tray then store in an airtight container until needed.

11 For the filling, first chop the hazelnuts very finely—using a mezzaluna or an electric grinder.

12 Lightly whip the cream and gently fold two-thirds of the chopped nuts into it.

13 Sandwich the meringue halves together with a generous spoonful of the hazelnut cream between each pair.

14 Press the remaining chopped hazelnuts into the cream filling at the sides before serving.

Desserts

meringue cuite and American meringue

There's more to meringue than the simple cakes shown in the chapter on meringue suisse. By using slightly different ingredients and methods you can make meringue cuite for magnificent meringue baskets and American meringue for luscious marshmallowy cakes.

A hazelnut meringue cake nears completion as the raspberries and cream are sandwiched between meringue.

Once you can make simple meringue suisse (as shown in the previous chapter) you have the basic knowledge and skills to try the slightly more complicated meringue cuite and American meringue.

Meringue cuite, or cooked meringue, is the mixture used for meringue baskets and shells. It is made when icing sugar and egg whites are beaten together over gentle heat. This process results in a meringue which is stable long enough to hold its shape after beating, so it can be piped. When baked, the meringue is hard, dry and powdery and always very white. When used to make a meringue basket, this texture provides a perfect foil to luscious cream or ice-cream and juicy fruit fillings.

American meringue has a marshmallow-like consistency, obtained by using more sugar than usual, and beating in vinegar and sometimes cornflour. American meringue is used to make delicious party cakes—such as hazelnut meringue cake and the great Australian classic, Pavlova—both perfect for serving when you have a lot of guests, because they can be made well in advance.

Both meringue cuite and American meringue will increase your dessert repertoire enormously. You will be surprised to see just how easy those apparently impossible meringue baskets and layered cakes are to make.

357

Step-by-step meringue cuite

250 g [9 oz] icing sugar
4 egg whites
pinch of salt
3 drops vanilla extract

1 Sift the icing sugar. Select a pan into which the bowl will fit, without touching water at the bottom. Add tepid water to pan.

2 Place egg whites in the bowl. Add a pinch of salt and stir. Whisk until foamy but not until stiff and standing in peaks.

3 Whisk in the icing sugar 5 ml [1 teaspoon] at a time. Whisk in the vanilla extract. Place the pan over low heat and position bowl.

INGREDIENTS FOR MERINGUE CUITE

As in meringue suisse, it is important that the ingredients for meringue cuite be used in the correct proportion to one another.

Egg whites

Egg white should be from large eggs at room temperature. Do not use very fresh eggs as the whites will be thin and less likely to beat into a stiff foam than the thicker whites of older eggs. Four egg whites is the smallest manageable quantity for meringue cuite and they should be placed in a scrupulously clean, grease-free bowl.

Sugar

Icing sugar is used for meringue cuite as it gives a thick, glossy meringue (ideal for piping) when whisked with egg whites over heat. Usually, 62 g [2¼ oz] of icing sugar is used per egg white. Be sure to sift the icing sugar before use as it can be lumpy.

Flavouring

Traditionally, meringue cuite is flavoured with vanilla. Two to three drops of vanilla extract are sufficient to flavour meringue cuite made with four egg whites.

INGREDIENTS FOR AMERICAN MERINGUE

American meringue is made from a thick mixture which falls between meringue suisse and meringue cuite.

Egg whites

Egg whites are used in the same way and in the same proportion as for meringue cuite.

Sugar

Caster sugar is used for American meringue cakes to help give a marshmallowy centre. Sugar is used in the same proportion in American meringue cakes as in meringue cuite.

Cornflour

Cornflour is used for American meringue cake in two ways. Firstly, it is used to dust the baking sheet or tin to prevent sticking, as described in the section on equipment. Secondly, it is whisked into the meringue to help dry it out during cooking and prevent the sugar 'weeping' which would make the cake too sticky. Usually 5 ml [1 teaspoon] cornflour is used per egg white, though this may vary. In some recipes containing ground nuts, which help absorb the sugar, cornflour may be omitted.

Vinegar

Achieving the soft, marshmallowy centre of American meringue cakes is aided by adding a little malt vinegar with the cornflour. The vinegar has no effect on the flavour of the meringue but changes the structure of the sugar, making the cake soft in the centre but crisp on the outside. In some recipes, you may find a mixture of vinegar and lemon juice being used. This makes the meringue very white. Usually 2.5 ml [¼ teaspoon] malt vinegar is used for every 2 egg whites. More vinegar may be used in Pavlovas as they should be very soft in the centre.

Flavourings

Vanilla extract is usually used to flavour meringue cakes in the same amount as for meringue cuite. Coffee essence may be used in the same way. In nut-flavoured meringue cakes, ground almonds or hazelnuts are folded into the mixture before cooking. The amount used varies from recipe to recipe. It is unwise to experiment with flavourings for meringue as the balance of the ingredients can be altered causing the meringue to fail.

1 Fit a piping bag with 12 mm [½"] star or eclair nozzle. Fill with meringue cuite.

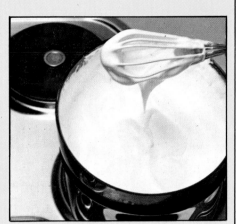

4 Whisk the meringue mixture over heat until it thickens. This will take about 8 minutes. When ready, it will leave a thick trail.

EQUIPMENT

You will need the basic bowl and whisk as given for meringue suisse in the previous chapter.

For meringue cuite, you will need a pan over which your bowl will fit, leaving enough room for water underneath. The water should not touch the base of the bowl. A double boiler is not suitable as the top pan is not usually large enough to allow the beating of air into the mixture.

To pipe meringue cuite nests and baskets, you will need a piping bag, a 12 mm [½"] eclair nozzle or a 12 mm [½"] star nozzle. You will also need a pencil and a compass or a plate of the diameter you wish the basket to be.

To cook meringue nests and baskets, you will need a baking sheet and some silicone-coated or greaseproof paper. The paper is spread on the baking sheet and lightly oiled before the meringue is placed on it. After cooking, the paper will peel away quite easily.

To cook meringue cakes, you will need a shallow sponge cake tin with removable base, about 20 cm [8"] in diameter. Always use a tin with a removable base as it is impossible to get meringue out of a fixed-base tin. The tin must be brushed with melted margarine, dusted with cornflour and base-lined with non-stick silicone **paper cut slightly larger than the base and trimmed at the edges.** Or use a baking sheet prepared with greaseproof lining as described for meringue cuite basket. Draw circles of the required size on the paper and spread over the mixture. Using a baking sheet does not give such neat cakes as using a tin.

MAKING MERINGUE CUITE

Making meringue cuite may be divided into four stages.

Sifting icing sugar

Icing sugar is almost always lumpy so it must be sifted before use. This is most important as the lumps would not dissolve in the meringue and would destroy the aeration.

After you have sifted the icing sugar, select a large bowl in which to whisk the meringue and a pan on to which it will fit, leaving enough room for water below. The water should be tepid and should not touch the bottom of the bowl.

Initial whisking

Add a pinch of salt to the egg whites and whisk until foamy but not stiff. Then whisk in the icing sugar 5 ml [1 teaspoon] at a time. Whisking in the icing sugar bit by bit in such small quantities ensures that it is all dissolved.

Whisking over heat

Place the pan containing the water over low heat and put the bowl in position over the water. Whisk the meringue until it is thick. This is the point when it will leave a thick trail on the meringue in the bowl when the whisk is lifted. It usually takes 10–15 minutes' beating to reach this stage with a balloon whisk or 8 minutes with an electric whisk. As soon as the meringue reaches this stage, remove from the heat.

Piping and cooking

Gently spoon the meringue into the piping bag, taking care not to crush the air out of it. Pipe as wished on to a prepared baking sheet. Meringue cuite is always cooked in an oven heated to 110°C [225°F] gas mark ¼ for 1–2 hours depending on the size. When cooked, remove from the oven and immediately gently peel the paper away from the base of the meringue. Cool on a cake rack before filling or decorating as wished.

Step-by-step to meringue nests

2 On a prepared baking sheet, pipe a filled-in circle 10 cm [4"] in diameter.

3 Using a 12 mm [½"] star nozzle, pipe a line on top of the circle. Pipe another line on top of this.

4 Bake for about 2 hours. Fill with fresh fruit and cream or ice-cream and fruit if washed.

MAKING AMERICAN MERINGUE

Making American meringue can be divided into 5 stages.

Whisking egg whites

Add salt to the egg whites, stir once and then whisk until the whites will stand in stiff peaks. Beating to a stiff stage is essential for this type of meringue or it will collapse when sugar is added.

Adding sugar

Whisk the sugar into the egg whites 5 ml [1 teaspoon] at a time, making sure one lot of sugar has dissolved and that it has been evenly distributed before you add the next. To test this, rub a little of the mixture against the side of the bowl with a knife. If the mixture feels granular then the sugar has not dissolved. Undissolved sugar is a great danger when making American meringue as it can give a weepy meringue which will stick stubbornly to the baking tray or

paper. Also, undissolved sugar in meringue can break down the aeration and the mixture will then collapse. Adding the sugar will take about 8 minutes.

Adding vinegar, cornflour and flavouring

The vinegar, cornflour and any liquid flavouring can be added to the mixture all at once and are quickly whisked in. Adding all at once rather than separately cuts down the whisking time and reduces the danger of destroying the aeration of the meringue.

Adding nuts

If the meringue is to have a nutty flavour, the nuts must be finely ground and folded in after the cornflour and vinegar. Fold the nuts in gently with a figure-of-eight movement, using a metal spoon or palette knife.

Cooking

Carefully pile the mixture into the prepared tin or tins and make a slight hollow in the centre. This will provide a space in which to put the filling. The temperature at which meringue cakes are cooked and the time for which

they are cooked varies from recipe to recipe. Generally speaking cakes containing nuts are cooked for the shortest time at the highest temperature and marshmallowy Pavlovas for the longest time at a slightly lower temperature, though this varies from recipe to recipe.

When the cake is cooked, remove from the oven but leave it for a few minutes to allow the meringue to shrink away from the sides of the tin. Then push up the tin base, remove the meringue from the base and peel away the paper from the base of the cake. Place on a wire cooling rack and fill when cold.

FILLINGS FOR MERINGUE CAKES AND BASKETS

Combinations of fruit and cream or ice-cream are the best filling for meringue baskets. Here are a few to try. Do not fill the baskets or nests until just before serving or the filling will soak into the meringue.

●Fill a large meringue basket with chocolate ice-cream and raspberries. Serve with a Melba sauce made from sieved raspberries sweetened to taste with icing sugar.

●For a refreshing dessert, fill individual meringue nests with strawberry water-ice and top with fresh strawberries.

●Sandwich meringue cakes together with whipped cream into which you have stirred fruit purée. Apricot, peach and gooseberry purée are all good, as are sliced bananas.

●Flavour the cream used to sandwich meringue cakes or fill baskets and nests with a few drops of liqueur of your choice.

●Fill meringue nests with vanilla ice-cream and serve with a cold chocolate or butterscotch sauce.

●For a ginger filling, stir chopped stem ginger and a little of the syrup into cream or vanilla ice-cream used for filling.

●Add interest to vanilla ice-cream by stirring in sliced fruit. Strawberries, peaches and grapes are all good.

Meringue cuite is used to make a meringue basket.

Step-by-step to a large meringue basket

⬒⬒⬒ *To make this basket, two quantities of the meringue cuite mixture given in the step-by-step instructions are used. Do not make both at once. The first is used to make the basket base and sides and the second to decorate. Make the first batch before step 1 and the second between steps 5 and 6. Meringue cuite will stay up longer than meringue suisse but should not be kept waiting where this can be avoided.*

1 Prepare two baking sheets, covering with oiled greaseproof or silicone paper. Draw two 15 cm [6″] circles on each piece of paper.

2 Fit a piping bag with a 12 mm [½″] eclair nozzle and fill. Pipe a circle, following pencil line. Fill in circle with meringue.

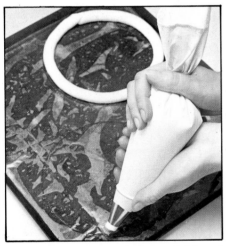

3 Now pipe around the outside of the remaining 3 circles so that the pencil line is covered and the centre is empty.

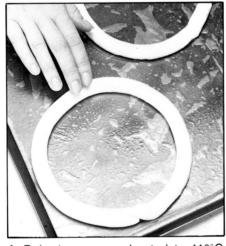

4 Bake in an oven heated to 110°C [225°F] gas mark ¼ for 50-60 minutes until dry and crisp. Make up second batch of meringue.

5 Gently peel away paper from hollow circles. Place the three circles on top of the solid base circle. Make more meringue.

6 Fit a piping bag with a 12 mm [½″] star nozzle. Fill with meringue and carefully pipe vertical lines all around the basket.

7 Pipe a decorative border around the base and top of the meringue basket to cover the ends of the piped lines.

8 Return to the oven and cook for a further 60 minutes to cook the outside piping. Remove when cooked and peel away paper.

361

Step-by-step to American meringue cake

4 egg whites
250 g [9 oz] caster sugar
3–4 drops vanilla extract
5 ml [1 teaspoon] malt vinegar
20 ml [4 teaspoons] cornflour
100 g [¼ lb] ground almonds

1 Grease and dust with cornflour a 20 cm [8"] loose-bottomed cake tin or line the base with oiled non-stick silicone paper.

2 Heat the oven to 190°C [375°F] gas mark 5. Place the egg whites in a bowl and whisk until they will stand in stiff peaks.

3 Beat in the sugar 5 ml [1 teaspoon] at a time. Test to see that the sugar has dissolved by rubbing mixture against the side of the bowl.

4 Whisk in the vanilla extract, vinegar and cornflour. Stop whisking as soon as amalgamated—about 2 minutes.

5 Fold the ground almonds into the mixture in a figure-of-eight movement, using a metal spoon. Stop folding as soon as amalgamated.

6 Pile the mixture into the prepared tin, levelling the top slightly and making a shallow indentation in the middle. Cook 40 minutes.

OR to make a layer cake, divide the mixture between two tins. Cook in the centre of the oven for 40 minutes.

7 Allow the meringue to shrink away from the tin then push up the loose tin base and peel the paper away from the meringue. Cool.

Desserts

water-ices

Cool and beautiful, water-based ices bring cool comfort when the temperature rises. Inexpensive and simple to make, they are a must to see you through the high days of summer or to serve as a cheering treat on the dark winter days.

When the temperature rises, so do the sales of commercially made ice-cream, depressingly tasteless and unrefreshing though it often is. A better way to cool down is to make your own ices. Despite the mystique that surrounds ice-cream making, there are no special techniques or equipment needed and anyone who can follow a recipe can make ices that put the bought product to shame.

The simplest point at which to start making ice-cream is with ices—granitas, water-ices and sorbets—elegant combinations of sugar syrup, flavouring and sometimes egg white, frostily tangy and very impressive to serve when guests are present.

All you need to make these ices is a refrigerator or freezer, some ice cube trays or a bread tin and a rotary or electric mixer—plus patience of course, because they do take time. The results however, are well worth waiting for—as you will agree when you've tried the recipes given here.

THREE TYPES OF ICE

There are three basic types of ice.
Granitas are the easiest of all to make, being simply a weak sugar syrup flavoured with tea, coffee or fruit juice. Granitas are a cross between a drink and an ice and are perfect served after a game has left you hot and bothered, or when you are feeling generally frayed and overheated.

Traditionally, granitas are served in a tall glass topped with cream. A long spoon is provided so the top half of the granita can be eaten. The bottom half is usually drunk.
Water-ices are made from stronger sugar syrup flavoured with fruit or vegetable juice or purée. After initial partial freezing, a small amount of egg white is beaten into the ice. It is then frozen again until firm, then beaten again, to break up ice crystals. After a final freezing, the ice is ready to use.

Water-ices may be served as a refresher—after a spicy dish such as a curry, as a first course if they are vegetable-based, or as a dessert.
Sorbets are the finest of ices. They are made when fruit purée or juice is added to a very strong sugar syrup. After this stage they are then made by exactly the same method as water-ices, except that a larger quantity of egg white is beaten in to give the finished ice a smooth, light texture.

In old cookery books, you may see sorbets referred to as sherbets. They were traditionally served as a refresher in the middle of a large banquet. Today, sorbets are usually served as a dessert, or simply as a cooler when the temperature is high.

EQUIPMENT

The most important piece of equipment for making ices is the freezing appliance.

Refrigerator

Ices can be made quite easily in the frozen food compartment of a domestic refrigerator. The refrigerator will need to be turned to its coldest setting, so move food you don't want frozen down to the bottom shelves. Or if you know your refrigerator rather overdoes things, remove food completely. The refrigerator must be turned down at least an hour before you make the ice.

Freezer

A freezer is the ideal place in which to make ices. The temperature is at a constant low so there is no need for adjustment. There is no need to set to fast freeze either, as the temperature will be quite low enough to freeze the ice. Another advantage of using a freezer is that you can make quite a large quantity of ice and store it until needed.

Ice-cream makers

Ice-cream makers are purpose built appliances which freeze the ice and stir it constantly so that a smooth result is obtained. This means that there is no need for vigilance on your part, and no need to beat between freezings. Unless you make ices and ice-cream in large quantities, it is not worth buying an ice-cream maker. Further details on ice-cream makers are given in the following chapter which covers making ice-cream.

Other equipment

If you are making the ices in a refrigerator, an ice-cube tray, with the divider removed, makes a good container. Alternatively, use a 450 g [1 lb] bread tin. This will fit easily into a frozen food compartment and will hold more than an ice-cube tray, saving you space and time.

If you are using the freezer, the ice can be frozen in a freezer-proof plastic or metal bowl. This can also be used for beating the ice in. If you are making the ice in the refrigerator, it will have to be turned out of the tray or loaf tin into a bowl for beating.

To beat up the water-ices and sorbets, and also to whisk egg whites, an electric whisk is best. Failing this a rotary or balloon whisk may be used. As well as these, you will need a heavy-based pan in which to make the syrup, a sieve to strain the syrup or make fruit purée (nylon mesh is essential as metal transfers flavour to fruit), a swivel-type potato peeler to remove citrus peel, a juice extractor to remove citrus juice and, if you have a freezer, rigid boxes in which to store the finished ice.

THE SYRUP

The syrup is the most important part of a water-based ice. It is made up of two parts, sugar and liquid.

Sugar

Traditionally cube sugar is used for making ices. This is mainly because it is easier to see when it has dissolved in the liquid. Caster sugar may be used instead and gives exactly the same results, besides being cheaper and more easily obtainable than cube sugar. White sugar is always used—brown does not give the ice a good colour.

The amount of sugar in any mixture to be frozen is crucial for a successful end result—too much sugar and the ice will refuse to freeze, too little sugar and it will set like concrete. Granitas have the least sugar of all ices. Water-ices and sorbets have more sugar to give them a smoother consistency.

The sugar is mixed with liquid and boiled for varying lengths of time to give the strength of syrup required. It is impossible to give a general rule on the amount of sugar to use as this varies from ice to ice and is worked out carefully in proportion to the natural sugar in the other ingredients.

Liquid

The amount of liquid varies between the three types of ices. Granitas have the most liquid and sorbets the least. The liquid is always water, except in the case of granitas where tea, coffee or a mixture of cider and water may be substituted. The liquid is always made into a syrup with the sugar and other flavouring.

MAIN INGREDIENTS

The main ingredient, which gives an ice its character, is the flavouring. This can be either fruit or vegetables, or the drinks already mentioned under liquids.

Fruit

Fruity ices are very pretty to look at and delightfully refreshing on a hot, sticky day. In an ice, the flavour of the fruit is sharp and fresh after the freezing process. Strongly flavoured fruits are best, so choose from raspberries, strawberries, lemons, limes, oranges, grapefruit, tangerines, black and redcurrants, blackberries, pineapple, peaches, nectarines, apricots or loganberries.

For granitas, only the fruits which purée into a juice (blackcurrants, redcurrants, blackberries, raspberries, loganberries, strawberries) and citrus fruit juices are traditionally used. Water-ices and sorbets may be made using any of the fruit given above.

Canned varieties of fruit may be used but, as one of the joys of homemade ices is the flavour of fresh fruit, this is not really worth doing. Frozen fruit is very good.

When using citrus fruit (oranges,

lemons, limes etc) the maximum flavour is obtained from the rind by boiling it in the syrup. The best way to remove the rind is to pare away thinly with a swivel-type potato peeler. The juice is squeezed from citrus fruit using a juice extractor and added to the syrup.

Raspberries, strawberries, loganberries, peaches, nectarines, apricots and pineapple can all be puréed when raw. All but pineapple can be puréed using a food mill or a sieve. Pineapple can only be puréed in a blender and must have all woody parts ruthlessly removed first. If you purée pippy fruit in a liquidizer, it will have to be sieved after to extract the pips.

Currants and blackberries must be cooked before they can be puréed. Stew in a little water but do not add sugar. All the sugar in these ices comes from the syrup. The fruit must be drained before being puréed.

Vegetables

Vegetable ices may be a new one on you but, odd though they sound, they are well worth trying. Unlike sweet ices, vegetable ices are usually served as a first course, or as a refresher after a spicy dish such as curry. There are very few vegetables suitable for making ices. Best are ripe tomatoes, cucumber, avocado pear, watercress and cooked carrots.

Tomatoes should be simmered until soft and then pushed through a sieve. They can be pulped in a liquidizer but you would have to go to the trouble of skinning and deseeding them before simmering.

Cucumber is peeled and liquidized. For the sake of colour, leave a little of the peel on. There is no need to salt cucumber first as its wateriness is needed to make up the liquid in the ice.

Avocados are halved, stoned and peeled before being pulped in a liquidizer. Mix the flesh with a little lemon juice to prevent discolouration. Carrots must be prepared and cooked before being liquidized or sieved. Watercress must be washed and any limp or yellowing leaves removed before being puréed in a liquidizer. Usually, lemons or oranges are used with watercress.

OTHER INGREDIENTS

The most important remaining ingredient is egg white, which is added to water-ices and sorbets to give a light consistency. Use the whites of large eggs. In water-ices only half an egg white is used for an ice to serve four people. This is about 15 ml [1 tablespoon] of white. If you don't want to be bothered by halving the egg white, make double the quantity of ice and use all the white. In sorbets, more egg white is added to give a smooth texture. Usually two egg whites are added to a four-portion serving.

For both water-ices and sorbets, the egg whites are whisked until they reach the stage where they will stand in soft peaks. They are added to ices after they have been partially frozen.

Another addition made after the ices have been frozen is liqueur. This may be added at the final beating or poured over the ice just before serving. About 15 ml [1 tablespoon] is enough for a four-portion ice if added at the final beating. If pouring over, pour over 5 ml [1 teaspoon] per serving. Choose a liqueur that complements the fruit used in the ice. Kirsch goes well with all fruits. Crème de cassis goes with blackcurrants, Drambuie with peaches, cointreau with oranges, apricot brandy with apricots and peach brandy with peaches.

Left, orange and lemon water-ice. Centre, strawberry sorbet. Right, blackcurrant sorbet—all perfect for a hot summer day.

THE BASIC PRINCIPLES

In order to make ices that taste and look good, it is necessary to understand the basic principles.

Making the syrup

This is the starting point for all ices. To make the syrup, first add the sugar to the cold liquid. Stir to start the grains dissolving and add any other flavourings specified in the recipe (usually pieces of citrus peel). Place over medium heat and bring to the boil, stirring.

As soon as boiling point has been reached, the syrup is simmered for the length of time stated in the recipe. The length of simmering time affects the strength of the syrup. The longer it is simmered, the stronger it will be. Syrups for granitas are simmered for the shortest time, syrups for sorbets are simmered for the longest time to concentrate the sugar.

The syrup is then removed from the heat and allowed to cool. If tea or coffee is being used, it is added to the syrup at this point to infuse while it is cooling. If something is infusing in the syrup, the pan is covered to accelerate the development of the flavour. The syrup is then strained and chilled. Chilling helps to speed initial freezing. After chilling, a fruit purée or juice, if used, is mixed into the syrup.

Initial freezing

After chilling, the syrup (now mixed with its flavouring) is poured into whatever container you plan to use for freezing it. It is then covered with a double layer of foil. This prevents the top freezing solid while the bottom remains soft. The ice is then frozen until it reaches the stage when it looks rather like slush. This takes about 30 minutes.

Beating

After this first freezing, the ice must be beaten. This breaks up ice crystals and gives a good consistency. If you are making the ice in ice-cube trays or a bread tin, turn it out into a kitchen bowl, scraping all the ice away from the sides. Stir until the ice crystals break up. If you are making a granita, continue stirring for about 3 minutes, until the ice is almost liquid again, then pour back into the ice-cube trays or bread tin and freeze again.

This operation is repeated twice more with a granita until a granular mush is formed. The granita is ready to serve when this stage is reached and must not be frozen any further.

If you are making water-ice or sorbet, this is the point where the egg white is added.

Adding egg white

The egg white should be whisked to

Step-by-step to granita

SERVES 4
100 g [¼ lb] coarsely ground continental roast coffee or 50 g [2 oz] strong tea leaves
75 g [3 oz] caster sugar
whipped cream
coffee beans (optional)

1 If using refrigerator, turn to its coldest setting and remove all food you don't want frozen.

2 Put 1.1 L [2 pt] water and the sugar into a pan. Stir once. Bring to boil over medium heat, stirring.

4 Strain into a jug. Cool, then chill. Pour into the ice-cube trays or a loaf tin.

5 Cover and freeze for 30 minutes. Stir (turn into a bowl if using trays), then cover and re-freeze.

6 Repeat this operation twice more at 30 minute intervals until a granular slush is formed.

the soft peak stage. The water-ice or sorbet is then added in spoonfuls and the ice is whisked well with an electric mix or rotary mixer between each addition so that all the white is amalgamated.

When all the white has been whisked in, the consistency should be that of a firm snow. The ice is then covered and re-frozen.

Second beating
Water-ices and sorbets must be beaten once more to break up ice-crystals. This is done after they have been frozen for about 1½ hours. Beat as above. In the case of sorbets, a liqueur is sometimes beaten in again at this stage.

Final freezing
The ice is then covered and frozen again until firm. When it reaches this point, turn the refrigerator back to

3 Boil for 3 minutes and then remove from heat. Stir in coffee or tea and leave for 15 minutes.

7 Turn into tall glasses and top with a whirl of cream. Decorate coffee ice with coffee beans and serve.

normal and leave the ice in the frozen food compartment, if not using right away. If you have a freezer, you may like to store the ice in a rigid plastic box.

STORAGE
Granitas must be eaten as soon as they are ready. If kept they will freeze too far and lose their characteristic granular consistency. Water-ices and sorbets may be stored in a freezer compartment or a freezer for six months. When the ice is ready, turn it into a rigid plastic box and cover. If using the refrigerator, turn it back to normal temperature before storing the ice in the frozen food compartment.

Before using sorbets or water-ices stored in this way, leave at room temperature for about 30 minutes to soften slightly.

SERVING
To look their best, ices should be shown off in your prettiest dishes. Granitas should be served in tall, sundae-type glasses with a long spoon. Water-ices and sorbets may be served in traditional ice-cream dishes, champagne or wine glasses or in fruit shells. Orange or lemon shells arranged on a bed of green laurel leaves look very pretty.

A filled pineapple shell makes a splendid centre-piece. Hollow out the pineapple shells so that all the flesh is removed. Purée to a pulp and use to make the ice to be contained in the shell.

To hollow out an orange or lemon, cut a thin slice off the bottom so that it will stand level. Cut a thicker slice off the top so that the flesh shows. Using a small spoon, scoop out the flesh. Use the juice for the ice. Pile the ice into the shell.

Ices are always served standing on a plate. This is because biscuits or wafers are traditionally served with the ice. Instead of serving crumbling and rather boring ice-cream wafers, serve elegant biscuits. Langues-de-chat, tuiles, sugared sponge fingers and shortbread are all very good. All can be bought from good grocers and delicatessens or you can make them yourself. Instructions are given in a later course.

Instead of sticking the traditional wafers in the ice, top with a swirl of citrus peel, a few finely chopped

walnuts or, for savoury ices, sprigs of fresh mint, basil or borage.

How much to serve
Ices are really more a refresher than a filling dessert. If serving after a meal, two ice-cream scoops per person, or the equivalent in tablespoonfuls, is fine. For a refresher, one scoop is enough.

When serving vegetable ices, serve one scoop or for a spectacular effect, turn the ice into a ring mould after the final beating. When it is frozen, turn out of the ring by dipping the rounded side quickly in hot water and then inverting on to a plate. Fill the centre with salad.

SERVING IDEAS
●For a refreshing dessert, serve strawberry granita topped with fresh strawberries and cream.
●Orange, tangerine and lime water-ices are all delicious. Use the same quantities as for the lemon ice in step-by-step to water-ice.
●For coupe Jacques, half fill a champagne glass with lemon water ice. Cover this with a layer of fresh, halved peaches which have been steeped in kirsch. Top this with strawberry ice and fresh strawberries.
●For peach coupe, peel a fresh peach. Divide into sections and remove the stone. Reassemble the peach and surround with lemon water-ice.
●For pineapple Parisienne, remove the flesh from a pineapple leaving the shell whole with just a lid cut off the top. Fill the shell up with alternate layers of raspberry sorbet and chopped pineapple pulp. Decorate the top with raspberries.
●Grapefruit water-ice makes an interesting change from ordinary grapefruit to start a meal. Make it in the same way and using the same quantities as the lemon water-ice shown in the step-by-step guide. Decorate with mint leaves.
●Try serving scoops of different-coloured water-ice or sorbet together. Good combinations are black and redcurrant, lemon and lime or lemon and orange, peach and strawberry, orange and raspberry.
●Lemon water-ice looks exotic and tastes delicious with a little crème de menthe poured over it.
●For an unusual first course, serve cucumber water-ice with prawns.

Step-by-step to water-ice

1 If using a refrigerator, turn to its coldest setting and remove all food you don't want frozen.

2 Pare the zest from 3 large lemons using a swivel-type potato peeler. Squeeze out the juice.

3 Put 850 ml [1½ pt] water, lemon zest, juice and 200 g [7 oz] caster sugar into a pan. Stir once.

5 Allow to cool. Strain syrup into a jug. Chill in freezer or refrigerator but do not freeze.

6 Pour the mixture into ice-cube trays or a bowl. Cover and freeze for 30 minutes until slushy.

7 Separate one large egg. Measure out half the white and whisk until it will stand in soft peaks.

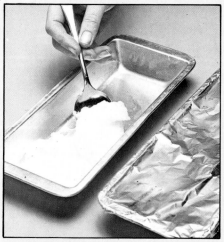

9 When a firm snow is formed, cover and return ice to freezer or refrigerator. Freeze for 1½ hours.

10 Remove from freezer or refrigerator, turn into bowl and beat again.

11 Put in tray, cover and freeze. When ice is firm, turn the refrigerator back to normal.

4 Place over medium heat and bring to the boil, stirring. Lower the heat and simmer for 5 minutes.

8 Remove the ice from the freezer or refrigerator. Stir, then beat ice into egg white in spoonfuls.

12 If storing in a freezer, pack into a rigid box. Leave at room temperature for ½ hour before use.

BLACKCURRANT LEAF WATER-ICE

⊠⊠⊠ *If you have a blackcurrant bush in your garden, this is an excellent way to make use of the aromatic leaves, which have the heady flavour of muscat grapes. Choose green unblemished leaves and reserve a few for garnish. The addition of green food colouring gives the ice a good colour.*

SERVES 4
4 large handfuls blackcurrant leaves
3 large lemons
200 g [7 oz] caster sugar
2-3 drops edible green colouring
1 large egg
4 bunches blackcurrants

1 If using the refrigerator turn to its coldest setting and remove all food you don't want frozen to the lower shelves.

2 Wash the blackcurrant leaves in cold water and drain on kitchen paper or in a salad spinner. Reserve a few of the best ones for a garnish.

3 Pare the zest from the lemons using a swivel-type potato peeler. Squeeze out the juice.

4 Put 850 ml [1½ pt] water, lemon zest, juice and sugar into a heavy-based pan. Stir once.

5 Place over medium heat and bring to the boil, stirring. Lower the heat and simmer for 5 minutes.

6 Remove from the heat and add the blackcurrant leaves. Stir so that they are all soaked in syrup. Cover the pan and leave to infuse for 30 minutes.

7 After infusion, strain the liquid, squeezing the leaves to extract all the flavour.

8 Stir in the green colouring. Chill in freezer or refrigerator, but do not freeze.

9 Pour the mixture into ice-cube trays or a bowl. Cover and freeze for 30 minutes until slushy.

10 Separate the egg. Just before you remove the ice from the freezer or

refrigerator, measure out half the white and whisk until it will stand in soft peaks.

11 Remove the ice from the freezer or refrigerator. If ice-cube trays were used, turn ice into a bowl. Stir the ice. Then beat the ice in spoonfuls into the egg white using either an electric mixer or a rotary whisk.

12 When a firm snow is formed, cover and return ice to the freezer or refrigerator. Freeze until firm (about 1½ hours).

13 Remove from freezer or refrigerator and beat again. Cover and re-freeze (about 1½ hours).

14 When ice is firm, turn the refrigerator back to normal and store in the frozen food compartment.

15 If storing in a freezer, pack into a rigid plastic box. Leave at room temperature for 30 minutes before use

16 Serve in scoops decorated with blackcurrant leaves and a little raw fruit.

Variations
● For geranium leaf ice, use sweet geranium leaves in the same way.
● For mint ice, use enough mint leaves to fill a 550 ml [1 pt] jug. Make in the same way as blackcurrant leaf water-ice.

APRICOT BRANDY WATER-ICE

⊠⊠⊠ *This is an ice to serve after a heavy main course. If you wish, skinned, stoned and chopped fresh apricots may be served with it. There is no need to add fruit to the ice; the apricot brandy provides all the flavour that is needed.*

Because there is no fruit in the ice to provide natural sugar, a larger amount of sugar than usual is used.

SERVES 4
1 lemon
350 g [¾ lb] caster sugar
150 ml [¼ pt] apricot brandy
1 egg

1 If using the refrigerator, turn to the coldest setting and remove all food you don't want frozen to the lower shelves.

2 Pare the zest from the lemon using a swivel-type potato peeler.

3 Put 850 ml [1½ pt] water, lemon zest and sugar into a heavy-based pan. Stir once.

4 Place over medium heat and bring to the boil, stirring. Lower the heat and simmer for 5 minutes.

5 Extract the juice from the lemon and add to the syrup. Allow to cool and then chill in the refrigerator for 10 minutes.

6 Strain the syrup and add the apricot brandy. Pour into ice-cube trays or a tin. Cover and freeze for 30 minutes until slushy.

7 Separate the egg. Just before you remove the ice from the freezer or refrigerator, measure out half the egg white and whisk until it will stand in soft peaks.

8 Remove ice from freezer or refrigerator. If the ice is in trays or a bread-tin, turn into a bowl. Stir to break up crystals.

9 Whisk the ice into the egg white, a spoonful at a time, using an electric or rotary whisk.

10 When a firm snow is formed, cover and return ice to the freezer or refrigerator. Freeze until firm (about 1½ hours).

Citrus ices look attractive served in shells. Lids can be made from the top of the fruit if wished, as shown for lemons.

11 Remove from the freezer or re-frigerator and beat again. Cover and re-freeze until firm (about 2 hours).

12 When ice is firm, turn the re-frigerator back to normal and store the ice in a rigid box in the frozen food compartment.

PINEAPPLE SORBET

Served in a pineapple shell, this ice makes a splendid centre-piece for a party. To make it look really effective, surround with fresh strawberries and mint leaves.

SERVES 4
1 medium-sized pineapple
175 g [6 oz] caster sugar
2 eggs

1 If using the refrigerator, turn it to its coldest setting, and remove all food you don't want frozen to the lower shelves.

2 Cut a thin slice off the bottom of the pineapple without cutting through to the flesh. Cut off the spiky top.

3 Run a knife around the inside of the pineapple to loosen the flesh from the skin. Hold the pineapple

upside down so that the flesh falls out. Be sure to do all this on a plate to save loss of juice.

4 Cut the pineapple into slices and extract the 'eyes' with the point of a knife.

5 Chop the pineapple into rough pieces. Place in a liquidizer and blend until pulpy.

6 Put 400 ml [¾ pt] water and sugar into a heavy-based pan. Stir once. Place over medium heat and bring to the boil, stirring. Lower the heat and simmer for 5 minutes.

7 Allow to cool. Strain the syrup into a jug. Chill in the freezer or refrigerator but do not freeze.

8 Mix the pineapple pulp and juice with the syrup. Pour the mixture into ice-cube trays or a bowl.

9 Cover and freeze for 1 hour until slushy.

10 Separate the eggs. Just before you remove the ice from the freezer or refrigerator, whisk the egg whites until they will stand in soft peaks.

11 Remove the ice from the freezer or refrigerator. Stir the ice then beat into the egg white in spoonfuls with a whisk.

12 When a firm snow is formed, cover and return ice to the freezer or refrigerator. Freeze until firm (about 1½-2 hours).

13 Remove from freezer or re-frigerator and beat again for 3-4 minutes. Cover and re-freeze (about 1 hour).

14 Pile the sorbet into the pineapple shell and replace the lid. Surround with fresh fruit of your choice and mint leaves.

Variations
● For blackcurrant sorbet, stew 450 g [1 lb] blackcurrants in water. Drain and purée. Make into a sorbet using 275 g [10 oz] caster sugar, 550 ml [1 pt] water, 30 ml [2 tablespoons] lemon juice and 2 egg whites.
● For raspberry or strawberry sorbet, use the same quantities as for blackcurrant but reduce sugar to 225 g [½ lb].

CUCUMBER GRANITA
Cool and elegant, cucumber granita is much more refresh-ing than a sweet drink or ice after a hectic game. Serve it in tall glasses decorated with sprigs of boragè or mint. Because cucumber is naturally watery, there is only a little water in this recipe. As this is a savoury ice, only a small amount of sugar is used.

SERVES 4
1 lemon
1 large cucumber
75 g [3 oz] caster sugar
sprigs of mint or borage
to garnish

1 If using the refrigerator, turn it to its coldest setting, and remove all food you don't want frozen to the lower shelves.

2 Pare the zest from the lemon, using a swivel-type potato peeler.

3 Put 150 ml [¼ pt] water, sugar and lemon zest into a pan.

4 Place over medium heat and bring to the boil. Lower the heat and simmer for 2 minutes.

5 Remove from heat and allow to cool. Strain into a jug. Squeeze the juice from the lemon and add to the jug.

6 Chill in the freezer or refrigerator for 10 minutes, but do not freeze.

7 Meanwhile, peel half the cucumber but leave the peel on the other half to give the granita a good colour.

8 Roughly chop the cucumber and purée in a liquidizer.

9 Stir the cucumber purée into the syrup. Pour the mixture into ice-cube trays or a bowl. Cover and freeze for 30 minutes until slushy.

10 Remove from the freezer or re-frigerator. If not in a bowl, turn into a bowl and stir for 3-5 minutes until almost liquid. Cover and return to the freezer or refrigerator.

11 Repeat this operation twice more at 30 minute intervals until the granita has become a granular slush. Serve immediately in tall glasses garnished with mint or borage.

Strawberry water-ice with melon balls

⬚⬚⬚ *Strawberry water-ice looks as luscious as it tastes and has the joy of being low in calories as well. Melon is a great friend to slimmers; some varieties contain only four calories per ounce. Here it provides an attractive colour contrast to the ice.*

Make sure your melon is ripe. Choose a cantaloupe or two small Ogen melons. A honeydew melon will do but it is more fattening.

SERVES 4-6
450 g [1 lb] strawberries
100 g [¼ lb] caster sugar
45 ml [3 tablespoons] lemon juice
45 ml [3 tablespoons] orange juice
1 cantaloupe or 2 Ogen melons
1 egg

1 Set the refrigerator to its lowest setting and remove food not to be frozen.

2 Measure 250 ml [½ pt] water into a pan. Add the sugar and stir once. Bring to the boil over medium heat, lower heat and simmer for 5 minutes.

3 Pour into a jug, leave to cool and then chill.

4 Wash and hull the strawberries, reserving 100 g [¼ lb] for decoration. Use a liquidizer or push the remaining 350 g [¾ lb] through a sieve to purée.

5 Mix the orange and lemon juice with the strawberry purée.

6 Mix the strawberry purée with the sugar syrup. If using a refrigerator pour into an ice-cube tray or loaf tin. If using a freezer you can leave the mixture in a plastic bowl. Cover and seal with a double thickness of foil or cling film and freeze for about 45 minutes until slushy.

7 Just before removing the ice from the freezing compartment, separate the egg white and reserve the yolk for future use. Whisk the white until it stands in thick peaks.

8 Turn the slush into a bowl if necessary and beat the harder outside into the softer inside. Then beat in the egg white a spoonful at a time.

9 Re-cover and freeze until the mixture again forms a slush (about 45 minutes).

10 Turn out the ice and beat as before. Return to freezing compartment and freeze until firm.

11 Make the melon balls using a melon baller, or cut it into chunks. Place these in individual serving dishes.

12 Ten minutes before the meal, remove water-ice from the freezing compartment and place on the least cold shelf of the refrigerator.

13 Scoop water-ice on top of the melon balls and decorate with one or two strawberries.

Desserts

home-made ice-cream

Genuine home-made ice-creams are the ultimate in luxury desserts. They are guaranteed to impress your guests and even the most self-indulgent can usually find room for something which looks so tempting and slips down so smoothly. Nevertheless, they are surprisingly easy to make and no special equipment is needed.

After sampling a genuine home-made ice-cream, most people find the confections of whipped fats sold commercially under this name inferior. A well-made ice-cream is one of the perfect ways of ending dinner.

The principles of making true 'ices'—granitas, water-ices and sorbets—from flavoured syrups and fruit purées are described in the previous chapter. In this chapter learn how to add cream to fruit purées to make creamy fruit-flavoured ice-creams and how to make custard-based rich ice-cream, best known as vanilla ice-cream and the basis of the delicious family of liqueur and nut ice-creams.

There are three basic types of ice-cream, each of which is made by a different method. The first two are the quickest and easiest. Custard-based ice-cream, the basis of the classic vanilla ice-cream, is a little more time-consuming but should present no problems if you follow the step-by-step instructions. To make any type of ice-cream you have only to combine two techniques already learned in previous courses and freeze the results.

Sophisticated apricot liqueur and sumptuous strawberry ice-creams are each decorated with the appropriate fruit.

Simple fruit ice-creams

The simplest type of ice-cream to make, fruit ice-cream is also one of the most popular. Who can resist a pink raspberry or dark blackcurrant ice-cream on a hot day? A fruit purée is made as already described in the previous chapter and whipped cream is simply folded into it. In effect this is the same as making a fruit cream as when making a fool or mousse base and then freezing it. The biggest advantage of this type of ice-cream is that little or no cooking on a hot stove is required.

Cream ices

This type of ice-cream uses a sorbet, as described in the previous chapter, as its base.

Fruit purée or juice is added to a very strong sugar syrup. This is then frozen and beaten in turns. For a sorbet the ice is finished by beating in egg whites to make a firm snow, which is then frozen. For a cream ice, however, egg white is not added but is replaced by lightly whipped cream. This is then frozen.

Rich ice-cream

This is the most time-consuming and expensive method of making ice-cream, but, as you might expect, it gives the most rewarding results! The custard is made with cream and eggs cooked together in a bowl over gently simmering water. There is a wide choice of flavourings. Additions, such as chopped nuts and fruit are made after the ice-cream has partially frozen. Alternatively, the ice-cream may be combined with puréed fruit, producing a result similar to a cream ice but rather richer.

EQUIPMENT

Like water-ices, ice-cream can be made perfectly satisfactorily in the frozen food compartment in an ordinary domestic refrigerator. This must be set to its lowest temperature one hour before the mixture is put into the frozen food compartment.

Sorbetières

Electric sorbetières (sorbet or ice-cream makers) are both labour saving and efficient. These are usually placed inside the freezer compartment of the refrigerator while the flex trails out to an electric plug. They do not themselves include any freezing device. A sorbetière with a 1 L [1¾ pt] capacity is a suitable size for most domestic refrigerators.

The big advantage of the sorbetière is that it has a constantly moving paddle, which stirs the ice while it is freezing. This prevents crystals forming. It also saves the cook time and trouble because there is no need to check the ice mixture at intervals or to beat it regularly.

Sorbetières must only be filled three-quarters full, as the mixture expands with beating.

Ice-cream buckets

These old-fashioned, hand-operated ice-cream buckets are effective but rarely seen nowadays. They have a large capacity but are hard work to operate. A handle is cranked to work a moving paddle called a dasher. Only fill the ice-cream compartment three-quarters full. To provide the freezing element, ice and freezing salt are added to the outer layer of the bucket.

Other equipment

The equipment used for making water-ices will also be needed for ice-cream. You will need:

- a heavy-based pan for making syrup
- a sieve for straining syrup for making the fruit purée
- a swivel-type potato peeler for peeling citrus zest or a citrus zester
- a juice extractor for citrus fruit
- a jug for cooling the syrup
- a whisk, preferably an electric one, for beating the ice and the cream
- 2 metal spoons
- a supply of aluminium foil to cover the ice-cream in the freezer
- ice-cream trays (with the dividers removed), bread tins or plastic boxes in which to freeze the ice-cream.

In addition to these, you will need extra items for ices containing cream. Two more bowls will be needed for beating the egg yolks and whisking the cream. Depending on your choice of ice-cream method, you may need a second, heavy-based pan for scalding the cream and a double boiler (or bowl plus a bain-marie) for cooking the custard.

Ice-creams are often made in fancy shapes as they mould better than water-ices. Jelly moulds of suitable size can be used, while kitchen shops sell special bombe moulds which enable you to produce gorgeous-looking desserts rivalling any chef's creation. If you intend to purchase one of these, make a note of the measurements of your frozen food compartment before you do, to be sure that it will fit in comfortably. If you own a freezer cabinet, the ice-cream can be frozen in this.

An ice-cream scoop is optional for serving but it does have several advantages over a serving spoon. Some models have a moving back wire, controlled by a switch which releases the ice-cream ball after it has been scooped. Dip this type into water periodically to warm it. Another type of scoop contains liquid with a very low freezing temperature, so that the metal does not become as cold as the ice and the ball of ice is easily released. Ice-cream scoops give the ice a ball shape, which many people find appealing.

INGREDIENTS
Cream and milk

Cream gives its name to ice-cream. Many commercial mixtures called ice-cream contain no cream whatsoever, but cream is an essential ingredient of home-made ice-cream. Thin or thick cream may be used according to individual recipes.

Thick cream is needed for simple fruit ice-creams and is added towards the end of ice-making. This is lightly whisked to give the ice-cream a thicker texture. It is important that this is whipped only to the soft peak

Although this equipment is not all essential for making ice-cream, it is labour saving and helps in presentation. **1** *Ice-cream scoops.* **2** *Sorbetière with bowl.* **3** *Dessert moulds.* **4** *Charlotte russe mould.* **5** *Electric whisk.* **6** *Freezer trays.*

stage. If it is whipped beyond this, it will turn buttery and this will affect the texture of the final ice-cream. Thin cream may be used for making the custard base of a rich cream ice.

Milk may be substituted for thin cream in the custard base of rich ice-cream as an economy or emergency measure. However, because it is thinner than cream, it tends to give a granular texture to the final ice-cream. Extra egg yolks are therefore usually added to counteract this. So, although milk might seem cheaper, the economy can be cancelled out. Use milk only in emergencies.

Eggs
Neither simple fruit ice-creams nor cream ices require the addition of either egg whites or of egg yolks.

Egg yolks, though, are essential for the custard base of rich ice-cream. It is the yolks that give vanilla ice-cream its golden glow. The richest ices are obtained by using only egg yolks but whole eggs may be used instead. The proportion to be maintained is two egg yolks or one whole egg. Thus, in an individual recipe, 4 egg yolks could be used or 2 whole eggs, or 2 egg yolks with one whole egg. For general purposes the last combination is probably most satisfactory.

The number of eggs needed in a recipe is determined by the thickness of the cream used. Thick cream already has quite a lot of body and therefore a smaller proportion of egg is needed to thicken it. A custard made with 550 ml [1 pt] thick cream needs only 2 yolks to thicken it. If you use thin cream, you will need more eggs to thicken it. A custard made with 250 ml [½ pt] thin cream and 250 ml [½ pt] thick cream needs 4 yolks or 2 yolks and one whole egg.

Extra yolks are needed to thicken milk, if this is used instead of cream. Use 6 yolks or 2 yolks and 2 whole eggs to make custard with 250 ml [½ pt] milk and 250 ml [½ pt] thin cream.

Beaten egg whites are rarely added to ice-cream. This is sometimes done, however, when a dense cooked fruit, such as apple, is being used as it lightens the texture of the final ice.

Sugar
Caster or icing sugar may be used for ice-cream, as with water-ices. One type—cream ices—also includes a sugar syrup, prepared according to the instructions in the previous chapter on water-ices.

As with all ices the proportion of sugar to other ingredients is most important. If too much sugar is used the ice will not freeze—too little, and the final result will be so hard that you cannot get your spoon into it.

Fruit
Fruit purées, made by the puréeing techniques of gentle cooking, then blending and sieving, are a super component of ice-creams, and give a smooth result. Weights given in recipes for purées refer to the weight of the made purée and not to the original weight of fruit. All excess liquid is drained from the purée and it is not sweetened as this might upset the sugar balance.

Chopped fruit—fresh, canned, glacé or dried fruit—and chopped peel may be added to ice-cream. These additions give it a more varied texture. However, it is important that these only be added when the ice-cream is near completion, otherwise the extra sugar will upset the balance and the ice-cream will not freeze.

Step-by-step to rich ice-cream

SERVES 4–6
250 ml [$\frac{1}{2}$ pt] thin cream
1 vanilla pod or 2–3 drops
  vanilla extract
2 egg yolks
1 whole egg
50 g [2 oz] caster sugar
250 ml [$\frac{1}{2}$ pt] thick cream

1 Set refrigerator to lowest setting and remove food to lower shelves. Chill ice-cream container.

2 Gently scald thin cream together with vanilla pod. Cover and allow to infuse for 15 minutes.

4 Pour the hot cream on to the beaten egg mixture in a trickle, stirring continuously.

5 Cook the mixture over hot, but not boiling, water. Stir continuously for about 15 minutes.

6 When cooked and thick, remove from heat. Add extract if used. Strain, leave to cool, then chill.

8 Just before removing the ice, lightly whip the cream to the soft peak stage.

9 Turn ice into bowl and thoroughly beat. Add cream and stir in. Cover and freeze (about 45 minutes).

10 Remove from freezer and beat thoroughly. Return to container, re-cover and freeze.

3 In the top of a double boiler, cream together the whole egg, yolks and sugar until thick.

7 Turn into the container. Cover with foil and freeze for 45 minutes or until mushy.

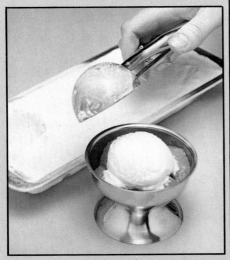

11 Remove from the refrigerator 20 minutes before serving, to allow ice-cream to soften slightly.

Other additions

Freezing tends to diminish flavour so that all mixtures to be frozen need to be well flavoured. Lemon and orange zest and juices and liqueurs are used to enhance fruit ices or may be used to flavour ice-creams by themselves.

Nuts are another attractive addition to ice-creams. One famous ice-cream, Nesselrode, uses puréed chestnuts; another well-known one is praline, made from ground caramelized unblanched almonds. Chopped nuts of almost every type give an attractive texture, as well as adding flavour, to ice-creams.

MAKING SIMPLE FRUIT ICE-CREAM

This method will make attractive ice-creams from raw soft fruit such as raspberries and strawberries as well as peaches, apricots and pineapple. Cooked fruit, such as black and redcurrants, gooseberries and apples may also be used. The fruit should be puréed. Prepare the fruit after first washing it and discarding any damaged parts. Fruit puréed in a liquidizer will add more texture to the final ice-cream. Fruit passed through a sieve will make a smoother ice-cream.

If the fruit is pippy, it should always be sieved after liquidizing to remove seeds. Sieving will also remove tops and tails from gooseberries (saving you kitchen time) making gooseberry ice-cream quick and economical.

Icing sugar blends in best with sieved fruit. Be sure to sieve the sugar before the fruit to save unnecessary washing-up.

The basic proportion for a fruit ice-cream is an equal quantity of fruit purée and cream. This however is varied for individual recipes.

As mentioned previously, a proportion of citrus juice is often added to bring out fruit flavours.

The method of making the ice is exactly the same as that of making any fruit fool or fruit mousse where cream is combined. When the fruit purée and cream have been combined, this mixture is then poured into the freezing tray, loaf tin or bowl. Cover this and place in the freezer compartment of the refrigerator.

Freeze for 45 minutes. When the ice-cream forms a partially frozen mush, remove from the freezer compartment. Tip it into a bowl (unless already in one) and beat thoroughly with a wooden spoon to break up ice crystals. Return to the refrigerator for a further 45 minutes. Remove the ice-cream and beat it a second time. Return to the freezer and freeze until firm. The ice-cream is then ready to serve or store.

MAKING A CREAM ICE

The inclusion of a syrup with the fruit purée makes these ice-creams rather longer to make than simple fruit ices and a little more tricky to freeze successfully. The results, however, are well worth it!

Make the syrup following the instructions given in the previous chapter on ices. The proportion of sugar to water varies from recipe to recipe as it is dependent on the fruit that is to be included with it. Equally the proportion of fruit juices or purée to syrup varies.

Start off by the sorbet method, described in the previous chapter, pouring the chilled combined fruit purée and syrup into the freezer tray. Cover and freeze for approximately 45 minutes until the mixture is mushy. Turn out into a bowl and beat.

Lightly whip the cream to the soft peak stage and incorporate this into the mushy ice. Return to the freezer tray, cover and re-freeze. After another 45 minutes turn out and beat once more to prevent the formation of ice crystals. Cover and freeze once more. The ice-cream is then ready for serving or storing.

MAKING RICH ICE-CREAMS

The most famous of all ice-creams—vanilla—is made from a custard base, containing cream (sometimes milk), eggs and sugar. When this is cool, make the additions, which may include fruit juices, puréed or chopped fruit, puréed, chopped or ground nuts, spices and liqueurs. Thick or thin cream is also added.

The custard is a rich form of a crème anglaise and is made by the method of cooking in a bowl over simmering water, whether milk or cream is used. Allow the custard to cool then chill.

The refrigerator is turned to its lowest setting, as for other ices, and the container should be chilled. Turn the cold custard into the container, cover and freeze for 45 minutes or until it becomes mushy. Then turn

out and stir the sides, which always freeze first, into the middle.

If thick cream is being in-corporated, lightly whip it to the soft peak stage and stir it into the ice mixture. If thin cream is being used this need not be whipped. Thin cream does not, however, give such a rich texture to the final ice-cream.

Any additions to be made to the ice-cream are made at this point, when it is partially frozen. This is important as chopped fruit contains extra sugar and liqueurs inhibit mixtures from freezing, so these must not be added until freezing is almost complete.

The mixture is then returned to the freezing tray, covered and re-frozen.

Dark, fruity raspberry and redcurrant ice-cream served with langues-de-chat.

After another period of 45 minutes turn the mixture out again and beat a second time. This is particularly important if thin cream is used as this has a greater tendency to create an ice-cream with granular texture. Freeze once more until the ice is firm. It is then ready to serve.

SERVING
Do remember to take ice-creams out of the freezing compartment (or freezer) some time before serving or it will be difficult to spoon it and

tongues may burn. The time needed for softening will vary with the recipe but soft-textured ice-cream should be removed about 15 minutes before serving. A firmer ice-cream should usually be removed at the start of the meal and put on the bottom shelf of the refrigerator.

Quantities
Ice-creams are generally eaten in small quantities. However, if the ice-cream is to be the family pudding at a meal where no first course is served, larger portions will be needed than for the end of a formal dinner. Ice-creams based on 550 ml [1 pt] of cream or mixed cream and fruit purée will serve four people generously or

six people with smaller servings.

Dishes

Ice-creams look very appetizing when attractively presented. Ice-creams made in bombe or jelly moulds may simply be turned out on to a plate. To release the ice from the mould, invert the mould over the plate and then place several dish cloths, which have been wrung out after soaking in hot water, over it. This is safer than standing the mould in hot water, when too much of the ice may melt. Loosen ice-cream from a straight-sided mould by working round it with a palette knife, which you have dipped in hot water.

If the ice-cream was made in a freezer tray, loaf tin or a bowl, scoop out into sundae glasses or cut glass bowls. For tinier, dinner party servings use individual soufflé dishes, petits pots (such as those used for petits pots de chocolat) or wine glasses. Glass shows off the pretty colours of ice-creams best and the long stems look elegant. A knickerbocker glory effect is easy to create in tall sundae glasses. Use three differently flavoured and coloured ice-creams and pile them in alternately. You may also use the hollowed-out fruit shells from which you have scooped the pulp.

Stand individual dishes or glasses on a side-plate. This will hold the dessertspoon (which could fall out of a glass) and any wafers or biscuits.

Wafers and biscuits

Wafers tucked into the top of ices are popular with children. For a dinner party, put a couple of biscuits on each plate when serving and pass more on a small dish. Tuile biscuits which can be home-made or bought from food stores are particularly delicious with ice-cream. Or try serving langues de chats.

Sauces

Sauces are a popular accompaniment to ice-cream; they add bulk and a contrast in flavour. If you have any fruit purée left over from making a simple fruit ice, put a spoonful of this over each individual serving.

Butterscotch and chocolate sauces, always firm favourites with children and adults alike, are popular accompaniments to vanilla and coffee ices. Coffee sauce is good served with chocolate ice-cream, and raspberry sauce is particularly de-licious with peach ice-cream.

STRAWBERRY ICE-CREAM

A favourite with everyone, strawberry ice-cream is simple to make and you will be astonished how much better it tastes than the shop-bought ice-cream with the same name. The orange juice is added to bring out the strawberry flavour.

SERVES 4–6
450 g [1 lb] strawberries
225 g [½ lb] icing sugar
half an orange
half a lemon
250 ml [½ pt] thick cream

1 Turn the refrigerator to its coldest setting an hour before you start and chill the container in which you will freeze the ice-cream.

2 Wash and hull the strawberries. Chop them roughly.

3 Sieve the icing sugar into a bowl.

4 Purée the strawberries by passing through a sieve or vegetable mill. If using a liquidizer, sieve to remove pips.

5 Measure out 250 ml [½ pt] strawberry purée and stir into the icing sugar.

6 Squeeze the orange and lemon on a citrus presser and add the juice to the purée. Chill the purée in the refrigerator.

7 Lightly whisk the cream to the soft peak stage. Fold this into the fruit purée and turn over until the two are mixed.

8 Pour into freezer tray, loaf tin or bowl. Cover with foil and put in the freezer compartment of the refrigerator for 45 minutes.

9 Remove the freezer tray from the refrigerator and turn the partially frozen mush into a bowl. Stir thoroughly, turning the frozen outsides into the softer middle.

10 Return to the freezer tray and re-freeze for 45 minutes.

11 Turn out the frozen ice-cream and stir vigorously once more to break up ice crystals.

12 Return the ice-cream to the freezer. After 45 minutes it will be ready for serving.

13 Remove the ice-cream from the refrigerator 20 minutes before serving to allow it to soften slightly.

Variation

Other fruit purées may be substituted for the strawberry.
●Gooseberry ice-cream is an unusual, economical and very successful ice-cream. Substitute 250 ml [½ pt] of gooseberry purée which you have flavoured with an elderflower head, for the strawberries and citrus fruit juices.

RASPBERRY AND REDCURRANT CREAM ICE

The combination of raspberries and redcurrants, which are in season at the same time, is delightful. This ice-cream is sharp and fruity, rather like a sorbet. Make the purée following the instructions in the previous chapter.

SERVES 4–6
550 ml [1 pt] mixed raspberry and redcurrant purée
225 g [½ lb] caster sugar
1 lemon or 1 orange
150 ml [¼ pt] thick cream

1 Turn the refrigerator to its coldest setting one hour in advance and chill the container for the ice-cream.

2 Put the sugar into a heavy-based pan with 150 ml [¼ pt] water and stir once.

3 Bring to the boil and let boil for 5 minutes without stirring.

4 Allow the syrup to cool. When cold add it to the fruit purée.

5 Meanwhile squeeze the lemon or orange. Add the juice to the fruit purée.

6 Pour the fruit purée into the chilled container, cover with a double layer of foil and freeze for 45 minutes until mixture has formed a partially frozen mush.

7 Just before removing the fruit purée from the freezer, lightly whip

the cream to the soft peak stage.

8 Turn the fruit mush into a chilled bowl. Stir briskly to break up the ice crystals, stirring the sides into the middle. Beat in the cream.

9 Return to freezing container, re-cover with foil and freeze ice-cream for a further 45 minutes.

10 Remove the ice-cream mixture from the refrigerator and beat once more to break up the crystals.

11 Re-cover with foil and freeze until firm.

12 Remove from refrigerator just before serving as this ice-cream is quite soft.

Variations
All the fruit used for sorbets and water-ices may be used for this type of ice-cream.

PRALINE ICE-CREAM
⊠⊠⊠ *The crunchy texture of toffee and nut is a pleasant surprise in ice-cream. It makes an interesting contrast if served with a smooth ice-cream.*

SERVES 6
550 ml [1 pt] basic rich vanilla ice-cream
175 g [6 oz] caster sugar
175 g [6 oz] unblanched almonds

1 Make up the basic vanilla ice-cream as described in the step-by-step recipe, steps 1–9.

2 To make the praline, place the caster sugar in a heavy-based pan and heat it gently until it melts. Stir with a metal spoon until the sugar turns brown (protecting your hand with an oven glove).

3 Quickly stir in unblanched al-monds. Pour the praline on to greased baking foil or a marble slab. Spread the mixture out thinly.

4 When cold break the praline into pieces and put them either into a mortar to be ground with a pestle or into a mixing bowl to be crushed with the end of a rolling pin. Alternatively, put small pieces into an electric grinder.

5 Mix the praline into the vanilla ice-cream at the final beating stage at step 10, and freeze until firm.

Variations
Numerous additions can be made to the basic vanilla ice-cream to turn it into a selection of inviting desserts, each magically different from the next. The additions are all made at step 10 of the step-by-step to basic vanilla ice-cream before the final freezing.

●For brown bread ice-cream, sprinkle 45 ml [3 tablespoons] of brown breadcrumbs on a baking tray. Scatter 15 ml [1 tablespoon] caster sugar over the crumbs and bake in a moderately hot oven until coloured. Remove from tray and cool. Add crumbs with 30 ml [2 tablespoons] rum to the vanilla ice-cream at the final beating stage. Make sure the crumbs are well dispersed in the ice-cream.

●For ginger ice-cream, add 75 g [3 oz] chopped preserved ginger together with 45 ml [3 tablespoons] of the syrup to the ice before final freezing.

●For a tutti-frutti ice-cream, chop 50 g [2 oz] glacé cherries, 25 g [1 oz] angelica, and 25 g [1 oz] mixed orange and lemon zest. Add these, with 25 g [1 oz] sultanas soaked in 45 ml [3 tablespoons] cognac, plus the cognac, to the ice-cream before the final freezing.

●For walnut ice-cream, chop 50 g [2 oz] walnuts. Add these, with 45 ml [3 tablespoons] Grand Marnier.

●For Oxford ice-cream, add 225 g [½ lb] coarse-cut marmalade to the ice-cream.

FRUIT AND NUT ICE-CREAM
⊠⊠⊠ *This ice-cream is made with milk but you could use thin cream and omit one of the whole eggs. Honey gives it a special flavour, while the fruit and nuts give it an unusual consistency.*

SERVES 6
250 ml [¼ pt] milk
60 ml [4 tablespoons] honey
2 medium-sized eggs
2 egg yolks
7.5 ml [1½ teaspoons] ground nutmeg
250 ml [½ pt] thick cream
100 g [4 oz] seedless dried fruit (raisins, sultanas and currants)
60 ml [4 tablespoons] chopped almonds or hazelnuts

1 Turn down the refrigerator to its coldest setting and move food that you do not want frozen down to the lower shelves. Chill the freezer tray or ice-cream container.

2 Put the milk into a small heavy-based pan. Add the honey and scald.

3 Remove top of double boiler and in it beat the eggs. Pour on the hot milk in a thin trickle, stirring continuously with a wooden spoon.

4 Put the pan containing the mixture on to the bottom of the double boiler containing the hot water. Do not allow the water underneath to boil but cook the custard gently stirring all the time. This will take about 15 minutes.

5 The custard is cooked when it will coat the back of the spoon.

6 Strain into a bowl and add the nutmeg. Cool then chill.

7 Pour the mixture into freezer tray or a loaf tin or bowl. Cover, and freeze for 45 minutes, when it will be mushy.

8 Just before removing from the freezer, beat the cream to the soft peak stage. Remove the mixture from the refrigerator and stir to remove ice crystals. Stir in the cream.

9 Return to the container and freeze for a further 45 minutes.

10 Remove from the freezer and beat the mixture once more. Add the dried fruit and chopped nuts and stir in.

11 Return to the container. Cover and freeze until firm.

APRICOT LIQUEUR ICE-CREAM
⊠⊠⊠ *Because fruit purée is added it takes rather long to freeze this ice-cream. Dried apricots are used and, as they have a rather strong flavour, the extra quantity of cream is needed for balance.*

SERVES 8

250 ml [½pt] thin cream
50 g [2 oz] caster sugar
1 vanilla pod or 2–3 drops vanilla extract
2 egg yolks
450 g [1 lb] dried apricots
50 g [2 oz] granulated sugar
15 ml [1 tablespoon] apricot brandy
250 ml [½ pt] thick cream

1 Cover the apricots with twice their volume of cold water. Add the granulated sugar, bring to the boil, cover and simmer for 40 minutes. Remove from the heat.

2 Leave the apricots in the covered pan to soak for five hours.

3 Turn the refrigerator to its coldest setting and move all food that you do not want frozen to the lower shelves.

4 Put the thin cream into a small heavy-based pan and scald. Add the vanilla pod, cover, and leave to infuse for 15 minutes.

5 Put the egg yolks into the top of a double boiler, add caster sugar and beat with a wooden spoon.

6 Remove the vanilla pod and pour the hot cream on to the eggs in a thin trickle, stirring all the time.

7 Put the upper pan or bowl over a lower pan of heated water. Cook gently, stirring all the time without allowing the water to boil underneath. The custard should take about 15 minutes to cook.

8 When cooked, the custard will coat the back of a spoon. If used add vanilla extract. Cool then chill.

9 Drain and purée the apricots in a liquidizer or by passing through a vegetable mill.

10 Stir the apricot purée into the cold custard mixture.

11 Turn the mixture into freezer tray, a loaf tin or a bowl. Cover and freeze to a mush, about 2 hours.

12 Just before removing the ice-cream, whip the cream lightly until it forms stiff peaks. Remove the ice-cream and beat briskly. Then stir in the cream and the liqueur. Return to the freezer tray, cover and re-freeze for a further 1½ hours.

13 Remove the ice-cream from the freezer and beat once more. Return to the container, cover and freeze until firm.

Glasses of ice-cream are refreshing for a special tea. Strawberry, ginger and apricot liqueur ice-cream are shown.

CHOCOLATE AND COFFEE ICE-CREAM GATEAU

This sumptuous and sophisti- cated ice-cream gâteau will end any dinner party on a note of perfection. Rich traditional chocolate ice-cream is married to a layer of tangy coffee ice-cream just before the final freezing. Decorated with cream and candles it's an unusual birthday cake.

You will need two freezing trays, loaf tins or plastic boxes for the initial freezing stages. In the final stage the ice-creams are sandwiched together in a cake tin 18 cm [7"] in diameter and 7.5 cm [3"] deep. You will find it easiest to unmould the ice-cream cake from a ring or push bottom cake tin. If you use a fixed bottom cake tin, work round the sides with a palette knife which you have dipped in hot water before unmoulding the ice-cream gâteau.

SERVES 12
550 ml [1 pt] thin cream
2 whole eggs
4 egg yolks
175 g [6 oz] caster sugar
100 g [¼ lb] plain dark chocolate
40 g [1½ oz] ground coffee
50 g [2 oz] icing sugar
550 ml [1 pt] thick cream
30 ml [2 tablespoons] curaçao
30 ml [2 tablespoons] Tia Maria or Kahlua

For the garnish:
150 g [¼ pt] thick cream
50 g [2 oz] unblanched hazelnuts (optional)
25 g [1 oz] grated chocolate (optional)

1 Set refrigerator to its coldest setting and remove food to lower shelves. Chill containers.

2 Gently scald thin cream over a low heat in a heavy-based pan.

3 In the top of a double boiler, beat together whole eggs, egg yolks and caster sugar until thick.

4 Pour hot cream in a trickle on to the beaten egg mixture, stirring all the time.

5 Cook mixture over hot, but not boiling, water. Stir continuously for about 15 minutes.

6 When custard is thick, remove from heat, strain and divide equally between two bowls.

7 Break chocolate into small pieces and melt in bowl over a pan of hot water over low heat.

8 Combine melted chocolate with warm custard in one bowl. Leave to cool.

9 Pour 150 ml [¼ pt] boiling water over coffee grounds and leave to infuse for 15 minutes.

10 Strain off the coffee grounds, add icing sugar to coffee and stir. When cold add to second custard.

11 Pour each custard into a separate freezing tray, cover with foil and freeze for 45 minutes.

12 Just before removing freezer trays, divide the thick cream into 2. Whip to soft peaks.

13 Turn out the chocolate. Stir, then beat in half the cream and curaçao. Cover, re-freeze (45 minutes).

14 Turn out coffee, stir, then beat in remaining cream and liqueur. Cover and re-freeze (45 minutes).

15 Remove chocolate ice-cream from the freezer, turn into a bowl and beat to break up crystals.

16 Spoon ice-cream into cake tin and level off the top. Return this to the freezer.

17 Beat coffee ice-cream, spoon on top of chocolate ice-cream and level off. Re-freeze until firm.

18 Remove from the refrigerator 20 minutes before serving and turn out on to a serving plate.

19 Decorate with whipped cream and chopped nuts or grated chocolate.

Pictures supplied by
Rex Bamber: 53; 56 7; 58 9; 60 1; 65;
  66 7; 289; 291; 292 3;
  335; 336 7; 342; 344;
Terry Calcutt: 216TC;
Phillip Dowell: 216CL;
Alan Duns: 21; 22 3; 28 9; 31; 32 3;
  36 7; 38 9; 40; 70 1; 89;
  90 1; 96; 98; 120 1; 127;
  129; 135; 136; 142 3; 151;
  167; 170 1; 174 5; 176;
  192; 193; 194 5; 196; 199;
  200; 205TL & TC, CL,
  BL & BR; 206; 207; 210;
  214 5; 216TL; 216TR;
  CR, BL & BC; 223; 224;
  225; 227; 235; 239; 242 3;
  294 5; 304 5; 306; 307;
  318; 319; 323; 356; 357;
  360; 373; 374 5; 378; 381;
Melvin Grey: 8 9; 20; 78; 99; 100; 101;
  104 5; 124; 125; 128;
  130 1; 132BR, BC & BL;
  133B; 197; 198; 202;
  221; 222; 233; 316;
  320 1; 322; 331;
Paul Kemp: 1; 11; 14; 41; 47; 48 9; 50 1;
  97; 102 3; 106; 107; 108B;
  145; 146; 147; 148; 149;
  150; 152 3; 166; 203; 204;
  205TR, CR C; 206 7;
  208 9; 212 3; 219; 220;
  244; 260 1; 263; 264; 265;
  266 7; 268; 272 3; 276;
  277; 278 9; 327; 328 9;
David Levin: 3; 4 5; 6; 10; 12 13; 15;
  30; 34 5; 43; 46 7; 54 5;
  62 3; 64T; 68 9; 72; 75;
  76 7; 79; 82 3; 92; 94 5;
  108; 109; 110; 114 5; 117;
  118 9; 132; 133; 138;
  140 1; 156; 157; 158 9;
  160; 162 3; 169; 172 3;
  181; 182 3; 185; 186 7;
  216(insert); 216C; 216BR;
  217; 218; 228 9; 230 1;
  236 7; 238; 241; 248; 250;
  257; 271; 274 5; 284;
  285; 296 7; 300; 301;
  302 3; 310 11; 312 3;
  314 5; 324 5; 332 3; 334;
  338 9; 340 1; 350; 351;
  358 9; 361; 362; 366 7;
  368 9; 376 7; 382; 383;
  384;
Peter Lloyd: 85; 86 7; 88;
Moulinex Ltd: 179;
Roger Phillips: 52; 80 1; 111; 112 3;
  116; 122 3; 126; 164 5;
  808 9; 345; 348 9; 352;
  353; 354 5; 363; 364;
  365; 370 1;
Iain Reid: 180; 188 9; 190 1;
Paul Williams: 281; 283; 287; 288;
George Wright: 17; 18 9; 44; 177;
  211; 245; 246 7; 249;
  252 3; 254 5; 258 9;